ECONOMIC PRINCIPLES

Seven Ideas for Thinking ... About Almost Anything

Douglas W. Allen

Second Edition

Custom Publishing

New York Boston San Francisco
London Toronto Sydney Tokyo Singapore Madrid
Mexico City Munich Paris Cape Town Hong Kong Montreal

Cover Art: *Glen the Rooster,* photographed by Alison E. Allen.

Printed in Canada

10 9 8 7 6 5 4 3 2 1

2009400080

MH

Pearson
Custom Publishing
is a division of

www.pearsonhighered.com

ISBN 10: 0-558-25248-6
ISBN 13: 978-0-558-25248-9

NOTE TO INSTRUCTORS

What does the world need another principles textbook for? That's a legitimate question, and the answer is mostly personal. I began teaching economic theory in 1982 as a teaching assistant. Within a couple of years I was lecturing and wondering why most textbooks were i) long, ii) similar in content, iii) boring, iv) expensive, and v) so darned politically correct. I got to the point where even the word "widget" bothered me. Several years later I co-authored a third year textbook with the intention of writing a book that would avoid most of the pitfalls in other books. No doubt every textbook writer starts with the same objectives. I discovered the publishing industry is structured in such a way that it is almost impossible to write outside the mold.

In order for publishers to make money on a book they have to cater to the "average" student, in the "average" class, being taught by the "average" instructor. They must keep an eye open for unconventional topics or missing chapters. They also have to worry about books "offending someone." Printing a conventional textbook is expensive and involves a substantial risk. It also involves significant costs to correct mistakes. All of these factors lead to the bland books we see in the market place.

With these thoughts in mind, I initially published this book as an electronic text. An electronic text is cheap, easy to change, and I had complete control over the book. With complete control I was able to avoid the marketing problem of a conventional textbook. When marketing a conventional book, publishers "fish" for customers by sending every potential teacher a free copy, followed up by a visit from a sales representative. In addition to the book there is a litany of "supplements": instructor guides, overheads, test banks, study guides, software, perhaps even Internet support. These supplements cost money and these costs get built into the price of the book. The bottom line is students pay over $100 for a typical textbook. So the second reason for writing and publishing an electronic book was to produce a basic book with a low price.

Unfortunately there turned out to be a major drawback to an electronic book. The Napster generation just stole it. One student would buy a copy and then just email it to all his or her friends. Others would post the book on pirate websites. In the end, the costs of trying to protect the copyrighted material exceeded revenues.

But all is not lost. Pearson understood what I was trying to do with my book and has arranged to publish the original book through its courseware division. By using this unconventional method of deliverying the book, editorial control remains with the author. In addition, the lower printing costs, and absence of supplements means that the book is still one of the lowest cost books on the market.

So much for history. What actually makes this book different from other introductory principle texts?

- First, the book is relatively short. I focus on the essential ideas in microeconomics. The book is not encyclopedic, and hopefully it doesn't read like a dictionary either.

- Second, the book is quite visual. To aid instructors and students the most important ideas are boxed. There are lots of graphs and tables.

- Third, the book is full of interesting examples, applications, and even jokes. I've avoided examples about widgets or gadgets, and most examples are real and (at least I think) interesting.

  One of the (few) advantages of growing older is having the luxury of time to go back and read the masters of economics. I found this quote from the preface of John Stuart Mill's first edition (1848) of his Principles book most interesting. In commenting on Adam Smith's *Wealth of Nations* he states:

  > The most characteristic quality of that work, and the one in which it most differs from some others which have equaled or even surpassed it as mere expositions of the general principles of the subject, is that it invariably associates the principles with their applications. This of itself implies a much wider range of ideas and of topics than are included in Political Economy, considered as a branch of abstract speculation. ... Except on matters of mere detail, there are perhaps no practical questions, even among those which approach nearest to the character of purely economical questions, which admit of being decided on economical premises alone. And it is because Adam Smith never loses sight of this truth; because, in his applications of Political Economy, he perpetually appeals to other and often far larger considerations than pure Political Economy affords — that he gives that well-grounded feeling of command over the principles of the subject for purposes of practice, owing to which the Wealth of Nations, alone among treatises on Political Economy has not only been popular with general readers, but has impressed itself strongly on the minds of men of the world and of legislators.

  I don't think this sentiment is any less true today.

- Fourth, the questions at the end of each chapter are a rich source of learning. I've avoided questions like "repeat what is on page 45," and have included questions that make students think. Each chapter has review questions (with answers), which students should be able to do on their own. Each chapter also has a large set of problems (with the odd-numbered ones answered). These questions are harder, and designed for groups to discuss and practice on.

- Fifth, the overriding emphasis is on *explanation*. There is the odd discussion of policy implications, but I've kept them to a minimum. This might offend some economists, but I believe the most important aspect of a principles course is to teach students how to think like an economist, and this begins with explaining behavior.

- Sixth, the book has not been edited for political correctness. I don't go out of my way to make gratuitous offenses, but I have no idea if the number of female names equals the number of male names, or if I've used enough examples outside my own personal culture ... I probably haven't. I've simply written a text to interest the reader, convince them economics is useful, and perhaps whet their intellectual appetite.

- Seventh, an entire part of the book is devoted to transaction cost economics. I believe the principles of economics apply not only to the volume and terms of trade, but also to how that trade is organized.

- Finally, this book is about economic principles, not mathematical details. There are several appendices to help those who want to learn more about the mechanics of the model. However, the entire book can be read (and understood) without reference to them. Years ago, after teaching a first year class production possibility curves, budget constraints, indifference curves, and demand curves, I came to realize that 90% of the students in the class only saw four downward sloping lines. They didn't have enough economic background to appreciate the difference between the curves. Since then I've found a focus on the key important ideas leads to much better prepared students for intermediate theory.

Over the years a few people have been very helpful to me in developing this book. I'd like to thank Suki Badh, Bogdan Buduru, Les Marshall, and Bill Sjostrom for their assistance and encouragement.

TABLE OF CONTENTS

Page

CHAPTER 1

INTRODUCTION

Let me tell you a story about Arthur Wellesley, the first Duke of Wellington. Everyone knows he led the British Army in their combined attack against Napoleon in the 1815 battle of Waterloo. However, did you know Wellesley had no formal military training? In fact, he didn't even want to be a soldier, he wanted to be a politician. Wellesley was the fourth son of a moderately wealthy family. Most of the family resources were devoted to one of his older brothers who was groomed from birth to be Prime Minister, and so one family problem was: what to do with Arthur? The solution was found in 1787 when the family purchased an ensign commission for him in the army. Today one joins the military voluntarily and receives a wage. The Wellesley family actually *paid* to have their son become a junior officer. However, Arthur never showed up for work. Not discouraged, the family bought him better and better commissions, so that by 1794 he'd moved up seven ranks to the position of colonel in charge of his own regiment. To that point he'd seen no military action and had received no military training. Unfortunately for Arthur, as colonel he had no choice but to assume responsibility and report for duty. His first attempts at leadership were against Napoleon in the low countries where he was quickly and soundly thrashed, but managed to find his way home. Later he was assigned to the Spanish peninsula to again fight Napoleon. This time his ability to form alliances and an innate sense of logistics eventually allowed him to oust the French Emperor. Of course, the story ends happily with the ultimate victory at Waterloo, the peerage, the prime-ministership, and all the fame and wealth that went with it.

What's so striking about this story is that someone would pay to be a soldier. What's even more striking is that virtually all of the officers in the British Army (and the other armies of Europe) purchased their commissions. Any Tom, Dick, or Arthur who wanted to lead an army only needed a few thousand pounds, and away they could go. What a strange institution. Strange as well, was that in the navies of Europe, one *never* purchased an officer's commission. There, a complicated set of patronage appointments were made, so that someone like Horatio Nelson could rise to the rank of admiral so quickly he never learned to sail very well. *Why do you think commissions were sold in the army but not in the navy?*

Sticking with the nautical theme, let me tell you another story. Admiral Sir Clodisley Shovell was leading five ships home from victory over the French near Gibraltar in 1707, when he encountered severe fog. Consulting his officers, he determined they were safely in open sea. However, on board was an ordinary seaman who had been keeping a record of the ship's position. Out of concern for his own safety, the seaman approached the Admiral to warn him of the shore close by. Admiral Shovell had the man hanged on the spot! Several hours later, four of the five ships ran into the Scilly Isles off the tip of England and 2000 troops (including the Admiral) were lost. *A tragic story, but why do you think they hung the poor sailor who was trying to save the ship?*

The problem for Admiral Shovell, and for any other sailor prior to the nineteenth century, was he couldn't tell where he was. Ever since the ancient Greeks, men at sea were able to tell what their latitude was by the position of the sun. But even by the time of Admiral Shovell they still had no way of knowing their longitude. The problem of longitude was perhaps the greatest scientific puzzle of the eighteenth century. Many of the greatest minds worried about it and tried to solve it. In fact, in 1714 the British Parliament set a prize of £20,000, a King's ransom, for anyone who could find a reliable method to determine the position of a ship at sea. The solution fell to a humble clock maker

John Harrison, who devoted his life to building four separate frictionless clocks, the last of which eventually became known as the Chronometer. The chronometer is a very precise clock, and works to determine longitude because once one knows the exact time at home and the exact time at sea, it is easy to figure out how far away home is. John Harrison's solution was so unusual, so bold, so ... unscientific that it took him over forty years to claim his prize. But there is no denying the fact he wouldn't have even tried to invent anything without the prize incentive. *Why did the king offer a prize? Why didn't he set up a university and pay people to invent a Chronometer?*

Maybe you don't like history or the military, and we've already gotten off to a bad start. Let me tell you a different story. LoJack is an anti-theft device used to recover stolen cars. It is a small box that sends out a radio signal so the police can track the vehicle if stolen. The manufacturer hides the box somewhere on the car, so a car theif can't find it and disable the thing. It sounds like such a great idea. If Nissan put it on every one of their cars, no one would steal a Nissan, they'd steal other cars. But this would force all car companies to put the device on, and car theft would be over! But manufacturers seem reluctant to do so. *Why do car manufacturers make sure every car has a radio, but they don't install a device that stops autotheft?*

One last little puzzle for you, if you can stand it. The birth control pill was, perhaps, one

women could engage in sexual behavior *and* control pregnancy. Not surprisingly, in North America during the 1970s there was massive adoption of "the pill" and it quickly became the first choice form of birth control. At the same time, the number of children born out of wedlock also started to rise to levels never seen before. *Could there be any relationship between the invention of a simple pill to prevent pregnancies, and a rise in pregnancies among women who were not married?*

Now here are two personal questions: *Do you find any of these questions interesting? Do you think of any of them as economic?* If you think these questions are interesting, then you're probably going to find this book interesting. If you think these questions are obviously economic, then you're probably too smart for this book and you should be reading something more advanced. If you like these types of questions, but can't understand how they relate to "Economics" then you're the person this book is aimed at.

1.1 What is Economics?

Everyone seems to have an incorrect notion of what an economist is. To test this hypothesis go ask a grocer, a barber, or your mother what an economist does. They'll probably tell you "an economist figures out what the interest rate should be"; or "an economist studies the business community." If you talk to my wife she'll tell you they're people who talk about money, but never have any. Most people know more jokes about economists than they know about lawyers. The general inability of the man on the street understanding what economics is, probably results from the few interactions people have with economists. For most folks, their understanding about economics comes from either the business page of the newspaper or from watching "economists" talk about the stock market on TV programs. From these sources we conclude i) economists have an answer for everything; ii) they only worry about financial markets, GNP, interest rates, inflation, and government debt; iii) economics involves a lot of facts that are hard to remember ... but probably easy to look up; and iv) economics is pretty darn boring!

Amazingly, economics isn't any of those things just mentioned. What is economics? Here it is:

> *Economics is a particular way of thinking about behavior.*

Notice I didn't say it was a way of thinking about "market" behavior, or "rational" behavior — economics is about any type of behavior, and it applies to *every* aspect of our life. Economics addresses issues like: why did the divorce rate increase so much in the 1970s and 80s? Why do firms use coupons, rather than just lower their prices and save printing costs? Why do we think only-children (those without siblings) are more "spoiled" than children with lots of siblings? Why can't parents sell their children? Why can't anyone sell their kidney or their driver's license? Why does Canada import oil and produce oil at the same time? Why are auto parts the largest export from Canada to the U.S. and yet also the largest import? Why is the optimal amount of pollution not zero? Why do people make investments (like planting an oak forest) that might take over 100 years to mature, when they only live to 70 or 80 years old? Why would some firms be non-profit and how do they stay in business when they compete against for profit firms? Why were some people in the 1800s allowed to duel with pistols while others would be charged with murder for the same activity? Why is wine so expensive at a restaurant? Why do women still, after so many years of feminism, earn less on average than men? Why were the American and Canadian frontiers settled with homesteads rather than land sales?

Some of these questions may appear more economic than others, but that's just because you're biased in your thinking. Like most people, you probably think economics is only about the business section of the newspaper when, in fact, it covers the entire thing. The great thing about economics is that once you learn the "model" you can answer all of the questions above, and hundreds more that are thrown at you. Economics is like having a general thinking tool box at your disposal. Ready for any problem that comes along.

1.2 The Economic Way of Thinking

If economics is a way of thinking about behavior, what is the nature of the economic way of thinking? A key feature of economic thinking is its formality; that is, economic thinking is constrained by a number of *explicit* assumptions that have come to be known as *economic principles.* These economic principles force us to see and interpret the world a certain way. Just like the case of the wife, who was married to a man who thought he was dead. The wife took the man to doctor after doctor, but no one could convince the man he was alive. Finally, one doctor asked the man: "does a dead man bleed?" "No" was the reply. Upon hearing this the doctor took his scalpel and cut the man's finger, which of course, started to bleed a great deal. "What do you know," cried the man "dead men do bleed!"

The dead man had a theory about himself: he thought he was dead. This theory influenced how he interpreted the events around him. Likewise, in economics, our model based on economic principles influences how we see the world. Many people think this, in and of itself, makes economics special, but in fact, it really just makes it a religion ... like all of the other sciences. That might sound like a ridiculous thing to say, so let me defend it a bit.

This book is about the set of assumptions called economic principles. Many of these assumptions are not observable or testable in any meaningful way, and ultimately economists accept them by faith (some economists don't really believe them, and you have to wonder why they ever became economists!). These principles, when put together, form a basic *economic model*, which in turn is what economists use to analyze everything from why vegetables are cheap in the summer, to why mules were used in southern U.S. agriculture but not in the north. Economists believe this model, ... they have faith in it. This is what I mean by "economics is a religion." If this were a book on sociology, biology, or any other subject, it would simply be about a different set of beliefs.[1] Again, this isn't the least bit unusual, because ...

> *Everyone uses "models" to function in life.*

It is important to realize everyone operates with some type of "model" in mind. It's like the three scientists (a physicist, biologist, and mathematician) who were watching a building when two people went in and three came out. "We must have made a measurement error" said the physicist. "No" replied the biologist, "there must have been some reproduction." "Well I don't know what's

---

[1] In an email exchange on the SFU campus, a member of the faculty from the physics department stated the following:

> In every introductory level course I teach in physics or astronomy I inform my students, among other things, that I am an atheist. I feel that definition of my frame of reference is necessary because knowledge of that frame may usefully inform a student's understanding of some things I will have to say while teaching, since I have the idea of Natural Law in the sciences which makes me intolerant, for example, of claims for miraculous events. I tell my astronomy students that when I ask, for instance, for the age of the Earth, I will expect a number nearer to 4.5 billion years than to six thousand. I emphasize that they need not *believe* what they write on my examinations, but I really do expect the doctrinally correct answer to be given. They must be able to explain the bases in radioactive clocks for these claims in a coherent manner even though they do in reality buy the rantings of some "Creation Scientists" who can explain them away. Moreover I tell them that I will not waste class time (but that I am willing to waste some limited out of class time) debating relative merits of our two world views. I do all of these things without the qualification of having taken even a single course in comparative religion and without ever having been an adherent to a religion, let alone a theologian qualified to discuss the nuances of transubstantiation or the unity of the Trinity.

That's about as religious as a scientist can get. The passion and honesty varies from one academic to another, but we all believe that our particular paradigm is true ... otherwise, why would we devote our lives to it?

going on," said the mathematician, "but if one more person enters the building it will be empty." Everyone interprets the world around them through a set of beliefs, and these beliefs we call a "model."

It would be impossible to interact with other humans or nature without some model to guide us. We all have a pretty decent model of local moving bodies. So much so I venture we all can imagine what happens if you jump in front of a bus moving 50 miles per hour! When it comes to explaining the way people behave, there is no shortage of models either. The sociologist, psychologist, and other social scientists all have different models. Feminists, marxists, and other "ists" have different models. And, of course, Joe Blow down at the local diner probably has a pretty explicit model of behavior as well. If everyone thinks with various types of models in mind, then the question comes up: what model should we think with? Hopefully, after reading this book you'll agree the economic model, or way of thinking, is particularly useful.

The point of having a good model is it makes us better thinkers. Consider the following riddle: *A cow starts walking along a mountain path at 9AM one morning, and eventually makes its way to the top of the mountain by 6PM the same day. The exhausted cow lays down for the night, but starts out early the next morning at 8:30AM and is down at the bottom by 2:00PM. Is there a spot on the path where the cow was at the same time each day?*

Hmmmm. That seems difficult to think about, and your first reaction is probably only by *chance* would such an unlikely event occur. But let's use a simple model to figure this out. Consider the graph below in Figure 1-1.

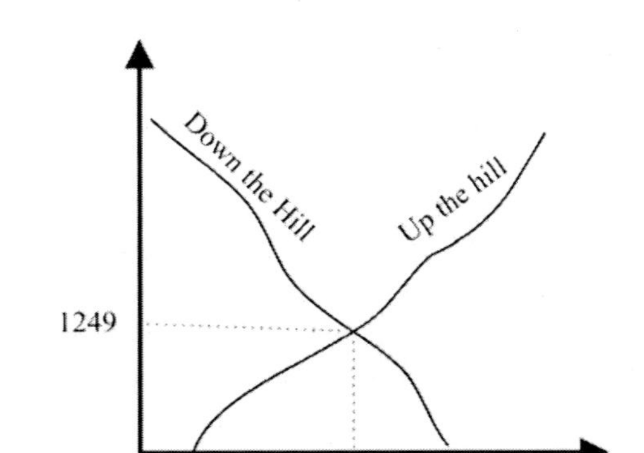

Figure 1-1
A Model of A Cow Going Up a Mountain

On the vertical axis is plotted the elevation of the mountain; on the horizontal axis is the time of day. The upward sloping line represents the trip on the first day, while the downward sloping line shows the trip on the second day. Clearly there is one spot where the two lines cross. This represents the same elevation and time for each day. Riddle solved!

However, the power of the model becomes clear when we extend it a little bit. What would happen if the cow didn't continuously go up the hill? Suppose the cow went up, then down, and then back up again? Would there still be a spot the cow was at the same time each day? Would there be more than one spot?

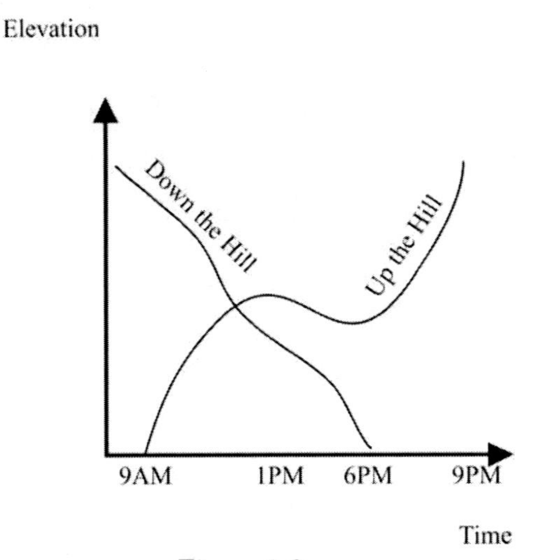

Figure 1-2
A Model of A Cow Going Up and Down and Up a Mountain

Figure 1-2 shows this simple change might make no difference to the answer. In Figure 1-2 there is still just one time of day when the cow is at the same elevation. However, if you can visualize it, it is also clear the upward sloping line *could* cross three times at most, meaning there could be three locations that satisfy the riddle. The point is, a simple little graph makes a seemingly intractable problem suddenly very easy to come to terms with.

The "cow on the mountain model" has a number of characteristics which make it attractive. The model is formal, testable, simple, and is consistent with the general facts of the world (that is, we didn't have the cow fly to the top!). In economics we'd like our model to be characterized by these features as well. These features are what make economics a ... science. Laying out our assumptions so they can be examined, creating models that can actually be tested and refuted, and coming up with theories which we believe are true, is all part of the scientific process. So sure, economics is a religion because we accept a lot of concepts on faith, but it is also scientific because we test our models and rely on logic to sift through the competing theories of explanation. Let's think a little more about these scientific characteristics.

1. Formality can be helpful.

A formal model is explicit about the assumptions it makes ... the model "lays all of its cards" on the table, so to speak. This doesn't mean the model is automatically great, or true, or useful. It just means we want to be honest about what we're assuming. By being honest with our assumptions, we'll have a better idea of where our model needs fixing when it fails to explain some behavior. There is a famous, in fact it is the most famous, joke about economists. The joke starts with three men stranded on an island with a can of beans and no can opener. The first man, a steel worker, proposes they open the can of beans with a rock. The second man, a physicist, suggests they magnify the sun's rays with his eye glasses until the can explodes. The third man, an economist, starts off his proposal by saying: "first, let's assume we have a can opener." Economists are constantly criticized for the assumptions they make, especially assumptions that seem unrealistic.[2] Everyone makes assumptions in life, just like the steel worker and the physicist, but like the economist on the island, we're going to be explicit about our assumptions.

2. Our model should be testable.

Aristotle had a beautiful model to explain the movement of planets: the earth was the center of the universe and all the heavenly bodies moved around the earth in perfect circles. It is a beautiful model, just as you can see in Figure 1-3.

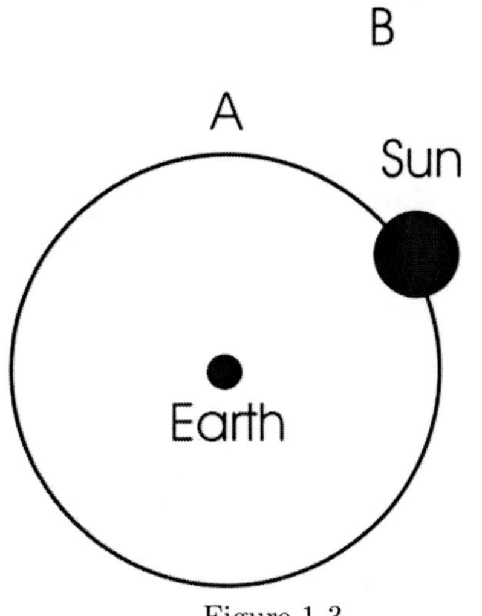

Figure 1-3
Aristotle's Model of Heavenly Bodies

There was just one little problem with this beautiful model, ... it was wrong! By wrong I mean it made predictions that didn't come to pass. Based on the model astronomers would predict the sun should be a point A in the sky, when it ended up at point B. What to do?

Having a model fail happens all the time because models are just simple representations of the world around us. Think about it. If a model was as complex as the world it was describing, it wouldn't be much use. Aristotle's model is extremely simple and was adequate for some purposes, but unfortunately it was false and of no use for navigation. But being false isn't such a bad thing. In fact, it is a good thing if you're interested in learning about something: a false model tells you what doesn't work. Knowing what doesn't work isn't the same as knowing the truth, but it's better than

---

[2] There is a long tradition in economics of defending unrealistic assumptions in economics. For example, it is true that unrealistic or even false assumptions can still lead to true conclusions. However, in this book I want to convince you most assumptions we'll make are true.

nothing. When a model is capable of being shown wrong, we say it is *testable.* Aristotle's model of the planets, though simple, was also testable.[3]

Having a testable model is one of our goals. Having a model fail, however, is a real bummer. Especially when you've spent half a lifetime investing in learning about the model. When models fail, the "scientist", "economist", or "Joe Blow down at the diner", is faced with a choice. They can either take the high road and reject the model, or they can take the low road and "insulate" their model from testing. Early astronomers insulated Aristotle's model by saying bodies like the sun moved in smaller epi-circles along the larger circular path. When this didn't work out, they simply added more epi-circles. You can see the result in Figure 1-4:

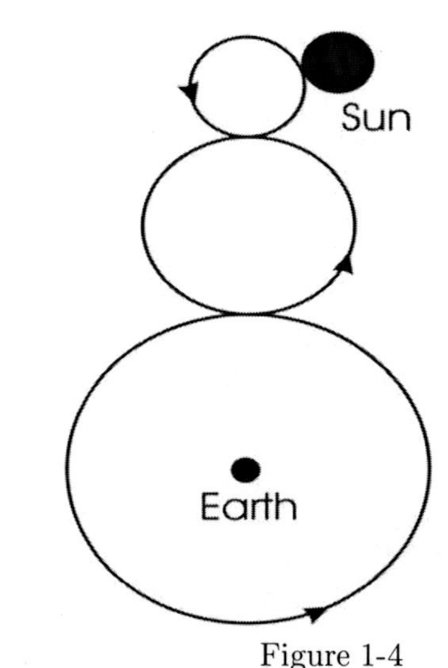

Figure 1-4
Aristotle's Untestable Model of Heavenly Bodies

No doubt this was known as the snowman theory of planetary motion. Though insulating a model from testing might comfort the model user, it ultimately is a useless exercise, and one that doesn't fool anyone in the long run. Perhaps you've heard the story of the college president who wants to improve the reputation of his school. He's told the best way to do this is to create a few elite departments. One advisor suggests it would be good to work on the mathematics department because it won't be too expensive, all they need is a pencil, some paper and a wastebasket. A second advisor suggests it would be even better to work on the economics department, since they don't even need wastebaskets!

---

[3] We don't want to get too involved in high foolutin' philosophy, but you probably know we can never tell if a model is True. To know if a model is actually true would require an infinite amount of knowledge which we will never have. A model can work and work and work, and though our confidence in it builds, the failure may just be around the corner. This is what is known as the "problem of induction".

A good model is one that potentially could end up in the wastebasket. It is ultimately of no use to say "it will either rain tomorrow or it won't". We want to shut this back door and have models make predictions that potentially could be wrong. These types of models are useful. Perhaps you'd like an actual economic example, rather than one from the Heavens. In a few chapters you are going to learn one of the most powerful ideas in all of social science. It is called the "law of demand." To put it crudely, this proposition will say that there is an inverse relationship between a good's price and the the quantity demanded by consumers. An *inverse* relationship. That means if we find a positive relationship the law of demand would be refuted. The law of demand is a testable model.

> *A testable model is a useful model.*

3. Simple Models are Better Than Complicated Models.

Other things being equal, we want a model to be simple and easy to use. The nice feature of the "cow on the mountain" model is it is so easy to think about and modify. The ugly feature of the "epi-circle" theory of planetary motion is it is so difficult to calculate where a planet should be. If we have two theories predict the same thing, but one is much more complicated than the other, then we want to pick the simpler one. Remember, a model is made for a purpose; we're ultimately trying to think systematically about social behavior. It's hard enough to do, so if we can do it with a simple model, then that's the road we want to take. Besides, if it isn't simple, how can we impress our boss at the annual Christmas party?

4. People are Fundamentally the Same

In 1776 modern economics got its start with the publication of Adam Smith's *The Wealth of Nations.* In it he stated:

> The difference of natural talents in different men is, in reality, much less than we are aware of; and the very different genius which appears to distinguish men of different professions, when grown up to maturity, is not upon many occasions so much the cause as the effect of the division of labour. The difference between the most dissimilar characters, between a philosopher and a common street porter, for example, seems to arise not so much from nature as from habit, custom, and education. When they came into the world, and for the first six or eight years of their existence, they were perhaps very much alike, and neither their parents nor playfellows could perceive any remarkable difference. About that age, or soon after, they come to be employed in very different occupations. The difference of talents comes then to be taken notice of, and widens by degrees, till at last the vanity of the philosopher is willing to acknowledge scarce any resemblance.
>
> [Book 1 Chapter 2]

Since that time economic models have been characterized by a particular view of mankind: *human beings are fundamentally the same across time and space.* This doesn't mean everyone is exactly the same. Rather it means our motives and natures are the same. More specifically, we're characterized by the economic principles we will be elaborating throughout this book. Hence, when an economist comes across a fact like the British use cloth napkins at dinner time, while most North Americans use paper napkins, he does not say "well, the British are just different than the North Americans. They're 'uppity', they like cloth, and they aren't smart enough to know the advantages of paper." Rather, the economist naturally thinks that since people in Britain and North America are fundamentally the same, it must be something in their local circumstances that manifests in the different choices over mouth wiping material.

John Stuart Mill, another early economist put it this way:

> Of all vulgar modes of escaping from the consideration of the effect of social and moral influences on the human mind, the most vulgar is that of attributing the diversities of conduct and character to inherent natural differences.
>
> [Book 2, Chapter 9]

Economists don't think the Swiss are genetically great watch makers, the German's born great engineers, or the Japanese naturally industrious. Rather, the economist views all people as having similar natures that obey certain economic principles. When people are placed in different situations with different opportunities, then they behave differently.

This basic assumption often puts economists at odds with certain groups of people, and in bed with others. In recent times feminists and aboriginals often have a hard time with economic principles because of the reluctance of economists to assume men and women or natives and non-natives are fundamentally different in terms of their preferences and what motivates them. On the other hand, in the 19th century Evangelical Christians formed a coalition with economists (like J.S. Mill) because they also believed all individuals are similar in nature. This latter partnership, in fact, gave economics the name of the *dismal science.*[4]

The story is quite interesting. Most people think the phrase "dismal science" comes from the common perception of Malthus. Thomas Malthus was a 19th century economist who believed population growth would outstrip the production of food, and as a result famine would eventually reign — dismal indeed. As it turns out, the phrase dismal science comes from a description of economics by Thomas Carlyle, a 19th century essayist. Carlyle was upset with economists like John Stuart Mill who, though not a Christian, had aligned himself with them in the anti-slavery movement. Carlyle, felt blacks were equivalent to cattle and therefore felt slavery was justified. Carlyle made the "dismal science" statement in an 1849 essay called "An Occasional Discourse on the Negro Question." In it he states:

> Truly, my philanthropic friends, Exeter Hall Philanthropy is wonderful; and the Social Science — not a "gay science," but a rueful — which finds the secret of this universe in "supply-and-demand," and reduces the duty of human

---

[4] The history of the phrase dismal science, along with the connection with the anti-slavery movement is found in David M. Levy, *How the Dismal Science Got Its Name: Classical Economics & the Ur-Text of Racial Politics*, University of Michigan Press, Fall 2001.

> governors to that of letting men alone, is also wonderful. Not a "gay science," I should say, like some we have heard of; no, a dreary, desolate, and indeed quite abject and distressing one; what we might call, by way of eminence, *the dismal science.* These two, Exeter Hall Philanthropy and the Dismal Science, led by any sacred cause of Black Emancipation, or the like, to fall in love and make a wedding of it, — will give birth to progenies and prodigies; dark extensive moon-calves, unnameable abortions, wide-coiled monstrosities, such as the world has not seen hitherto! [emphasis added]

Exeter Hall was the center of the Christian anti-slave movement. Carlyle was complaining that economists, with their notions of similarity of men, were in tow with the Christians who opposed slavery. And he was right, they were a coalition. The economists, as we will see, viewed all people as greedy. The Christians viewed all people as sinners. Either way, they both treated all people as fundamentally the same.

Today, issues of explicit slavery are no longer an issue. But the issue of treating all people the same still is. When faced with observations of different behavior — either across time, across space, or across cultures — we do not want our arguments based on assumptions that people are different in fundamental ways. We're all human, and as humans we are all characterized by certain traits.

1.3 Economic Principles

So what is the *economic* model? What are these assumptions I've been alluding to? At this point all I'll do is list some of them — I'm not even going to spell them out. As you read through the book, refer back to Table 1-1 and see if it starts to make more sense.

ASSUMPTIONS	CONSTRAINTS		
Maximization	Prices		
Substitution	Income		
Demand	Customs	$\Longrightarrow$	Predictions
Cost	Laws		
Etc.	Etc.		

Table 1-1
The Economic Model

In the left hand column we have our assumptions, which from now on we're going to call *economic principles.* These are a collection of ideas that ultimately we'll accept on faith as true. Over the course of the book I'll try to convince you they are true by appealing to your own experiences, evidence others have gathered, and any other rhetorical tool I can muster, but eventually you'll have to accept or reject them on your own ... there is no absolute measure of their truthfulness. In the middle column are listed a number of "constraints". These facts of life are generally observable, and include such things as prices, incomes, laws, peer pressure, and the like. Constraints interact with our principles and together they produce a prediction which we hope explains something we're interested in.

You might be starting to think that economics is rather mechanical. Sure, you have to accept some fundamental principles on faith, but after that you just build a model and away you go. Quite often engineering and other physical science students struggle with economics, and they are puzzled because they realize that on the surface economic models are quite simple mechanically. "Surely if I can do differential equations in a dynamic setting, I can breeze through an economics course" they think. Their error, however, is to ignore the last aspect of economic thinking. Economics is part religion. Economics is part science. But economics is also part art. It takes talent and intuition to play with the ideas we call economic principles. Each idea by itself is quite simple, but they fit together in many different ways. Like a piano with 88 simple keys, an economic argument in the hands of a master makes beautiful music. Many of the questions at the back of each chapter are designed to develop economic intuition. In the words of Dr. Evil of Austin Power fame, "stroke them, pet them, but do not eat them mini-me." Think about these questions, discuss them with other students, roll them over in your mind. In doing that, you will not only learn what the economic principles are, you'll learn how to use them and how to think ... about almost anything!

1.4 The Roadmap

This book is organized in three parts. Part I goes through each one of the economic principles, the basic budget constraint, production, exchange, and equilibrium. Together these concepts make up the basic *neoclassical model* of economics. This model is the basic tool used by every economist to understand the volume of trade and the terms or prices trade takes place at. It is basic, but don't be fooled, it is very powerful. Part II examines some standard complications to the basic model. It looks at choice over time, labor markets, non-competitive markets, and competition policy. Finally, Part III introduces a different type of question: how does trade get organized? This last question introduces us to the concept of transaction costs, and completes the introduction to economic principles. There is an appendix to this chapter to help you out on some of the arithmatic of the book. Glance at it now just to see some of the issues covered. When you come to the topics later in the book, you can come back to the appendix if you need some help.

REVIEW QUESTIONS

1. A traditional definition of economics is "The study of the allocation of scarce resources among competing means." How does this relate to the definition provided in this chapter?

2. What is the difference between a "model" and a "theory"?

3. Is there anything unscientific about making assumptions and assuming they are true?

4. What does it mean to say a theory is "falsifiable," "testable," "operational"?

5. In the chapter it was argued that people are assumed to be fundamentally the same. How can economists hold to such a notion when people are so different? That is, some are short, others tall. Some people are women, others are men. In what dimensions do we assume people are the same?

6. Why do you think Admiral Shovell had the sailor hung for keeping track of his position?

7. As you begin to learn how to think like an economist, it is important to keep in mind how different this approach is to other fields in social science. Roger Schank, a psychologist and computer scientist, stated the following regarding choices.

   > I do not believe that people are capable of rational thought when it comes to making decisions in their own lives. People believe they are behaving rationally and have thought things out, of course, but when major decisions are made — who to marry, where to live, what career to pursue, what college to attend, people's minds simply cannot cope with the complexity. When they try to rationally analyze potential options, their unconscious, emotional thoughts take over and make the choice for them.

   What does the economist mean by "rational"? How do you think economists deal with "unconscious, emotional thoughts"?

8. It has been suggested that one way to reduce traffic congestion in Vancouver would be to allow people to drive into the city on odd numbered days if they have an odd numbered license plate, and allow people to drive into Vancouver on even numbered days if they have an even numbered license plate. For example, if your license plate was ECO 103, you could drive into Vancouver on March 1, 3, 5, etc. If you were a commuter into Vancouver, what might you do to avoid the restriction?

Review Question Answers

1. *The definition given in this chapter is much more general, but entirely consistent with this more traditional definition. Almost all human behavior is about "allocating" something. When you decide what to purchase at a store you're allocating your income (which is scarce) across a set of goods. When you play football, you're allocating time (which is scarce) to that sport instead of some other activity. We'll see in the next chapter that scarcity and competition are implications of our first economic principle: maximization.*

2. *Generally speaking, we think of a theory as "couched" within a model. We have a theory of gravity, but in order to test it we need to build a model. The model may be physical or theoretical, but the model contains a number of assumptions which must be satisfied for a proper test of the theory. For example, in a few chapters we'll have introduced something called "the law of demand." We can think of that as a theory. But in order to test this theory we'll need to know what prices and income are. We'll have to understand the context in which it is being applied. All of these extra things are part of the model. This is, in part, what makes testing theories so difficult. When a test fails, did it fail because the model wasn't right (e.g., we assumed income was 100k, when in fact it was actually 50k) or was the theory itself flawed. In this book we will be fairly loose with the distinction between model and theory.*

3. *Not at all. In fact, every body of knowledge necessarily rests on a set of assumptions.*

4. *All of these things refer to a situation where the model could be wrong. If we have a theory that predicts it may or may not snow tomorrow, then that theory is true by definition. It is a tautology. Such a theory is not testable, operational, or falsifiable.*

5. *The economist means that everyone is the same in terms of the principles of behavior. For example, in the next chapter we will assume that everyone is greedy. The economist assumes everyone is that way, regardless of their skin color, religion, sex, location, or age. The economist does not assume that everyone faces the same constraints in life, or that people are identical in every respect.*

6. *In the age of sail, when death at sea was common, food was poor, and living conditions left something to be desired, mutiny was an ever present reality. One of the key methods of preventing mutiny, was to have only those in command aware of the tools of navigation. If the ordinary seamen could determine where they were, then they could find safe refuge. By keeping the seamen ignorant of location, the navies of the world raised the cost of mutiny.*

7. *By "rational" the economist only means people make consistent choices. This means economists believe people have preferences. They believe people can rank bundles of goods. That is, I can tell you if I like a movie and popcorn more or less than a Starbucks coffee or a Tim Hortons donut. Economists don't have anything to say about "unconscious, emotional thoughts." They play no role in an economic model.*

8. *This policy was tried in Mexico City. After a couple of years it was discovered that people increased the number of vehicles they owned. Instead of owning a $40,000 car, a commuter would own two $20,000 cars, and would make sure one had an even plate and the other had an odd plate. Perhaps you came up with other methods to avoid the restriction. The more you came up with, the more likely you're a natural born economist!*

PART I
EXCHANGE AND PRODUCTION

Part I of this book analyzes some very famous problems in economics. First, we'll be interested in *trade.* We want to know why people trade, how much they trade, and what determines the terms of that trade. Second, we'll be interested in *production.* We'll look at costs and output, and we'll see what the conditions are for the optimal level of output. Finally, we'll put these ideas together and discuss competitive markets. Once we've built our basic model we'll analyze market behavior (like taxes or quotas) and non-market behavior (like home heating or bargaining). The material covered in Part I entails the fundamentals of the economist's bag of tools.

CHAPTER 2

MAXIMIZATION

What motivates people? What makes us do the things we do? Is it some type of emotion like love or hatred, some sense of higher calling like altruism or religious faith, or are we hard wired in some instinctive way? For an economist there is only one source of motivation: greed. Adam Smith, in the *Wealth of Nations* put it most famously in the following words:

> But man has almost constant occasion for the help of his brethren, and it is in vain for him to expect it from their benevolence only. He will be more likely to prevail if he can interest their self-love in his favour, and show them that it is for their own advantage to do for him what he requires of them. Whoever offers to another a bargain of any kind, proposes to do this. Give me that which I want, and you shall have this which you want, is the meaning of every such offer; and it is in this manner that we obtain from one another the far greater part of those good offices which we stand in need of. It is not from the benevolence of the butcher, the brewer, or the baker that we expect our dinner, but from their regard to their own interest. We address ourselves, not to their humanity but to their self-love, and never talk to them of our own necessities but of their advantages.
>
> [Book 1, Chapter 1]

Today economists call this "self-love" maximization, but that's almost a marketing strategy to tone things down a bit. The bottom line is that economists view all behavior as effort to improve one's "situation" or "well being". Economists have a word to describe this well being: *utility.* Individuals get utility from things they value, whether friends, food, or fun. When economists say that people are maximizers (greedy) they mean people try to get as much utility as possible.

PRINCIPLE #1

Maximization: *All individuals are always motivated by greed.*

What a depressing way to start a theory of human behavior. In fact, if you meet anyone who rejects the economic way of thinking, 9 times out of 10 they reject it because they simply can't accept this as a universal motivation. It's either the greed aspect of maximization they don't like, or its the "all" and "always" parts. It's bad enough that economists think people are greedy, but why must it be so ubiquitous? Even a lot of economists tone things down a bit and often say that people are "self-interested" not greedy. By self-interest some economists simply mean greed, which means at best its a politically correct distinction without a difference. Others think of self-interest as including actions like altruism, which means it includes literally everything and so at worst "self-interest" is a subtle way of opening up the back door of non-testability. We're going to be honest and upfront and call maximization for what it really is: greed. Don't despair, though, economics is about *explaining* behavior, not condoning actions or suggesting hedonistic lifestyles. Keep in mind that what we're after is a model that's good at helping us understand the world around us, and if that means starting with a "darker" motivation, so be it.

Let's start thinking about maximization by considering what it is not. Maximization doesn't mean that people are always smart or correct. Thomas Watson, chairman of IBM in 1943 was a great business man, worried about maximizing the profit of his fledgling computer company all the time, but he also said "I think there is a world market for maybe five computers." Bill Gates, now one of the richest men in the world, no doubt still remembers his 1981 remark that "640K ought to be enough [memory] for anybody." And H. M. Warner, part owner of Warner Brothers and no stranger to making money, once quipped in 1927 "who the hell wants to hear actors talk?" Individuals are greedy, and though that greed might drive them to learn, experiment, and think about an issue, there's no guarantee they'll be right. Smart and dumb people are greedy. Quite often, as students go on in economics and come face to face with some tough mathematical maximization problem, they come to believe that only smart people can solve such problems. It just ain't so.

Greed also doesn't mean that "more is always preferred to less". To say that people always want more of some good is to say that they are never satisfied ... they're nonsatiated. Quite often economists make this assumption just to make their technical models work better, but it isn't a necessary tool in our tool box, and certainly shouldn't be confused with maximization. You can probably think of lots of things that you don't want more of, but that doesn't mean you're not selfish.

Greed is the bedrock assumption for economists. It's what makes an argument "economic" and what makes economists so unpopular with others at a cocktail party. For an economist there is no other motivation for individual behavior. For example, a non-economic argument could be one based on *altruism.* Altruism, practically by definition, is non greedy behavior. When the general public observes Mother Teresa spending her life working with orphans and lepers they see a woman behaving altruistically, someone who unselfishly gives of herself to others. The economist is more skeptical. They see someone doing the best they can under a given set of circumstances, and someone who achieved a great deal of fame in the process (not to mention the Nobel money). Arguing over whether Mother Teresa was an altruist or not is ultimately futile since any given behavior is consistent with greed or altruism; that is, in and of themselves, both motivations are unobservable. For example, when someone walks to the middle of a high bridge and jumps off, were they maximizing? Anyone can say "yes, the gains to jumping were greater than the costs." And when someone helps another, it is easy to offer an explanation that somehow the return to helping is greater than the cost.[1] Still, this is the first economic principle, so if it is directly unobservable, why would economists want it?

Maximization is held so strongly by economists because it has several implications that are so strongly observed in the world around us. These include scarcity, exchange, and equilibrium. All of these concepts will be developed in this book, but they merit some introduction now.

---

[1] In biology, the theory of evolution is based on maximization. Biologists have no problem coming up with maximizing explanations for all types of apparently "altruistic" behavior shown by one species to another.

2.1 Scarcity

People confuse scarcity with rarity all of the time. When something is rare, it simply means that it is in short supply — there isn't much of it around. Lots of things are rare: sunshine in November in Vancouver or Dublin is rare; the anthrax virus is rare; multiple murders by strangers with hockey sticks are very rare. To be scarce means more than to be rare. To be scarce means that more people want a good than is available, when the good is free.[2] When a good is scarce it might also be rare, but it doesn't have to be. If you live in Seattle, Washington, tickets to the Washington Huskies football games are scarce, but they aren't that rare (the stadium holds almost 80,000 people). If you live in Manchester, England, the same could be said about Manchester United soccer matches (Old Trafford stadium seats about 76,000 people). Likewise, just because something is rare, doesn't mean that it is scarce. The anthrax virus is rare, but since no one wants it, it is not scarce.

> *Scarcity exists when the price of a good is zero and people want more than is available.*

Scarcity is a result of greed. When everyone is greedy — always striving to improve their utility — and when the world is a place of relatively fixed endowments where goods are produced by the sweat of the brow, scarcity is just a fact of life. If people were just content with what they had, or if the disaster in the garden of Eden had never happened, we wouldn't live in a world of scarcity ... there would be ample for everyone.

Scarcity has several implications that we're all familiar with. Since the world is full of scarcity, there just isn't enough of everything to go around, and what's more ... there never will be enough. This is the paradox of the western world. The west lives in a society with abundant riches. Our streets aren't paved with gold, but compared to many places on earth, Westerners are the kings and queens of consumers. And yet, are we more content than others? Hardly. Do we have "enough" yet? No. As a student, you've probably had a thought like "if I could just make $50,000 a year, I'd be laughing." Or maybe the number is $100,000, or perhaps even a million dollars. When I was a student, I remember $30,000 was a wage one could aspire to. Alas, it doesn't matter what the number is you pick, when you get there you only want a bigger number. And it doesn't stop with money. The kids never behave well enough, appreciate their parents enough, the wife is never (fill in the blank) enough. It's never enough. You know it, and that's maximization at work in your life.

One of the facts of life that results from scarcity is that we are faced with making choices. Since there is never enough of things we want, both as a society and individually, the only way we can get more of one thing is to give up something else. If I want more income to buy a new car, then I have to give up some of my spare time in order to work more. If the government of British Columbia decides to spend more money on health care, then it means less money is available for education and other government services. Milton Friedman made this fact famous when he said "there's no such thing as a free lunch", and he was right; it is unavoidable.

---

[2] We'll see later on that this means scarce goods always have a positive price.

2.2 Equilibrium

The most difficult implication to understand about maximization is equilibrium. By equilibrium economists mean a situation where no one wants to change their behavior. Consumers settle on a bundle of goods to buy, firms settle on prices to charge and quantities to produce, families settle on a specific number of children, etc. As we'll see in later chapters an equilibrium will always be reached when individuals and firms maximize. People finish trading and producing when all of the potential gains from doing so are exploited. To put it crudely, and to borrow a gambling metaphor, no money is left on the table when there's an equilibrium. The reason is quite simple: if people get together to increase wealth, and they don't fully exploit every opportunity to do so, then they haven't maximized.

One of the easiest examples to understand equilibrium is rush hour traffic. When someone leaves their office to head home in the evening, there are often several ways home. At the very least, if they are taking the freeway home, then there are several lanes on the freeway, all leading in the same direction. Which lane should be taken?

Well, in equilibrium, it doesn't matter which lane you take. When you enter the freeway, suppose the left lane is traveling faster. As a maximizer you'll want to get home as quickly as possible, just like everyone else, so you switch into the left lane. However, by switching you slow that lane down a little and increase the speed of the right lane. If there is still a difference in speed someone else will do the same thing and move into the left lane. Again the speed in the left lane slows a little and the right lane speeds up. The end result, the equilibrium, occurs when each lane is moving at the same speed. When all the lanes are moving at the same speed, there are no more gains from switching ("trading") lanes: all the gains from trading lanes have been exploited. As a result, when you enter the freeway, it doesn't matter which lane you take, they'll all get you home at the same time.

"The Margin"

Economists often analyze equilibrium with a concept called "the margin". In the above example an economist might say: "there's no marginal benefit to changing lanes in equilibrium." What this means is that the marginal or incremental lane changer is indifferent between changing lanes and staying put.

Indifference: *letting someone else choose for you.*

Someone who is indifferent between two options is neither better nor worse off with either option. There once was a lazy, but quick thinking, lad who was down on his luck. He decided to go to his rich uncle for a loan. "I don't give my money away" declared the rich uncle, "but I'll tell you what. I have a man come by and cut my grass for $20. I'll give you $25 for the same job." "Let the man keep the job," said the poor nephew, "but I'll take the $5." Now that's exploiting the concept of indifference.

Once we understand the marginal person in traffic, it makes sense to talk about the "intra-marginal person." This is the person for whom there is some gains from trading lanes. Suppose that everyone is in the right lane on the freeway heading home. The first person to switch to the left lane is certainly better off. So is the second, third, and forth driver. Perhaps the two lanes don't equalize in speed until the 3033rd driver moves over. The first 3032 drivers are "intra-marginal", while the 3033rd driver was the marginal one. For the marginal driver, the gains from moving over to the other lane just equal the costs. As a result that driver is *indifferent* between driving in either lane. We will see this concept over and over again.

Using Economics to Make Lots and Lots of Money

Unfortunately, the concept of equilibrium that results from maximization, has one nasty little implication. There is no way a student of economics can use an economic model to "save the world" or more hedonistically "make abnormal profits." Let's start with the concept of making a lot of money, piles of money, ... without working too hard for it. If you go to any party over the next couple of weeks and tell someone that you're taking an economics class, you'll almost be guaranteed to have someone ask: "what do you think will happen to the interest rate next week?" or "is now the time to get back into technology stocks?" The question might vary a little (what's a good mutual fund to invest in, what's going to happen to GNP or the inflation rate), but the drift will be the same. Everyone thinks that if we could just "understand" the economy we'd all be rich.

And why shouldn't people think this way, since everyday we're bombarded with pitchmen telling us that they're rich because they do understand how the world works. We turn on the TV and we see show after show with "professionals" telling us everything about the future, from politics to real estate prices. Whether it's Tommy Vu or Wall Street Week the story is the same. In fact, let's take two examples.

Figure 2-1 is the cover of a 69 page booklet that arrived in my mailbox . Inside you read about Ken Roberts, investor/author/publisher, who asks the question: "In the next 10 years: where are home prices headed? where are car prices headed? ... where are medical costs headed?" If we want, we "can learn how to make money no matter what is happening in the world." Inside are testimonials from "real people" about how they've managed to turn $400 into $4000 in just a few weeks, and how investing the Ken Roberts way has given financial freedom to so many. In fact, Jan R. of Arkansas writes: "...I never thought I would be close to [my father]. You have brought us together ... Thanks a million times over." A fortune, peace of mind, and even reconciliation, and all you have to do is pay $195 for the manual and course! Inside, Mr. Roberts gives a hint at some of the valuable lessons you'll learn. Page after page contains pictures of stock market price graphs with little arrows showing you where he bought and where he sold. It turns out, that in order to make money, all you have to do is buy low and sell high! Amazing, why didn't I think of that?

When faced with the likes of Mr. Robert's booklet, the skeptical economist asks: "why is Mr. Roberts willing to sell me such information for a mere $195?" Could it be that Mr. Roberts actually makes his money selling books rather than pick up easy money on Wall Street? The principle of maximization, with its implication of equilibrium tells us, of course you won't get rich with Mr. Roberts.

Its not just that there are no $500 bills lying around Wall Street, unfortunately, there aren't any easy grades lying around either. Figure 2-2 shows a leaflet that was distributed around campus

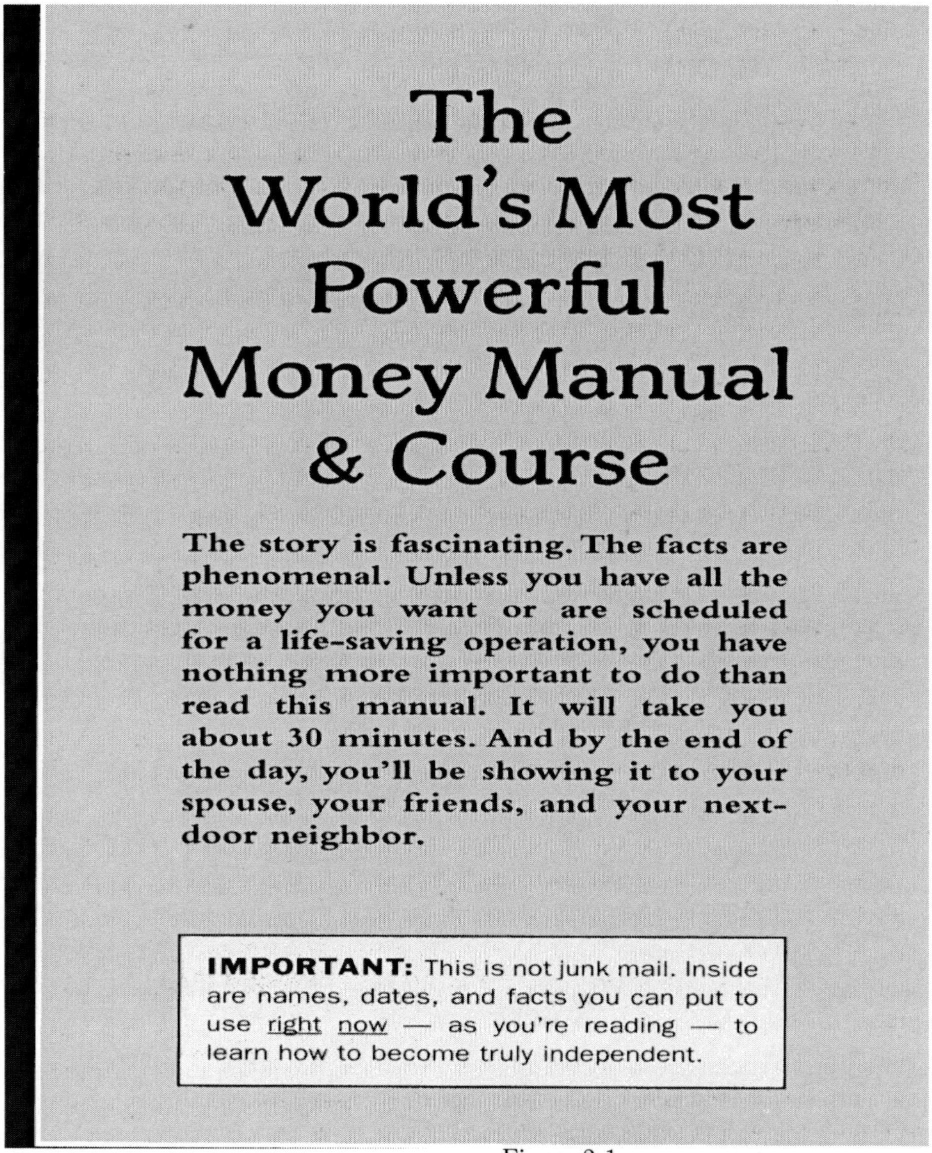

The World's Most Powerful Money Manual & Course

The story is fascinating. The facts are phenomenal. Unless you have all the money you want or are scheduled for a life-saving operation, you have nothing more important to do than read this manual. It will take you about 30 minutes. And by the end of the day, you'll be showing it to your spouse, your friends, and your next-door neighbor.

> **IMPORTANT:** This is not junk mail. Inside are names, dates, and facts you can put to use right now — as you're reading — to learn how to become truly independent.

Figure 2-1
Making Money Without Trying

a few years ago, stating something similar to Ken Robert's investment strategy. For a mere $25 a student can obtain an easy "A" (the equivalent of a first in Britain). Although I didn't purchase the Ken Robert manual, I did buy the cheating book by Michael Moore, ... just in case. As expected, it offered just enough information that the author couldn't be arrested. The first 39 pages claim that cheating is OK because: everyone does it; nobody finks; professors don't care; university is a rip off anyway; and you have to cheat in life, so you might as well practice now. The last half of the book is devoted to how to copy answers from the person beside you. It contains real gems like: sit by a friend, develop hand signals, and wear a hat. Like Mr. Roberts, there's no real secret here either.

To make "easy" money, obtain a "free" A grade, or get the girl/boyfriend of your dreams without trying is to earn an above normal rate of return, and in equilibrium, these do not exist. It would be like getting on the freeway tonight and being the only person in your city to notice that no one is in the left lane.

We must be skeptical of anyone suggesting they have a sure way of making money. The thing is, if anyone is in possession of such knowledge, why aren't they using it themselves? Why does Mr. Roberts let us in on his little investment secret for a mere $195? If his claims are true he could be infinitely wealthy by exploiting the knowledge himself. It just doesn't make any sense. When someone gives you advice about how to make money, that's probably what it is worth ... nothing. At the very least, you should check out their own asset position before you take any action.

Perhaps you're wise enough to know that forms in the mail announcing you've just won a million dollars if only you'll send $20 to claim your prize, are bogus. But are you wise enough to know that no one at your university can give you this type of information as well ... not even your local economics professor? If any economist knew the price of corn next week, he'd have a Faustian knowledge that would lead him to infinite riches, and he sure as shootin' wouldn't tell you.

Harold Demsetz, a great economist at UCLA, learned this lesson the hard way. In telling the story of how he left the University of Chicago for UCLA he states:

> The second reason for moving to UCLA was financial. I had joined a small group of business school colleagues in the purchase of long-term treasuries. We were speculating heavily, having put up only 5 percent of the price of the bonds. The rate of growth of the money supply had turned down. Being strong believers in monetary theory, we expected the economy and interest rates to turn down also. Interest rates did not fall immediately, or for a very long time after our purchase. I found myself sending margin to my broker as frequently as one feeds a pet dog. My proverbial "shirt" was lost. Reuben Kessel dryly observed that we still have a lot to learn about interest rates. Were Reuben still alive, he would be pleased to learn that my understanding of interest rates has improved considerable. Now, I lose a much smaller fraction of my wealth speculating on changes in these rates (which are sure to come).
>
> [p. 9, 1988][3]

---

3 Harold Demsetz, *Ownership, Control, and the Firm* (New York: Basil Blackwell, 1988).

Cheating 101:

AS SEEN ON TV

The benefits and fundamentals of earning the "Easy A."

Finally a helpful book for students has been written exploring the benefits and techniques for cheating. Learn the best and safest methods of ensuring good grades with the least amount of effort. This innovative work addresses cheating as a realistic issue on campus and helps students examine the best routes for academic short-cuts in classes that are anything but educa-'ional and important. Take charge of useless time wasted studying. Read how the best win in the classroom and conquer meaningless exams and term papers.

Order this unique book and start getting better marks immediately!

PROBLEM SOLUTION

This is the opportunity you have been looking for! Don't let it pass you by. Grab a pen now and order the book that is taking North American campuses by storm and start enjoying University.

O.K. This is what I have been looking for! Here is my $19.95 (please add $5.00 for taxes and postage). Pleas. rush me a copy of Cheating 101. Make check or Money Order payable to: CONCERNED MARKETING CO..ORATION.

NAME______

ADDRESS______

CITY______ PROV.____ Postal Code ______

Mail to:
CMC
P.O. Box #6004
6417 Fraser Postal O tlet
Vancouver, B.C.
V5W 4B5

Figure 2-2
Cheating 101

Perhaps I still haven't convinced you yet. Of course people like Mr. Roberts and Mr. Moore are not to be trusted, and Mr. Demsetz, well he's just one guy. If you want to make money you have to really know what you're talking about. If you still think like that, consider the case of Long Term Capital Management. This was a company started by Wall street insider John Meriwether, and two Nobel prize winning economists: Robert Merton and Myron Scholes. LTCM managed to get people to invest 4.8 billion dollars with them. They would use this money to buy up to 160 billion dollars worth of stocks and bonds, plus derivatives (fancy word for fancy financial contracts) worth 1 trillion dollars on paper. That's trillion, not billion. LTCM was the poster child for hedge fund companies in the mid 1990s. People were dumping money at the front door of headquarters just to get a piece of the action. And what was the action? LTCM was attempting to capitalize on tiny spreads in financial markets around the world. They were, according to one executive, "picking up nickels and dimes off the sidewalks."

LTCM might work as follows. Suppose there were two United States treasury bills, one that matures in 29 years another that matures in 30 years. Suppose also that a difference in yield exists between the two bonds, perhaps 50¢ . What LTCM did was bet that this difference would disappear, since the two bonds are essentially the same. They would bet by selling short on the low yielding bond and buying the high yielding one. On a 1 million dollar bet they would make $5000 ... hardly anything to write home about. But wait, with 4.8 billion in the bank, they took out loans in the form of margins. They would buy the 1 million worth of bonds with only $10,000 on margin. Now the $5000 is a 50% return.

Alas, it turned out there not only aren't $500 dollar bills on the sidewalk, there weren't any nickels and dimes either. Instead of converging, many of these spreads started to diverge. LTCM lost money, banks started to call the margins, and 4.8 billion quickly became 600 million. With almost 1 trillion in derivatives, the Federal Reserve Bank actually stepped in and bailed LTCM out. Even Nobel prize winners can lose money ... big time.

Using Economics to Save the World

Perhaps you're not interested in making money. Perhaps you're more idealistic and you want to save the world ... or at least work in the urban planning department of your local city. Can economics tell you what type of social programs are best for your area? Whether or not rent controls on apartments are a good thing or a bad thing? What the optimal rule for the Bank of Canada is for the money supply? Many economists would say "Yes!!". Alas, we cannot, at least not if we're going to stick with our principle of maximization.

When the economist assumes that everyone is always greedy then, as mentioned, all gains from trade are maximized. If they weren't then the individuals didn't maximize and something is seriously wrong with our logic. Our model will always be based on the idea that individuals have done the best they can. How then, can an economist come along and say that he knows a better way? It is impossible.[4]

Not that a little faulty logic has ever stopped economists from continually doing this. In fact,

---

[4] This seems to explain why business students generally hate economics. The business major rejects the notion of equilibrium. Every business major thinks they'll invent a great mouse trap, they never assume that the best trap is already invented.

the profession is littered with stories of policies gone wrong, with often tragic outcomes. There is an old joke of an engineer, a doctor, and an economist all arriving at the gates of Heaven only to find out that the one spot available is being allocated to the person with the oldest profession. "That's me!" says the doctor. "Eve was created from Adam through a surgical procedure." "Hold on," said the engineer. "God created the Heavens and Earth from chaos, and that was an engineering act, so I get to go in." "Not so fast," said the economist. "Where do you think the chaos came from?". Economists get the policy wrong all the time because their model is not designed to do policy implications. The economic model is designed to explain behavior, not tell people what to do. When people behave inconsistently with what an economic model says they should do, then it's time to scrap the model, not tell people to change their behavior!

2.3 Why Believe in Maximization?

If maximization can't make abnormal rates of return nor save the world, why keep the maximization assumption? On what grounds do economists hold such faith to it? The word "maximization" also makes it sound as if people are calculating machines, constantly assessing the costs and benefits of everything. Just by introspection we know that this doesn't seem right. When I got up this morning I poured myself a bowl of Raisin Bran, just like I do most mornings. I didn't think about it in any calculating way. I didn't try to maximize any function or perform a complicated optimization problem.

> *Economists believe in maximization because it works.*

The first reason why economists believe that individuals are motivated by greed is because it seems to generally explain so much behavior. For example, we've already seen that greed provides an explanation for scarcity. As we go through this book, we'll see that the principle of maximization helps us understand trade, pricing, and institutions. When something works, it's wise to pay attention to it.

Understanding the world around us isn't simply a matter of philosophical interest. Economists can make a pretty decent living as consultants because understanding markets is a valuable skill. Firms want to know what the characteristics of the demand for their products are. Governments want advice on the distributional effects of economic policies. And legal firms want economic advice in anti-trust law cases that involve complicated pricing practices. Thus, if the principle of maximization is the correct way to think about the world, we want to use it even if it doesn't save the world or produce abnormal rates of return.

> *Economists believe in maximization because it is the only type of behavior that survives.*

A more subtle grounds for accepting the principle of maximization is that if people did not maximize then they wouldn't survive. Greed has a survivability characteristic similar to the concept of natural selection. Most biologists believe that any animal that has a characteristic that allows it to out compete other animals will tend to survive and proliferate until eventually it is the only type of animal left. Likewise, individuals compete with other individuals, both at an individual and firm level. Those individuals that behave in a maximizing way survive and proliferate. Those that do not die out. In the end all we are left with are individuals who are maximizers.[5] Let's start with some silly examples and work up to some more serious ones.

Gary Larson retired years ago from producing his famous cartoon *The Far Side.* One of my favorite cartoons could have been called "How not to catch a saber toothed tiger." The cartoon showed the feet of two cavemen who were standing *inside* a large box trap. A box trap is a box tilted up at one end with a string tied to a rope. The one who sets the trap, waits in a bush, and when an animal comes along and enters the trap to eat a treat left there, the string is pulled and the box falls on the animal. In the cartoon, a saber tooth tiger is approaching the trap and the caption reads: "Shhh, Zog, I think I hear one coming!". The humor of the cartoon comes from the fact that Zog and his buddy are about to be eaten! This is non-maximizing behavior if ever there was any. Suppose that there was another pair who just happened to stand outside the trap when using it. They stood outside not because they thought about it, but just by some fluke they stood outside. That pair would end up surviving, and if they continued to stand outside the trap when using it, and why wouldn't they ... they aren't thinking about it, they would continue to survive and would show their children where to stand as well. Since only maximizing strategies survive, the only thing we observe is trappers standing outside their traps. The rest get eaten or starve to death, just like poor old Zog.

The point is, maximizing behavior survives whether you are aware of what you're doing or not. Lots of people are successful in life, even though they don't know why what they do is successful. Perhaps you recall seeing a movie called *Phar Lap.* It was the story of an unbeatable Australian horse, named Phar Lap appropriately enough, who was owned by a trainer with a strange view of how to train horses. This trainer thought that the best way to condition a horse was to work it to the point of death. If the horse stopped working, then he'd beat the crap out of it. As it turned out, when he owned Phar Lap he won every race, and he would brag to others about his superior methods of training. Once he sold Phar Lap, he went broke because all of his other horses died in the training program. The maximizing strategy of winning a horse race in Australia at the time was to own Phar Lap. The fact that the trainer didn't understand this didn't make him less successful. Just because you're rich and successful doesn't mean you're smart, it only means you're doing the maximizing strategy ... a fact of life poor faculty members remind themselves of every morning.

We should not reject the principle of maximization because in our hearts we don't think of ourselves as greedy, opportunistic, cold calculating machines. Nor should we reject it because no one in our lives admit to maximizing anything. We are the people who survived, and what we're doing is the maximizing strategy whether we know it or not. I can safely predict that everyone reading this book has eaten nutritious food over the past thirty days. I can predict this because only those who did so would be alive right now to read the book. Those who starved themselves, or those who started to consume gasoline instead of water, simply are not around. Likewise, when an economist looks at a firm, he is confident that the firm is maximizing its profit, whether the firm's owner is aware of it or not. Had the firm not maximized profits, it would have gone out of business ... driven out by other firms that were doing the maximizing strategy. Since maximization is the only strategy

---

[5] This argument was first articulated by Armen Alchian in "Uncertainty, Evolution, and Economic Theory" *Journal of Political Economy* (1950).

that survives, economists assume that all individuals are maximizers. It is a little like the first law of biology: If your parents didn't have any children, then you probably won't have any either.

What is being maximized

We've talked a great deal about the process of maximization and what it implies. But what are people maximizing? Economists use a funny word to capture the object of a consumer's maximization: utility. Every time you consume any bundle of goods, you get utility or satisfaction from that bundle. Consumers try to get as much utility as possible. When we discuss firms, the object of maximization is more observable: profit. profit is simply the difference between revenues and costs.

Consumers maximize utility, firms maximize profits.

2.4 The Panglossian Dilemma

Taking maximization seriously leads to a conclusion that many simply find unacceptable: everything must be optimal ... in its own way. When selfish individuals go about to produce and exchange in such a way that all gains from trade are maximized, then no better outcome is possible. If a better outcome was possible, then the individuals didn't maximize and we have a contradiction.

Have you ever complained about something? Perhaps you wish that there was a pizza restaurant closer to your home. "Darn!" you're always saying, "I wish there was a closer pizza restaurant near my home." People complain all of the time and this would suggest that the world is not optimal. Well, the question is: why don't you invest in a restaurant? Perhaps you say "no one will lend me the money." But why will the banks, your friends, and your parents not lend you the money? Is it because you cannot guarantee that you will pay it back and there is some cost of risk in opening up a restaurant? If so, then this cost must be factored in and now perhaps the restaurant doesn't look like such a good investment.

To say that the world is optimal doesn't mean that the world is perfect or that we cannot imagine a better world. It simply means that the world we live in is the best we can do under the circumstances. If you don't agree with this, then you're an entrepreneur, not an economist, and you should go make your fortune.

2.5 Summary

The principle of maximization is the first and most fundamental idea in economics. Every economic model, no matter how simple or complicated, assumes people are maximizing. So important is this idea that without it an argument simply is not economic. As we've seen, maximization has a number of implications. We live in a world of scarcity. If goods were freely available, we would demand more than is supplied. Furthermore, we live in an equilibrium. Markets out of equilibrium are markets where the gains from trade are not maximized. Equilibrium means that economic knowledge can only earn a normal rate of return — it cannot lead to easy fortunes or solutions to economic problems. Finally, the principle leads to the counter intuitive result that the world is optimal.

REVIEW QUESTIONS

1. What is the difference between assuming people are maximizers and assuming people are never satiated (ie. more is preferred to less)?

2. Is there any behavior at all, which we can confirm is not the result of maximizing behavior? In other words, is maximization, by itself, testable?

3. If something is scarce, is it a good? If something is a good, is it scarce?

   Scarce = good but good not always scarce.

4. Why is "choice" the result of scarcity?

5. What is the difference between "intra-marginal" and "marginal"?

6. Why would maximization survive over other forms of motivation?

7. A physicist once said "It seems to me that given this model of economics every greedy economist should be wealthy, since he knows the switches and levers." Why does the physicist not understand the proper role of economic theory?

8. A student sent his professor the following email:

   > I just finished your Economics course, and you discussed at the beginning of the semester how you can never find money just laying around, because the people before you had already found it and taken it for themselves....I just wanted to let you know that while Christmas shopping today at the mall ... I stumbled across a $20 bill just laying in the middle of the food court floor!!! Being the maximizer I am, of course, I picked it up. Perhaps, if you're lucky...you CAN find money just laying around!

   What does this story highlight about the nature of our *equilibrium* model?

9. A bumper sticker reads: "Remember: Pillage *then* burn." How does the humor of this sticker depend on the principle of maximization?

10. What is the character's motivation in the song *Mercedes Benz* by Janis Joplin:
    Oh Lord, wont you buy me a Mercedes Benz?
    My friends all drive Porsches, I must make amends.

11. *Fly Like An Eagle* by the Steve Miller Band is a great song, but a little lacking in terms of economics. What economic reality is missing from the following:
    Feed the babies who dont have enough to cat
    Shoe the children with no shoes on their feet
    House the people livin in the street
    Oh, oh, theres a solution

PROBLEMS

1. Two bedouins are arguing in the desert that their camel is the worst in all of Arabia. The fight goes on for some time before one of them thinks up the following bet. They will race their camels to an oasis two miles away, the last person to get there wins — his camel obviously being the slowest. The men mount their camels, and start the race. Several hours later, a wise man (who understood maximization) comes by and asks the men why they are sitting on their camels, going nowhere in the hot sun, when there is an oasis two miles away. The men get off, tell the wise man their problem. The wise man whispers two words to the men, and they immediately race off (on the camels) to the oasis. What did the wise man tell them?

2. Alexander Pope once wrote: *In spite of pride; in erring reason's spite, One truth is clear; whatever is, is right.* Is Pope's conclusion consistent with the principle of maximization?

3. I had a neighbor one time who planted an entire orchard of fruit trees at a 45 degree angle under the theory that they would bear more fruit. What common observation would make an economist skeptical of such a claim? As it turned out, all of his trees died, but he could have been a genius who really did discover how to increase fruit yields. What does this suggest about the economists ability to judge innovations in general?

4. A classic scene in Old West movies has the old prospector running into town yelling "Gold! Gold! I've discovered Gold!" Given the principle of maximization, what's wrong with this scene?

5. The whole world knows how a small handful of men were able to hijack four airplanes on September 11, 2001 and use them as bombs to kill thousands of people. Explain how a small number of hijackers use the principle of maximization to gain control over 40 to 60 people?

6. One of the most useful things one learns in economics is "Friedman's Law for Finding Men's Washrooms." This Law states: Men's rooms are adjacent, in one of the three dimensions, to ladies' rooms." Why is this an application of the principle of maximization?

7. "When I go to McDonalds, I can buy as many Big Macs as I'd like. Therefore, they are not scarce." True or False, explain your answer.

8. Are beautiful sunsets a scarce good? Briefly state why or why not.

9. It is a "well known fact" that the correlation between investor return and education level for stock brokers is negative — better brokers usually have less education. Is this consistent with the notion of maximization or a refutation of it? That is, do you think those brokers that went on to college would have been better brokers by not going?

10. In the *Silmarillion*, J.R.R. Tolkien (author of the *Lord of the Rings*) provides a history of Middle Earth. Of the many tales, one is told of the Numenoreans — high humans who didn't die until they were several hundreds of years old, and who prospered almost beyone measure under the watch of elvin kings and the Valar (angel like beings). Eventually, the Numenoreans (of whom Aragorn was a descendant) become upset over their mortality, and wonder why they cannot live forever like the elves. Some Valar messengers are sent to talk to them. The end of their conversation is written:

> [Valar] "... and so it is that you die. Thus you escape, and leave the world, and are not bound to it, in hope or in weariness. Which of us therefore should envy the others?"
>
> And the Numenoreans answered: "Why should we not envy the Valar, or even the least of the Deathless? For us is required a blind trust, and a hope without assurance, knowing not what lies before us in a little while. And yet we also love the Earth, and would not lose it."

Explain what economic principle is driving the Numenorean behavior.

11. Tom Middleton is a money expert who writes syndicated columns for a number of outlets, including *MSN Money.* In his column for February 26, 2008 his headline was "Financial Stocks: The Stars of 2008" the subheading was "Several top fund managers think its time to buy." He, and these other experts, turned out to be very wrong. By October of 2008 the Dow Jones average had lost almost 25% for the year. Why, given the principle of maximization, should no faith have been put in what these guys said in the first place?

Review Question Answers

1. *Maximization is a motivation. It is the reason why people do things — at least that's what economists think. Nonsatiation, is just a matter of preferences, and many times it isn't true. I might have some allocation in my life which is an absolute bliss point. If I ever reach this point, I would be in heaven. To have such a point would be a violation of "more is preferred to less." But as a maximizer I would want to reach such a point! Thus there is no contradiction in being a satiated maximizer. However, in this book we'll generally assume there's always something individuals want more of.*

2. *I don't think so, at least not until we can peer into the hearts of men and measure motivation. If you pick any type of behavior whatsoever, it is easy to come up with a maximizing explanation. If a person jumps into a blazing fire to save some people, we can say "he's no altruist, he just wants to be famous ... pure greed." Whether or not you find this plausible or not is beside the point. Maximization, just by itself, is not a testable theory. It is consistent with everything.*

3. *If something is scarce, then it must be a good. If it is scarce, then people want it, which is the definition of a good. If something is a good, it may not be scarce. Water is a good. But you may be in a situation where there is so much water, that it is not scarce.*

4. *When goods are scarce it means that there is more wanted than is available. This the definition of scarcity. Hence, a choice must be made over who gets how much of the good.*

5. *Marginal means "small change." So when someone makes a small change to their behavior we call it "marginal." We'll see throughout the book that people already in a market make marginal changes to their behavior when prices change. Often in economics we refer to the last unit consumed or produced as the "marginal unit." In this sense, those units consumed or produced before the last unit are the "intra-marginal" ones. For example, if a consumer is purchasing 10 apples per week. The 10th apple is the marginal apple, and the other nine are the intra-marginal ones.*

6. *To maximize is to do the best under the given circumstances. If you do less than the best, and someone else does better, then that person will out compete you. He'll gather more food, make more weapons, and eventually overpower you in some dimension. If you do not copy the maximizing strategy you or your business will simply disappear and we won't observe that type of behavior anymore. The principle of maximization is equivalent to the biological theory of "survival of the fittest."*

7. *Economic theory is not a license to print money. Economic theory is used to explain human behavior. Even if economists did understand all there was to human behavior (and believe me, we're a long way from that!) knowing the "switches and levers" doesn't help you get rich any more than understanding physics helps you to be a great pool player. One of the implications of our model based on maximization is that the gains from trade are fully exploited. This means the economist cannot use the model to find non-exploited gains from trade. It is an unfortunate aspect of logic.*

8. *Our model says that in equilibrium there will be no money lying around on the floor of a mall. Our model doesn't have much to say about how an equilibrium is reached, but in the context of money on the floor, we get to an equilibrium by having someone pick up the money. Clearly,*

this student was part of the equilibrium process. It was because of his actions there was no money on the floor in equilibrium.

9. *If you burn before you pillage ... there's nothing left!*

10. *The person in the song is motivated by maximization, but notice it is exercised not just over what is consumed, but also relative to what others consume. As if greed is not enough, we also worry about "keeping up with the Jones." That is, we worry about our relative consumption. For the most part, we'll ignore this even darker side of the human spirit.*

11. *It all sounds nice, but it ignores the fact we live in a world of scarcity. There's never enough and choices must be made. Providing shoes, food, and shelter are all good things. If there was a costless solution, as the song suggests, we'd have used it by now. That's dismal.*

Odd Numbered Problem Answers

1. *Switch camels.*

3. *This is a true story, and the neighbor was a biologist with a theory of different types of sap in fruit trees. The economist should be skeptical because driving past commercial orchards one never sees trees planted on an angle. Tree producers have a strong interest in finding the best environment for growing trees, and it seems reasonable they would have tried this procedure, even by accident over the past several thousands of years. Still, this could have been the proverbial "better mouse trap." It shows that economists have no tool to evaluate innovations. On the contrary, the principle of maximization tends to make us quite skeptical.*

5. *Every hijacker makes it known that the first person to attempt a takeover will be killed. Often the hijackers make a demonstration that they are willing to kill by killing someone randomly. Collectively there is no way a group of hijackers could stand an assault by 40 to 60 people, but of course, no one wants to be the first one to attack. If there is no first person, there's no attack and the hijackers gain control. This is a major problem with getting infantry to fight in battles, and most infantry formations are designed to make sure the first mover is not at such a disadvantage.*

7. *If Big Macs were not scarce, then they would be free. They are not free, therefore, they are scarce. This question can be used to get the students to start thinking about prices, price taking, demand, and supply, before any of these things are introduced.*

9. *This observation makes it appear students who enter college get taught information which makes them a worse broker. However, this question is really about maximization and self selection. If, given the principle of maximization, an instructor can't teach anyone how to be a great stock broker, those who are naturally good at it will not go to college. If they are good at it and stay in the business, then you get the observed correlation.*

11. *The bottom line is that there is no crystal ball for the future, and if there was, the result of acting on it would eliminate any systematic trading gains. The stock market prices move in a random pattern, with occasional enormous moves up and down. Since it is a random pattern, these experts can offer no valuable advice.*

CHAPTER 3

SUBSTITUTION

The second important idea in economics is the principle of substitution. The principle of substitution simply states that everyone is willing to trade some amount of one good, for some amount of another. All goods are substitutes when they all provide us with some amount of enjoyment. If a good doesn't provide a person with enjoyment (what economists call "utility") then the item isn't a good, its a bad.

PRINCIPLE #2

Substitution: *everyone is willing to trade some amount of one good for some amount of another.*

If we were to put it crudely, the principle of substitution essentially states that everyone has their price. If I want you to give up something, then all I have to do is give you enough of some other good, and you'll part with what I want. Like the principle of maximization, substitution is hardly a noble characteristic, but in terms of explaining behavior it is very successful.

We run into substitution everyday of our lives. Children at a dinner table are often bribed with dessert if they'll just eat a little bit more broccoli and carrots. Essentially the parents are exploiting the child's willingness to trade a bad thing (broccoli) for a good thing (dessert). If the parents resort to threatening a spanking to get the child to eat the broccoli, again they are exploiting the child's willingness to trade one bad thing for another. When a shopper goes to Safeway for some fruit, but notices that mangos are $2.40 each, while plums are a mere $.20 per pound, they tend to buy more plums and fewer mangos. The fact that different types of fruit satisfy the shopper's desire means that he views plums and mangos as substitutes. In fact, if fruit was really expensive, the shopper would consume, more of some other type of food, like cookies, and less fruit. There's no end to what goods substitute for others.

Before we go on, three things need to be said. First, substitution is an act of the will. One is *willing* to substitute one good for another. The principle of substitution isn't referring to forced consumption, but rather addresses what people are willing to do. Second, the principle of substitution only says that everyone is willing to substitute one good for another, but it doesn't say how much. It might take a twelve plum payment to get you to give up one mango, but for me it might take 60, or perhaps 2. It is just a matter of taste, and there's no reason why tastes are the same across people. The principle of substitution only states that if you want me to give up one mango, there is some amount of plums (or other goods) you can give me that will make me do it. Third, there is a relationship between what someone is willing to pay and what someone is able to pay. To be able to pay for something, literally means that you have enough resources (income) to make the payment. Just because someone is able to pay for something, doesn't mean he's willing to do so. You're no doubt able to purchase illegal drugs, but I would guess you're likely unwilling to do so. If you are willing to pay for something, then you must also be able to pay for it. It makes no sense to say you're willing to pay for something when you can't afford it. People get the relationship between ability and willingness to pay mixed up all the time. It is far better to watch a person's actions than listen to their words. Consider the following story:

> A taxi driver from the Bronx dropped off a passenger one day and then immediately felt sicker than he had ever felt in his life. Fearing that he might be mortally ill, he drove immediately to Park Avenue, where he had seen signs for the offices of many doctors. Locating an office, the cabbie burst in demanding to be seen at once. The receptionist, fearing the man might die, called a doctor, who concluded it was a simple case of indigestion. "How much do I owe?" asked the cabbie to the receptionist. "Oh, $150 will do," she replied. "$150!" shrieked the cabbie. "That's highway robbery, that's outrageous, that's out of the question." The cabbie kept on yelling and making such a fuss that the doctor finally came out to calm him down. Finally he said "just pay what you think you should." "Fine," said the cabbie, "here's $15." The doctor took the money, and before the cabbie left he said "You know, Park Avenue is the most expensive place in New York for doctors, and you must know that. Why did you come here?" "Listen doc, when it comes to my health, price is no object."

With those three thoughts in mind, consider some possible objections to the principle of substitution. "I don't care what you pay me, I'll never give up my life." People say things like this all of the time. Let's think of "giving up my life" in two ways: dying now, or shortening your lifespan. In terms of the latter, there are just a million ways we trade-off years of life for other goods. Consider all of the vices you have in your life. Perhaps you smoke, drink excessively, eat a lot of pizza (for breakfast), drive too fast, sleep with multiple partners, drink too much coffee, and don't get enough sleep ... sounds like the average undergraduate lifestyle. Anytime you engage in such behavior you reduce your expected lifespan. Why do we do such things? Because in doing them we get enjoyment from the activities. Essentially we're trading off one good for another: satisfaction now for a shorter life later.

"Fine" you say, "but there's no amount of any good you could give me that would make me kill myself". Perhaps, but what this might mean is that the price is simply very high. Quite often when people are tortured they beg to be killed rather than endure the torture. The terrorists who bombed the World Trade Center were willing to trade what they believed would be future in paradise for a suicide mission on that day. Other people have given their life for friends, family members, defending their faith and the like. No one gives up their life for any amount of potato chips, but for some price we do find examples.

If a person is willing to trade their own life against some other good, perhaps they are unwilling to trade, say, their child's life or their parent's life for some amount of other goods. Again, in terms of life expectancy, we do this all the time. If I drive my children to school, rather than have them ride the bus I increase the probability of a fatal car accident in exchange for more convenience. One of the most spectacular examples of endangering children's lives came about in the late 1980s in Seattle. A local hospital was charging its patients by the day, and the day began at midnight. Every evening a group of women in various stages of labor gathered in the parking lot, and rushed the emergency room at the stroke of twelve. You can just imagine the tortured men and women, waiting anxiously through each contraction, knowing that if they could just hold off a few more minutes they could save themselves $600. Although the hospital eventually solved the problem by charging patients by the hour, it still provides a remarkable example of a parent's willingness to trade-off their newborn child's welfare for a few hundred dollars.

In an old Calvin and Hobbes cartoon, the two characters are having a conversation "If I've learned one thing in life," says Calvin, "It's that everyone has his price. Raise the ante high enough and there's no such thing as scruples! People will do anything if the price is right." "What's your price?" says Hobbes. "Two bucks cold cash up front" replies Calvin. "I don't know which is worse. That everyone has his price, or that the price is always so low" quips Hobbes. Indeed, when we start to look around, the principle of substitution doesn't seem that surprising. It is only surprising how low the price is. The TV show 60 Minutes had a segment where an office in a hotel was set up across from a state legislature in order to pay legislators to vote a certain way on a piece of legislation. The producers of the show set the price at something like $5000 thinking they might get one or two takers. To their surprise, at one point the elected officials were actually lined up outside the hotel room door.

I had a Canadian friend who was adamant she could never live in the United States, so great was her malevolence for the country. Yet all it took was a cute American boy to get her to change her mind. In all religious faiths, no matter how seriously and sincerely the individuals take their beliefs, they all agree sin continues in their lives as they substitute the pleasures of obedience for the pleasures of the flesh. No matter what aspect of our life we treasure, the truth is some sell out at high prices, others at low ones — but everyone sells out at some price.

3.1 Trade-offs are Everywhere

The key to understanding substitution is to realize that we constantly make trade-offs in our life. If we want a nicer home in the country, we have to drive an old Honda Civic; if we want newer, more fashionable clothes, we have to give up eating at our favorite Chinese food restaurant every Friday. We want to get our homework done, but it's hard work with payoffs down the road, laziness has immediate rewards. To say that trade-offs are made everywhere is to say that nothing, when it comes to our actions, is sacred ... we are willing to sacrifice everything.

Most of the time our substitutions are innocent enough, and strictly a matter of personal choice. However, quite often when we trade-off one thing for another we hurt other people, and as a result we sometimes make promises not to substitute or we pay penalties for doing so. Consider the marriage vow to "forsake all others." This is a promise not to substitute another individual for your spouse. Of course, people cheat on their spouse all the time, but they do so with some penalty, and that penalty surely discourages some cheating. Note though that even though a married individual may not commit adultery, at the margin, they are constantly forsaking their partner for things like a golf game, time with the kids, or "girls night out." Substitutes are everywhere.

At a social level we often create institutions that try to limit the type of substitutions people make. Many laws are designed to restrict behavior and prevent us from substituting into choices that would hurt others. Traffic laws, for example, impose costs on trading speed for safety.

Although everyone makes trade-offs, it is important to understand that not everyone makes the *same* trade-offs. There was an old Rabbi and a Priest who played chess every Thursday for many years. One day the Priest asked the Rabbi "have you ever eaten pork." The Rabbi got a little uncomfortable and finally admitted he'd tried pork when he was younger. "But" said the Rabbi, "have you ever been with a woman?" The Priest became very uncomfortable, but finally admitted he'd been with a woman, when he was young, before he took his vows. "Ah" said the Rabbi, "it's better than pork, isn't it?" Priests and Rabbis are both religious men who make different trade-offs in their lives. Everyone has different preferences, and these manifest in different amounts of goods we're willing to trade-off. Some students are willing to buy this book; that is, they are willing to sacrifice consumption of other goods they could have had with the money. Other students are not willing to buy this book, which means they prefer the consumption of other goods. Everyone has different tastes or preferences.

3.2 The Fallacy of Priority in Consumption

How often have you heard comments like "Every Canadian needs adequate health care"; "Our freeway needs to be expanded to handle the increased traffic flow"; or "Unless new reserves of water are found, the current supply will not meet our needs."? Each one of these statements contains the notion of *necessity* and each one ignores the concept of substitution.

To say that an individual "needs" something is to say that there is a priority in consumption and that an individual will not live if the need is not met. To have a priority in consumption would imply that individuals first satisfy their most important need (say breathing), then satisfy their second need (say eating), then their third (say housing), and so on until their income is exhausted or they run out of needs. Though common, such a view grinds against the way individuals actually behave. People desire many goods simultaneously and they generate utility from combinations of goods. Different combinations can generate the *same* amount of satisfaction. Like the logger who was convicted of killing and eating a seagull. When asked by the judge what the bird tasted like the logger replied: "Not bad, sort of a cross between a spotted owl and a bald eagle.[1]

Look around in the building you're currently sitting in. Perhaps you're at home, at school, or at the campus coffee shop. Safety is something that everyone values, but look around. How safe is the building you're currently in? How many fire exits are there? If there's one, why aren't there two or three? The reason is that though safety is of value, other attributes of the building are of value as well. The building's appearance, its ability to function, and of course its cost (the value of other consumption) are all important. No one designing a building considers only one aspect. The different parts of the building are traded off in such a way that the value of the building is maximized.

Trade-offs, trade-offs, trade-offs. This trait of human behavior is neither good nor bad in and of itself. It is simply a fact that every thing we desire, from love, honesty, beauty, truth, virtue, cars, wine, and song, are all substitutable ... at least at the margin.

---

[1] The actual combinations individuals consume depends on their preferences and on the prices they face ... but now we're getting ahead of ourselves.

3.3 Marginal Value

An important idea that comes from the principle of substitution is *marginal value.* Marginal value (MV) is the maximum amount an individual is willing to sacrifice, or give up, in order to obtain an additional amount of another good. For ease of discussion we'll assume that the additional amount of the other good is one unit. Hence the marginal value is the maximum amount one is willing to give up of one good to get one extra unit of another good.

> **Marginal Value:** *the maximum amount of one good an individual is willing to sacrifice to obtain one more unit of another good.*

Marginal values exist because people are willing to substitute one good for another. They are important because they provide a measure of value for goods. For example, if Sally is willing to give up 5 apples for one hot dog, then the marginal value of the hot dog is 5 apples. Notice that value is measured *in terms of other goods.* Value is a *relative* concept, and only has meaning in terms of one good relative to another. If Sally was willing to give up 7 bananas for one hot dog, then her marginal value of hot dogs, in terms of bananas would be 7.

In order to understand marginal value, we must understand the concept of *indifference* which was raised in the last chapter. Suppose Sally is offered two different bundles of goods, as shown in Table 3-1.

Sally

	Apples	Hot Dogs
A	2	6
B	3	4

Table 3-1

Suppose that Sally tells us she is indifferent between the two separate bundles. By indifferent she means that she is willing to let anyone else choose which bundle she will consume. Suppose that Sally actually has bundle A (2,6). If Sally is to increase her apples to 3, what is the *maximum* number of hot dogs she is willing to sacrifice? The answer is 2, and this 2 is the marginal value of the third apple.

Let Sally have a friend named Tamara who is indifferent between the two bundles in Table 3-2.

Tamara

	Apples	Hot Dogs
A	2	6
B	3	2

Table 3-2

It should be clear that the MV of the third apple for Tamara is 4 hot dogs. To the economist we would say that Tamara likes apples more, at the margin, than Sally because she is willing to sacrifice more to get an extra one.

Most of the time, when an economist speaks of marginal value, they say it is the maximum number of dollars one is willing to sacrifice in order to obtain the next apple, or whatever. This is only done for convenience. The dollars simply represent other goods and are not valued in and of themselves. As mentioned, value is based on sacrifices of real goods.

3.4 Exchange

Exchange or trade takes place every day in our lives. Often the trades are formal and legal, like when I fill up my car with fuel and have to pay the gas attendant. Other times the trades are very informal and not enforcable at law, like when I tell my son I'll take him to a movie if he helps me mow the lawn. Very seldom do two or more people get together when some type of trade doesn't take place. Even a conversation can be thought of in terms of an exchange. In fact, we tend to avoid conversations that are "one-sided"; that is, where no exchange takes place.

There are two big misconceptions about trade: trade takes place because one party has "too much" of something; trade involves exchanging items of "equal" value. Both of these statements are wrong. Trade doesn't take place just because someone has a surplus of something. If, as our first principle states, we're all maximizers, then it is unlikely that we ever think we have too much of anything. In my entire life I've never owned more than one car at a time, yet that hasn't stopped me from trading several of them. On the other hand, I've often had too many dandelions in my yard and yet I've never managed to trade any of them.

Trade does not occur just because someone has a surplus.

Likewise, trade never happens when individuals value goods equally. When people value goods equally, there is no point to trading. People engage in trade only when their *marginal* values are different. When marginal values are different, trade can make everyone better off.

> *Trade takes place when individuals have different marginal values*

Let's consider another set of bundles of apples and hot dogs for Sally and Tamara — the ones shown in Table 3-3.

Sally			**Tamara**		
Apples	Hot Dogs	MV	Apples	Hot Dogs	MV
9	13		5	17	
		5			2
10	8		6	15	
		4			1
11	4		7	14	

Table 3-3

The table shows three bundles of apples and hot dogs for both Sally and Tamara, and as before, let's assume that Sally is indifferent between her three bundles, and that Tamara is indifferent between her three. Also, let's assume that Sally actually has the middle bundle of (10,8) and that Tamara has the middle bundle (6,15). Finally, note that the marginal value of apples in terms of hot dogs is listed for each.

If Sally and Tamara know one another, will they trade with one another? Since their marginal values at the bundle they are endowed with are different, the answer is yes, they will engage in trade. Sally and Tamara might come up with their own terms of trade (price), but to make matters easy let's assume that the price at which they can trade is 1 Apple = 3 Hot Dogs. This price is pulled out of the air, to help you understand the example, try another price.[2]

The first thing to note is that Sally has a MV for apples of 4, which means that she's willing to sacrifice up to 4 hot dogs to get one more apple. Since she can purchase an apple for 3 hot dogs, she certainly will try to increase her amount of apples. Tamara on the other hand, only has a MV for apples of 1 hot dog. In fact, the MV of giving up one apple for her is 2 hot dogs. Since she can sell an apple for 3 hot dogs, this obviously would appeal to her. In fact, Tamara will trade one apple to Sally in exchange for 3 hot dogs. This would leave Sally with a bundle of (11, 5) and Tamara a bundle of (5,18). Since Sally was indifferent between her starting bundle and the third one in the

---

[2] See if you can figure out the limits on the price such that each person is not made worse off because of trade.

table (11, 4), she is better off with the new bundle. Likewise, since Tamara was indifferent between her starting bundle and the first one (5, 17), she is also better off with the new bundle.

> *Mutual voluntary trade makes both parties better off.*

Think about this result for a moment, because it is quite remarkable. Without increasing the total amount of goods available to consume, both people were made better off with trade. Why? Because they both valued the goods differently. The person with the higher marginal value for apples (Sally) got more apples, while the person with the higher marginal value for hot dogs (Tamara) got more hot dogs. Wealth was created in the form of a higher level of utility by rearranging the combinations of goods that each consumed. Furthermore, all that was required was for each person to know what they liked, and for a price to exist. No third party was required to make the exchange for the individuals, they were able to do it on their own.

The fact that mutual voluntary trade is beneficial to all parties involved is one of the most fundamental ideas in economics, and it is an idea that many people oppose very strongly. Have you ever heard comments like the following: if Canada exports logs to Japan, this is bad because it exploits our resources at home, but if Canada imports logs from say the United States this is bad because it creates unemployment in our forests. Or what about this: if Canada imports American TV programs this is bad because it destroys our culture, but if we export our cultural products to the US it is also bad because our product becomes Americanized and we lose our identity (eg. there are too many American hockey teams, its not a Canadian sport any more!). Sentiments like this simply ignore the fact that mutually voluntary trade makes both parties better off. Trade has costs, no doubt about it. When Sally trades with Tamara she had to give up three hot dogs. However, she gained an apple which was worth more. There's no point in just looking at costs when discussing trade. The benefits must also be considered, and more than this, we know that the benefits with mutually voluntary trade exceed the costs.

3.5 Summary

The second principle in economics is substitution. Though it is easy to admit substitutes exist, the relentless application of the idea to all goods is harder for some to swallow. Individual behavior speaks otherwise, however. In all things, important and un, we demonstrate our willingness to trade one thing for another. Nothing is sacred according to the way we act towards all things we value. From substitution we get the concept of marginal value: the maximum we are willing to sacrifice to obtain one more unit of a good. With the concept of marginal value we saw that trade takes place when these marginal values are different.

REVIEW QUESTIONS

1. In your own words, what is the principle of substitution?

2. When you go to a store and purchase something like a shirt, what are you substituting for what?

3. When you go to work, what are you substituting for what?

4. Is the principle of substitution related to the principle of maximization?

5. How is marginal value related to indifference?

6. Do people trade things of equal value? Is this fair?

7. Adam Smith, the founding father of modern economics, articulated a theory called "the labor theory of value." He said "Labour is the real measure of the exchangeable value of all commodities .... Labour alone ... never varying in its own value, is alone the ultimate and real standard by which the value of all commodities can at all times and places be estimated and compared." How does this relate to the theory of value articulated in this chapter?

PROBLEMS

1. At a local gym a fellow walks up to the equipment counter and asks "how much to rent a squash racket?" The girl behind the counter says $3.50 per hour. To which the reply is "I can't afford that." What did the fellow really mean?

2. Reintroducing wolves into Wyoming has led to reduced numbers of cattle, elk, and other animals. This is an example of what economic principle?

3. As mentioned above, Adam Smith articulated a theory called "the labor theory of value," by stating the amount of effort that went into the production of a good is the best measure of a good's value. When a student comes up to a professor and complains about a grade, stating "...but I worked so hard on this assignment, it must be worth something" what theory of value is implicit in the student sentiment?

4. A poster of the leaning tower of Pisa reads: "Mediocrity: It takes a lot less time and most people won't notice the difference until it's too late." Explain in terms of the principle of substitution.

5. Complete the following conversation:

Kessel: When people say that they cannot afford something, they really mean that they prefer to buy something else.

Stigler: I can't afford a battleship.

Kessel: You could rent one for a short period, say 10 microseconds.

Stigler:

6. "Some goods are so necessary, there are no substitutes for them. Gasoline is one such example. No matter what the price people still have to travel to work." What are some ways people substitute out of gasoline when the price increases?

7. School Boards throughout the province of British Columbia are being required to upgrade their buildings to withstand serious earthquakes. Do increasing the earthquake standards on school buildings necessarily make schools a better place? What are some things that are likely to be sacrificed by doing this?

8. "Anything worth doing is worth doing well." Comment from an economic point of view.

9. The Boeing 767 uses less than 110 pounds of fuel per seat per 1000 miles. The older 727 uses 155 pounds. The Boeing 767 costs far more per seat to purchase, however. Which of the planes should an airline purchase if it is interested in efficiency? Does the price of fuel affect the answer?

10. In 2007 a guilty murder verdict was handed down on Nelson Hart in Newfoundland. He was the father of two daughters who drowned in a lake. He had claimed he had a seizure during the

time. Four years later, he confessed to killing them during what the RCMP call a "Mr. Big" operation. In this type of sting operation, the police have a suspect, but not enough evidence to convict. An undercover cop befriends the suspect, and offers him a job. Then another, and another. The jobs are easy and pay well, and eventually the suspect realizes he's involved in "illegal activities." He's eventually told that he's been working for a crime syndicate, which is headed up by "Mr. Big" — a Godfather like figure. This can go on for years. Finally, the suspect is told there is a really big job he's needed for, but he has to meet "Mr. Big." He's told to never mess with him, and always tell the truth. When the day finally comes, Mr. Big challenges the suspect over his "police problems," and tells him if he doesn't come clean, they are through. In the case of Mr. Hart, he confessed (on tape) and was convicted.

a. If Mr. Hart really believed that Mr. Big was who everyone said he was, and if Mr. Hart really believed that the job would pay better than all his past easy jobs, then what are the incentives faced by Mr. Hart over what to tell Mr. Big? How is this an example of substitution?

b. Given your answer to (a), what problems does this pose to the jury?

11. Vancouver, like most cities in North America, is surrounded by suburbs. To get to the city commuters have to cross one of several bridges on relatively small freeways during the morning rush hour. It is constantly heard that the solution to congested traffic is to "have one more bridge" or "more lanes of freeway". However, consider two observations. First, since the mid 1990s a number of freeway improvements have taken place (carpool lanes, interchange upgrades, new exits, etc), and the congestion issue has not gone away. Second, when one looks at the traffic in a town like Portland, Oregon where there are approximately the same number of people, but the freeway system is much larger, the rush hour times are similar. How is it that rush hour times are not reduced when freeway capacity is increased? (Hint: the city of Vancouver has a higher population density than cities like Seattle, Portland, or Los Angeles which have larger freeway systems.)

12. Assume the following bundles of goods are given to John and Mary:

	John			Mary		
	Meat	Fruit	MV Meat	Meat	Fruit	MV Meat
a)	0	12		0	16	
b)	1	8		1	10	
c)	2	5		2	5	
d)	3	3		3	1	

i) Calculate the MV of meat for both.

ii) Assume that John and Mary are indifferent between their respective combinations a,b,c, and d, and that the price of one meat is three and one-half fruit. If both start at combination c, show how they both can be made better off by trading.

Review Question Answers

1. *Well, I don't know what your own words are, but mine are in the box on page 38!*

2. *You're giving up some money, in exchange for the shirt. Money is not valued for its own sake, however. That money could be used to purchase any other commodity. So, in fact, when you buy the shirt your sacrificing some other good that has a price equal to the shirt.*

3. *You're giving up some leisure time for dollars. Again, the money is only an intermediary good, so you're really giving up leisure time in exchange for goods to be purchased with the income.*

4. *People could still be maximizers even if they were unwilling to trade one good for another. (Economists have a name for this type of idealized behavior: consumption in fixed proportions.) Likewise, someone might be willing to trade one good for another, even though they were motivated by something other than maximization. Thus the two principles are independent of each other.*

5. *We use the notion of indifference to calculate marginal value. To find marginal value we need to know what the maximum amount is you would sacrifice to obtain more of some good. But to find this, we need to know those bundles with which you are indifferent.*

6. *People trade when they value things differently at the margin. If the marginal values are the same, then they will not engage in trade. To trade things of different value seems "unfair." However, both people are made better off by the exchange, and that is the true measure of whether or not the trade will take place or not. As economists, we are not interested in what is fair or not, as if we could tell what is. Rather, we're interested in explaining behavior.*

7. *It is clearly a different theory, and one that was eventually rejected by economists. The value of a good is not determined by the amount of labor that went into its production. Value is based on sacrifice. Even Smith's notion that labor "never varying in its own value" is rejected by fact. You know this from your own experience.*

Odd Numbered Problem Answers

1. *He really meant "I'm not willing to pay that much for a racket." Everyone has access to $3.50.*

3. *The student is following the labor theory of value, which is quite entrenched in everyday thinking. Grades (should be) based on the quality of an answer, not how long it took to reach the answer. Refutations of the labor theory of value abound.*

5. *As I recall, Stigler said he couldn't afford a battleship for a year. The point being, there are some things in life we literally can't afford. Kessel though makes the good point that most of the time people confuse willingness and ability to pay.*

7. *Upgrading for earthquakes costs dollars that come from the school board budgets. Hence, a better protected school is one with fewer other resources like teachers, computers, and library books.*

9. *The efficient one critically depends on the price of fuel. The 767 only becomes profitable when fuel costs are high.*

11. *When a new lane is added to a freeway it lowers the driving time for a given amount of traffic. However, the volume of traffic never stays the same. If the commute time is lowered, there are fewer car pools and fewer people taking the bus which immediately adds to congestion. People in the suburbs might decide to start work in the city, surrounding municipalities decide to develop more subdivisions, and people move from the city to the suburbs as the freeway grows in size. The result is an amount of congestion practically the same as before the expansion.*

3.6 Appendix: Mapping Preferences

We all think differently. Some of us like verbal arguments, others see the world through mathematics. In the appendices of this book I'm going to present some of the arguments in terms of graphs. I'll also go into a little more depth into what lies behind the ideas in the chapter. This material is intended to supplement the chapter material, and I hope it helps your understanding. If you find the appendix material more confusing than helpful, then maybe you're just a verbal type person and you should just skip them.

Chapters 2 and 3 described two key aspects of preferences that economists believe characterize everyone. Everyone is a maximizer and everyone is willing to make trade-offs. In making trade-offs people don't view goods as unique, but rather as inter changeable to some extent.

It turns out we can represent these two ideas in a graph. As the book moves along, subsequent appendices will develop this graph a little more. The graph is called an "Indifference Map". That's a fancy name, but it really is quite simple. An indifference map basically shows an individual's values he places on any bundle of goods. In the end it will look something like a contour map of a hillside ... but we're getting ahead of ourselves.

Let's start by making things simpler. Let's assume that there are only two goods: mangos and bananas. Let's assume that we are interested in the preferences of Shauna, who likes mangos and bananas, and who is as greedy as they come. What would her preferences look like?

Well, preferences are going to be graphed, so we have to start with a graph. Consider Figure 3-1.

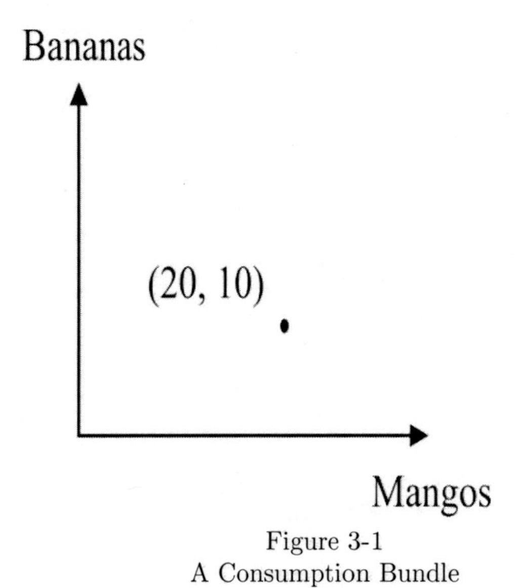

Figure 3-1
A Consumption Bundle

Notice what is on the axes: the two goods, mangos and bananas. The first problem students have with graphs is not paying attention to what is on the axes and what the units are. In this case both axes have one of the goods on them, and the units are just the number of goods. Notice also, that a bundle of goods is represented by a point. In Figure 3-1 the bundle (20,10) is graphed. This point represents the bundle of 20 mangos and 10 bananas. Can you figure out where the bundle (10,20) would be?

Now our girl Shauna likes mangos and bananas, so she certainly will like 20 mangos and 10 bananas. Who wouldn't? But the question is, how would Shauna feel about this bundle compared to some other bundle? Figure 3-2, shows a number of other potential bundles. The original bundle is labeled 'A', and two other bundles are labeled 'B' and 'C'.

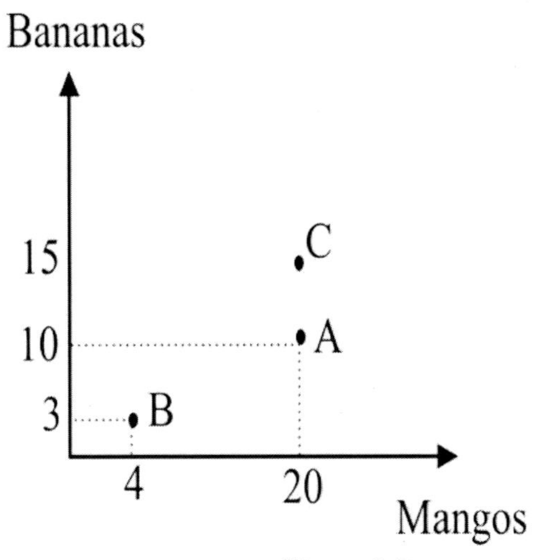

Figure 3-2
Three Consumption Bundles

Since Shauna is a maximizer she likes it when her fruit basket is full. So she likes bundle A better than B. Bundle B has less of both fruits in it. If we presented Shauna with two baskets of fruit, one with 20 mangos and 10 bananas, and the other with 4 mangos and 3 bananas, she wouldn't have any problem telling us which one she wanted. And as economists, we wouldn't have any problem predicting which one she wanted. Bundle B! ... Just kidding to see if you were paying attention. She would prefer A over B.

There is a third bundle in Figure 3-2. Bundle C has 20 mangos and 15 bananas. How will Shauna feel about this one? Clearly she will also prefer bundle C to bundle A. Now pick a point in the space, ... any point. Can you tell how Shauna would feel about it compared to bundle A?

There are only three options. Either Shauna prefers A to your bundle, prefers your bundle to A, or she thinks they are both the same. If she thinks they are the same, then she is indifferent between the two bundles. The concept of indifference is the key to mapping out Shauna's preferences.

What we'd like to do is connect all of the dots (bundles) for which Shauna is indifferent. We know the line can't be upward sloping because this would mean connecting points like A and B, and we've just argued that Shauna likes A more than B. So if we connect points of indifference, the line must be downward sloping. Such a line is called an Indifference Curve, and it is shown in Figure 3-3.

In the next chapter's appendix we'll attach some numbers to the indifference curves. The numbers don't mean much, but they help us rank which curve represents a higher level of satisfaction or utility. You'll see that the further the indifference curve is from the origin, the higher the level of utility.

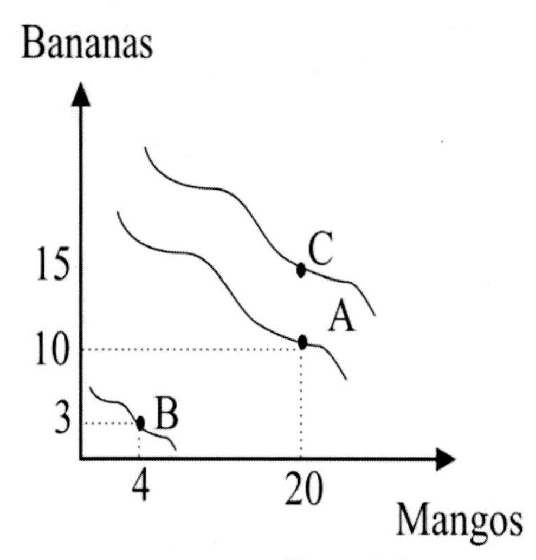

Figure 3-3
Three Indifference Curves

For now these don't look like much. Our principle of maximization tells us that they must be downward sloping, and our principle of substitution allows us to connect the points, but we can't say too much else. In the next chapter we'll put more restrictions on these curves and in the next appendix we'll see how they can be used to derive a demand curve.

CHAPTER 4

THE LAW OF DEMAND

4.1 Diminishing Marginal Value

Think of something you really like. Perhaps you've fallen in love and you really like that person. When you first met your current "special person", do you recall how you'd do anything to spend time with them. Miss work... no problem. Skip your brother's 12th birthday party... he'll have other birthdays. Lie to your parents on where you're sneaking off to... you've lied to them before. If you're like most people you are willing, and often do, make tremendous sacrifices to be with your new love.

Now, fast forward to the present. Perhaps you've dated for a year or two, perhaps you've even married your sweetheart. Do you still long to spend the same amount of time together? Are you sooooo willing to sacrifice time with your other friends, time at school, or time on your career, just to be with this one person? The answer is absolutely not. If you've never experienced this scenario, ask yourself if you're willing to sacrifice a lot to spend more time with your parents, your brother or sister, or someone else who you've spent much time with.

Perhaps love isn't your thing. If you're human though, one thing you'll be needing is some water. Everyone needs some water to survive, but most of the water we consume has nothing to do with survival. Any one stuck in a desert, or on a lifeboat in ocean, knows that when it comes down to having water for survival purposes, it is worth an incredible amount. For those who live in arid places like Arizona or New Mexico, there's enough water to live on, but driveways are swept and lawns kept to a minimum. In arid climates people value water at the margin more, and they use water-recycling gadgets, low flow toilets, water softeners for better washing, automatic faucets, and water is often charged for. For those who live in Vancouver, where there's "water water everywhere" and every drop can drink, water is treated as if it was worth nothing. Everything from cars, homes, and driveways get washed, kids run through sprinklers, hot tubs are refilled weekly, taps are left running, water is free in restaurants without asking, toilets use 5 gallons per flush, lawns are watered without restrictions, heavy industrial users of water move in, and leaks in the water system are not repaired.

This phenomenon holds for everything. The more you have of anything, the less you are willing to give up to get more of it. Economists call this *the law of diminishing marginal value,* and it is our third economic principle. Let's be a little more careful with our definition:

PRINCIPLE #3

Diminishing Marginal Value: *The maximum one is willing to sacrifice at the margin for a good, per unit of time, declines the more one has of that good — other things held constant.*

Let's take this definition apart a little. Notice the "maximum one is willing to sacrifice at the margin" is simply the definition of marginal value, so the definition says MV falls the more you have. The "per unit of time" part of the definition means that we're talking about a rate of consumption and not a total amount. For example, diminishing MV means the MV of eggs *per week* falls, the more eggs *per week* you consume. Finally, the "other things held constant" means that when the amount of the good increased, nothing else (like your income, other prices, preferences, ... nothing) changed. If we ignore the "other things held constant" caveat, then some obvious things become mysteries. On September 10, 2001 the price of a ride to the top of the Sears tower in Chicago cost \$12, and there was a line of people waiting to go up. On September 12, 2001 the price was lowered to zero. Yet, reportedly, very few people went up the tallest building in Chicago on the 12th. That seems puzzling until you remember the world changed a little on September 11th. So the law of diminishing marginal value is a very specific thing.

Thus far we have made three assumptions regarding the nature of human preferences: every one is greedy (maximization), everyone has their price (substitution), and everyone values a thing less at the margin the more they have of it (diminishing marginal value). From just these three principles we've already been able to draw several conclusions. First, we live in a world of scarcity. Second, voluntary exchange makes everyone better off. We're almost ready to discuss the really big implication of these ideas. However, before we can introduce demand functions, we need to make a slight detour and discuss incomes and prices.

4.2 (Real) Income and (Relative) Prices

We're going to make some very simple assumptions about incomes and prices in order to analyze choices individuals make. First, we're going to assume that people have fixed incomes, and cannot borrow any money from the bank to enhance that income. Second, we're going to assume there are only two goods: 1 and 2. The prices for these goods are known: p_1 and p_2.

These prices, furthermore, are going to constitute the entire cost of goods 1 and 2. There are no additional time costs, no entry fees, or no costs imposed on or by third parties. Budgets and prices obviously constrain individuals on what they are *able* to consume. If someone says "I can't afford a new motor home," then they mean the cost is greater than their income. That's pretty obvious, but the phrase "I can't afford it" gets abused all the time.

One of the most important things to understand about economic decisions is that they depend on *real income* and *relative prices*. Real income is a measure of how many actual goods one can consume, and is given by the nominal income an individual has (just the number of dollars) divided by some type of price level. You are probably familiar with the consumer price index (CPI), which is a complicated index used to measure real income. For us, we're going to measure real income with a simple formula:

$$Real\ Income = M/p_2.$$

In this formula M is simply the number of dollars the consumer has, and is called the nominal income. For our price level, we're simply going to use the price of our other good, good 2. In measuring real income this way it becomes apparent the level of real income depends on the price index used. To use the real income measure above means real income is measured in terms of how much good 2 can be consumed. If we had calculated real income using the price of good 1 we would have measured it in terms of the amount of good 1 consumed. For example, if you have \$250 and

prices are $p_1 = 10$ and $p_2 = 5$, then real income in terms of good 2 is 50, and is 25 in terms of good 1. This means at most the consumer could consume 50 units of good 2 or 25 units of good 1. Real income is a measure of a consumer's purchasing power in terms of goods.

Economists are interested in real income because changes in it cause changes in behavior. Any Canadian is well aware of the fact that the Canadian dollar trades at about \$.63 for a U.S. dollar. That is, it only takes 63¢ American to buy one loony. Does this mean the standard of living is necessarily lower in Canada? Well, not generally. What we really need to know is the real income of a Canadian versus an American. The first thing one notices when looking at nominal salaries between the two countries is that often the Canadian ones are higher for a given occupation. But the prices in Canada are generally higher as well. If you live near the border, check out the price of Big Macs on either side. At the time of writing they are around \$3.80 Can and \$2.20 U.S. It's not clear which real income is higher.[1] If you live in one city and are considering a job in another, you don't just think about the salary the company is willing to pay you. You'll want to know about the cost of housing, food, and taxes in the new community. In other words, you want to know about the *real* income you'll face.

Nowhere is this more true than in the context of inflation. Inflation is an increase in the money supply relative to the amount of goods and services available in an economy, and it causes all prices to go up... including wages. In a pure inflation the prices of all goods might go up by 10%, but if incomes go up by 10% as well, no one is better off or worse off. Real incomes have not changed.

Relative prices are like real income in that they measure how many other goods one must sacrifice to obtain more of another good. We will represent relative prices by:

$$Relative\ \ Price = p_1/p_2.$$

In other words, we will measure the price of good 1 in terms of how much of good 2 must be given up. If the price of good 1 is \$15 and the price of good 2 is \$3, then the relative price is 5. That means, every time a person buys one unit of good 1, they could have purchased 5 units of good 2.

Like real income, economists are interested in relative prices because people respond to them rather than nominal prices. Again returning to the example of inflation, all prices since WWII have generally increased. A Chevy Nova in 1978 cost \$6000, whereas a similar car today costs around \$20,000. Given that all prices have increased, including incomes, it would not be correct to say that the amount sacrificed for the car has more than tripled.

A relative price is a physical exchange rate of one good for another. For convenience, prices will most often be denoted in terms of dollars. Hence a price of \$12 really means that \$12 worth of other goods are being exchanged for one unit of the current good. Unless otherwise stated, we'll assume that the price of good 2 remains the same. Hence any change in the nominal price of good 1 will mean that its relative price has changed as well.

---

[1] Truth be told, real incomes are higher in the U.S. The point, however, is that one simply cannot compare the nominal incomes across the two countries.

> *Behavior depends on Real Income and Relative Prices, not nominal income and nominal prices.*

When people believe their behavior depends on nominal incomes and prices, rather than real income and relative prices, economists say they suffer from "money illusion." They think their wealth has gone up or down because their nominal income has gone up or down. A humorous example of money illusion and real income is found in Mark Twain's classic story *A Connecticut Yankee in King Arthur's Court*, where the hero attempts in vain to convince a group of workers the difference between real and nominal values.

> "In your country, brother, what is the wage of a master bailiff, master hind, carter, shepherd, swineherd?" The smith's face beamed with joy. He said: "With us they are allowed the double of it! And what may a mechanic get — carpenter, dauber, mason, painter, blacksmith, wheelwright, and the like?" "On the average, fifty milrays: half a cent a day." "Ho-ho! With us they are allowed a hundred! With us any good mechanic is allowed a cent a day! I count out the tailor, but not the others — they are all allowed a cent a day, and in driving times they get more — yes, up to a hundred and ten and even fifteen milrays a day."
>
> And his face shone upon the company like a sunburst. But I didn't scare at all. I rigged up my pile-driver, and allowed myself fifteen minutes to drive him into the earth — drive him all in — drive him in till not even the curve of his skull should show above ground. Here is the way I started in on him. I asked: "What do you pay a pound for salt?" "A hundred milrays." "We pay 40. What do you pay for beef and mutton — when you buy it?" That was a neat hit; it made the color come: "It varieth somewhat, but not much; one may say 75 milrays the pound." "We say 33. What do you pay for eggs?" "Fifty milrays the dozen." "We pay 20. What do you pay for beer?" "It costeth us 8.5 milrays the pint." "We get it for 4; 25 bottles for a cent. What do you pay for wheat?" "At the rate of 900 milrays the bushel." "We pay 400. What do you pay for a man's tow-linen suit?" "Thirteen cents." "We pay 6. What do you pay for a stuff gown for the wife of the laborer or the mechanic?" "We pay 8.4.0." "Well, observe the difference: you pay eight cents and four mills, we pay only four cents." I prepared, now, to sock it to him. I said, "Look here, dear friend, what's become of your high wages you wee bragging so about, a few minutes ago?" — and I looked around on the company with placid satisfaction, for I had slipped up on him gradually and tied him hand and foot, you see, without his ever noticing that he was being tied at all. "What's become of those noble high wages of yours? — I seem to have knocked the stuffing all out of them, it appears to me."
>
> But if you will believe me, he merely looked surprised, that is all! He didn't grasp the situation at all; didn't know he had walked into a trap, didn't

discover that he was in a trap. I could have shot him, from sheer vexation. With cloudy eye and a struggling intellect, he fetched this out:

"Marry, I seem not to understand. It is proved that our wages be double thine; how then may it be that thou'st knocked therefrom the stuffing? — an I miscall not the wonderly word, this being the first time under grace and providence of God it hath been granted me to hear it."

Well, I was stunned; partly with this unlooked for stupidity on his part, and partly because his fellows so manifestly sided with him and were of his mind — if you might call it mind. My position was simple enough, plain enough; how could it ever be simplified more? However, I must try:

"Why look here, Brother Dowley, don't you see? Your wages are merely higher than ours in name, not in fact." "Hear him! They are the double — ye have confessed it yourself." "Yes, yes, I don't deny that at all. But that's got nothing to do with it; the amount of the wages in mere coins, with meaningless names attached to them to know them by, has got nothing to do with it. The thing is, how much can you buy with your wages? — that's the idea. While it is true that with you a good mechanic is allowed thou three dollars and a half a year, and with us only about a dollar and seventy-five—" "There — ye're confessing it again, ye're confessing it again!" "Consound it, I've never denied it I tell you! What I say is this. With us, half a dollar buys more than a dollar buys with you — and therefore it stands to reason and the commonest kind of common sense, that our wages are higher than yours."

He looked dazed; and said, despairingly: "Verily I cannot make it out. Ye've just said ours are the higher, and with the same breath ye take it back." "Oh, great Scott, isn't it possible to get such a simple thing through your head? Now look here — let me illustrate. We pay four cents for a woman's stuff gown, you pay 8.4.0., which is 4 mills more than double. What do you allow a laboring woman who works on a farm?" "Two mills a day." "Very good; we allow but half as much; we pay her only a tenth of a cent a day; and—" "Again ye're conf—" "Wait! Now, you see, the thing is very simple; this time you'll understand it. For instance, it takes your woman 42 days to earn her gown, at 2 mills a day — 7 weeks' work; but ours earns hers in 40 days — two days short of 7 weeks. Your woman has a gown, and her whole 7 weeks' wages are gone; ours has a gown, and two day's wages left, to buy something else with. There — now you understand it!"

He looked — well he merely looked dubious, it's the most I can say; so did the others. I waited — to let the thing work. Dowley spoke at last — and betrayed the fact that he actually hadn't gotten away from his rooted and grounded superstitions yet. He said, with a trifle of hesitancy: "But — but — ye cannot fail to grant that two mills a day is better than one."

"Shucks! Well, of course I hated to give it up. But alas, it didn't crush. No, I had to give it up. What those people valued was high wages; it didn't seem to be a matter of any consequence to them whether the high wages would buy anything or not."

When the relative price of good 1 goes down, it means that for a given amount of real income, the opportunities to consume good 1 increase. Think about it. If you've got $100 and goods 1 and 2 cost $5 and $4, then the maximum amount of good 1 you can consume is 20 units. If the price of good 1 falls to $2, then the maximum amount of good 1 available to consume is 50 units. Now the question is, if the price of good 1 falls, and the amount a consumer is *able* to buy increases, will the consumer be *willing* to consume more? The amazing answer to this is yes, and this universal reaction to a change in price is called the Law of Demand.

4.3 The Law of Demand

The law of demand is, perhaps, the most powerful idea in economics. In this section I'm going to introduce you to the concept and discuss how it is related to diminishing marginal values, relative prices and real incomes, but the basic definition of the law of demand is pretty simple:

> **Law of Demand:** *There is an inverse relationship between a good's price and the quantity demanded, other things held constant.*

The easiest way to proceed is to visualize what this relationship looks like. Figure 4-1 is a graph of a demand curve.

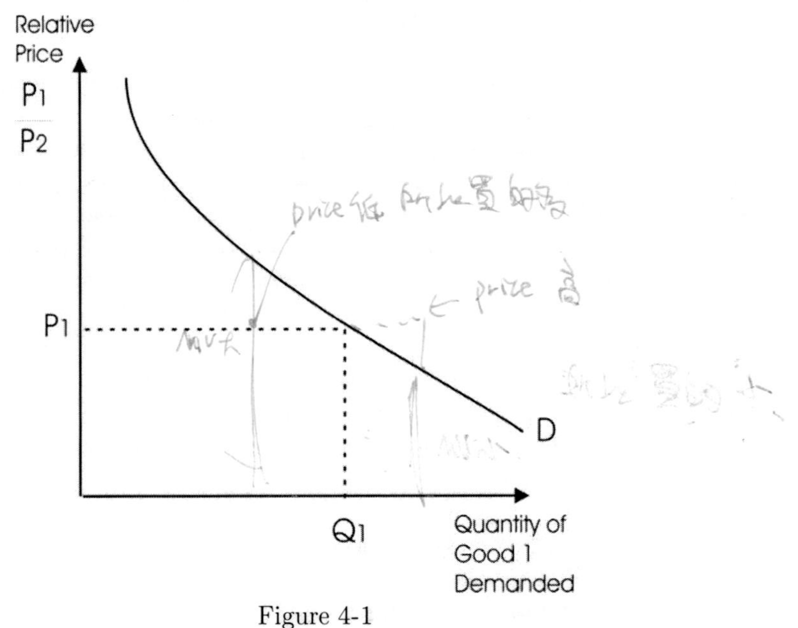

Figure 4-1
A Demand Curve

Notice that the relative price of good 1 is on the vertical axis, and that the quantity of good 1 demanded is on the horizontal axis. For convenience we'll often write the relative price simply as P, especially when referring to a specific price as in the graph, but keep in mind this is not a nominal price. Figure 4-1 has a demand curve that is not a straight line. Although the demand curve can take on any shape — as long as it is downward sloping — for additional convenience we'll often draw them as simple straight lines.

The law of demand states that there is an inverse or negative relationship between the price and quantity of a good demanded, but why is this so? Why is the demand curve downward sloping? It lies this way because of our three principles we've assumed thus far. A demand curve tells us the *maximum* amount someone is willing to spend for incremental units of good 1, other things constant. But this is, by definition, the marginal value, and we know that marginal value diminishes the more one has of good 1. Thus, the height of the demand curve is not just equal to the price, it is also equal to the marginal value, and the more of a good one has, the lower the marginal value is. This means that the demand curve must slope downwards.

As a consumer moves down their demand curve the process of substitution is taking place. When the relative price of good 1 falls, consumers use more of this good to generate utility for themselves. As they substitute into this good, they substitute out of other goods. Thus, when you go to the grocery store and you notice that mangos are only 25¢ each, you buy a lot of them and cut back on the seedless grapes and other fruits that haven't changed in price. This doesn't mean you stop buying other fruits, it just means that you buy less of them and more mangos.[2]

But there is more than just substitution going on with the demand curve. There is maximization! In Figure 4-1, when the price is P_1, the consumer demands a quantity of Q_1. Any less than this amount and the consumer's marginal value would have been higher than the price. Hence the consumer would want more. Any more than this amount and the consumer's marginal value would have been less than the price. Hence the consumer would want less. This means the price quantity combination (Q_1, P_1) is an equilibrium for the consumer — the consumer has maximized his utility by choosing Q_1 when faced with price P_1. At this equilibrium it is true that the relative price of the good is equal to the marginal value.

A consumer is in equilibrium when Relative Price = Marginal Value.

To find the equilibrium quantity then is quite easy. For any given price you just draw a horizontal line until it reaches the demand curve. That quantity is the *quantity demanded* by the consumer when he faces that price.

---

[2] It's not always true that less of other goods will be consumed. More on this in the next chapter.

4.4 The Law of Demand is Everywhere

The law of demand is one of the most useful ideas you'll ever learn, and it explains so much of the world around us. For example, you've probably noticed that vegetables and fruit are cheaper when they are in season than when they are out of season. Why is that? The answer is the law of demand. When there is lots and lots of fruit around, every individual has a low marginal value of fruit. In order for farmers to get consumers to eat the extra fruit, it is necessary to lower the price. When consumer's face a lower price they consume more fruit because they maximize their utility by equating the lower price to their marginal value.

You may have seen the law of demand in action at local gas stations. Have you ever noticed how many cars line up for gas when there is a price war? When there is a price war the "price of gas today" is cheap relative to the "price of gas tomorrow." When consumer's face a lower relative price, they consume more, and there are line ups at the gas station.

You've probably seen the law of demand at work in department stores. Have you ever been in a K-Mart store when the "Blue Light Special" happens? A clerk with a flashing blue light on a high pole walks through the store. Where the clerks stops, those goods are marked down by some drastic amount. Usually there are so many people following the blue light one has to avoid being stampeded. If the law of demand didn't hold, we wouldn't observe mobs of people following the blue light promise of lower prices. In fact, imagine what the Blue Light Special would be like if demand curves were upward sloping: "Attention shoppers, follow the Blue Light, where it stops ... all prices doubled!" Not likely.

If you live close to the American border (and what Canadian doesn't), you might have noticed a change in your cross border shopping habits over the past ten years. In the late 1980s the exchange rate between the US and Canadian dollar was around 83¢ . At that price many Canadians crossed the border to do grocery and clothing shopping. In fact, several shopping malls and gas stations were built just on the US side of the border to accommodate this shopping. However, over the last decade the Canadian dollar has depreciated considerably relative to the US dollar. At an exchange rate of 63¢ , many fewer Canadians are willing to cross the border to do their shopping. A falling exchange rate is the equivalent to a rise in the price of US goods. Given the law of demand, when consumers face a higher price they reduce the amount they consume. After the bombing of September 11, 2001 security at the border crossings increased considerably. This lead to longer crossing times. The increased waiting time is another component of the cost of US goods, and this increase in the wait further reduced the amount of shopping done in the US. All according to the law of demand.

Not all applications of the law of demand are so straightforward and obvious. Sometimes the law of demand can be very subtle. Several years ago in Seattle a grocery store called Tradewell launched an advertising campaign against its main rival Safeway. In the ad an interviewer approaches a customer coming out of the Tradewell store and inspects what groceries have been purchased. In the ad you can hear the interviewer mumble to himself "Okay, you've got a box of Corn Flakes, a dozen eggs, some lettuce, ... oh, some chocolate bars... etc." After doing this the interviewer says "Let's go over to Safeway and buy the *exact* same bundle, and see if the total bill is higher." Sure enough, the next clip shows the customer coming out of Safeway with the same bundle of goods and the bill is higher. No matter who came out of the store the result was always the same and the commercial always ended with the interviewer saying "and there you have it folks; Tradewell, where you always trade well for the lowest prices."

Now a skeptic might think the entire affair was simply staged. However, the experiment is actually a clever exploitation of the law of demand. When a consumer goes to Tradewell they face a host of different products and prices. The consumer has a demand for each good, and for a given set of prices they maximize their utility by choosing quantities of goods that set their marginal values equal to the prices they face. Given that every consumer is a maximizer, this process cannot be improved upon. This maximization process involves tradeoffs. If cream cheese is on sale at Tradewell the consumer substitutes into cream cheese, and away from goods that have higher prices. If chocolate bars are particularly expensive at Tradewell the consumer substitutes out of chocolate bars and into sweets with lower prices. Hence, when the customer comes out of Tradewell, the bundle of groceries is biased towards goods that were low in price at Tradewell. Assuming the prices of identical goods at Safeway and Tradewell are not identical (because of in-store specials and the like), if you force a customer to buy the Tradewell bundle at Safeway it *must* cost more.

Let's consider this case a little more carefully. Suppose the two stores each carry the same items and each have the same regular prices, with the only difference being that different items are on sale throughout the week. For example, both Tradewell and Safeway might carry Captain Crunch cereal for \$5 a box, but for one week Tradewell might have it on sale for \$3. Similarly Safeway might have meat on sale for \$8 a package, while the package costs \$10 at Tradewell, and a box of frozen peas might be \$9 at Tradewell, but only \$7 at Safeway. How could one ever tell which store has the cheapest prices?

For simplicity, let's suppose that the consumer has the same demand for each one of the goods, and that the demand is given by the simple function:

$$Q = 11 - P.$$

This equation means that if the price of Captain Crunch is \$5, then the consumer wants 6 boxes (11 minus 5). If the price of meat is \$8, then consumer wants 3 packages. Looking at Figure 4-2 we can see how much the consumer would demand at Tradewell and how much he would spend.

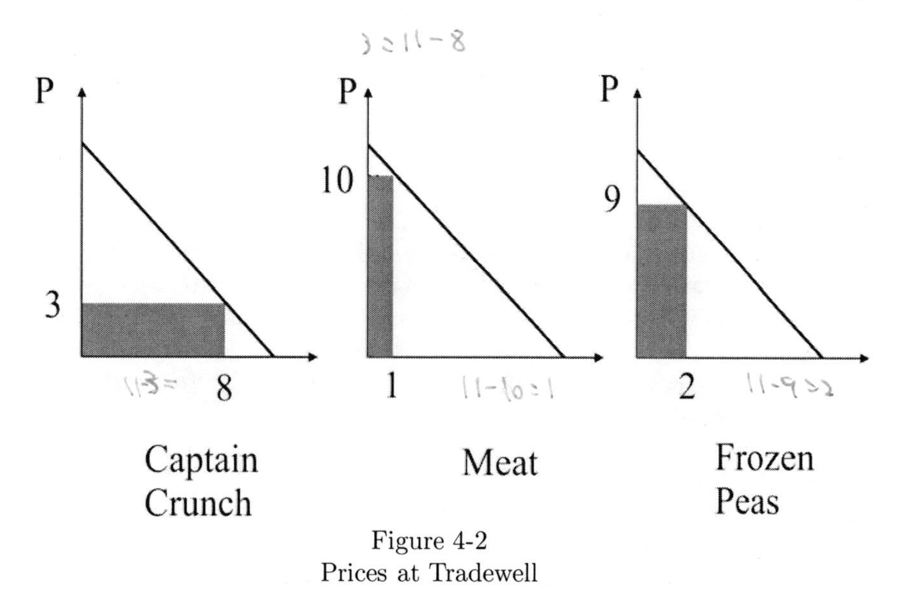

Figure 4-2
Prices at Tradewell

The shaded areas on the graph tell us how much the consumer spent on each good at Tradewell. For example, the consumer spent \$24 on Captain Crunch (3×8). Can you figure out how much the consumer would have spent at Safeway? We can take the information from the graph and put them into Table 4-1.

TABLE 4-1

Shopping at Tradewell

	Price	Quantity	Total Spent
Captain Crunch	3	8	24
Meat	10	1	10
Frozen Peas	9	2	18
Total Spent			$52

Shopping at Safeway
with Tradewell Quantities

	Price	Quantity	Total Spent
Captain Crunch	5	8	40
Meat	8	1	8
Frozen Peas	7	2	14
Total Spent			$62

When the consumer shops at Tradewell they spend a grand total of $52, but when we force the consumer to buy the same bundle at Safeway the total expenditure shoots up to $62. The reason is quite simple. At Safeway Captain Crunch is not on sale, yet we're forcing the consumer to buy as if it was. Likewise, the other two goods are on sale at Safeway, and yet we're forcing the consumer to ignore these lower prices. By compelling the consumer to not maximize, the consumer ends up doing worse.

The irony of this whole affair is that if Safeway did the same thing with their customers, they would have found total expenditures were always lower at Safeway. To check your understanding, work through the problem with the consumer shopping at Safeway first, and then force the consumer to shop at Tradewell with the Safeway bundle. Under this case the consumer spends $82 in Safeway and $84 at Tradewell. Obviously this is not a wise procedure for determining which store has the lower prices, but it is a great example of how tricky the law of demand can be.[3]

---

[3] There is obviously a limit to how far the prices at the two stores can diverge before this experiment will not work. For example, if Safeway was giving its food away (that is, if every price was zero) then every bundle would be cheaper at Safeway. The Tradewell ad was relying on the assumption that prices at Safeway will on average resemble prices at Tradewell.

4.5 Direct, but Objectionable Examples of the Law of Demand

Although we experience the law of demand constantly in our daily lives, most non-economists are uncomfortable in applying it to everything. When the price of sugar goes up, everyone agrees that the consumption of sugar will fall, but what if the good in question is gasoline, insulin, or sacred native territory?

We often hear people say gasoline is a necessity. "How could consumers use less gas when the price goes up? It's a necessity!" Yet when gas prices increase, consumers have no problem consuming less gas. They car pool, use the car less often, buy a smaller car, move from a two car to a one car family, take the bus, purchase a motor cycle, get a push lawn mower, stop washing their hands with gas, stop starting fires with gas, convert to solar power, and on and on.

Gasoline is something we might consider essential until we take a closer look at our own driving habits, but what about the case of insulin? Insulin is a miracle drug for people who suffer from diabetes, a condition where a pancreatic hormone for regulating sugars is lacking in the body. Diabetics need insulin to live, but the amount of insulin required is not fixed, and is still subject to the law of demand. There are many things a diabetic can do to help their condition. Changes in diet and the combination of different foods, for example, can alter how much insulin is needed. Exercise and weight loss are important factors in controlling insulin resistance. And reducing stress also alleviates some of the diabetic problems. Dieting, exercise, and avoiding stress are things that take time and effort. If insulin is cheap, the diabetic will use insulin as a substitute for these activities. As insulin becomes more expensive, the diabetic will use less insulin and substitute into different meals, sports, and occupations. As a result the law of demand holds for a drug like insulin, just like it holds for gasoline. The same holds for every other type of good you can imagine.

Essentially, to deny the downward slope of the demand function is to deny the principle of substitution. For every good there is a substitute, which means when the price of something goes up, people substitute into other goods that provide utility at lower relative prices. Substitutes are everywhere, and so demand curves are always downward sloping.

Still, many people are not convinced. What would the law of demand say about mandatory seat belt laws? If a seat belt lowers the drivers chance of getting hurt in an accident, then there should be more accidents! "Wait" you cry. "No one wants to get into an accident." Of course not. But everyone wants to get places faster and listen more to the music on the radio than pay attention to the car at the next intersection. As objectionable as it strikes us, the truth of the matter is that when seat belt laws are introduced there are more accidents, more passenger injuries, and more pedestrians hit. Lowering the cost of driving poorly, leads to more poor driving. If you don't agree with this, consider the following thought experiment: how safely would you drive, if instead of the nice airbag in your car, there was a 6 inch dagger coming out of the steering wheel, pointed right at your chest? Sobering thought, isn't it?

The list goes on and on. Here's one that many find very objectionable. In over 30 of the United States, individuals are able to carry a concealed handgun and use it in their self defense. The individuals with weapons have to be trained, acquire a permit, and cannot have a criminal record. Survey results show that these weapons are pulled out (not necessarily shot) about 2 million times each year to prevent crimes. The number of individuals in any given state that actually apply for a weapon is quite small, between 2% and 4%. However, even with this low take up rate the effects on crime are quite large. It turns out that violent crime rates fall with the introduction of right to carry laws. Murder rates in these states fell by 8%, rape by 5%, robbery by 3%, and aggravated assault by 7%. Interestingly, for crimes that involved stealth, such as burglary, crime rates increased. Who are these armed vigilantes? They tend to be older, female, and well educated.

This pattern of behavior is consistent with the law of demand. If a criminal is going to engage in an activity where he or she now stands a slight chance of running into a weapon, the cost of crime increases dramatically. Given the small number of individuals that actually carry a weapon, it might seem unreasonable that there should be such a large effect on crime. However, what if you knew that the chance of a serious car accident was 2%? That is, in the next 50 times behind the wheel, you would probably be involved in a serious accident that might kill you. No doubt you would stop driving. Unlike driving, the benefits to most crimes are not very high. Hence it is not unreasonable that the effect of the law should be so large. Also note the fact that criminals substitute into crimes of stealth where they are less likely to run into people, suggests that even criminals act according to our principles.

One additional finding is worth noting. Concealed weapon laws had a much larger impact on protecting women than men. When an additional woman carries a concealed hand gun it reduces the murder rate by about 3 to 4 times more than when an additional man carries a concealed handgun. This no doubt reflects the larger marginal gain of a hand gun to a woman than to a man. Criminals prey on those they think will be the easiest victims. Robbing an elderly woman is much easier than taking on a large adult male. The marginal benefit of women carrying weapons, then, is much greater.

All of this is simply a direct implication of the law of demand. However, many people find the suggestion that more guns can lead to less crime verging on insanity. Still, let's push the implications of the reasoning even further. After the terrorist attacks of September 11, 2001 there was a tidal wave of suggestions on how to improve the safety of airlines. Sky marshalls were suggested. But given the hundreds of thousands of flights each day, it was quickly realized that the employment of so many marshalls would have a prohibitive cost. Locking the pilots in the cabin has been suggested. But the problem is that the promise to not open a locked door, when a flight attendant has their life threatened, is not very credible. More security has been added to airports, but spot testing has already shown this to have little effect and leads to bombs made to avoid detection. Recently a plot was stopped in England where liquid bombs were being placed in shampoo containers. What would be a cheap, effective deterrent?

What would happen to a hijacker's ability to take a plane if a random and unknown 2% of the passengers were licensed to carry a concealed hand gun? Suppose the guns were designed such that they wouldn't pierce the plane's envelope. The answer is that the plane would probably never be taken over. The only way a small group of people can hold a large group hostage is to exploit each individual's personal desire to live. The hijackers simply let the crowd know that the first person to attack them will die, and no one wants to be the first person. However, when the first person is armed with a weapon of their own, and have the element of surprise on their side, it is difficult to see how the hijacker could win. At the very least, policemen and other individuals we allow to carry weapons all the time should be allowed to carry their weapons on board. In fact, they should fly for free! Such a policy would seem to raise the price of hijacking so much there should be no hijackings. Yet, try to make this suggestion at your next social gathering and see how people start to move away from you. The law of demand often has direct, but unpopular implications.

4.6 Indirect Evidence for the Law of Demand

The famous investments of the Hunt brothers during the late 1970s in an effort to corner the silver market is an interesting case of indirect evidence for the law of demand. In the summer of 1979 the price of silver was \$8/ounce. Throughout the 1970s a wealthy Dallas oil man Nelson Bunker Hunt and his brother William Herbert had been accumulating silver, and by the summer of 1979 had control of 42 million ounces. Beginning in the fall of that year, the price of silver began to rise sharply, and by January 1980 the price of silver was an unprecedented \$50/ounce. The Hunt brothers, by this time had gained control of 280 million ounces of silver — equivalent to the annual world silver production. On the surface, the Hunt brothers look like an exception to the law of demand — as the price increased, the quantity of silver they demanded increased. In fact, the Hunt brothers were just an example of behavior commonly known as speculation. Is speculation a counter example to the law of demand?

It turns out that speculation is a nice example of downward sloping demand curves. Recall that demand depends on the relative price (p_1/p_2), not the nominal price. With speculation the two prices that matter are the price today and the expected price tomorrow of the good in question. In the case of the Hunt brothers, they were not so much concerned with the price of silver on a given day, but what they thought the price would be in the coming weeks. We might think of the relative price as: $P_{\text{today}}/P_{\text{tomorrow}}$. If the price of silver today is \$8, and you expect the price tomorrow to be \$8, then the relative price is 1, and a certain amount of silver is demanded today. But if the expected price of silver tomorrow is \$50, then the relative price today is 8/50=.16. Silver is an absolute bargain today and the quantity demanded today increases. Just as shown in Figure 4-3.

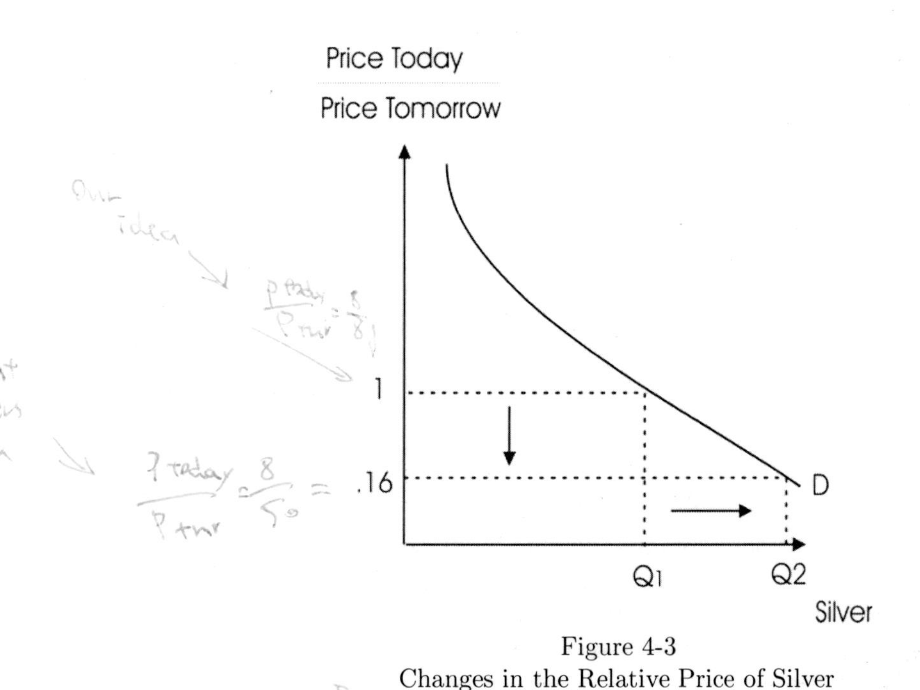

Figure 4-3
Changes in the Relative Price of Silver

A speculator is by definition someone who thinks the price tomorrow will be higher than the price today. Thus when the price of silver rises today, but the investor thinks it will rise even more tomorrow, then the relative price today actually falls! Given the law of demand, the speculator should buy more today. Rather than being a counter example to the law of demand, the Hunt brothers are actually a testimony to it.

An even more subtle example of the law of demand is called the Alchian-Allen theorem, after the two economists who first articulated it. Suppose there is a commodity called leather sandals made in Spain, which can be broken down into two goods: high quality sandals, and low quality sandals. In Spain the high quality sandals sell for $10, while the low quality ones sell for $5. In other words, the relative price in Spain of high quality sandals is 2 pairs of low quality sandals. Further suppose that in order to ship the sandals to North America it costs $10/pair independent of the quality. The relative price in North America is now 20/15=1.33. Now the relative price of high quality sandals is down from 2 to 1.33. As Figure 4-4 shows, the law of demand predicts that there will be a higher proportion of good sandals relative to bad sandals consumed in North America than in Spain.[4]

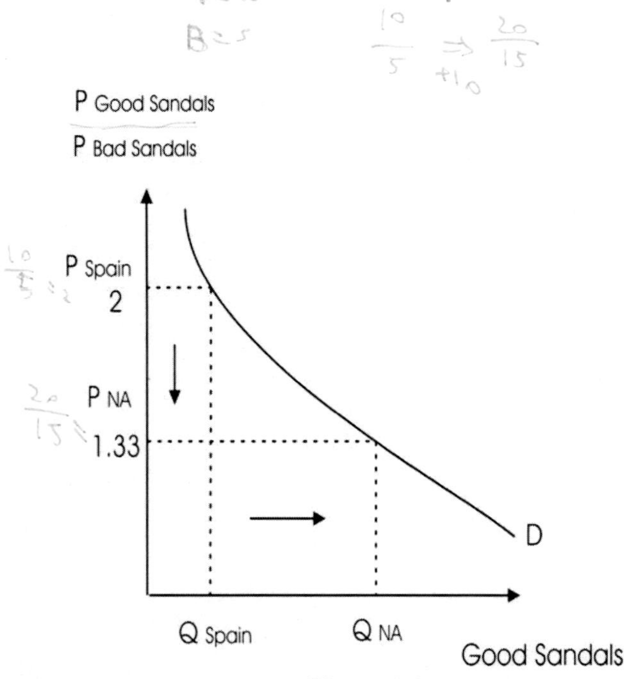

Figure 4-4
Transportation Charges and the Demand for Good Sandals

This is a remarkable result and holds for all goods that are traded over large distances. In fact, the Alchian-Allen theorem is often called "shipping the good apples out" because of the observation that the better apples grown in the Pacific Northwest find their way to distant parts of North America that do not grow apples. In general, the foreign place consumes less of the good, but a

---

[4] A further implication of the law of demand comes from the relative consumption of other goods to sandals. Since both types of sandals are more expensive in North America relative to other goods, North Americans should consume fewer Spanish sandals than people in Spain.

higher fraction of their consumption is of high quality. Many examples of this relative price effect abound: Alaskans eat less beef than Texans, but more of it is deboned; Canadians drink less French wine than the French, but the proportion of expensive wine is higher; New Yorkers consume fewer grapes than Californians, but they consume a higher proportion of high quality grapes; and on and on. Essentially what is happening is consumers are substituting into the relatively cheaper commodity, even though both goods are becoming more expensive. The critical lesson here is that moving up and down a demand curve involves substitution.

> *A fixed charge applied to a high and low quality good, lowers the relative price of the high quality good, and results in a higher relative consumption of the high quality good.*

This result of a change in relative prices goes beyond mere transportation charges. Whenever there is a fixed charge added to two separate prices, it lowers the relative price of the high quality good. Hence couples with children go out less often, but to more expensive events, than similar couples without children because they must pay for a baby sitter and the baby-sitting fee is independent of where they go. For example, suppose there is a discount movie house that charges only \$1 per show, and a first run movie theater that charges \$8 per show. Before a couple has children, the relative price of the expensive theater is 8. That is, the couple sacrifices eight low quality movies for every high quality movie they see. Once the couple has a child they must pay a baby-sitting fee which is independent of the type of movie they attend. If the baby-sitter charges \$20 for the evening, then the relative price of the two types of entertainment becomes $28/21 = 1.3$. Now the relative price of the expensive movie falls a great deal. Instead of giving up eight low quality movies, they essentially give up one. Faced with this choice, the couple will substitute into the higher quality of entertainment. Because both prices have gone up, however, the couple will demand less movies overall.

As with transportation charges, the number of examples one can imagine that involve fixed charges is only limited by your imagination. For example, nice homes are built on expensive lots rather than cheap ones because the fixed lot cost lowers the relative price of the expensive home, gold bindings only go on hardback books not paperbacks because the fixed printing cost lowers the relative price of the hardback book, and tailored suits use more expensive cloth than suits sold off the rack because the fixed tailor fee lowers the relative cost of the expensive cloth. All are examples of changes in relative prices brought about by fixed charges, and how these bear on the law of demand.

You might be wondering, if the high quality items tend to be shipped out, why do you have to go to Maine to get a great lobster, or Vancouver to get a great salmon? The answer, of course, is just the law of demand once again. It doesn't really matter if the salmon gets shipped to you, or you get shipped to the salmon — there is still a fixed transportation charge. Let's suppose that you are traveling from Chicago to Vancouver for the sole purpose of sitting down at the Pan-Pacific Hotel dining room and eating the best salmon in the house. Suppose there are two Salmon prices on the menu: high quality, costing \$50, and low quality costing \$25. Suppose also your travel costs are \$1000. The relative price for you of the good salmon is $1050/1025$. The relative price for a local Vancoverite is 2. Since your relative price is extremely close to one, you buy the expensive salmon. Now you know the reason why travelers often return home boasting about the food on their adventures.

4.7 Total Value vs Marginal Value

If the height of the demand curve at a given quantity is the marginal value, then the area under the demand curve up to that quantity must be the *total value.* For example, if the consumer is willing to pay $12 for the first apple, and $10 for the second apple, then the value of two apples would just be the sum of $22. Consider Figure 4-5, where we'll think of marginal value in its discrete form: the value of each additional apple. Notice in this figure the labeling on the vertical axis is simplified to P_1 rather than the relative price.

> *Total Value: the maximum amount one is willing to pay for a given quantity rather than have none at all.*

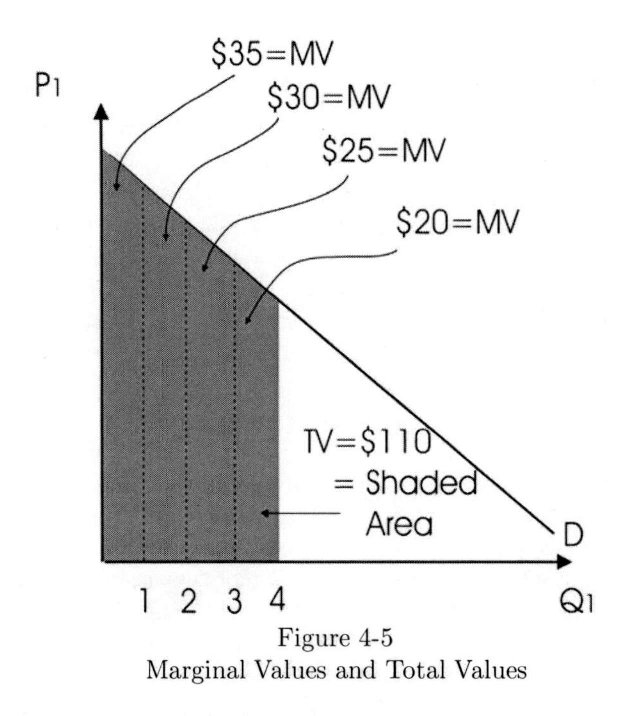

Figure 4-5
Marginal Values and Total Values

In Figure 4-5 the consumer is willing to pay $35 for the first unit of good 1. This means that the marginal value of the first unit is $35. For the second unit the consumer is willing to pay $30. This means that in order to go from having one unit to two units the consumer is willing to pay an additional $30. However, it also means that the consumer is willing to pay $65 for two units, rather than have none at all. The $65 is the consumer's *Total Value* of two units. Notice that the marginal value continues to fall the more the consumer demands. For the third unit the marginal value is $25, and the fourth unit only has a marginal value of $20. However, the total value continues to rise: $90 for three units, and $110 for four units. The total value for 4 units is shaded in Figure 4-5. This inverse relationship between marginal and total value is a fundamental property of demand curves.

There is an inverse relationship between total value and marginal value.

Total value is just the sum of all the marginal values, and is graphically represented as the area *under* the demand curve. The difference between marginal and total value explains a number of paradoxes that arise in life over the ambiguous use of the word value. For example, a 19th century paradox of value arose from the observation that falling grain prices always accompanied a bumper grain harvest. If more grain is always better, why did the price fall, indicating that consumers valued the grain less? The answer, of course, is that more grain increases the total value, but lowers the marginal value. Since prices equal marginal values, not total values, the prices also fall.

This is what is commonly known as the water-diamond paradox, after a stylized example. Water is necessary for life while diamonds are of only minor importance, yet water is generally very inexpensive and diamonds are pricey. Similarly, you may have noticed that at various times Coca-Cola sells for two to three times the price of gasoline, yet most of us think that gasoline is more valuable than Coke. Once again, we see an abuse of the term value. As shown in Figure 4-6 where the total value is the shaded area, gas has a high total value and a low marginal value, while Coke has a high marginal value and a low total value. If people were given the choice: you must give up either gasoline or coke, they would certainly abandon the latter.

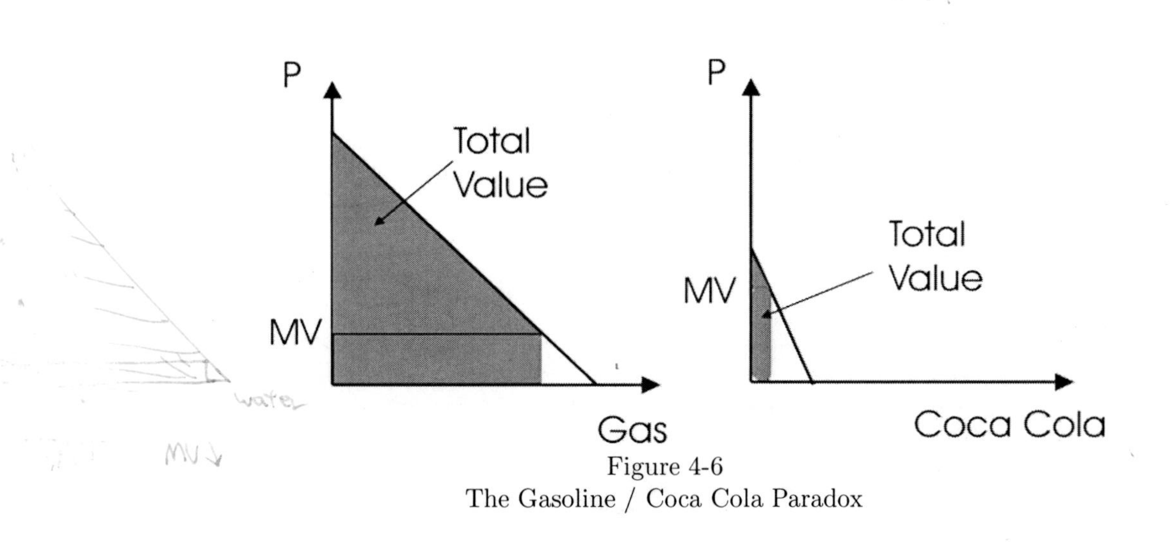

Figure 4-6
The Gasoline / Coca Cola Paradox

The difference between MV and TV has a number of daily personal applications. Have you ever had a near fatal experience? Perhaps you had a serious car accident or a close friend or relative almost died? At those times many people sense a reevaluation of the things they value, and express sentiments like "it really makes you appreciate what is important in life." People make vows to spend more time together, take time off work, smell the roses, etc., and yet when the tragic moment passes, they tend to live as they always did. What is going on?

The answer lies in the difference between MV and TV. Most of our lives are spent at the margin. We divide our time and income up and we choose to spend an hour here, a dollar there. Thus it is natural for us to often think about values in terms of marginal values because in choosing optimal quantities we set MVs equal to prices. In tragic moments though, when a child suddenly disappears, your parents are caught in a house fire, or life flashes before your eyes, you are faced with an all or nothing situation. Now you have to make decisions based on total values, not marginal ones. Things, like children or parents, that had high total values and low marginal values become much more important than they were before. When life returns to normal, we again go about our days making marginal decisions.

One final point to be made about marginal values is that they tend to equalize across people and goods when prices are equal. Figure 4.7 shows the author's demand curves for old Seinfeld episodes and The Simpsons. Each show takes thirty minutes and plays at approximately the same time of day, so for the sake of argument the price in terms of hours is equal across the two shows. Given the cost of watching the shows, I watch 12 hours of Seinfeld each week and 1 hour of the Simpsons. Clearly I have a higher total value for Seinfeld because the area under the demand curve for Seinfeld (up to 12 hours) is larger than the area under the demand curve for the Simpsons (up to the 1 hour). But notice that the marginal values of each show (the height of the demand curves at 12 and 1) are equal. As long as the MV of a Seinfeld episode is greater than its price, I'm better off consuming an additional episode. The same is also true for Homer and his family. The optimal amount to watch is determined when the relative price equals the marginal value. Since the price is the same for both shows, the MV for each show is equal, which means that at the margin I'm indifferent between the two shows. This equalizing across the two margins is the result of maximizing behavior and occurs for the same reason that the speed of traffic across the lanes on a highway tend to equalize. Can you see why?

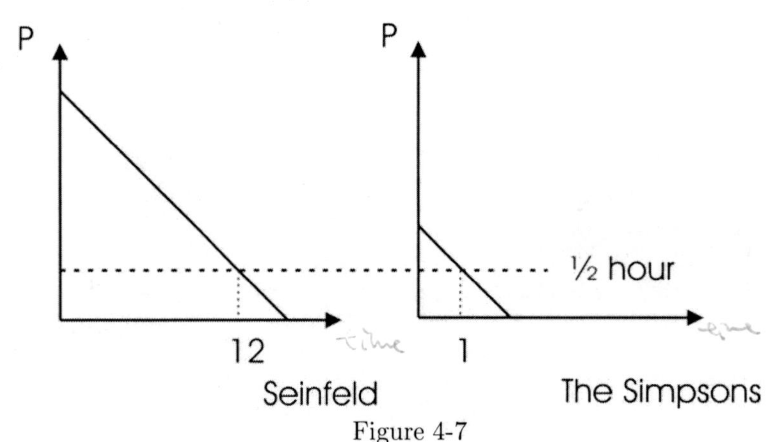

Figure 4-7
Equal Marginal Values When Costs are the Same

4.8 **Total Expenditure and Consumer's Surplus**

If the area under the demand function is the total value a consumer places on a good, then we can divide this area into two parts. Consider Figure 4-8, which simply repeats Figure 4-1. When the consumer buys a quantity of Q_1 at a price of P_1, he spends an amount of $P_1 \times Q_1$. This amount is equal to the consumer's total expenditure — it's how much the consumer spends, and is equal to the boxed area on the graph. On the other hand, if the area under the demand curve is how much the consumer is *willing* to spend, and the bottom shaded rectangle is how much money the consumer *has* to spend, then the difference between these two is the "surplus" the consumer gets from consuming. This consumer's surplus is the triangular area above the total expenditure.

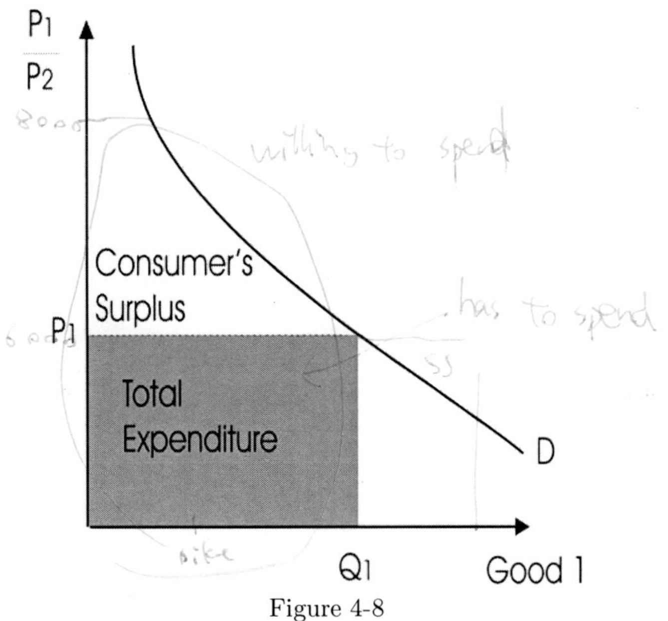

Figure 4-8
Consumer's Surplus and Total Expenditure

For example, suppose you want to buy a motorcycle, let's say the new Yamaha V-Star cruiser. If you're like my friend Mike you might be willing to pay $8000 for such a bike. The $8000 is the total value of the bike to Mike. However, the bike only sells for around $6000. If Mike buys the bike, his total expenditure is $6000, and his consumer's surplus is $2000. That $2000 represents how much better off Mike is from buying the bike rather than not having it at all. In other words, the consumer's surplus is a measure of the gains from trade to the consumer. As such, it is a very valuable tool for assessing various issues involving trade, and it is something we will use over and over again.

One application of consumer's surplus can be found in the Tradewell/Safeway example. Recall what's at issue is which store offers the better prices. The experiment conducted by Tradewell failed to determine an answer, but one solution would be to examine the total consumer's surplus at each store. Figure 4-9 shows the demand for each good, along with their prices and consumer's surpluses at each store.[5] The consumer's surplus at Tradewell is $34.50, while at Safeway it equals $30.50. Thus we see that Tradewell does offer the better deal overall.

---

[5] Recall these demand curves come from the equation $Q = 11 - P$. We're just assuming this simple demand curve applies to all three goods for simplicity. Having complicated demand

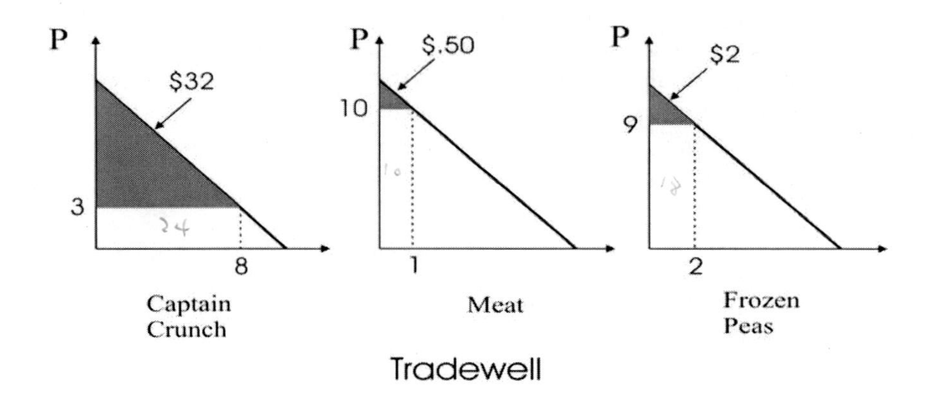

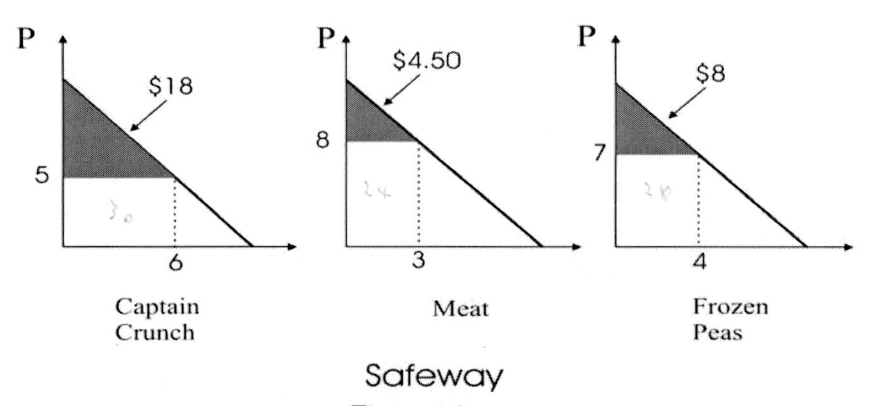

Figure 4-9
Consumer's Surplus at Tradewell and Safeway

4.9 **Summary**

This chapter has introduced you to the *law of demand*, one of the most significant ideas in all of social science. The law of demand, with its simple, intuitive relationship between prices and quantities, has many subtle and strong implications. Like the principle of substitution, the law of demand applies to anything people value. Furthermore, as we saw with speculation and shipping the good apples out, the law of demand has many indirect implications as well. Throughout the rest of the book we will use the concepts of this chapter many times.

---

curves, or different demand curves for each good would be more realistic, but it wouldn't change the fact that the best way to determine which store has the better prices is to use consumer's surplus.

REVIEW QUESTIONS

1. Tom is talking to Emily: "Yesterday I went to a movie and the price was $12. Do you know I have to work 1.5 hours to pay for that movie, and I could have bought a t-shirt with that money." Identify the nominal prices of movies and t-shirts, the relative price of movies to t-shirts, and Tom's nominal wage in this statement.

2. If the price of American dollars falls relative to the Canadian dollar, do more Americans or Canadians cross the border to shop?

3. Suppose an individual's demand for potato chips is given by the equation: $Q = 35 - 5P$. What is the quantity demanded when the price is $10, $7, $6, and $3?

4. From question (3), if the price was $3, what would be the total amount spent on potato chips? What would be the consumer's surplus? What would be the total value?

5. Is it inconsistent for a parent to yell at their child to "stop bugging them" one minute, but then get upset if the child goes missing the next?

6. What economic idea was King Solomon getting at when he said:

   Let your foot rarely be in your neighbor's house, lest he become weary of you and hate you.

   Proverbs 25:17

7. Fred has an income of $10,000 per month. There are two goods to consume with prices $p_1 = 50$ and $p_2 = 100$. What is Fred's real income in terms of good 1. What is his real income in terms of good 2? What is the relative price of good 2 to good 1?

8. Below are some lyrics to the classic Barry White tune "Can't Get Enough of Your Love, Babe" Are these lyrics consistent or inconsistent with our principle of diminishing marginal value?
   I've heard people say that
   Too much of anything is not good for you, baby
   But I don't know about that
   Darling, I can't get enough of your love babe ...

9. Consider a consumer with an ordinary demand for some product. Will it always be true that the consumer's surplus is greater than the total expenditure on the good if the demand curve is inelastic.'

10. Mr. Lear has three daughters. The oldest was a little cranky one day and so Mr. Lear decided to cheer her up with a game. "Come my child, we shall talk. Ask me any question you wish, and I will grant you an answer." "Okay," the daughter responded, "your three daughters have been sentenced to death, but you can save one of them. Who do you choose?" "My goodness" Mr. Lear quietly responded, wishing he'd never played the game. What economic concept was the daughter trying to elicit from her father?

PROBLEMS

1. In Joni Mitchell's 1973 hit song *Big Yellow Taxi* she has the famous lyrics:
   Don't it always seem to go
   That you don't know what you've got till it's gone?
   They paved paradise and put up a parking lot.

   How would you interpret these sentiments using the economic ideas discussed in this chapter?

2. "Currently the criminal sentence for growing marijuana is independent of the quality. Therefore, if the drug became legal we would expect the level of quality to increase." True, False, Uncertain, Explain.

3. "Water is so precious for life, and without it everything dies. Therefore, we must treat it with care and look after it. Unfortunately, we abuse water. We waste it watering our lawns, flushing out toilets, and washing our cars." If water is so valuable, why are we so frivolous with it?

4. Children are fond of asking parents "What's your favorite 'blank'?" Where they may be asking about a color, television show, or morning cereal. What notion of value are they implicitly using? If you ask a child, however, what is their favorite toy, friend, or parent(!), they often say "all of them are my favorite". What notion of value are they using in this answer and why would they give this answer?

5. Suppose that a large company owns an underground parking lot that has spots currently worth \$200/month. Initially the company provides the parking for free to its employees with the condition that they are not allowed to sublet the spot. After a change in management, the company removes the free parking privileges and charges the employees \$200/month for the spot. If there are only two types of cars (good cars that rent for \$1000/month and bad cars that rent for \$500/month), what would you predict would happen to the average quality of car parked in the lot after the increase in fee?

6. What does the law of demand predict will happen to the number of abortions when abortion is made legal? How would you respond to the comment: "the law of demand doesn't apply to desperate women seeking an abortion."?

7. In the 1970s the United States adopted a policy to reduce speed limits to 55 miles per hour on its freeways in order to save fuel. Speed limits on secondary roads were not changed. If we think of the cost of using different roads simply in terms of the amount of time it takes to get from point A to B, what did this policy do to the relative price of using freeways versus using secondary roads? Driving on freeways is much safer than driving on a secondary road. What impact do you think the 55 mph speed limit had on the overall death rate from car accidents in a given state?

8. Every country in the western world has some type of safety net system to help the poor. In creating such laws it is necessary to define who the poor are. In an effort to obtain the money in such plans, what types of substitutions do you think will be made by some individuals if the poor are defined as:

   a. individuals with an income less than \$13,000.

b. single parents.

c. blind people.

9. Provide a law of demand type explanation for why urban families have fewer children than rural families.

10. Why do you think women and seniors are more likely to participate in volunteer activities like churches, the red cross, and fraternal societies, than men and people under 65?

11. Most life insurance policies are void if the policy holder commits suicide within a short time of obtaining the policy. These probation periods are usually either 12 or 24 months. How many months after a policy has been taken out do you think coincide with the highest for number of suicides? Which number of months do you think have the lowest?

12. We often hear expressions like "free to choose"; economics is often called "choice theory"; in religious circles there are debates about "freewill". Given our basic principles of economics would you say that individuals have freewill? How would you reconcile this with the following quote from a national newspaper regarding the sensational Lorenna Bobbit marriage case: "Lorenna Bobbit had no choice but to cut off her husband's penis. She was abused from the beginning of the marriage, and enough was enough."

13. "It wouldn't matter if you raised the price of gas to $5 per gallon, consumption of gas would not change, because people need gas." Does this make any sense? Use a graph in your answer.

14. British Columbians have the highest per capita use of real Christmas trees than any one else in North America. The head of the Christmas Tree Grower's Association says this is due to "our love of real trees". What is a better explanation

15. The ancient mariner said "Water, water, everywhere, and all the boards did shrink. Water, water, everywhere, nor any drop to drink." (For those of you who don't know, the mariner was on the ocean.) Would there have been a water-diamonds paradox for the ancient mariner? Explain.

16. When I lived in Seattle I attended the University of Washington Husky football games regularly. Now that I live Vancouver B.C. (100 miles away), what do you think has happened to (i) the quantity of live Husky games I attend and (ii) the quality of seat I now sit in? Briefly explain your answer.

17. It has been reported that Canadians on average spend more money on perfume than they do on post secondary education. Would this mean that Canadian's value perfume more than education?

18. In Spain good sandals cost $6, while cheap ones cost only $3. Spanish sandals, however, are subject to a $12 duty and shipping fee when brought into Canada. Predict the relative consumption of good and cheap sandals, here and in Spain. What about the relative consumption of sandals to other goods, here and in Spain?

19. At some public hearings over their decision to allow various firms to use "dirty" fuels, like coal,

as a substitute for natural gas. At a hearing a spokesman for the Canadian Lung Association got up and said "When you can't breathe, nothing else matters". In what sense was this person confusing marginal and total value. Draw a graph to explain your answer, and be careful to indicate what is on the demand curve.

20. It is often observed that when a "war on drugs" takes place, the number of deaths by overdose increases. How is this a subtle implication of the law of demand?

21. Fact number one: the price of gas throughout most of the 1990s was about \$2 per gallon; in 1980 the price was about \$1.20 per gallon; and in 1972, the price was about 40 cents per gallon. Fact number two: in the 1970s there was a massive movement towards small cars with four cylinder engines (Pintos, Hondas, Toyotas, etc.). Fact number three: in the 1990's there was a large movement towards larger vehicles with six and eight cylinder motors (eg. SUVs, Vans, Suburbans, etc.). Why would there be in increase in the demand for large gas consuming vehicles when the price of gas increased? Make sure this answer can also explain why there was a move towards small vehicles in the 1970s.

22. Suppose that in 1985, the prices of steak and potatoes were, respectively, \$3 and \$.50 per pound. In 1995, after some inflation, the prices became \$4 and \$.60, respectively. If we ignore income effects and assume there are no other goods, would you expect this person's consumption of steak and potatoes to have changed?

23. I get paid, like most people, once every two weeks. Like most people, I spread my income around so that I consume about the same everyday. I don't go from "feast to famine". Using the appropriate graph, show why this behavior is consistent with economic principles.

24. Prior to unleaded gasolines all cars used leaded gas, with the more expensive gas containing more lead. It turned out that lead was a major pollutant, and in the 1960's, in an effort to mitigate pollution a tax of \$.10/gallon was placed on all gas in the hope that it would reduce the level of gas consumption and lower the amount of pollution. Can we say, unambiguously, that such a tax would lower pollution from leaded gasoline? Why or why not?

25. Joe's, an impoverished student, has a demand for meat given by

Price	12	11	10	9	8	7	6	5	4
Quantity Demanded	1	2	3	4	5	6	7	8	9

In the market place the price of meat is \$8. However, the government has introduced a "meat stamp" subsidy program for students. Students can purchase \$1 of meat stamps for \$.50. Each student is limited, however, to how many meat stamps they can buy. At most Joe can buy \$80 worth of meat stamps (for \$40).

a. Assuming Joe cannot trade meat and meat stamps (that is, he must use them for his own meat consumption), how much meat will Joe buy and at what total expenditure?

b. What is the consumer's surplus to Joe of being able to purchase meat stamps? That is, how much better off is Joe when he is allowed to buy the meat stamps?

c. If Joe can resell the meat stamps to non-students, how much meat will Joe buy?

d. Which case would Joe prefer, the case where he must use the stamps, or the case where he is allowed to sell them? Why?

26. Once I took my children skating. Afterwards my eldest daughter bought a hot chocolate, and by the time we reached the car, she still had not finished. "You'd better not spill that in my car" I told her. Sure enough, 5 seconds later, she spilled the drink on her lap and on the seat. I got angry, and she replied, "You love your car more than you love me!" I responded that this was partly true, and then told her why. What economic concepts did I tell her about?

27. Video Jones (VJ) likes to play arcade games. There are two arcades in the town where he lives. No other close substitutes are available. Arcade A and Arcade B differ only with respect to the way they price their games. Arcade A charges 50 cents per game, with no admission charge. Arcade B charges 40 cents per game after customers pay a weekly admission fee of $5. Reproduced below is a portion of VJ's demand schedule for arcade games.

Price	Games/Week
$.55	25
.50	50
.45	75
.40	100
.35	125

a. In order to gain the most from his purchase of arcade entertainment, which arcade should he patronize? (Assume VJ's demand schedule is not affected by payment of a weekly fee.)

b. Suppose Arcade B raised the weekly admission fee to $11. If VJ purchased from Arcade B, would he receive any consumer surplus? In this case would he purchase from Arcade A or Arcade B?

28. Does the fact that garbage men make more money than the average high school teacher mean that society values garbage removal more than education? If not, what does it mean?

29. Many seminars are presented by job candidates for faculty positions in the economics departments of North American universities. Typically, several current faculty members go out to dinner with the candidate after the seminar. If the department were to subsidize this activity by reimbursing current faculty a flat amount, say, $15.00 per dinner, how would this affect:

a. The number of dinners attended by faculty?

b. The quality of the dinners, ie. would the subsidy lead to consumption of more costly, or less costly dinners?

30. "In 1979–80 the Vancouver real estate market went crazy. People would buy properties, the price would rise, then they would buy more. The demand for housing was upward sloping!" What's a more reasonable explanation that is consistent with the law of demand?

31. Explain the economics behind the following quote from the newspaper: "Among the reasons for a larger, more expensive home is the lot cost. Just two years ago, lots in some areas sold for $60,000. It doesn't make sense to build a $50,000 home on lots that cost up to $150,000 today."

32. Parents use a number of methods to discipline their children. Two long standing methods are to spank or withhold goods. How do you think the frequency of spanking varies with income within the family? (Hint: What happens to the number and quality of goods to withhold from children as income changes?) When parents withhold toys and other goods, do they want to exploit a child's marginal value or total value?

33. The Israelite King Solomon (*c.* 1000 BC) was one of the wealthiest men of all time. He had over 1000 wives, 40,000 horses, and many mansions. Yet despite all of this he claimed that life was pointless, and that "Vanity of vanities, All is vanity!" Why would someone with so much, have such a dim view of life?

34. In their song "Homeward Bound", Simon and Garfunkel talk about a singer on the road who has grown tired of the road. In part they say:
    Everyday's an endless stream
    Of cigarettes and magazines
    And each town looks the same to me
    The movies and the factories
    And every stranger's face I see
    Reminds me that I long to be ... Homeward bound

    Why would they say something like this when most people think that traveling is fun and singing before hundreds of adoring fans would be an adrenaline rush?

35. The documentary movie "Alone in the Wilderness" (shown about once every 3 months on PBS) is the true story of Dick Proenneke who moved to the remote Twin Lakes region of Alaska in 1967 with only a few hand tools and a small 16mm camera. With this camera he filmed himself building his cabin from scratch, finding food in the wild, and using his ingenuity to solve the daily problems that arise when all alone in the wild. It is a fascinating show, and PBS airs it every time they have a fundraising drive. On these drives, the host invariably says something like "Dick Proenneke wasn't the type of person who didn't enjoy the company of people. In fact, if anyone ever dropped by for a visit, he was known to be very friendly and a great host." Using the ideas of marginal value and total value, why is Dick Proenneke's behavior towards visitors still consistent with a claim that he didn't really enjoy the company of people?

Review Question Answers

1. *The nominal price is $13. When Tom talks about how long he'd have to work for the movie, he's using the notion of real income. When he compares the movie to how many shirts he could buy for the same money, he's using the notion of relative price.*

2. *American dollars have become cheaper. The quantity demanded will, therefore, also increase. This means more American goods will be purchased, and more Canadians will cross the border to shop in the United States.*

3. *If the price is $10, then nothing will be demanded. Likewise at a price of $7. When the price falls to $6, then the quantity demanded is* $35 - 6 \times 5 = 5$. *Therefore 5 bags of chips are demanded. At a price of $3, there are 20 bags demanded.*

4. *If the price was $3, then* $3 \times 20 = \$60$ *would be spent. The triangle above this price is* $\$4 \times 20/2 = \$40$. *So consumer's surplus is $40. The total value is the sum of these two, so total value is $100.*

5. *No, it is not inconsistent. The marginal value of the child might be very low, but the total value could be enormous.*

6. *Clearly he is referring to diminishing marginal values. Two neighbors might be good friends, but when one spends too much time at the other's home, the marginal value of the time together could become negative. Recall on the TV show Seinfeld that Jerry enjoyed his friendship with Kramer, but was not always happy to see him as he barged through the door.*

7. *The real income in terms of good 1 is 10,000/50=200. Real income in terms of good 2 is 10,000/100=100. Clearly the level of real income depends on the price you use in the denominator. This means that the concept of real income is ambiguous. The relative price of good 2 to good 1 is 2. Every time Fred buys a unit of good 2, he could have had 2 units of good 1.*

8. *This is inconsistent with DMV. We get enough of the people we love all the time.*

9. *This is false. If the price gets high enough then total expenditure can exceed consumer's surplus in the inelastic section of a demand curve. To see this, draw a straight line demand curve. Now start with a price of zero. Clearly CS is greater than the TE. Now raise the price. Keep doing this all the way until the elasticity is unitary. Can you see where TE became larger than the CS?*

10. *By adjusting the time he spends with his three daughters, Mr. Lear equates the marginal value of each. However, the oldest one was trying to determine for which daughter Mr. Lear had the highest total value. Sneaky daughter.*

Odd Numbered Problem Answers

1. *She's talking about the difference between marginal and total value. When there are lots of trees around, we enjoy them, but behave towards them based on the value of the marginal tree. When all of the trees are gone, we realize we had a paradise, and we miss the total value we once had.*

3. *For many communities around the world, water is not very valuable at the margin. In Vancouver, where it rains 60 inches in a year, and where the snow pack provides storage for the summer, water is used at zero marginal costs. As a result, it gets used for many frivolous things. In Mesa Arizona, where water is much more scarce, water is more valuable at the margin and is used more sparingly. This says nothing about the total value of water in Vancouver or Mesa.*

5. *This is a "shipping the good apples out" type of question. The cost of parking has increased by $200/month because there is no subletting allowed. Hence, the average quality of car should increase.*

7. *It raised the relative price of using the freeway. Freeways often are not as convenient as secondary roads, but we use them to go faster. It has been shown that lowering the speed limit on freeways marginally lowers deaths, but the number of deaths on secondary roads go up, as does the total death rate.*

9. *Wages for women tend to be higher in urban centers. Since children are time intensive for women, higher wages mean the cost of children are higher. Hence urban families have fewer children, closer together than rural families.*

11. *The 13th and 25th months have the highest rates of suicide, and the 11th and 23rd months have the lowest.*

13. *The statement is arguing the elasticity of demand is zero. That is, there are no substitutes for gasoline. This of course is false, and when the price of gas increases, there is a fall in the quantity demanded. In the figure, for any demand curve with some elasticity there will be a fall in the quantity demanded.*

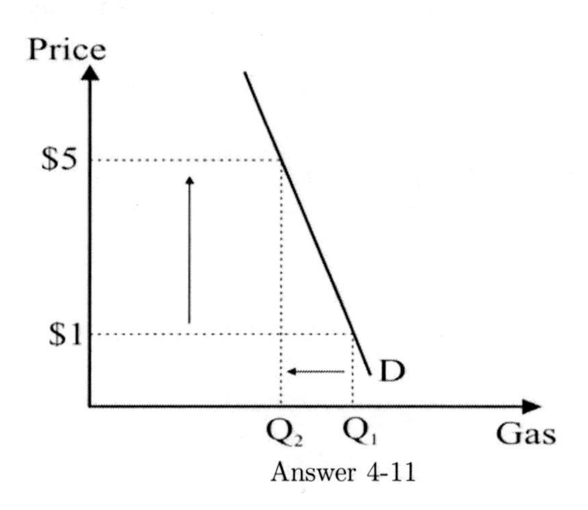

Answer 4-11

15. *No. The mariner had no freshwater, and would have paid much more for a glass of water than for a diamond.*

17. *No, it only means they spend more. The total value placed on post secondary education could be higher.*

19. *Allowing more dirty fuels means there is less clean air to breath, it doesn't mean there is no clean air to breath. If we think of dirty fuels as adding to the cost of consuming clean air (because one has to move, buy filters, etc), then we have:*

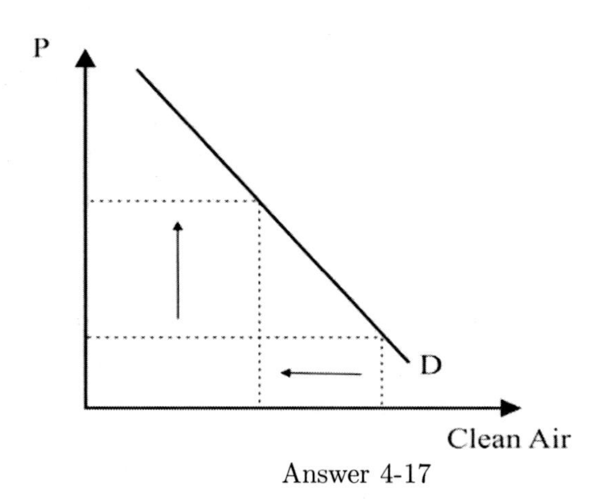

Answer 4-17

21. *So, over time the nominal price of gas increased, but there was a movement towards smaller, then larger vehicles. The real price of gasoline was higher in 1974 than it was in 1986. Thus in the 1970s there was a serious movement to develop cars with better gas mileage. From the mid 80s until the mid 90s there was a continual fall in the real price of gas, and this led to the demand for more powerful cars.*

23.

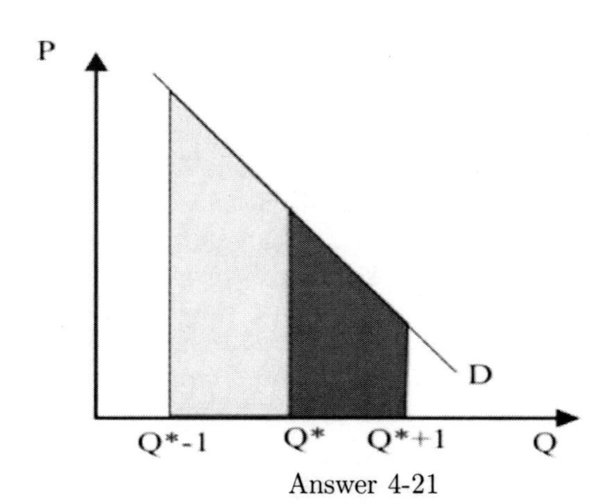

Answer 4-21

Suppose I have two days in between paychecks. If I consume $Q^* + 1$ on the day I get paid, and $Q^* - 1$ on the day I don't, then on payday my total value is the area under my demand curve up to $Q^* + 1$. On the day I don't get paid my total value is the area of the demand curve up to $Q^* - 1$. If I consumed the same each day, the total value for the two days would be two times the area under the demand curve up to Q^*. Hence we have to compare the two shaded areas to see which methods gives me the highest value. Since my MV is falling, I don't get as much marginal value on feast days as I do on famine ones. Thus, I should consume the same each day.

25.

a. *The price is now \$4 for the first 10 units. Joe will buy 9 units at this price for \$36.*

b. *The total consumer's surplus without the stamps is \$12.5. With the stamps the CS is \$40.5. So he is better off by \$28 with the stamps.*

c. *Now he'll buy 10 units of meat. He'll sell 5 units at \$8, and consume the other 5.*

d. *Joe prefers the case where he can sell the extra five units of meat for \$40. This makes him \$12 better off.*

27.

a. *He should go to B. With arcade A he only gets a surplus of \$2.5. With Arcade B his surplus is \$5 (\$10-\$5).*

b. *Now he has a surplus of \$-1, at arcade B. So he should go to A.*

29.

a. *This lowers the price of dinners relative to other activities, so more will go.*

b. *The subsidy raises the relative price of expensive dinners, so less costly dinners will be ordered.*

31. *This is the third law of demand again. The expensive lot lowers the relative price of an expensive home.*

33. *It is one of the great ironies of life. Those with much are often the least happiest. The highest suicide rates in the world are in wealthy western countries. In a nation like poorest Chad, suicide is almost unheard of. In the case of Solomon, he had so much wealth that his consumption was constrained almost only by the amount of time in a day. Whatever he wanted he got, and in vast quantities. The result was that the marginal value of his 40,000th horse, was probably zero. As was his marginal value of just about everything. Since we mostly live life at the margin, this meant he felt most of life was pointless and unenjoyable. Of course, this does not mean he was not a maximizer. On the contrary, his behavior was the result of maximization. Solomon always had the option of giving everything away, but he never did that.*

35. *Even someone who hates people, but never sees any will have a high marginal value for the first*

interaction. Dick Proenneke only saw another human once every 10-12 months. Of course he'd be nice to them. If one of them ever suggested they wanted to build a second cabin on the lake, he probably would have had a different reaction.

4.10 **Appendix: Deriving a Demand Curve**

The Indifference Map

If you recall from the Appendix to Chapter 3, we were discussing how to draw or map the preferences of the ficticious Shauna. We found a way to represent her preferences in a two dimensional graph, and based on the principles of maximization and substitution all we could say was that the lines connecting all of the bundles for which she was indifferent were downward sloping (and didn't cross).

In Chapter 4 we've added two more pieces of information. First, we've discussed the third principle of economics, diminishing marginal value. As we'll see soon, this imposes some shape on Shauna's indifference curves. Also, we've introduced the idea of a budget constraint. Together, all of these assumptions will generate a demand curve.

Starting with the principle of diminishing marginal value, consider Shauna again who has bundle B in Figure 4-10 with 15 mangos and 15 bananas.

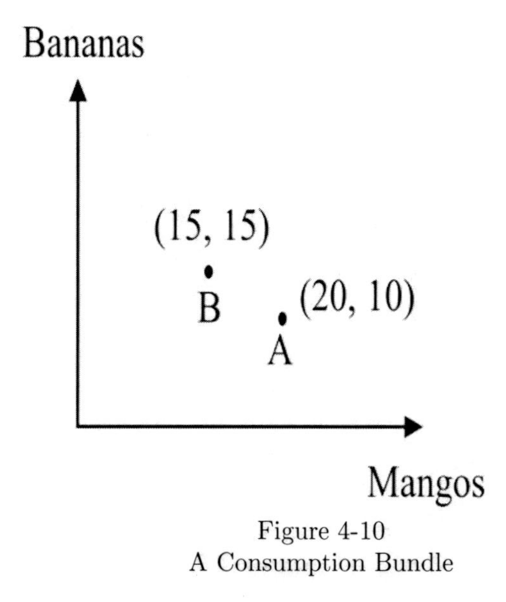

Figure 4-10
A Consumption Bundle

If Shauna is indifferent between bundles A and B, then each of these points would lie along the same indifference curve. But where would a third point lie? Shauna's marginal value for mangos as she moves from B to A is 1 banana. That is, she's willing to sacrifice 5 bananas at most to get another 5 mangos. In other words, the slope between points A and B is Shauna's marginal value. How many bananas would she be willing to sacrifice if increased the number of mangos to 25? Would she give up another 5 bananas?

The answer is, of course, no. The more mangos she has, the fewer bananas she is willing to sacrifice to get more of them. Perhaps she'd only be willing to give up 3 bananas at most. This would mean that her point of indifference would be C in Figure 4-11.

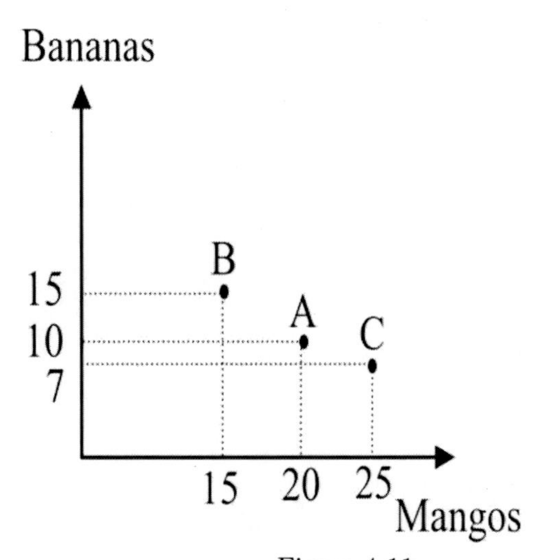

Figure 4-11
Three Indifferent Consumption Bundles

Notice the shape these three bundles are starting to trace out. If we plot all of the points indifferent to B, and which satisfy the principle of diminishing marginal value, then we get the following convex indifference curve:

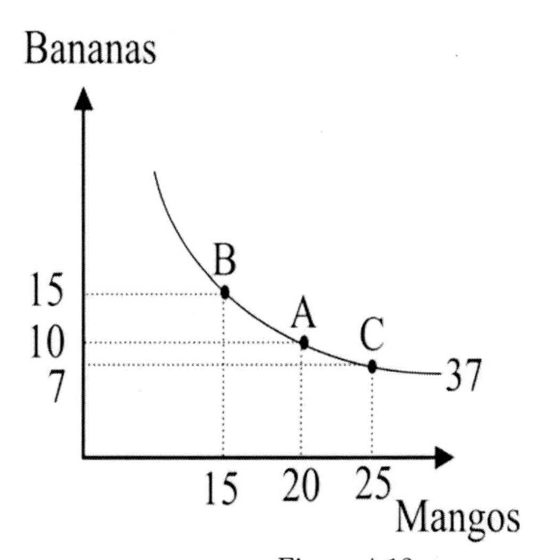

Figure 4-12
An Indifference Curve

It is a convention in economics to assign an arbitrary value to this curve. In this case the number 37 has been assigned. This number simply represents the level of satisfaction Shauna receives when she consumes bundle A, B, C, or any other bundle located on the indifference curve. If we had chosen any other point not on this indifference curve, then we could have found the bundles indifferent to that one, and we could construct another indifference curve. If we did this for every bundle in the

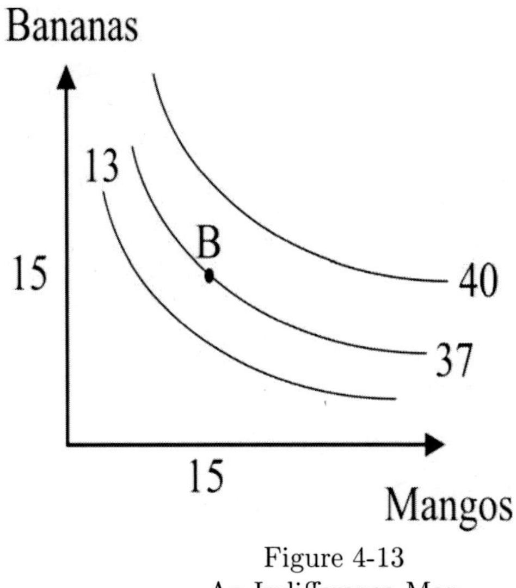

Figure 4-13
An Indifference Map

space, we would have a complete mapping of Shauna's preferences. The next figure simply shows three of them. As before, they are downward sloping, smooth, and do not cross.

Notice that the other two indifference curves also have numbers assigned to them. These are almost arbitrary. The numbers don't mean much, but they must be increasing as Shauna moves away from the origin. The meaning of this is that Shauna prefers to have more goods rather than less. Hence she prefers bundle B over D because the level of satisfaction she gets at B is 37, while the level of satisfaction she gets at D is only 13.

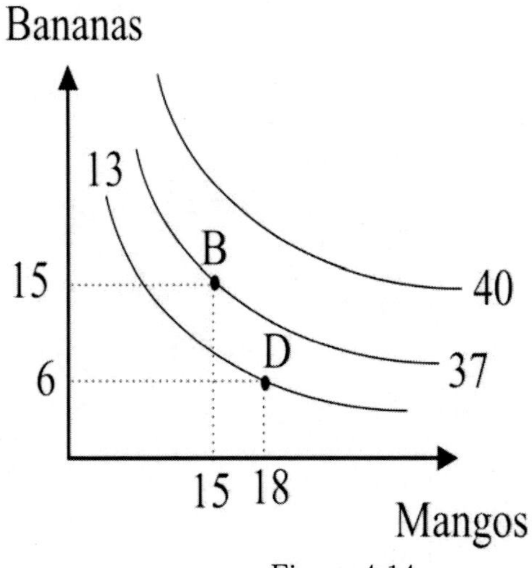

Figure 4-14
An Indifference Map

The Budget Constraint

Let's leave aside Shauna's preferences for a moment. Chapter 4 noted how choices are constrained by the income and prices. To keep things simple, we'll continue to assume that Shauna only consumes mangos and bananas, and that these prices are given by p_m and p_b. If Shauna has a nominal income of \$100, and she spends all of this income on these two goods, then we can think of her budget constraint as:

$$100 = p_m Q_m + p_b Q_b$$

where Q_m and Q_b are the quantities of mangos and bananas Shauna chooses. We can rewrite this equation in the simple "slope-intercept" form everyone learns in high school. Solving for Q_b we get:

$$Q_b = 100/p_b - p_m/p_b \times Q_m.$$

The first term on the right is real income, while the second term includes the relative price. As mentioned in the chapter, this equation shows that the quantity of bananas that Shauna can consume depends on real income and relative prices. If we graph this straight line in the same space that we graphed the indifference curves, then we get Figure 4-15.

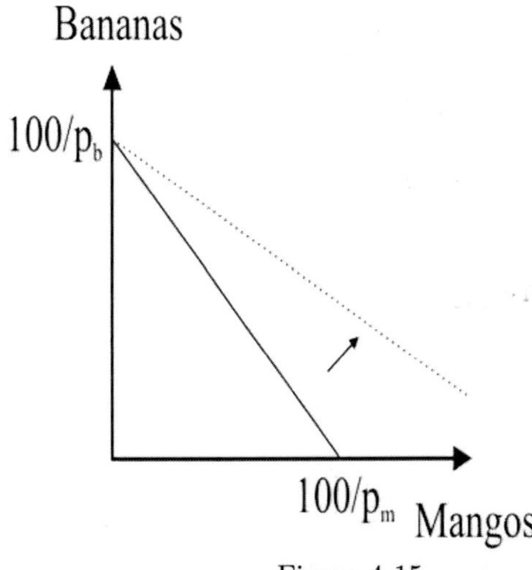

Figure 4-15
A Budget Line

The intercepts of the budget line are just the two measures of real income. We can interpret these intercepts as the maximum amount of bananas or mangos that Shauna could consume. More importantly, the slope of the budget line is the relative price (plus a negative sign). Any change in income or prices leads to a change in the budget line. Notice in Figure 4-15 the dashed line is rotating around the vertical intercept. Can you tell what must have changed to have caused this? ... If you said the price of mangos went down, then you'd be correct. If the price of mangos became cheaper, the budget line would have become steeper and still rotated around the vertical axis. Can you draw a new budget constraint with a higher income? With a higher or lower price for bananas?

The Demand Curve

As argued in the chapter, the demand curve results from combining the three principles of preferences with the budget constraint. Given a budget, Shauna wants to achieve the highest level of satisfaction possible. This means she wants to reach the highest indifference curve she can given her budget and prices she faces. The solution to this problem is shown in Figure 4-16.

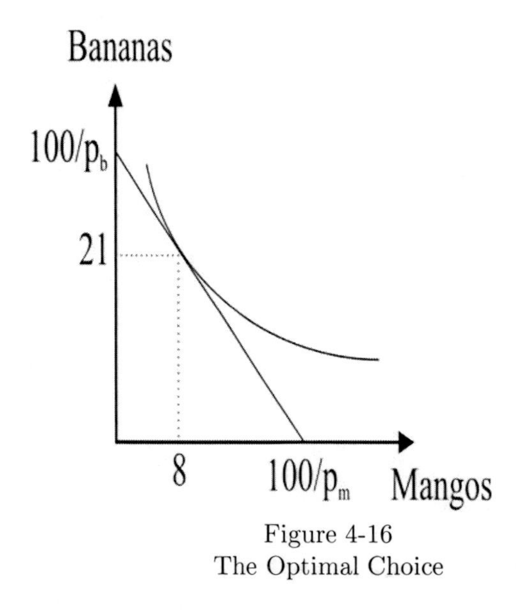

Figure 4-16
The Optimal Choice

When Shauna is consuming 21 bananas and 8 mangos, she has maximized over her preferences. She can't do any better. Sure there are indifference curves higher than this one, but she can't afford them. Sure she could choose a bundle somewhere else along the budget line, but these are on a lower indifference curve. This bundle is the best she can do under the circumstances.

But what happens if the price changes? Suppose the price of mangos changes? Suppose it falls? Well, Shauna then has a new budget line, and given her new circumstances she tries to get on the highest indifference curve once again. We see this in Figure 4-17.

Now notice what has happened. When the price of mangos fell, Shauna consumed more mangos. If that sounds like the law of demand to you, it should, because it is! The law of demand follows from the three assumptions we've made about preferences combined with the budget constraint. Change preferences, income, or prices, and there will be a subsequent change in the demand curve. But these changes are a matter for the next chapter. When you look at Figure 4-17 it doesn't look like a demand curve, and that's because it isn't. Figure 4-17 just has all of the information in it to draw a demand curve. A demand curve has the relative price on the vertical axis, not bananas. A good exercise would be to take the information from Figure 4-17 and on another graph with the relative price on the vertical axis and quantity of mangos on the horizontal, draw out the demand curve.

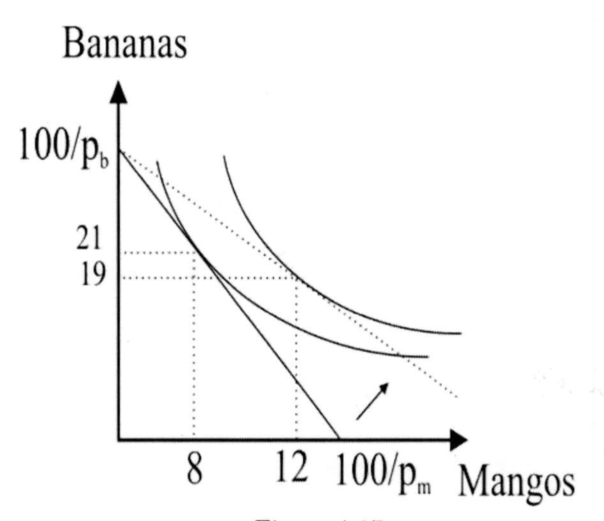

Figure 4-17
The Optimal Choice With a Change in Price

Knowing how a demand curve is derived is an advanced skill, but it also helps us understand behavior better. We can see that the optimal point of consumption is always along the budget line. This means that a person always spends all of their money. Wait! you say, what about savings? Some people save, that's true enough. But for us we can just treat savings as another good and all income is spent on consumption and savings.

Just for some fun, consider the following lyrics from ABBA's song *Money, Money, Money.* The song starts off with the singer complaining that they work day and night to pay the bills, and there's never any money left over for themselves. The singer dreams fo finding a wealthy man so they wouldn't have to work anymore because:

I wouldnt have to work at all, Id fool around and have a ball...
Must be funny ...
Always sunny
In the rich man's world

The first part of the song makes perfect economic sense. We work to pay the bills. That's sad, but it is just a product of living in a world of scarcity. There's never a penny left over because we're always on the budget constraint. As maximizers we always spend what we get. Even when we save, we're just postponing consumption until later. But lead singer Anni-Frid Lyngstad gets off track with the rest of the song. It's only a dream, but in fooling around and having a ball she'd soon find out she would be back on the budget constraint, and life wouldn't always be sunny in the rich man's world. When we earn $15,000 per year, we imagine that life would be set earning $100,000 per year. Yet when you talk to someone who earns a large income you find that they face scarcity just as much as the rest of us ... they just consume more stuff.

CHAPTER 5

TECHY ISSUES OF DEMAND

5.1 Changes in Demand

Very few of the simple things in a book on the principles of economics confuse students as much as the distinction between *changes in demand* and *changes in the quantity demanded.* It is unfortunate the language of each statement is so similar when the concepts are so different.

A change in demand refers to a *shift* in the demand curve. When the demand curve shifts out to the right, we say there is an increase in demand. When the demand curve shifts in to the left, we say there is a fall in demand. Examples of changes in demand are shown in Figure 5-1.

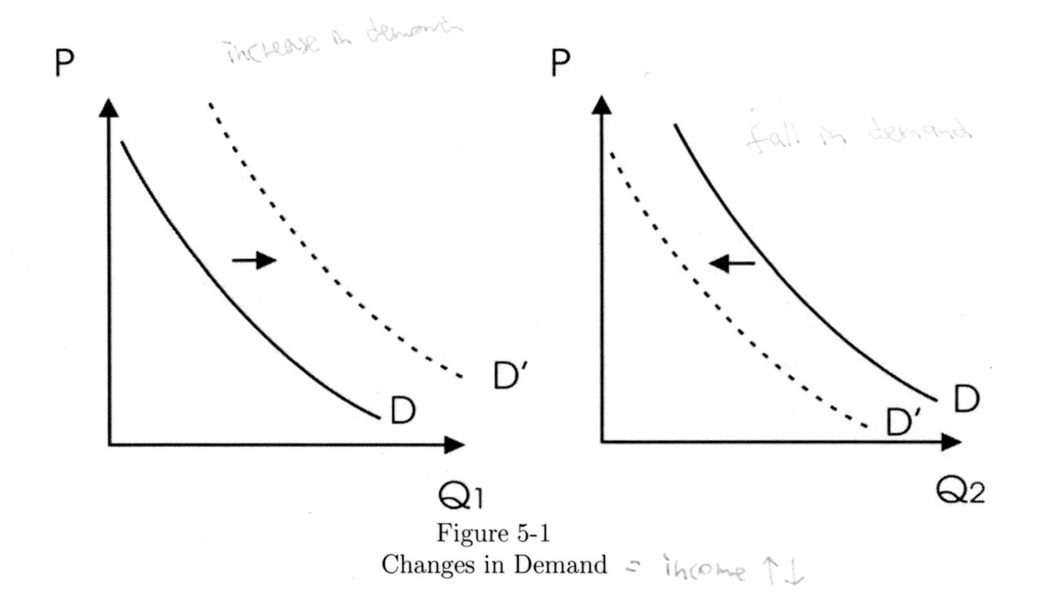

Figure 5-1
Changes in Demand

In the left hand graph the demand curve has shifted to the right, meaning there is an *increase* in demand for good 1. In the right hand graph the demand curve for good 2 has *decreased.* Both of these shifts are what economists call "changes in demand."

You might be wondering: what brings about a change in demand? Recall in the discussion from last chapter that demand curves depended on our principle of diminishing marginal value, which in turn depended on the phrase "other things held constant." Three exogenous parameters implicitly held constant in the discussion of demand were income, the prices of other goods, and tastes or preferences.

Changes in Demand result from changes in exogenous parameters.

Changes in Tastes

Let's start with individual tastes. Clearly everyone has different tastes for different things. You like Pepsi, I like Coke. Some people are vegetarians, but other people won't let anything green touch their plate unless its jello. Whatever the dimension, whether colors, flavors, people, or cars, all of us are simply bent in different directions. For example, there was once a personal advertisement which read: "Farmer, 35 years old, looking for wife between age 30 and 35 who owns her own tractor. Send replies to box number 12, and include picture of tractor." To be more explicit, having different tastes simply means that we have different marginal values *and* different rates at which those marginal values might diminish. That is, everyone's demand curves have different heights and slopes. Although each of us satisfies the first three principles of economics, there is still plenty of room in our theory for everyone to be different.

The left hand graph in Figure 5-1 has an initial solid demand curve in it simply called D. The height of that demand curve is the marginal value that individual places on good 1. If, for whatever reason, a person suddenly liked good 1 more than previously, what would happen to the marginal value? Practically by definition, the marginal value would increase. In other words the demand curve would shift up and out. So an increase in the taste for some good would lead to an increase in the demand for the good. Likewise a decrease in the taste for some good, would lead to a decrease in the demand, similar to the right hand graph in Figure 5-1.

Economists seldom talk about changing tastes because we simply can't observe them. In other words, economists generally assume tastes are constant and don't change over time. Most of the time this seems like a reasonable thing to do. My tastes for most goods I consume seem reasonably constant over time. However, if one is considering changes in consumption over an individual's lifetime, then changes in taste seem inevitable. When I was a child I couldn't stand ethnic foods, but now I love them. No doubt you've noticed changes in your own tastes as you've moved into adulthood.

Changes in Income

By now you might have caught on that changes in demand result from changes in those things "held constant" when drawing the initial demand curve. If you're thinking that way, then keep it up because you're right. When we draw a demand curve we assume that an individual's income is held constant. But what if an individual's income goes up? What happens then?

The answer, unfortunately, is that it depends on the nature of the good. Some goods are what economists call "normal." For these goods an increase in income leads to an increase in demand, just like the left hand graph in Figure 5-1. Thus, if clothing was a normal good, when your income increased, you would buy more clothing — makes sense.

However, when your income increases you might actually buy less of some goods. If you do, then economists call these types of goods "inferior" goods. For example, if your income goes up you might buy fewer canvas shoes and more leather shoes. The canvas shoes would be inferior and the leather shoes would be normal.

Normal Goods: *When income increases the demand for normal goods also increases.*

Inferior Goods: *When income increases the demand for inferior goods decreases.*

Changes in Other Prices

The last thing we assumed was being held constant was "other prices," or the price of good 2 in our simple case. When the prices of other goods change there is a relatively complicated impact on the consumer. First, when the price of good 2 changes, this changes the relative price p_1/p_2. Hence if good 2 becomes cheaper, then the relative price of good 1 increases. As a result, people substitute out of good 1 and into good 2. This is our old friend the *substitution effect.* However, if you recall, demand also depends on the level of real income, which we defined as M/p_2. So when the price of good 2 changes it changes the level of real income. As we've just seen, when real income changes sometimes we increase the consumption of good 1 and other times we decrease consumption, depending on whether good 1 is normal or not.

What this all amounts to is that we cannot say what will happen to the demand for good 1 when the price of good 2 changes. Sometimes the demand will increase, other times the demand will decrease. As with changes in income, however, we can categorize the different effects. If the demand for good 1 increases when there is an increase in the price of good 2, then the two goods are called "substitutes". So, for example, if the demand for butter increases when the price of margarine increases, then we would say that butter and margarine are substitutes. If, on the other hand, the demand for good 1 decreases when there is an increase in the price of good 2, then the two goods are called "complements." Hence, if the demand for bread decreases when the price of butter increases, we say that bread and butter are complements.

Substitute Goods: *When the Price of good 2 increases the demand for good 1 also increases.*

Complement Goods: *When the price of good 2 increases the demand for good 1 decreases.*

The use of the word "substitute" in this context is an unfortunate historical accident. In chapter 3 we noted that all goods are substitutes for one another in that they all provide utility and people are willing to trade anything they value for some amount of anything else they value. We will basically stick with our chapter 3 definition, and will explicitly note when we switch to this more detailed definition of a "substitute."

You may also have noticed there really are no testable implications that come out of changes in demand curves. When one of our parameters (tastes, income, or other prices) changes, essentially anything can happen. In terms of explaining behavior, then changes in demand are not very useful unless we know i) what the change was, and ii) what the nature of the good is. Sometimes economists have a very good idea on whether a good is normal or not, or whether it is a complement or not. For the purposes of learning the principles of economics, however, these empirical matters are generally beyond our concern.

5.2 Changes in Quantity Demanded

A change in demand is a shift in the demand curve that results from a change in a parameter. A *change in the quantity demanded* is a movement along a demand curve that results from a change in the price of the good. Let's refer to Figure 5-2, to help us understand the difference.

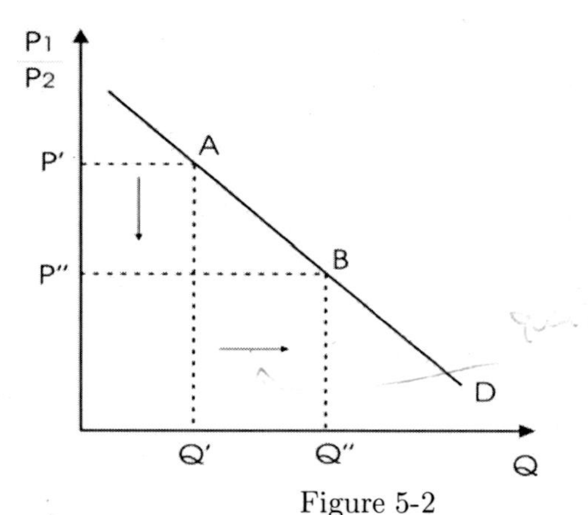

Figure 5-2
Changes in the Quantity Demanded

When the relative price of good 1 is P' then the equilibrium quantity of good 1 that the consumer demands is Q'. When this price falls to P'', the *quantity demanded* increases to Q'' — this is the law of demand. Notice that the demand curve did not shift; that is, there was no change in the demand curve. This is because income and other prices have not changed. The fall in price resulted from a fall in the price of good 1. Although the demand curve did not change, there was still a change in the quantity demanded.

Changes in Quantity Demanded result from changes in the relative price.

This distinction is important because without it people get themselves in all types of trouble. When we hear someone say "fall in demand," we want to know whether this is in reference to shift in the demand curve or a fall in quantity demanded. When we finally get to understanding how prices are determined, this distinction will be crucial.

5.3 Elasticity

We have seen how the quantity demanded of a particular good responds to a change in an exogenous variable like income or other prices; however, how do we compare measures of responsiveness? To make meaningful comparisons we need a unit-free measure — one that is not based on a particular measure like quarts or gallons. In this section we will develop a general unit-free measure of responsiveness — known as *elasticity* — that economists use in a variety of contexts. There's an old joke about a wife who always cuts her husband's meat before he eats it. "Would you like me to cut your steak into four pieces or eight?" she asks one night at dinner. "Oh, four tonight dear," he replies. "I'm on a diet." A characteristic of elasticity is a little like that joke. Although elasticity is a very useful tool, a number of its elements are quite arbitrary, and can influence the actual number you end up with as your answer. In learning about elasticity, try to keep in mind the economics behind the arithmetic.

Also when learning about elasticity, keep in mind the following three step procedure. First, generally speaking, elasticity is a percentage change of a dependent variable due to a percent change of an independent variable. Second, when it comes to prices and quantity demanded, keep in mind that the quantity demanded depends on price (not the other way around). Therefore, the quantity demanded is the dependent variable and price the independent variable. Finally, once you understand this relationship, simply apply the given formula.

The Own Price Elasticity

Suppose that you were working for a firm that sells rolls of unfinished paper to various clients around the world, and suppose that your boss has come to you and told you that they're thinking of lowering the price of each roll by 36¢ and they expect that sales will increase by three million rolls — given the law of demand. Your boss then asks you: Is that change in quantity demanded big? Will it increase or decrease revenue? Furthermore, suppose your boss tells you that he wants to know if this change in quantity demanded is big relative to sales of finished paper, which has fallen in price by $2 per tonne. Wouldn't it be nice if there was some type of standardized measure of demand that would be independent of the unit of prices or quantity, and which could easily tell you what will happen to revenues when there is a price change? Well, elasticity is such a concept.

The Own Price Elasticity measures the percentage change in the quantity demanded of good 1 ($\%\Delta Q_1$) for a given percentage change in the price of good 1 ($\%\Delta P_1$). The formula for elasticity is quite simple:

$$E_{11} = \frac{\%\Delta Q_1}{\%\Delta P_1}$$

$$= \frac{\Delta Q_1/Q_1}{\Delta P_1/P_1}$$

$$= \frac{\Delta Q_1}{\Delta P_1} \times \frac{P_1}{Q_1}.$$

The subscripts on E tell us that we're dealing with the price and quantity of good 1. The last expression is quite informative. It says that the own price elasticity is equal to the inverse slope of the demand curve (the first term) multiplied by the relative sizes of the price and quantity. It is important to remember that an elasticity is *just a number.* From this simple little equation any negative number is possible, although it is a convention in economics to drop the negative sign. Before we get to what these numbers mean, let's do a simple example. Consider Figure 5-3 where several prices and quantities are listed along the demand curve.

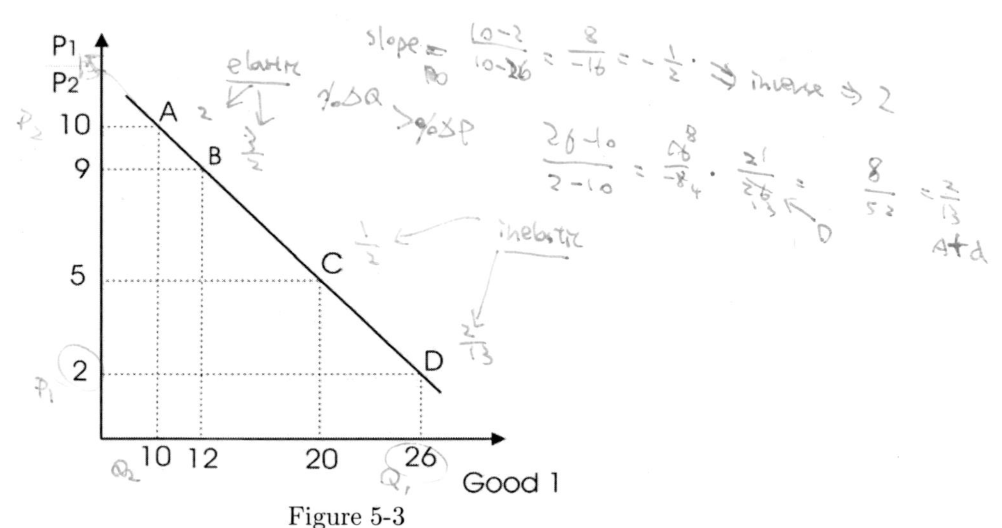

Figure 5-3
Elasticity Changes Along the Demand Curve

The slope of this demand curve is $-1/2$, (or $1/2$ as we'll treat it) which means that $\Delta Q_1/\Delta P_1$ is 2. Since the demand curve is linear, this 1/slope term of the elasticity formula is always 2. Which means to calculate the elasticity of demand at any point we simply have to multiply this number by the fraction P_1/Q_1. Hence at point A the elasticity is 2; at B the elasticity is 18/12 or 3/2; at C the elasticity is 1/2; and at point D the elasticity is 2/13. Notice that the elasticity is falling as we move down the demand curve. Also notice that even though the demand curve has a constant slope, the elasticity is not constant.

But what do these numbers mean? The own price elasticity takes on three types of values (ignoring the negative sign). If the number is greater than 1 the demand curve is *elastic.* This means the percentage change in quantity demanded is larger than the percentage change in price. A small change in price leads to a relatively large change in the quantity demanded. If the number is equal to 1 the demand curve is *unitary elastic.* This means the percentage change in quantity demanded equals the percentage change in price. A change in the price leads to the same relative change in quantity demanded. Finally, if the number is less than 1 but greater than 0 the demand is *inelastic.* Now the percentage change in quantity demanded is smaller than the percentage change in price. This is every seller's dream — a large change in the price leads to a relatively small change in the quantity demanded. Figure 5-4, draws some extreme cases of demand elasticities to get the point across.

The three graphs in Figure 5-4 are quite unrealistic. The left hand side graph is an example

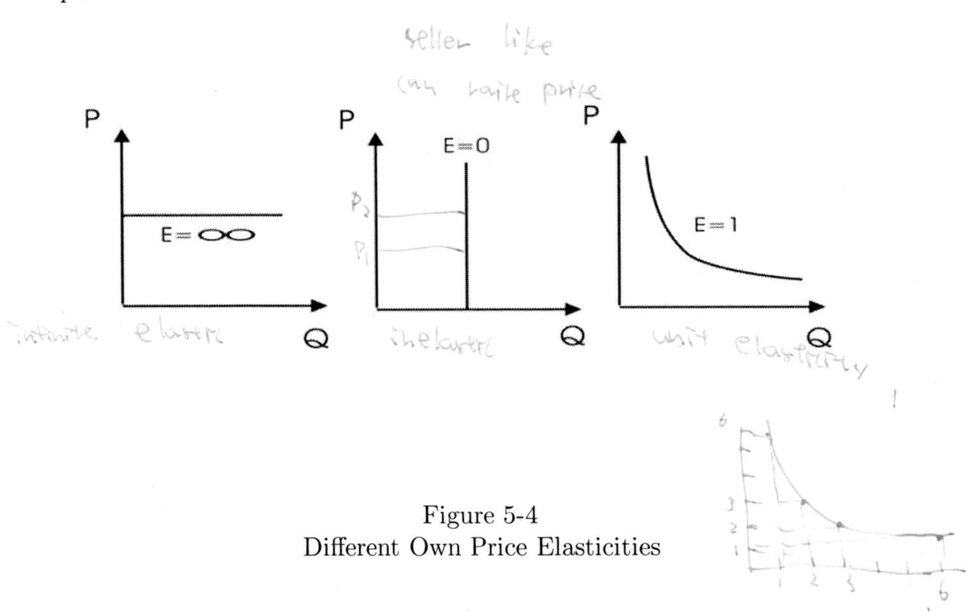

Figure 5-4
Different Own Price Elasticities

of infinite elasticity. This would be the case where a slight rise in price leads to nothing being sold, and a slight fall in price leads to the whole world at your doorstep. Such a demand would suggest a perfect substitute exists for the good, and so consumers are unwilling to tolerate any increase in price. The middle graph represents the case of perfect inelasticity. Here any rise in price results in the same quantity demanded. No matter what the price, consumers demand the same amount. Such a demand curve violates our principle of substitution which states that as the price increases consumers substitute into other goods. It also violates our notions that people have finite wealth levels. At some point, as the price of a good increases enough, you run out of money and have to buy less of a commodity. The final graph is a very special case as well. If the demand function happened to take on the following functional form: $k = p \times q$, where k is just some constant number, say 16, then the elasticity of demand is unitary everywhere.

Until this point we've been calculating elasticities at a *point* along the demand curve. This is very simple to do when the demand curve is a straight line, but requires some calculus (don't worry... we won't do any calculus) when the demand curve is non-linear. It is also possible to calculate the elasticity between two points on a demand curve, whether the demand is linear or not. In doing so one is actually calculating an *average* elasticity between the two points. This type of elasticity is called an *arc elasticity* as opposed to a point elasticity. Although the same formula is used, there is a minor complication in deciding which price and quantity combination should be used. Should the initial price/quantity be used, the terminal price/quantity, or some price/quantity combination in between. Which one is used will slightly alter the answer you get, but the bottom line is that the choice is quite arbitrary. For example, we could calculate the elasticity of demand between points A and D in Figure 5-3 using point D as the reference point.

$$E = \frac{26 - 10}{10 - 2} \times \frac{2}{26} = \frac{2}{13}$$

Similarly we could calculate the elasticity of demand between points A and D in Figure 5-3 using the average price and quantity as our reference point.

$$E = \frac{26 - 10}{10 - 2} \times \frac{6}{18} = \frac{2}{3}$$

The arc elasticity is easy to calculate relative to the point elasticity when the demand curve is not a straight line because it only requires two data points. On the other hand, the arc elasticity is just an average, and is not very accurate. Which one you use depends on the information you have, the complexity of the demand curve, and how good you are with numbers. What we gain for ease, we lose in accuracy since it is only an average... a classic case of substitution.

> *Arc Own Price Elasticity is an average elasticity between two points on a demand curve.*

Elasticity and Total Revenue

One of the useful aspects of own price elasticity is it tells us quite a bit about how total revenue and price move together.[1] When the demand for a good is elastic then total revenue and price move in the opposite direction. A fall in price, leading to a large change in quantity demanded, leads to an increase in total revenue. When the demand is inelastic, total revenue and price move in the same direction. A rise in price leads to a small fall in quantity demanded, and this leads to an increase in revenue.

Suppose the demand for a product is $Q = 12 - P$, where Q is the quantity demanded and P is its price. The table below lists several points along this demand curve.

TABLE 5-1

Elasticity and Total Revenue

Price	Quantity	Elasticity	Total Revenue
11	1	11	11
9	3	3	27
7	5	1.4	35
5	7	.71	35
3	9	.33	27
1	11	.09	11

Notice how total revenue increases as the price initially falls, but as price continues to fall and as the elasticity continues to get smaller the total revenue eventually falls as well. To see if you understand this relationship recalculate the elasticities and total revenues assuming the demand curve becomes $Q = 16 - P$ and $Q = 12 - 2P$.

Income Elasticities

---

[1] Total revenue is how much the seller generates from a sale. Total expenditure is how much the consumer spends. Without taxes the two are identical.

When income changes there is a shift or change in demand which will lead to a change in the quantity demanded for any given price. We can measure an income elasticity of demand the same way we measure an own price elasticity. The only difference is that now we replace the price term with income, and now it is important whether or not the answer is positive or negative. The income elasticity is given by

$$E_{1M} = \frac{\Delta Q_1}{\Delta M} \times \frac{M}{Q_1}.$$

Where ΔM is the old income minus the new income, and ΔQ_1 is the quantity demanded at the old income minus the quantity demanded at the new income. As mentioned before, when income changes we can say nothing about whether the demand for good 1 will increase or decrease. This even holds across people. Joe might respond to an increase in his income by buying more fresh fish while another person — say Rena — may respond to an increase in her income by buying less of it. For Joe fresh fish is a normal good, while for Rena it is an inferior good. Nevertheless, we can get a good idea of whether, for the average consumer, a particular good is normal or inferior by using aggregate data to compute an average income elasticity of demand. The income elasticity of demand is the elasticity of quantity consumed per capita with respect to per capita income. In empirical studies of income elasticity of demand for a good, aggregate data is used to compute an average demand function. Then, this average demand function is used to compute various average elasticities, including the income elasticity of demand.

A normal good has a positive income elasticity: $E_{1M} > 0$

An inferior good has a negative income elasticity: $E_{1M} < 0$

Cross Price Elasticities

If we want to measure the response in quantity demanded of good 1 with respect to a change in the price of good 2, we can calculate a cross-price elasticity of demand in a similar way we calculated the other elasticities. The cross-price elasticity of demand for good 1 with respect to the price of good 2 is given by the formula:

$$E_{12} = \frac{\Delta Q_1}{\Delta P_2} \times \frac{P_2}{Q_1}.$$

Where ΔP_2 is the old price of good 2 minus the new price, and ΔQ_1 is the quantity demanded at the old price minus the quantity demanded at the new price. When this number is positive the goods are "substitutes" and when this number is negative the goods are "complements."

A complement has a negative cross price elasticity: $E_{12} < 0$

A substitute has a positive cross price elasticity: $E_{12} > 0$

5.4 Elasticity Miscellany

Knowing arithmetic doesn't make you a mathematician, but every mathematician must know arithmetic. The same is true for elasticity. Just knowing the formulas and relationships doesn't make you an economist, but it's pretty hard to think like an economist without knowing what elasticity is. Let's consider some "economics" of elasticity.

Elasticity and the definition of goods

Let's go back to own price elasticity, which is by far the most interesting and useful elasticity concept. As alluded to, the size of the elasticity is a reflection of the degree to which substitutes exist for the good: high numbers mean more elastic and more substitutes. But this is really just a reflection of how the good is defined to begin with. Suppose a good is defined very broadly: say food. If data is collected on average food prices and quantities, and an elasticity of demand is calculated, what would you expect the number to be like? One would think the demand would be quite inelastic since there are few decent substitutes for "food." If on the other hand, the good was a box of *Special K* cereal, then we would expect the demand for such a narrowly defined good to be very high. Other cereals, hot cereals, eggs and bacon, fruit, and all the other things people can eat for breakfast are great substitutes. So the elasticity of demand is sensitive to how the good in question is defined.

Less obvious is the relationship between the budget share for a good and its elasticity. Some goods are expensive and use up a large fraction of one's budget. Housing, car payments... alimony are large expenses. Snacks, pens, and flowers for the wife are small expenses. When a good takes up a large share of the budget then it will tend to have a larger elasticity. Changes in the price of large ticket items have a big effect and induce a larger quantity response. On the other hand, when the price of bubble gum doubles, it has little impact on my budget and therefore a smaller impact on the quantity demanded.

Elastic Demand: *Lots of substitutes. Large budget shares.*

Inelastic Demand: *Small numbers of substitutes. Small budget shares.*

Elasticity in two seconds

It turns out there is a nifty little graphic trick to determine the point elasticity for any linear demand function. Figure 5-5 shows how it works.

Suppose we wanted to calculate the elasticity of the demand curve at point C. If we draw a horizontal line from point C, back to the vertical price axis, we see that the vertical axis can be divided into two segments: A and B. It turns out that the elasticity at point C is equal to A/B; that is, the distance A divided by the distance B. This is a very handy tool for determining the relative elasticity of any

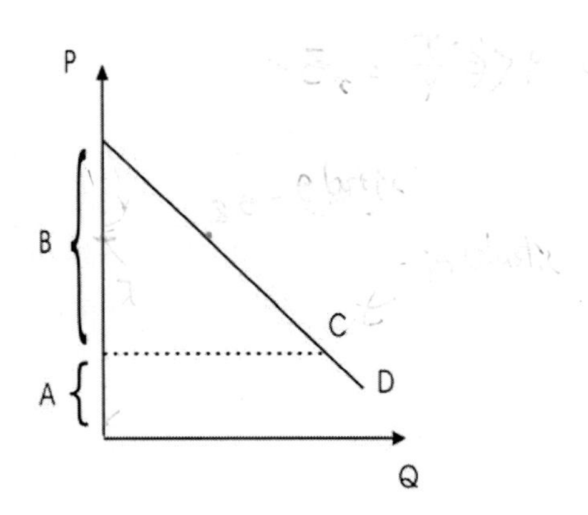

Figure 5-5
Eyeball Calculations of Elasticity

two demand curves plotted on the same graph.[2] From Figure 5-5 it is clear that $A < B$, and as a result we can say that the demand is inelastic at point C.

Suppose two individuals, Verlyn and Carla, each have a demand for hot dogs, and these demands are represented in Figure 5-6. At a given price, say P', which demand curve is more elastic? That is, is the elasticity greater at point E or F?

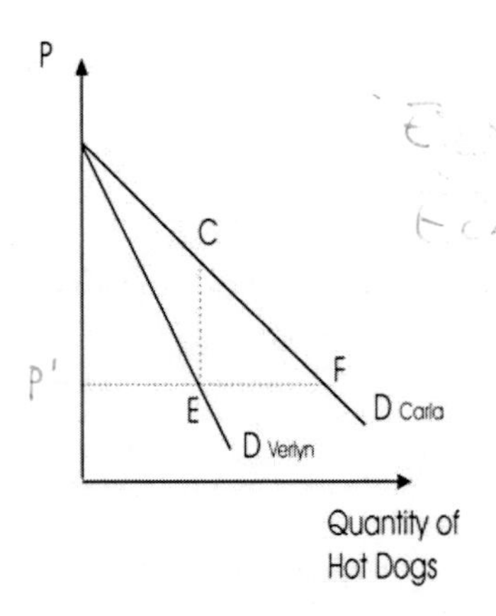

Figure 5-6
More Eyeball Calculations of Elasticity

---

[2] If the demand curve is non-linear then there is a slight complication. You simply draw the tangent line to point C and continue this line back to the axis as if it were the demand curve. You then calculate the distances as just stated.

If we use our little trick we can see that the elasticity is the same at both points. To check your understanding, what can we say about the elasticity at point C?[3]

The Second Law of Demand

There is an empirical regularity that economists and others have observed for so long it has come to be called the Second Law of Demand (the first law being the inverse relationship between price and quantity... just in case you've forgotten already!). The second law of demand states that long run demand curves are more elastic than short run demand curves.

Second Law of Demand: *long run demand curves are more elastic than short run demand curves.*

One of the problems in understanding the second law of demand is what's meant by "long run." Most often economists view the long run as a long period of time, when permanent changes are made, and adjustments are made slowly. Likewise short run would mean a short period of time, with temporary changes and quick adjustments. Still others refer to the long run as the period when the most choices can be made, and the short run as a period when many of our choices are fixed or constrained. It's all quite confusing.

Fortunately for us we don't have to worry too much about such details. We'll think of the long run as meaning periods of time when people make permanent and flexible decisions. Most importantly, in the long run more information is available to make decisions. In the short run, the opposite will be the case. If we think of the long run as a situation in which "other things are changing", then we recognize that the demand curve must be shifting over the long run.

Let's think about the demand for gasoline. In 1971 there was a certain demand for gasoline based on the nature of cars, homes, and other factors. In 1971 gasoline was quite inexpensive and lots of people purchased large amounts of gas. I recall, in 1971, my parents often saying "let's jump in the car and go for a drive." "Sunday drives" were a North American pastime in the 60s and early 70s when gas was cheap. Figure 5-7 shows the demand for gas in 1971.

Even though most of you were born a decade after the Arab oil embargo of 1973–74, it was such a dramatic and watershed moment in popular North American culture that you've no doubt heard all about it. Over night the price of gas went up dramatically. What was the response? Individuals cut back the amount of gas consumption, according to the first law of demand. Again this is shown in Figure 5-7 by a movement from point A to B.

Initially all people could do was reduce their driving, turn the heat down in their homes, and car pool a little. But over time a number of things began to change. Insulation was installed in homes that were never insulated. New types of insulation were produced. Pipes were insulated,

---

[3] It's greater than at E or F.

crawlspaces had floors concreted over, and windows became double paned. In my neighborhood a family built a home in the side of a hill, with every wall but the front one covered by Earth! New cars were invented (the Honda civic), and existing cars became smaller and more fuel efficient. Carpool lanes were built and 55 mph speed limits were imposed. Wind, solar, and other forms of energy were developed. Pools became covered with thermal blankets. All of these innovations *decreased* the demand for gasoline, and the demand curve shifted left as in Figure 5-7. At the 1974 price the quantity demanded of gasoline fell to point C. This shift left, caused by the long run adjustments in behavior brought on by the increased price is the Second Law of Demand.

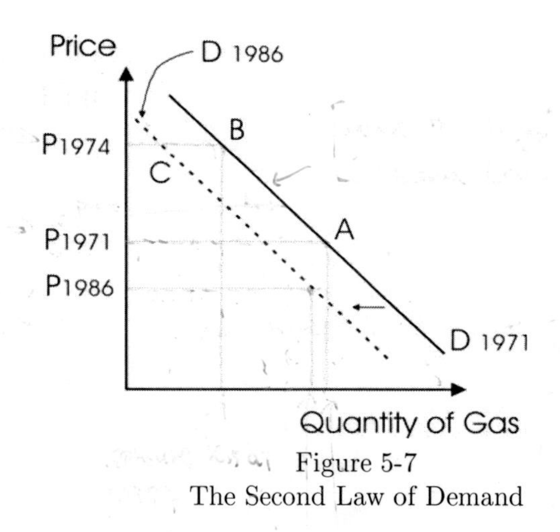

Figure 5-7
The Second Law of Demand

The case of gasoline is interesting because by 1986 the real price of gasoline was at 1966 levels. With this fall in price came increased uses in gasoline. Small muscle cars and SUVs developed, car pool lanes dropped the required passengers from 3 to 2, and interest in alternative energies waned. Although there were these first law of demand effects, the use of gasoline never returned to the 1971 levels. Why? Because when the price of gasoline induced second law of demand changes, these effects were permanent. The insulation put in houses in 1975 was not ripped out in 1986. So even though homes were warmer in 1986 than in 1975, they were heated more efficiently.

5.5 Summary

In chapter 4 we discussed the fundamental inverse relationship between price and quantity, and noted this was called the law of demand. In this chapter we've discussed some of the more technical aspects of demand, starting with the distinction between changes in demand and changes in the quantity demanded. The former results from changes in exogenous parameters assumed to be held fixed, like tastes, income, and prices. The latter results from changes in relative prices. When any of these things change, the subsequent changes in demand can be expressed in unitless numbers called elasticities. These elasticities are simply numbers used to describe how responsive demand is to changes in prices, incomes, and other prices. Elasticity numbers depend critically on how the good is defined. The second law of demand states that over time demand curves become more elastic.

REVIEW QUESTIONS

1. What does it mean to say a variable is exogenous? Endogenous? For a demand function, what are the exogenous and endogenous variables?

2. Are there any testable implications with respect to demand curves resulting from changes in income?

3. If good 1 is inferior, will it more likely be a complement or a substitute to good 2?

4. Why does the elasticity of demand change along a linear demand curve? Does it change along a non-linear one?

5. What is the relationship between elasticity and substitutability?

6. What is the difference between point and arc elasticity?

7. Suppose an individual's demand function is given by the equation $Q_1 = 60 - 2p_1 + 4p_2 + M$.

   a. Are goods 1 and 2 substitutes or complements?

   b. Is good 1 normal or inferior?

   c. Does the demand curve obey the first law of demand?

8. "Smoking and coffee is a Bosnian tradition. If you have cigarettes you have coffee. If you have coffee, you have cigarettes." What is the sign on the cross-price elasticity of demand for coffee with respect to the price of cigarettes in Bosnia? Are cigarettees substitutes or complements?

9. "The cross price elasticity of demand is the change in the quantity of good x divided by the change in the price of good y." T/F/U. Explain.

10. "All goods cannot always be inferior at the same time." T/F/U. Explain.

11. As we move along a linear demand curve the elasticity of demand changes. The elasticity of demand also tells us something about the available substitutes for a good. Does this mean that the number of substitutes changes as a consumer moves up or down their demand curve?

PROBLEMS

1. Using the little graphical trick discussed in section 5.4, show that the demand curve for 1986 in Figure 5-7 is more elastic at every price than the demand curve in 1971.

2. "The quantity demanded can change, even though the demand has not changed, but if the demand changes, then the quantity demanded must also change." True or False. Use a graph in your answer.

3. Suppose Barbara spends her entire income on two goods, diet coke and bagels. Her demand curve for diet coke is inelastic. If the price of diet coke rises, will she consume more or less bagels? Show graphically what happens.

4. Transit buses, on a local San Francisco run carry 1000 passengers a day who are each charged \$.50. The marketing Dept. feels that by raising the price to \$.75, ridership will decline by 200 persons to 800 passengers a day.

   a. What is the estimated elasticity of demand for buses on the run if quantity demanded falls to 800?

   b. Does this increase in price increase Transit's revenue on these trips? Why?

   c. Suppose ridership at the new price is only 100 persons per day. What is the actual elasticity?

   d. Given the true elasticity, should the transit authority stick with the \$.50 price or raise it to \$.75 (ignore cost issues)?

5. Answer the following True/False, with a brief explanation why.

   a. "A straight line demand curve has a constant slope and therefore a constant elasticity."

   b. "If total revenue is constant along a demand curve, then the demand is infinitely elastic."

6. Suppose you own a movie theater and most of your costs (the band, security, the land rental, etc.) are independent of how many people show up. What is likely to be the point elasticity of demand at the price you decide to charge?

7. The city of Toronto currently charges \$12 per week for garbage pick up, and you can put out as many cans of garbage as you like. On average people put out three cans per week. The township is thinking of switching to a plan where each can must have a "tag", and these tags cost \$4 each. If the switch is made, what will happen to the amount of garbage collected?

8. In a response to suggesting that drugs should be made legal, William Bennet (one time director of the Office of Drug Control Policy in the U.S.), stated the following: "Drugs would become much cheaper — at least one-fifth the cost. Then five times as many people could and would buy them. We would then have five times as many addicts." What assumption is he making about the average elasticity of demand for drugs?

9. It has been reported that business rents in Manhattan have increased since the destruction of the trade center towers. They have increased so much, that the total rents in the city are higher than they were before. Does this mean that the trade center towers were making a negative contribution to the city? Use a graph in your answer.

10. "The demand to view the *Mona Lisa* painting is completely inelastic because there is only one, and the artist is long dead" True/False/Uncertain. Explain.

11. Suppose an insect destroys 20% of every grower's raspberry crop. As a result, the price rises from 25 cents to 50 cents per pound. Did the total value of the crop increase?

12. In 1977 Brazil was supplying about one third of the world's coffee exports. When a frost wiped out about 75% of Brazil's 1977 crop, the world price of coffee rose about 400%. What was the approximate price elasticity of demand for coffee. Was the demand elastic or inelastic?

13. You are given the following demand curve: $Q = 14 - P$. The table below contains several points along this demand curve.

    a. Calculate the elasticities over the segments indicated in the table and the total revenue at those points.

P	Q	Elasticity	Total Revenue
11	3		
9	5		
7	7		
5	9		
3	11		
1	13		

    b. Graph the demand curve and label the elasticities along the demand curve. Now, using a separate graph, draw the total revenue curve against quantity. Label the elasticities along this curve.

    c. What is the relationship between TR and elasticity?

    d. Assume the demand curve shifts to the right with two more units sold at every price. Recalculate the elasticities for the price intervals, (3-5), (5-7), (7-9), and (9-11).

    e. Is the new demand curve more or less elastic than the old at each price? At each quantity?

14. Forestry economists have been estimating various elasticities for wood for years. They have found the following: softwood short run demands are very inelastic; the long run cross-price elasticity of BC softwoods, with softwoods from other parts of the world is quite high; and the long run cross price elasticity of softwoods with other woods is positive, but not as high.

    a. Do these make sense?

    b. BC and the Pacific Northwest, happen to be very productive in producing high quality timber (old growth, clear wood). Not only this, but our forests are generally much better at regenerating itself than many other forests (especially tropical ones) around the world. Given this, and the elasticities mentioned above, what happens globally when land is set aside from logging in BC? That is, what happens to the price, to the supply of wood, by other countries, and to the amount of wood cut down elsewhere.

    c. In what sense are the "friends of Clayquat Sound" (a large tract of forest on Vancouver Island that is now protected from logging) also the "enemies of the Amazon rain forest"?

15. Can the demand for a good be inelastic everywhere?

16. When the price of X is 100, the quantity demanded is 100. Calculate the relevant arc elasticities of demand for the following changes (assuming they are all independent of each other, and using the initial point in your calculations).

    a. When the price of X changes to 50, the quantity demanded increases to 250.

    b. When the price of good Y goes from 5 to 10, the quantity demanded of X increases to 120.

    c. When the person's income changes from $10,000 to $20,000 the quantity demanded of X falls to 80.

17.) Suzy has a demand for yoga given by P=15-3Q. What is the elasticity of demand at price $9. Is this elastic or inelastic? At what price is total expenditure maximized? What is the elasticity at this price?

18. In 2008 the 2010 Vancouver Olympic Committee released the prices for the various future events. In the press release they stated that two of their goals were to "avoid having empty seats" as has happened at past Olympics, and to make sure that many tickets were given away through lotteries. It was also stated that efforts would be made to avoid having tickets fall into the hands of scalpers. Why is it that if you give tickets away through lotteries, but prevent resale, you are likely to end up with empty seats? Why would this not happen if tickets were allocated strictly through prices?

19. The tune *If I had a Million Dollars* by the *Barenaked Ladies* is a simple song that works around the children's line "If I had a million dollars, We... whatever." According to the singer they would take a limousine to the store rather than walk, they wouldn't wear a green dress (because that would be cruel), and they wouldn't eat Kraft dinner:
But we would eat Kraft Dinner
Of course we would, we'd just eat more

And buy really expensive ketchups with it
That's right, all the fanciest like... dijon ketchups

Based on this, which goods are normal or inferior?

20. Prior to the opening of the Golden Ears bridge across the Fraser River in the summer of 2009, policy wonks in the government were trying to figure out the effects of a toll of $2.00/trip. Suppose the quantity demanded at $2.00/trip is 100,000 trips/hour.

    a. If the price elasticity of demand for bridge trips is −2.0, what is the effect of a 10% toll increase on bridge traffic?

    b. What is the effect on toll revenue?

    c. Without doing any arithmetic, how would your answers have changed if the elasticity had been −.5? Explain.

21. Over the past century incomes have increased and fertility rates have fallen. What does this suggest about the income elasticity of chilren?

22. In the fall of 2008 much of the Western world went into a recession. During this time various people commented on industries that are "recession proof". One such proposed industry is the movie industry. Apparently gate receipts go up in recessions, not down.

    a. If this is true, what would this suggest about the overall income elasticity for the demand for movies?

    b. Another casual observation people make about the movies is that "better" movies are made during recessions and depressions than in boom times. Let's assume by "better" that critics generally mean movies that appeal to more mature audiences (e.g. fewer "slasher", "action", or "movies with Paris Hilton" in them). Given the answer in (a), why might this be so?

23. Metro-Vancouver spans the city of Vancouver and various suburbs. The Metro-Vancouver regional district has the authority to place taxes on gasoline to pay for transit in the region. When a 6 percent tax is placed on gasoline it has been observed that in areas close to the center of the region there is about a 2 percent fall in the quantity demanded. In areas close to the borders of the region, there is about a 35 percent fall in the quantity demanded.

    a. What are the elasticities of demand for gasoline in the center of Metro-Vancouver and at the borders?

    b. Why would there be such a difference in elasticity?

24. Suppose a demand curve for good x is given by $Q_x = 60 - 2P_x + 0.5P_y - 0.1M$ (For those of you who don't like math, don't be afraid that this demand curve looks complicated because P_y and M are in it, just plug the values in).

a. If $P_y = 10$ and $M = 100$, graph the demand curve and show the quantities demanded for $P_x = 20$ and $P_x = 10$. Calculate the own price arc elasticity over this price range using the average price and quantity as your base.

b. Assuming that $P_x = 10$ and that $M = 100$, suppose the price of P_y goes from 10 to 20. Calculate the cross price elasticity of demand for goods x and y. Are they complements or substitutes?

c. Assuming that $P_x = 10$ and that $P_y = 10$, suppose income changes from \$100 to \$200. Calculate the income elasticity of demand for good x. Is x a normal or inferior good?

Review Question Answers

1. *An exogenous variable is determined "outside" the model. It is a given. Thus in our model we take tastes, incomes, and other prices as given. Our model does not tell us where they come from. An endogenous variable is one that is determined "inside" or "by" the model. For the moment we are taking the own price as exogenous, but as we develop the model this variable, along with the quantity exchanged, will become endogenous.*

2. *At the general level of our model, there are no testable implications. When income changes the demand curve could shift in or out (the same is true of changes in tastes or other prices). In order to make this testable we would need to know what type of good we are dealing with (e.g., whether the good is normal or inferior).*

3. *Suppose the price of good 2 goes down. The substitution effect will cause the consumer to purchase more good 2 and less good 1. When the price of good 2 falls, however, the real income increases. Since good 1 is inferior this causes the consumer to purchase even less good 1. Thus both effects work together: price of good 2 goes down, less good 1 is purchased. They are substitutes.*
   if P_2 ↑

4. *You must keep in mind that slope and elasticity are not the same thing. Along a straight line demand curve the slope is not changing, but the elasticity (which is the inverse slope multiplied by a weight) is. Essentially the percentage changes in price and quantity are not constant as you move down a linear demand curve. There is one case (the rectangular hyperbola case) where a non-linear demand curve has a constant elasticity. However, other non-linear demands have changing elasticities as you move down them.*

5. *Generally speaking, the more elastic a demand curve is, the better are the substitutes.*

6. *A point elasticity is an exact elasticity. It measures the percentage change in the quantity demanded when there is an extremely small change in price or income. An arc elasticity is an "average" elasticity over a discrete change in prices or income.*

7.
   a. *The goods are substitutes because when the price of good 2 increases, so does the demand for good 1.*

   b. *Normal. When income increases, so does the demand for good 1.*

   c. *Yes. When the price of good 1 increases, the quantity demanded of good 1 falls.*

8. *It is negative. The two goods are complements.*

9. *False. The cross price elasticity of demand is the* **percentage** *change in the quantity of good x divided by the* **percentage** *change in the price of good y.*

10. *True. If there is an increase in income it must be spent on something. If all goods were inferior, then you would buy less of everything when your income goes up.*

11. *The actual number of goods available doesn't change. What changes is the willingness of a consumer to substitute one good for another. When gasoline prices are high consumers are more willing to substitute from cars to public transit. The public transit, however, was always available.*

Odd Numbered Problem Answers

1. *As can be seen in Figure 5-1, the elasticity at point 1 along the 1986 demand curve is A/B, while the elasticity at point 2 on the 1971 demand curve is A/B'. Since the distance A is the same in both cases, the 1986 demand curve is more elastic.*

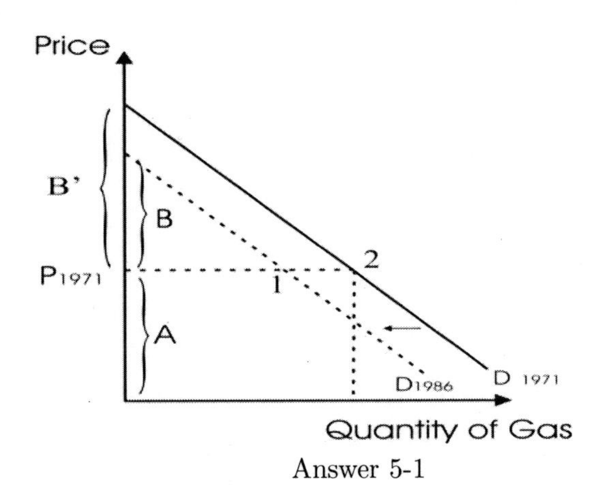

Answer 5-1

3. *Since the demand for Diet Coke is inelastic an increase in price leads to more income spent on this good. This means there is less income available for Bagels, which results in a shift inwards for the demand for bagels. Shown in Figure 5-1.*

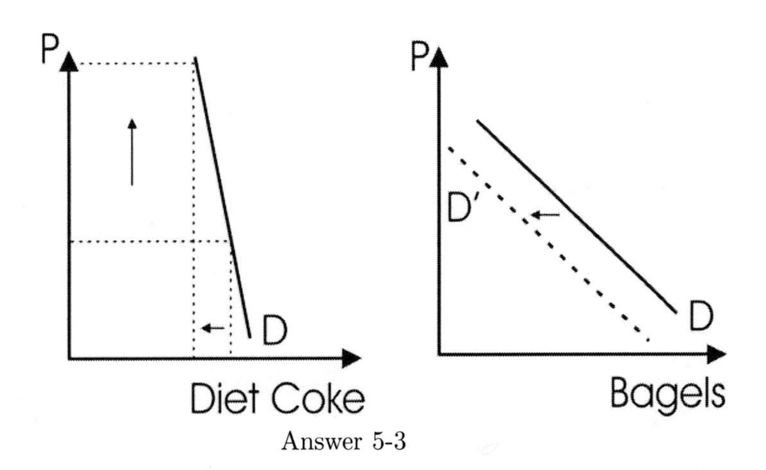

Answer 5-3

5.

   a. *False. It has a constant slope and a changing elasticity. This follows from the definition of elasticity.*

b. *False. If the demand curve is infinitely elastic, then the more the firm sells, the higher the revenue.*

7. *Unless the demand for garbage pickup is perfectly elastic, the amount of garbage picked up must fall and people will spend less than $12 per week on their garbage.*

9. *No, it only means the demand for commercial space is inelastic. From Figure 5-9 when the twin towers are destroyed, total rents increase, but total consumer's surplus goes down.*

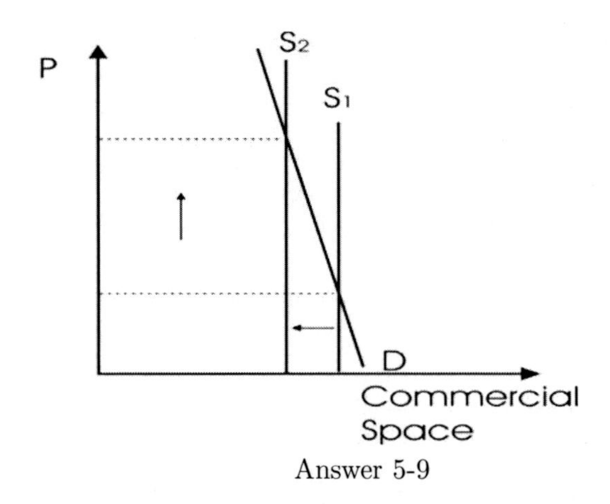

Answer 5-9

11. *No, the total revenue increased, but since there is less crop there must be a lower total value.*

13.

a.

P	Q	Elasticity	Total Revenue
11	3	3.66	33
9	5	1.8	45
7	7	1	49
5	9	.55	45
3	11	.27	33
1	13	.07	13

b.

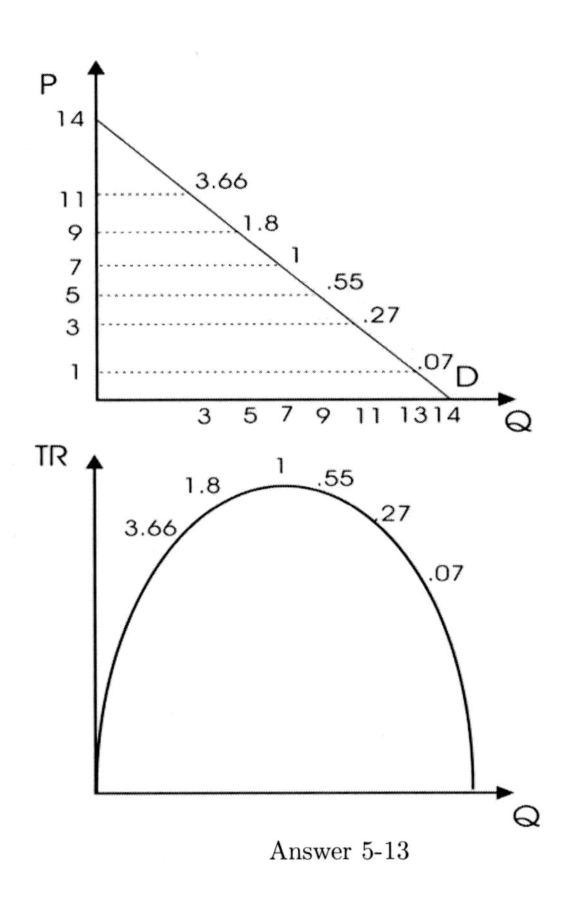

Answer 5-13

c. *When the demand curve is elastic and price is falling, TR is increasing. When the demand curve is inelastic and price is falling, TR is also falling.*

d.

P	Q	Elasticity	Total Revenue
11	5	2.2	55
9	7	1.28	63
7	9	.77	63
5	11	.45	55
3	13	.23	39
1	15	.06	15

e. *At every price the demand curve is less elastic. At every quantity the demand curve is more elastic.*

15. *No. Eventually the consumer would run out of income and the demand would become elastic.*

17. *The elasticity is* $-1/3 \times 9/2$, *which equals* -1.5. *This is elastic. Total expenditure would be maximized when price is \$7.50. The elasticity is* -1 *at this point.*

19. *Walking to the store is inferior, while limousines, kraft dinner, and dijon kechups are all normal.*

21. *That they are inferior. Many economists argue that although the quantity of children is inferior, the quality is normal. Hence, as incomes increase people have fewer children, but the "quality" of children (in terms of the levels of their human capital) is higher.*

23.

   a. *The elasticity in the center is* $-.33$, *and the elasticity around the border is* -5.83.

   b. *There is such a difference because the jurisdictions just across the borders do not have the tax. Since gasoline outside Metro-Vancouver is a perfect substitute for gasoline inside the border, the elasticity of demand is very high close to the border. It is not infinite because people have to travel to the farther away stations.*

5.6 Appendix: Arithmetic Issues

Discrete vs Continuous Variables

Students are constantly confused by the difference between discrete and continuous variables, so if it bothers you, know that you are not alone. For the purpose of introducing a new concept, it is often useful to start with a discrete example. However, once the concept is known, it is often easier to analyze a problem using continuous variables. Thus economic textbooks are constantly switching from one to the other, and it does get confusing after awhile.

A *discrete* variable is one that takes on only whole number values: $1, 2, 3, 4, 5...n$. In economics we often use discrete numbers when we're talking about people or goods. It doesn't make much sense to talk about 3.5 people, nor does it make much sense to ask your grocer if you can buy 1/3 of an apple.

A *continuous* variable is one that takes on any real (positive) value. A continuous variable could have a value of $1, 2, 2.5$ or 2.5698732. When you purchase gasoline for your car, you can stop the pump at any time up to two decimal places, you don't have to buy 1, 2, or 30 gallons exactly. We would consider the gasoline purchase, then, a continuous variable.

For now that may be all you need to know. You should stop reading this appendix now and return to its various sections when you are having problems in the text that are related to discrete vs. continuous variables.

Discrete vs Continuous Variables And Demand Curves

When we are using a discrete variable our graphs tend not to be smooth. Consider Figure 5-8, which shows a demand curve for a good which can only be purchased in discrete units. The demand curve is downward sloping like it should be, but it isn't a "curve." Rather the demand function has "steps." Each step tells us how much the consumer would have paid at most in order to purchase that discrete unit. Thus, the consumer would pay \$25 for the first unit, \$20 for the second, etc. The demand function is not smooth because the good itself is not continuous. The lumpiness in the nature of the good, leads to the step like shape to the demand function.

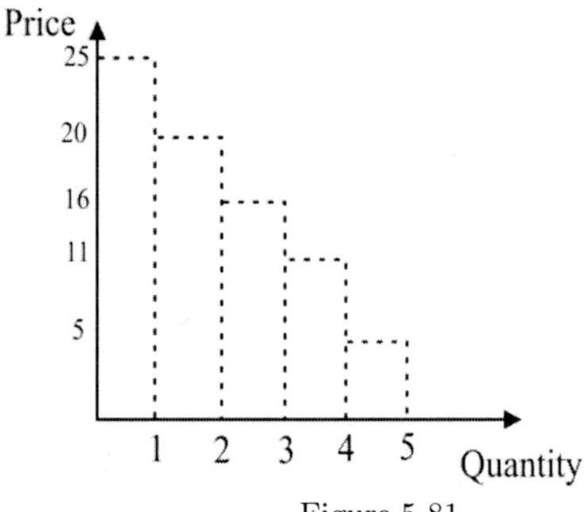

Figure 5-81
A Discrete Demand Curve

When a variable is continuous, our graphs start to take on smooth shapes. In Figure 5-9, we have a good which is continuous, and as a result the demand function is a smooth curve. We like to work with smooth curves because they're easy to draw and can be represented by nice mathematical functions. In addition, even for goods which must be purchased in discrete units, when we aggregate up across all of the people in a market, the discreteness goes away... at least in a practical sense.

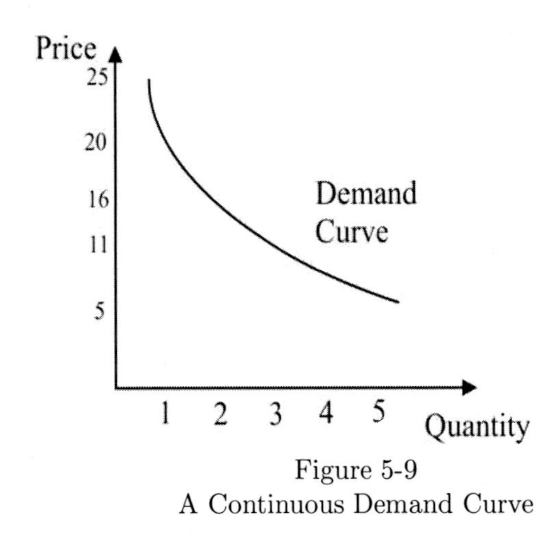

Figure 5-9
A Continuous Demand Curve

Discrete vs. Continuous Variables and Elasticity

The difference in discrete vs. continuous variables comes up in the context of elasticity. Consider the case of own price elasticity: the percentage change in the quantity demanded of a good, divided by the percentage change in its own price. When a variable is discrete, we have no choice but to measure the elasticity across a discrete segment of the demand function. If the good can only be purchased in units of 1,2, or 3, etc., it makes no sense to find the elasticity at a point. As a result, we need to calculate an *arc* elasticity. However, even if the good can be consumed in a continuous fashion, we may still want to calculate the elasticity over a discrete (read "large") price change. Consider Figure 5-10 where we have two points on a demand function. These points may have come from the demand function in Figure 5-8 or from Figure 5-9, in either case we are going to calculate the elasticity over a discrete distance.

Since we are moving a discrete distance along the demand function we must calculate the elasticity using the formula:

$$E_{11} = \frac{\%\Delta Q_1}{\%\Delta P_1}$$

$$= \frac{\Delta Q_1/Q_1}{\Delta P_1/P_1}$$

$$= \frac{\Delta Q_1}{\Delta P_1} \times \frac{P_1}{Q_1}.$$

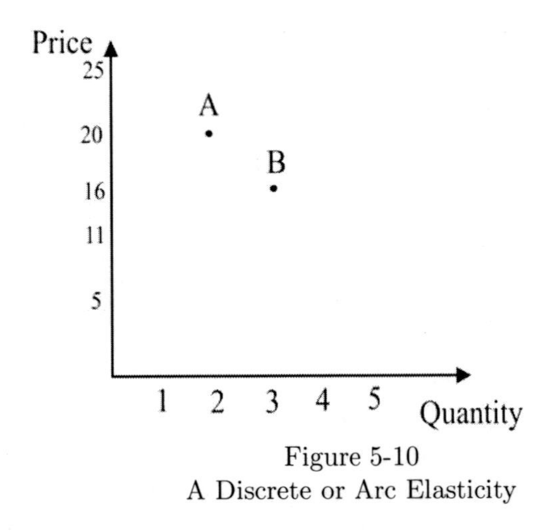

Figure 5-10
A Discrete or Arc Elasticity

The Δ in this equation means "discrete change." The dilemma here, as mentioned in Chapter 5, is that with a discrete elasticity there is an ambiguity over what price and quantity to plug into the formula. Should it be the price and quantity at point A, or B, or some price and quantity in between? The answer is, there is no answer. It also isn't a big deal, it is just the ambiguity that arises over measuring elasticity over a discrete range.

If we did not consider a discrete range for measuring the elasticity, then we would be measuring the elasticity at a point, say point A in Figure 5-10. The advantage of using point elasticities is the ambiguity goes away. The disadvantage is that the Δ gets replaced by a derivative sign. This is only a problem if you haven't had calculus. Since I'm assuming you have not, we just won't go there.

Discrete vs. Continuous Variables and Marginal Values

The other place students get confused over this issue is in the discussion of marginal value. A marginal value is the maximum the consumer is willing to pay for a *change in the quantity* of the good. The key is, how big is this change in the quantity? If it is a large change, then the marginal value is discrete, if it is an extremely small amount, then the marginal value is continuous.

The best way to see this is to consider Figure 5-11. In the left graph the consumer must make a discrete change in the consumption of the good. Hence the consumer moves from 3 units to 4 units. As a result, the marginal value is the area under the demand curve from 3 to 4. On the other hand, in the right graph the consumer is able to make a continuous change in the consumption of the good. This means the consumer can move from something like 3.99999 to 4 units. As a result, the marginal value is the area under the demand curve from 3.99999 to 4, which in a practical sense is just a vertical line as shown. In the left hand graph we say the discrete area is the marginal value of the *fourth* unit. In the right hand graph we tend to say the height of the demand curve is the marginal value of the fourth unit.

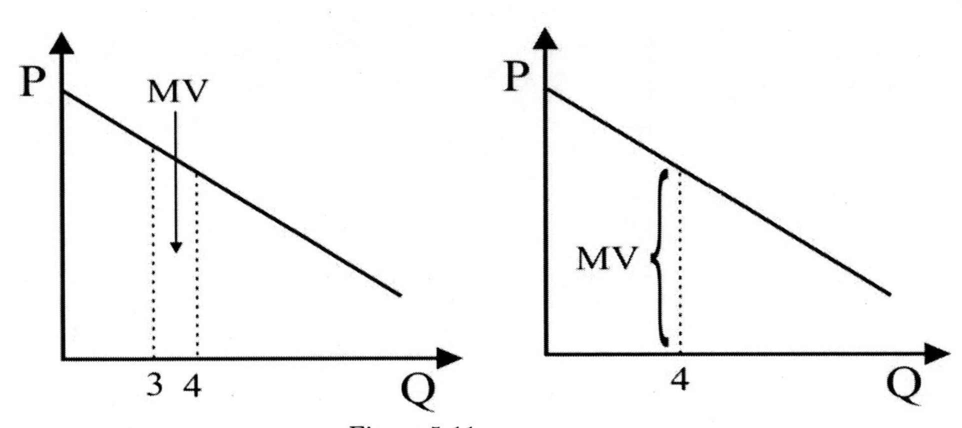

Figure 5-11
Discrete vs Continuous Marginal Value

CHAPTER 6

EXCHANGE WITHOUT PRODUCTION

6.1 **Trade with Just Two People**

In chapter 3 we saw that voluntary exchange led to both parties being made better off. With our new tool "the demand curve" we can now analyze trade in a very powerful and more complete way. The key to using demand functions in understanding trade is to remember that the height of the demand function is the marginal value — the maximum amount an individual is willing to pay for more of the good. As we saw in chapter 3, when marginal values are different, trade takes place. This means that when the heights of two individual demand curves are different, trade will take place.

Let's think of two people who live next door to each other: Nelson and Darlene. Darlene has chickens that produce 20 eggs each week no matter what, while poor ol' Nelson doesn't own any chickens and buys his eggs from Darlene. Let's assume that the price for each egg is 10¢ . The demands for Nelson and Darlene are shown in Figure 6-1. D_N is Nelson's demand curve and D_D is Darlene's. Note this would be Darlene's demand curve whether or not she had any chickens.

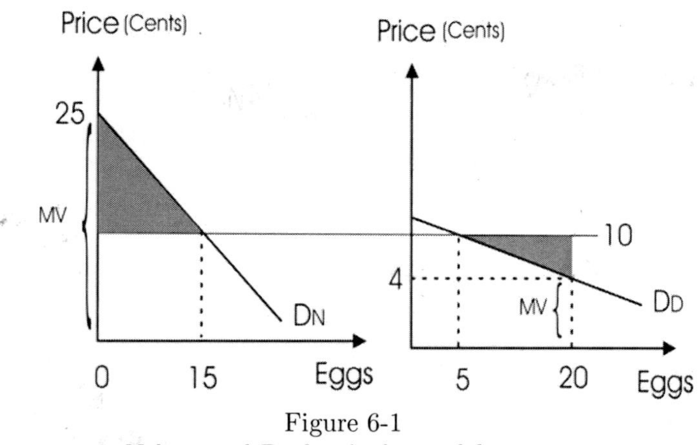

Figure 6-1
Nelson and Darlene's demand for eggs

Since Nelson has no eggs of his own, his MV is 25, the height of his demand curve above 0. For Darlene, who has 20 eggs each week, her MV is 4, the height of her demand curve above 20.

Since Nelson is willing to pay 25¢ for his first egg, and the price is only 10¢ , Nelson will clearly buy an egg. For this first egg Nelson gains consumer's surplus of 15¢ (25-10). But his MV is greater than the price for the second egg as well, and the third, and the fourth ... all the way up to 15 eggs. When Nelson purchases the 15th egg his MV is just equal to 10¢ , which just equals the price. As we've seen before, Nelson is now at an equilibrium, he doesn't want to consume any more or less eggs.

What about Darlene. When Nelson offers 10¢ for the first egg, she takes it because her MV is only 4¢ . This makes her 6¢ better off. However, when she sells an egg her MV begins to increase, but until she has only 5 eggs remaining the price remains higher than her MV. At 5 eggs Darlene is also in a position where her MV is equal to the price of 10¢ which means she's in an equilibrium as well.

The shaded area in the left hand graph represents Nelson's *consumer surplus*, which was briefly discussed in section 4.8. The area of this triangle is $1.12, which is the amount of wealth Nelson gains from entering trade with Darlene. He would have been willing to pay this amount to gain access to the 15 eggs, but he didn't have to — hence it is surplus to him.

The shaded area in the right hand graph is Darlene's *seller's surplus* — a whopping 45¢ . This is the amount of wealth Darlene gains from entering trade with Nelson. Seller's surplus is just the difference between the total revenue Darlene gets and her total value of the eggs she sold; that is, it is the price times quantity traded, minus the area under her demand curve.

Consumer's Surplus: *Total value minus the total expenditure of the consumer.*

Seller's Surplus: *Total revenue minus the total value of the seller.*

The sum of consumer and seller surplus is called the *gains from trade*. The amazing thing about voluntary exchange is not just that both parties are made better off. The amazing thing is that the total gains from trade are *maximized*. In the case of Nelson and Darlene, there is no other combination of eggs which leads to a larger sum of seller's and consumer's surplus. The maximization of the total gains from trade is a direct implication of our first principle of economics: maximization. Yet the result is important enough to have its own name: the Theorem of Exchange.

Theorem of Exchange: *All gains from trade are exhausted at the margin.*

The phrase "exhausted at the margin" means that in equilibrium there are no gains from increasing or decreasing the quantity traded. In our little egg example, there are no gains from moving away from the (15,5) distribution of eggs between Nelson and Darlene. At the initial allocation of (0,20), there were lots of gains from trade at the margin, which is why it wasn't an equilibrium, and why Nelson and Darlene were not content to stay at that combination. If you recall the discussion of which freeway lane to take home in chapter 2, you'll note that the same logic was used there. People switch lanes in traffic until there are no gains from switching lanes.

The other amazing feature about exchange is that the gains from trade were maximized without the aid of any third party. Both Nelson and Darlene acted on their own and in their own selfish interest. In doing this they ended up making each other better off. This was one of the great insights of Adam Smith: private vice can lead to public virtue. We don't get good service at our local Domino's Pizza because the owner is altruistic or because the Pizza police are watching. We get good service because it behooves the owner of Domino's Pizza to provide it. When I'm served well, I return. I get utility from the meal, the owner makes a profit. The gains from trade get maximized.

It isn't quite correct to say this trade takes place without the aid of a third party. Many times economists (especially right-wing ones) forget about a little "helper" that sneaks in under the proverbial table. What happened in our egg example is that an *institution* came to the aid of Nelson and Darlene. This institution is called the *market* and the key aspect of a market is the *market price.* For the next several chapters we're going to assume that the market price works for free. Perhaps it's not too surprising that an allocation mechanism that works for free achieves an outcome that maximizes the gains from trade. Regardless, this assumption is what defines the branch of economics known as *neoclassical economics.* In the third part of the book we'll see what happens when we relax this assumption and assume that the market price is not free.

In the meantime we need to know how this market price is determined. To begin with, since we only have two trading people, we'll start with a little graphic method that provides a lot of intuition about supply. Then we will work at creating a model of market demand and supply.

6.2 Determining Price with Two People

Consider Figure 6-2. This figure is a three sided box, with the width of the box equal to the total amount of goods available. If we stick with our Nelson and Darlene scenario, the width of the box is 20 eggs. The left hand vertical axis is just the vertical price axis for Nelson, while the right hand vertical axis is the price axis for Darlene. Where things get tricky is in the interpretation of the horizontal axis. If we move from left to right it is just the number of eggs that Nelson gets. If we move from right to left it is the number of eggs that Darlene gets. Essentially there are two scales on the horizontal axis. The way we create this graph is to *rotate* Darlene's demand curve around its vertical axis and then impose it on top of Nelson's. Hence, Nelson's demand curve still looks the same, but Darlene's demand curve is backwards and upward sloping. Although it looks upward sloping, there's still an inverse relationship between price and quantity for Darlene. The more eggs Darlene has, the lower her MV is because for her the quantity of eggs increases from right to left ... get it?

What we see from this graph though is the determination of the equilibrium. Where the two demand curves intersect determines the equilibrium price and quantity. When the price is equal to 10¢ it is true that both individuals have a MV equal to the price, and therefore, both individuals have the same MV. Also, it is clear that the gains from trade are maximized at this intersection.

To say that the gains from trade are maximized is to say that the exchange is *efficient.* Efficiency often refers to "technical" efficiency, which in the lay sense usually doesn't mean anything more than "faster" or "stronger". People think that a chain saw is more efficient than an axe, a tractor is more efficient than a horse. If you study economics, the second comment people make to you after the one on "what's the interest rate next week," will be something based on a misconstrued notion of efficiency. On one occasion I was painting some trim on a house with a group of friends.

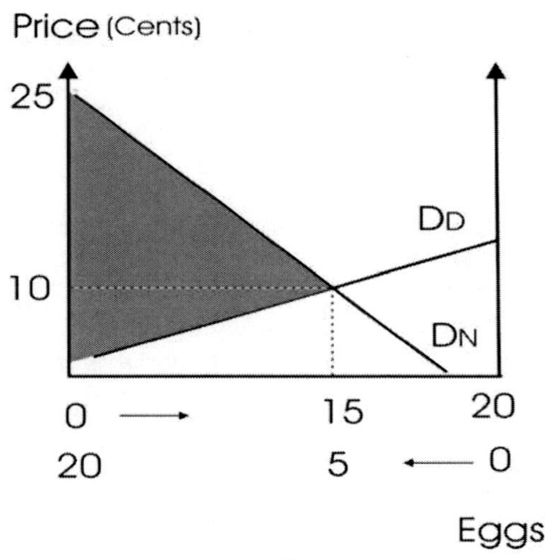

Figure 6-2
Determining the Equilibrium Price

One of my friends came up to me and said "You'll appreciate this, I'm going to use a roller ... its way more efficient!" What he meant to say was it was faster. When he was done, it took several of us to clean up the mess he'd made getting paint all over the side of the building. It was faster; it wasn't more efficient.

> *Efficiency means the gains from trade are maximized.*

Figure 6-2 provides some intuition for a result that we're going to develop in future chapters: supply curves slope upwards. Nelson views Darlene's demand curve as essentially his supply curve. If he wants more than 15 eggs, he'll have to pay more than 10¢ because Darlene's MV increases the more eggs Nelson gets. Generally speaking, supply curves are upward sloping because demand curves are downward sloping. When more is produced in one industry, that means fewer resources are available for use in other industries. Hence the MV of those resources increases in those other industries, and therefore they start to cost more to acquire in the industry that wants to produce more. Alas, we're getting way ahead ourselves here.

Figure 6-3 shows what would happen if Darlene's chickens suddenly started to produce more eggs each week. Suppose that instead of 20 eggs, she was getting 30 eggs each week. In terms of the graph, the width of the box now expands to 30 eggs. This means that Darlene's demand curve shifts to the right. When this happens the intersection with Nelson's demand curve also shifts to the right and Nelson consumes more eggs (22) and the price of eggs falls (to 7¢). Clearly Nelson is made better off by this development, and this is shown by the increase in his consumer's surplus. The gains from trade for Darlene have increased as well, and so as we might expect, an increase in the amount of eggs available has increased the total gains from trade.

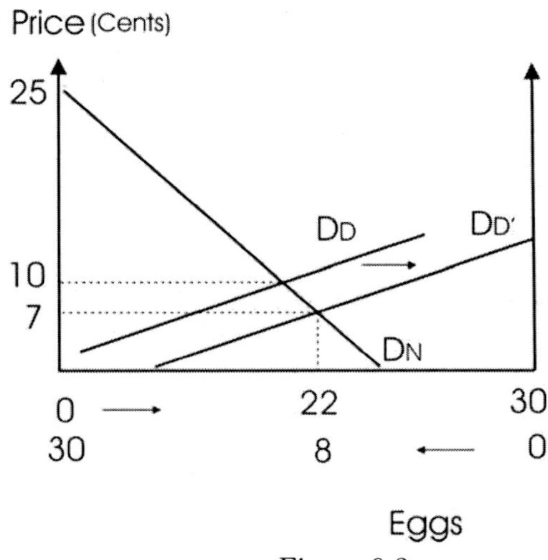

Figure 6-3
A Change in the Supply of Eggs

A Digression on Efficiency: Pareto Optimality

In this book we are going to use the definition of efficiency often attributed to Alfred Marshall, a famous British Economist of the late 19th and early 20th centuries. That is, for us efficiency means to maximize the gains from trade. Quite often, especially when lots of people are involved, some type of action or policy improves the overall amount of wealth in an economy, but reduces the amount of wealth for some individuals. For example, when Canada signed onto the NAFTA trade agreement with the United States and Mexico, it increased the wealth of the country, but hurt some producers who formally had tariff protection from cheaper foreign competition. Even though some individuals were hurt by NAFTA, it was efficient it increased the gains from trade.

An alternative definition of efficiency is called Pareto Optimality. A movement from state A to state B is said to be Pareto optimal if at least one person is made better off by the move and no one is made worse off. Pareto Optimality is a stronger condition than Marshallian efficiency, and as a result any thing which is Pareto optimal is efficient, but the reverse is not true. For example, Canada signing the NAFTA would not be Pareto optimal because some individuals were made worse off. Pareto Optimality is mostly used in welfare economics. Since our concern is explaining human behavior, and since we believe this behavior is best explained by the pursuit of maximizing the gains from trade, we will not use the concept of Pareto Optimality.

6.3 Market Demand and Supply Curves

Although the above method of determining the equilibrium price and quantity traded is very intuitive, the double labeled axis is a little cumbersome, and if we want to add more traders to the model, things would get downright ugly. A better way to determine the equilibrium, and the one we'll consider for the rest of the book is the use of *market demand and supply* curves.

This might sound a little intimidating, but it is really quite simple. Until now we've considered *individual* demand curves. These curves tell us the quantity demanded by a given individual for a given price. They also tell us the individual's marginal and total value for any given quantity. A market demand curve is simply a *horizontal* summation of all the individual demand curves in a given market. A market supply curve is simply the sum of all the individual supplies in a given market. The area under the market demand curve will tell us the total value of all the consumers in the market.

Consider Table 6-1 which lists the points on the demand curve for Miriam and Gayle, two people interested in homemade crafted ornaments. For simplicity, these two amount to the entire market for crafted ornaments.

TABLE 6-1

Individual and Market Demands for Crafts

Price	Quantity Demanded by Miriam	Quantity Demanded by Gayle	Total Quantity Demanded
10	0	0	0
9	1	0	1
8	2	0	2
7	3	1	4
6	4	2	6
5	5	3	8
4	6	4	10

Both of the demand curves are simple straight lines (with slopes of -1), but Miriam's is larger due to her strong preferences for things crafty. Note that when the price of the ornament is $10, neither one of them demand any. Thus the total amount demanded is also zero. When the price falls to $9 Miriam buys 1 craft, but Gayle still buys none and the total amount demanded by the market is just 1. In fact, until the price hits $7, Miriam is the only person in the market, and as a result the market demand will just be her demand curve.

However, notice what happens when the price goes to $7. At that price Gayle buys one ornament and Miriam buys 3, which means that the total quantity demanded is 4. At every lower price the market demand is the sum of the quantity demanded by each individual. If Miriam and Gayle's friend Barb decides to join them, then the market demand would simply be the sum of the three individual demand curves. It doesn't matter how many people join the market the market demand curve is always the sum of quantities demanded by those in the market.

These individual demands and the market demands are drawn in Figure 6-4. Notice that the market demand curve is more elastic than the individual demand curves.

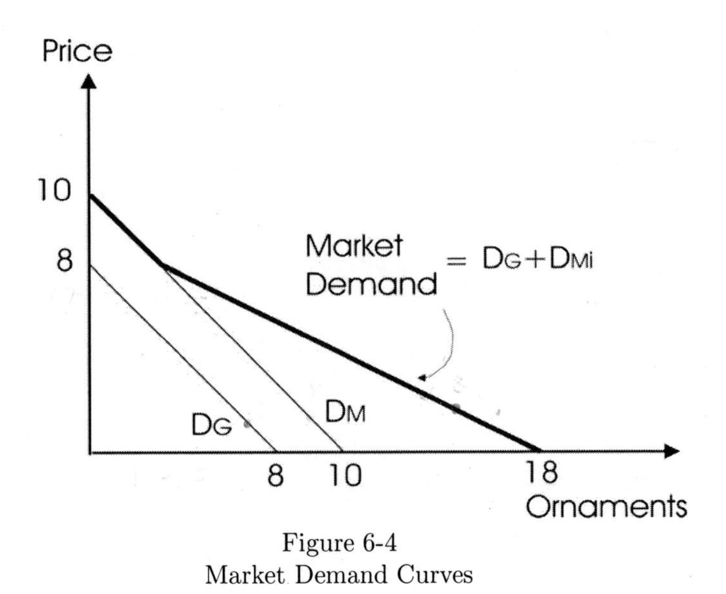

Figure 6-4
Market Demand Curves

Market demand curves are more elastic than individual demand curves.

Now for something important ... pay attention. Why is the market demand curve more elastic? The reason is that a market demand curve is downward sloping for two reasons. First, when the price of the good falls, everyone who is *in the market* buys more because they substitute out of other goods and into this cheaper one. Second, marginal individuals who were just indifferent to buying ornaments at the higher price now enter the market when the price is lower. These two effects have special names. The first effect is called the intensive margin; the second effect is called the extensive margin.

6.4 Unit Demand Curves (A Special Case)

To help understand the extensive margin, let's consider a special case. There are many things in life, which for various reasons, you only do once or own one of. In most societies we only have one spouse at a time, most people own only one house, furnace, and table saw at one time. It's hard to be pregnant twice at the same time, you register for school only once, and you have only one driver's license. In such situations economists say that individuals have *unit demand curves.* These are special demand functions that simply tell us the total value a consumer has for the first unit of a commodity. Figure 6-5 shows two unit demand curves for hot water tanks in the first two graphs.

Notice that the demand curves are simple rectangles — just the amount one would pay for one unit. Notice also that these two individuals have different total values for the hot water tanks. The first person is willing to pay $1000 while the second person is only willing to pay $750. Presumably a market would be made up of hundreds or thousands of individuals, all with different unit demands for hot water tanks.

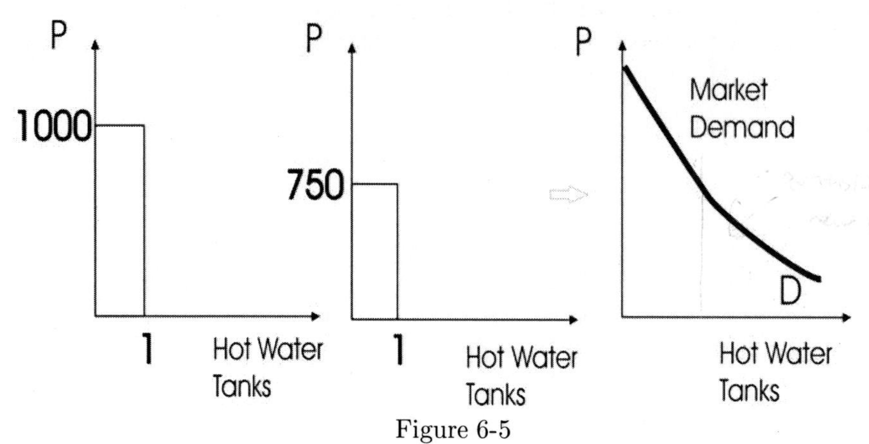

Figure 6-5
Individual Unit Demand Curves and Market Demand

What does this mean for the market demand curve? Remarkably, the market demand curve looks just like it would if the individuals all had demand curves that were downward sloping. The reason is that although there are no intensive margin changes in the quantity demanded, there are still extensive market changes. As the price of the hot water tanks falls, more individuals enter the market. Thus the graph on the far right of Figure 6-5 shows a downward sloping line. Every extra unit that is sold represents a new consumer entering the market. The last consumer to enter the market is called the *marginal consumer* because that person receives no consumer's surplus. Those *intra marginal* consumers in the market get consumer's surplus, but the last person does not. Those people who have low unit demands; that is, their total values are still lower than the price, simply are not in the market.

The notion of market demand curves based solely on unit demands on the part of consumers is extraordinarily useful because it allows us to extend the law of demand at a market level in situations where it might not make sense to use it at the individual level. For example, economists would predict that lowering the cost of divorce would increase the divorce rate. For any individual couple, they either get divorced or they don't. A divorced couple cannot divorce a second time. Furthermore, when the cost of divorce goes down, not everyone gets divorced ... most still stay married. But some marginal couples, just indifferent to being married or divorced now become divorced when the cost of divorce falls, and this is predicted by the market demand curve.

The same would be true about predictions regarding crime. Raising penalties for crime won't mean that every criminal ceases such activity, but some of them do ... the marginal ones. Likewise, if the cost of crime goes down, some individuals engage in crime, but not everyone goes out and commits a murder! Consider university enrollment. When the price of tuition goes down, most people don't change their behavior, but the marginal students now enroll. Changes in the extensive margin mean that the market demand curve is downward sloping, even when individuals can only make a dichotomous "in or out" decision.

6.5 **Market Supply**

Since we're talking about exchange in an economy where supply is just fixed, the calculation of market supply is trivial. Every individual is endowed with some amount of the good in question (this endowment could be zero), and this means the individual supply curves are simply vertical lines. It doesn't matter what the price is, no more or less can exist. To find the market supply curve, we simply add these sums up horizontally. This is shown in Figure 6-6.

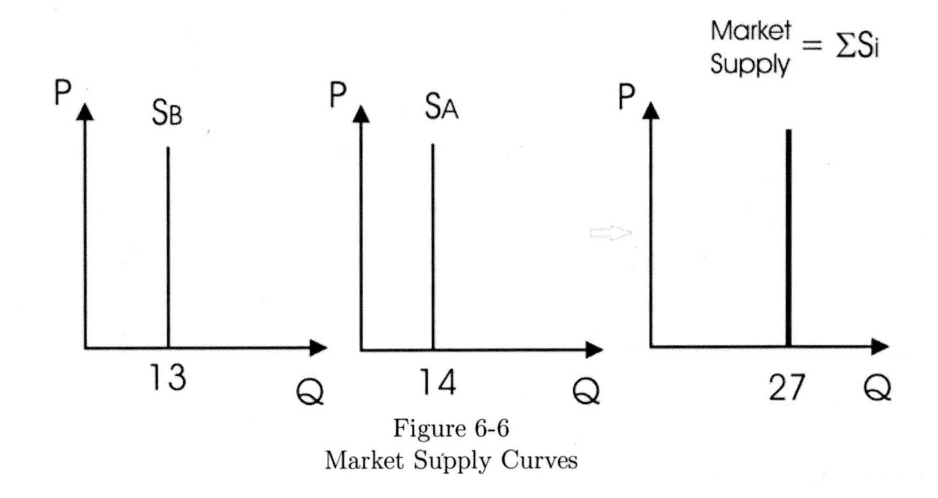

Figure 6-6
Market Supply Curves

To find the equilibrium price and quantity is now quite simple: it is determined by the intersection of the market demand and supply curves, as shown in Figure 6-7.

> *Equilibrium price and quantity are determined by the intersection of the market demand and market supply curves.*

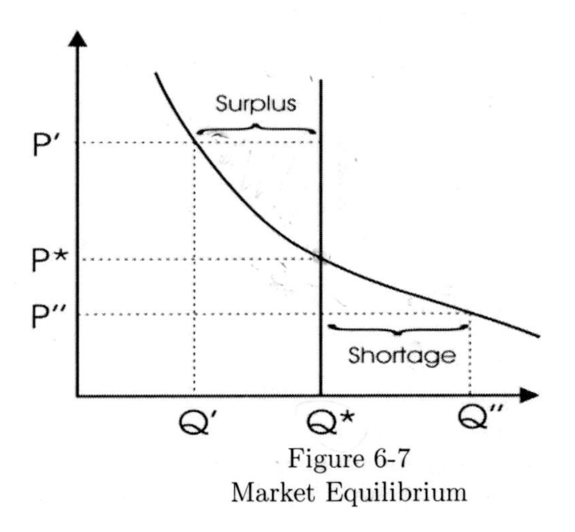

Figure 6-7
Market Equilibrium

When the price is P^*, the total quantity demanded equals the total quantity supplied. If the price was greater than this, say P', then the total quantity demanded falls, as every individual substitutes out of the good to some extent. Since the quantity demanded at this high price is less than the quantity supplied, a surplus exists. Market pressure will result in the price falling back down to P^*. If the price was lower than the equilibrium price, say P'', then the quantity demanded would increase beyond the quantity supplied, and a shortage would result. Again as consumers competed for the good, they would bid the price back up until it once again equaled P^*. At the equilibrium price each individual is in an equilibrium because the price is equal to their marginal value.

We can now see what happens to the equilibrium price and quantity when demand and supplies change. Figure 6-8 shows four graphs. The top two graphs show what happens to the equilibrium price and quantity when the supply increases or decreases. The bottom two show what happens when the demand curve increases or decreases.

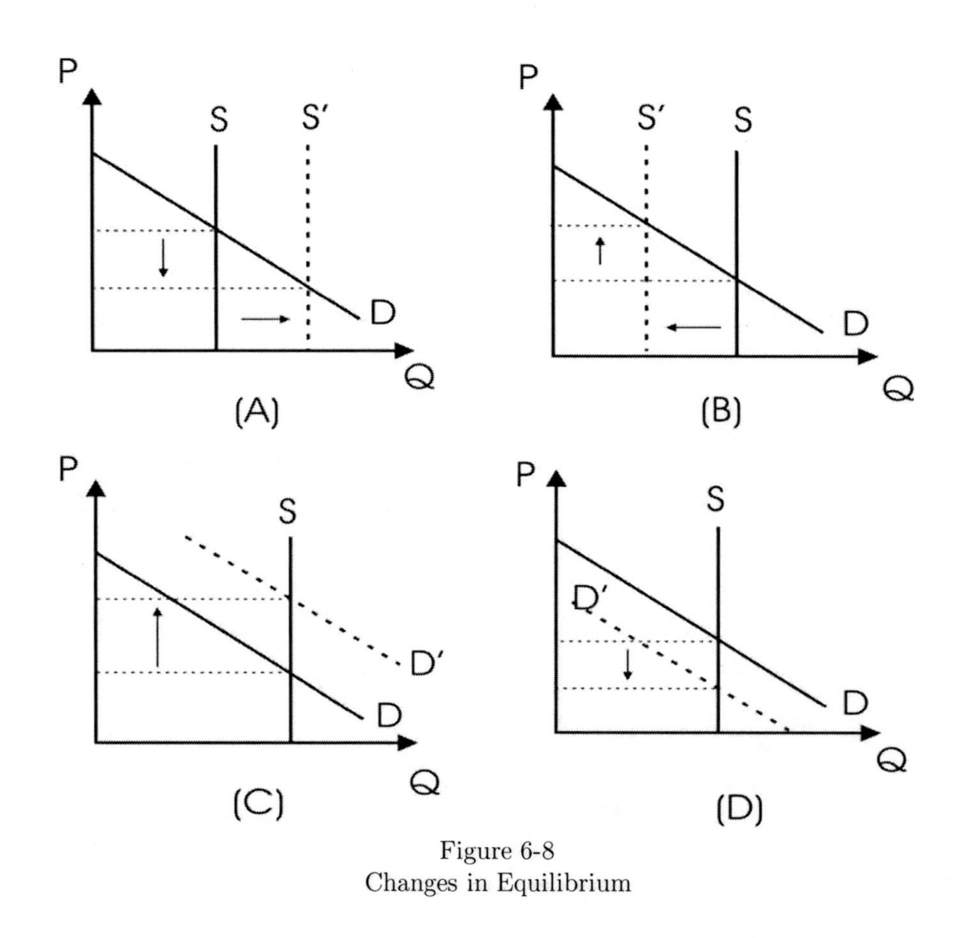

Figure 6-8
Changes in Equilibrium

In panel (a) the supply curve increases and this leads to a fall in price and an increase in the quantity demanded. Notice, and this is important, when the supply curve shifts there is a change in the quantity demanded, but there is no change in demand. A shift in the supply curve does not cause the demand curve to shift. Why does the price fall? If it did not fall there would be a surplus of goods available. At the original price the consumers are not willing to purchase all of the new supply. Hence the price must fall because at the new larger supply the marginal value of consumers is also lower.

Panel (b) shows a similar situation with a reduction in supply. Now the equilibrium price increases and the quantity demanded falls. Had the price not risen there would have been a shortage, since at the original price consumers demand more than the new lower amount supplied. The rise in price "clears the market" and guarantees that the quantity supplied equals the quantity demanded.

Panel (c) shows the results of an increase in demand when the supply curve is vertical. Since the supply is fixed, there is no change in the quantity demanded, only an increase in price. Panel (d) shows that when the demand curve shifts down there is a subsequent fall in the price. The movements in prices and quantities when there is a shift in either demand or supply is what the average person casually refer to as "the laws of supply and demand." Well, let's hope this is what they're referring too!

6.6 Exchange with Market Demand and Supply

Let's suppose that we have another small market of two individuals: Rich Mr. Redekop and Poor Miss Mach. Both of the individuals happen to own some rooms in which they live. Miss Mach has 2 rooms, while the wealthy Mr. Redekop has 15. However, each has a demand for rooms that is similar to their endowments. Mr. Redekop has a large demand, while Miss Mach has a much smaller one. These demands and supplies, along with the resulting market demand and supplies are drawn in Figure 6-9.

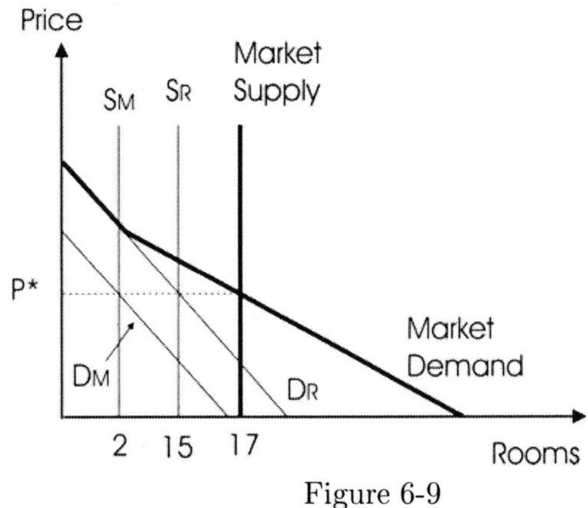

Figure 6-9
Equilibrium in the Room Market

I've drawn these curves purposely a certain way, such that at the equilibrium price, P^*, Miss Mach just happens to demand 2 rooms, and Mr. Redekop just happens to demand 15 rooms — their very endowments. Is the price P^* an equilibrium price? At the price P^* the marginal value of rooms for Miss Mach is equal to the price and equal to the marginal value of rooms for Mr. Redekop. There is no other allocation of rooms that could increase the total surplus. So this is an equilibrium.

Now, suppose tragedy strikes. Poor Miss Mach. In an effort to save a little on electricity she was burning candles one night while doing Mr. Redekop's laundry for a few extra dollars. She fell asleep from exhaustion and the candles caught the sheet she was using for curtains on fire. Luckily Miss Mach escaped unharmed with the laundry, but the two rooms were destroyed. Did I mention it was Christmas Eve?

What happens now in this market? Suddenly the market supply has gone from 17 to 15 rooms, and all of these rooms belong to Mr. Redekop. With no rooms to live in Miss Mach's marginal value for rooms has increased and is now higher than Mr. Redekop's. As a result she is willing to rent rooms from him. Figure 6-10 shows the post fire situation. At the new intersection of market demand and supply we see that Miss Mach now demands 1 room, and Mr. Redekop is willing to give up this room. The new consumer surplus for Miss Mach is shown as the shaded area under her demand curve. Notice that this is smaller than her consumer's surplus before the fire, but it is larger than the consumer's surplus she would get if she could not rent a room. In fact, in that case her surplus would be zero. The shaded area just above Mr. Redekop's demand curve is the seller's surplus he gets from renting the room. This is the amount of rent for the room minus the marginal value he placed on the room when he consumed it himself (the area under his demand curve for the 15th room). Thus Mr. Redekop is made better off by the misfortune of Miss Mach.

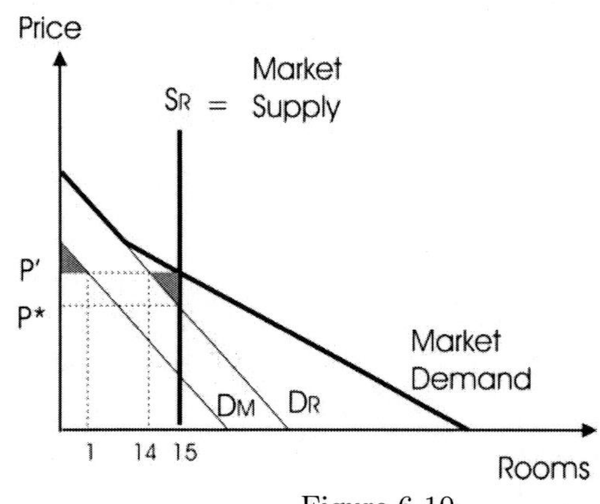

Figure 6-10
Equilibrium with Fewer Rooms

Perhaps you're thinking "such is the injustice of market efficiency." Well, no, such is the injustice of homes burning down. The market price mechanism actually made the situation better. Suppose that in anticipation of Mr. Redekop's opportunistic increase in rental prices, the local government passed a law preventing rents from increasing, just after the fire occured. Mr. Redekop could rent out a room, but it would have to be at the original price of P^* — no price gouging allowed!

What would be the result of such a move? The result would be Mr. Redekop would not rent out a room. Why should he? If he rents out a room at price P^*, his marginal value increases, which means that the value he places on the room is higher than the rent he'll receive. Since Mr. Redekop is greedy, just like Miss Mach, he won't do anything that makes him worse off. But if Mr. Redekop won't rent out the room, then poor Miss Mach is stuck with living on the street. The good intention of the law has had the unintended consequence of hurting the very person it was supposed to help.

When markets work well at allocating goods, preventing the market from working by restricting the movement of prices will lower the total gains from trade.

The real point of this melodramatic section is to help you realize what is behind the concept of a market equilibrium. When the market supply and market demand intersect an equilibrium results not just because the total amount supplied just happens to equal the total amount demanded. In addition to this, every individual is also in equilibrium. Each consumer sets their marginal value equal to the price, and every consumer is content to stay at this quantity because it maximizes their utility and maximizes the gains from trade.

6.7 Applications

Rent Control

With our market model we can analyze all types of things in the world around us. Let's consider rent control when there is a fixed supply of housing available. At various times and in various jurisdictions rent control has been a popular public policy. Essentially what a rent control does is restrict the rent of an apartment from increasing above some ceiling amount. For the purposes of simply demonstrating the price effects, let's assume that the government is perfectly able to enforce the rent control. Hence, landlords and tenants are not able to pay money under the table in order to get around the law.

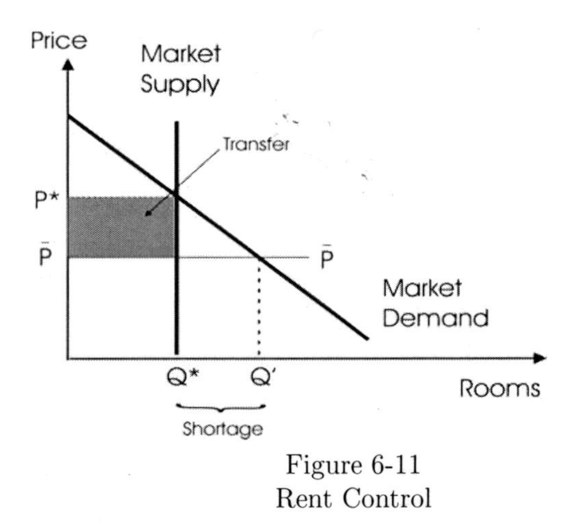

Figure 6-11
Rent Control

Figure 6-11 shows a rental market where the local government has imposed a price ceiling of $\bar{P}$, which is below the equilibrium price of P^*. The simple result of this is a shortage of apartments is created. At this low price the quantity demanded increases beyond the fixed supply of rooms. The impact is that people would line up or otherwise try to compete for the rooms that are hard to get. The second effect is that for those people lucky enough to get rooms, there is a *transfer of wealth*. This is shown as the shaded area in the figure. This transfer was wealth that used to be seller's surplus and is now consumer's surplus. It results from the fact that the rooms are rented at the lower price. There's a lot more to rent control than these two effects, but we'll have to wait to complicate our model with production before we can analyze them.

This is the first mention of wealth transfers, and more needs to be said about them. A true wealth transfer takes a given amount of money from one person, say $100, and gives it to someone else. Many wealth transfers in the real world don't work this smoothly. When you donate money to a nonprofit firm like CARE or UNICEF, for every dollar you give, perhaps 60¢ actually gets transferred to the intended recipient. In a true wealth transfer nothing is lost in the transfer. Economists are prone to consider true wealth transfers as neutral in terms of efficiency, because the changes they cause in utility are unobservable. Some people think any wealth transfer from rich people to poor people must increase efficiency because a dollar should be worth more to people who don't have very many. But people who think this way usually aren't rich! Consider the ficticious case of Scrooge and Cratchet in Dicken's *Christmas Carol*. If we took a dollar from rich Scrooge and gave to poor Cratchet, no doubt the latter would be filled with joy. However, Scrooge would be beside himself with angst, and it's not clear if the gain to Cratchet would exceed the loss to Scrooge. As much as we might detest the likes of Scrooges, the point is well taken. In this book we'll stick with the convention of considering true wealth transfers as neutral with respect to efficiency.

Just Lucky

Have you ever seen a graph like the one in Figure 6-12 in a newspaper or book? Quite often these graphs are couched in discussions of the global warming, environmental degradation, and the general end of the earth. The argument usually goes something like: up until now we've been lucky that the supplies of natural resources have been sufficient to meet the consumer demands. However, in the future, as demands continue to grow and as the world's fixed resources begin to decline, shortages are inevitable. Demand will outstrip supply.

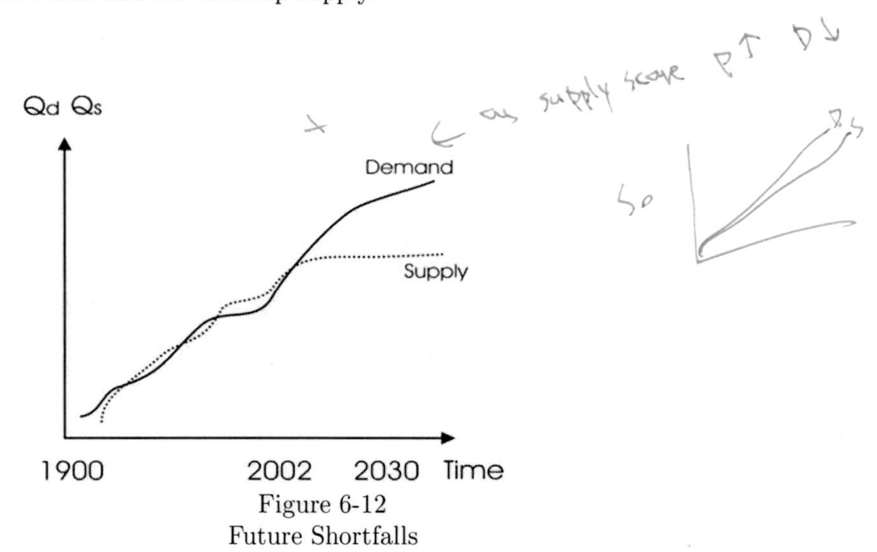

Figure 6-12
Future Shortfalls

What's wrong with this type of analysis is it ignores the equilibrating role of prices. It was no fluke supplies of natural resources just happened to meet demands over the past centuries. As resources become more scarce, prices rise. These rises in prices cause reductions in the quantity demanded until an equilibrium is reached. The equilibrating effect of changing prices means that quantities demanded will always equal quantities supplied. It's not luck ... it's equilibrium.

6.8 Prelude of Things To Come

In the next chapter we will start to discuss costs and production. The next two chapters will have the purpose of understanding the supply curve, and in particular, understanding why it is upward sloping. Before we do so, however, it may be of some use to simply assume the supply curve is upward sloping and consider our example of rent control in order to better understand markets and exchange.

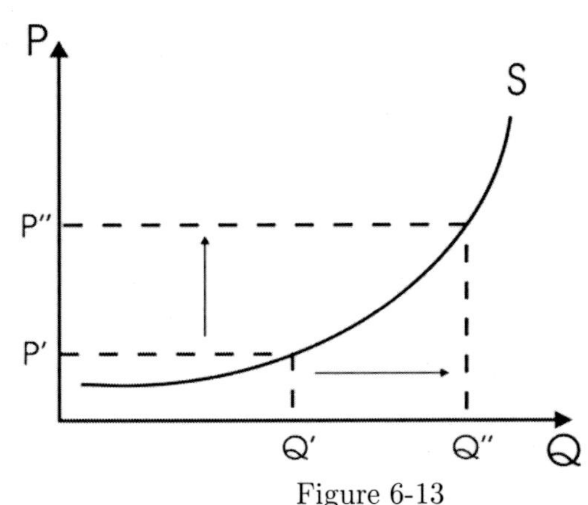

Figure 6-13
An Upward Sloping Supply Curve

What does it mean, at a market level, to say a supply curve is upward sloping? Visually it is quite simple and is shown in Figure 6-13. Basically a supply curve tells us how much of the commodity Q will be supplied to the market at a given price. When the price is P' then Q' is supplied. When the price rises to P'' then the amount of the commodity supplied to the market increases to Q''. In other words, there is a positive relationship between the price of a commodity and the amount suppliers (often firms) are willing to take to the market. When supply curves are upward sloping the equilibrium price and quantity are still determined by the intersection of supply and demand, just as in Figure 6-8. The only difference is that changes in price now induce a change in the quantity supplied as well as a change in the quantity demanded.

Let's consider the example of rent control again, this time using an upward sloping supply curve. Now when rental rates increase there is an increase in the number of rooms available to rent, and when there is a decrease in rental rates, there is a decrease in the number of rooms to rent. Consider Figure 6-14. Before there was any form of rent control the rental on rooms was P^* and a total number of rooms Q^* was both supplied and demanded. When the rent control is put on the rental rate is legally set to $\bar{P}$, which means the quantity demanded increases to $\bar{Q}$. This is the same as before. The difference now is that suppliers of rooms *remove some rooms from the market.* When the market price for a room falls, room owners convert some of the previously rented rooms to other uses. For example, they may just use the room for a guest room, or a shop, or sewing room. There are many uses for rooms, and the landlord will seek the best one. This fall in the quantity supplied of rooms to Q' means the marginal value those rooms actually rented increases to P'. Anyone who actually rents a room at these lower prices is getting a great deal, and those who do not have a room are willing to pay up to P' to get one. If you're a *Seinfeld* fan, you may recall the episode where George is trying to get a new apartment in his building which is rent controlled. Those in charge of renting the room out are going to give it to an old man because he survived a ship sinking at sea. George gives them a brief outline of his life and easily proves he has a more pathetic life and deserves the apartment. In the end the apartment goes to another person who simply bribed the superindendent of the building. Such is what happens under rent control.

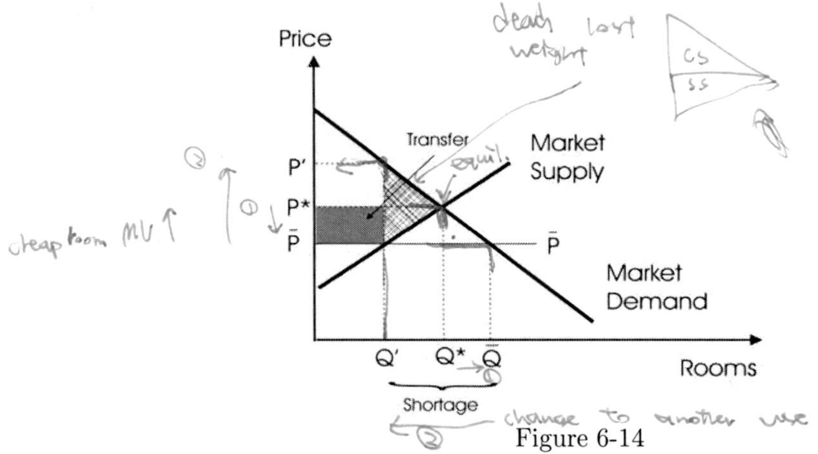

Figure 6-14
Rent Control With Upward Sloping Supply Curves

When the supply curve is upward sloping, the rent control has more significant impacts. Notice with an upward sloping supply curve the shortage of apartments is larger. Notice also there is a reduction in the number of units available to rent because of the rent control. This means there is a loss of consumer and seller surplus from the reduction in trade. This loss is represented as the cross hatched area in the figure. We'll discuss this area more in chapter 9, but it is called a "deadweight loss." A deadweight loss is different from a transfer of wealth. This is a loss of surplus, which no one acquires. Thus from figure 6-14 we would say the rent control made some sellers and buyers worse off by the amount of the deadweight loss.

6.9 **Summary**

This chapter has examined trade when people are simply endowed with goods and are unable to change the supply of what they have. Using demand curves we again saw that trade takes place when people have different marginal values. We also saw that trade stops when marginal values are equal, and this condition is met when market demand and market supply are equal. When a trading equilibrium is reached, the gains from trade (the sum of consumer and producer surplus) are maximized.

Changes in any of the factors that are normally held constant, like changes in incomes, other prices, tastes, or supplies, will lead to shifts in either the market demand or supply curves. These shifts then lead to changes in the equilibrium prices and quantities. Any increase in demand leads to an increase in price and quantity. Any increase in supply leads to a fall in price, but an increase in the quantity traded.

Although we briefly introduced the notion of an upward sloping supply curve at the end of the chapter, in the next two chapters we will examine issues of production before we return again to markets and supply curves.

REVIEW QUESTIONS

1. Explain how exchange can make both parties better off, even when there is no production?
2. How is the Theorem of Exchange just an implication of the principle of maximization?
3. If trade between two people makes them both better off, will trade between three people always make all three better off?
4. What is the difference between the extensive and intensive margins?
5. If there is an excess supply, what forces will cause the price to fall?
6. If there is an excess demand, what forces will cause the price to rise?
7. In real markets we see prices moving up and down all the time, does this mean the market is out of equilibrium?
8. When Doug finally finished the renovation on his house he had 20 Hardie Boards left over. Brian lives next door and has a demand for Hardie boards given by P=450-3Q. If Doug is the only supplier, what would be the equilibrium price? If the local hardware store sells the boards for $9 each, how many would Brian demand? At this lower price, what would his consumer's surplus be?

PROBLEMS

1. What is wrong with the following statement: "If the price of housing goes up to $500,000 then no one will be able to afford it."

2. When asked why a hand carved mask was so expensive, the owner of the store said "Because it takes so many hours to make it." Provide a better answer.

3. When you find someone who eats hot dogs at a ball park, the person invariably says "da dawgs, dey alvays taste great!". Assuming that hot dogs don't really taste better at the ball park (but knowing that they cost twice as much as they normally do) what would explain this observation (that is, why would we observe a large fraction of the hot dog consumers in the park saying that the hot dogs taste great relative to hot dog consumers at home or elsewhere)?

4. "Trade occurs when two people value different goods equally. In this sense, trade is fair because equally valued goods are being traded." True, False, explain.

5. Person A has demand curve $D_a = 8 - P$, while person B has demand curve $D_b = 13 - P$ for some good. Person A owns 7 units, while person B only owns 4.

    a. What is the equilibrium price at which trade takes place?

    b. Who is a net seller, who is a net buyer, and by how much?

6. Analyze the following statement using our economic model: "The threat of sexually transmitted diseases (stds) has increased the demand for prophylactics, but this increase in demand has raised prices of prophylactics. At the higher prices demand falls and in the end fewer prophylactics are used, and stds become more common."

7. If the gains from trade are exhausted or will be, why do individuals trade at all? Aren't individuals better off with gains rather than having their gains exhausted? Briefly explain.

8. "The wages in Mexico are significantly less than those paid in Canada. Therefore Canada will gain from trade with Mexico, but not the other way around." True/False, explain.

9.. Mr. A and Mr. B have the following respective demands.

$$P^a = 25 - 5X, \qquad P^b = 11 - X$$

    a. Graph them on separate graphs.

    b. Mr. A has no X's while Mr. B has 10 X's. What are their marginal and total values at these quantities? Using either method discussed in the chapter, determine how much each will have after trade? What will be their marginal values at these quantities?

10. Suppose you are in charge of a toll bridge that is essentially cost free. The demand for bridge crossings Q is given by $P = 12 - 2Q$.

a. Draw the demand curve for bridge crossings.

b. How many people would cross the bridge if there were no toll?

c. What is the loss of consumer surplus associated with the charge of a bridge toll of $6.

11. What economic principle is Robert Frost discussing below?
Two roads diverged in a yellow wood,
And sorry I could not travel both
And be one traveler, long I stood
And looked down one as far as I could
To where it bent in the undergrowth;
Then took the other, as just as fair,
And having perhaps the better claim,
Because it was grassy and wanted wear;
Though as for that the passing there
Had worn them really about the same,
And both that morning equally lay
In leaves no step had trodden black.
Oh, I kept the first for another day!
Yet knowing how way leads on to way,
I doubted if I should ever come back.
I shall be telling this with a sigh
Somewhere ages and ages hence:
Two roads diverged in a wood, and I —
I took the one less traveled by,
And that has made all the difference.

A literary critic, commenting on this poem said "The poet's 'difference' is in him from the beginning, long before he sets out on his career. The road that Robert Frost took was not only the 'different' road, the right road for him, but the only road he could have taken." Who is the better economist, Frost or the Critic? Why?

12. Whistler is an international ski resort with a relatively fixed supply of housing at any time. Recently a home renting 70 beds for $700 per month for each bed was shut down for violating fire codes. The mayor of the town stated it was morally wrong to charge so much for one bed in a room with nine other beds, and if it were up to the mayor, all such bunk houses would be shut down. Who would be hurt by such a by-law? Who would benefit?

13. "The law of demand says that when the price of something falls, more should be consumed. But when the price of vacations falls, I still just take one vacation per year." How does the law of demand fit in this circumstance?

14. In the summer of 2003 the interior of the province of British Columbia experienced the worst forest fire season in recorded history. In the city of Kelowna, over 200 homes were destroyed by fire. In a CBC radio interview a Kelowna city councillor made the following statement: "Since the forest fires of the summer there has been an enormous increase in the cost of rental housing in the city. Two hundred and thirty people lost their homes to forest fires, and these people have to live somewhere. It will take a long time before the supply of housing equals

demand." Assuming the councillor meant to say "It will take a long time before the quantity demanded of housing equals the quantity supplied," what is wrong with his economic logic?

15. One of the common traffic rules car drivers must know is how to proceed at a four-way stop. This happens in intersections where drivers from all directions must stop and then proceed on a "first come, first served" basis; that is, the first person to the intersection goes first, the second person goes second, etc. If there is a tie, the person on the right goes first. Suppose a busy intersection has a four-way stop procedure, is such a rule Pareto optimal? If not, do people proceed along lines which are Pareto optimal?

16. Before there were charitable trusts in England, it was a common practice for the rich to buy all available grain in years of bad harvest, and then sell it back to the poor at half price. The poor were allowed to buy as much as they wanted at this reduced price. For this question, let's assume that three things are true: the poor are the only ones who consume grain, they end up buying as much as they want at the reduced price, and that the reduced price is half what the rich paid for the grain.

    a. In a graph, draw the poor's demand for grain, an initial (vertical) supply curve, and a new (vertical) supply curve for the bad crop. Show the bad crop equilibrium price assuming there is no interference by the charitable rich.

    b. With a new graph, now assume the charitable rich enter the market. Represent this as an increase in demand. Show the new price, and the price the poor now pay. Assume it is still a bad crop.

    c. Are the poor or anyone else helped by this scheme? Briefly explain.

17. An article in the Globe and Mail claimed that NASCAR auto racing is a "waste of fuel in an age when gasoline prices are over $1 per litre." Is it?

18. "One man's junk is another man's treasure." What economic idea does this cliche reflect?

19. Billy Dean, in the song *We Just Disagree*, states the couple needs to just drop the dispute:
    'Cause we can't see eye to eye.
    There ain't no good guy,
    There ain't no bad guy.
    There's only you and me and we just disagree.

    In this chapter we've looked at how two individuals can come together and exchange. In what way are the conditions for exchange a case of not seeing eye to eye? How does an exchange resolve the problem of just agreeing to disagree?

20. Angie has 12 cookies, and a marginal value curve described by $P = 45 - 3Q_A$, while Benny has 0 cookies, and a marginal value curve described by $P = 44 - 2Q_B$.

    a. Draw a three sided trade diagram, with Benny's marginal value curve going from left to right, and Angie's going from right to left. Be careful to state how wide the diagram is in terms of units of cookies. Draw both marginal value curves in this diagram.

b. How might we interpret Angie's marginal value curve in this context? What are their marginal values before trade?

c. After trade, how many cookies do each of them have? What is the marginal value of each person after trade?

d. If we assume that all cookies traded at a price equal to the final marginal values, what are the consumer and seller surplus from trade?

21. Suppose a little economy has ten people in it. Each person has a unit demand for cars, which means that each person is willing to pay x_i for one car, but zero for a second. The demands for each person are given below in the table.

Person	1	2	3	4	5	6	7	8	9	10
x (in 000's)	20	30	40	20	60	10	50	70	5	30

a. In the graph on the left below I want you to graph person 7's demand curve. In the graph on the right I want you to graph the market demand curve. Be extremely careful to label everything and accurate in your graphing.

b. Now suppose that the market price for cars is $40,000.

Who is the marginal consumer?

Who are the intra-marginal consumers?

Which individuals do not buy a car?

c. Now suppose that the price decreases to $30,000. What is the arc elasticity of demand? Is the demand elastic or inelastic?

REVIEW QUESTION ANSWERS

1. *When two people exchange goods, the flow is from low valued users to high valued users. Surplus is generated because the two parties value the goods differently at the margin. Hence, production is not necessary for the generation of wealth, a redistribution from low to high valued users also generates wealth. As a corollary, if there is a forced, involuntary redistribution of goods in an economy, this must lower wealth.*

2. *When people are maximizers they trade because it makes them better off. As long as there are gains to be had, they keep trading. This process only stops when all the gains from trade are exhausted at the margin, but this is the Theorem of Exchange.*

3. *No. When a third party enters a trade arrangement, he is likely to displace one of the other traders. If he has a higher or lower marginal value of a good then he will start to receive or trade that good. As a result, even though the total gains from trade will increase with more traders, not everyone will be happy about it. This means having more traders is not usually Pareto Optimal. Can you think of when it would be?*

4. *The extensive margin refers to individuals entering or leaving the market. The intensive margin refers to those already in the market who now buy a little more or less.*

5. *An excess supply means inventories increase. That is, those with the goods have a low marginal value for them, and those without the goods have a high marginal value. Maximization is the force that will drive the price down until the marginal values are equal.*

6. *The answer is essentially the same as in (5).*

7. *Our model is an "equilibrium" model. That is, it assumes the "economy" moves from one equilibrium to another instantaneously. Hence, fluctuating prices are interpreted as movements from one equilibrium to another due to some changes in the demand or supply curves.*

8. *Setting the supply equal to the demand we get $P = 450 - 3 \times 20$, and therefore $P = 390$. Those would be expensive boards. If the price is 9 dollars at the store then Brian would buy 147, and his consumer's surplus would be \$32,413.5.*

Odd Numbered Problem Answers

1. *Prices are determined by supply and demand. A demand curve is based, in part, on one's ability to pay. Therefore, if the price is $500,000 then someone is willing and able to afford that price.*

3. *The observations we see are a biased sample. Only those people who value goods greater than the price purchase, and only those firms with costs below the price produce. At the ball park, only people who love hot dogs are willing to pay the high price. They would say any dog tasted great. At a birthday party where the hot dogs are free, everyone consumes them and many people will say they are gross ... even though they may be fresher and better than the hot dogs at the ball park. For the same reason you won't find anyone coming out of a Brittany Spears concert saying it was a bad show. Any fan willing to stand in line for two days and pay several hundred dollars for a ticket would love any Spears performance.*

5.

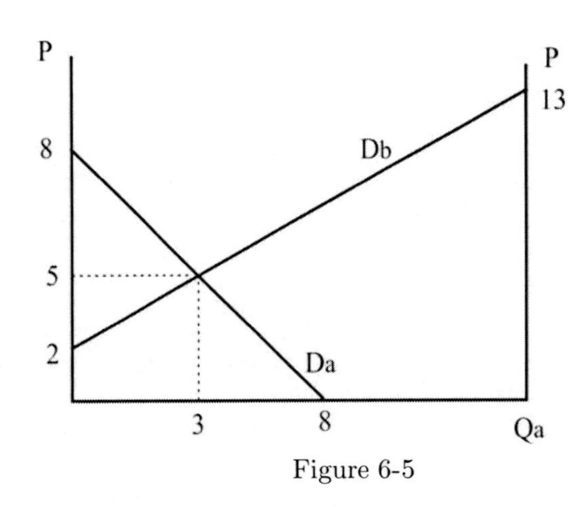

Figure 6-5

a. *The easiest way to solve this problem is to make a box 11 units wide, and solve the two equations. From the graph we see the equilibrium price is $5, and person A demands 3 units, while person B demands 8 units.*

b. *Person A is a net seller of 4 units, and person B is a net buyer of 4 units.*

7. *The gains are exhausted* **at the margin**. *When this happens the total gains from trade are maximized.*

9.

a.

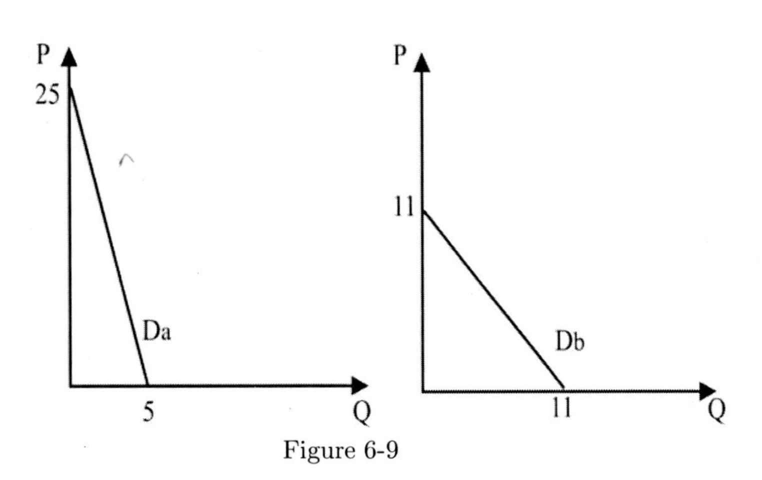

Figure 6-9

b. *When Mr. A has no X's his MV is 25 and his TV is zero. If Mr. B has 10 X's, then his MV is 1, and his TV is 60. After trade Mr. A will have 4 units and Mr. B will have 6. The MV of each will be 5.*

11. *Frost is pointing out life is full of choices, a very economic notion. The critic seems to be suggesting Frost had no choice. This gets at a deep philosophical issue which is nicely raised at this point. What is the nature of choice? If we have preferences and constraints, and if we are driven by maximization, then in what sense do we choose? Are we a computer program, like Maple, where once the parameters are punched in an optimal "choice" spits out? Maple has no choice but to pick a certain outcome, are we, like Frost's critic, made to make choices like this? I think not. Unlike Maple, we make choices because we want to, not because we must make them. We have the ability not to do the optimal strategy. Frost* **could have** *taken the other road, he just didn't want to. And that makes all the difference. Frost was the better economist.*

13. *There's no such good as a "vacation". People take time off, they actually go places, buy trinkets, etc. What good actually fell in price? If the cost of taking time off falls, then people will take more time off. They may take one vacation, but it will be longer. If flights away fall in price, the person might take one vacation, but will fly further away. And so on. Whatever the dimension of price reduction is, there will be increased consumption along that margin.*

15. *It generally is not Pareto Optimal. If you have four cars at an intersection, the two cars going in opposite directions can go at the same time. This means four cars go through in the time it takes two cars under the legal rule. This happens all the time at four way stops, and no one gets mad because no one is harmed and some benefit.*

17. *If people like to watch NASCAR (there's no accounting for tastes!) and are willing to pay the price of admission (which has to cover the cost of fuel), then this is an efficient use of fuel.*

19. *The necessary requirement for an exchange is a difference in marginal values. In a fundamental way a difference in marginal values reflects a difference in the desires over how to use a good. If you eat the apple, you get the value, if I eat the apple I get it. When we use the phrase "let's just agree to disagree" what this means is that the problem has not been resolved. Exchange is a very important solution to the problem "who gets what?" Society would starve to death if we just agreed to disagree over who gets to eat. Through exchange there is not only a resolution, but the outcome sends goods to those who value them the most.*

21.

   a.

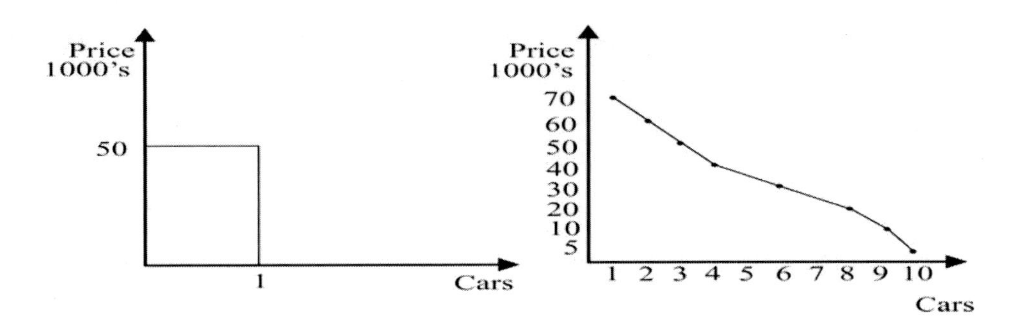

   b. *Person 3.*

Persons 5, 7, and 8.

All the others: 1, 2, 4, 6, 9, and 10.

   c. *The arc elasticity is −7/5 which is elastic.*

CHAPTER 7

COST AND COMPARATIVE ADVANTAGE

7.1 What is Cost?

There's a not so famous story of a Nobel prize winning economist who sits down on an airplane seat beside a Nobel winning Doctor. "Tell me" says the Doctor to the economist, "what is one simple and important idea in economics that's not obvious?" The economist thought for a moment, and couldn't come up with anything. Later, after he'd left the plane, the economist realized he should have said "Cost." The concept of cost is one of the most important and valuable ideas in economics, yet the profession has done such a bad job in marketing its true meaning that the general public has a very confused idea as to what cost means.

Let's pause and consider what cost is. Ask the man on the street, "what is cost?" and the response is almost universal — "what you pay for something". In other words, the layman's notion of cost is "historical cost". This answer is reinforced by the accountant's use of historical cost as their measure of cost. Although it's possible for historical cost to equal the true cost, historical cost is often completely irrelevant in measuring actual costs, and as a result, often bears no relation to current prices or behavior. Your parents may have paid a trivial price for their home thirty years ago, even though it might be worth a small fortune today. The original price has no bearing on how they value the property today. Perhaps you've purchased a car for $10,000, only to find out it is rusted-out, and needs major repairs. The $10,000 you paid is irrelevant to what the car is worth, and irrelevant for how you will behave with respect to the car. A firm may own an asset that has long been fully depreciated on the accountant's books, but is still a valuable piece of equipment. The firm will treat the equipment as valuable, even though the accountant tells them it is worth nothing. In all of these examples, the historical cost is irrelevant.

Economists refer to costs as *opportunity cost.* Opportunity cost is the value of the next best alternative, and is often independent of historical cost. When you decide to do something, like ride your bike, you give up the opportunity to do hundreds of other activities. Each one of those activities has a value. The highest valued activity, is the cost of riding your bike. To be even more concrete, suppose instead of riding your bike you could see a movie worth $20 or study another course worth $15. The cost of riding then is $20.

To help understand this notion of cost, keep in mind opportunity cost always refers to an action. In our casual speech we say things like "how much does the book cost?", but such a statement literally does not make any sense. What we should say is, "how much does it cost to *buy* the book, *read* the book, *write* the book" and so on. Actions imply there is a forgone alternative, and therefore a cost. If there is no action or choice taken, then there can be no cost.

Likewise, if there is no alternative, neither is there a cost. The most common linguistic mistake made in this regard, is with respect to time. We say things like "my time is money", or "my time is valuable", or even "I'm a high time-cost person". As with the case of the book, these are examples of sloppy language — time is not a cost! Time marches on and there is nothing we can do about it. What is costly is what we do with our time. If I sleep in, I forgo having breakfast. The value of the lost breakfast is the cost of using my time between 7:00-8:00AM for sleeping. When we say an individual is a high time-cost person, what we really mean is the value of the alternative uses of this person's time are high. Opportunity cost is our fourth economic principle.

> **PRINCIPLE #4**
>
> **Opportunity Cost:** *the value of the highest forsaken alternative.*

7.2 Adding Up Costs

Opportunity cost critically hinges on the value of the *next best* alternative, not the value of all the alternatives. At this moment, what is the cost to you of reading this chapter? Perhaps you could be working right now for $18 per hour? Perhaps you could be at a party, or eating lunch with friends. If you think about it, the set of things you could be doing right now is very large. The cost of reading this chapter is not the sum value of all these activities. Rather it is the value of the single alternative activity you value the most.

This is not to say several values are never added up to arrive at the cost of an activity. Suppose the final exam for this course is only three days away — on a Friday. On Tuesday night there are three mutually exclusive things you can do besides study. Ranking them from most to least preferred you can (i) go to a party, (ii) go to a movie, or (iii) watch an old Star Trek episode. On Wednesday night you could (i) go to a party, (ii) visit your Mom, or (iii) get some sleep. On Thursday night you could (i) go visit your priest, (ii) do the laundry, or (iii) go to yet another party. If you decide to study all three nights, what is the cost? It is the value of two parties and one visit to the priest. It is not the value of every single activity, nor the value of the single highest activity. Cost is the value of the highest forsaken alternative, and the key to understanding it is to determine the true alternative. For example, suppose you buy a hot-dog at a sidewalk vendor for $1.50. Is the $1.50 a cost? Absolutely, since the money could have been spent on anything else, including the most valuable alternative. Suppose in addition to the money, you had to wait for 10 minutes, and what you could do with this time was worth $2. Is this part of the cost of the hot-dog? Absolutely, because in deciding to purchase the hot-dog, you are deciding to forgo the time as well as the money.

As a final example, consider the cost of your education. The tuition is an obvious sacrifice, and is part of the cost of your education. When you pay tuituion, that money could have been spent on your next best alternative. In addition to your tuition, the amount of income you sacrifice to come to school is also a part of the cost of your education. By being in school you are out of the workforce, and this constitutes a major cost of education. What about your books, are they part of your education cost? If you wouldn't have bought them otherwise (which is probably true for all your books but this one!), then yes they are a cost. What about the rent for your apartment, is it a cost of your education? This is a little trickier. If, by going to school, you had to move and increase your rent, then this *increase* in rent is a cost of education. Presumably, you would have been renting something had you not gone to school, so if your rent does not change, then it is not part of the cost of your education.

7.3 Costs and Bads

It is a common mistake to always think of costs as a bad thing and to confuse costs with bads. In every decision good things and bad things come along with that decision. The bad things, however, are not the costs of the decision... unless they influence the value of the next best alternative. Hence, sweat, toil, and pain, unless they affect the value of alternatives, are not costs. For example, suppose there are two mutually exclusive choices: you can purchase a swimming pool for your home or purchase a new car. There are good things about the swimming pool — you can exercise, cool off, brag to your friends and family, etc., and these may be worth $15,000 to you. However, there are also some bad things — the neighbor kids are always over, you worry about pets drowning, etc., and perhaps these "bads" are worth $\$-2,000$ to you. The difference of $13,000 is the total value of the pool, namely the amount you would be willing to pay to have one. Suppose the car also has good and bad features about it, and the difference of $9,000 is the total value of the car. What is the cost of having the pool? It is not the value of the bads ($2,000), it is the forgone value of the car ($9,000).

When we think of costs always as "bads," we miss the fact that increasing costs can sometimes be a good thing! Suppose an individual is working for the Microsoft corporation in Seattle Washington, and has a salary of $160,000. Then one day Corel Software offers him a job for $300,000 in Ottawa. The cost of staying in Seattle, namely the value of the next best alternative, has gone up because the worker now gives up a higher salary in Ottawa. However, we wouldn't want to say the worker is worse off because his costs have increased. He is clearly better off with the new job offer. Any increase in outside opportunities is an increase in cost, but this type of increased cost is a good thing because it represents an increase in wealth. The employee who has zero opportunity costs of staying at his or her job is not exactly in a strong bargaining position.

When a competitive firm pays workers $10 per hour it does so because these workers could earn $10 per hour at some other activity — the firm must pay the workers their opportunity cost. When you read about marginal costs and supply curves, keep in mind the cost of producing an additional unit ultimately reflects the value of the inputs in their next best use. Hence, though the term "opportunity" will usually be dropped in the rest of the text, the costs relevant to a firm are still opportunity costs.

7.4 Sunk, Avoidable, Fixed, and Variable Costs.

For economists there are three critical distinctions among different types of costs. The first is the difference between ordinary costs of production and transaction costs. Transaction costs are costs that arise when individuals try to cheat one another in an exchange. Shoplifting is a transaction cost, but so are the extra wages paid for shirking workers. This distinction is central to Part III of the book, but for Parts I and II we simply ignore these types of costs and assume all transaction costs are zero.

The second distinction is between sunk (unavoidable) costs, and avoidable costs. Sunk costs are costs that have no bearing on economic decisions because nothing can be done about them. When your mother told you not to cry over spilled milk, she was recognizing the lost milk was sunk, gone, ... history. Avoidable costs, on the other hand, are costs that need not occur and can be avoided. If you buy an ugly lamp, and later lament your decision, the cost is not sunk if you can resell the lamp for what you paid for it. People base their decisions on avoidable costs, not sunk costs. Sunk costs are costs that once incurred, cannot be recovered. Avoidable costs are costs that need not be incurred.

The third distinction made among costs is the difference between fixed and variable costs. A fixed cost does not vary with output, while a variable cost changes when the level of output changes. When you turn the light on in your room to do some reading, the cost of the electricity is independent of how much reading you do. In this sense, the electricity would be a fixed cost. In the next chapter we introduce the inputs of labor and capital into our production model. Labor will be allowed to vary and hence labor costs will be variable costs. The capital will be usually assumed fixed, and so the capital costs will be fixed costs. Fixed costs do not vary with output, variable costs do change with output.

Sunk Costs: costs that cannot be recovered.

Avoidable Costs: opportunity costs that are not sunk, they can be recovered or avoided.

Variable Costs: costs that change when output changes.

Fixed Costs: lump sum costs that do not change with output.

Costs can be sunk and either fixed or variable, or they can be avoidable and either fixed or variable. In other words, any combination is possible. Table 7.1 provides some examples.

	Avoidable Cost	**Sunk Cost**
Fixed Costs	Heating	Advertising
Variable Costs	Metal	Firm Specific Press

Table 7-1

Suppose you own a factory which makes a special auto part for the engines in General Motors cars. Let us consider some of the costs in your factory. The cost of heating the factory space is a fixed cost, since it does not change with the number of parts produced. The heat bill is also avoidable because you can shut the heat off at any time. Similarly, your parts may require some metal to build them. The metal is a variable cost because the more parts you make, the more metal you use. The metal is also an avoidable cost because if you stop producing parts, you don't have to use any metal. Any advertising done is a sunk fixed cost. You cannot get the investment back and the advertiser doesn't charge based on output. Finally, there may be a special stamp or press used in producing the part, and this stamp may wear out the more you produce. Because it wears out it is a variable cost, and because it is only used by this firm it is a sunk cost — no other firm would pay anything for the special stamp.

Although any combination of the different types of costs is possible, for the remainder of the book, unless otherwise stated, we will make the standard assumption that all fixed costs are sunk, and that all variable costs are avoidable. This is a strong assumption, but one made only to make the presentation simpler and easier to understand.

7.5 Comparative Advantage

We saw in earlier chapters how individuals could be made better off by trade when they valued goods differently. Now we want to ignore differences in values for a moment and focus in on gains from trade that result when individuals have different costs for different activities. When individuals have different *marginal costs*, then they gain from trade.

> *Individuals with different marginal costs gain from trade, even when marginal values are the same.*

Marginal costs are the incremental opportunity costs from increasing output by one unit.[1] Once we start talking about marginal costs, we're clearly talking about a world where people can make things. Producing things is a complicated process. There is the physical aspect of production; that is, the labor, skills, and resources used in the actual product. There is also the organization of production; that is, the firm, the boss, and the contracts used to combine the various physical inputs. To start with, we're going to assume most of these complications away and consider the simplest production processes. In the end, we're going to see that even in the simplest cases, supply curves are going to be upward sloping.

Consider a married couple, Jon and Elaine, who have two household tasks to accomplish: clean the kitchen, and cook the meal. Jon is very fast at both activities, in fact, he's faster than Elaine in both of them. The times it takes Jon and Elaine to do these two tasks is given in Table 7-2.

	Cleaning	Cooking
Elaine	60 minutes	80 minutes
Jon	40 minutes	20 minutes

[1] Technically, marginal costs are the change in costs for any given change in output, but for ease of language we'll think of marginal costs as the costs of one more unit.

Table 7-2

Because Jon is better at both activities, we say Jon has an *absolute advantage.*

> *An absolute advantage means you are more productive in all activities.*

Generally speaking people tend to naturally think in terms of absolute advantage. We think the United States shouldn't bother to trade with Niger, Bangladesh, or Haiti because those poor countries couldn't possibly offer the United States anything. Any product produced in those countries could no doubt be better produced in the United States. That's probably true. The United States probably has an absolute advantage over thousands of goods over dozens of countries. But here's the catch: absolute advantage doesn't tell us anything about who will produce what goods.

What we need to know is *comparative advantage*, which is a concept based on opportunity costs. To have a comparative advantage in something means you are the least cost producer, even though you may not have an absolute advantage.

Consider Jon and Elaine above. Jon is twice as good at cooking as he is at cleaning. When he does one cleaning of the kitchen he could have cooked two meals. On the other hand, when Elaine does the cleaning, during that time she could only have cooked 3/4 of a meal. Jon sacrifices more meals when he cleans, therefore, Jon is a high cost cleaner. To turn it around, if Elaine were to cook, she would sacrifice 1.33 cleanings, while Jon only sacrifices 1/2 of a clean kitchen for every meal he cooks. So, although Jon is the high cost cleaner, he's the low cost cook. Thus Jon has a comparative advantage in cooking, and Elaine has a comparative advantage in cleaning.

> *Everyone has a comparative advantage in something.*

Notice Elaine doesn't have an absolute advantage, but she does have a comparative advantage. This is the reason why small poor countries are able to trade with large rich ones. There are some activities at which they are the low cost producers.

> *A comparative advantage exists, even though an absolute advantage may not exist.*

Suppose Jon and Elaine start off thinking they should take turns cleaning and cooking. Over two days, Jon will spend 60 minutes doing housework (40 minutes cleaning, 20 minutes cooking), while Elaine will spend 140 minutes doing her work. The total time spent doing chores in the household is 200 minutes. Now suppose the two decide to specialize according to their comparative advantage and trade jobs one for one. So Jon does all the cooking and Elaine does all the cleaning. Now Elaine, over a two day period, spends 120 minutes on housework, and Jon spends only 40, for a grand total of 160 minutes. By specializing they both are made better off, and they saved 40 minutes of time.

Your own experience no doubt confirms this simple reasoning. Consider households made up of some combination of men and women. Most of these households divide their labor up according to comparative advantage. Men often do outside work, automotive repairs, and the more physical jobs in the household, women tend to do the cleaning, cooking, and laundry. Even after 50 years of feminist sensitivity training, one's hard pressed not to find this. But even if you find a household where the woman changes the oil in the car, you can bet the male of the household is not changing it as well — he'll be doing some other activity he's specialized in. By specializing according to comparative advantage, both parties to the exchange are made better off. To do otherwise would simply raise costs. Consider how long it would take Jon and Elaine to do their chores over a two day period if they specialized according to their comparative *disadvantage* — 240 minutes.

7.6 The Gains from Specialization

It is hard to underestimate the gains from specialization according to comparative advantage. Consider the famous section in Adam Smith's *Wealth of Nations*

> To take an example, ... the trade of the pin maker; a worker not educated to this business, ... could scarce, perhaps with his utmost industry, make one pin in a day, and certainly could not make twenty. But in the way in which this business in now carried on, not only the whole work is a peculiar trade, but it is divided into a number of branches, of which the greater part are likewise peculiar trades. One man draws out the wire, another straightens it, a third cuts it, a fourth points it, a fifth grinds it at the top for receiving the head; to make the head requires two or three distinct operations; to put it on is a peculiar business, to whiten the pins is another; it is even a trade by itself to put them into the paper; and the important business of making a pin is, in this manner, divided into about eighteen distinct operations. ... I have seen a small manufactory of this kind where ten men only were employed, and where some of them consequently performed two or three distinct operations. But though they were very poor, and therefore but indifferently accommodated with the necessary machinery, they could, when they exerted themselves, make among them ... upward of forty-eight thousand pins in a day.

To go from making 20 pins in a day to making 48,000 is simply amazing. In fact, none of the pleasures we enjoy in life could be achieved without everyone being highly specialized. Take any product, no matter how primitive, and odds are you have no idea how to make it. Forget your computer, what about the little yellow pencil you have in your pencil case? Any idea how to make that? How would you know what wood to use? What would you use to cut the tree down, how would you take the tree and turn it into a small piece of wood? What about the paint and little gold letters, how would you make those? And the graphite shaft, who even knows what graphite actually is, let alone where it comes from and how you make it so skinny. And let's not even get started on the metal ring and little rubber eraser. When it comes right down to it, we have no clue how to make a pencil. And yet, we can go to our local book store and buy one for under a dollar. The more you think about it, the more remarkable it is. Probably thousands of people were able to combine their specialized skill to come up with a pencil that costs almost nothing.

Specialization doesn't just mean goods become cheaper. The forces of specialization can be strong enough to influence culture as well. Perhaps this effect has been no greater than in the Prairies of Canada and the Great Plains of the U.S. where specialization in agricultural communities is changing the rural landscape. In 1920 approximately 30% of people in North America lived on farms, while today less than 2% do. What allowed for this dramatic shift was the tremendous changes in technology in planting and harvesting grain. These changes were possible due to the introduction of tractors, combines, and paved roads in rural communities. Whereas one farmer, in the 1920s could barely manage to farm 300 acres on his own, today a farmer can easily manage 10,000 acres. A farmer in the 1920s would have raised mixed livestock as well as grain, but today livestock are raised on specialized farms and feed lots, and farmers specialize in certain types of grains. As farmers specialized and lowered the costs of farming, they became bigger and the local communities began to get smaller and smaller. The result has been a steady decline in rural populations, and in some provinces like Saskatchewan, a fall in total provincial population. Any individual who tries to farm the old fashioned way, is simply driven out of business by the larger more efficient and specialized farmers.

You've probably noticed other effects of specialization around you. Consider your college instructor. If someone is a professor of engineering, they probably know very little about economics. If you have a professor of micro economics, that person probably knows little about macro economics. Professors specialize in specific types of knowledge because it is the only way to push the frontiers of knowledge. The person who knows a little of everything is a lot of fun at a cocktail party, but they'll never win the Nobel prize. Jack-of-all-trades in academics never get tenure because they can't compete against the low cost specialist.

If you're from a smaller community, you've probably noticed there is much less specialization than in large urban centers. This is because the amount of specialization is limited by the size of the market. If a barber lives in a town of 65 people, he'd probably starve to death if he only cuts hair for seniors. In fact, he'd probably starve to death if he was just a barber. The size of the market is just too small to support someone so specialized. I have a cousin, who lives in a very small community in rural Saskatchewan, she not only runs the local store, but she's also the postmaster and owns an antique business. On the other hand, I have a friend in New York City whose full time, and well paying job, is to assess the risk of a particular type of insurance transaction. Incomes in large cities are greater than those in rural communities, in part because the larger markets allow for so much greater gains from specialization.

7.7 Comparative Advantage and Marginal Cost Curves

Comparative advantage means production takes place at least cost. Those people producing one good, who sacrifice the least in terms of other goods, are the ones who produce the good first. To see how this leads to a supply curve, let's consider another example, this time with three people.

Sue, Charles, and Daphne are all capable of producing two goods: machine guns and spinach. The amounts of each good they can produce in a given day are given in Table 7-3. Sue, for example, can produce at most 8 machine guns *or* 4 units of spinach. She cannot produce both 8 guns and 4 spinach because she is constrained by how much time and other inputs she has.

	Machine Guns	Spinach
Sue	8	4
Charles	3	3
Daphne	1	2

Table 7-3

As in the example of Jon and Elaine, we see Sue has an absolute advantage over the other two. She can produce more of either good in one day than the other two can. In calculating who has the comparative advantage though, we must recognize this is a two-by-two concept. Thus it should be clear that Sue is the low cost gun maker, sacrificing only 1/2 of a unit of spinach for every gun she makes. Daphne is the high cost gun maker, losing 2 units of spinach for every gun made. Charles, on the other hand, who has costs of 1 unit of spinach for every gun made, lies in between the other two. Compared to Sue, he is the low cost spinach producer. Compared to Daphne he's the low cost gun maker. This is no problem. The key is we can rank the individuals from low cost to high cost producers. Efficient production requires the low cost producers produce the good first, followed by the next lowest cost person, etc.

Figure 7-1 shows how many machine guns and spinach could be produced by these three, assuming they always specialize according to their comparative advantage.

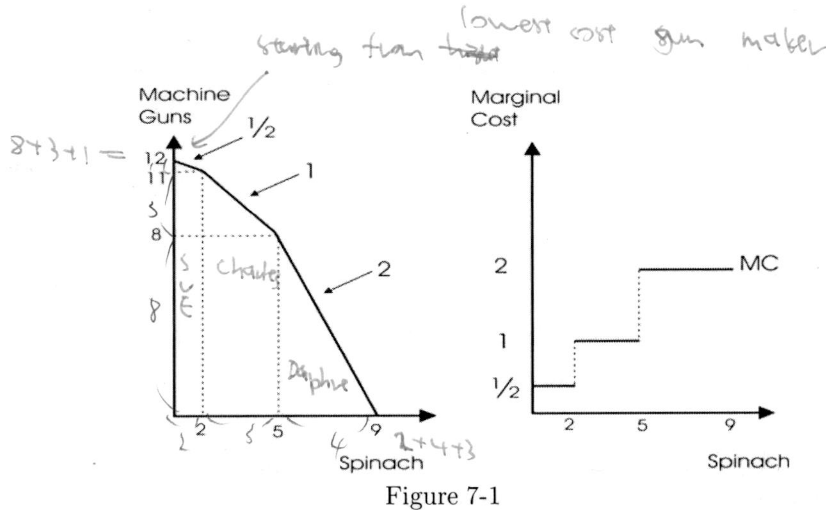

Figure 7-1
The Marginal Cost Curve

The graph on the left is called a *Production Possibility Curve* and it tells us the maximum amount of both goods this little economy can produce. If everyone works building guns, then at most 12 guns per day can be made (8+3+1). If everyone works in the field producing spinach, then at most 9 units of spinach can be made (2+3+4). The curve that lies in between these points contains the combinations of goods the economy is capable of producing if everyone specializes at what they are least cost at. Hence, if the combination 11.5 guns and 1 unit of spinach are to be produced, Daphne, the low cost spinach producer makes the spinach. If Sue were to make the spinach there would be a reduction of 2 guns, rather than just 1/2 of one gun. If more than 2 units of spinach are wanted, then Charles is the second person into the field. It is only if more than 5 units of spinach are wanted that Sue reduces the number of guns she makes and starts to produce spinach.

The slope of the production possibility curve at any point tells us the marginal cost of producing one more unit of spinach. This cost moves from 1/2 to 1, from 1 to 2. If we graph this slope against the amount of spinach produced we get the graph on the right which is the marginal cost curve for producing spinach. The *height* of this curve is the marginal cost of producing a given quantity. Notice this curve is upward sloping. Why? Because the low cost individual produced first, and the highest cost person produced last.

Can you see what will happen to the marginal cost curve if the number of people in the economy starts to get larger? Figure 7-2 shows what happens. As the number of producers increases, each individual has a smaller and smaller impact on the total amount produced. This means the production possibility curve becomes smooth, and the marginal cost curve looses its "step" shape. As a result the marginal cost curve is continuously upward sloping.

Marginal cost curves can slope upwards because different individuals have different costs of production.

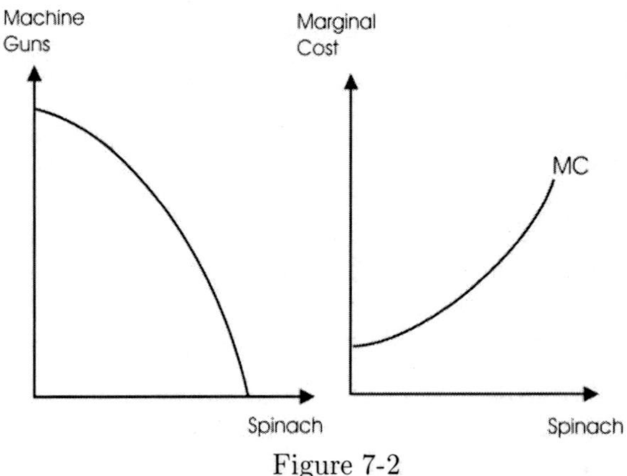

Figure 7-2
The Marginal Cost Curve with Lots of People

7.8 Marginal Costs and the Supply Curve.

The height of the marginal cost curve is the incremental cost from increasing output by an infinitesimal amount. If we think about marginal cost in a discrete sense, the marginal cost would be the area under the marginal cost curve between two different levels of output. If the difference in the levels of output was one unit, then the marginal cost would be the cost of producing one more unit.

$$Marginal\ cost = \frac{\Delta TC}{\Delta Q}$$

Total cost

Given this definition of marginal costs, the area under the marginal cost curve must be the total costs (ignoring any sunk costs). This is shown in Figure 7-3.

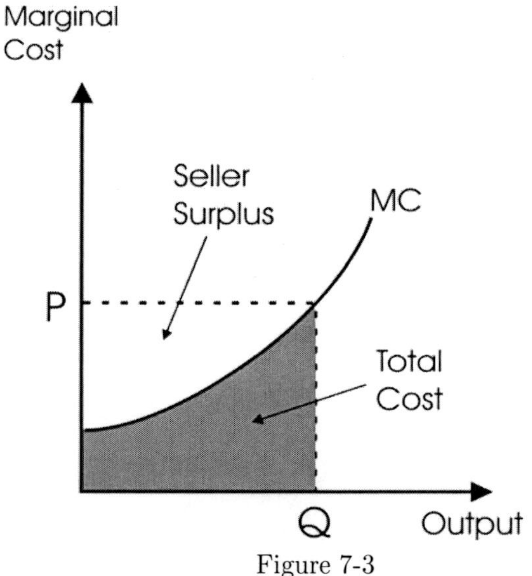

Figure 7-3
Marginal Costs, Total Costs, and Surplus

Since the total revenue is price times quantity, and since the area under the marginal cost curve is the total cost, then the difference between these two (revenue − cost) is the seller's surplus. This surplus is often called a rent. A rent is an amount that could be taken away from the producer and the same output would still be produced.

In Figure 7-3 there is a price listed on the vertical axis. At this price, the amount Q will be supplied because those producing this good are made better off in doing so. In other words, they achieve some surplus or rent. The rent on the marginal unit produced is zero, and this is where production stops. To produce any more would make the producers worse off because the marginal costs would be more than the price. In other words, when the price is equal to the marginal cost, there is an equilibrium for the producers. At this point the producers have maximized their surplus. When the price increases, more is produced because this again sets price equal to marginal costs. Hence, the marginal cost curve is the supply curve of these producers.

7.9 Summary

Unlike earlier chapters, in chapter 7 we started to talk about production. We began with a discussion of opportunity cost — the value of the highest forsaken alternative. Opportunity is not easy to think about because we are so used to thinking about cost as "what we paid for something." What we pay is often the relevant cost, but many times it isn't. To understand behavior, we need to understand opportunity cost.

In addition to opportunity cost we discussed the related concept of comparative advantage. Comparative advantage is what comes out of combining maximization with opportunity cost — everyone is better off when they specialize in production according to their least cost activity. When individuals produce this way, marginal cost curves are upward sloping because the low cost individuals produce first. The more output produced, the higher the costs are. Since we assumed that any individual has constant costs, movements along the marginal cost curve are *extensive changes* — costs change because different individuals are producing the good. In the next chapter we'll consider intensive changes that lead to increasing marginal costs.

REVIEW QUESTIONS

1. Why do you think accountants mostly use historical cost in keeping books?

2. If opportunity cost is the value of the next best alternative, why would you ever add up costs? That is, wouldn't there just be one next best alternative?

3. Why is a "bad" not the same thing as a "cost?"

4. In what way is comparative advantage a combination of the principle of maximization and the definition of cost?

5. What might be some reasons for why there are gains to specialization?

6. Is there any difference between the two concepts of cost and price?

7. In a year, Country A can produce 600 cars or 300 buses, while country B can produce 400 cars or 300 buses. This means that country A has the comparative advantage in producing buses and an absolute advantage in producing cars. It also means that if the price of 1 car was 1/3 of a bus, both would be made better off by trade." True, False, Uncertain, Explain.

8. It would appear that the 2010 Vancouver Olympics are going to cost around $2 billion dollars, rather than the first estimated $600 million. Let's suppose that if the citizens of Vancouver had known this initially, they would never have gone ahead with them (probably a realistic assumption). However, now that the new cost estimates are in, they're continuing on with the Olympics. Does this make sense? Would it matter to know that much of the cost of the Olympics is already spent, underway, or legally committed?

9. Alison is getting married, and the guest list is growing (much to her father's dismay). Initially there were to be 200 guests, but now the other family wants to add 30 names. The good news is they are willing to pay for the extra people. But how much should they pay? Alison thinks the total costs of 230 guests should be divided by 230 people, and then multiply this number by 30. Her father thinks they should take the total cost of 230, minus the total cost of 200.

   a. What "cost" names would you give to each calculation?

   b. Are the two methods the same? Why or why not?

10. Recently Vancouver was rated as "one of the most expensive cities in the world." A local television station interviewed a teacher who had just moved from Quebec to Vancouver. He had just paid $265,000 for a 400 square foot apartment in Vancouver, after selling a house in Quebec for $100,000. Towards the end of the interview he said "But I would never move back." For this person, which city is the most expensive place to live: Vancouver or his home town in Quebec?

PROBLEMS

1. Zane hates doing his income tax, but his wife Isabella loves doing it for him. Is it more costly for Zane to do his income tax, than for his wife?

2. Suppose a fishing equipment retailer buys 30 new lobster traps that have the special feature that they collapse and are therefore easy to store on dock. Suppose he pays $2 000 for the traps, but after one month he has sold no traps, and suspects it is because of a news release that the traps are also collapsing under water and releasing the lobsters! The only good news is that a local school has offered to buy the lot for $2100 for holding class supplies. The retailer has checked out the scrap yard and discovered that the traps are worth $560 as junk metal. In order to make his decision the retailer calculates his costs.

Wholesale costs	$2 000
Interest charges	20
Handling and Advertising	230
Display Space	110
Total Cost	$2 360

   Since it is bad business to sell below cost, our retailer decides to turn down the offer from the school. Did he make the right decision?

3. In 1950 those living in the Republic of Ireland were a demographic outlier. Compared to other western countries, the family sizes were much larger, wives stayed home more, contraception was not used, age at first marriage was higher, and divorce was unheard of. Incomes were also very low. No doubt most of this was due to the strong presence of the Catholic Church in Ireland. The Catholic Church is just as strong in Ireland today, but with rising incomes, what do you think has happened to family sizes, contraception use, divorce, etc in Ireland now compared to other western countries?

4. Given the answer to (3) what types of pressures do you think the Catholic church is under regarding the use of contraceptives, divorce, etc? At one time (prior to 1930) the Anglican church did not allow the use of contraception. In many churches today there is a debate over the legitimacy of homosexual unions. Do you think religions have an impact on the costs and benefits people face in day to day living, or do you think the costs and benefits of daily life have a bigger impact on religion?

5. Consider a society whose only worker is Helen, who allocates her production time between cutting hair and baking bread. Each hour per day she devotes to cutting hair yields 4 haircuts, and each hour she devotes to baking bread yields 8 loaves of bread. If Helen works a total of 8 hours per day, graph her production possibilities curve.

6. A bumper sticker reads "Eliminate Government Waste — At Any Cost". Does this make sense economically?

7. The Professor (on Gilligan's island) was better at everything than Gilligan, and yet Gilligan still performed a lot of tasks on the island. This demonstrates the difference between what two economic ideas?

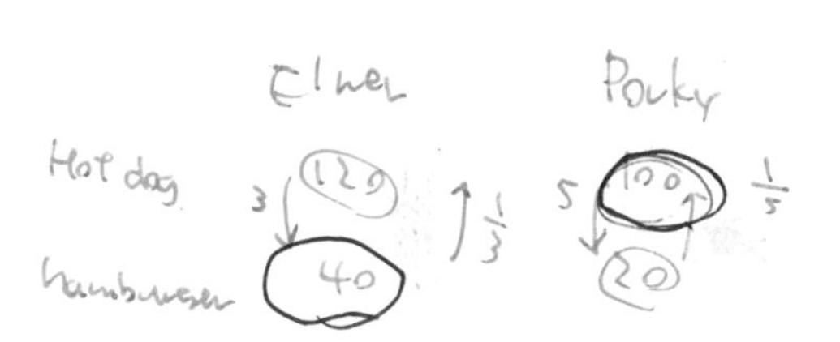

8. In one hour Elmer Fudd can make 120 hot-dogs and 40 hamburgers. Porky Pig can make only 100 hot-dogs and 20 hamburgers in the same time. Which one has a comparative advantage in the production of hot-dogs, and why?

9. By taking an airplane one can go from Toronto to Montreal in one hour. The same trip takes five hours by bus. If the air fare is $500 and the bus fare is $50, which would be the cheaper mode of transportation?

10. The city of Vancouver has about 2 million people in it, and is located next to the mouth of the Fraser River. The delta of the Fraser river has some of the best soil in the world for growing crops and yet most of it is not used for farming; it is used for warehouses, airports, and housing. Explain why the best soil in the province of British Columbia is not used for farming.

11. Suppose you live in Chicago and the Black Hawks finally make it to the Stanley Cup finals. If people are willing to pay $1000 for a ticket with a face value of $100 to see one of the games, and someone gives you a ticket, what does it cost you to attend the game?

12. Complete the following table (note the marginal cost of $1.10 lies in between the quantity 1 and 2). Average cost is defined as Total Cost, divided by Quantity.

Quantity	Total Cost	Marginal Cost	Average Cost
1	1.00		
		1.10	
2			
3	3.36		
4			1.20
5			1.25

13. Biologists tell us that females of every species are more selective of mates than males. If sex and reproduction cannot be separated, why would this be so? For humans would you think that women would be more selective of mates before or after the invention of the birth control pill?

14. Why are waiting lines longer in poorer neighborhoods?

15. "In Japan a great deal of agriculture is done on carefully terraced hill sides, while on the Canadian prairie there is a far more wasteful use of land."

   a. Is it true the Japanese use their land more efficiently?

   b. How would you explain this different pattern of farming?

16. Suppose you work in a firm that provides you with free parking, along with the condition that you can sublet the space if you want to. What is the cost of parking?

17. Recent changes have made it harder to get a drivers license in BC. Although you can still apply at 16, there are more restrictions and the tests are harder. For the sake of argument, suppose

this delays the acquisition of a license for 1 year. What effect will this have on the high school completion rate for students in BC?

18. There is an old cliche that states "you can't have your cake, and eat it too". Is this consistent with the principles of economics we've looked at so far? Explain your answer.

19. How long will you search for a $50 bill that you lost in your bedroom, if the value of your time is $5 per hour? Suppose that you know with certainty that it is lost in your bedroom, that the value of your time remains at $5 per hour no matter how long you look, and that you must look for the money in order to find it.

20. One day my kids wanted to go to Kid's city (essentially a private indoor playground that you pay to use). I told them, of course, they would like to go, because I was paying for it. I then told them that they could have a choice: they could go, or they could stay at home and have the money for admission. In this case, what economic concept am I exploiting to guarantee an efficient decision?

21. Should the casualties already incurred in a war be taken into account by a government in deciding whether it is in the national interest to continue the war? Explain.

22. Women participate in religious activities (as measured by the amount of hours per week) more than men do. Why would this be? [Hint: don't say "women are more religious!"]

23. The following statement made by a rather fashionable young woman was over-heard (paraphrased): "Honestly, I've never met a good looking punker. I don't mean their style of dress, make-up, and jewelery [which she obviously found distasteful], but basically I think their looks are below average." Granted beauty is in the eye of the beholder, but there are conventions for good looks ... there seems to be something of a common denominator in the women of Playboy, fashion magazines, TV shows, and movies. Anyway, for the sake of argument, lets take the young woman's observation as fact. Would it make economic sense? That is, would "ugly" people become punks before the women on Bay Watch?

24. Suppose you recently made a confection which called for one cup of buttermilk. The smallest container of buttermilk you could find was one pint (two cups). Having made it, you have one cup of buttermilk left. You do not like to drink buttermilk, but there is another dessert you could make which would use up your remaining cup. Suppose the pint of buttermilk originally cost 50 cents and the other ingredients for the dessert cost $2.50. The value you place on the dessert is $2.70. Should you make the dessert? Why?

25. Suppose there are two identical gold bars that you own. The only difference between them is how you acquired them. One bar was won as a prize the other you purchased.

    a. What is the difference in the cost of retaining ownership in the two bars?

    b. Will there be any predicted difference in the use of the bars?

26. The following table shows the amount of corn and wheat that two countries could produce if they devoted all of their resources to that good. That is, England for example, could produce at most 200 units of Wheat or 400 units of Corn. Assume that there is a linear transformation

from one crop to another, meaning the cost of producing more corn is always a constant amount of wheat sacrificed.

	England	Germany
Wheat	200	300
Corn	400	900

Suppose both countries are currently devoting half of their resources to the production of corn and half of their resources to the production of wheat. What would be the total amount of wheat and corn produced? If they now specialize to their comparative advantage, and if wheat production is to be held at 250, what would be the total increase in corn production?

27. When Tom takes a nap, he always gets a cramp. Does the cramp make it more costly for him to take a nap than if he didn't get a cramp?

28. Why are there so few gas stations in the center of large cities? With such heavy traffic one ought to be able to do an excellent business.

29. The acres of grass surrounding the Taj Mahal in Agra, India, are often cut by young women who slice off handfuls with short kitchen blades. Is this a low or high cost way to keep the lawn mowed?

30. You have the following three options for your building:

    a. rent as restaurant for $1200/mo.

    b. sell as warehouse for $1400/mo.

    c. rent as bookstore for $700/mo.

    What is the cost of each action?

31. Airlines always try to over book their flights. If a situation arises where not enough seats are available, then the airline bids for passengers to be bumped to another flight. As compensation to bumped passengers, the airline supplies an additional ticket for any flight over the next year. Suppose an average airfare is worth $300. It seems likely that many passengers would be willing to wait for $100 (quite often the wait is only 1 or 2 hours, and many times there is a fight to get bumped). Why would the airline pay so much when it could pay less with cash?

32. Professor Sneed got to be the Marshall at the Hogsworth graduation ceremony. On his way back to his office (dressed in a spectacular regalia) a student approached him, and they had the following conversation:

    Student: "You just love strutting around in that hat."

    Sneed: "Absolutely!"

    Student: "How much did that outfit cost, anyway?"

    Sneed: "$600, but I used my professional development money to pay for it."

Student: "So, it didn't cost you anything."

At this point Sneed walked away. Professional development money is a budget of about \$1000/year, that each Hogsworth faculty gets to pay for journals, travel, computers, paper, books, and regalia. Do you think this student needs to learn some economic principles?

33. At one point during an economics principles course, in which I was using this on-line book, I asked a student what they thought of the book. "Great" was the reply, "I really like the price, and I appreciate not having to line up at the bookstore to buy the book." Why would "not having to line up at the bookstore" probably not be a benefit of purchasing an on-line book? Under what circumstances would it be?

34. Suppose you have the option of going to one of two concerts: U2 or the Rolling Stones. You would be willing to pay \$100 to see U2, but only \$80 to see the Rolling Stones. The price of U2 is \$40 and the price of the Stones is \$65. You know that U2 has underpriced their tickets and a line up is expected. The value of your time in line is \$10. There will be no line for the Rolling Stones. Unfortunately, you have flat feet, and standing in a line is painful. The pain goes away as soon as you leave the line, and you'd be willing to pay \$5 to avoid the pain.

    a. What is the cost of going to U2? What is the net value of going to U2?

    b. What is the cost of going to the Rolling Stones? What is the net value of going to the Rolling Stones?

    c. Which concert will you go to?

35. In the novel *Candide* by Voltaire, Candide and his companion Martin are about to reach the coast of England when they have the following conversation:

    > 'You know England,' continued Candide, after a pause: 'are they as mad there as they are in France?' 'Yes," said Martin, "but their's is another kind of folly. You realise, of course, that these two nations are fighting over a few acres of snow on the borders of Canada, and that they spend more money on this glorious war than the whole of Canada is worth.'

    What is it about the costs of war that might make a country spend more on a war than the value of what is being fought over?

36. Commercial rents in Vancouver have risen dramatically over the past 6 years. As a result, many firms are moving out to the suburbs of Richmond, Surrey, and Langley. Not only do firms that rent their facilities move, but firms that own buildings in Vancouver have moved as well. Why would a firm that owned its own building not ignore the increases in rental prices?

37. If you want to place a 30 second advertisment on the CKNW radio station, it will cost you \$4000 on Wednesday morning before 8AM, and it will cost you \$12,000 on Wednesday afternoon between 4–6PM. The radio station uses the same resources to air the advertisement in the morning as it does in the afternoon (ie. it pays the engineers, workers, the same, it uses the same equipment, etc.). Does this mean the radio station earns a higher profit in the afternoon?

38. Suppose three countries were self sufficient and produced along a straight line production possibility curve. The maximum amounts of clothing and cars each can produce by using all of its resources are as follows:

	Canada	Mexico	United States
Clothing	6	15	30
Cars	20	20	30

   a. What is the cost of a car, expressed in terms of clothing, in each country? Which is the low cost producer of cars?

   b. Draw the world's production possibility curve if the three countries find themselves in an open economy.

39. Suppose someone is caught committing a crime. Suppose the judge can either give the criminal a fine or a jail sentence. The criminal is indifferent between the two punishments. Does each punishment have the same opportunity cost to society?

40. The turn of the 21st century saw a rapid rise of the Canadian dollar relative to the American dollar. By the fall of 2007 the Canadian dollar was at an all time high with an exchange rate of almost 1.10. As this happened various Canadian firms relying heavily on exports to the United States started to make noise that they might go out of business. Parliament even entertained various ways these firms might be subsidized to avoid bankruptcy. This is just one example of bankruptcy, which happens daily in our country. Bankruptcy is obviously a bad thing from the firms point of view, but socially speaking, does bankruptcy cost society as a whole?

41. Bruce Chang owns his own bookkeeping firm, and runs it out of the basement in his home.

   a. Bruce claims that his firm is low cost because he doesn't have to pay any rent for an office. Is this true? Briefly explain.

   b. Bruce has recently turned down an offer to be a postal worker for $55,000 per year. His income from bookkeeping is $48,000 per year. Is his bookkeeping business profitable?

   c. Bruce loves to be his own boss, and this is worth $10,000 per year to him. Does this change your answer to (b)? How so?

42. You've neve heard of the Hanson brother's singing group and you have no feelings for them one way or another, but just the same you've won a ticket to their concert. You are sure you could resell the ticket for $50. Lucky for you, your favorite band the New Old Kids on the Block have reunited and are also performing on the same night. Believe it or not these two events are your only options for the evening! Tickets to see the New Kids are $80. On any given day, you would be willing to pay up to $100 to see the New Kids. Assume there are no other costs of seeing either performer. Based on this information,

   a. what is your opportunity cost of seeing the New Kids, and why?

b. Your friend loves the Hanson brothers and would be willing to pay $60 for a ticket, but she has also won one. She has the same willingness to pay for the New Kids as you do. Which concert will she go to and what is the cost?

43) It takes a wife 60 minutes to clean the house and 150 minutes to mow the lawn. It takes the husband 200 minutes to clean the house and 180 minutes to mow the lawn.

a. Who has the comparative advantage in what activity? Who has any absolute advantage?

b. Suppose the couple have company coming over in 2 hours, and both the house and lawn need work. If they specialize according to their comparative advantage, and if the wife helps out her husband when she is finished her first task, will they get done in time?

44. It is amazing, but you have won another free concert ticket, this time to see *Sparkling Apple.* No one has ever heard of this band, which explains why it has no resale value. The Backstreet Boys, are also performing on the same night, and (believe it or not) on this night this is your next-best alternative activity (what a loser!). Tickets to see the Backstreet Boys cost $80. On any given day, you would be willing to pay up to $100 to see the Backstreet Boys. Assume there are no other costs of seeing either performer. Based on this information,

a. What is the opportunity cost of seeing Sparkling Apple? 20

b. What is the smallest amount that seeing Sparkling Apple would have to be worth in order for you to go to their concert? 20

Review Question Answers

1. *Opportunity costs are not always observable to third parties. For accountants it is critical to be consistent and accurate ... even if incorrect. Thus historical cost is often a more appropriate measure of cost for them. Accountants do a number of things to try to correct for this. The concept of "goodwill" is an attempt to cost out the value of an entrepreneur; the use of the term "net income" rather than "profit" to reflect the fact that true costs are not considered; and special formulas for adjusting depreciation of capital (e.g., sum of years digits) to reflect the true value, are just three examples of accounting corrections to historical cost figures.*

2. *There is only one next best alternative, however, that alternative may involve a collection of sacrifices. Hence these sacrifices must be added up to put a value on the forgone alternative.*

3. *A "bad" is something that generates a negative level of satisfaction or utility. When you step in dog crap, that's a bad thing, but it isn't a cost until it effects your alternatives. "Bads" influence the value you place on something, like walks in the park where there are lots of dogs, but they don't change costs unless they also change the value of alternatives.*

4. *When people maximize they go about their activities in a cost minimizing way. For example, when you go to school, you generally take the route that minimizes your travel time. So maximization implies cost minimization. Comparative advantage basically says that in order to maximize output you should produce according to the minimum opportunity cost. Hence it is a combination of the two ideas.*

5. *Perhaps the most important is learning. Consider most jobs around the household. If you've ever had to hang a door, repair a wall, or do some plumbing or electrical work, you'll know the first time doesn't always work out too well and takes forever. And why wouldn't it, you don't have a clue what you're doing. If you do any of these tasks a second time, however, it generally goes better, and by the third time you're an expert. You learn over time. However, there are other gains as well. Every task has set up and take down costs. By specializing you can minimize the number of times these non-productive activities have to take place. Also, specialization often results in different types of capital being used. If you paint one door you use a brush. If you paint 1000 doors, you get a compressor and a spray gun.*

6. *Yes. Price is determined by the intersection of a demand and supply curve. As we are learning, the supply curve is related to cost. So, in equilibrium the price of a good is equal to its marginal cost, but the two concepts are different.*

7. *It is false on both counts. Country A has a comparative and absolute advantage in producing cars, and that price does not make both better off trading.*

8. *It might make sense if there are large costs already committed to the project. These sunk costs must be incurred anyway. At the same time, the value of the Games might have increased.*

9. *Alison wants to use an average cost measure, while her father wants to use marginal costs. The two will not likely be the same. If there is a spare seat at the reception table adding one more guest will only cost the price of the meal, and the marginal cost will be lower than the average cost. However, if adding one more guest means adding another table, then the marginal cost of the extra person will be higher than the average cost.*

10. *This is a common mistake people make. They look at the cost of a house and say "wow, it is expensive to live here!" However, they forget that people live in places they like because lots of value is generated. To live in Vancouver is to enjoy skiing, beaches, mountains, multiple cultures, and all with no humidity. When you live in Quebec you sacrifice living in Vancouver. This particular person clearly places a higher value on life in Vancouver than in Quebec. Therefore, for this person, the high cost location is Quebec, not Vancouver.*

Odd Numbered Problem Answers

1 *Cost is about alternative, not hating or liking. The cost for Zane and Isabella depends on their alternatives. Zane might be an aging academic, with nothing better to do, while Isabella might be an international fashion designer with extreme demands on her time. Under these conditions Zane would be the low cost income tax doer.*

3. *With rising incomes, especially for women, the cost of having a large family has increased a great deal. Thus family sizes are smaller, more contraception is used, and children are born closer together. Divorce is now common in Ireland.*

5.

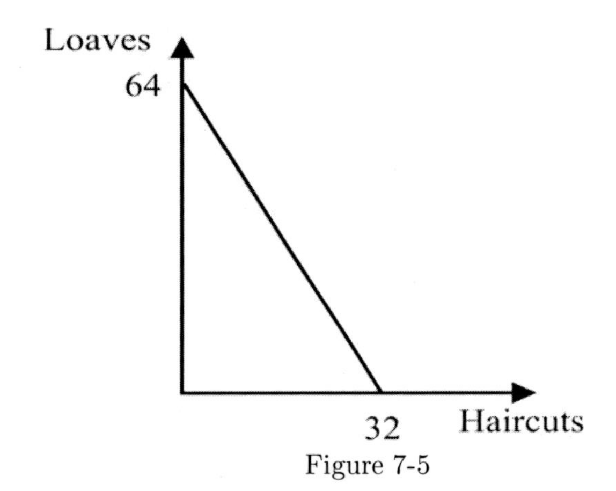

Figure 7-5

7. *The Professor had an absolute advantage in everything, but Gilligan still had a comparative advantage in many tasks.*

9. *It depends completely on the cost of time. A high time cost individual would find the bus trip very expensive.*

11. *$1000.*

13. *Sex for a female is much more costly when it leads to reproduction. Not only must a female carry the offspring and care for it after birth, but females have few eggs relative to male sperm. Reproduction with one male precludes mating with other males, while this is not true for males. Many studies have been done regarding the selection of mates after the introduction of the pill, and it appears that women do select differently.*

15.

a. *No, they use their land more intensively.*

b. *The price of land is much different. In the Fraser Valley of British Columbia, for example, the value of land is very high and we see very intensive use of the land (greenhouses, high valued crops, etc). On the prairies, where land is very cheap, we see much less intensive agriculture.*

17. *Having a driver's license increases one's opportunities for employment. Better employment opportunities lead to higher costs of staying in school. Thus the delays in getting a license lower the costs of staying in school and should lead to higher completion rates.*

19. *You'll look until you find it (assuming it is worth looking for) because the time spent looking will be sunk. I know you want to say 10 hours, but this is wrong.*

21. *No. These costs are sunk. The real issue is how many more casualties will occur in order to meet the objective of the war.*

23. *It is lower cost for an ugly person to damage the market value of their body than for a person with a valuable body. Yes it does make economic sense.*

25.

    a. *Nothing.*

    b. *No.*

27. *No, not unless the cramp prevents him from doing things. Cost depends on alternative values, not on pleasure.*

29. *It must be a low cost method, or else it wouldn't be used. In India wages are low and labor intensive methods of production are used. In North America where wages are high, more capital intensive methods are used.*

31. *It is paying its customers a ticket that has no cost to them. When a plane takes off with an empty seat it is simply lost revenue. Adding a passenger does not alter the cost of the flight. Hence giving a ticket away for a flight that is not full has no cost. Whereas, to give away $100 costs the airline $100.*

33. *If the student had to go to the bookstore to purchase books for other classes anyway, then not having to go there to purchase this particular book is not a benefit of an on-line book. It would be a benefit if this course was the only course the student was taking, or the only course which required a textbook, or the student made a unique trip to the bookstore for every book she needed.*

35. *The resources devoted to battle, once used, are sunk costs. If a king felt that one more bullet would result in victory the bullet would be used, even if it meant the total costs were about to become greater than the total value of the assets fought over.*

37. *No, the radio station doesn't earn a higher profit. The cost increases because other firms are willing to pay more during those times. Therefore, for the station to rent air time to one firm means it sacrifices more in the late afternoon.*

39. *No, the costs are not the same. A fine amounts to a transfer of wealth from the criminal to*

the state. When someone is put in jail we sacrifice not only the resources required to put and keep the criminal there, but also the lost productivity of the criminal. So the real question is: why don't we just fine criminals rather than put them in prison? You might find an answer in one of the last chapters of the book. You might also be interested to know that prisons are a relatively modern invention (about 200 years old).

41.

a. *Bruce might have a low cost firm, but not because he doesn't have to pay rent for an office. If his basement could be used as a suite to earn income, this this lost income is a cost. If his basement could be used as a play room for his family, then the dollar value of the lost utility of the room is a cost. The economist wants to know all of the costs of his business, not just his cash expenses.*

b. *Well now we know that his business is not profitable. The opportunity cost of his time is greater than the income from his business, and we're not even including the cost of the basement space.*

c. *Yes this does change the answer to (b). Now the benefits to his business are* \$58,000 *per year, which is greater than his alternative occupation. Again, we're ignoring the cost of the basement.*

43)

a. *The wife has the comparative advantage in cleaning, the husband in mowing. The wife has an absolute advantage in both activities.*

b. *They can do it! The wife cleans for 60 minutes and gets the house ready. In that time the husband has mown 1/3 of the lawn. In the next hour the husband will mow another 1/3, so the question is, can the wife mow 1/3 of a lawn in 60 minutes? She can mow 6/15 ¿ 1/3, so it will get done with time to have a drink before the guests arrive.*

CHAPTER 8

PRODUCTION WITH DIMINISHING MARGINAL PRODUCTS

In the last chapter we saw when individuals had different abilities the supply curve at the market level was upward sloping. By specializing in activities in which they had a comparative advantage, low levels of output are produced by the low cost individuals. As more and more output is produced, the cost of producing this output increases as different individuals with higher costs join production. If you recall, however, each individual was always equally productive, no matter how much of any particular good they produced. In other words, the cost of production for an individual was always constant. This was apparent in the flat individual marginal cost curves in Figure 7-1.

In this chapter we're going to reverse the assumptions on the homogeneity of productive inputs. That is, rather than assuming different people have different productivities, every individual will be assumed to be equally productive. However, unlike the last chapter where a given individual was always equally productive, now each person's productivity will change depending on how much they produce. Once again, we will show that under this set of assumptions, the supply curve is again upward sloping. Essentially the last chapter was looking at changes in cost along the *extensive margin*, while this chapter will consider changes in costs along the *intensive margin*. At the end of the chapter we will bring both of these movements together and discuss the general supply curve of a firm where productivity varies across inputs and with intensity of use the inputs.

8.1 The Production Function

Let's start by considering the process of production a little more carefully. Producing an output requires some inputs: land, workers, machines, other raw material, and most importantly, some type of organization. In a small, single person firm, the individual coordinates production by himself. In large firms, the organizational structure is extremely complicated. Until we reach Part III of this book we're going to assume away all such organizational issues, and claim output is produced by simply combining various inputs. In other words, output is simply given by a *production function*. A production function tells us the maximum amount of an output for a given amount of inputs. As unrealistic as it seems, this production function will describe the economic "firm."

> *A production function tells us the maximum amount of an output for a given amount of inputs.*

To keep things even simpler, we'll assume there are only two inputs: labor (L) and capital (K). Labor is an input that hardly needs introduction. When you apply your physical effort to a task, you're providing labor to some type of production. By capital, economists refer to long lived assets that generate income. A tractor is capital, and when used provides services that generate income. Land is a form of capital, and generates rents over time for its owner. Ironically, people can also be capital. When a person invests in education, for example, they increase the productivity of their labor services, and therefore increase their income. Hence, economists often speak of *human capital.* Since we're generally only going to look at one input at a time, it is enough for us to think of labor as being the human input and capital as being the non-human one. If we consider Q as the quantity of output produced, then our production function is given by:

$$Q = f(L, K)$$

This is a very "engineer" like relationship. Simply combine a certain quantity of labor and capital and presto, output appears. It reminds one of the story of the Russian immigrant who comes to America and enters a grocery store. He's reading the labels of the products: "Instant Potato Powder ... just add water. Powdered eggs ... just add water. Chocolate cake powder ... just add water." Then he comes across another product: "Baby powder". The man looks up and exclaims "what a country!" We shouldn't worry too much about this presto technology, or "black box" production function as some call it. The model we're developing is intended to explain movements in the volume of trade and the price of trade, and for this purpose the simple production function is entirely adequate. When it comes to issues of explaining why firms are organized differently, we'll see this procedure is not adequate and we'll have to complicate the model.

Constant Returns To Scale

The production function has certain properties. First of all, when all of the inputs are increased, the amount of output increases. Generally speaking we have little to say about *how much* output will change when all inputs change. It would make some philosophical sense if doubling all inputs doubled the output. After all, if you do something once, you should be able to repeat the procedure and get the same outcome. Consider the situation in Figure 8-1.

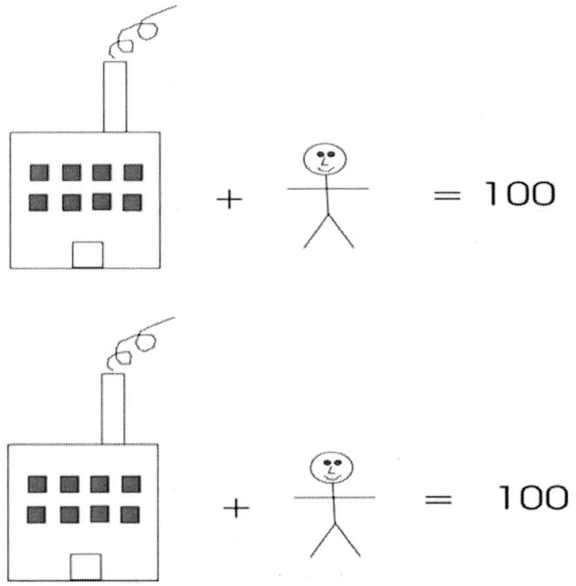

+ = 100

+ = 100

Figure 8-1
Replication and Constant Returns to Scale

In Figure 8-1 we have a factory as one input, and a person as the other input. When these two inputs are combined in a production function they yield 100 units of output. If we could double both of these inputs exactly, and combine them once more, then we should also get another 100 units. Hence, there is something appealing to the idea that doubling all inputs always leads to a doubling of output. When this happens it is said the production function is characterized by *constant returns to scale.*

> **Constant Returns to Scale:** *a doubling of all inputs leads to a doubling of output.*

The debate over the returns to scale in production is a very old one. There is a famous dialogue between the 19th century economists Pareto and Walras. Walras, who was theoretically opposed to the notion of constant returns existing everywhere, apparently stated to Pareto, "if you doubled all of the subways in Paris I doubt you would double the volume of rides." To which Pareto is claimed to have said "yes, but you didn't double the Paris." The problem with directly testing for constant returns to scale is we can never be sure we've literally doubled everything exactly. Inputs are hard to measure, and we're never sure two inputs are always identical. Constant returns to scale is an assumption we'll make for convenience, but not one we'll use too much. Much more important is the second characteristic of production functions.

Diminishing Marginal Products

From the production function we can calculate two other functions: the marginal product and the average product. The marginal product is defined as the change in output when a single input changes. Hence, the marginal product of labor would be the change in output when labor is changed. The marginal product of capital would be the change in output when capital is changed. The average product, on the other hand, tells us the output per unit of an input. Thus, the average product of labor is the total amount of output, divided by the total number of labor units used. Likewise, the average product of capital is the total amount of output, divided by the total units of capital used. Formally these functions are given by:

$$\mathrm{MP_L} = \frac{\Delta Q}{\Delta L}$$

$$\mathrm{MP_K} = \frac{\Delta Q}{\Delta K}$$

$$\mathrm{AP_L} = \frac{Q}{L}$$

$$\mathrm{AP_K} = \frac{Q}{K}$$

It is important to keep in mind that when you calculate a marginal product, only one input is changing. The others are held constant. The production function has an important property with respect to marginal products. When the amount of only *one* input increases, and all other inputs are held constant, then output also increases, but eventually at a decreasing rate. Since these increases in output are called *marginal products,* this property is called diminishing marginal products, and it is our fifth principle of economics.

PRINCIPLE #5

Diminishing Marginal Products: *increases in one input, other inputs held constant, lead to increases in output at a diminishing rate.*

The principle of diminishing marginal products is another idea, like the law of demand that has been noticed for centuries. For example, in agriculture, when labor is added to a fixed amount of land, crop output increases, but very quickly the effects of diminishing returns are felt. Output increases, but at a slower rate. Figure 8-2 shows both a graph of the production function in the top graph, and the resulting marginal product curve in the lower graph.

In the top graph the production function drawn is often called a "three stage production function." The first stage is where output is increasing at an increasing rate. The second stage is where output is increasing at a decreasing rate. Finally the third stage is where output is actually decreasing. The first and third stages seem consistent with common sense, but the principle of diminishing marginal product states that stage II must exist. As we'll see shortly, the firm will always operate in stage II, and never in stage I or III.

The production function in the top graph of figure 8-2 takes this shape because the ratio of labor to capital is changing as we move from left to right. Output depends on the labor to capital ratio. Since capital is held fixed, low levels of labor mean there is "too much" capital for the small units of labor. Imagine a situation where there is a large machine, perhaps a steam engine tractor. When there is only one unit of labor applied to the tractor some output is produced, but not very much. When a second labor is added to the tractor output increases a great deal because one can keep the fire going while the other drives and makes sure enough water is in the boiler. When a third person is added to the tractor output might increase even more. As the amount of labor increases relative to the fixed amount of capital this effect goes away. Eventually, as you add more and more labor units to the tractor, output increases, but at a decreasing rate — stage II. If we keep adding units of labor output eventually falls as workers simply get in each other's way. If it makes sense there could be too much capital or too much labor, then in between the two extremes the capital labor ratio must be about right. Hence, the principle of diminishing marginal products essentially says region II must exist. Output never continues to increase at an increasing rate.

The bottom graph in figure 8-2 plots the *slope* of the top graph. The slope of the production function is the marginal product. The production function is steepest as it moves from stage I to II. At this level of labor L_1, the slope of the production function is 10 units of output. This is the marginal product of L_1 units of labor. The production function is flat when it reaches a maximum between stages II and III, which means the marginal product is zero. Notice when output is increasing at an increasing rate in stage I, the marginal product is increasing. When production is increasing at a decreasing rate in stage II, the marginal product is positive but decreasing. In stage III the marginal product is actually negative. The marginal product curve tells us how much each unit of labor contributes to output. For example, when there are L_1 units of labor being used,

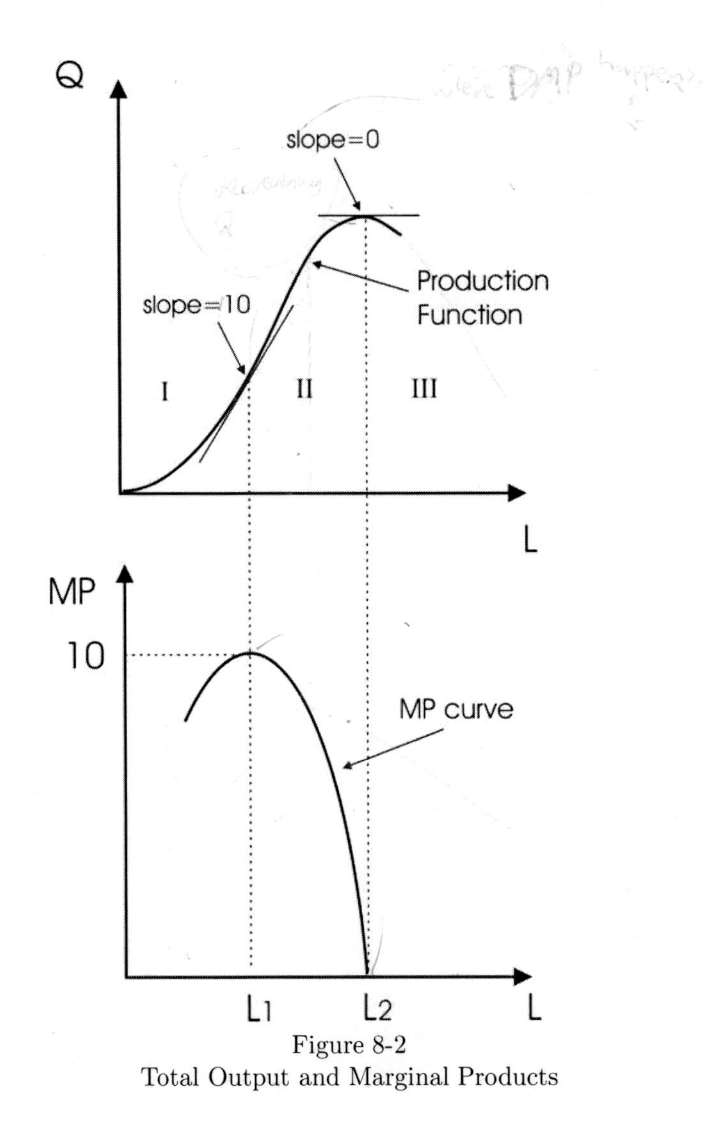

Figure 8-2
Total Output and Marginal Products

the last unit of labor contributed 10 units to output. When L_2 units of labor are used, then the marginal product is zero — the last worker contributes nothing.

8.2 Marginal Products and the Demand for Labor

The notion of marginal products is valuable in part because it tells us what the demand for labor is when other inputs are held fixed. Suppose our output is eggs. The production function tells us how changes in the amount of labor applied to a farm determines the number of eggs produced. Suppose the local wage rate for egg collectors is 4 eggs per hour. How many hours of egg collecting time should a farmer hire? Consider Figure 8-3, which shows the marginal product of an egg collector. For simplicity the marginal product curve is drawn as a straight line.

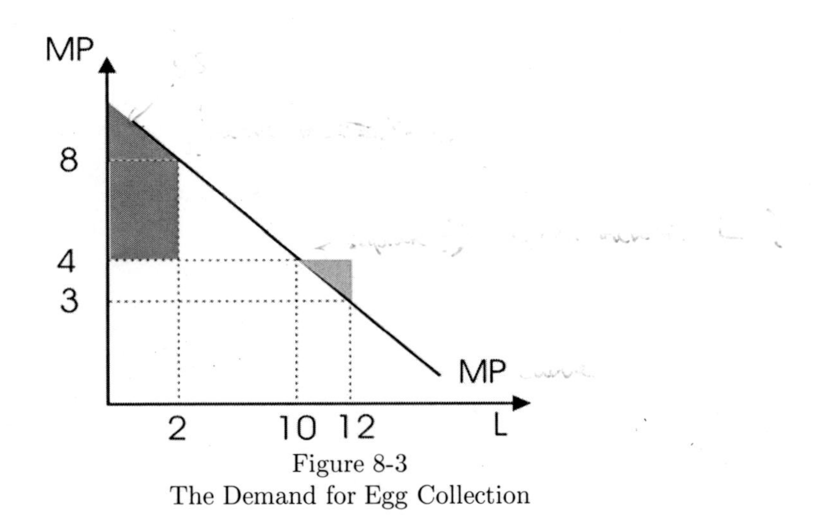

Figure 8-3
The Demand for Egg Collection

When the farmer hires two units of labor he only pays 4 eggs for each unit. However, the marginal product of the second unit of labor is 8 eggs. Hence the farmer receives more eggs than he pays out and is better off. In fact, the farmer receives a surplus of eggs equal to the dark shaded region above 4 eggs and below the marginal product curve. Since the farmer is demanding labor, this is his consumer's surplus for labor. We've seen this logic before. The farmer certainly isn't going to stop hiring units of egg collecting labor at 2. If the farmer hires labor up to 10 units he will maximize his surplus of eggs. At a "wage" rate of 4 eggs per unit, the farmer will then demand 10 units of labor. If the farmer stops short of this amount then he fails to maximize his surplus, and if the farmer hires more than this amount, say 12 units of labor, then the farmer's surplus would be lower by the lightly shaded triangle. The marginal product schedule in figure 8-3 is the demand for labor in terms of real goods (eggs in this case). Notice the upward sloping segment of the marginal product curve is irrelevant. If each additional hour hired led to more and more eggs, the farmer would continue to hire, until eventually he reached the downward sloping part. Likewise, the negative section of the marginal product curve is irrelevant as well. Why would a farmer hire workers who made a negative contribution? Thus the positive downward sloping portion of the marginal product curve is the only relevant section for a profit maximizing firm. This section corresponds to stage II of the production function.

Rather than think of the demand for labor in terms of the real goods provided by labor, we could convert the entire exercise in terms of dollars. The wage to the labor would not be in eggs, but would be some number of dollars per hour. We'll call this wage rate w. In terms of output, rather than the amount of eggs that get produced, we measure the *value of the marginal product.* The value of the marginal product is the price of the output (the price of eggs in this case) multiplied by the marginal product. It tells us the how much the change in output is worth.

The value of the marginal product is: Price × the Marginal Product.

Hence the demand for labor is generally shown in Figure 8-4. For a given wage rate, the quantity demanded of labor is where that wage intersects the demand curve. Notice if workers become more productive, (that is, if their marginal product increases) the demand curve for labor will increase. Notice also if the price of the output increases, then the demand for labor will increase as well. If the supply curve of labor is fixed, or generally upward sloping, then this means the wage will increase in both of these cases. People who earn high wages earn them because they are either good at what they do, or what they produce is very valuable, or both. On the other hand, if someone is very productive, perhaps the best rock picker in the whole world, but people don't value rock picking, then that person will earn a low wage.

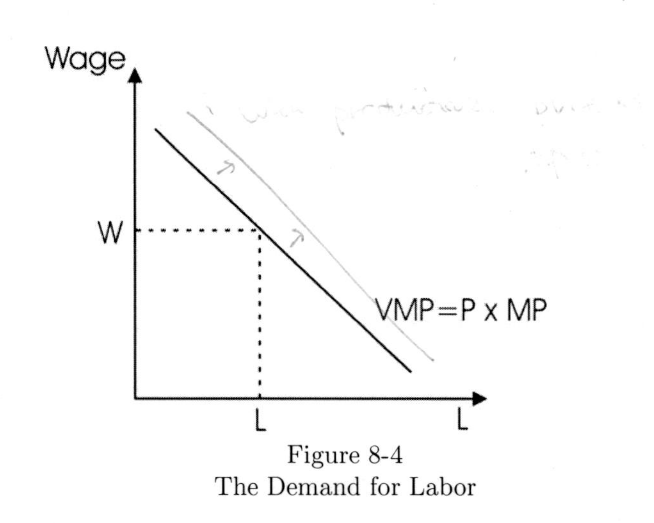

Figure 8-4
The Demand for Labor

The Demand for Capital and Variable Inputs

If we had held the amount of labor constant and varied the amount of capital instead, all of what we have said about labor would have followed for capital. There is a marginal product for capital, just as there is for labor. Under these conditions the demand for capital would also be the marginal product curve for capital, and it would be true that in equilibrium the rental price for the capital would have to equal the value of the marginal product of capital. Everything follows through.

Things do get a little tricky, however, when both labor and capital are allowed to vary. Fortunately for us, since we're not concerned with technical details in this book, we can focus in on a few simple outcomes. First, it is still true the demand curves for inputs are always downward sloping, even when both inputs are allowed to change. Second, it is still true in equilibrium, the firm hires labor and capital until the value of the inputs marginal products is equal to its price.

Suppose we stick with our simple case of two inputs (L) and (K), suppose the per unit price of these are w and v, and suppose the price of the output produced is P, then profit maximizing conditions are:

$$w = P \times MP_L$$

and

$$v = P \times MP_K.$$

Namely, the input price equals the value of the marginal product for each input. These equilibrium conditions are graphically shown in Figure 8-5. The height of the demand curve for each input is equal to the value of the marginal product of that input. It should be obvious by now that when the equilibrium conditions are met the firm's surplus is maximized.

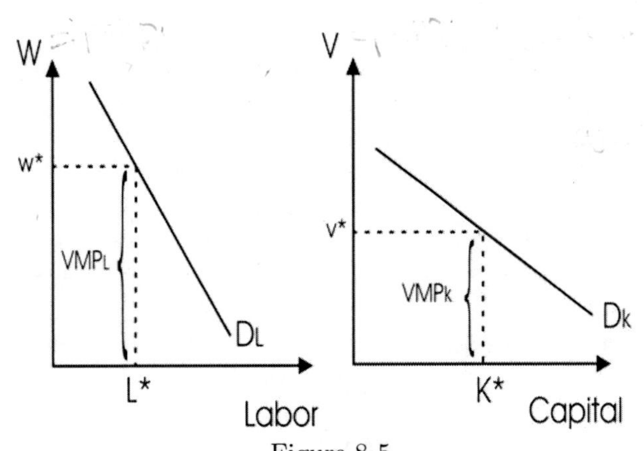

Figure 8-5
The Demand for Labor and Capital

If we take the equilibrium conditions and divide one by the other and then manipulate the terms a little bit, we get the following:

$$\frac{MP_L}{w} = \frac{MP_K}{v}$$

This is a very interesting and powerful expression. It says the marginal product per dollar the firm spends must be equal across the two inputs used to produce output if the firm is to use inputs efficiently. Now think about this for just a moment, because it makes perfect sense. If a firm has an input that gives a big boost to output and doesn't cost very much, and it has another input that makes a marginal contribution to output and yet is relatively expensive, then the firm will make more money if it hires more of the first input and less of the second. As the firm hires more of the first input, its marginal product starts to get smaller according to principle #5. For the same reason, as the firm hires less of the second input, its marginal product starts to get bigger. Eventually the marginal product per dollar will equalize, and the firm can hire no better combination of inputs.

> *When firms maximize profits they equalize the marginal product per dollar across all inputs.*

We've seen this result before when we talked about the consumer's marginal value across goods. Whenever a person (whether a consumer or producer) makes a decision involving several margins (how many apples and oranges to buy, how much labor and capital to use) the benefits per dollar across these margins must be equalized in order to maximize — whether we're maximizing profits or utility. Most notably, maximizing the benefits per dollar under these conditions does not mean the *average* products per dollar are equalized. However, when people talk about productivity, they often refer to average productivity, and as a result mistakes in logic often follow. Consider the following applications.

In the early 1990s the Toronto Blue Jays baseball team achieved a remarkable thing by winning back-to-back World Series. They were unable, however, to win three times in a row. In virtually all cases of professional sports teams, dynasties are rare and short lived. What prevents a wealthy team owner from accumulating all of the stars on one team and winning year-in, year-out? Before we answer that question, consider an analogous one. In World War II, submarines sank almost 90% of the boats sunk in the war. They were by far the most important weapon in a Navy's arsenal. Given this, why would Navies invest in other types of vessels? Why not just have submarines?

To answer both questions, consider the relevant production functions and marginal products. The marginal product of a single hockey star to a given club is quite large. When Wayne Gretzky was traded to the Los Angeles Kings, he almost single handedly turned the team around, and within a couple of years they made it to the Stanley Cup finals. However, given diminishing marginal products, the marginal product of a second star player is lower than the first — even though he may be the same quality. Likewise for the third, fourth, and fifth star. The more stars on a team, the lower is their marginal contribution. For teams without a star, the marginal product is very high. As a result, poor teams without stars are able (and willing) to pay more for the marginal star player on the good team, and this draws some star players to the poor team. In the process the marginal products of the various quality sports stars get equalized across teams, and no single team systematically tends to dominate.

The same answer applies to the submarines. Submarines were very effective on average, but at the margin their contribution could be quite low. If the Navy must make a decision between the 1000th submarine and the 1st battleship, it is quite possible the marginal product of the latter is higher than the former. When the marginal products of the different weapons are equalized, there are necessarily larger numbers of those weapons with the higher total product — in this case, more submarines.

The great power of economics is that you don't have to learn a new theory every time a different situation arises. Can you use the notion of diminishing marginal products to explain the practice of triage by medical doctors in war time? Under triage patients are divided into three categories: those who will get better without attention; those who will get better with attention; and those who will die no matter what is done. Although it is a crude system, triage is an attempt to equalize marginal products across patients. The marginal product of the first and third categories is close to zero, and as a result the Doctors concentrate on the second group of patients. By working on patients who have a chance of winning they are applying their services where their marginal products are highest.

8.3 Marginal Costs Again

We will return to our study of marginal product curves when we analyze input markets more closely. In the meantime, our concern is to explain why supply curves are upward sloping. In the last chapter we saw there was an extensive margin explanation for this. When individual inputs are different, maximization implies the low cost inputs are used in production first. The more produced, the more costs increase because those inputs not well suited for production start to be used.

In this chapter we've been assuming all labor inputs are identical, and all capital inputs are also identical. Hence we do not have the above extensive margin reason for increasing marginal costs. However, we do have the principle of diminishing marginal products, which states that as more labor is used in production for a given amount of capital, the labor is less productive at the margin. This *intensive margin* also implies marginal costs are upward sloping. Consider Figure 8-6.

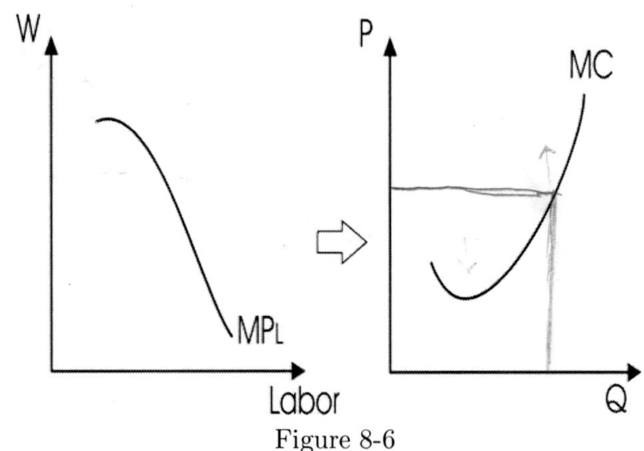

Figure 8-6
The Marginal Product and Marginal Cost Curves

The marginal cost curve is *inversely* related to the marginal product curve. They are not exact mirror images of each other, but when one is rising the other must be falling, and vise versa. The intuition is rather straight forward. Keeping in mind labor is paid a fixed amount, consider what happens to marginal cost when the *marginal product* is increasing in stage I. An increasing marginal product means that for every unit of labor added to production, output increases by more than it did for the unit before. If the first unit of labor contributed 10 units to output, the second unit might add 20 units to output, and the third unit might add 30 units to output. If each unit of labor costs \$25, and if there were no other inputs, then the total cost of 10 units is \$25, or \$2.50 per unit, the total cost of 30 units is \$50, or \$1.67 per unit, and the total cost of 60 units is \$75 or \$1.25 per unit. These costs per unit are the average costs, which are clearly falling, but what is happening to marginal costs? Marginal costs are the change in costs divided by the change in output. Hence the marginal cost of going from 10 to 30 units is 25/20=\$1.25. The marginal cost of going from 30 to 60 units is 25/30=83¢ . Clearly the marginal cost is falling.

The opposite is the case for when the marginal product is diminishing in stage II. When the marginal product is diminishing, the output each individual unit of labor contributes is falling. However, the firm continues to pay each worker the same wage, even though the marginal product is falling. Therefore, the cost per unit of output must increase when the marginal product is falling. Table 8-1 contains a more specific example of what we've being considering. In this trivial example it is clear that when the marginal product is falling, the marginal cost is increasing. As labor is added to a fixed level of capital, output increases at a decreasing rate. We see this in the steadily declining marginal product numbers. The cost of labor is \$10, so as labor increases, costs increase as well. But look what is happening to marginal costs. They increase. Marginal costs are increasing because each additional unit of labor contributes less and less. The marginal cost curves can be upward sloping when all units of labor are the same, just as long as production experiences diminishing marginal products.

L	TP	MP	TC	MC
1	10		10	
		8		1.25
2	18		20	
		7		1.42
3	25		30	
		6		1.67
4	31		40	
		4		2.50
5	35		50	
		3		3.33
6	38		60	
		2		5.00
7	40		70	
		1		10
8+	41		80	

Table 8-1
The Inverse Relationship Between MP and MC

Differences in Inputs and DMP

Thus we've shown the principle of diminishing marginal products implies marginal cost curves are upward sloping, even when the quality of inputs is held constant. What happens though, when we combine the assumptions of last chapter with the principle of diminishing marginal products? When both inputs vary in terms of quality and when diminishing marginal products are present, then marginal cost curves slope upwards for both reasons. Thus the marginal cost curve slopes upwards for both extensive and intensive reasons, just like the market demand curve. As the amount of output produced by a firm increases, costs increase at the margin both because higher cost inputs are eventually used, and because increased use of an input when other inputs are held fixed lead to falls in the marginal products of those inputs.

Consider figure 8-7. As we move from points A to B to C, the costs at the margin are increasing. They increase for two reasons. First because not all inputs are the identical and the inputs used to produce at point A are "better" (lower cost) than those used at point C. Second, the costs also increase because at point C, more of every type of input is also used, and thus their marginal products are lower.

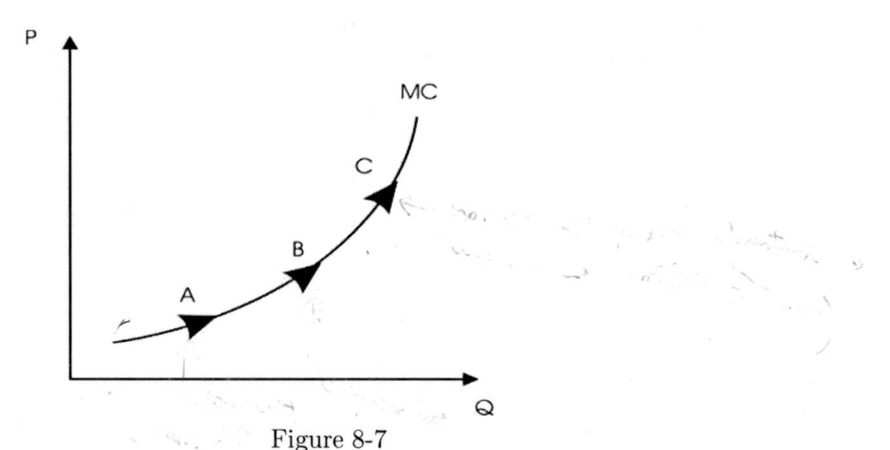

Figure 8-7
Marginal Costs with Extensive and Intensive Margins

8.4 Average Cost Curves

The most important idea of this chapter is what lies behind the marginal cost curve, and what explains its positive slope. In the next chapter, however, it will be necessary for you to understand one other type of cost curve: the average cost curves. Whereas the marginal cost curve tells us the change in total costs for a change in output, the average cost curves tell us the cost per unit. In this sense, they are an easier type of cost to think about.

There are three types of average costs we will worry about. First there is the average total cost, or simply the average cost. This is the total cost of a given level of output, divided by the level of output. Second, there is the average variable cost, which is the total average variable cost divided by the level of output. Finally there is the average fixed costs, which is the total fixed costs divided by the level of output.

$$\textit{Total Costs} = TC = TVC + TFC$$

$$\textit{Average Total Cost} = AC = TC/Q.$$

$$\textit{Average Variable Cost} = AVC = TVC/Q.$$

$$\textit{Average Fixed Cost} = AFC = FC/Q.$$

Average Fixed costs is very straight forward. Since a fixed cost is just a lump sum of money, as output increases, the average fixed cost contiuously falls. Suppose you built a rail line for 10 million dollars of fixed costs. If you only ran one train on the line, the average fixed cost would be

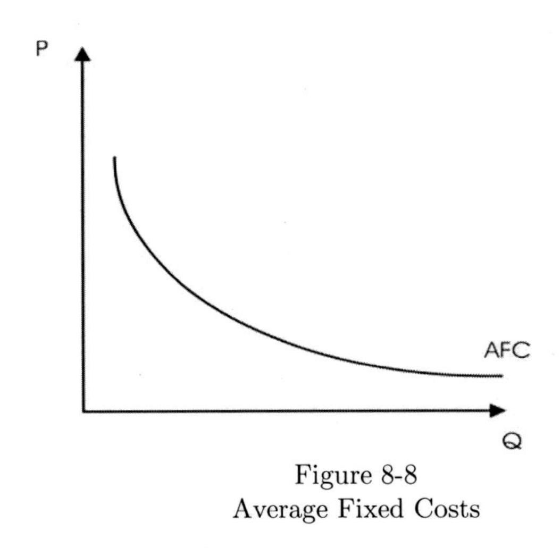

Figure 8-8
Average Fixed Costs

10 million dollars per trip. If you ran two trains, the AFC would be 5 million per trip, and four trains would bring the AFC down to 2.5 million, and on and on. The AFC is graphed in Figure 8-8.

Average Variable and Average Total costs are not quite as simple as the AFC. In order to understand them, it is best to return to our three stage production function found in Figure 8-2. Recall in stage I ouput is increasing at an increasing rate as the labor input increases at a constant rate. This must mean the average cost per unit of output is falling. As production moves through the second stage, ouput is increasing, but at a decreasing rate. Eventually, the average cost per unit begins to rise. This means, as output increases the average variable and average total cost curves will be U-shaped, and will have a minimum. These average cost curves are shown in Figure 8-9.

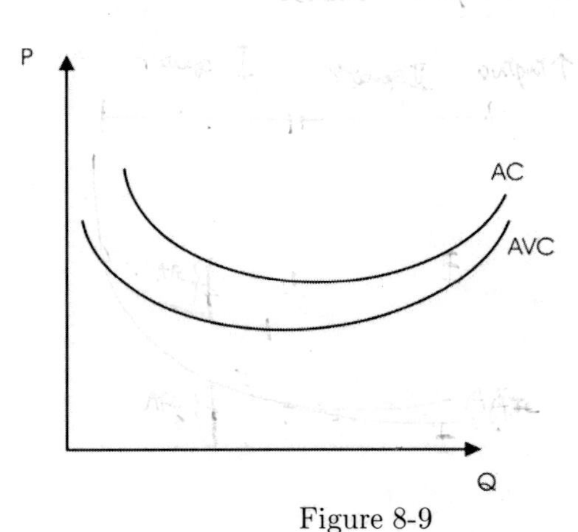

Figure 8-9
Average Total and Variable Costs

Notice the AVC and AC curves have a shorter vertical distance the larger the output. Can you tell why? Recall total costs is just the sum of the variable costs and the fixed costs. This means the AC=AVC + AFC. In other words, the vertical distance between the two curves is just the AFC. Since this is always falling with output, the vertical distance is getting smaller.

Tin Cans and Card Board boxes.

In the next chapter we'll see that an individual firm will always want to minimize their average costs. That is, a firm wants to produce a product for the lowest possible cost per unit. This is part of the firm's profit maximizing strategy. If a firm is making a given product, it will make more money if it produces this product at the lowest possible cost.

There is a wonderful application of this in storage containers. The next time you visit your local grocery store, take a walk down the canned goods section. You'll notice, that most of the cans have a particular shape — the relationship between the height and diameter of the can is relatively constant. This turns out to be an implication of cost minimization, and a little thought to the matter might help your intuition of production.

Let's suppose a tin can has the general shape of panel (a) in Figure 8-10, where D is the diameter of the can and H is its height. Let's also suppose there is no wastage in making the side piece of tin, but the top and bottom must be cut from a square piece of tin and this leaves some waste, shown as the shaded area in panel (b) of Figure 8-10. It is a simple mechanical problem (which we will ignore) to show that the cost minimizing amount of tin for a given volume is H=1.27D. That is, in order to use the minimum amount of tin for a given volume requires the height of the tin to be about 25% bigger than the diameter.

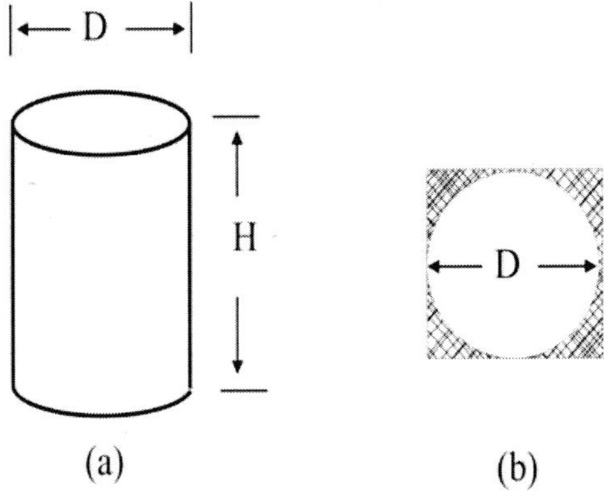

Figure 8-10
The Cost Minimizing Can

A walk down the canned goods isle shows about 90% of the cans satisfy this relationship. Soup, beans, vegetables, fruit, and spaghetti, all seem to satisfy this rule. There are two big exceptions, however. Pop cans, are too tall, and tuna cans are too short. This means there must be some other aspect to these cans, other than size, which matter to consumers in order for producers to produce a more expensive can. For pop cans the answer is quite obvious. Many times people drink straight from the can. A can with the relative dimensions of a soup can is too thick to comfortably hold in your hand. So the can is made thinner and taller to accommodate this.

Why would tuna cans, though, be so short? To think about this, consider the types of contents in these short tins: tuna, salmon, cat food, and other meat products. The problem with putting meat in a can is the bacterium is not killed by simple canning procedures. To can meat it is necessary to can it under 10-15 pounds per square inch pressure. When the meat cools down inside the can there is pressure placed on the walls of the can. A can shaped like a soup can would likely collapse under this pressure, and so the can is made shorter and stronger. Often these cans have "ribs" in the tin which increase their strength. Interestingly, cat food comes in short cans, while dog food generally comes in tall cans. It turns out cat food is mostly made of meat, but dog food is mostly cereal based.

If you walk down the cereal isle in any grocery store, you'll notice cereal is never sold in cans, nor is it sold in cylindrical containers. The shape of the container often depends on the method used to pack the contents. Contents under pressure or packed under heat often require a cylindrical container for strength. For a given volume of content, a cylindrical container also minimizes the cost of container material. However, a cylindrical container wastes shelf space, while rectangular boxes can utilize shelf space more effectively. Here again we see predictable tradeoffs by firms trying to minimize costs. When the value of the contents and the cost of the container material fall relative to the value of shelf space, the goods are more likely to be sold in boxed form. Cereals, like Corn Flakes and Cheerios, dish soap, and items sold close to the check out stand seem to conform to this pattern. Exceptions abound at every turn in a grocery store, of course, because of the huge variety of items being sold, but our simple understanding of cost minimization and trade-offs between different inputs seems to explain a great deal of packaging at the local store.

8.5 Summary

This chapter has been one of the more technical ones, and one where many issues have been left unsaid. What is important is your understanding of why a marginal cost curve is upward sloping. At the beginning of the chapter the concept of a production function, along with a marginal product curve was developed. The shape of this curve came from our fifth economic principle, namely that marginal products were diminishing. It was briefly discussed how these marginal product curves related to the demand for inputs into production, but their main purpose was to generate a marginal cost curve. Although not proven, the marginal cost curve is inversely related to the marginal product curve. Marginal costs, when all inputs are homogeneous, increase because the more of an input is used, the less productive it becomes at the margin. At the end of the chapter we showed how allowing for different quality of inputs does not reverse the slope of the marginal cost curves. Whether for extensive or intensive reasons, the marginal cost curve is upward sloping. We also provided a brief definition of the average cost curves. In the next chapter we move on to an analysis of the output decision of the firm, and the determination of the market supply curve.

REVIEW QUESTIONS

1. In Chapter 7 it was shown that marginal cost curves were upward sloping. In this chapter it was also shown that marginal costs curves are upward sloping. What is the relationship between the two explanations?

2. Does a production function have anything to do with the price of inputs?

3. Suppose you have a square piece of property measuring 100 feet by 100 feet (or 100 meters by 100 meters if you like), and you decide to fence it in. You've got 10,000 square feet of property. Now double the sides of the property so it is 200 feet by 200 feet. Now you're going to use twice as much fencing, but you've got 40,000 square feet fenced in. Is this an example of constant returns to scale?

4. Why is it that only stage II of the production function is really relevant to study? That is, why would firms not operate in stage I or III?

5. What does the demand for an input depend on?

6. Why would a firm have to choose the least cost method of producing a good. Do you think this argument applies to firms like churches or universities?

7. Do "Too many cooks spoil the broth?"

8. How about this cliche, is it consistent with production theory? "You can't make an omelet without breaking eggs."

PROBLEMS

1. Every book publisher sells far more principles books than advanced books because the principles class sizes are so large. Why would publishers even bother publishing books for classes that have only 10 students?

2. Is it more efficient to build dams with lots of labor or lots of machines?

3. If you've ever used a drive up window for banking, you've probably noticed that the buttons have Braille dots on them. This is puzzling because blind people don't drive cars and don't use drive through banking. Why is it that keypad buttons on drive up automatic teller machines have Braille dots?

4. "We want the best person for the job" Does that mean we want the person who can perform the job best?

5. You own a hardware store, and your accountant tells you that based on profit per square foot, home appliances are much better than tools. Does this mean you should expand the home appliances section at the expense of the tool section?

6. In your computer lab what can explain why the productivity of the network laser printer falls as more computers are connected to the print queue?

7. Does an owner of a firm hire additional workers if the cost of the worker is greater than the average product of the worker?

8. If the total cost of producing 8 units is $53, and the marginal cost of producing the 9th unit is $10, what are the total costs of producing the 9 units?

9. If $w/MP_L > v/MP_K$ then what will a profit maximizing firm do in terms of the amount of labor and capital it uses?

10. Consider the following production function: $Q = 2K + L$ where Q is output, K is capital and L is labor. For positive amounts of labor and capital, what are the marginal products of capital and labor?

11. Suppose a firm has a production function that is characterized by the three stages described in this chapter. Suppose the firm is using 20 units of labor. At this level of input, the marginal product of labor is 50 and the average product is 30.

    a. What is the level of output?

    b. Is the Marginal Cost Curve upward or downward sloping?

    c. Is the Average Variable Cost curve increasing or decreasing?

12. A firm is using 10 workers, and their average product is 200 units. Suppose the marginal product of labor is 250 units. In answering the questions below, explain your answers briefly.

a. How much output is the firm producing?

b. Is the marginal cost curve increasing or decreasing?

13. From the production function it is clear that output is produced using different factors of production, like labor and capital. Depending on the price of each factor, the firm could make its output with different combinations of the inputs. Use this basic idea to explain why strategic bombing in wartime has generally been unsuccessful. Strategic bombing is where a country targets specific sites to hit. For example, in WWII the Allies bombed German railways and ball-bearing plants to destroy German manufacturing; during the Vietnam War the US bombed the Ho Chi Minh Trail to stop arms moving from north to south. In both cases manufacturing continued and arms still flowed south.

14. Here's a question for discussion. In the song *Youngstown* by Bruce Springsteen he laments a common sentiment that workers are underpaid. He says that from the Monogaleh valley, the Mesabi range, and the Appalacchia coal mines, it is always the same old story:
    Seven-hundred tons of metal a day
    Now sir you tell me the world's changed
    Once I made you rich enough
    Rich enough to forget my name

    It turns out that labor's share of value-added in the nonfinancial corporate sector in North America is around 74%. If labor receives the bulk of the value added in production, why do you suppose these sentiments exist? Is there anything about labor versus capital that can cause this?

15. Are the following statements true or false:

    a. If the average product is increasing, the marginal product must be less than the average product? __________

    b. If marginal product is negative, average product is negative. __________

    c. If average product is positive, total product must be rising. __________

    d. If total product is increasing, marginal product must also be increasing. __________

    e. If the marginal product equals the average product, then total product is maximized. __________

16. This question has to do with marginal products.

    a. When firms hire workers, they equate the wage they pay to the __________

    b. Thus, when workers become more productive, other things equal, the demand for their services shifts __________

    c. As long as the supply of these workers is not infinitely elastic, their wage will be __________.

d. In football the player with the highest marginal product is almost always the quarter back (QB). Not surprisingly, the QB is almost always the highest paid player on a football team. In front of the QB is the offensive line. On the left side is the left tackle position (LT), and on the right side is the right tackle position (RT). RT and LT are not perfect substitutes. Most QBs are injured when they are hit from their blind side. This means, if a QB is right handed his blind side comes from his left. If a QB is left handed, his blind side is from the right. Now, the question: if a QB is right handed what would you predict is the value of the marginal product of the RT versus the LT? Which one do you think earns more money? [in fact, this player is almost always the second highest paid player on the team!]

17. You own a pizza shop and you use both labor and capital to make your pizzas. Currently the marginal product of labor is 5 pizzas per hour, while the marginal product of you capital is 2 pizzas per hour. You pay your labour $10 per hour, and your capital costs you $5 per hour. The price of pizza is $2.50. Is you little shop using its inputs efficiently? Explain.

18. Complete the following table,

Total Output	Total Fixed Cost	Total Variable Cost	Total Cost	Marginal Cost	Average Fixed Cost	Average Variable Cost	Average Total Cost
0		$0					
			10				
1							
2		18			5		
3		23					
4						6.5	

19. Writing in 1795, Patrick Colquhoun made the following comment on the harsh criminal laws of England:

> *... by the Laws of England, there are above one hundred and sixty different offenses which subject the parties who are found guilty, to death without benefit of Clergy. This multiplicity of capital punishments must, in the nature of things, defeat those ends, the attainment of which ought to be the object of all law, namely, the prevention of crimes.*

Colquhoun was referring to the *Black Act* which made vast criminal acts, from the minor to the major, subject to a punishment of death. Colquhoun was right in noting that having a blanket massive punishment often had the opposite effect on crime.

a. Why would making "death" the punishment for everything from littering to murder often lead to more serious crime? Use the economic concept of marginal cost in your answer.

b. Ironically, Colquhoun's sentiments contrast with commonly expressed opinions today, which constantly claim that we have too much crime because all punishments for crime are too low. Is it possible that both Colquhoun and modern commentators could be right? Namely, would it be consistent with the economic ideas you have learned that universally low punishments can lead to crime problems as well? Use the law of demand in your answer.

20. Complete the following table,

Total Output	Total Fixed Cost	Total Variable Cost	Total Cost	Marginal Cost	Average Fixed Cost	Average Variable Cost	Average Total Cost
0		$0					
1						10	
2		30					
3							80/3
				20			
4					5		

21. Are the following statements true or false:

a. If the marginal product is increasing, the average product must be increasing?

b. If marginal product equals the average product, then the marginal cost equals the average variable cost.

c. If average product is negative, total product is negative.

d. If total product is increasing, marginal product is diminishing.

e. If the total product is maximized then average product equals zero.

Review Question Answers

1. *In chapter 7 every individual was assumed to be different in terms of their costs of producing goods, but for a given individual the cost of producing each unit was the same. Thus, marginal cost curves were upward sloping because the low cost individuals produced first. In chapter 8 we are assuming every person is the same in terms of their productivity, but when they produce more goods they become subject to diminishing marginal products. Thus there are two reasons for why marginal cost curves are upward sloping.*

2. *No. A production function is a technical relationship between the amounts of inputs and the amount of output. There are no prices involved.*

3. *This is not a case of constant returns to scale, and in fact, it is really the most important type of exception. Here when you double the input (fencing) you square the output (area). Hence we have what is called increasing returns to scale.*

4. *In stage I there is really too much capital for the amount of labor being used. Every time the firm adds more labor, output increases at an increasing rate, so it always makes more money by increasing output. Thus the firm ends up in stage II. In stage III there is too much labor. The firm is paying for workers who are making a negative contribution. Clearly the firm would be better off reducing the number of workers at the firm, and ending up in stage II.*

5. *It depends on the price of the output and the inputs marginal product.*

6. *If they didn't they would soon find they could not compete with other firms that were. This must hold for all firms in a competitive environment, even if they are technically nonprofit. A church that does not minimize costs will not be able to provide the same services as a similar church that is not wasting money. Parishioners will see their contributions are more productive at the other church and will leave. At a public university, if the state is constantly willing to subsidize the extra costs, then non cost minimizing behavior is possible.*

7. *They could. If you continue to increase the number of cooks for a given kitchen, then eventually the marginal product becomes negative. That is, the soup has someone's hair in it!*

8. *It certainly is. It takes inputs to make outputs. As much as we like to think otherwise, there's no free lunch.*

Odd Numbered Problem Answers

1. *Even though the average product of a principles book is higher, at the margin an advanced book with limited sales might contribute more than a principles book. The publishing company is equating the value of the marginal products of all its books (assuming they cost the same), even though this implies drastically different sales for the different types of books.*

3. *There are fixed costs in producing the banking machines. To create a different banking machine without the Braille dots would increase these costs, but would produce no benefit. Sighted people don't care if Braille dots are present. This sort of thing is found all over. Cars, for example, come with thousands of "standard features" like wheels, locks, heaters, and seats because to customize each car over issues that almost everyone wants is costly without producing a benefit. At one time heaters in cars were an option, but since most people ordered them, it was cheaper to simply make all cars with heaters.*

5. *No. This only tells you what the average product is for each department. What you want to know is the marginal product.*

7. *No. Under such circumstances the firm would be better off to shut down.*

9. *This says the cost per marginal product of labor is greater than the cost per marginal product of capital. A firm would want to hire less labor and more capital under such circumstances.*

11.

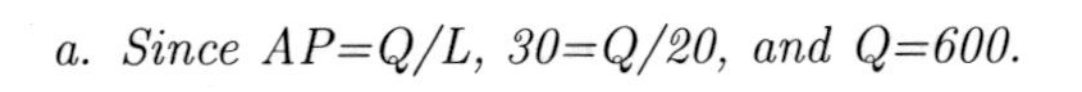

   a. *Since AP=Q/L, 30=Q/20, and Q=600.*

   b. *Since MP>AP, the MP might be increasing or decreasing. This means we can't tell whether the MC curve is upward or downward sloping.*

   c. *Since MP>AP, the AP must be increasing, therefore, the AVC is decreasing.*

13. *Strategic bombing generally assumes that there is one way to accomplish a task. However, when you bomb one trail, the enemy uses another. The ability to substitute in production makes effective targeted bombing difficult.*

15. *They are all false.*

17. *The firm should be equating the marginal product per dollar between the two inputs. As it stands the marginal product per dollar for labor is .5 and the marginal product per dollar for capital is .4. Thus, the firm is not using its inputs efficiently, it should be using more labor.*

19.

   a. *The problem is that you make the marginal cost of a second crime equal to zero. Hence, if a person commits a crime, then they have every incentive to commit others as long as the benefits are greater than zero. For example, if someone kidnaps another person for ransom, they have an incentive to also murder their victim to prevent identification.*

The idea of having increasing punishments for increasing crimes is called the principle of "marginal deterrence."

b. *Yes it is consistent. By having death the punishment for many crimes the cost of the first crime is extremely high. By the law of demand, fewer people commit crimes. The problem is that of those who commit crimes under this system, they commit more serious ones. The net effect is ambiguous.*

21. *The first question is false in general, but true for the types of production functions we draw. The rest are True, True, False, and False.*

8.6 Appendix: Deriving Cost Curves

The Marginal Cost Curve

The point of Chapter 8 is to understand what lies behind an upward sloping supply curve. We've seen that supplies are upward sloping because inputs have differences in comparative advantage, and because inputs experience diminishing marginal products. This appendix is intended to show you the mechanical relationships between the various cost curves mentioned within the chapter. It is hoped that understanding the mechanics may help you understand the economics of cost curves. However, some students find the mechanics more confusing than helpful. You'll have to be your own judge on that.

Let's begin again with the production function, graphed in panel (A) of Figure 8-1A, which tells us the maximum amount of output the firm gets for a given amount of labor, holding capital constant.

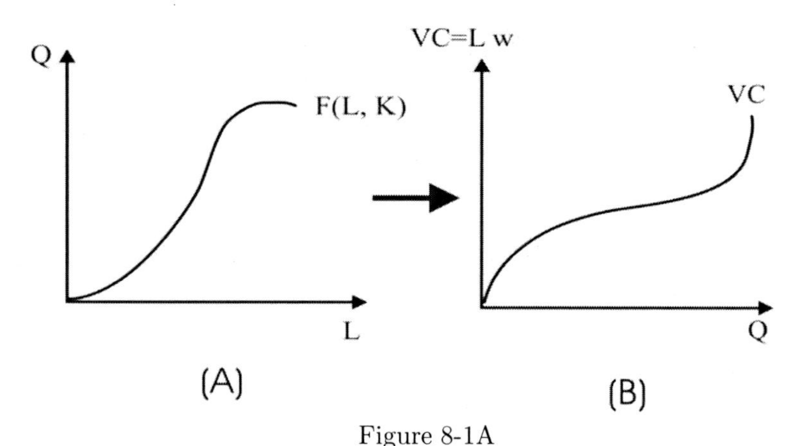

Figure 8-1A
The Production Function and Variable Cost Function

Now, in your mind I want you to do a little thought experiment. Let's multiply L (the amount of labor) by w, the wage rate. That would give us $w \times L$, which equals the variable costs. Next I want you to imagine rotating the entire graph (axes and all) in panel (A) of Figure 8-1A around the 45° axis. After such a maneuver, we now have variable costs on the vertical axis and output (Q) is on the horizontal axis. Can you picture that? In your mind the new figure should look like panel (B) in Figure 8-1A.

The variable cost function is a mirror image of the production function, with a little stretch depending on the wage rate. Once we have this total variable cost curve, we can determine what the marginal costs are. By definition, marginal cost is the change in variable costs when there is a change in output. We can write this as:

$$\text{MarginalCosts} = \frac{\Delta \text{VC}}{\Delta \text{Q}}$$

If you think about this equation, the marginal cost equation takes the form "rise over run" and is a slope of some type. A slope of what? The slope of the variable cost function. If we let ΔQ get really small, then the marginal cost is the slope of the variable cost curve at a given point.

In Figure 8-2A the variable cost curve is plotted with a number of tangency lines. The slopes of these lines are the slopes of the VC curve at the tangency point, and therefore, the value of this slope is the marginal cost for that level of output.

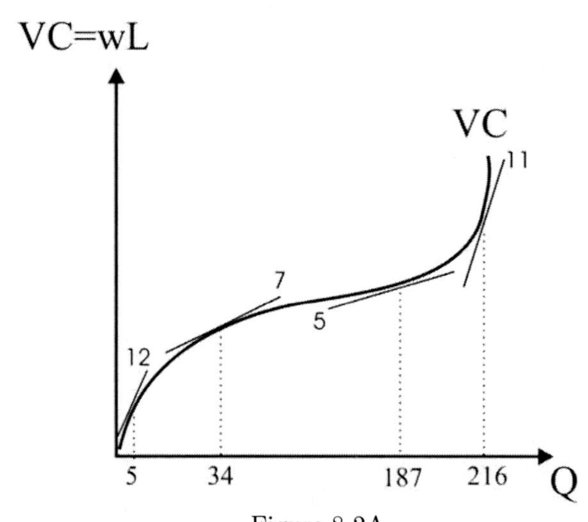

Figure 8-2A
The Slope of the VC Curve is the Marginal Cost

As you can see from the figure, when the firm is producing 5 units of output the marginal cost of that output is $12. When the firm produces 34 units the marginal cost is $7, and when the firm produces 216 units the marginal costs are $11. The actual numbers are just made up, but notice the shape of the VC curve means that the marginal cost starts out very high, falls, reaches a minimum, and then starts to rise again. This is the shape which was described in the chapter and shown in Figure 8-6.

The Average Cost Curves

We know that $TC = VC + FC$. That is, the total costs of the firm are equal to the variable costs plus the fixed costs. We know what the variable cost curve looks like, but what would the fixed costs look like if they were plotted against output? Well, by definition the fixed costs are fixed. They don't change when output changes. Hence they would be a flat line. Suppose for the sake of argument the fixed costs were $100. In Figure 8-3A both the variable and fixed costs are plotted, along with their vertical summation.

The important point to see here is that the total cost curve is simply a parallel shift up of the variable cost curve, by the amount of the fixed costs. Because the shift is parallel, the slope of the total cost curve is the same as the slope of the variable cost curve for every level of output. Hence the slope of the total cost curve is also the marginal cost.

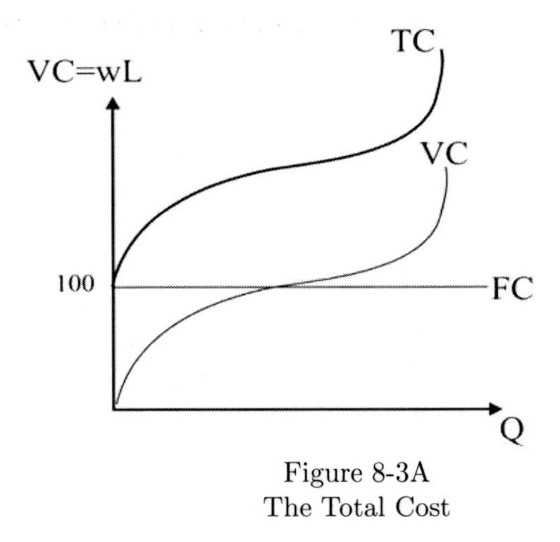

Figure 8-3A
The Total Cost

Once we have all of the cost curves, we can graphically show how to derive all of the average cost curves. An average cost takes the general form "costs divided by output." Hence, the average total costs (often abbreviated as just AC) is given by:

$$AC = \frac{\text{TotalCosts}}{\text{Q}}$$

Now consider Figure 8-4A, where the total cost curve is drawn, along with a straight line from the origin to point A.

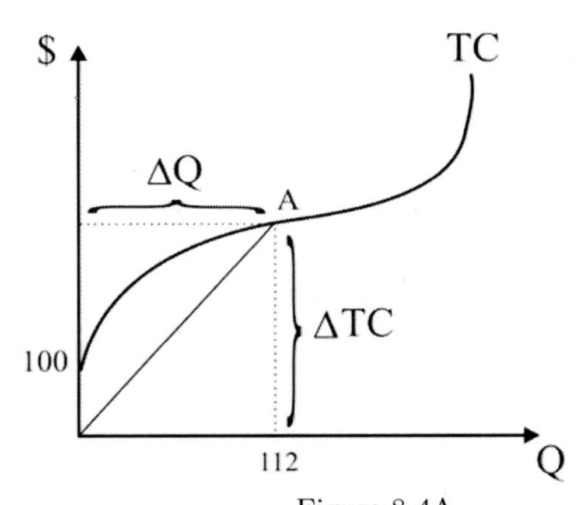

Figure 8-4A
The Average Total Cost

The slope of the straight line is "rise over run," but this is just $\Delta TC/\Delta Q$. In other words, the slope of this straight line is the average total costs of output level 112. If you drew a bunch of lines from the origin to a given point on the total cost curve, then the slope of that line would be the average total cost at the corresponding level of output. Notice what would happen to the values of these slopes as we start with low levels of output and move to higher ones. The average cost would be very high, would fall, would minimize, and then start to increase.

Let's use this method to figure out the average fixed costs. In Figure 8-5A we have our Fixed Cost curve flat at $100, and we have a series of lines from the origin to various points on the fixed costs.

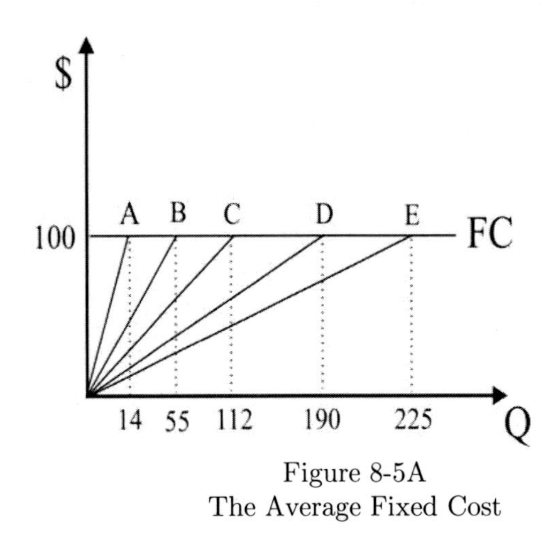

Figure 8-5A
The Average Fixed Cost

When the firm produces 14 units of output the AFC is 100/14 or $7.14. When the firm produces 55 units the AFC is 100/55 or $1.81. If we continue down the other cases we get AFCs of $.89, $.52, and $.44. As output increases the average fixed costs just gets smaller and smaller. If we were to graph these values against output, then we would get Figure 8-8 in the chapter.

If you're still reading, it is time to put it all together. Figure 8-6A shows all of the cost curves in the upper panel and the corresponding average and marginal cost curves on the bottom panel. For one level of output the relevant slope lines and values are drawn in the top panel and labeled in the bottom. It is left as an exercise for you to choose other levels of output and assign values for the average and marginal costs that make sense.

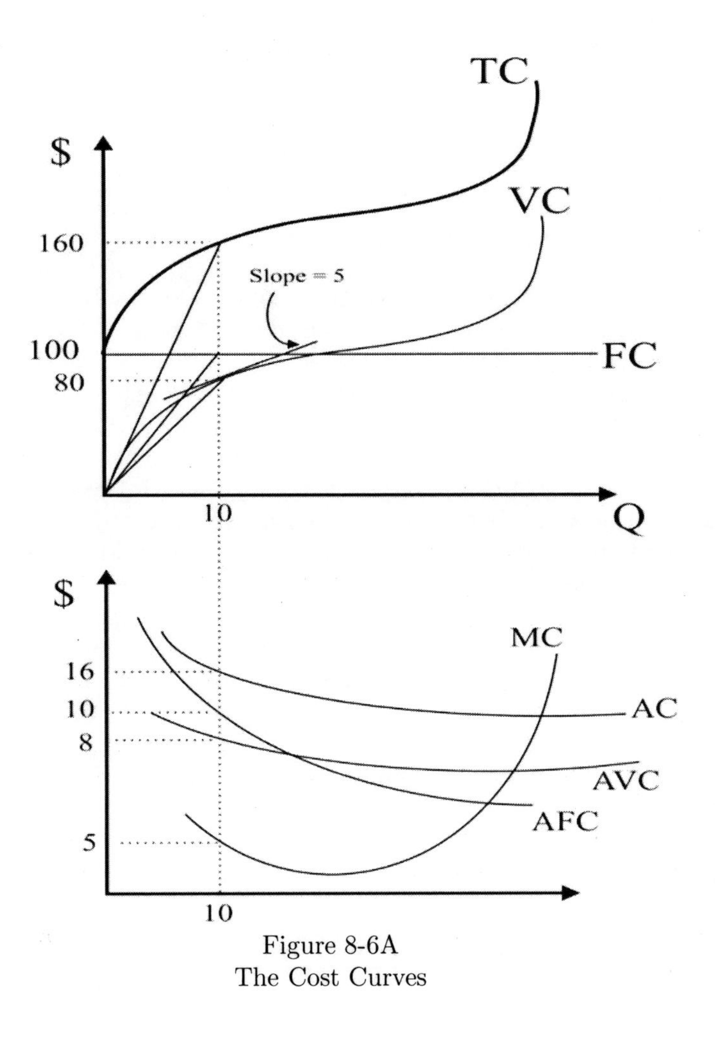

Figure 8-6A
The Cost Curves

CHAPTER 9

THE COMPETITIVE FIRM AND MARKET SUPPLY CURVES

Now that we've discussed the concept of opportunity costs, comparative advantage, and diminishing marginal products, we're ready to discuss the competitive firm. By "competitive" economists refer to a highly stylized set of conditions that describe a certain market structure. Normally when we hear the word competitive we think of rivalry. A competitive race is one where one racer is up against several others, and the winner is determined by the relative speed of each racer. This is not what a competitive market means. A competitive market is characterized by several features. First, all firms are *price takers*. A price taking firm is one that has no impact on its price, in part because it is so small relative to the size of the market. The wheat farmer in Saskatchewan or Nebraska can produce all of the wheat he wants, but his output is such a small contribution to the world supply of wheat he has no impact on the price of wheat. Whatever the world price of wheat is, the individual farmer simply takes it as given. Second, all competitive firms ignore their rivals, and make output decisions based only on prices. Since any individual firm has no impact on price, every firm simply ignores the actions of other firms in the industry. If one farmer decides to plant his back forty in corn rather than wheat this year, his neighbors simply ignore this action in deciding how much land they should plant in wheat or corn. Finally, and this is related to the other two features, there is no strategic behavior on the part of firms. Since every firm has no impact on price, they don't waste time thinking "if I plant the back forty on corn, then my neighbor will think I know something about the wheat market, and he'll plant corn. But I don't want him to plant corn, I want him to plant soybeans, so perhaps I should pretend I'm planting soy, ..." Owners of competitive price taking firms don't think this way.

The Competitive Firm: *each firm is price taking, ignores its rivals output decisions, and doesn't engage in strategic behavior.*

To say that a firm is price taking is to say something very specific about its demand curve. As far as the firm is concerned, its demand curve is flat and just equal to the price. This is shown in figure 9-1. The price for the product is determined in the market for this commodity, and the firm simply takes this price as given and assumes it can sell all it wants at that price. If the firm were to charge just a penny more than this price, then no one would buy from the firm and the quantity demanded would be zero. If the firm charged a penny less than the market price the world would beat a path to the firm's door. This means the elasticity of demand for the price taking firm is infinity. In other words, consumers think of one competitive firm as being a perfect substitute for every other price taking firm in that industry.

When a firm considers the market price as its demand curve, then the demand curve is also equal to the marginal and average revenue for the firm. Marginal revenue is the change in total revenue divided by the change in output. Average revenue is the total revenue divided by the level of output. When the price of the good is fixed, then both the marginal and average revenue just

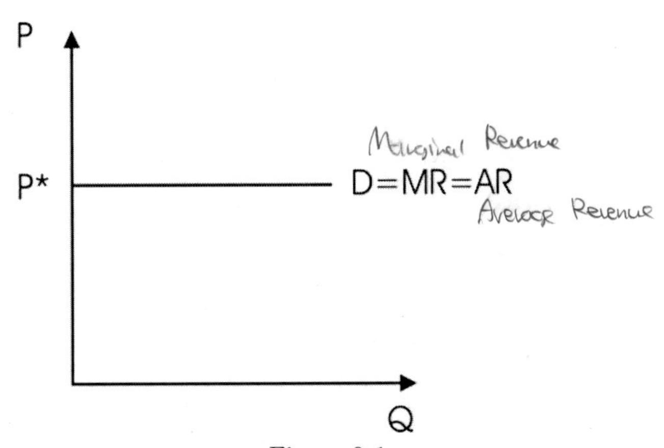

Figure 9-1
The Demand for A Perfectly Competitive Firm

equal the price. For every unit that is sold the total revenue simply increases by the price. We can show this with a simple example in Table 9-1. In the table the price of the good is \$10. When the firm sells one unit its revenues are \$10; when it sells two units revenues are \$20, and so on. Every time output changes by one unit, the total revenue changes by \$10. Hence the marginal revenue is also \$10. Likewise, when output is 7, total revenue is \$70. Therefore average revenue is \$70/7=\$10.

> *Marginal Revenue: a change in total revenue divided by a change in output:* $\frac{\Delta TR}{\Delta Q}$
>
> *Average Revenue: total revenue divided by total output:* $\frac{TR}{Q}$

> *For a price taking firm the demand curve is the price, the marginal revenue, and the average revenue.*

9.1 The Profit Maximizing Level of Output

Let's suppose that a competitive firm has a production function for producing shoes as discussed in the last chapter, and that its level of capital is fixed at one unit. Furthermore, let's suppose that the price of this fixed capital input is zero, so that the firm has zero fixed costs. All of the costs the firm has are variable costs that result from changes in the amount of labor used to produce shoes.

Quantity	Price	Total Revenue	Marginal Revenue	Average Revenue
1	10	10		10
			10	
2	10	20		
			10	10
3	10	30		
			10	10
4	10	40		
			10	10
5	10	50		
			10	10
6	10	60		
			10	10
7	10	70		
			10	10
8	10	80		

Table 9-1
The Relationship Between Total, Marginal, and Average Revenue

The firm is a price taker and faces a price of \$10 for every pair of shoes it sells. How many pairs of shoes should the firm make and sell if it wants to maximize its profits?

First we should note that the firm's profit is equal to the total revenue minus the total costs. Total costs are equal to the total variable costs plus the total fixed costs. Hence we can write profit as:

$$\text{Profit} = TR - TC.$$

Since we are going to assume that all variable costs are *avoidable* and all fixed costs are *sunk*, then the *rent* a firm earns is equal to total revenue minus the total variable costs. We can write rent as:

$$\text{Rent} = TR - TVC.$$

The distinction between rent and profit is confusing and important. The easiest way to understand it is to remember that rent is equal to the sunk costs of the firm in equilibrium. Rent is the amount of money that could be taken away from the firm, and the firm would continue to produce. In the shoe example we've started, the sunk costs are zero ... at least initially.

Our shoe example is shown in Figure 9-2, where the upward sloping marginal cost curve intersects the U-shaped average variable cost curve at its minimum point. The profit maximizing level of output is where the marginal cost equals the price.

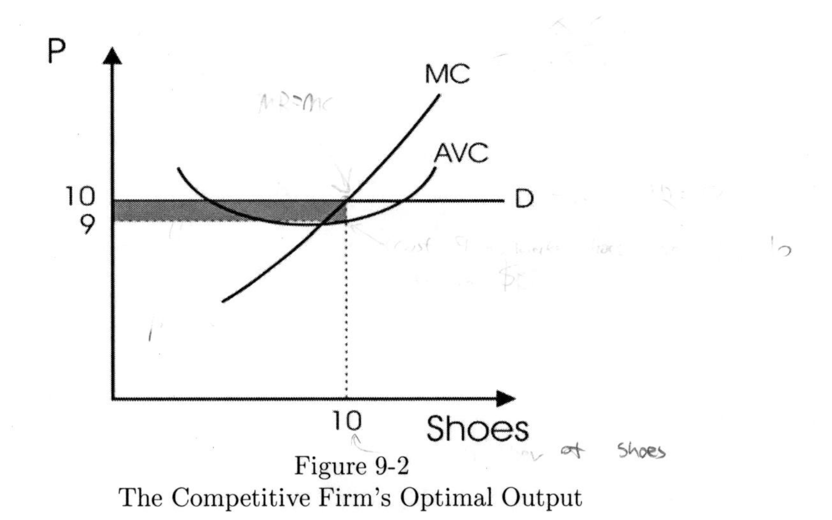

Figure 9-2
The Competitive Firm's Optimal Output

> *Profits are maximized when marginal cost equals price.*

In the our shoe case this happens when 10 pairs of shoes are produced. Had the firm produced fewer than 10 pairs of shoes, say 9 pairs, then the marginal revenue of shoes would be greater than the marginal cost. This means the firm makes a positive contribution to profit by producing the 10th pair of shoes. Since the firm wants to maximize profit, it produces 10 pairs of shoes rather than 9. If the firm produced more than 10 pairs of shoes, say 11, then the marginal costs would be greater than the marginal revenue, meaning that the 11th pair of shoes lowers profits. Hence, 10 pairs of shoes maximizes the profits of the firm, and this occurs where marginal revenue equals marginal costs.

Notice when the firm produces 10 pairs of shoes, the average variable cost (AVC) of 10 shoes is $9. This means that each pair of shoes costs $9 (remember there are no fixed costs). Since the average revenue is $10, the firm makes a profit of $1 per pair of shoes, or $10 profit. This is shown as the grey area in Figure 9-2.

Figure 9-2 is drawn under the assumption that the price of capital is zero. Suppose that the price of capital rises to $10, so that the cost of one unit of capital is $10. This cost eliminates the profit of the firm because the variable cost (VC) of $90, plus the $10 fixed cost (FC) just equals the $100 of revenue the firm makes when it produces 10 pairs of shoes. This result is shown in Figure 9-3.

Several technical things need to be noted in Figure 9-3. First, notice that the average total cost curve (AC) lies above the average variable cost (AVC) curve. This is because the difference between the two is the average fixed cost (AFC).[1] Since AFC is just the FC divided by output, the larger

---

[1] This is a little confusing, but keep in mind that its just arithmetic. Since $TC = VC + FC$, if

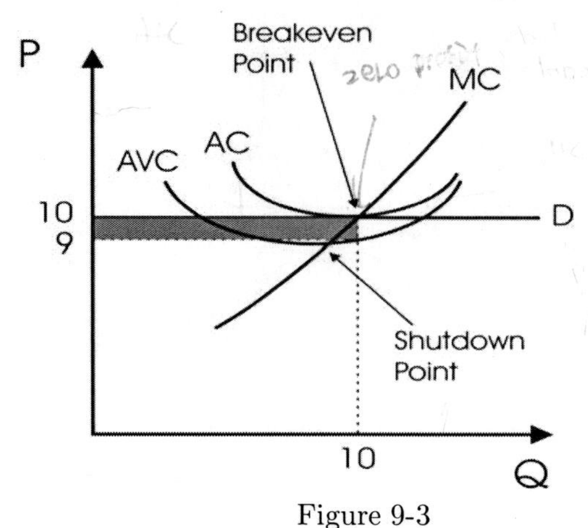

Figure 9-3
Profits with Fixed and Variable Costs

the output is the smaller AFC is. Hence the difference between the AVC and the AC curves gets smaller and smaller as the number of shoes produced increases.

Second, notice that the MC curve again intersects the AC curve at the minimum point. Furthermore, the AC at 10 pairs of shoes is $10, which is equal to the price, which tells us that the firm is earning zero profits. In fact, from our definition of profits and rents, we see now that the grey area in Figure 9-3 is no longer profit but rent. The distinction is important. If the price of shoes were to fall, say to $9.25, the firm would lose money. The $9.25 would cover the labor costs of producing the shoes, but the firm would not make enough money to cover the fixed costs of capital. Would the firm stay in business? At first glance you might think, no. Why would a firm stay in business if it loses money. However, keep in mind that the fixed cost is *sunk*. There's nothing the firm can do to get this money back. So as long as the firm covers its variable costs, the firm stays in business. When the time comes to reinvest in the capital (e.g., update equipment), if the firm still cannot meet this expense, then the firm will go out of business. If the price of shoes falls below the minimum AVC point, then the firm goes out of business because it can avoid incurring the labor costs. As long as the firm earns a rent it will stay operating. Hence the minimum point of the AC curve is called the *break even point* because profit is zero there, and the minimum point of the AVC curve is called the *shutdown point* because at this point the rent is zero.

Breakeven point: the minimum of the AC curve.

Shutdown point: the minimum of the AVC curve.

Since output is zero if the price falls below the shutdown point, and since the firm produces a quantity determined by P=MC above this point, the supply curve of the individual firm is the marginal cost curve above the AVC minimum point.

---

we divide the equation by the level of output we get $AC = AVC + AFC$.

> *The firm supply curve is the MC curve above the shutdown point (min AVC).*

This is shown in Figure 9-4. Notice that since the supply curve lies above the AVC curve, it always lies on the upward sloping part of the MC curve. This means that supply curves are always upward sloping. Increases in prices for the firm's product always leads the firm to produce more.

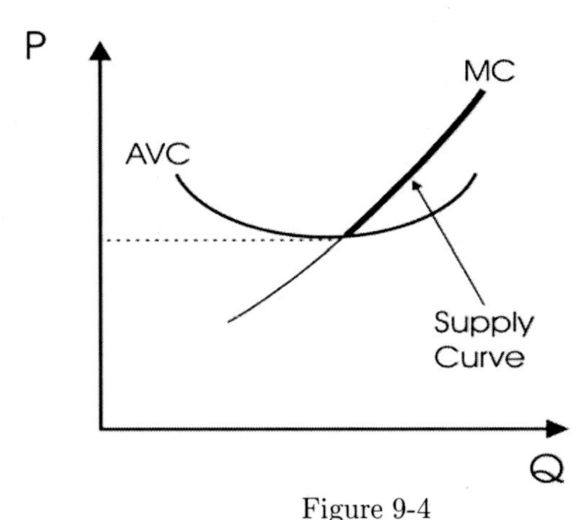

Figure 9-4
The Supply Curve of the Firm

Shifts in Cost Curves

The cost curves of the firm are not fixed, but depend on several factors. Any thing that changes one of the fixed costs will shift the AC curve, but will not shift the MC or AVC. These latter to cost curves depend on the opportunity costs of the firm, not the sunk costs. Anything that changes the variable costs of the firm will shift the AC, AVC, and the MC of the firm.

The marginal cost curve depends on three things: the level of output, the price of the inputs, and the production function. When the level of output changes there is a movement along the marginal cost curve; it does not shift. We can see this in Figure 9-5.

When output is 90, the MC is $4, but when the level of output increases to 100 units, the MC increases to $5. The increase in MC is a result of moving along the curve, not from any shift in the curve.

If an input price (like a wage rate) changes or there is a change in technology, then the MC curve will shift. Generally speaking, if an input becomes more expensive this will shift the MC curve up. Hence, if a tax is placed on labor, the firm will find it more expensive, at the margin, to produce output and the MC curve shifts up. On the other hand, if there is a technological change that changes the marginal product of an input, then the MC will shift. If there is a change that makes labor *more* productive, then this will shift the MC curve *down*. That is, the advance in

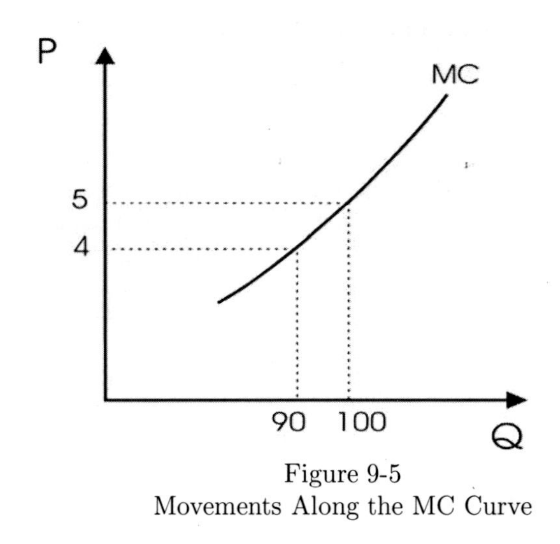

Figure 9-5
Movements Along the MC Curve

technology makes it cheaper for the firm to produce output. Anything that lowers the marginal product of labor will have the effect of increasing the MC curve.

One relatively easy parameter change to analyze is the effect of a tax on cost. A government can impose two types of taxes: lump sum taxes and per unit taxes. A lump sum tax is one that does not vary with the output of the firm. In other words, it is a fixed cost. A per unit tax is one that varies with the level of output and is, therefore, a variable cost. Figure 9-6 shows the impact of a lump sum tax on a firms costs.

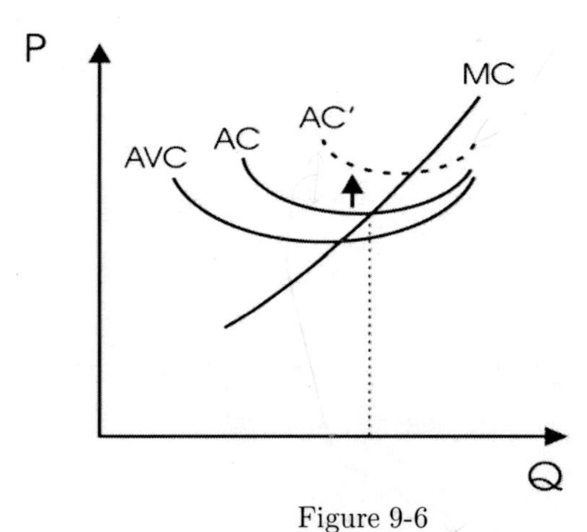

Figure 9-6
Effects of a Lump Sum Tax

The lump sum tax increases the AC curve to AC', but the other cost curves remain in place. This is because a lump sum tax doesn't effect the cost of producing an additional unit. One way to think about the costs of the firm is that there are now three types of average costs: the average variable costs, the average fixed costs, and the average lump sum tax. Together these three cost curves make up the new average total cost curve AC'. The AC curve will increase by the average lump sum tax.

If the tax is $1000, then the AC will shift up by $1000/Q. Clearly, by influencing the average total costs, the lump sum tax will influence the profits a firm makes.

When the firm faces a per unit tax, then all of the cost curves will increase. An example of a per unit tax would be $2 per unit.[2] Figure 9-7 shows the effect of such a tax. Since the tax influences the variable costs, the marginal cost curve shifts up. It turns out to shift up by an amount *equal to the tax*, which in this case is $2. This would seem to make perfect sense. Every time the firm produces a unit of output it not only has to pay for the costs of production, it must now also pay the $2 tax. The AVC curve also shifts up, and also shifts up by the amount of the tax. Again, this makes sense. If the firm produces 20 units then the total tax bill will be $40, and the average tax is $2 per unit. If the AVC curve shifts up by $2, then it must be the case that the AC curve also shifts up by $2.

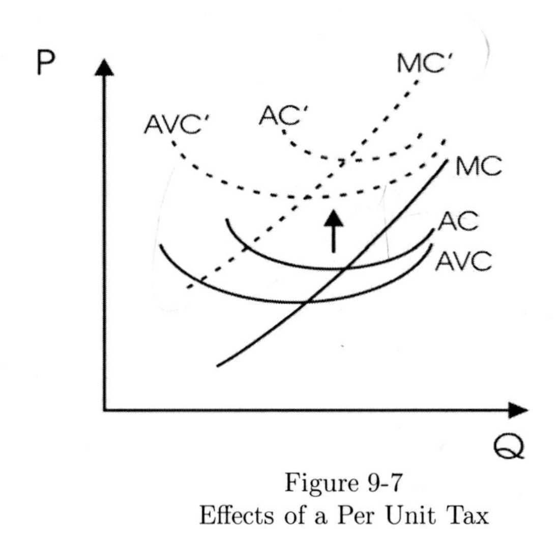

Figure 9-7
Effects of a Per Unit Tax

9.2 Profits of the Firm

Nothing is more confusing for students than the concept of economic profits. It is simple enough to say that "profit is equal to total revenue minus total costs." But let's keep in mind that total costs include opportunity costs and sunk costs, and doesn't just include the *cash flow* of the firm. All costs are accounted for in total costs.

For example, suppose you owned a little bicycle repair shop. After the first month in business you tally all of your receipts and find out that you've brought in $36,000. After you deduct the

[2] Most taxes that we face as consumers are a type of per unit tax, namely the *ad valorem* tax. These taxes charge a percentage of the value of the purchase. Thus a sales tax might charge 5% of the value of goods bought. The effect of such a tax is to increase the MC, AC, and AVC curves as well.

rental for the shop, the wages for your employee, the price you paid for parts, and all the other costs that involved a cash outlay, you end up with $4000 in your pocket. Would this money be considered a profit?

If you're understanding the concept of opportunity cost, then you should recognize the firm must also cover the cost of the entrepreneur's time ... namely you. If you sacrifice working for another bicycle shop for $3000 a month, then the firm made a profit of $1000. However, if you sacrifice working at another firm for $5000 a month, then the firm lost $1000. The alternative use of the entrepreneur's time might not be the only implicit cost to the firm. The firm might be exposed to risk, and risk requires a yield in order for someone to hold it. Running a bicycle shop is a risky business compared to working for someone else, and as a result this cost should also be factored in.

The bottom line is when an economist talks about economic profit, he's referring to the difference between all revenues and all costs. Consider how different this is from the accountant's income statement. On an accounting income statement there is a list of expenses. Most of these expenses are monthly cash flows like salaries, benefits, rent, office supplies, etc. However, some of the expenses include things like "depreciation" of capital assets. To the economist the true depreciation of a capital asset is its fall in value; that is, the change in the opportunity cost of holding the asset. The accountant, however, has no idea what this is, and so just uses an arbitrary formula for calculating the cost. Likewise the accountant ignores differences in risk, and ignores opportunity costs that do not have a cash flow. Thus the accountant's income statement is not a statement reflecting the firm's profits. Thus, a firm could have a positive number on the bottom of an income statement, but still make zero economic profit.

If we understand what an economic profit is, then the question must be asked: what is the *equilibrium* profit of the firm? Every firm wants to make as much profit as possible, but the firm is constrained by the demands of the consumer, *and* the behavior of other firms in the industry. It turns out the pursuit of profit on the part of all firms leads to the counter intuitive result that all economic profits are zero in equilibrium. We've assumed the market is full of lots of small firms. How similar these firms are determines how profits get driven to zero, but in either case (through costs or price changes) the result is the same.

> *In equilibrium, each firm must earn zero economic profit.* ≠ accounting profit

All Firms are Identical

Let's start with the assumption that every single firm is identical in every respect and no firm has any sunk costs. Under these conditions the marginal costs of every firm would be identical, as would the AVC. Furthermore, the AVC curve would equal the AC curve, since there are no fixed/sunk costs. Suppose, that a situation like the one in Figure 9-8 existed for 10 firms who just happened to be the only firms in the market, even though there are plenty of potential firms just like them not producing.

This firm, and the 9 others just like it, are experiencing an economic profit. The revenues they receive not only cover *all* of their opportunity costs, they exceed them by the amount of the shaded area. The owners of this firm are better off being in this market by the amount of $100. But this

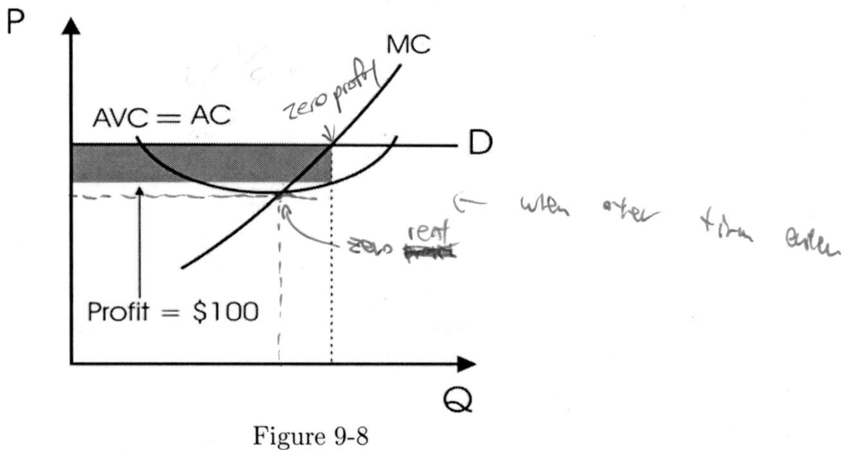

Figure 9-8
Out of Equilibrium Profits

can not be an equilibrium because there exists a host of other identical firms just as eager to have this $100 as these firms are. These firms, on seeing the profits to be had, *enter* the industry. When they enter the industry they increase the supply of goods available and this lowers the equilibrium price of the good. This process happens until all firms in the industry earn zero profits. As long as profits exist, firms will enter and prices will fall until the profits are eliminated.

But how can firms stay in business if they earn zero profits? If you find yourself asking this question, then you've got to go back and reconsider what profit is and how it relates to opportunity costs. When the firm earns zero profits it is covering all of its costs, including the return on capital, risk, and the opportunity costs of time of the owner running the firm.

If the ten firms we started out with were earning a loss, would anything have been different? No. Instead of firms entering the industry some firms would have just *exited* instead. When firms exit, the market supply starts to fall and prices increase. This increase in price would continue until all losses were eliminated or all firms left and no market existed. The result though is the same: profits are zero in equilibrium.

Firms Differ in Sunk Costs

When we assume that all firms are identical, the process of equilibrium is quite easy: prices simply adjust. When we assume that firms can be different we not only end up with countless possibilities, but the process that eliminates profits becomes a little more complicated. To keep things simple, let's only consider the case where firms differ in terms of their sunk/fixed costs. In this case each firm has a different marginal cost curve, but we'll assume they have the same slope. To keep things even more simple, let's suppose the fixed input is the "talent" of the entrepreneur. Let's suppose the output is hot dogs, and some people are just born great vendors and others less so. Having a lot of hot dog talent means that the AVC of producing hot dogs is lower than a firm whose owner doesn't have a lot of hot dog talent. The *fixed cost* is just the value of this talent, which doesn't vary with the number of hot dogs produced.

Let's begin with an out of equilibrium scenario where the price of "hot dog talent" is zero. Since fixed costs equal the value of the talent times the amount of talent, every firm has zero fixed costs even though they have different levels of the fixed talent. Thus, each firm has a different AVC curve, but AVC=AC. Once again 10 firms are in the market, and two of them are drawn in Figure 9-9.

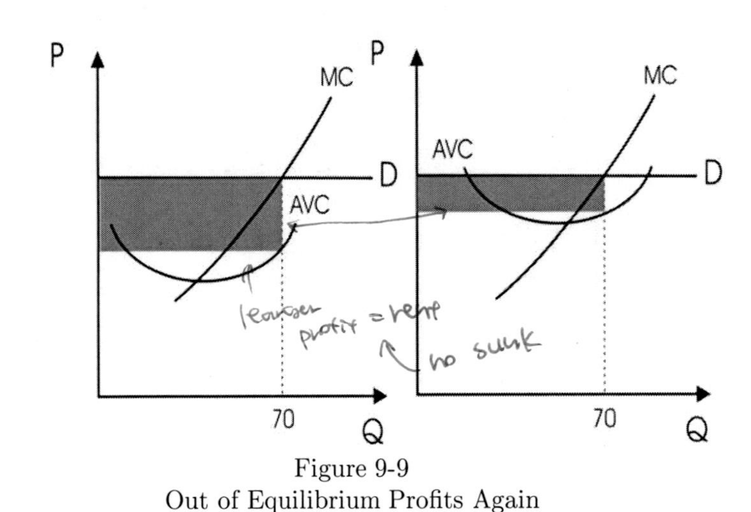

Figure 9-9
Out of Equilibrium Profits Again

The firm on the left has an entrepreneur with more talent than the firm on the right. As a result the firm on the left is earning a larger profit than the one on the right. In any event, both of them are earning profits and outside firms are going to be looking in thinking "we want some of that action." If the other firms also differ in terms of their talents; that is, if they differ in terms of their levels of fixed costs, then profits will be eliminated through two forces. First, as other firms enter the market, output will increase and prices will fall, just as before. However, there will also be a demand for this hot dog talent. Firms will offer individuals with such talent a higher and higher wage for these people to work for their firm. As these wages increase, the fixed costs of the firm increase. These increases in fixed costs do not change the AVC curve, but they do change the AC curve, as we've argued above.

Hence, when profits exist, entry by other firms will tend to lower the price, and increases in the cost of the sunk/fixed asset will tend to raise AC ... until the profit is eliminated. Which effect is larger will simply depend on the distribution of talent. If there is lots of talent, then the price fall will dominate. If there is almost no talent for making hot dogs, then the AC curve increase will be larger and the owner of this talent will become wealthier. With hot dog production, it is likely the price does most of the adjusting. With hockey players, where talent is quite limited, the AC would appear to do most of the work. The equilibrium is drawn in Figure 9-10.

Notice that each firm, though it now earns zero profits, earns a rent. This rent is the payment to the special fixed factor that causes the AVC curve to be lower.

9.3 The Market Supply Curve

We're now ready to talk about the market supply curve. In earlier chapters, where there was no production, the market supply curve was simply the sum of the individual endowments. It is

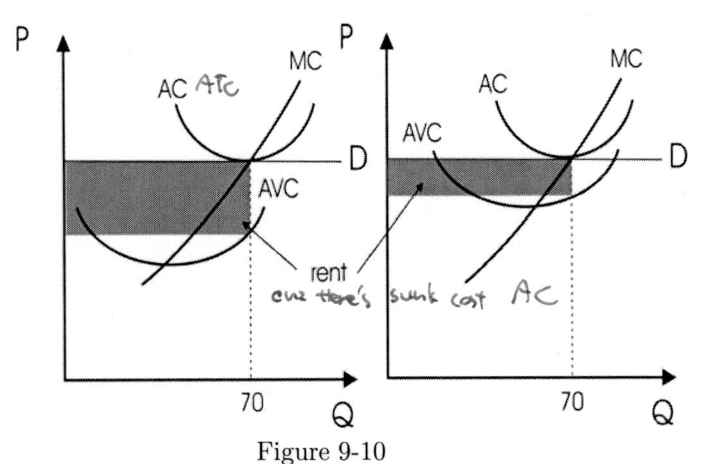

Figure 9-10
Equilibrium Profits with Different Firms

still true that the market supply curve is just the sum of the individual supply curves of each firm. However, in summing up individual supply curves we still need to account for the market structure, or the distribution of firms. As in the section just above, we'll make two simple assumptions: either all firms are identical, or they differ only in terms of their fixed costs.

In Figure 9-11 a series of identical firms is shown. Each has the same AVC=AC, and the same MC. Furthermore, we can assume that there are plenty more of these firms where they came from. We can ask ourselves, what would happen if the price were to rise just a little above $\bar{P}$, the price equal to the minimum AC point? If the price were any higher, then every firm would be earning a profit, entry would occur, output would increase and price would fall back to $\bar{P}$. If the price were below $\bar{P}$, then every firm would make a loss and would leave the market ... nothing would get produced. If nothing got produced the price would again rise back to $\bar{P}$. In other words, in a world like this, the price can never be anything but the minimum of AC. Technology is completely determining the price. In such a world, the market supply curve is the sum of the output each firm produces in equilibrium (equal to $\bar{Q}/N$ which is the total amount supplied divided by the number of firms), and is just a flat line. The elasticity of supply is infinite.

In a market where every firm is identical the equilibrium price and quantity are determined in a special way. It is still true that the equilibrium is found where the market demand and supply intersect each other. However, as just mentioned, the price is determined by the supply curve, which in turn is determined by the cost curves of the firms. The quantity traded, on the other hand, is determined by the market demand curve. When demand increases, the volume of trade increases. This increase in quantity is accomplished by firms entering the market. When demand decreases the volume of trade decreases through firms exiting the market. Changes in demand have no impact on price in this situation.

The case of identical firms is a very special one. When firms differ, even if it is just in terms of the size of fixed costs, then we get a much more standard result. Figure 9-12 shows the derivation of the market supply curve when firms differ. The first firm is the firm with the largest sunk/fixed cost, while the nth firm is the one with zero fixed costs. Presumably there are a number of firms in between these two extremes. Let's consider what happens to the firms as the price moves from

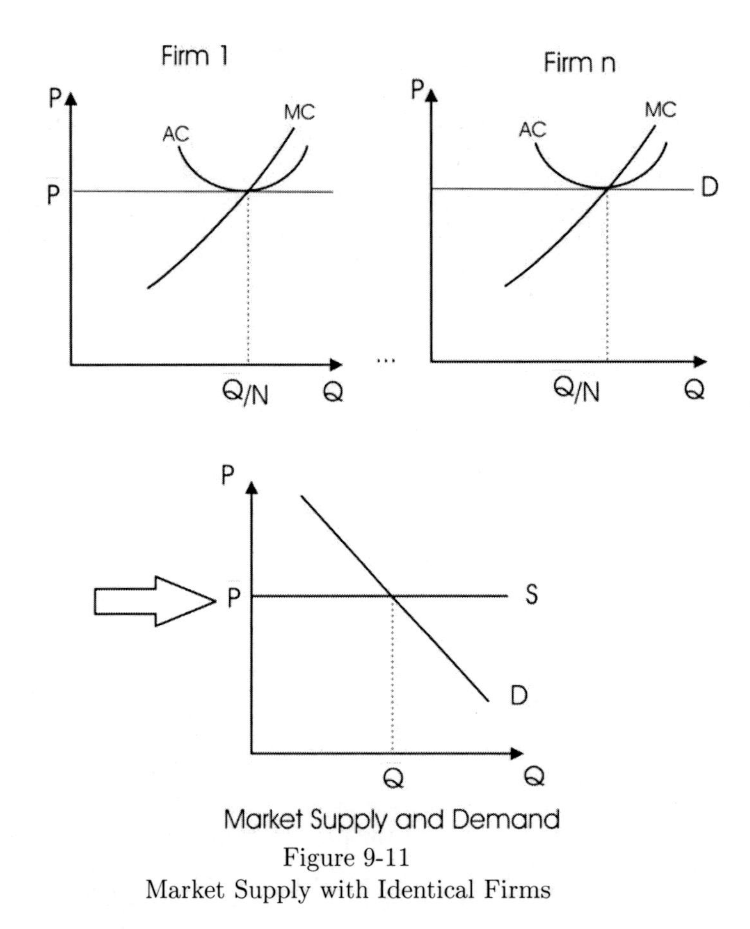

Figure 9-11
Market Supply with Identical Firms

very low to higher. When the price is low enough, only the first firm will be in the market because the price is above its shutdown point but below the shutdown point of the other firms. As the price increases, the first firm increases its output (ie. it moves along its supply curve), and eventually the second firm enters the market. As the price continues to increase the firms already in the market continue to produce more, and more and more firms enter the market. The market supply curve, then, is the sum of all the individual firm supply curves and will be upward sloping.

The nth firm in the market earns no rent. The intra marginal firms all earn a rent. The rent for the first firm is shown as the shaded area in the top left graph. When these rents are added up over all the firms in the market they equal the shaded region above the market supply curve and below the price. This area is called either the rent or seller's surplus, and represents the gains from trade on the production side.

Figure 9-12 shows how a market supply curve is constructed when the firms only differ in terms of their fixed costs. Had firms differed more, for example had their marginal cost curves differed as well, the basic result would have remained the same. The market supply curve would have changed its shape, but it still would have remained upward sloping. Hence, in general the market supply curve is upward sloping.

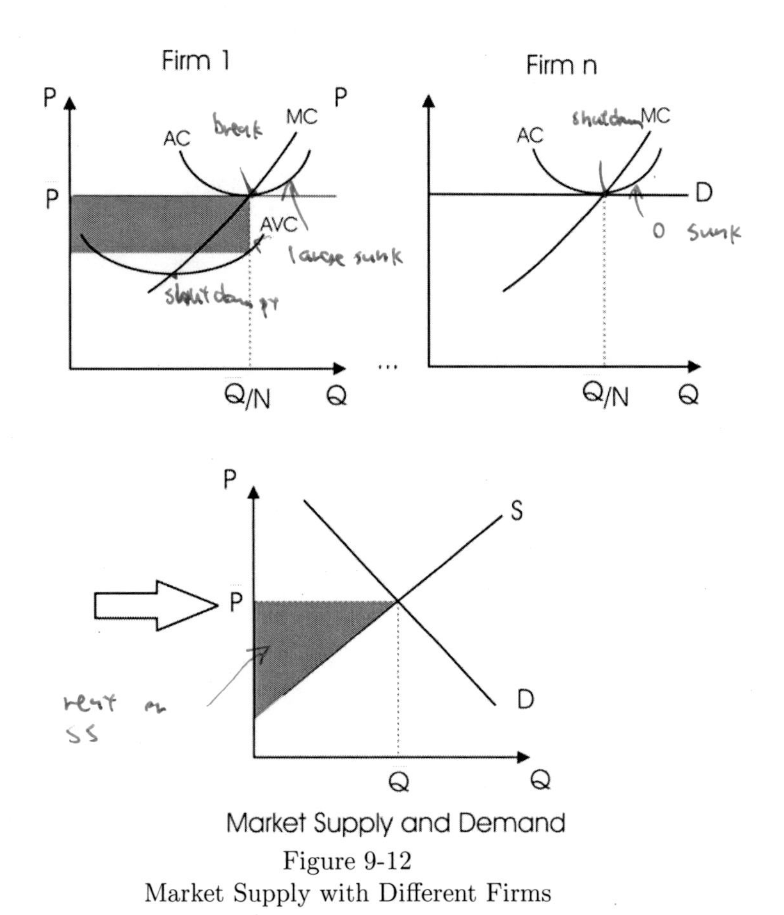

Figure 9-12
Market Supply with Different Firms

9.4 Summary

The competitive firm is characterized by its price taking. Firms that have no bearing on their price only choose how much output to produce, and they maximize profits by producing until their marginal costs equal the price. At this level of output the profit of the firm depends on the average costs. When a firm is making a profit, it is not an equilibrium situation. Other firms will be attracted by the profit and will either enter the industry and lower the price, or will bid for the special input that allows profits. In either case, an equilibrium is reached when profits are zero. This result is counter intuitive, until one realizes that profit is the difference between all revenues and all opportunity costs.

A firm will not produce output unless the price it receives covers its variable avoidable costs. Any price below the minimum average variable cost curve means the firm will shut down. When the price equals the minimum of the average total cost curve, then the firm is breaking even and earning zero profits. How profit is driven to zero depends on the structure of competition. Generally speaking profits are eliminated through a combination of changes in output prices and increases in costs. When we sum up the individual firm supply curves we obtain a market supply curve. This market supply curve is upward sloping, except in the very restrictive case where every single firm is identical in every way. Now that we understand how a market supply curve is generated, we have completed the neoclassical model. In the next chapter we will spend some time using this model to explain different types of behavior.

REVIEW QUESTIONS

1. Why would a firm stay open, even though it is making a loss? Have you ever seen a dumpy roadside motel which always has a vacancy sign outside, why wouldn't such a place shut down?

2. Why might a firm sell a product "below cost"? For example, a pizza restaurant might sell a first pizza at regular price, and sell a second one for $1. Or a fancy hotel might have "off season" rates at only a fraction of their regular rates. Or an airline might let you fly free if you have enough points.

3. How can a firm have zero profits in equilibrium?

4. What is rent? How is it different than profit?

5. Even though the marginal cost curve is not always upward sloping, and even though the supply curve is equal to the marginal cost curve, how is it that the supply curve is always upward sloping?

6. Are profits maximized when revenues equal cost?

7. "In equilibrium rent is the payment to the fixed factor of production." True, False, or Uncertain?

8. Oingo Boingo, in their song *Capitalism* emote there's nothing wrong with profit and wanting to live nice:
   I'm so tired of hearing you whine about the revolution
   Bringin' down the rich
   When was the last time you dug a ditch, baby!

   According to our model, is there anything wrong with making a profit? If a firm or person does make a profit, does that mean the wealth was taken from someone else? Do profits mean that prices are higher?

PROBLEMS

1. Answer the following questions about cost functions as True or False, and provide a graph in your explanation.

   a. The difference between AVC and ATC is the fixed cost.

   b. When AC is falling, MC is also falling.

   c. If workers become 10% more productive, then MC remains the same but AC falls.

   d. If for any given amount of labor output is higher by 10 units, then MC remains the same and AVC decreases.

   e. FC continuously fall with output.

2. Assume that a perfectly competitive firm has MC=AVC=$12, MC=ATC=$20, and MC=MR=$24. On the basis of this information, can we tell what level of output will the firm choose? Is the firm making a profit? Is the firm making a rent?

3. You own a cigar company in Cuba. You produce 999 boxes of cigars per year. Your average costs per box is $1.00. Jean Chretien offers you $5.00 to produce an extra box so that he can give it to his best friend George W. Bush. If you accept his offer your average costs per box will be $1.01. What should you do?

4. Which firms are hurt the most when a lump sum tax is put on an industry: those intra marginal firms earning a rent, or those marginal firms that earn no rent?

5. Suppose the following statement is true: "When Q is 300, MC is $75, ATC is $65, and AP of labor is 30." Under these conditions what is the level of labor hired, and is ATC rising or falling?

6. "The law of diminishing marginal product says that the more workers you hire, the less they produce at the margin. How can the twelfth worker hired be less productive than the third worker hired, even if they have the same skills?" Let's assume that the workers do have the same skills. What is wrong with the statement?

7. Why is it that "superstars" like hockey players and baseball players (and university professors!) are spread out evenly among teams? That is, it never seems to pay for a team to have all the best players, (or it never pays one university to have all the best academics). What is going on?

8. A price taking firm makes air conditioners. The market price of one of their new air conditioners

is \$120. Its total cost information is given in the following table:

Air Conditioners/day	Total Cost/day
1	100
2	150
3	220
4	310
5	405
6	510
7	650
8	800

How many air conditioners should the firm produce per day if its goal is to maximize profits?

9. Suppose that a firm had two plants, each with different marginal costs. Using a graph, show how you would construct the marginal cost curve for the firm as a whole. Draw in a price for the output, and show on your graph how much output would be produced at each plant. What is true about the marginal costs at each plant in equilibrium?

10. Complete the following table (fractions are ok).

Q	FC	VC	AVC	TC	MC	AC
20			100	6000		
30						
					250	
40						300

11. Farmers have long recognized that "bumper crops" are not always a great thing in terms of their revenues.

    a. In terms of the elasticity of demand, why would this be so?

    b. Would it ever be in the interests of a single farmer to reduce his output in an effort to raise price?

    c. In point form, list three problems farmers would face if they tried as a group to restrict output.

12. The government decides to tax all firms by \$1000. This is a one time lump sum tax. What exactly will happen to a) the Marginal Cost of each firm? b) the Average Cost of each firm? c) The Average Variable Cost of each firm? d) the Average Fixed Cost of each firm?

13. A firm that faces a unit elastic demand curve, has constant marginal costs, and zero fixed costs would want to produce how much? (Assume the firm could only produce in discrete units).

14. Complete the following table:

Qs	FC	VC	AVC	TC	MC	AC
					250	
10			100	2500		
20						
					145	
30						195
40		5500				
50		6500				
60		7500				
70		8650				
80		10100				
90		12000				
100		14500				

15. A bumper sticker reads: "People not profits: Smash Capitalism" Comment.

16. If there is one peanut seller in the park, is he a price taker?

17. "Mr. Black, the grocer, buys his bread at 15¢. What price should he charge in order to make a profit of 50%?" Why is this good arithmetic, but bad economics?

18. What is the difference between a profit and a rent? If a firm is interested in maximizing profits, why would it stay in an industry if profits are zero?

19. Suppose an industry is perfectly competitive, with an extremely large number of identical firms. Each firm has a U-shaped average cost curve which has a minimum at 10 units of output. There are no sunk costs. The value of average costs at this minimum is $6.

    a. If the market demand curve is given by $P = 1000 - .2Q$, how many firms will there be in the industry?

    b. What is the total market consumer's surplus?

c. What are the total market rents to the firms?

20. "It is possible that a firm may have falling average total costs for every level of output, but still have a constant (flat) marginal cost." True, False, or Uncertain?

21. A purely mechanical question. If the marginal cost of a single firm is given by $MC = 2q + 1$, find the horizontal summation (or the supply curve) if there are ten firms.

22. In 1995 Pierre Omidyar created the consumer-to-consumer trading company "eBay." As everyone knows, eBay allows buyers and sellers from around the world to meet in an electronic market place and make trades. Search engines, ratings of trading histories, and various other eBay details make trading very inexpensive. On a supply and demand graph for, let's say old Elvis albums, show what happens to the volume of trade, the prices to consumers and suppliers, the deadweight losses, and the costs of trading, when eBay gets introduced to the market. Explain the graph you draw.

23. Wal-Mart is a giant among retail outlets and accounts for major fractions of toy, grocery, and clothing sales in the United States and Canada. Wal-Mart's success is partly due to increases in productivity through many innovations in their operation. The result has been a fall in local retail prices between 5-8 percent when a Wal-Mart moves in.

    a. In a graph draw a production function for an average retail outlet (call it K-Mart) and one for Wal-Mart. Assume it has the three stage shape laid out in Figure 8-2. Make sure you label everything carefully.

    b. Now on another graph draw the Marginal and Average Total Cost curves for K-Mart and Wal-Mart.

    c. Briefly, what happens to the marginal product of labor at Wal-Mart compared to K-Mart?

    d. When Wal-Mart moves into a community, there is often very little change in wages for store clerks. Given your answer to (c), what would explain the relatively constant wages for store clerks?

Review Question Answers

1. *Because it would be minimizing its losses. If a firm has sunk costs, the shut down point is below the zero profit point. Hence the firm would lose the sunk investment if it shuts down, but at least covers part of it staying open. Dumpy motels stay open because the few patrons they get cover their marginal cost. Eventually, as the place literally falls apart, the motel is not replaced and the firm shuts down.*

2. *Because it is covering its marginal costs and perhaps some of its sunk costs. The marginal cost of a pizza probably is close to £1, especially if the ingredients have been prepared and cannot be stored. Off season rates cover the marginal costs of the hotel, not the fixed/sunk costs. The marginal cost of a plane seat that would have gone empty is zero.*

3. *It has zero economic profits. The key to remember is the average cost function includes all costs, including the opportunity costs of the entrepreneur, the cost of risk, etc. Economic profit is not the same as accounting net income.*

4. *Rent is revenue minus opportunity costs. Profit is Revenue minus all costs.*

5. *The supply curve equals only the upward sloping part of the marginal cost curve above the minimum average variable cost curve.*

6. *No, when marginal revenues equal marginal cost.*

7. *True. In equilibrium the rent is equal to the sunk costs, which is the payment to the fixed factor.*

8. *There is nothing wrong with profits according to our model. Profits are merely the difference between revenues and costs. Raising revenues or lowering costs are both good things. Profits arise from the creation of wealth, so they do not accrue at the expense of others. Firms persue profits by offering their customers a good deal. This means the existence of profits tend to lower prices.*

Odd Numbered Problem Answers

1.

a. *False. The difference is the* **average** *fixed cost. This follows from* $ATC = AVC + AFC$.

b. *False. See the graph. In the dark segment of the MC curve, between* Q_1 *and* Q_2*, the MC curve is rising while the AC is falling.*

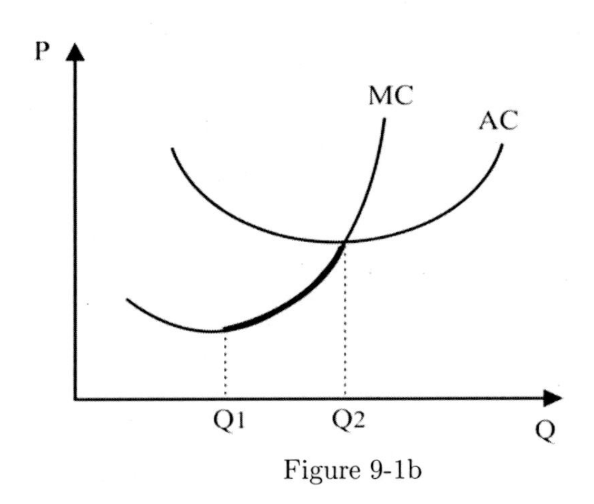

Figure 9-1b

c. *False. A 10% increase in productivity will change the worker's MP, which will change the MC curve and the AC curve.*

d. *True. The marginal product doesn't change, therefore the MC remains the same. However, the average product increases, so the AVC curve must fall.*

e. *False. The AFC continuously falls with output.*

3. *By producing the extra box total costs increase by \$11. Since this is greater than \$5 you should turn the deal down ... if there are no consequences from turning a Prime Minister down!*

5. *Since AP=Q/L, there are 10 units of labor hired. Since the MC¿ATC the ATC must be rising.*

7. *The marginal contribution of superstars falls the more a team has. This means the first superstar on a team is worth more than the tenth superstar. As a result, a team with few superstars will be willing to bid away the tenth superstar on another team. In the process there is an equalization. The distribution won't be exactly equal because teams differ from city to city.*

9.

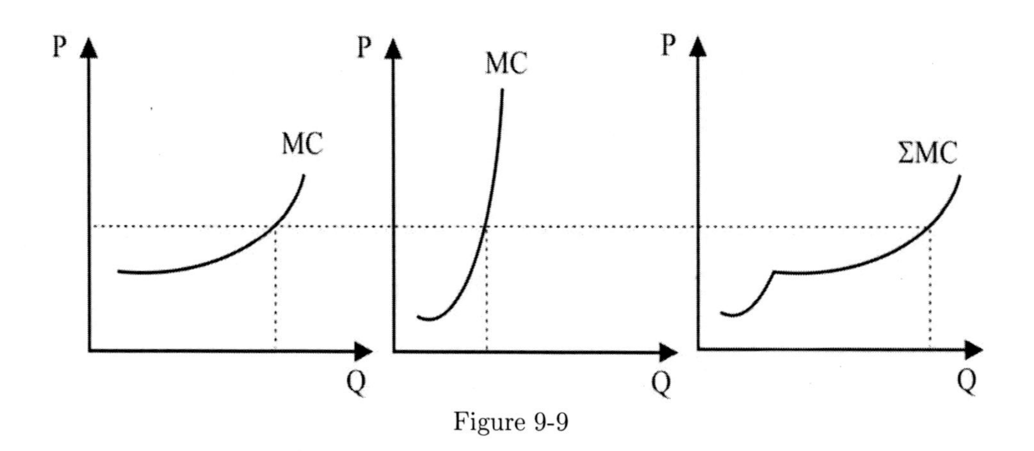

Figure 9-9

The MC curve for the firm is simply the horizontal summation of the individual firm MC curves. The MC cost of each plant will be set the same.

11.

a. *If the elasticity of demand is low, then a bumper crop leads to a great fall in price and a fall in revenue.*

b. *No, because the farmer is just a price taker and has no impact on the price.*

c. *They would face cheating problems within the group, as individual farmers tried to produce more. They would face competition from entry as new farmers produced the crop. And they would face the second law of demand as consumers found better substitutes for the product.*

13. *The firm would produce 1 unit. Producing anymore increases costs without increasing revenues.*

15. *Profits accrue to people and people own capital, so the sticker is slightly inconsistent.*

17. *Mr. Black is a price taker. He takes his price as given.*

19.

a. *The market supply curve is flat at 6 dollars because every firm is identical. Hence to find the total amount produced we just equate the supply and demand curve:* $6 = 1000 - .2Q$. *Thus Q equals 4970 units. Since each firm produces 10 units, there must be 497 firms.*

b. *Total market consumer's surplus is the area under the demand curve above 6 dollars. This is given by (994 times 4970)/2* = *\$2,470,090.*

c. *None of the firms earn any rents.*

21. *The supply curve equation would be* $MC = q/5 + 1$.

23.

a.

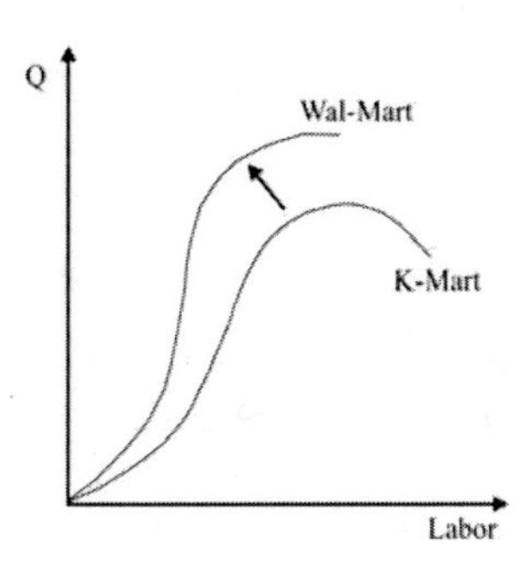

b.

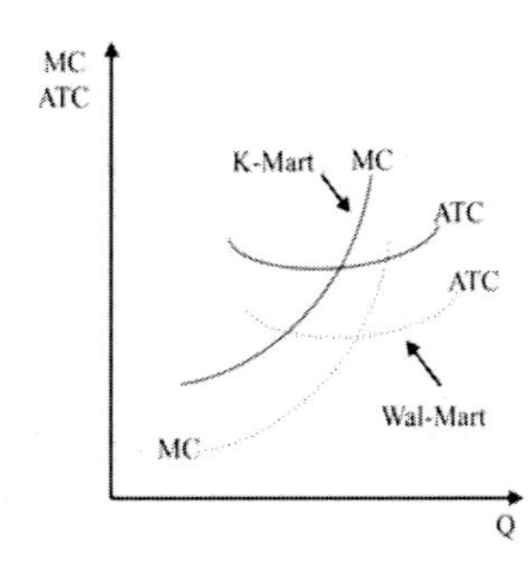

c. *The increased productivity translate into a higher marginal productivity for the workers at Wal-Mart.*

d. *The elasticity of supply for Wal-Mart clerks is very elastic. Hence an increase in the demand for clerks is met with a large increase in employment, but very little change in the wage.*

CHAPTER 10

APPLICATIONS OF THE NEOCLASSICAL MODEL

10.1 Market Equilibrium

We've come along way in just a few short chapters, and it's time to put everything together. We started off with the first principle of economics — maximization. Maximization is what motivates everyone in an economic model. For consumers the principle means they choose bundles of goods in order to maximize their utility. We saw this was equivalent to maximizing their consumer's surplus: the difference between what they would have been willing to pay and what they had to pay. Graphically, the consumer's surplus is the difference between the height of their demand curve and the price they faced. Firms maximized their profits, and this amounted to maximizing their producer surplus, which equaled the difference between their revenues and costs. Graphically, this difference was the area above the supply curve and below the price they faced.

This equilibrium is summarized in Figure 10-1. Maximization for consumers meant they equated their marginal values to the price of the good. Maximization for firms meant they equated their marginal costs to the price of the good. Hence, since firms and consumers face the same price, it must be true that in equilibrium the marginal value of consumers equals the marginal costs of firms. This means that in equilibrium the market demand curve intersects the market supply curve. It is clear from Figure 10-1 that this equilibrium maximizes the gains from trade: the sum of consumer's and producer's surplus.

In equilibrium, MV=MC.

We also know what shifts each of these curves. Any change in the price of other consumer goods, changes in consumer incomes, or changes in tastes will shift the market demand curve and leave the supply curve unchanged. Any changes in input prices, or changes in technology will shift the supply curve and leave the demand curve unchanged. When one of these curves changes there is a movement to a new equilibrium. Our model assumes this movement is instantaneous. Hence there are no dynamic movements in prices — the market moves immediately from one equilibrium to another.

This chapter is intended to pause and consider the equilibrium neoclassical model we have developed thus far. What makes this model so general is its ability to apply to almost anything. In building the model we put virtually no restrictions on the nature of the quantity produced and traded. All that is required is for it to be something people value. As a result, people not only have demands for soap, cars, and dishwashers, they also demand valuable non-market goods as well, like friendship, spouses, and children, or churches, blood, and clean air. Likewise, in developing the concept of price, our only restriction was in terms of willingness to sacrifice. We often use a

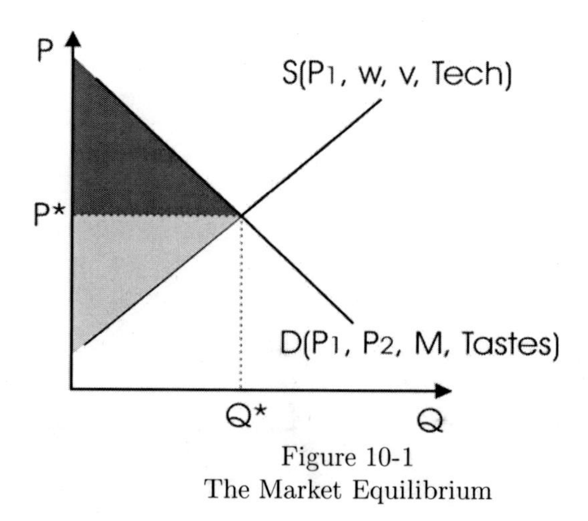

Figure 10-1
The Market Equilibrium

dollar price simply for convenience, but our model assumes that the "price" is the amount of other valuable things forgone. Hence our model can analyze markets for all types of things in life, even when formal markets do not exist.

10.2 Shifts in Supply and Demand

Let's consider what happens to equilibrium price and quantity when market demand and market supply shift. As mentioned, the market demand function for a good can shift for a number of reasons. Tastes may change, causing a shift in market demand. For example, in the 1980s, there was apparently no demand for "grunge" clothing, the "stair-master" exercise machines, or the student back packs that became popular in the 1990s. So, too, the price of either a substitute or a complement for the good may change, causing the market demand for that good to shift accordingly. If the price of a substitute for good 1 goes up, then the market demand function for good 1 will shift upward and to the right. For example, if coffee becomes more expensive, the demand for tea will shift upward and to the right. If the price of a complement goes up, the opposite will occur. For example, if a ski-lift ticket becomes more expensive, the demand for ski-equipment rentals will shift down and to the left.

Suppose for some reason the demand function for good 1 does shift up and to the right. Then both the equilibrium price and quantity will increase. This can be seen in panel (iii) of figure 10-2, where the initial equilibrium is point A and the new equilibrium is point B. If, for some reason the demand function for good 1 shifts to the left, as in panel (iv) of figure 10-2, then the equilibrium price and quantity both fall.

Let us turn now to changes in market supply. Again, a number of factors can cause a shift in the market supply function. Technological change — the development of more efficient production processes, for example — can cause shifts in market supply functions. So can changes in the prices of inputs. If the price of a variable input goes up then the market supply functions will shift upward and to the left. For instance, the dramatic increases in the price of crude oil in the 1970s caused a shift in the supply functions for a whole range of plastic products, including plastic cups, because crude

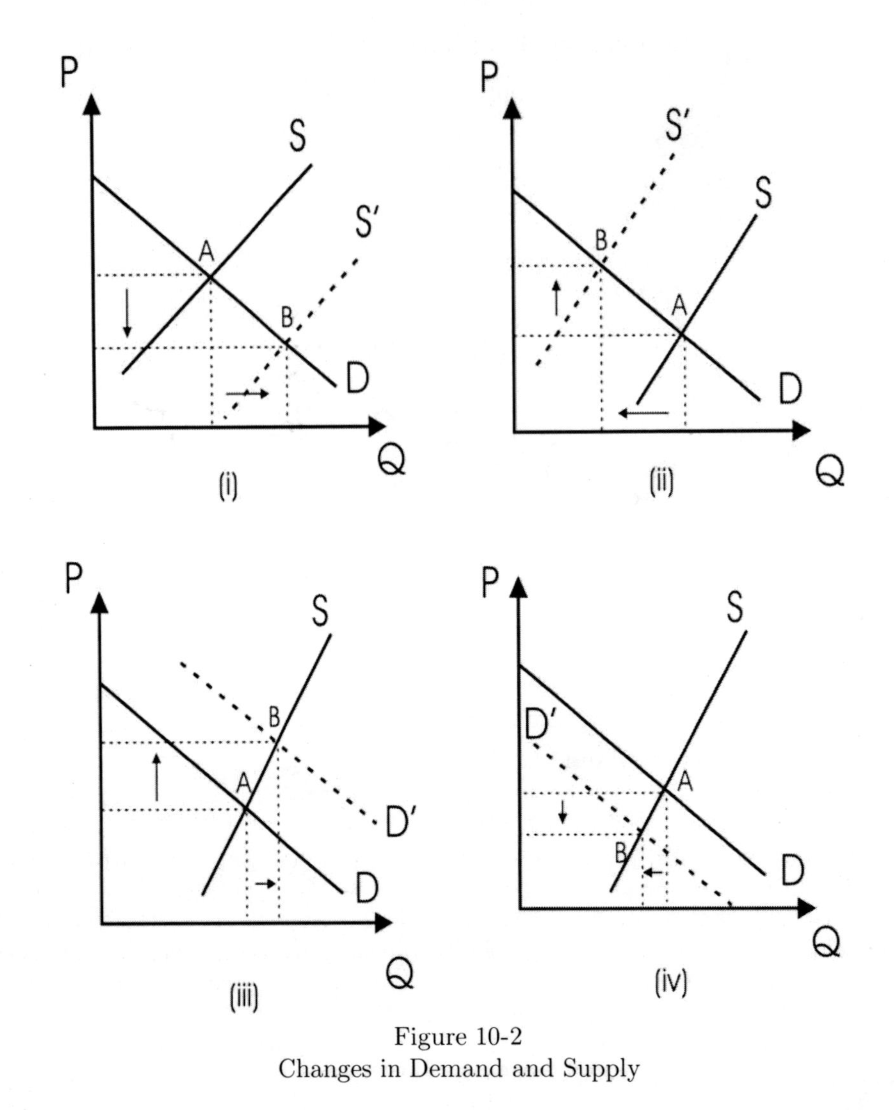

Figure 10-2
Changes in Demand and Supply

oil is an essential input in the production of many plastics. Suppose, then, that the market supply function does shift up and to the left, as in panel (ii) of figure 10-2. Given the downward sloping market demand curve the equilibrium price will increase and equilibrium quantity will decrease. If the supply curve had shifted to the right as in panel (i) of figure 10-2, then the equilibrium price would have fallen and the equilibrium quantity would have increased.

Increases in demand lead to movements along the supply curve, an increased equilibrium price, and an increased equilibrium quantity.

Increases in supply lead to movements along the demand curve, an increased equilibrium quantity, but a decreased equilibrium price.

We saw this basic movement in prices in Chapter 6 when the supply curve was vertical and no production took place. These movements in prices and quantities in response to changes in market demand and market supply result from maximization and the competitive allocation of resources. An equilibrium occurs where "supply equals demand" because at that quantity all consumers have equal marginal values (and therefore have no incentive to trade), and all firms have equal marginal costs (and therefore have no incentive to shift production).

It is easy to draw these curves and to shift them around. The hard part is to see how they manifest in the world around us. Have you ever been to Europe and noticed the differences in house construction? Homes in Europe are mostly made of stone, concrete, and bricks. Most notably, they tend not to use a wood frame construction. In North America a stone home is rare, and most homes are made of dimensional lumber covered with plaster board. This reflects the relative prices of building materials. In North America we have vast supplies of softwood timber, while in Europe this is not the case. The increase in supply here lowers the price of wood, and as a result we use wood for applications that are not used elsewhere. Over time the price of wood in North America has been increasing, caused by increases in both domestic and foreign demand for wood, and by reduced supplies of timber. As a result, we use wood for fewer applications now than in the past. Wood used to be a common fuel for heating homes, but this is no longer the case. As hard as it is to believe, white oak was used for railway ties in the 19th century, and these ties are now made of cheaper wood or concrete.

When demand and supply curves shift they cause the above changes in prices and quantities. The actual size of these changes depends on the elasticities of demand and supply. The more inelastic the demand and supply curves, the more the price changes relative to the quantity. The opposite is true when the curves are more elastic. For example, in the winter of 1998 Quebec suffered a disastrous ice storm that knocked out power lines and electricity for weeks. Two years earlier in 1996, hurricane Fran hit North Carolina and caused a similar amount of destruction. Generally speaking there is much less inter-provincial trade in Canada than inter-state trade in the U.S. This is due to poorer trade routes in Canada and to government restrictions on trade between provinces. This essentially makes the supply of repair goods and services more elastic in North Carolina than in Quebec. These differences are shown in Figure 10-3. Predictably, there were huge changes in prices for generators and repair parts in Quebec and virtually no changes in prices in North Carolina. Corresponding to this, there were large changes in the volume of repair goods sent to North Carolina (new reports showed freeways congested with tractor trailer units heading to major centers), while in Quebec CBC Radio was hosting shows across the country for donated goods!

Prices are Determined by Supply and Demand

One of the most profound things you can learn from the simple demand and supply model we've developed is that prices and quantities are *determined* by the intersection of supply and demand curves. Prices don't fall from space, they aren't determined by costs alone, they come from the competitive interaction of consumers and producers.

A lot of very smart people just never get this point. For example, in 1972 a group of social and physical scientists published a book called *The Limits to Growth.* It was a volume produced by a group of academics who had gathered at a conference in Rome. Later this group became known as "The Club of Rome". The book sold over 9 million copies in almost 30 different languages. The book had, and continues to have, a tremendous impact on the way many people think about the future and natural resources, even though it contains a flawed analysis of the way markets work.

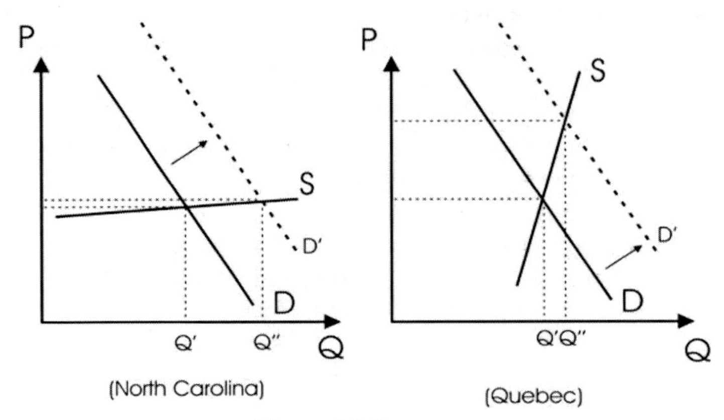

Figure 10-3
Different Elasticities Lead to Different Outcomes

The book *The Limits to Growth* made many bold predictions. Tin and silver were to be completely exhausted by the mid 1980s, other precious metals were to be depleted by the 1990s, and population and pollution were to grow unchecked — eventually terminating life as we know it. The basic reason for these calamities was that our industrialized world uses up resources that are presumably fixed, and so eventually we must run out.

Although this line of reasoning has been going on since the time of Malthus in the 19th century, it continues to go on today. In 1980 U.S. president Jimmy Carter commissioned the Global 2000 report which predicted "barring revolutionary advances in technology, life for most people on earth will be more precarious in 2000 than it is now." An article by Robert Kaplan in the February 2002 Atlantic monthly called "The Coming Anarchy" has been causing a stir in government circles by again making grim forecasts on the future.

As we saw in Chapter 6 the catastrophic predictions of the Club of Rome never came true because prices and quantities are endogenously determined in the competitive model. When the demand for a resource like tin increases, there is a movement along the supply of tin, and the quantity of tin demanded and supplied both increase. At the new equilibrium, supply still equals demand. Had the price not increased, more tin would have been demanded and less would have been supplied, and there would have been a shortage. However, the rise in the price acts to equilibrate the quantity demanded and supplied.

When people write books like the *Limits to Growth*, or *The Population Bomb* by Paul Ehrlich, about the coming shortages of our limited planet, they make several fundamental mistakes. The first, as just mentioned, is to ignore the role of the price mechanism in directing consumption and production. The second, is to ignore long run impacts. Over time, demand curves tend to become more elastic, given the second law of demand. The increased elasticity is a result of improved knowledge of substitutes. When the price of commodities increase because of reduced supplies these high prices induce individuals to begin exploring new substitutes. This mitigates the initial price increase, and in essence reduces the scarcity problem. In addition, there are long run effects on the supply side as well. At high prices firms seek new methods of production and new sources of inputs. In the 19th century the great social scientist Stanley Jevons predicted that England's growth would soon terminate because the reserves of coal would soon be exhausted. As the price of coal increased, however, new reserves were found, better extraction and transportation methods were developed, and eventually oil replaced most uses of coal. This process of innovation tends to increase the elasticity of supply over time, which tends to mitigate the initial rise in price.

Human history provides one example after another of exogenous shocks resulting in high prices, followed by the development of new substitutes, new methods of production, and new sources of supply. In spite of growing world populations, output in goods and services have easily grown faster. Mortality is down, life expectancy, literacy and consumption is up. We don't live in paradise, but the world is healthier, safer, and wealthier than it was 20 years ago. Necessity may be the mother of invention, but it is the equilibrating movement of prices that signals to individuals to move into action. Our equilibrium model suggests we should be optimistic about the future of the planet, not doomsayers.

Futures Markets

Movements in prices not only save us from the disasters resulting from over exploitation of resources, prices act as social coordinators for all types of goods, most of which we never give a second thought to. In the Pacific Northwest area of North America (Washington, Oregon, British Columbia) a major agricultural product is apples. When the harvest is done in late summer some of the apples get shipped to markets around the world for immediate consumption, but many are put into storage for consumption over the coming year until the next harvest. How do people decide how many apples to put into storage? Who bears the consequences if too many are put into storage, or not enough? One thing is clear: in any fruit market in North America one can eat apples all year long, and though the price fluctuates over the seasons, the change in price is quite minimal given that apples are only harvested once a year.

Apple growers don't store apples over the winter. Nor does McDonalds store apples for their apple pies. Apples are stored by thousands of people through commodity markets. Why would someone store an apple? At harvest time the price of apples falls because the supply of apples is large. In the winter, when the supply of apples has fallen the price is expected to increase. *Speculators*, in anticipation of the higher price in the winter time, purchase apples in the fall and store them for resale later in the year. They do this by simply calling a broker who arranges the storing space, insurance, etc. They do it because they hope to make a profit in the apple commodity market.

Apple speculators decide on their own when they want to sell their apples. Their decision depends on the price apples are selling today (called the spot price) and the price they expect to get in the future. If the demand for apples increases today, then the spot price of apples increases. This reduces the incentive for speculators to hold apples, and they sell more today. If the expected future price of apples increases, then speculators hold on to their apples, and save them until they are more valuable to consumers ... and themselves. But how does the speculator know what the future price will be? It turns out there is a market for apples that approximates the future price: *the futures market.* A futures market is where people agree on contracts *today* to deliver a certain quantity at a given price, in the *future.* This future price is today's best guess at what the price will be in the future. As new information is learned, the futures price changes.

You can look up futures prices in the financial section of almost any newspaper. It will tell you the spot price today and the futures price for various times in the future. If the harvest takes place in September, the futures price will increase over the year until the next harvest. This increase in price over the year is sufficient to cover, on average, the cost of storage, insurance, and interest costs of investment in holding the apples over the time period. Anyone who thinks the futures prices are wrong, and buys or sells futures, stands to make a fortune if correct ... or lose if incorrect. Suppose apples are currently selling for $6 a bushel at harvest, but the May futures price is $6.75. If you believe that the May price will actually be $7 (because you think over the next year someone is finally going to prove an apple a day keeps the Dr. away) then you should buy now a May futures contract for say 10,000 bushels. These apples will be delivered and paid for by you next May. In the meantime, you wait. If the May spot price turns out to be $9, then you get to buy your 10,000 bushels at $6.75 and sell them at $9, making a smooth $22,500 profit. If, on the other hand, the price falls to $6 a bushel, they you have to pay the $6.75 and sell at $6, losing $7500.

If you're not the only one who thinks the price next May will be higher than the current $6.75, then others will join you in bidding for May futures. This increase in demand will raise the price of May futures. At this higher price it is more profitable to store apples, and so more are taken out of the spot market and put into storage. In this way the futures market allocates goods from the spot market to the future. The result is quite amazing. Thousands and thousands of people are involved in futures markets, no one tells them what to do. The result is I end up eating apples in December at a cost that basically reflects the cost of storing an apple from September to December. Those speculators who are good at their job make lots of money, and consumers are rewarded with goods available at the right time. Those speculators who are bad at their job end up misallocating apples throughout the year, and they are punished by losses. Markets are social coordinators because the prices allocate goods in a decentralized fashion.

10.3 Trade One More Time

Before we move on to different types of applications, we should look at trade one more time. In Chapter 3 we saw that when individuals have different marginal values, they gained from trade. In Chapter 6 we saw this trade took place until the marginal value of the traders was equalized. In Chapter 7 we saw that when individuals or firms had different marginal costs, they could also gain from trade and that trade would take place until the marginal costs were equal across individuals or firms. Now, with our equilibrium supply and demand model we can put it all together.

Suppose Tom and Gary are two cattle farmers who, though living next to each other, do not trade. Both Tom and Gary produce and consume pigs, and their demand and marginal cost curves are shown in Figure 10-4.

Since both Tom and Gary essentially eat what they produce, they are simultaneously consumers and producers. Their surpluses are shown as the grey shaded areas. Tom produces and consumes 10 pigs, while Gary produces and consumes 11. It is clear from the graph that each produces pigs until their marginal value equals their marginal costs. In other words, both farmers are behaving efficiently. On the other hand, it is also obvious that the marginal values and costs across the two farmers are not equal, which means they can both gain from trading with each other. Suppose a market develops for these two. The market supply would simply be the summation of the individual marginal cost curves, and the market demand curve would be the summation of the individual demand curves. Both farmers can buy and sell as many pigs as they would like at the market price. The equilibrium outcome is shown in Figure 10-5.

The market equilibrium shown on the far right graph produces an equilibrium price of P^*. Gary, who is the low cost producer of pigs, increases his production to 20 pigs until his marginal cost equals this price. Gary does not consume all of these pigs, however, since he only demands 9

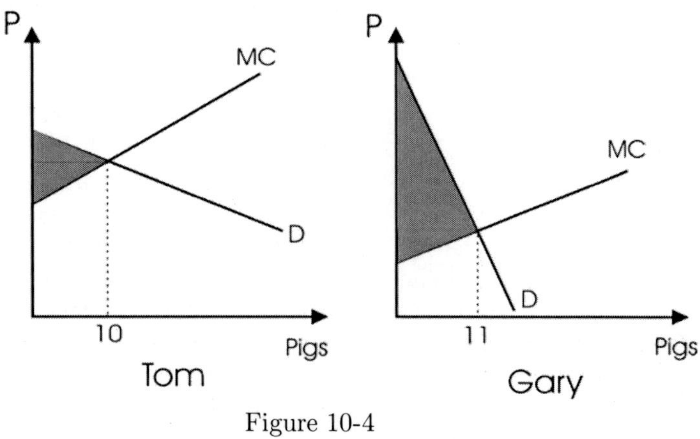

Figure 10-4
No Trade for Tom and Gary

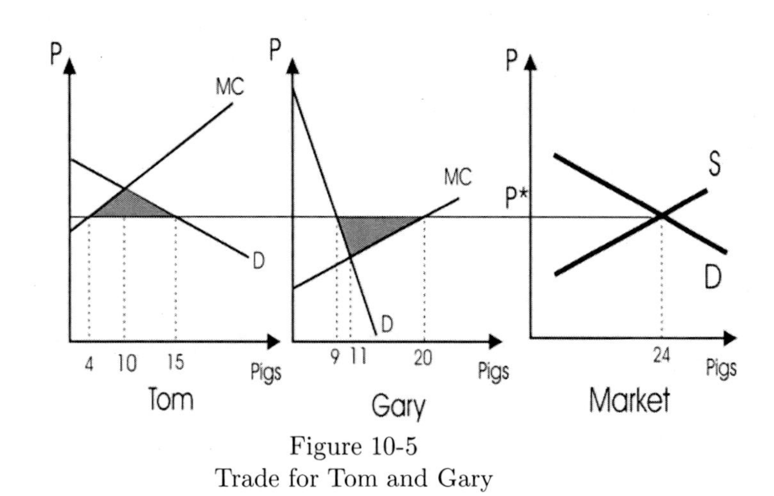

Figure 10-5
Trade for Tom and Gary

pigs at this higher price. The 11 extra pigs get traded to Tom. When Tom sees the new price P^* he wants to increase his consumption of pigs because the price is lower than his marginal value. He increases consumption to 15 pigs, but cuts down his production to only 4 pigs. The extra 11 he consumes come from Gary. The *net* gains from trade are shown as the shaded areas in figure 10-5. Tom is better off as a consumer of pigs, while Gary is better off as a seller. Notice now that once again the marginal values and marginal costs of each individual are equal. However, now also notice that the marginal costs of Gary are equal to the marginal costs of Tom, and their marginal values are equal as well. In other words, the trade is efficient and the gains from trade are maximized.

A market allocates goods such that the low cost producers (at the margin) produce the goods, and the high valued users (at the margin) consume the goods. The remarkable thing about this allocation is that each person acts independently of the other and only requires knowledge of the price to make decisions.

10.4 Taxes

In Chapter 9 we analyzed the different effects a lump sum and a per unit tax had on a firm's cost curves. Now we want to analyze the effects of these taxes in the context of our supply and demand model. We will see that our model provides a result that is almost counter-intuitive, and goes against what our common sense might first suggest. For example, we might think that in terms of tax revenue, it does not matter what goods get taxed. After all, if the government is faced with two goods to tax, each with a current volume of trade of 10,000 units, then a $1 tax per unit placed on either good should raise $10,000 in revenue. However, this is not the case. We might also think that if the government puts a tax of $1 per unit on a good that the price of the good must rise by $1, but this is not the case either! Finally, we might think that it matters a great deal whether or not the consumer is taxed at the point of consumption or the firm is taxed at the point of production. Yet again, our model suggests otherwise.

Let us begin by considering only the effect of a $1 per unit tax on a group of firms in a particular industry. Recall that a per unit tax means that for every unit of output produced, the cost of production is increased by the amount of the tax. Hence the marginal costs of production increase by the amount of the tax, in this case by $1. If every firm in the industry is taxed by the same amount, then the market supply curve must also shift up by the amount of the tax.

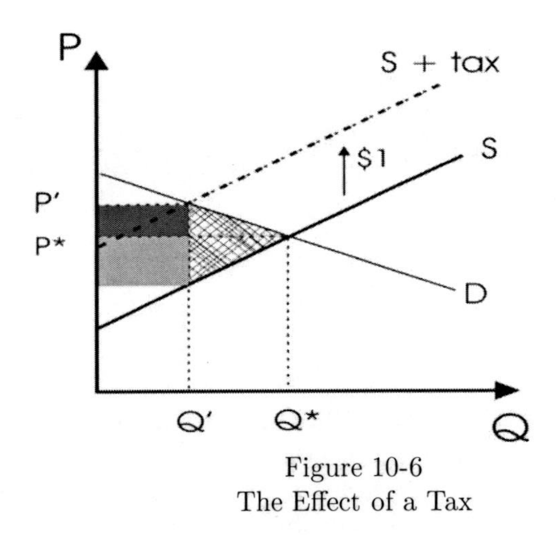

Figure 10-6
The Effect of a Tax

Figure 10-6 shows the effect of an imposition of a $1 per unit tax placed on all firms. Before the tax, the equilibrium price and quantity are P^*, Q^*. Since the tax shifts the supply curve up by $1, the new equilibrium price and quantity are P', Q'. Several things are immediately apparent from Figure 10-6. First, it is clear that as long as the demand curve is not perfectly inelastic, then the price will not increase by the full amount of the tax. In this case, though the tax increased marginal costs by $1, the price clearly goes up by less than this amount. As firms raise the price, consumers substitute out of the good being taxed and into goods that have become relatively cheaper. This substitution hinders the ability of firms to pass the tax on to consumers, and as a result, prices rise but by less than the amount of the tax.

> *A \$1 tax per unit raises price by less than \$1 as long as the demand curve is not perfectly inelastic.*

A second feature of the graph in figure 10-6 is that since price does not rise by the full amount of the tax, the consumer does not pay all of the tax revenue. The relative tax burdens are shown by the shaded regions. Consumers pay an amount of taxes equal to the dark shaded area. The area is defined by the increase in price they face $(P' - P^*)$ multiplied by the amount of the good they purchase, Q'. On the other hand, firms do not receive the price P', but rather receive $(P' - 1)$. Therefore the amount of the tax that the firms pay is given by $[p^* - (P' - 1)]Q'$, which is equal to the light shaded area.

A third feature of the graph is that the level of output traded has been reduced from Q^* to Q'. This fall in the amount of trade causes a "deadweight loss" to result. The concept of a deadweight loss is used by economists to denote a loss of wealth, or an inefficiency. A deadweight loss is wealth that should exist (because marginal values are greater than marginal costs) but does not exist for some reason, in this case because of taxes. The total deadweight loss in this case is the lost consumer's and producer's surplus caused by the reduced output, and is given by the crosshatched triangle. This should be considered a cost of taxation.

> *A per unit tax increases the equilibrium price by less than the amount of the tax, and creates a deadweight loss.*

The effect of a per unit tax on the amount of tax collected and on the incidence of who pays the tax, depends critically on the elasticity of demand. Figure 10-7 shows two markets which have an identical per unit tax placed on the firms. In panel (A) we see that the demand curve is very inelastic. This good has very few substitutes and as a result, the bulk of the tax is passed on to the consumer in the form of a higher price. If the demand curve were perfectly inelastic, then the entire tax would have been passed on. Notice that in the case of panel (A), there is also very little reduction in the amount of the good that is traded. As a result there is only a trivial deadweight loss, and the amount of tax revenue is almost equal to the original traded volume times the amount of the tax.

On the other hand, panel (B) shows a much different situation. Here the demand for the good is highly elastic. There are many substitutes for this good, and as a result consumers are quick to substitute into other goods when the price increases. This means consumers pay very little of the tax. In addition, when the demand curve is relatively elastic, there is a relatively large reduction in the volume of trade, and therefore, a relatively large deadweight cost from the tax — shown again as the crosshatched area.

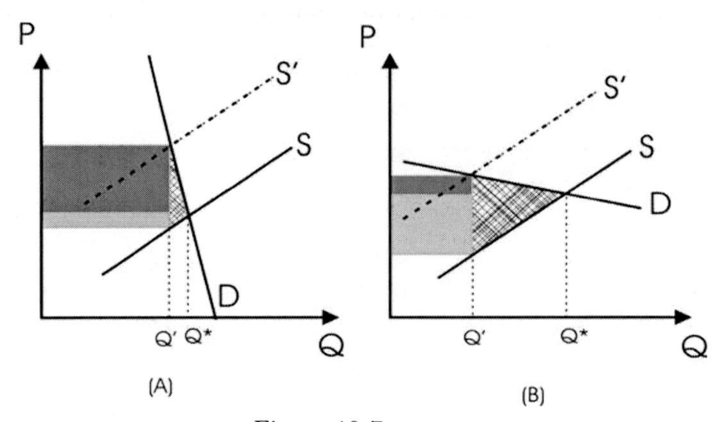

Figure 10-7
Taxes With Different Elasticities of Demand

The deadweight loss is created because output is being reduced. If you'll recall our discussion of firms and market supply curves you'll remember that output changes along the supply curve because firms change how much they produce, and because firms enter and leave the market. When a tax is put on, the marginal firms will leave the industry as a way of avoiding the tax. If the demand curve were extremely elastic, a per unit tax might have the effect of every firm leaving the industry. This sounds incredible, but it essentially means that if consumers have a perfect substitute for a good, then that good cannot be taxed without the firms ceasing production. For example, there are no gas stations on the Canadian side of the border with the United States. The differences in taxes between the two countries, along with the fact that American gasoline is identical to Canadian gasoline in the eyes of consumers, means that no one would buy gasoline from the Canadian station.

Differences in elasticities of demand can explain a great deal of tax policy. Governments look for goods with low elasticities of demand to tax, because if consumers and/or producers can avoid the tax, then tax revenues obviously fall. This explains why consumers firmly believe that if a good gets taxed, they're likely to pay. Historically, one of the most commonly taxed goods was salt. Not surprisingly, throughout the centuries, salt had a very low elasticity of demand, and before refrigeration, was used for more important things than flavoring food. In modern times it is fashionable to tax gasoline, alcohol, and tobacco. All of these goods have relatively low elasticities of demand. What we never see is the taxation of a particular brand of gasoline, beer, or cigarette. If the government suddenly decided that it wanted to tax Bud Light Beer, it would quickly find itself with zero revenue. Not only would consumers switch immediately to other light beers, but Budwiser would cease to produce that particular brand as well.

> *Who pays the tax depends on the elasticity of demand. Lower elasticities lead to consumers paying a larger fraction.*

When we say "producers" pay part of the tax, we need to remember production invovles all types of inputs. Consider a tax on cars. Cars are produced in factories along an assembly line, with parts produced elsewhere, made from raw inputs obtained from other firms. Once cars are produced they are shipped, and then sold by retail outlets. Which one of the hundreds of thousands of producers actually ends up paying for a tax on cars? Any inputs that can move to other industries without facing any costs of moving, would do so in order to avoid paying any of the tax. Moving inputs, however, is not costless, and some inputs will find it better to pay the tax than move elsewhere. Those inputs specialized to producing cars will pay for more of the tax than inputs not so specialized. As we've mentioned, these differences in producers is summarized by the upward slope of the supply curve. The more elastic the supply curve, the better options the inputs have in other industries, and the less tax they will bear. An industry with a fixed supply curve is one where the inputs cannot escape, and hence they will bear the entire tax. An industry with a perfectly elastic supply curve is one where the inputs have equal opportunities elsewhere and consumers will bear all of the tax.

> *Who pays the tax depends on the elasticity of supply. Lower elasticities lead to producers paying a larger fraction.*

Taxing Consumers

We have been examining taxes in the context of a tax on the firms at the point of production. An alternative form of taxation would be a sales tax placed on the consumer. One question we might ask is: would a tax of $1 per unit placed on the consumer lead to a different equilibrium price and quantity than what we just observed with producers? The answer, quite surprisingly, is no!

Consider Figure 10-8 which shows the effect of a sales tax on the demand curve. The demand curve tells us the maximum consumers are willing to pay for the good. When a tax is put on, consumers are still only willing to pay at most the height of their demand curve. As a result, the demand curve that the *firm perceives* shifts down by an amount equal to the tax. For example, if a consumer is willing to pay $10 for the first unit and the tax is $1, then the most that the firm can receive is $9. Hence, a sales tax has the result of lowering the demand for the good by the amount of the tax.

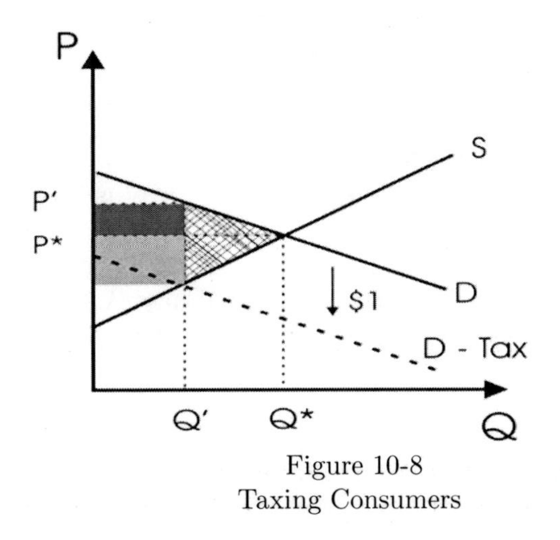

Figure 10-8
Taxing Consumers

As with the case of the producers, however, the price received by the firm does not fall by the amount of the tax. Rather, as is shown in Figure 10-8, the price to the consumer rises to P, and the price to the firm falls to $(P - 1)$. The difference between the two prices is the amount of the tax. Since the demand curve falls by the amount of a tax when consumers are taxed directly, and the supply curve shifts up by the amount of a tax when firms are taxed directly, the impact on price and quantity is identical. In other words, it does not matter if consumers are taxed or producers are, the outcome is the same. Not only this, but the incidence of who pays the tax is also the same, with the relative shares of tax burden again depending of the elasticities of demand and supply.

One of the general lessons of the analysis of taxation is that changes in costs are not fully borne by the firm or the consumer in general. These changes in costs, however, need not just result from taxes. When an industry experiences an increase in shoplifting, due to a change in the nature of the product for example, this raises the costs to the firms in that industry and some of those costs will be passed on to consumers. Workers may demand firms be forced to offer employees medical and dental coverage, but again this will partially be offset by slightly lower wages. How much consumers and workers pay depends on the elasticities involved, but the bottom line is there's no free lunch.

10.5 **Quotas in Agriculture**

A great number of agricultural policies can be analyzed with our simple supply and demand model. For example, farmers have been very successful in lobbying governments to establish farm programs. In Canada only about 4% of the population live on farms, yet in 1986 about 8 billion dollars were transferred from governments to farmers. These transfers accounted for almost 43% of agricultural income. One question that comes to mind is, do these farm income policies simply amount to transfers of wealth from non-farmers to farmers, or are there economic losses that result from them?

One type of agricultural policy is the farm quota. A government issued quota is essentially a license for a particular farmer to grow a specified amount of some crop or animal. Quotas are common for turkey, chicken, egg, and milk production. Most of the quotas in Canada were introduced during the 1970s. Figure 10-9 shows the effect of a quota on the turkey market. Prior to the quota a price of P^* existed. At this price, each individual turkey farm was earning zero profits, and there was no incentive to leave or enter the industry. At the price P^*, there are Q^* turkeys supplied, which amounts to Q^*/n turkeys per farm on average. When the quota is introduced only those farmers that have a quota can supply the market. The entire purpose of a quota is to raise the price of turkeys, and so the total supply must fall below Q^*. Suppose that quota allows for Q' turkeys in total, or Q'/n per farm on average. At that supply, the market clearing price is P'.

An effective quota reduces the quantity supplied and raises the price to consumers. At the new price the marginal value of turkeys is greater than its marginal cost. As a result the quota leads to a dead weight loss equal to the crosshatched triangle. This loss is made up of a loss of consumer surplus and a loss of producer's surplus, resulting from the reduction in turkeys produced. But there is also a transfer of wealth from consumers to producers equal to the grey shaded area. This transfer results from the higher price that consumers now face for purchasing turkeys. Hence consumers are unambiguously hurt by the quota. On the other hand, the farmers benefit from the quota because presumably the transfer from the higher price is greater than the loss from reduced output.

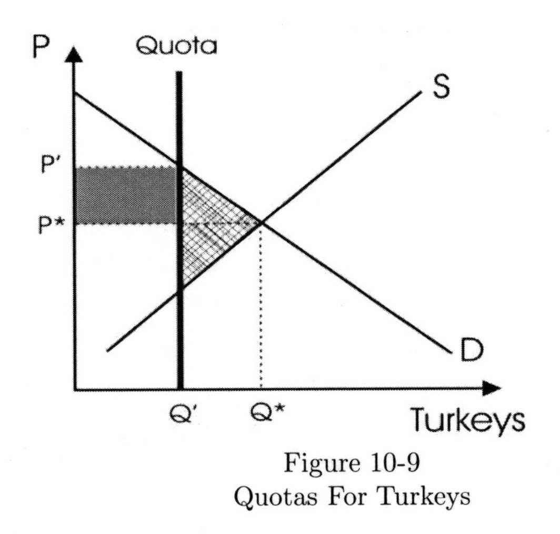

Figure 10-9
Quotas For Turkeys

Quotas introduce a number of distributional problems for farmers. Under perfect competition farmers decide to enter the industry and what number of turkeys to produce based on the price of turkeys. At the higher price P' more farmers want to enter the industry than the quota will allow, and for every individual farmer with a quota there is an incentive to produce more than their individual quotas allow. Since the price mechanism is ruled out as a solution to this problem, farmers must decide how to allocate the smaller output Q' to the farmers that are still producing and how to keep new farmers from entering. Fortunately for the farmers, the problem of preventing entry is taken care of by the government, which enforces the quota. However, the problem of allocating the reduced output to the existing farmers remains. An additional problem is deciding whether some farmers with quotas should leave the industry or not. Given that output has been reduced, only the lowest cost producers should remain. However, if the quotas are allocated evenly among all existing producers, then the high cost producers remain in the industry. Our model does not indicate how these distribution problems are solved, but to the extent the solution is costly, the net benefits of the quota to the producers are reduced.

As a method of raising incomes to farmers, quotas have an additional drawback. Suppose that the quota is introduced as a complete surprise to a group of farmers. Overnight they find that if they obey their quota and reduce their production the price will rise and their incomes will increase. To these farmers, the quota is like a gift from Heaven. The quota allows them to earn an economic rent year-in, year-out. If the farmer wished to sell his quota to another farmer, however, what price would he set for it? Clearly he would charge what it is worth, the present value of the stream of rents. But if he charges this amount, this means that the subsequent farmer who purchases this quota is now earning a zero profit return. The quota has simply increased his costs of entering the business, and in fact, the quota is now necessary for him to avoid losses. Hence, when a quota is sold to another farmer, the value of the quota is transferred completely to the original farmer. This problem is called the transitional gains trap, and points to how difficult it is to actually improve the incomes of farmers with quotas.

10.6 Warm Houses in Cold Climates[1]

The competitive model often yields surprising solutions to puzzling observations. Take, for example, the case of home heating. Anyone who has lived in a climate like Ottawa in the winter knows the meaning of the word cold! Winter temperatures are often 30 degrees below zero, which is cold in both Fahrenheit and Celsius. On the other hand, winters in Vancouver are very mild in comparison. Seldom does the temperature fall below freezing, and when it does it is short lived. Given the differences in outside temperatures, what would you expect to be the inside temperatures of the homes?

Common sense might tell you that in cold locations where people have to spend a lot on heating, the inside temperature would be colder, with the opposite happening in warmer climes. However, just the opposite tends to happen. Homes in cold climates have hotter indoor temperatures, other things equal, than homes in warmer climates.

Before we can explain this, some basic facts about the nature of home heating are necessary. Heat inside a house flows, like water down a hill, to the cooler outside air. The walls of the house slow down this flow, depending on how well the wall is insulated. The rate of heat flow also depends on the difference between the outside and inside temperatures. Anyone who has ever camped in a poorly insulated cabin in the winter knows that as the temperature outside falls the cabin becomes more drafty inside. Often, as the difference in temperature increases, you can hear the heated air whistle through the cracks in the doors and windows as it escapes outside.

It turns out that we can write the heating cost function in a very simple form:

$$TC = P_h B(T_i - T_o)$$

where P_h is the price of heat, T_i is the temperature inside, T_o is the temperature outside, and B is the "barrier" to heat loss. The size of B depends on how well the home is insulated as well as the shape and size of the home. If a home is poorly insulated, or if the home has a large surface area exposed to the outside due to the style and size, then B is a larger number. This cost function is very simple, since total costs are linear with respect to the inside temperature. Figure 10-10 draws three different cost functions representing three different homes. TC_1 is a poorly insulated home that has an outside temperature of 32 degrees Fahrenheit. Notice that if you wanted to have the inside temperature to be 32 degrees it costs nothing, you just open the window. TC_2 is the identical house to house 1 in terms of insulation, but the outside temperature is now 70 degrees. Notice that for a given inside temperature house 2 will have a lower total cost of heating because nature is "adding" 38 degrees to the home's heat. TC_3 is a better insulated home which also has an outside temperature of 32 degrees. Compared to home number 2, home number 3 starts heating sooner, but the marginal cost of an additional unit of heat is lower due to the better insulation. For high inside temperatures, it is possible that home number three even has a lower total heating bill.

Now lets see if we can resolve the paradox of warm houses in cold climates. Suppose there is an identical house in Ottawa and Vancouver, and that the only difference is the outside temperature. Let the Ottawa house be house 1 and the Vancouver house be house 2. Furthermore, let's suppose

---

[1] This example is taken from David Friedman "Cold Houses in Warm Climates and Vice Versa: A Paradox of Rational Heating." *Journal of Political Economy* 95 1987.

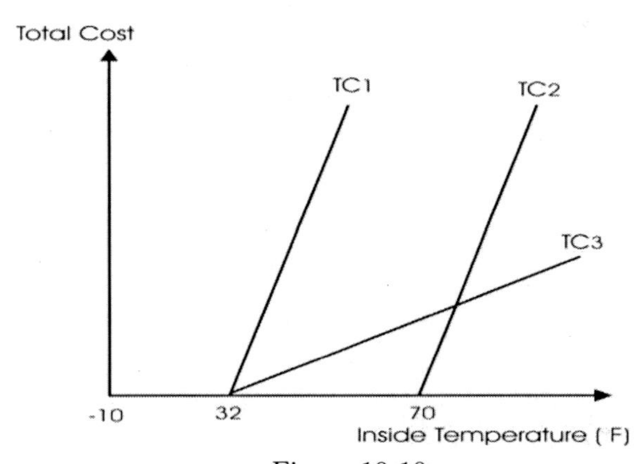

Figure 10-10
Total Costs of Heating Different Homes

that the demand for heat is identical for both homes; that is, at a given price residents in both places want the same inside temperature. Figure 10-11 shows the optimal temperature for each house. Since both homes are identical, they both have identical marginal costs of heat. Notice that the marginal cost curves are flat because the total cost curves are linear. Each additional unit of heat costs the same for both homes. Since each home has the same marginal cost of heat, both home owners heat their homes to the same temperature. The only difference is that the home in Ottawa heats sooner and has a higher total heating bill.

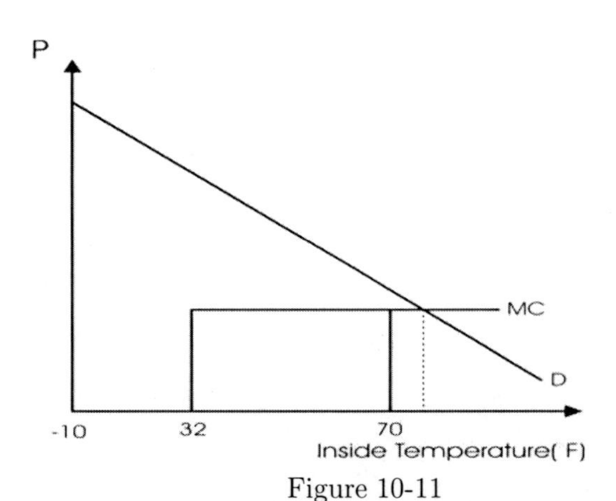

Figure 10-11
Optimal Temperatures for Identical Homes

But why should we assume that the homes in Vancouver and Ottawa are identical? What would be true for the demand for insulation in Ottawa versus Vancouver? In Ottawa a little insulation saves a lot of money because more heating is being done. Likewise, homes in Ottawa will more likely be designed to lower the value of B because there are so much more benefits. In other words, homes in Ottawa are more likely to have cost functions like home number 3 in Figure 10-10. Figure 10-12 shows the heating situation for homes number 2 and 3. The home in Vancouver is cooler because at the margin it is more expensive to heat. In Ottawa homes are not only better insulated, they are made of brick rather than wood, they are two stories with basements rather than ranchers and split-levels, they have smaller windows, no cathedral ceilings, and often share walls with homes next door. All of these features lower the marginal cost of heating and lead to higher inside temperatures. It is a very subtle application of the supply and demand model, but houses in cold climates have warmer inside temperatures because they are better insulated and designed to lower the marginal cost of heating.

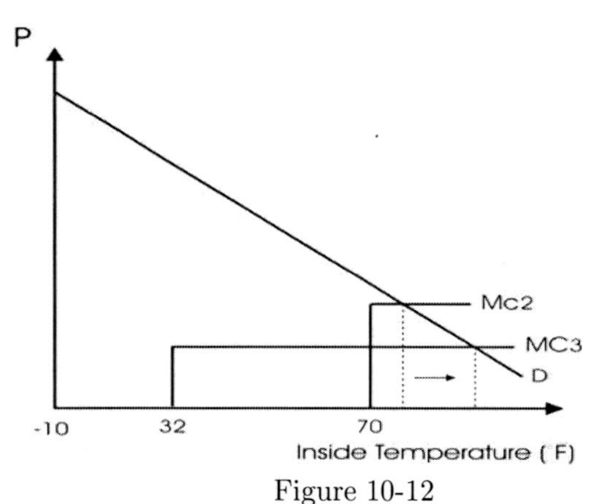

Figure 10-12
Optimal Temperatures for Different Homes

10.7 Criminal Behavior

Although there are many aspects of crime that are beyond the simple model of supply and demand, there is a great deal that can still be understood. The use of economics to understand criminal behavior and the criminal law strikes many as incongruous. After all, are criminals not irrational, acting on impulse and upbringing? This may be the common view of the criminal, but for the economist, as always, we assume that crime is the result of maximization. Ultimately the proof is in the pudding. To the extent that economics can explain this type of behavior, it is consistent with rational criminals.

When saying criminals are subject to economic analysis, we are saying the quantity of crime depends on the costs and benefits of crime, and that criminal behavior takes place when the benefits are greater than the costs. Criminals, like everyone else, participate in this type of "employment" because they earn more than they can in other, more socially desirable, methods of employment. When the costs of crime increase, the amount of crime should fall. When the benefits of crime increase, the amount of crime should increase. As economists, we do not claim everyone is engaged in rational criminal behavior. We only claim that as the cost of crime is reduced, those committing crime will commit more, and that some individuals will find it in their interests to become criminals.

Figure 10-13 shows a simple supply and demand model where the horizontal axis measures the quantity of "crime" committed. The demand curve is downward sloping because the marginal benefits of committing a crime fall with increased criminal activity. This results from diminished marginal productivity in crime. For example, suppose one was engaged in tax evasion. The first efforts at such crime might yield high payoffs as the obvious places to cheat are exploited. However, the more tax evasion one is involved in, the lower the return, as it becomes more and more difficult to find tax loopholes to exploit. The supply of crimes is upward sloping, demonstrating the rising marginal costs of production. One of the major costs of crime is the forgone income from legitimate employment. Those who have a comparative advantage in crime will have low alternative earnings. These are the first individuals to engage in crime. As the returns to crime increase, others are induced into the industry, but these people naturally have higher opportunity costs. In equilibrium the amount of crime is where the marginal benefits equal the marginal costs.

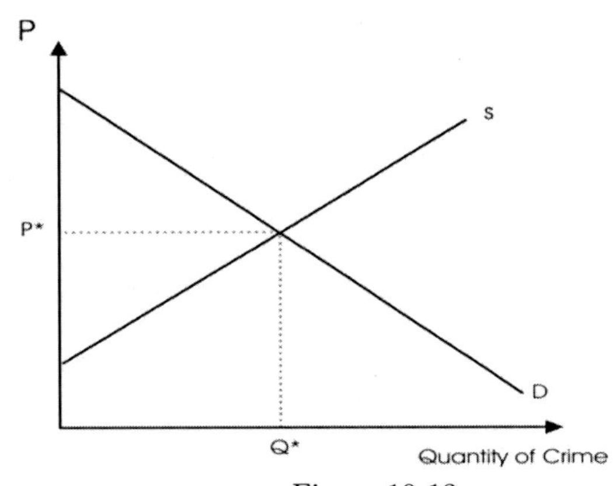

Figure 10-13
The Optimal Amount of Crime

This simple model suggests two methods of reducing crime. The first is that the net benefits can be reduced. Societies make all kinds of provisions that attempt to achieve this goal. One of the most common is to impose penalties for crimes and to create an environment where there is some positive chance that a criminal will get caught. When a criminal is anticipating a crime, he or she will compare the expected penalty (the amount of the penalty times the probability of getting caught) with the expected benefit. If the expected penalty is too high, then the crime is not committed. The other method of reducing crime is to raise the opportunity cost of crime. If employment opportunities improve, or if one is eligible for social services given no criminal record, then the costs of crime increase, and again there will be less crime. Here again, most societies have parts of their social safety nets designed to discourage low-income individuals from engaging in crime.

In terms of penalties, it is important to note that both the size of the penalty and the chance of detection are under social control. Penalties can always be made more severe, and more police and detection devices can be employed. In situations where the chance of detection is very small, as in cattle rustling in the old west or late-night muggings in large cities, the penalties tend to be high in order to compensate for the low probability of getting caught. It may seem that the rational thing to do is to spend very little on detection and simply make penalties enormous. For example, we could have the death penalty for jay-walking! However, there are a number of costs of this type of penal system. First, occasionally mistakes are made in detection. If mistakes are made, we wouldn't want to have only extreme penalties. Second, by having one penalty the principle of substitution is ignored. If the penalty of a crime is always death, then anyone about to be caught goes to extreme lengths to get away. Kidnappers are more likely to kill their victims if the penalties are the same for murder and kidnapping because it reduces the number of witnesses to their crime at no cost to them. More generally, with extreme penalties, criminals have a clear incentive to kill witnesses. An example of this lack of marginal deterrence is found in prisons with inmates who have no chance of ever being released. They often become extremely violent and difficult to keep under control because the maximum penalty has already been imposed.

In Chapter 4 we touched on an example of how increasing the penalty of crime can reduce the amount of crime is found in the recent fascinating work of Lott and Mustard, who have been studying the "right to carry" gun laws of the United States.[2] This study provides a nice example of using the economic model to understand crime. The murder rate in the United States has been in the news for many years because it is so high compared to other countries. Interestingly, the murder rate in the United States is closely tied to legislation regulating and enforcing the use of drugs and alcohol. In the 1930s, murder rates in the United States peaked during prohibition, which banned alcohol consumption. When this law was repealed the murder rate collapsed, and then slowly began to climb again. By the 1980s, murder rates in some states were as high as during the height of prohibition, and were undoubtedly related to the new war on drugs that began in the 1960s.

During most of this time, it was illegal for a private citizen to carry a concealed hand-gun. However, throughout the 1970s a number of states passed laws that allowed ordinary citizens to carry concealed weapons, and to use them in self defense. As mentioned in Chapter 4, the number of individuals in any given state that actually applied for a weapon was quite small, between 2% and 4%. However, even with this low take up rate the effects were quite large. Lott and Mustard have found that all violent crime rates fell with the introduction of right to carry laws. Murder rates fell by 8%, rape by 5%, robbery by 3%, and aggravated assault by 7%. Interestingly, for crimes that involved stealth, such as burglary, crime rates increased.

This application indicates that there is evidence that many criminals do behave in ways that are consistent with our general model. As a society we design our laws in light of this model. Laws are made such that there is marginal deterrence, repeat offenders get larger sentences, and young offenders get lighter sentences (in order to raise the cost of future crime by not destroying their future earning ability).

10.8 The Marriage Market

Marriage is a complex institution which legally regulates the terms of formation and dissolution of a union between a man and woman. Though there can be marriages without children, most people marry for the purpose of raising their own children. Marriages involve the state, family members, often the church, and even friends and larger social groups. Marriage is mostly about how production in the household is organized, and as such is a topic better left for the last section of this book. However, if we're willing to make some very strong assumptions, and think about the entire marriage market as opposed to specific relationships, we can see that our current model can tell us a few things regarding the volume of marriages and the (implicit) terms of trade.

To begin with, let's assume individuals are free to marry whomever they wish, and that all benefits and costs from marriage accrue to the couple. Historically, women were the property of their

---

[2] John Lott Jr. and David Mustard, "Crime, Deterrence and Right to Carry Concealed Hand-guns." Journal of Legal Studies 26, 1997.

fathers, and upon marriage their ownership transferred to their husbands under the legal doctrine of coveture. Even today, we can't say only a husband or wife receives all the benefits or costs of marriage, as many grandparents will attest. But we'll make this assumption anyway.

Second, let's assume every marriage is monogamous, and everyone is homogeneous. That is, all males are the same and all females are the same. We'll also assume it is possible for a price for a spouse to exist. This price is either negative or positive. In a western society we don't have explicit prices for a spouse, but we do have implicit ones. When a couple gets married, they bring assets, human capital, and expected future earnings with them. To the extent one person brings more than others, that person is paying the other spouse. If a wife pays a positive price to obtain a husband, then by definition the husband pays a negative price to obtain a bride. To keep matters simple, we'll assume there is an explicit price for a spouse.

Third, let's assume that everyone wants to get married in order to engage in some type of household production. This production might be the raising of children or simply producing the mundane daily goods of food, shelter and clothing. Under these circumstances we might expect a market situation as shown in Figure 10-14. In this graph we've drawn the demand and supply curves for wives such that at the equilibrium A, the price of the spouse is zero. *Keep in mind there would be a symmetrical graph for the market for husbands, since the supply of wives is the mirror image of the demand for husbands.*

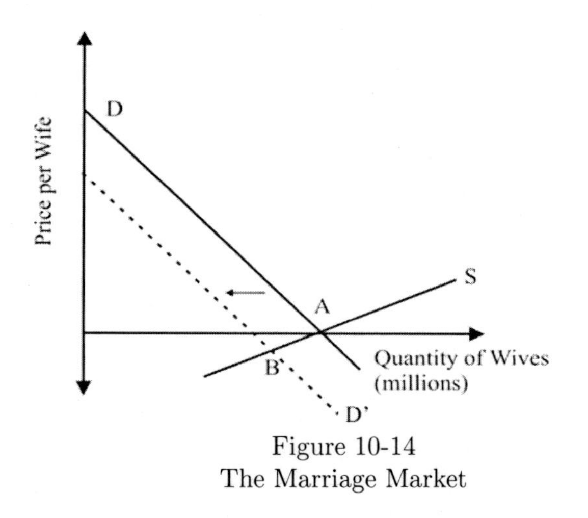

Figure 10-14
The Marriage Market

Now let's consider what happens in such a market when there are shocks to either the supply or demand for wives. Suppose, for example, a large war breaks out and most of the eligible men in a town leave to fight. The effect would be a fall in the demand for wives, and is shown as a movement to equilibrium B. This fall in demand means the price of wives becomes negative, or which is the same thing, the price of husbands becomes positive. In a western culture where prices are implicit, how might this fall in price manifest? Women would find they would have to promise men more things in order for them to agree to marriage. Perhaps more of the household duties would be assigned the wife, perhaps the husband would have more say in the number of children, where the couple lives, and what the relative shares in the marriage would be. One form of competition women might engage in when the terms of trade go against them is pre-marital sex. Historically sex was much more costly for women to engage in than men. Even today women bear most of the costs of sex when a pregnancy arises. As a result women tend to be less willing to engage in pre-marital sex than men. When the price of a wife falls, however, one form of payment to men might be to engage in sex before marriage. There is a humourous scene in the beginning of the movie *The Englishman Who Went Up a Hill and Came Down a Mountain* starring Hugh Grant, where the local minister is chastising the loose morals of the townsfolk while the local boys are off fighting in WWII. As the camera pans the congregation almost every young woman is seen holding a baby with red hair. Later we learn the only male left in town is the red headed bar keeper!

What would happen to this market if instead of a war, the number of eligible females in society fell? Since women often marry men a few years older than they are, this can happen when age cohorts are not the same. For example, if a large birth rate is followed by a small one, by the time the women of the small group are of age to marry, they will be in relatively small numbers to those men in the large group slightly older than them. Such situations happened in North America during the 1930s and the 1980s. According to the simple model, the supply of wives is reduced, and the price of wives increases. Now potential husbands must pay more for a spouse than previously. This might arise in terms of commitments to allow the wife more say in the marriage. It might also manifest in more commitment from the male prior to the marriage. Males, under such circumstances are more likely to commit to marriage, and less likely to pressure the woman to engage in pre-marital sex. Both the 1930s and 1980s were conservative times in the popular culture.

Our simple little marriage market model cannot explain much about marriage. However, it does tell us how changes in the sex ratio in the population of men and women of marrying age effects the terms of trade in marriage. To test your intuition, consider what would happen if polygamy were made legal. Polygamy is where a husband is allowed to legally have more than one wife. Our intuition might suggest this would make women worse off, after all, who would want to share a husband. But consider the model. Polygamy increases the demand for wives, and this raises the price of wives. Some wives will accept being the second wife because the price paid to them compensates for the reduced attention they get from sharing. Those wives in a monogamous marriage are much better off because they too receive the higher price. Those males with only one wife are made worse off.

There are only a few examples of widespread voluntary polygamy in history. One important case was the Mormon experience in Utah during the 19th century. Studies have shown that opposition to polygamy at the time did not come from women in Utah or the rest of the U.S., but from unmarried men in Utah and males outside the state. When Utah was granted statehood, one of the conditions was that polygamy be made illegal. This restriction was placed by the U.S. congress, made up and elected by men in the states other than Utah. An interesting counterfactual question is: had women been allowed to vote in the 19th century, would polygamy have been made illegal?

10.9 **Summary**

The neoclassical model presented in this chapter is the fundamental tool in an economist's tool kit. Its usefulness stems from its relative intuition and its applicability to a vast number of situations. The model assumes that there are many consumers and producers engaged in efforts to maximize utility or profit, and in this process the gains from trade are also maximized. The competitive model does not depend on the type of good we happen to place on the horizontal axis. If the competitive conditions are met for consumers and producers, then anything that is valued can be analyzed with this model. This means not only can we apply the model to market situations, like the effect of a tax on the price of orange juice, but we can also apply the model to nonmarket transactions like marriage, religion, or crime. This chapter completes our analysis of the basic neoclassical model. In Part II of the book we extend this model to two important applications and consider what happens when firms are no longer price takers.

REVIEW QUESTIONS

1. Explain why a competitive market produces efficient outcomes in terms of the allocation of resources?

2. Does cost determine price? If something becomes more costly, won't the price increase?

3. In the spring of 2004 gasoline prices in Canada hit $1.00 per liter. At that magical price almost everyone was paying attention to the pricing of gasoline, and many noticed that the price at every station was essentially the same. Many called for a public investigation into collusion on the part of the gasoline retailers. Does the same price at different outlets mean there is collusion?

4. Are speculators parasites on the economic system? Are they getting rich at the expense of others in an economy?

5. From a deadweight loss point of view, is it better to tax goods with inelastic demand or elastic demand?

6. There was a time before guns. Prior to the 15th century, hand guns and affordable muskets did not exist. Do you think this was a safer time or a more deadly time?

7. In a market with infinite elastic demand and normal upward sloping supply, will a per unit tax lead to an increase in price, but an increase that is lower than the tax?

8. Can a firm in a perfectly competitive market earn positive rents in equilibrium?

9. "LoJack" is a stolen vehicle recovery device that allows stolen vehicles to be tracked by police. The thief doesn't know whether a car is equipped with the device or not, nor does he know it has been activated when he steals the car. What would you predict would happen to rates of auto theft in areas where LoJack is commonly used? What would be the effect of LoJack on auto break-ins, where thieves break into cars to steal what is inside rather than take the car?

10. Gasoline retail price analysist are stumped. From January to August of 2008 retail gasoline prices rose by amost 25%, but total retail sales of gasoline only increased by just over 10%. "We don't understand it, especially since every summer more people tend to drive a lot more" said one analyst. Can you set the analysts straight?

PROBLEMS

1. For a given home that is being heated, will individuals be constantly adjusting their thermostat based on the temperature outside?

2. Suppose the demand and supply of chickens is given by:

$$Q_d = 20,500 - 250p$$

$$Q_s = 5000 + 100p$$

   a) Graph the demand and supply curves and determine the equilibrium price and quantity.

   b) Suppose a quota of 4000 chickens is imposed. What will be the new equilibrium price? What is the loss to consumers? What is the net gain, if any, to producers?

3. Suppose a tax of $1 per pound is put on apples. (Be very brief in your answers).

   a. What will happen to the output of peanuts and the price to the sellers of peanuts? Draw a graph as part of your answer.

   b. Given that apples grow from plants that last a long time, and are not costless to remove, what will happen to the value of apple land?

   c. What will happen to the value of general farm tractors?

   d. What will happen to the value of specific apple growing equipment?

4. For each long distance call anywhere in Canada, a new phone service will charge users 30 cents per minute for the first 2 minutes and 2 cents per minute for additional minutes in each call. Tom's current phone service charges 10 cents per minute for all calls, and his calls are never shorter than 7 minutes. If Tom's dorm switches to the new phone service, what will happen to the average length of his calls? Provide a supply and demand graph in your answer.

5. Tofu was available in 1977 only from small businesses operating in Chinese quarters of large cities. By 2003 tofu had become popular as a high-protein health food and is widely available in supermarkets throughout Canada. At the same time, production had evolved to become factory based using modern food processing technologies. Draw a diagram with demand and supply curves depicting the market for tofu in 1977 and the market for tofu in 2003. What does the model predict about the price and quantity of tofu over time?

6. Suppose the BC government were to import heating oil to Vancouver Island at a price of \$2/gallon and make it available to residents for \$1/gallon. If an Islanders' demand for heating oil is given by $p = 6 - q$, where p is the price per gallon in dollars and q is the quantity in millions of gallons per year, what is the increase in consumer's surplus from the subsidy. What is the net loss to society from the government's subsidy policy? Provide a graph in your answer.

7. In 2000 the BC government estimated that 1 million Salmon were missing from the Fraser River. This created a debate over what has happened to the fish. Some people argued that the fish were poached (caught illegally) and then sold, while others argued exceptionally warm ocean water killed the fish before they could reach the river. Knowing that 1,000,000 fish is a significant number in terms of the total quantity caught and sold, how could you look at the BC fish market and tell if the 1,000,000 missing fish were caught illegally or killed by nature? (You must draw a demand and supply graph as part of your answer. Label it carefully.)

8. "Medical costs would be lower if the government paid for tuition, because then the Drs would not need to recoup their investment." True or False, comment.

9. Suppose a city places a "green-belt" area around itself that effectively kills any future development. What will happen to current housing rental rates, future housing rental rates, and the current price of housing? Briefly explain why.

10. Would exchange ever be possible if all people had the same preferences?

11. Renters of apartments in Vancouver must pay three times as much as renters in Halifax. Suppose the BC government decides this is unfair and offers subsidies in the form of rent controls to Vancouver renters. Draw a graph of the situation and carefully explain what would happen if this were to take place.

12. "Hockey players are crazy if they think the NHL can survive free agency. Salaries will go out of the roof, and teams will bid so high for a few outstanding players, that they will be financially ruined." This comment was made in the Vancouver Sun almost 15 years ago. Salaries have risen a great deal, and yet the NHL has survived. What is the mistake made in the analysis?

13. Why is it that the prices of some goods increase during times of heaviest consumption while others go down?

14. "The Premier is wrong about the effect of taxes on the consumption of cigarettes. Now that the the tax on cigarettes is lower it is true that the demand for cigarettes will increase, but this increase in demand will drive the price of smoking up, and in the end there will be little change in the amount of smoking done." Comment.

15. Canada pension contributions are paid one-half by employers, and the other half is withheld from employees' paychecks. Does this mean that the employer and the employee in fact each share half the burden of the tax? What would determine their respective shares? Draw a graph to explain your answer.

16. Draw a market demand and supply curve, making sure you label the graph carefully. Suppose the government passes a price floor law that states the price of the good cannot fall below a certain price. Draw this situation in your graph. What is the new quantity demanded? Quantity supplied? Is there a shortage or a surplus?

17. The following equations are the market demand and supply schedules before the imposition of

a sales tax.

	Supply	Demand
Good X	$Q^s = P$	$Q^d = 10$
Good Y	$Q^s = P$	$Q^d = 10 - P$

Assume that there is an imposition of a tax of $2 on each good sold. Graph the demand and supply curves before and after the tax for each good. On each graph, shade in the tax incidence for the producers and the consumers.

18. "A decrease in supply will lead to an increase in the price, which will decrease demand, thus lowering price. Thus, a decrease in supply will have little effect on the price of a good." True or False, explain.

19. Given the following demand and supply schedules, find the market equilibriums algebraically.

    a. $Q = 16 - 4P$ and $Q = 2P - 2$.

    b. $Q = 20 - 2P$ and $Q = 4P - 4$

    c. Now graph them. Do you get the same answer?

20. (This is a long hard question.) An industry consisting of 1,000 firms produces a standardized product. Each firm owns and operates one plant, and no other size of plant can be built. The variable costs of each firm are identical and are given in the following table; the fixed costs of each firm are $100.

Output	TVC	Output	TVC
1	10	13	101
2	19	14	113
3	27	15	126
4	34	16	140
5	40	17	155
6	45	18	171
7	50	19	188
8	56	20	206
9	63	21	225
10	71	22	245
11	80	23	266
12	90	24	288

The industry demand curve is $pq = \$255,000$. Calculate the marginal and average costs of a firm, and the demand schedule of the industry for prices from $10 to $20. (The MC equation is $MC = q - 2$).

a. Draw the supply curve — that is, the sum of the marginal cost curves — and demand curve of the industry on the same graph. Read off the equilibrium price and quantity. Calculate the same price and quantity algebraically.

b. Draw the cost and demand curves of the individual firm on another graph. Explain their construction.

The government now unexpectedly imposes a tax of \$4 per unit on the manufacture of this commodity. The tax becomes effective immediately and remains in effect indefinitely. Assume (1) no changes in the economic system other than those attributable to the tax; and (2) none of the changes due to the tax has any effect on the prices of productive services used by this industry.

c. Draw the new supply curve and the demand curve of the industry. What is the new equilibrium price?

d. Draw the new cost curves and demand curve of the individual firm.

e. Why can the price not remain as low as \$15? Why can it not rise to and remain at \$19?

21. A markets demand function is given by $Q^d = 40 - .5P$, and the market supply function is given by $Q^s = (1/3)P - 10$.

    a. Draw the demand and supply curves, and calculate and label the market price and quantity on the graph.

    b. Calculate and label the consumer surplus and the producer surplus.

    c. If the government imposes a \$10 per unit tax on producers, draw the old and new demand and supply curves.

    d. Calculate the new price and quantity, and the new consumer surplus and producer surplus.

    e. What amount of the tax bill is paid by consumers, and what amount is paid by producers? Who pays more of the tax bill and why?

22. In the spring of 2007 gasoline prices in Canada continued to increase and reached as high as \$1.40 per litre. A Vancouver newspaper asked individuals if they thought prices should be regulated. Everyone said yes. Here are some of their quotes:

    "For the people it should be regulated, because how many can afford it?"

    "The cost of gas is getting too high. We have to earn a living and it's getting hard to make a living with these prices."

    "This is getting ridiculous. The price keeps going up and there's no standard."

"I don't think the prices should go as high as the oil companies want."

State how each statement is inconsistent with the neoclassical model of price determination.

23. "If the demand curve is unitary elastic everywhere, and the elasticity of supply is infinite, then consumers will bear all of the burden of a per unit tax." True, False, or Uncertain?

24. Wheat is grown all over the world. In Canada the supply curve (in millions of bushels) is $Q_s = 0.3 \times P$, and the demand curve is $Q_d = 2.4 - 0.5P$.

    a. If Canada did not engage in international trade, what would be the equilibrium price and quantity? Shade in the consumer and seller's surpluses on the graph.

    b. If the price wheat on the world market was $1.5, and there was no domestic tariff on wheat, draw the new equilibrium. Show the new consumer and seller surpluses, and the level of imports.

    c. Suppose the Canadian government placed a tariff of $0.5/bushel on wheat. Show the effect of this on a new graph below. Show the tariff revenue and any deadweight losses. Compare the sum of CS and PS here with that in (b), and explain any difference.

25. Suppose there are 1000 identical potential firms for a market, and they have rising marginal cost curves and U-shaped average cost curves. The minimum point on the average total cost curve is $10. There are 200 firms actually in the market. The market demand curve is given by $P = 1010 - .5Q$.

    a. What would the equilbium price and quantity be?

    b. How much is each firm producing?

    c. If a per unit tax of $5 is placed on the good, what is the new price?

26. The figure below shows two graphs. The one on the left shows the market demand for oats. The equilibrium price is $3 per bushel, and at this price there are four billion bushels produced.

    a. Gary is a small oat farmer in Lone Spruce Saskatchewan. He only plants a few hundred acres of oats each year. Using a solid line, draw the demand for oats for farmer Gary on the graph on the right.

    b. Now suppose the federal government places a $1.50 subsidy on oats. Using dotted (or different colored) lines and arrows, show on a graph similar to the one above what happens to both at the market level and for farmer Gary in the new equilibrium. [Don't worry about calculating an exact equilibrium price and quantity, just show it qualitatively. That is, make up some new prices and quantities consistent with a subsidy.]

    c. On another graph based on the one in (b), shade in any gains or losses, transfers, and deadweight losses on the market graph that result from the subsidy.

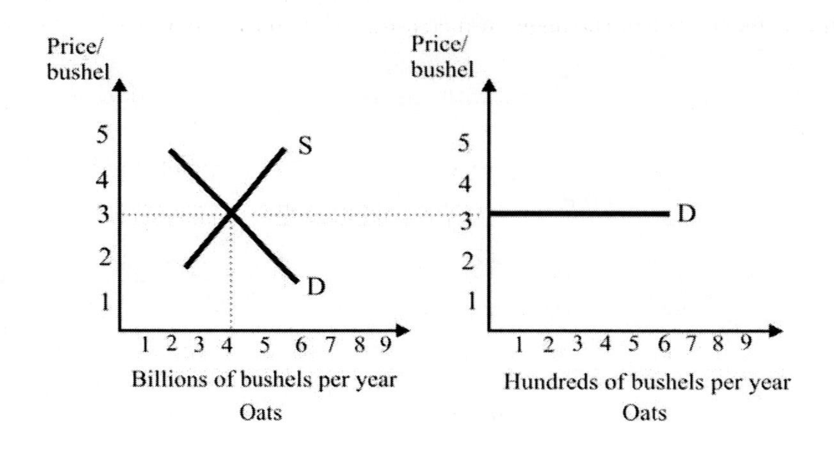

27. In 1974 the socialist government of British Columbia created the Agricultural Land Reserve. The ALR prevents farmers from subdividing their land for housing or business. The Independent Contractors and Businesses Association states that "it's time to free up land from the ALR so more homes can be built for Vancouver's growing population."

    a. Is "more land" necessary for "more homes?"

    b. If the ALR was removed, and the land became available for housing, what would likely happen to the price of a home in Vancouver?

    c. Given your answer in (b) does this necessarily mean that the ALR should be removed?

28. The government is considering placing a \$4 per unit tax on either Harry Potter books or Ikea clocks. The supply and demand curves for each market are given as:

    Harry Potter books: $Q^d = 200 - 20P$ and $Q^s = P$

    Ikea clocks $Q^d = 100 - 2P$ and $Q^s = P$

    a. On a single graph, draw and label the two demand curves and supply curves.

    b. Using your economic intuition, explain which good should be taxed if the government wants to maximize tax revenue?

    c. On another graph, show what would happen to the supply curve if a \$4 tax was placed on, and shade in the two different tax revenues.

    d. On which good should the government impose the tax if it wants to minimize efficiency loss? Explain why.

29. A local radio morning man said the following when Vancouver housing prices fell by 20% in the fall of 2008: "Sure the price of housing is falling, but we know that this causes an increase

in demand for housing. When the demand increases, this will lead to a rebounding of the local prices." Does the local radio man have his story right?

30. In Canada there is a universal health care system that provides "free" care to citizens and prevents doctors and hospitals from charging user fees. Users of the system face large delays in receiving care and often are on wait-lists for months. On the other hand, there is no universal dental or animal care in Canada, and no such wait-lists exist to see a dentist or a veterinarian. Why would universal free care lead to people having to wait?

31. Accounting professors earn more than English professors at most universities. Explain this with a supply and demand graph.

Review Question Answers

1. *In a competitive market those who value goods the most are the ones who get them, and those who produce the goods at the lowest cost are the ones who make them. Hence the gains from trade are maximized and the outcome is efficient.*

2. *Costs do not determine prices. Prices are the endogenous outcome of the interaction of supply and demand. Costs, however, lie behind the supply curve. Therefore, when costs change, the supply changes and this will generally lead to a change in price. The change in price, however, will not generally match the change in costs. This will depend on the various elasticities.*

3. *This is the great irony of competitive markets, they result in all firms selling at the same price, just like collusive firms! The Canadian Competition Bureau has investigated the oil and gas industry three times over the past 15 years and has never found evidence of collusion.*

4. *No. A speculator is one who prevents the premature use of resources. By holding onto an asset, like a piece of land, the speculator keeps it out of use until the most valued use comes along. This increases wealth, even though on the surface it looks like the speculator is making money by doing nothing. No one seems to worry when the speculator is wrong and loses money.*

5. *You want to tax those goods with an inelastic demand. If the demand were perfectly inelastic, then the deadweight loss would be zero.*

6. *Historians claim that "medieval England was boisterous and violent." In the thirteenth century they estimate 18-23 homicides per 100,000 people. This had fallen by two thirds by the end of the eighteenth century. In 1900, London had only 2 murders in a city over 1 million people. There are lots of factors going on, but the increase in the use of guns held by individuals, did not come along with an increase in violence. Starting at the turn of the twentieth century, England started to restrict the ownership and use of guns in self-defense.*

7. *If the demand is infinitely elastic, then it is flat. This means there are perfect substitutes for the product. Hence a tax will be absorbed completely by the seller. There will be no increase in price, but there will be a large reduction supplied.*

8. *Absolutely. If the firm has any sunk costs it will earn rents in equilibrium. The equilbrium is where profits are zero, not rents.*

9. *Fewer cars should be stolen in areas where Lojack is used because it raises the cost of theft. However, more breakins should happen as thieves substitute into that activity. Why do you think manufacturers don't advertise that their cars have Lojack? That is, they could advertise: "Buy a buick and never worry about your car being stolen."*

10. *No problem. The demand for gasoline has increased, but the supply is relatively inelastic.*

Odd Numbered Problem Answers

1. *No. They set the temperature based on the demand and marginal cost for heat. So unless either changes based on the temperature outside, the inside temperature remains the same.*

3.

   a. *There will be an increase in the price of apples. If apples and peanuts are substitutes, then the demand for peanuts should increase, causing an increase in the price of peanuts.*

   b. *The value of the land will fall as the owners absorb the tax.*

   c. *Nothing.*

   d. *The value of this equipment will fall for the same reason the value of apple land falls.*

5.

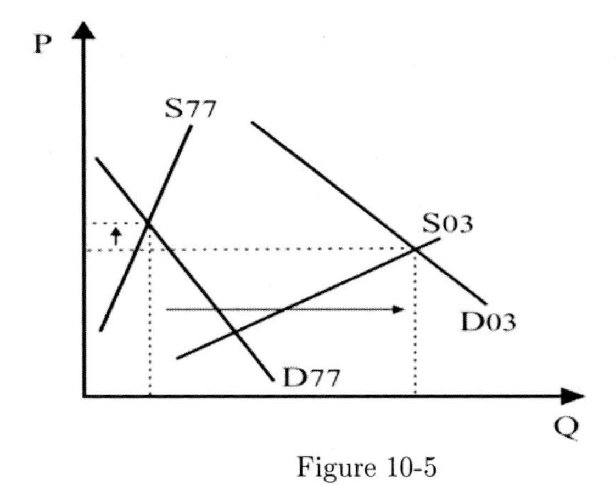

Figure 10-5

Both the demand and supply curves shift out. This leads to an ambiguous change in the price, but a predicted increase in the quantity traded.

7. *If the fish died at sea, it would reduce the supply of salmon and raise the price. If the fish were caught illegally and sold, there would be no change in supply and no change in price.*

9. *Assume the area is growing so the green belt is a binding constraint. The current rental rates will not change since they are determined by the current demand and supply of rental housing. Future rates are expected to increase, however, since growth in demand will lead to higher prices. These higher future rental prices will be capitalized into the price of current homes and so the price of a house will increase.*

11.

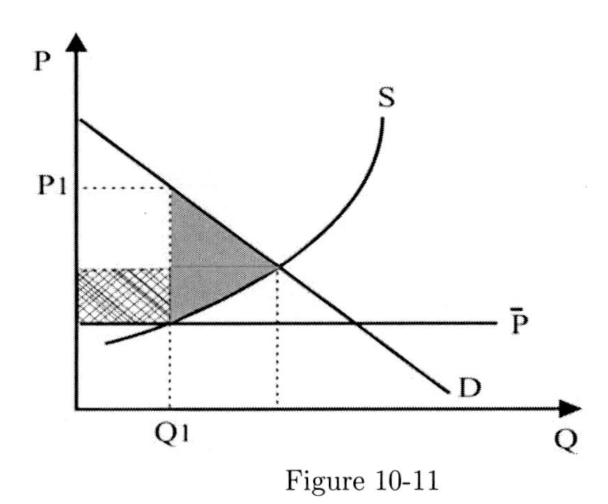

Figure 10-11

When the rental price is lowered to $\bar{P}$, suppliers of rental housing reduce their supply to Q_1. This creates a shortage of rental housing. At this lower supply, the marginal value of rental housing is P_1. People desperate for a place to live will be willing to pay this much to get an apartment. They may pay this in terms of key deposits, rented furniture, waiting in line, or some other method. If the rent control is binding, then there is a deadweight loss equal to the dark triangle. If those who rent the apartment only pay the price $\bar{P}$, then they get a transfer equal to the crosshatched area. How much they actually get depends on the nature of the competition for the apartments.

13. *It depends what drives the increased consumption. If the supply increases, then prices fall. If the demand increases, then prices go up.*

15. *The actual shares depend on the elasticities of supply and demand.*

17.

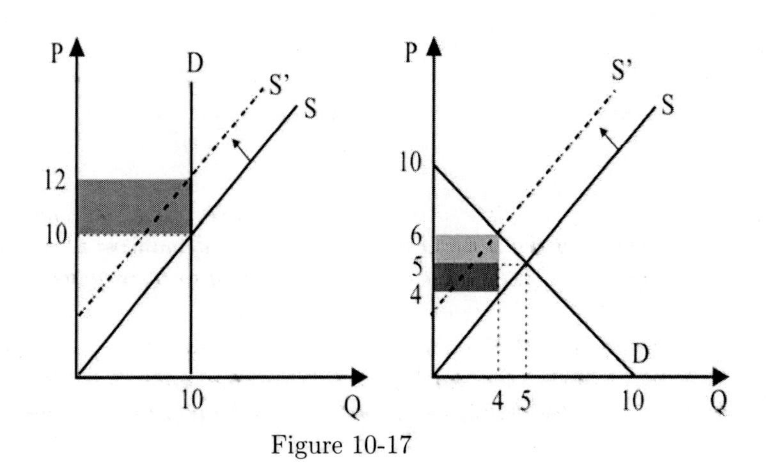

Figure 10-17

19. *For (a) P=3, Q=4. For (b) P=4, Q=12. Yes, you get the same answer.*

21.

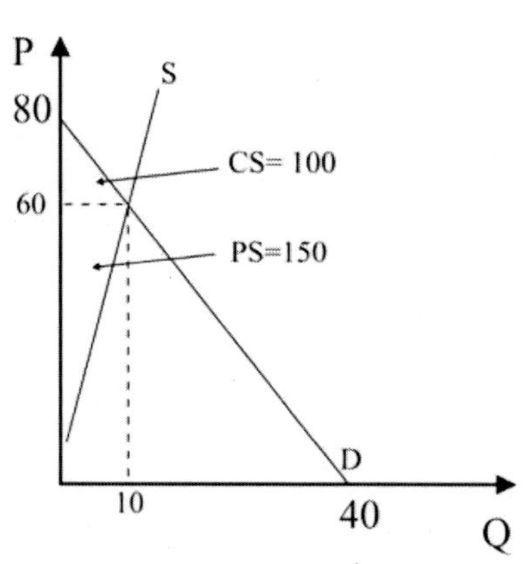

Figure 10-21a

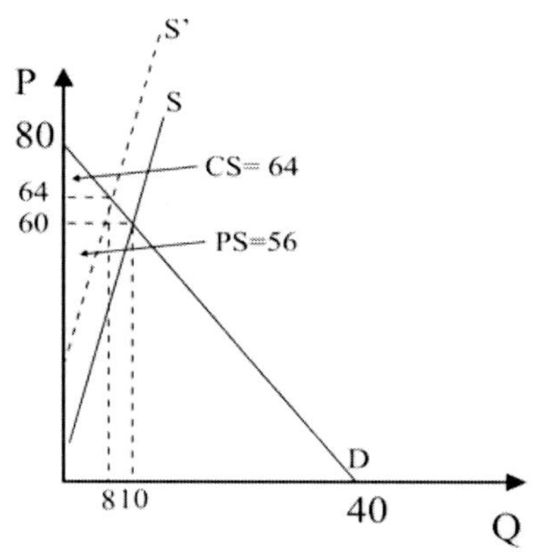

Figure 10-21b

After the tax the price increases by only 4 dollars. Meaning the firm pays most of the tax. This happens because the supply curve is so steep.

23. *If the demand curve is unitary elastic everywhere it is shaped like a rectangular hyperbola. If the elasticity of supply is infinite, then it is flat. If a tax is put on, then the flat supply curve shifts up by the amount of the tax and the consumer bears all of the burden of the per unit tax. The elasticity of demand is irrelevant (just a red herring to trick you!).*

25. *The market supply curve is flat at a value of £10. Therefore the equilibrium price is £10 and the equilibrium quantity is 2000. Each firm is producing 2000/200= 10 units. If a £5 tax is placed on the good, then the supply curve shifts up by £5 and the price also increases by £5 to £15.*

27.

a. *No. Anyone who has been to Hong Kong, New York, or even downtown Vancouver knows that density can be increased by building up.*

b. *It would go down.*

c. *No. The increased sprawl has many negative consequences that are not capitalized into the housing prices. We would want to consider a comparison between the total costs and benefits of removing the ALR.*

29. *This is a classic case of confusing a "shift in demand" with a "change in the quantity demanded." The fall in prices was caused by the recession and the collapse of the financial market. This meant a fall in the demand for housing. Given this fall, the price falls and we reach a new equilibrium. That's the end of the story.*

31. *Accounting professors have higher opportunity costs than English professors because business firms are willing to hire them. This means the supply curve for these professors is lower than for English professors, other things constant. Also, since people can earn a living with accounting easier than with English, the demand for these professors is also likely to be larger. Both effects work to raise the wage of accounting professors relative to English professors.*

PART II
EXTENSIONS OF THE NEOCLASSICAL MODEL

Now that the basic economic model is complete, Part II extends the analysis in different directions. Every chapter in this second part involves minor differences in assumptions or topics. Chapters 11 and 12 are simply extended applications of the basic model. Chapter 11 considers what happens when a consumer's choice over consumption is extended over time, rather than just across goods. We'll see that a few simple adjustments allow us to analyze interest rates, captial values, and markets for loanable funds. Chapter 12 looks at the market for labor services and analyzes policies and issues such as minimum wages and why some individuals are paid more than others. Chapter 13 changes our assumption of price taking and assumes that firms are price makers rather than price takers. Finally, Chapter 14 looks at the incentives for firms to collude and act like price makers, and touches on the law and economics of competition policy.

CHAPTER 11

CHOICE OVER TIME AND THE INTEREST RATE

11.1 The Interest Rate

In the model developed over the past 10 chapters, time played no role. Consumers were faced with the problem of choosing between different goods, but those goods all existed at the same time. For example, should they buy grapes or potato chips? ... today. However, in life many decisions, if not most, also involve choices over time. For example, to eat grapes now means they will not be converted to wine and consumed later. Decisions made regarding education and careers are intertemporal because they involve how time will be spent over the next several years. Decisions to spend money today instead of saving it for a future use is an intertemporal decision. A farmer's decision to sell off his herd today, rather than wait for the new calves next spring, is an intertemporal decision. In fact, when you think about it, most of what you do is a type of investment, and all investment decisions are intertemporal.

Making a choice over time involves comparing goods today with goods in the future. As always, to make things simpler, we'll often convert this to a problem of comparing sums of money at different points in time. Hence, in comparing the choice between becoming a professor or a cabinet maker, we can compare the different streams of earnings that the two occupations would earn over a lifetime. To be a professor involves a long period of training during which very little income is earned, but it promises a high annual income once training is completed. In contrast, cabinet making involves a much shorter training period, but the annual income of a journeyman cabinet maker is small relative to that of a professor. A person who faces the choice between these occupations needs to compare the two income streams. But how does an eighteen-year-old student trying to choose an occupation go about comparing two such different streams of earnings?

The key to making such comparisons is the interest rate. The interest rate is a price that allows us to translate future values into current values. Interest rates sound mysterious and complicated, but they are simply prices. Quite often, one hears the remark that "interest is the price of money". not true
This is not true. The price of one dollar is one dollar, not a number like 10%. The interest rate is the price of borrowing money. In fact, money doesn't even need to exist for there to be interest. Interest is the price paid for early consumption of one good in terms of another. In other words, it is just a relative price.

> *The interest rate is simply the price of early consumption.*

If the interest rate is just a price, then it must be determined in a market. If it is determined in a market, then it must be determined by the supply and demand in that market. In the second part of this chapter we'll examine this market explicitly. Before we do that, however, we want to examine how the interest rate allows us to compare values over time. It turns out that the price of durable goods depends on the interest rate, and we'll look at a number of examples.

11.2 The Value of Durable Goods

Some goods, like a raspberry, don't last very long. Leave a picked raspberry on the table for a day or two and there isn't much edible when you return. On the other hand, if that berry is converted to jam, jelly, or juice, it could last a long time. Not only could a jar of jam be saved for a rainy winter morning, but once opened it can last for some time still. Jam, as compared to the fragile berry, is a durable good. A durable good is simply one that yields a service now and in the future. Some durable goods yield services for a very long time. A good table saw or set of wrenches could last a life time. Of course, some durable goods, like the jam, may only last a few weeks.

When one buys a durable good, the price paid reflects the future service yields as well as the current ones. Anyone who buys a house, for example, is paying for all the future shelter services the house will provide. That's why the price of a house is so much greater than one month's rent. But what is the relationship between the stream of services over time and the price today? How does the price of wheat seed depend on the future crops that can be generated from that seed; how does the price of an agricultural quota that allows farmers to charge higher prices depend on those future revenues; or how does price of a piece of wood depend on how long the wood will last?

You might be thinking that all you have to do is add up all of the future values and this determines the current price. Thus, if a cedar deck provides services of \$100 for 12 years, then the price of the deck should be \$1200. Unfortunately, this simple procedure generally is not true. The \$1200 is too big for two reasons. The first is because people are impatient. The second is because most current services can be converted into more future services, making current services more valuable than future ones.

Impatient People

In earlier chapters we discussed characteristics of individual preferences like maximization, substitution, etc. We now introduce yet another assumption about human tastes: impatience. If you ask someone, "would you rather have an apple now, or the same sized apple one year from now" everyone always picks the apple today. There could be a host of reasons why this is so. Perhaps the person doesn't trust you'll give the apple a year from now; perhaps they think you'll forget. Regardless, people prefer goods today rather than goods in the future. This means that the marginal value of the same good today is always greater than the marginal value of the same good in the future. The old proverb, "a bird in the hand is worth two in the bush" could be interpreted to mean the same thing. If we want to get someone to defer their consumption, then we'll have to pay them. Perhaps for two apples next year, you'll give up having an apple today. This is the sixth principle of economics, which is often called the rate of time preference.

PRINCIPLE #6

Rate of Time Preference: *Other things equal, people always prefer a good today, rather than in the future.*

Children seem to have a huge rate of time preference. When the ice cream truck rolls around on a summer day, you can ask a child "I'll give you three ice creams of your choice tomorrow, if you don't have one today" and they always turn it down! Turning down a 300% return over 24 hours is an enormous case of impatience, but children just want everything today. This often causes large frictions between parents and their children. Teenagers engage in all types of hazardous behavior (smoking, pre-marital sex, fast driving) in part because they discount the future so heavily. "Living for today" might mean skipping classes at school or spending money on clothes rather than saving for college. Although a parent is hard pressed to convince even their teenagers to save their money (ie. postpone consumption), at every age people demonstrate impatience.

When people are impatient, future services of durable goods are valued less than if they were available currently. If there are two different apple trees — one that will bear fruit in 5 years, and the other that will bear fruit in 10 — then assuming the quality of apples are the same, impatient people will value the first one more. In other words, they value the slow growing tree less. For this reason, it would be improper to simply add up the value of future services to get the current price of a durable asset.

Investment Productivity

When current goods are not consumed, they can be used to produce future goods. This is called *investment.* An amazing feature about our world is that many things grow. Not consuming a large Douglas Fir tree today, means that next year there will be an even larger tree to cut down. Farmers who hold back 100 bushels of oats from the crop this year can plant those oats and reap enough oats to pay all of the expenses and still have more than 100 bushels next year ... perhaps 110 bushels. This extra 10 bushels of oats is the *net productivity of investment*, and it's what the world calls *interest.*

When an asset can be transformed today, such that it will yield much more in the future through growth, it is better to have the asset today (so you could invest it) rather than have it in the future and miss the investment opportunity. For this reason again, it would not be correct to simply add values over time to get the current price.

11.3 Present Values

The key to understanding the relationship of future and current values is, as mentioned, the interest rate. As we just saw, 100 bushels of grain can grow to 110 bushels, and the 10% premium is the interest rate. We can write this in an arithmetic form: \$1 will grow to a future value of $\$1(1+i)$, where $i = 0.10$, at the end of the specified period. The i in this little equation is the interest rate: the rate of growth of the investment. More explicitly we can say that

$$FV = PV(1 + i)$$

where FV is the future value of the investment, and PV is the present value of the good. Given this simple formula, we can calculate the present value of a lump sum simply as $FV/(1 + i)$. In other words, the present value of \$1 one year from now is $\$1/(1 + i)$. For example, \$1 a year from now is only worth approximately 90.9¢ today if the interest rate is 10%.

> *The Present Value of a lump sum future payment is FV/(1+i).*

The above formula would be good for calculating the price of a jar of jam, or a bottle of wine where the future value is a one time consumption. So if a bottle of wine is worth \$100 next year, and the interest rate is 8%, then today you would pay $\$92.59 = 100/(1 + .08)$. But how would we calculate present values if there is a *stream* of future amounts that must be discounted? For example, suppose we wanted to know the present value of double paned window that will provide better insulation and heat savings year after year?

Suppose we have the following income stream: $(M_0, M_1, M_2, ..., M_T)$. Income M_0 is received today, income M_1 is received one year in the future, and so on. First let us calculate the present value of M_t — income that is received t years in the future. The key to this calculation is the following definition: the present value of M_t is a sum of money 'PV' such that, if we were to invest PV today at interest rate i, it would be worth M_t in t periods. Suppose, for example, that you deposit \$1 in your savings account at interest rate i. At the end of one period, your balance will be the original dollar plus interest i on that dollar, or $\$(1 + i)$. At the end of two periods, your balance in dollars will be

$$FV = (1 + i)^2 = (1 + i) + i(1 + i).$$

The first expression on the right, $(1 + i)$, is the balance at the end of the first period, and the second expression on the right, $i(1 + i)$, is the interest earned in the second period. As you can easily verify, at the end of t periods, the balance will be $(1 + i)^t$. Therefore, \$1 invested today at interest rate i will be worth $(1 + i)^t$ in t periods.

Now we can use this result to find the present value of M_t. If you deposit 'PV' in your savings account today, then at the end of t years you will have $PV(1 + i)^t$. But this sum must be equal to M_t, since 'PV' is the present value of M_t. By solving the following equation for PV, we have the present value of M_t.

$$PV(1 + i)^t = M_t.$$

Solving for PV we have,

$$PV = M_t/(1 + i)^t.$$

As you know, if today you invested PV at interest rate i, you would have M_t in t years. Alternatively, the maximum sum your banker would lend you today in exchange for a payment of M_t in t years is PV. In these two senses, then, PV today is equivalent to M_t in year t.

With the help of this formula, we can calculate the present value of income stream $(M_1, M_2, ..., M_T)$[1]

$$PV = M_0 + M_1/(1+i) + M_2/(1+i)^2 + ... + M_T/(1+i)^T.$$

Calculating the value of this stream is rather tedious because each value of M is different. When each value of M is the same it is made easier. Such a simple income stream with equal payments is called an *annuity*. If the annuity lasts forever it is called a *perpetuity*. When a perpetuity is discounted at a constant rate of interest, an incredibly simple and useful present value formula results:

$$PV = M/i.$$

This simple formula closely approximates the PV of an annuity, especially when the annuity lasts for more than 20 years and the interest rate is above 10%. The present value of annuity streams beyond 20 years or discounted at interest rates greater than 10% are so small this formula comes quite close to the true value.

To help understand this arithmetic, consider the following example. Suppose an income stream A consists of \$0 today, \$6,000 one year from today, \$19,000 two years from today, and then stops. Income stream B consists of \$13,000 today, \$7000 one year from today, \$0 two years from today, and then stops as well. Which income stream has the larger present value? Hopefully, you now realize that we can't just add up the numbers. If we just add them up the first income stream would be worth \$25,000, and the second one would be worth \$20,000. What we need to know is the interest rate in order to compare them. Suppose the interest rate was 5%. The present value of income stream A would be:

$$PV_A = 0 + 6,000/(1+.05) + 19,000/(1.05)^2$$

$$= 22,947.84.$$

The present value of income stream B would be:

$$PV_B = 13,000 + 7,000/(1+.05) + 0/(1.05)^2$$

$$= 19,666.67.$$

Thus we see that the two streams are not equal, and at this low interest rate income stream A is worth more. What's happening is the interest rate is *discounting* the future values. The one that yields the most money up front is being discounted the least, but since the interest rate is so low it makes little difference. The greater the interest rate, the greater this discounting is, and the more valuable income stream B is compared to stream A. For example, if the interest rate were 20%, then PV_A would be \$18,194.44, while income stream B would be worth \$18,833.33. Notice when the interest rate goes up, both present values go down, but A goes down by more. At an interest rate of 20% the income stream B is actually worth more, even though it yields fewer nominal dollars. Can you see what the present values are if the interest rate were 0%? Now stream A is worth \$25,000 and stream B is worth \$20,000. This is the only time when it is correct to simply add values across time.

---

[1] Where M is received at the end of each year.

Value of Lotteries

Many lotteries in the U.S. boldly announce that the winner will walk away with a substantial prize, followed by a brief statement that payments are made annually for a period like 20 years. If you were told that you had won $1,000,000, but that you would receive this in 20 installments of $50,000 over twenty years, would you have won a million dollars? If the interest rate was more than zero, the answer is no. What the lottery is offering you is a $50 000 annuity, not a 1 million dollar lump sum payment. In order to convert the annuity to current dollars we need to calculate its present value. Suppose the interest rate was 10%. The value of the first payment is $45,454=50,000/1.1. The value of the last payment in twenty years is only $7,400 in current dollars! If we calculate the value of the entire annuity, it amounts to $425,500 — not quite half the value of the stated prize.

Calculating the value of an annuity by hand is quite painful, and fortunately there are several methods to ease the burden. First, most calculators do the job in seconds. But if you don't have a calculator, you can consult a present value table. Tables 11-1 and 11-2 are two such tables. The first table gives the present value of a future lump sum payment of $1 for various interest rates and various years. The second table provides the present value of a $1 annuity for various interest rates and various years. Together, these two tables can calculate the present value of some complicated income streams.

Using these tables is quite easy. In our lottery example the winnings are $50,000 for 20 years. To find the present value of this annuity, we go to Table 11-2, row 20 years, and column 10%. There we find the number 8.51. We multiply this by the $50,000 and we get: $425,500. The answer above. If we won $1,000,000, but it was paid as a lump sum after 20 years, then the present value of this would come from Table 11-1, row 20 years, and column 10%. This present value would be $.148 \times \$1,000,000 = \$148,000$. From the tables you can notice the more distant the payment is off in the future, and the higher the interest rate, the lower is the present value.

If you didn't have a calculator or a set of tables handy, you can still get a pretty good ball park estimation of annuity present values by using the simple perpetuity formula. Twenty years isn't quite forever, so we only get an approximate value, but it is amazing how close you can come. In this case we would have come up with $500,000=50 000/0.1, which is quite close to $425,500, and easy enough to do in your head. The higher the interest rate and the longer the annuity, the more accurate this formula becomes. It's a good formula to keep in mind when you want to impress you new boss with how good you are with figures.

Wealth

A fundamental issue that arises in many policy circumstances is *how can the material well-being of different individuals be compared?* Perhaps the government is interested in redistributing income through tax policy, and wishes to know what groups of individuals are most in need. Perhaps there is a legal case of age discrimination, and the court must assess which group has been harmed over time by the difference in pricing. What would be the most appropriate measure?

Consider three different people: Brenda, Jane, and Sarah. Brenda is a bright 21 year old university student who plans to be a computer programmer. She goes to school full time, has $23,000 in student loans, and works summer's planting trees in BC forests for $8,000 a season. She knows programmers start at a relatively low salary of $45,000 per year, but that this eventually find PV = one payment (lump sum)

TABLE 11-1: Present Value of a Future $1.

Year	3%	4%	5%	10%	15%	20%
1	.971	.962	.952	.909	.870	.833
2	.943	.925	.907	.826	.756	.694
3	.915	.889	.864	.751	.658	.578
4	.888	.855	.823	.683	.572	.482
5	.863	.822	.784	.620	.497	.402
6	.837	.790	.746	.564	.432	.335
7	.813	.760	.711	.513	.376	.279
8	.789	.731	.677	.466	.326	.233
9	.766	.703	.645	.424	.284	.194
10	.744	.676	.614	.385	.247	.162
11	.722	.650	.585	.350	.215	.134
12	.701	.625	.557	.318	.187	.112
13	.681	.601	.530	.289	.162	.0935
14	.661	.577	.505	.263	.141	.0779
15	.642	.555	.481	.239	.122	.0649
16	.623	.534	.458	.217	.107	.0541
17	.605	.513	.436	.197	.093	.0451
18	.587	.494	.416	.179	.0808	.0376
19	.570	.475	.396	.163	.0703	.0313
20	.554	.456	.377	.148	.0611	.0261
25	.478	.375	.295	.0923	.0304	.0105
30	.412	.308	.231	.0573	.0151	.00421
40	.307	.208	.142	.0221	.00373	.000680
50	.228	.141	.087	.0085	.000922	.000109

TABLE 11-2: Present Value of an Annuity of $1 at the end of Year.

Year	3%	4%	5%	10%	15%	20%
1	.971	.962	.952	.909	.870	.833
2	1.91	1.89	1.86	1.73	1.63	1.53
3	2.83	2.78	2.72	2.48	2.28	2.11
4	3.72	3.63	3.55	3.16	2.86	2.59
5	4.58	4.45	4.33	3.79	3.35	2.99
6	5.42	5.24	5.08	4.35	3.78	3.33
7	6.23	6.00	5.79	4.86	4.16	3.60
8	7.02	6.73	6.46	5.33	4.49	3.84
9	7.79	7.44	7.11	5.75	4.78	4.03
10	8.53	8.11	7.72	6.14	5.02	4.19
11	9.25	8.76	8.31	6.49	5.23	4.33
12	9.95	9.39	8.86	6.81	5.41	4.44
13	10.6	9.99	9.39	7.10	5.65	4.53
14	11.2	10.6	9.90	7.36	5.76	4.61
15	11.9	11.1	10.4	7.61	5.87	4.68
16	12.6	11.6	10.8	7.82	5.96	4.73
17	13.2	12.2	11.3	8.02	6.03	4.77
18	13.8	12.7	11.7	8.20	6.10	4.81
19	14.3	13.1	12.1	8.36	6.17	4.84
20	14.9	13.6	12.5	8.51	6.37	4.87
25	17.4	15.6	14.1	9.08	6.46	4.95
30	19.6	17.3	15.4	9.43	6.57	4.98
40	23.1	19.8	17.2	9.78	6.64	5.00
50	25.7	21.5	18.3	9.91	6.66	5.00

rises to over $100,000 if successful. Brenda loves programming, and believes she'll be successfully employed until she retires. Jane is 40, divorced, and a mother of two. She works part time as a sales representative and makes $31,000 per year. From the divorce she obtained the $200,000 family home, mortgage free, but she doesn't see any change in her future income prospects. Sarah on the other hand is 65. Her 71 year old husband of 43 years died two years prior, and she lives alone on the family farm. Sarah never worked off the farm her entire married life. The farm was purchased in 1963 for only $7000, but given its close location to Vancouver, it is now valued at $1,000,000. Sarah and her husband always saved and spent within their means, and she has some modest savings which provide some interest income. Her total income, including all pension income is just $16,000 per year.

How can the material well-being of these three individuals be compared? Looking at their yearly incomes would be one method, but it seems inappropriate given the other factors mentioned like age and assets. Brenda and Sarah have lower incomes than Jane, but Brenda has a bright future and Sarah has a valuable piece of property. An additional complexity is that Brenda's income all lies in the future, while Sarah's is mostly in her past. The problem of comparing the material well-being of one type of life-style to another seems very difficult to deal with. Fortunately, there is a relatively easy solution: consider the *wealth* levels of the three individuals.

The distinction between *wealth* and *income* is relatively straight forward once you understand the arithmetic of discounting. Everyone is familiar with the concept of income. Income is a *flow* of dollars from a stock of capital. If the capital is embodied in a person,[2] then income takes the form of wages, salaries, or other forms of labor income. If the capital is physical, then income is in the form of dividends, interest, or sale of goods stemming from the use of the physical capital. Income is relatively easy to measure, and as a result is often used to measure standards of living. On the other hand, wealth is a *stock*, and is related to income. By definition, wealth is *equity plus the present value of the stream of income an individual earns over their lifetime.* As we've already seen, a present value is the sum of income over the lifetime discounted by the appropriate interest rate.

Wealth: Assets − Liabilities + The Present Value of the Future Income Stream.

If we go back to our three individuals of Brenda, Jane, and Sarah, the best way to compare their material well-being would be to look at their wealth levels. These would be as follows:

Brenda's Wealth = −$23,000 + Present Value of income stream ($8000, + ... $45,000 + ... $100,000)

Jane's Wealth = $200,000 + Present Value of income stream ($31,000 + ...)

Sarah's Wealth = $1,000,000 + Present Value of income stream ($16,000 +...)

Who has the highest wealth level depends critically on the interest rate and the length of time the income is earned. Suppose Brenda expects to earn $8000 for two years, $45,000 for 12 years, and $100,000 until she retires. She also expects she'll die at 65 like all the women in her family. Jane,

[2] This is what economists call "human capital."

on the other hand, thinks she'll earn \$31,000 until she retires, but expects to earn \$15,000 until age 75 when she thinks she will die. Finally, Sarah expects to earn \$16,000 until she expects to die at 90. If interest rates are expected to be 12% then the wealth levels are:

$$\begin{aligned} \text{Brenda's Wealth} &= -23,000 + 8000/1.12 + 8000/1.12^2 + 45000/1.12^3 + ... \\ &\quad + 100000/1.12^{15} + ... + 100000/1.12^{44} \\ &= \$377,549 \end{aligned}$$

$$\begin{aligned} \text{Jane's Wealth} &= 200,000 + 31000/1.12 + 31000/1.12^2 + ... + 31000/1.12^{25} \\ &\quad + 15000/1.12^{26} + ... + 15000/1.12^{35} \\ &= \$450,582 \end{aligned}$$

$$\begin{aligned} \text{Sarah's Wealth} &= 1,000,000 + 16000/1.12 + 16000/1.12^2 + ... + 16000/1.12^{25} \\ &= \$1,125,440 \end{aligned}$$

At the high interest rate of 12% Brenda, who has all of her income in the future, is actually the poorest. Sarah, even though her income is relatively low, is actually the wealthiest. A different interest rate would have drawn a different conclusion. Had the interest rate been 2% the wealth levels would have been: Brenda (\$2,169,306), Jane (\$887,287), and Sarah (\$1,312,320). The lower interest rate clearly benefits Brenda.

The Problem with Ignoring the Wealth/Income Relationship

To measure standards of living social scientists often use individual income. This is mostly done for three reasons: (i) income is correlated with standards of living, (ii) income is relatively easy to accurately measure, and (iii) income does a reasonably good job as a proxy for wealth when individuals are *with-in the same stage of the life-cycle.* However, there are several shortcomings to the use of income as a measure of economic well being. First, standards of living do depend on the level of assets an individual has, not just their income. Consider, for example, two people with identical incomes but who have a different housing stock. One person may have inherited their large home, the other may rent a small apartment. The standard of living is clearly higher in the former, even though their incomes are the same. Second, higher levels of asset holdings for a given level of income, can always be converted to income through sale. Indeed, the above home owner could convert their housing asset to an income flow by either renting it out or earning interest through selling the home and investing the funds. Now, with the same level of assets, the former person has a higher income and a higher standard of living. Finally, owned assets can be used as a source of liquidity in financially stressful times. Sudden unexpected liabilities can be met through sale of assets and as a result consumption flows can remain relatively undisrupted. As a result, the true measure of living standards is an individual's wealth level, not their income.

An example of the inadequacies of income as a living standards measure is found with Statistics Canada Low Income Cut-off (LICO), which many use as a measure of the number of poor individuals in the country. The LICO measures the fraction of the population that spends a given percentage of their *income* on goods Statistics Canada deems necessities (eg., food, clothing, etc.).[3] Statistics Canada emphatically states that LICO is not a measure of poverty, despite its common use as such.[4] The reason LICO is a poor measure of poverty is that it includes individuals like students and elders, who in any given year might have a low income, but either have high incomes in the future or assets that are not yielding income. Thus an elder like Sarah with one million dollars of non-income bearing land, but a pension income of $16,000 per year, might spend a significant fraction of the $16,000 on food and clothing. However, it violates the common-sense notion of poverty to call her poor, even though she might qualify by the LICO definition. Only using income to compare material well-being will almost always be inappropriate, and is certainly so when comparing individuals at different stages of the life-cycle. Retired individuals clearly experience a decrease in income, but this does not make them poor *per se*, as witnessed by the fact many people actually look forward to retirement.

Rates of Return

Suppose a gold bar is currently selling for $1000 and is expected to sell for $1200 one year from now. What is the expected rate of return on the gold bar? The rate of return is given by the difference in the two prices divided by the current price, or:

$$R = (p_1 - p_0)/p_0,$$

where the subscripts represent the two years. In the case of the gold bar, the rate of return is $20\% = (1200 - 1000)/1000$. The more important question is, what rate of return would we expect on an asset like a gold bar in equilibrium? In answering this question, let us ignore any aspect of risk and assume that all investments have equal risks. Let us further assume that there is no utility found in holding gold bars per se. That is, they are valued strictly for their financial rate of return.

Under such conditions the rate of return on the gold bar must equal the rate of interest! Suppose that it did not, and that the rate of interest was only 10%. Given that gold bars yield a

---

[3] The actual fraction spent on necessities has varied over time. In 1959 a family was required to spend 70% of its income on necessities before it was considered below the cut-off. By 1992 this fraction had fallen to 54.7%. This reduction in the fraction increases the number of families below the cut-off.

[4] According to the Statistics Canada:

> Recently, there has been extensive and recurring media coverage of Statistics Canada's low income cut-offs (LICOs) and their relationship to the measurement of poverty. At the heart of the debate is the use of the LICOs as poverty lines. Statistics Canada has clearly and consistently emphasized, since their publication began over 25 years ago, that the LICOs are quite different from measures of poverty.

return of 20%, people will begin to invest in gold bars, and in so doing they will drive the price today up. This takes place until the current price is \$1110. At this price the rate of return is equal to $R = (1200 - 1110)/1110 = 10\%$. If the current interest rate had been 30% rather than 10% then individuals would have sold gold bars and driven down the current price until the rate of return again equaled the interest rate.

In equilibrium, and ignoring risk, rates of return must equal the rate of interest.

This equalization of rates of return across assets is another application of the principle of maximization, and in principle is no different than our example of traffic moving at the same speed across different lanes, or the example of equal MV's over old Seinfeld and Simpsons episodes. In equilibrium one asset cannot systematically be yielding a higher rate of return than other assets.

The television show *60 Minutes* once ran an episode on some decrepit manufacturing plants in England. The show mostly consisted of visiting various plants that were using very old machines for producing clothing, porcelain, and the like. Some of the machines in use dated back to the industrial revolution. The driving theme of the show was that these ancient techniques were inefficient, and without a massive injection of capital, England would cease to exist as an industrial power. Ignoring their melodramatic conclusion, the show still raised an interesting question: how is it that firms can use old machines, trucks, computers, and the like and still stay in business?

The answer is that the prices for these used pieces of equipment adjust until the rates of return are equal to those on the newer equipment. If you were starting a business and you had to decide between two computers to purchase, the price you would be willing to pay would be the present value of the stream of income each machine would generate. The more productive the computer, the larger the income stream it yields, and the more you are willing to pay. In this way, the differences in productivity are *capitalized* into the price of the computers, and as a result, their rates of return are equal. Firms that use old equipment pay less for the equipment. These lower costs just compensate for the lower productivity. Firms that use newer equipment pay more for it and these higher costs are just compensated for by the higher productivity. The rates of return must be the same in both cases.

As another example, suppose you own two stocks: A and B. Stock A has had a great previous week, increasing by 50% in value. Unfortunately stock B has done very poorly, and has fallen in value by 30% over the last week. If you want to sell one of the stocks, and if you are only concerned with the rate of return, which stock should you sell? ... you should be indifferent!

The stock prices were adjusting to reflect the future streams of income of each company. For company A there must have been good news regarding the future profits of the firm. With this news the current price of the stock increased until these future profits were capitalized into the price. For company B the news must have been bad, and this bad news was capitalized into its stock price. As we have seen, the prices adjust until the rates of return are the same, and so as an investor, you should be indifferent between them.

The preceding discussion is important enough to consider more carefully. Our assumption of maximization, when applied to rates of return on different assets, predicts that past movements in prices have no bearing on future price movements. All information about interest rates and future expected incomes are capitalized into the current price and the past prices are irrelevant. A great example of this is found in the movie *Wall Street*, starring Michael Douglas and Charlie Sheen. The Sheen character impresses his boss, Michael Douglas, by passing on some inside information that allows him to make some money on a stock deal. Sheen then stays up night after night tracking stock prices in an effort to repeat his insightful advice — all to no avail. In the end he discovers that the only way to make an above normal return is to engage in illegal activity. Keep this in mind the next time you get a hot tip on a stock based on its past market performance.

If the preceding is true, why are the returns to many assets so obviously different? One reason is that assets have different risks involved, and more risky assets must pay a premium in order for individuals to invest in them. However, it is not difficult to find assets with similar risk, still with much different rates of return. At your university, for example, more students apply for admission into the accounting program than the philosophy department because the financial rate of return is higher for accountants. Degrees in dentistry, medicine, law, and engineering all give higher financial rates of return than do degrees in drama, history, education, and political science. How is this so?

> *In equilibrium, differences in rates of financial return reflect differences in non-financial factors like risk and utility.*

Part of the answer is that many assets yield utility as well as income, and it is the total rate of return that must be equal across assets, not just the financial rate of return. For example, suppose there are two assets: gold bars that yield a financial return of 10% and yield no utility; and a painting, that yields a financial return of 10%, and a utility return of 3%. Could this be an equilibrium? No, because at a return of 13% the painting is too good of a deal. The price of the painting must rise until its financial rate of return is 7% and its total rate of return is 10%. The opposite is true for an asset that yields disutility. That is, if holding an asset is dangerous, distasteful, or painful, then its financial return must be higher in order to compensate. So take heart that dentists get paid so much ... it is simply the price of boredom, smelling bad breath, and knowing that no one wants to come visit you.

11.4 The Equilibrium Interest Rate

We now have a handle on the relationship between asset prices and the value of the stream of services they provide. This relationship depends critically on the rate of interest, but the question is, how is the rate of interest determined? As with all prices, it is determined by the intersection of demand and supply curves.

The interest rate is determined in the market for loanable funds. This is the market people borrow and lend in for early consumption, and is shown in Figure 11-1. The horizontal axis has on it "current consumption" which we can think of as the number of dollars people have for spending on goods today. The vertical axis has one plus the interest rate, which is the price of current consumption. The demand for current consumption is positive because people are impatient, given our sixth principle. We want consumption now, rather in the future, other things equal. The height of this demand curve shows how much we are willing to sacrifice in terms of future consumption to consume now. That is, it is the marginal value of current consumption. The supply curve for current consumption is positive and upward sloping because it reflects the opportunity cost of investment and diminishing marginal product of investment. When we consume goods today, we cannot invest them, and this is a cost. The more we consume today, the less there is to invest, and the greater is the cost. Hence the supply curve is the marginal cost of current consumption. Together these determine the equilibrium interest rate i^*.

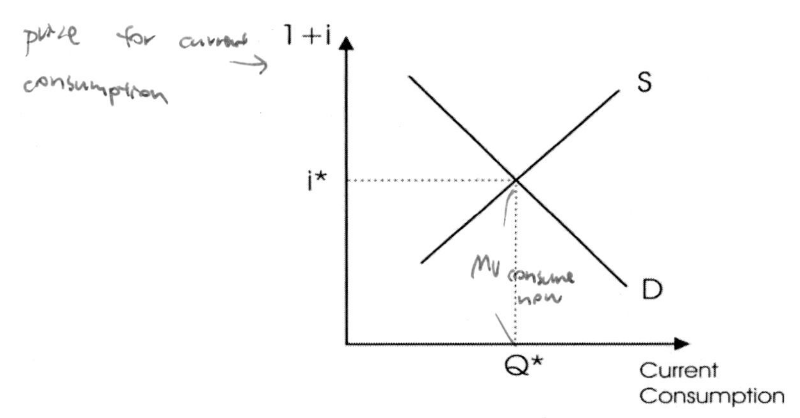

Figure 11-1
The Equilibrium Rate of Interest

Changes in the interest rate come about by changes in the demand or supply curve. If the demand for current consumption increases, then the interest rate increases. If the supply of current funds decreases, then the interest rate increases once more. Thus, if many people in the world thought that the earth was going to end tomorrow, these people would become much more impatient. Why put off consuming anything if the earth won't be here? Such a belief would shift the demand curve way out, and the interest rate would increase. On the other hand, if things in the world start to grow faster, then the opportunity cost of consuming today increases. So if trees start to grow faster, the supply curve of current consumption starts to shift left, and the interest rate increases.

A Note on Nominal and Real Interest Rates

As with most prices mentioned in this book, this chapter has been assuming that the interest rate is the *real* interest rate, even though it has been couched in terms of dollars. By real interest rate, we mean the amount of real goods one must sacrifice to obtain more current consumption. A *nominal* interest rate is denoted in terms of dollars, and is the amount of dollars one must sacrifice in order to obtain dollars of current consumption. The two rates of interest are equal, as long as there is *no inflation*. As noted in Chapter 4, inflation is an increase in the overall price level. If the inflation rate is 17%, then all prices are moving up at 17% per year.

When someone holds a real asset, like real estate, the rate of inflation is quite neutral. Prices go up, but the price of the land goes up as well, and there is no change in wealth. However, when one holds cash, its value falls with inflation. For example, if I hold \$1000, and face a price of \$50 for some pants, I could purchase 20 pairs if I wanted to. However, if there is an inflation, and the price of the pants jumps up to \$100, the money in my wallet stays the same at \$1000. Hence now I can only buy 10 pairs of pants at most. Inflation amounts to a depreciation rate on cash holdings.

Thus, when people hold cash and there is a threat of inflation, they demand a premium over the real rate in order to compensate for the expected inflation depreciation. As a result the nominal rate of interest is equal to the real rate of interest, plus the expected rate of inflation. If we let the real rate of interest be r, then we have the simple formula:

$$i = r + \text{expected rate of inflation}$$

For us we'll just assume that the expected rate of inflation is zero, and as a result the real rate of interest will equal the nominal rate.

11.5 Summary

In one respect the analysis of markets over time is a simple application of the basic neoclassical model. This chapter essentially only changed the analysis from exchange and production choice between two goods at a point in time, to choices of exchange and production of the same good over time. Yet, we've seen that this is an elaborate application indeed. This simple change leads to all sorts of extra behavior we can discuss and consider. The first issue dealt with in the chapter was simply how stocks and flows are related. Capital assets have prices that depend on the flow of services they provide. We saw that it was appropriate to discount this flow to arrive at the price of the asset. This discounting depended critically on the interest rate. The interest rate was the price of current consumption, which, like all prices, was determined by supply and demand.

REVIEW QUESTIONS

1. Why is the interest rate not the price of money?

2. Does the interest rate have a huge impact on the price of short lived goods, like clothing?

3. What is the present value of $10 sixteen years from now, if the interest rate was 15%?

4. What is the present value of a stream of $10 per year for 25 years if the interest rate was 4%?

5. Suppose you've worked for a firm for 6 years and have made contributions to your pension fund amounting to $12,000. Your employer has made matching funds, so your total pension is at $24,000. For the sake of argument, suppose it will earn 4% for the next 30 years. Suddenly you've been offered a job by a different firm, and you have to choose whether or not to pull your contribution out of the pension fund to invest yourself (the $12,000) or keep the entire $24,000 in the fund and redeem it 30 years from now. What should you do?

6. If you announce today that you intend to save all your income for the next year, what happens to the value of your wealth now?

7. Often simple nominal income is used as a measure of living standards. For example, in an article entitled "A Fact Sheet on the Economics of aging in Canada," the Law Commission of Canada (2005) stated:

   > Seniors are still considerably worse off than the average population. In 1991, 22% of persons 65+ were living below the poverty line, compared with 17% of all Canadians. Differently put, persons over 65 made up less than 11% of the population but over 13% of the poor. The result of this imbalance is that in 1995 nearly half of Canada's poorest families were headed by senior citizens. The picture hasn't changed in recent years. In 1997, seniors had an average income of just over $20,000 compared with well over $30,000 for those 35-54 and $26,000 among those in the 25-34 and 55-64 age ranges.

   Is it necessarily true that "seniors are still considerably worse off than the average population" *because* they have low incomes?

8. Statistics Canada calculates a number called "net worth" which is equal to the value of all assets minus the value of all liabilities. It is essentially a person's equity. Should a person's net worth be considered part of their wealth? If one were only to look at net worth numbers (and ignored future income streams) would there be a bias when comparing seniors to young adults?

9. Consider the lyrics to Queen's song *I Want It All*:
   I'm a man with a one track mind
   [...]
   So I'm living it all, yes I'm living it all

And I'm giving it all, and I'm giving it all
[...]
I want it all, I want it all, I want it all and I want it now

Is Freddie Mercury, Queens lead singer, expressing any economic principles?

PROBLEMS

1. Recently Bell labs announced the invention of a battery that potentially could replace gasoline engines for cars. A caller to a local radio show stated that this invention would never hit the market and would be suppressed because too many people stand to lose if the oil industry goes out of business.

    a. What is wrong with this caller's comment?

    b. Under what conditions (assuming the battery does exist) would the battery be used?

2. Sam is a mushroom farmer. He invests all his spare cash in additional mushrooms, which grow on otherwise useless land behind his barn. The mushrooms double in weight during their first year, after which time they are harvested and sold at a constant price per pound. Sam's friend Dick asks Sam for a loan of $200, which he promises to repay after 1 year. How much interest will Dick have to pay Sam for Sam to be no worse off than if he had not made the loan?

3. You have a friend who is a potter. He holds a permanent patent on an indestructible teacup whose sale generates $30,000/year more revenue than production costs. If the annual interest rate is 20 percent, what is the market value of the patent?

4. The following was in the *Wall Street Journal.* "Indoor sprinklers can save on insurance rates by providing added protection. By one estimate the savings over 30 years would pay for the system, but high-rise buildings are often built by speculators who plan to sell them far sooner than that."

    a. Why is the fact that builders soon sell the buildings irrelevant?

    b. Suppose a sprinkler system costs $30,000 to install and produces savings in insurance premiums of $1000 per year. How many years of such savings would be required to justify the expenditure?

5. Sam and Bob are very different people. Sam likes to eat, drink, and be merry, and let the future care for itself. He thinks the world is going to disintegrate in a few years anyway. Bob is only 21 but is already planning for his retirement. How do people like Sam benefit from people like Bob, and vice versa?

6. What effect would you expect the rate of technological innovation in a society to have on the level of interest rates? Why? Use a graph in your answer.

7. One auto dealer offers you a car for $20,000 cash. Another offers you the same car for $22,500, but you can pay in one year. Under what condition would you be indifferent?

8. Your dad has $100,000 to invest and is considering a stock that is expected to yield about $10,000 per year in dividends. If you advise purchase of stocks that pay out no earnings as dividends, your dad complains there will be no income. How would you explain that there still is an income of $10,000 per year?

9. Why would people plant trees that take 150 years to harvest when the average person only lives 70 years?

10. A piece of land is expected to sell for $100,000 in five years, and currently sells for $30,000. The current interest rate is 2%. What is expected to happen to the interest rate over the next five years?

11. Comment on the following sentence (taken from a Federal Reserve Bank publication). "Everything has a price. And money is no exception. Its price — the interest rate — is determined in the marketplace where money is borrowed and lent".

12. You purchase for $900 a $1000 government bond maturing one year from the date of purchase.

    a. Will you make a profit if you hold the bond to maturity?

    b. Will you make a profit if there is a sharp, general increase in prevailing interest rates a week after your purchase?

13. You have recently purchased some shares of General Motors (GM) common stock, and also some GM bonds with a maturity date of 30 years from now. The stocks pay dividends according to how much profit (in the lay sense) GM is expected to make, while the bonds are promises to pay a certain fixed dollar amount each year. Explain how each of the following events would affect the price of GM stocks and the price of GM bonds.

    a. Passage of a new law reducing the level of anti-pollution devices required in new cars.

    b. A sudden, widespread increased desire for earlier availability of goods.

14. People in a certain nation are anticipating having a war in the future. The economists there, who don't have too much concern about human sufferings, are only interested in what will happen to the interest rate.

    a. suppose people figure that they don't have a great chance of surviving the war. Will the interest rate increase or decrease?

    b. If it is expected that goods and property will be destroyed during the war but no people will be killed, how will this affect the interest rate?

15. I bought two stocks on Jan. 1, 2002. By August one had risen in price, while the other had fallen. If I want to sell one stock, which one should I sell. (Hint: don't add any more information to the problem).

16. Two refrigerators are available for purchase. One costs more to buy but less to operate.

	Price	Oper. Costs/year
A	$400	$100
B	340	120

At what interest rate would you be indifferent between the two machines if they last three years?

17. You own both stocks and bonds issued by Natural Fruits, Inc., an apple-growing corporation. A stock's price depends on the future flow of profits for the firm. A firm's bond price only depends on the market interest rate. Explain the effects on: i) the price of apples now and in the future; ii) the value of your shares of stock and; iii) the value of your bonds, of the following events:

    a. an increase in the real rate of interest.

    b. an increase in the nominal rate of interest, due to anticipated higher inflation.

    c. the announcement by the government of an available new hybrid that will increase the number of apples per tree, when these new trees reach maturity in 10 years.

18. Currently in the US, interest on a home mortgage is deducted from income when calculating federal income taxes. How would the removal of this provision affect the wealth of

    a. current home owners?

    b. prospective home owners?

    c. people in the construction business?

19. If everyone lived forever, what would the interest rate be?

20. In 1975 the BC government passed a law allowing farmers to pay considerably less property tax than other land owners. This law is still in effect today. A real estate person was heard stating "The great thing about buying acreage in BC, is that you don't have to pay property tax on small farms". Although this is technically true, in what sense do purchasers in 2002 have costs similar to those who pay the full tax?

21. What form would the rate of interest take in a society that used no money but depended entirely on barter for the exchange of goods?

22. "Save it," somebody says. "Don't sell it. It's not worth much now, but in 20 years it will probably be worth five times as much." Should you save it or sell it?

23. Every year publishers come by my office and try to convince me that their textbook is the one I should adopt, and in the process they always leave me a complimentary copy to look at. About a week later a used-book wholesaler comes by and asks if I have any books to sell. I usually give him my complimentary copies. The publisher doesn't like it when I do this, but they don't mind too much because they keep sending me books. Recently, one of them sent me this neat poster for my wall, that proudly says "I don't sell my Professional review copies!"

    a. Publishers don't like the used book market. Suppose they could invent a new ink that would disappear as soon as the book is sold a second time. Would their profits go up or down?

b. Why do you think the publisher doesn't want me to sell the books he gives me, given your answer to part (a)? Why does he give me the copies anyway?

24. The government borrows money by selling at auction $1,000 bonds, payable in two years, with no interest payments. The market interest rate is 10 percent.

    a. How much will the bonds sell for? You must provide a formula for the calculation.

    b. Even though the bonds do not "pay interest" (the buyer receives $1,000 when the bonds mature and nothing before that), buyers still end up receiving interest on their inve stment. Explain.

    c. What interest rate are buyers of the bonds actually receiving on their investment? Explain.

    d. What will happen to the wealth level of bond holders if, immediately after the bonds are sold, the market interest rate unexpectedly falls to 5 percent?

25. If you invest $60 today, and one year from now you get back $240, what rate of interest did you earn? Now suppose you don't get the $240 until two years from now, what rate of interest do you earn?

26. Suppose your wealth level today is $191,633, and the interest rate is 3.97%. If you consume all of your income for the next five years, after five years what will be your wealth level?

27. Raisins are made from drying grapes; that is, they take longer. Suppose the price of raisins relative to the price of grapes went up. What would that tell us about what happened to the rate of interest? What would this change in the interest rate do to the profitability of producing raisins? Explain both answers.

28. Documents from a 13th century English estate reveal that the value of its flock of sheep was £56. The profit from wool, cheese, and lambs produced in a year were £23. Suppose the expectation was that this yearly stream of profits would continue forever.

    a. What estimate of the interest rate would you make for the 13th century? (Be explicit about the formula you're using.)

    b. Using our simple model of interest rate determination, speculate on why the interest rate was likely so high? [hint: do you think there was a lot of borrowing or not so much in 13th century England?]

29. Recently there has been a "subprime mortgage crisis" in the US. Lending institutions were lending money to individuals who would normally not qualify for a prime mortgage. As the economy slowed in certain regions of the US many loans were called and families have lost their homes when they have not been able to pay back the mortgage. Interestingly, these loans are being called "predatory" and and "exploitive." Demands are being made for legislation that would prevent them from happening in the future. Were the lending institutions exploiting the borrowers? Would a law preventing the loan have made the borrowers better off?

30. Jared is thinking about two different careers. Career A starts immediately and can earn him \$50,000 per year for thirty years. Career B requires some training. The training costs \$1000 for the first year. For the next 9 years the job pays \$30,000 per year. For the next twenty years the job pays \$80,000 per year. If the interest rate over the next 30 years is expected to be 5%, which job will make Jared wealthier. Use the tables in the text, assume the values are all realized at the end of the year, and calculate the wealth levels of both careers.

31. In the past a common practice for selling a home was to allow the buyer to "assume the mortgage." This meant that the buyer would be able to take over the existing mortgage of the seller. The advantage of doing this was that the existing mortgage might have a lower interest rate than current mortgages. Suppose that a seller of a home has an interest rate of 3% on his existing mortgage and it is locked in for the next 5 years. Suppose also that the best interest rate buyers can get for a new mortgage is 6%. If the mortgage is assumed by the buyer, who benefits: the buyer or the seller? Explain.

32. You are 18 years old. You believe that for the next four years you will earn −\$10,000 per year as you go to school. Then you believe you will earn \$20,000 per year for the next 10 years. Then you believe you will earn \$80,000 for the next 30 years and then you will retire. Assuming these payment come at the end of each year, calculate your expected wealth if the interest rate is expected to remain constant at 15%.

Review Question Answers

1. *The price of one dollar is $1. The interest rate is a percentage. It doesn't make any sense to say it is the price of money. What people mean when they use this phrase is "the interest rate is the price of renting money."*

2. *No, the interest rate will have no significant impact on clothing already made.*

3. *$1.07. Not very much is it?*

4. *$156.00.*

5. *So the issue here is, do you sacrifice $12,000 now for the opportunity to invest money on your own. The critical issue is, how much could you earn investing on your own. If you could earn 10%, then the $12,000 will grow to $208,800 in thirty years, but at 4% the $24,000 will only grow to $77,000 in thirty years! Surprised? Only if you failed to earn over 6.7% would you be better off leaving the money in the pension fund.*

6. *Assuming you don't save it under your matress, your wealth will remain the same.*

7. *It is clearly false. Seniors have low incomes because they are retired. However, they have had a lifetime accumulating assets and paying off their liabilities. Therefore, the "equity" part of their wealth is large, even though the present value of their income might be low. In terms of equity, or net worth, senior citizens are at the top of the distribution.*

8. *Yes. Wealth is net worth plus the present value of future income, so it must be included. Just looking at the net worth term will provide a biased measure of wealth. Seniors have had a long time to accumulate net worth, while young adults have not. Hence a 22 year old, and a 65 year old who have the same wealth level, would necessarily have different net worths.*

9. *Duh, yeah! There's just a little maximization and rate of time preference going on here.*

Odd Numbered Problem Answers

1.

   a. *If the battery yields a stream of income which is greater than the stream of income generated from gasoline engines, then those in that industry will not be able to pay enough to keep the battery off the market.*

   b. *It would only be used if it was profitable to use it. The battery might exist, but it may be too expensive to produce, or it produces too little power. There are many battery powered cars around in 2003, yet none of them can effectively compete against the traditional motor.*

3. *$30,000/.2= $150,000.*

5. *Sam is likely a net borrower. He borrows funds to consume now, and pays the loan back with interest later on. Bob is a net lender. He supplies funds now to earn interest for later on. Goods cannot literally travel through time. To borrow goods from the future means you borrow from someone else right now. Thus, without people like Sam, Bob would have a hard time saving today.*

7. *If the interest rate was such that $20,000 = $22,500/(1+i), then you would be indifferent. If the interest rate was higher, you would take the delayed payment.*

9. *Because the value of the tree is capitalized into its price. Therefore, at 70 years of age the tree can be sold, or be used as collateral for a loan.*

11. *The price of money is the number on the currency. That is, a dollar sells for a dollar. The interest rate is the price of early consumption, not the price of money.*

13.

   a. *If this increases the profitability of GM, then stock prices increase, but bond prices remain unchanged.*

   b. *Interest rates increase, the bond price falls. The future earnings are also worth less, so stock prices fall as well.*

15. *You should be indifferent. Prices have adjusted until the rates of return are expected to be the same.*

17.

   a. *no change in the price of apples now. If this leads to fewer trees being planted the price in the future could increase. Stock prices will fall, and so will the value of bonds.*

   b. *The real price of current and future apples remains the same. Stock prices increase, bond prices decrease.*

c. *The current price remains the same, future prices decrease. Stocks and bonds remain unchanged.*

19. *Many fiction writers seem to thing immortals become very patient and interest rates go to zero. I personally think nothing would happen. On the demand side you'd still prefer goods today rather than tomorrow.*

21. *It would still be a percentage, but it would mean the amount of real goods you would have to pay back on a loan.*

23.

   a. *The value of the secondary market is capitalized into the price of the first book. So if it costs more to produce the self destructing book, then it will not be worth making.*

   b. *Just because the second market price is capitalized into the price, doesn't mean he won't benefit from another sale. Suppose purchasers anticipate selling the book, but after reading it they decide to keep it. This amounts to a windfall for the publisher. They send me books because the marginal cost of sending is zero, and the cost of it ending up on the resale market is offset by the slight chance I might adopt it.*

25. *In general* $FV = PV(1+i)^t$, *so if you get the money at the end of one year we have* $240 = 60(1+i)$ *or i=3. This means you earn 300 percent. If you have to wait two years the return is 100 percent.*

27. *If the price of raisins increases relative to the price of grapes, then the interest rate must have fallen. Raisins are "in the future" and if a future value increases relative to the present value, then interest rates must be lower. This would increase the profitability of growing raisins, relative to grapes.*

29. *In our neoclassical model it makes no sense to restrict the capital funds market. Borrowers and lenders get together because they expect gains from trade. Any restrictions will just lower wealth. In a world of uncertainty it still makes no sense. In such a world, ex post, some deals will go bad, but ex ante borrowers and lenders expect to gain from the inter temporal exchange. The only time it might make sense is if cheating of some type might be taking place in the market place. This topic is covered in later chapters.*

31. *It seems only natural to think that the buyer will benefit from this exchange because he get a mortgage at a better rate. However, there may be many potential buyers competing for the house and only one seller with a mortgage at 3%. In such a case, the lower mortgage payments will be capitalized into the price of the house and the seller benefits from the ability to transfer the mortgage. On the other hand, if there are many sellers with this option, and few buyers, then the surplus will be transfered more to buyers than sellers.*

CHAPTER 12

LABOR MARKETS

All chapters thus far have analyzed the markets for final goods. Those goods might have been baseball gloves and hockey sticks, or consumption today versus tomorrow, but in any event the final consumer was doing the demanding and firms were doing the supplying. Now we want to extend our analysis to input markets, especially labor markets.

When we analyze input markets, output markets cannot be completely ignored, since an input's value to any firm depends on the price the firm can charge for its output. Because of this, the demand for an input is often called the "derived demand," to reflect the value of the input is partially derived by the value of the output. For example, demand for leather seats for cars or assembly line workers depends on the output price of the automobiles. This chapter will develop the model of equilibrium price and quantity in a perfectly competitive input market. As we analyze the resulting allocation, we will deepen our understanding that competitive markets are efficient. That is, in competitive markets, resources are successfully allocated to their most valuable uses. Once comfortable with the basic model, we will move on to labor market applications.

12.1 The Demand for Labor

Chapter 8 discussed one element of labor markets — an individual firm's demand for labor. In that chapter we saw that the demand for labor or capital was always equal to the value of the marginal product of that factor. This can be seen in Figure 12-1.

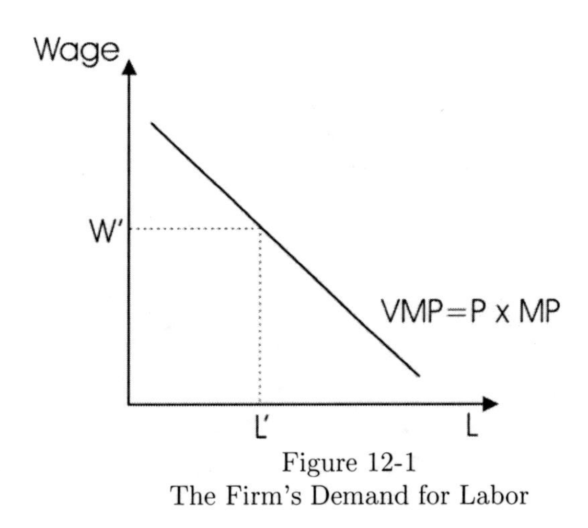

Figure 12-1
The Firm's Demand for Labor

The demand for labor tells us how much a firm is willing to pay for a given input. Hence, for L' units of labor, the firm is willing to pay W'. Conversely, for a wage of W' the firm demands a quantity of labor equal to L'. The willingness of a firm to pay for labor comes from two sources: the marginal product and the price of the output. The more productive a worker is, the higher is the marginal product, and the more the firm is willing to pay. Likewise, the higher the value of the output of the worker, the more the firm is willing to pay. Given that the firm pays each worker a fixed wage rate, the firm maximizes its "consumer's surplus", if you will, by choosing workers until the wage rate equals the value of the marginal product.

> *Profit maximizing firms hire workers until the wage equals the value of the marginal product:* $w = p \times MP$.

Changes in wage rates lead to changes in the quantity of labor any firm demands. When wages are high, firms hire fewer workers, because large numbers of workers would lead to low marginal products and losses for the firm. When wages are low, firms increase the number of workers they hire. Changes in the level of *other inputs* leads to shifts, or changes, in the demand for labor. For example, better libraries and other research services at a given university make professors more productive in their research at that university, and increase the demand for their research services at that university. It is no surprise to find high demands for research professors at those universities with large amounts of complementary inputs to research. Changes in the level of capital can also act as a substitute for labor, and can shift the demand curve for labor inward. Hence, the introduction of robotic arms in assembly line production, might lower the demand for assembly line workers. As always, it is the case that we can make no predictions about shifts in the demand curve when there are changes in the "other things constant" category. But one thing is clear: the demand for labor is downward sloping and lower wages lead to more workers hired.

Every firm will have a demand for labor and other inputs used in the production of its outputs. If the demand curves of the firms are summed up over each input, then this yields a market demand curve for that input. You'll notice there is nothing new here — the market demand curve is calculated exactly the same way all market demand curves are arrived at. The derivation of market demand curves is shown in Figure 12-2, where for simplicity it is assumed there are only two firms demanding labor in this market.

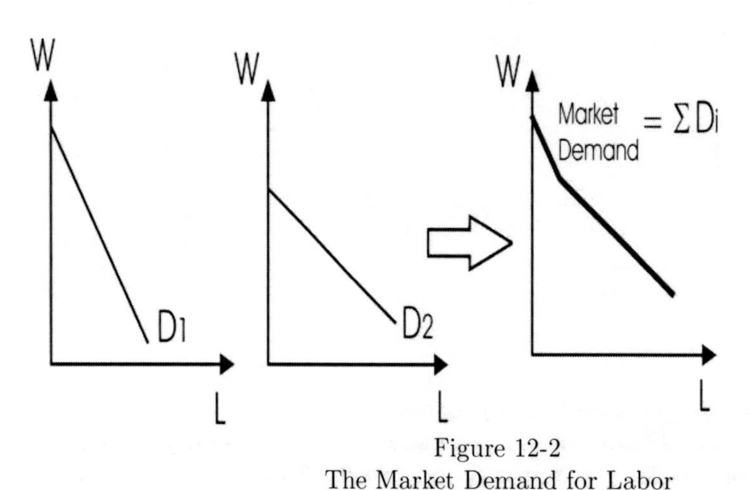

Figure 12-2
The Market Demand for Labor

The market demand for labor is made under our normal set of assumptions for a competitive market. That is, a perfectly competitive input market is characterized by firms that are price takers; that is, firms cannot have any significant impact over the price they pay for labor. Essentially we are assuming once again that the number of input demanders is large enough and each demander is small enough so that no individual firm hires a significant portion of the total quantity traded.

12.2 The Supply of Labor

Now let us turn to the supply of labor which depends on the decisions that individuals make about how much of their time to spend at work rather than do leisure-time activities. At any given time, about 60–70% of abled bodied adults are either working in the labor force or seeking employment. This number has remained quite stable for the past century, although for certain subgroups, like women, the number has changed over time. At the turn of the century less than 25% of women were in the workforce, while today over 50% of women are working. This change in the participation rate of working women no doubt reflects the increased education of women, changes in household technology (like appliances and ready made meals), changes in birth control methods, and rising wages. In addition to workforce participation, a large class of workers not usually counted in official statistics are those (mostly) women working at home as spouses and parents.

One of the critical factors in deciding to enter the workforce is the wage that is offered. Wages are the opportunity cost of leisure activities. When someone takes an hour to spend sailing or playing tennis that they could have used to generate income, that income is the cost of the time used for sailing or tennis. Since leisure is a good, valued like all other goods, it is subject to the principles of economics outlined in our earlier chapters. Thus the law of demand applies to leisure as it applies to apples and oranges. When the cost of leisure goes up, people substitute out of leisure and into work. Thus, when the wage rate goes up, people spend more time in the labor force, other things equal.

The economics of labor supply imply that entering the workforce is a choice. People decide all of the time whether or not they should take one job or another, go to school, travel, or become married and specialize in household production. At times the choices people make might be incredibly constrained, perhaps to the point where it appears one is forced, but fundamentally, labor market participation is a choice we all make. Quite often we hear in the press "there are not enough jobs" or "this government created 5000 jobs." This is a fallacy. If you recall, one of the basic implications of the principle of maximization is that our life is characterized by scarcity. We always want more of just about everything. We want more schools, roads, and shopping. We want better movies to watch, sports teams to cheer for, and bigger homes and gardens. When more and more goods are always wanted, it must be the case that there is a surplus of jobs to do. There are never too few jobs, ... there are too many! The problem for an economy is how should the scarce labor available be allocated among the limitless number of possible jobs in such a way as to maximize the wealth of that economy. Thus labor supply is a constrained choice we make, but one that is not constrained by the number of jobs available.

12.3 The Market for Labor Services

As complicated as the issue of labor supply is, one basic truth is that the supply curve is upward sloping. Pay people more, and more hours of work will be forthcoming. If we add all of these individual supply curves up, we get a market supply curve for labor. Figure 12-3 shows the market demand and supply curves for labor.

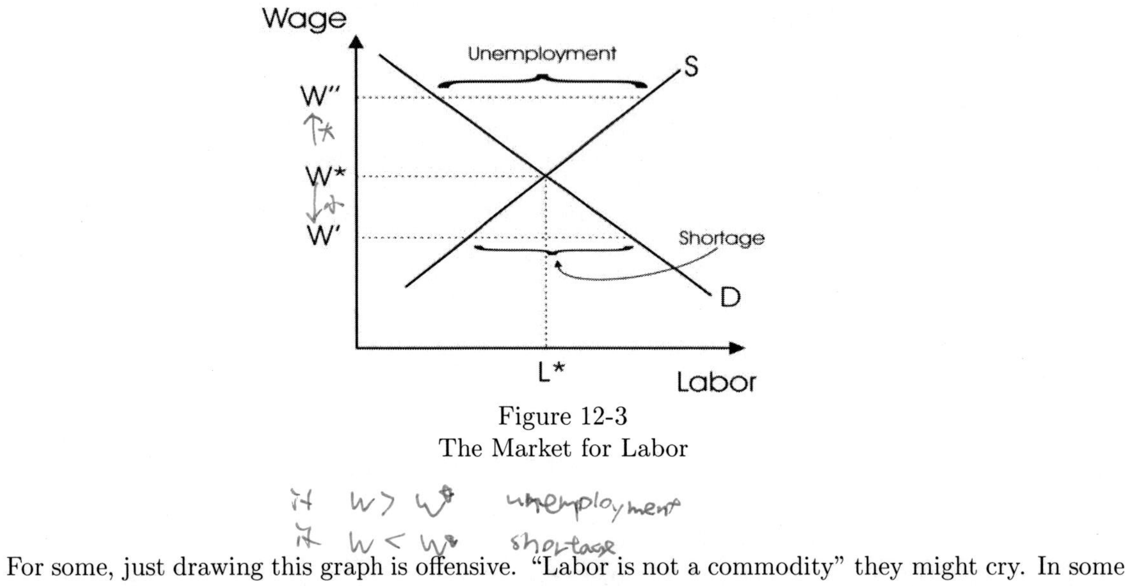

Figure 12-3
The Market for Labor

For some, just drawing this graph is offensive. "Labor is not a commodity" they might cry. In some regards, they are right. When we decide to enter the workforce, it is a personal decision, and one that is likely entered into with a lot of thought and consultation with family, teachers, and people in the market already. Much of our personal identity is tied up in our occupation, and for many our jobs are a source of pride. Labor contracts can be complicated and involve negotiations, legal documents, and friendships. Furthermore, the age of slavery is over and it is illegal the world over for a firm or individual to completely own a human being. Instead firms "rent" worker services, and pay for it by the hour, for example. However, as true as this is, labor services are bought and sold everyday. In fact, income from labor services accounts for about 80% of the value of all goods and services produced in countries like Canada and the United States. So although the procedure for buying and selling, say, legal services, is different than for buying a jug of milk, the forces of demand and supply are still acting. Labor services can be understood as a commodity.

Figure 12-3 shows the equilibrium wage and quantity of labor as W^* and L^*, which are determined by the intersection of demand and supply. One of the first things we can see from this graph is that the level of *unemployment* is a function of the wage. At the equilibrium wage rate, there is no unemployment. Only when the wage rate is above the equilibrium wage W^* does unemployment begin to exist. Furthermore, the higher the wage rate is, the greater the level of unemployment is. So often in the media we read about unemployment as an exogenous force. Unemployment is said to be structural, cyclical, chronic, etc. Though the circumstances for unemployment change all of the time, the fundamental reason for unemployment is a wage that is higher than equilibrium.

Likewise, shortages of workers result from wages that are below the market clearing levels. The wage W' in Figure 12-3 is such that the quantity demanded of labor services is greater than that supplied. As a result a shortage exists. The province of British Columbia, over the past several years, has experienced tremendous shortages of doctors and nurses, especially in remote towns and regions. Hospitals have closed, hours of operation have been limited, and services cut back as a result of this shortage. In response to this a number of suggestions have been made to solve the problem: train more nurses and doctors, force nurses and doctors to start their careers in remote rural communities, and other non-price solutions. The key to the solution, however, is to simply let the wages in these communities rise to the point where private doctors and nurses are willing to work there.

Labor markets work the same way other markets do. Figure 12-4 shows two examples. In panel (A) the demand for labor has increased, and as always this means a movement to a new equilibrium with a higher wage and level of employment. Hence, when a new sports league starts up, as in the case of the WHA, XFL, or Arena Football, competition for the scarce athletic talent increases and wages are driven up. In panel (B) the supply of labor has fallen, and as in output markets, this leads to a reduction in trade and higher prices. One of the great reductions in the supply of labor came during the Black Death. Starting around 1350 AD and ending *c.*1500, populations in Europe were reduced from 1/3 to 1/2 by the Black Death. This drastic reduction in the supply of labor led to large rises in wages at the time. As the population recovered relative to the amount of land and capital available, wages fell.

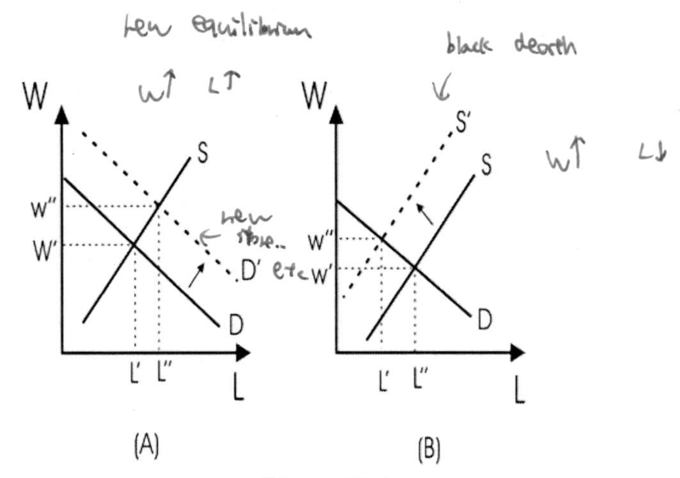

Figure 12-4
Changes in the Demand and Supply of Labor

12.4 Income Differences

It is a fact of life that our personal incomes are not equal. Many over the centuries have felt this a social injustice and have attempted to rectify the situation. Others, have taken matters into their own hands and have engaged in theft or conquest to change the distribution of income. Every morning on radio sports casts across the country, commentary is made on ridiculous salaries and bonuses paid to professional sports athletes. No matter what side of the issue you are on, it is important to understand why salaries differ across individuals. Understanding might change your mind on whether incomes should be equalized by force, or it might help you think up a better way to equalize them.

Incomes are determined by supply and demand. It can't be stressed enough how counter-intuitive this is to most of us. Many have "justice theory of wages." In our mind we often think about some occupations being more important than others in a deep justice sort of way. Firefighters, policemen, medical doctors, and other people who save lives, so the justice theory goes, should be paid well. Inventors of pet rocks, game show hosts, and middlemen, are people we think we can do without, and therefore should not earn large incomes. When we look around we see some musicians earning millions of dollars and others singing on the street corner. None of this seems fair according to our notions of justice through wages. Still others of us have a "working theory of wages." According to this view, those people who work really hard should make more money. If someone digs a ditch and sweats a lot, we think that person should have a higher wage than the lumber broker who just talks on the phone four hours each day. Alas, neither of these views is correct, and the proof is in the pudding — they are rejected by the evidence we see around us every day.

Differences in Supply

One reason wages and incomes vary is due to differences in supply. If throwing a football accurately for 80 yards while under the pressure of 300 pound men charging to crush you was a common skill, and if simple arithmetic knowledge was hard to come by, then professional quarterbacks would likely be paid less than bookkeepers. If, over night, the number of lawyers increased by tenfold, then the salary of lawyers would fall below bookkeepers as well, since with so many lawyers there marginal value would also be low.

People invest in their human capital all the time in order to meet shortages in labor supplies for various markets. In the university you attend, there are no doubt more business and computer majors than English and history majors. The computer and business majors, seeing the relative wages for computer scientists versus English teachers, are attempting to increase the supply of workers in business and computers. In fields where talent is difficult to acquire, the wages will tend to remain high because people can't easily train to enter the market. Some occupations simply require a natural talent one is only born with. Great singers, musicians, and actors, all earn huge rents because they have a gift no others can exactly acquire. Could these talents be produced at no cost, the incomes in these occupations would simply equal their next best alternatives.

Differences in Risk

Some occupations come with a large amount of risk attached to them. If you become a real estate agent your income is more variable than if you become a janitor. If risky occupations paid the same income as other safer occupations, no one would enter them. As a result, competitive pressure raises the incomes to compensate for the increase in risk. Entrepreneurs often bear large amounts of risk. As a result, they often earn incomes that seem out of line with their more visible contributions to the firm. Government jobs, at least in the past, often provide security of tenure and as a result government workers often earn less than their counterparts in the private sector. Differences in risk work through the supply function. Workers are less willing to supply labor in risky occupations, and this raises the wage and reduces employment.

Differences in Productivity

When one worker is much more productive than another worker, the wage will reflect this because the demand for the more productive worker will be greater. For most occupations, though we might personally feel otherwise, the difference in performance between people is not that great. Consider a job like a secretary. One person might be better at filing and answering the telephone than another, but the difference is likely not to be great. Furthermore, the difference probably has little bearing on the productivity of the firm. As a result, in many low level jobs differences in productivity means little in terms of income. However, for high level jobs differences in performance could have huge consequences for the firm. A president of the company might make better decisions than someone else only some of the time, but this slight margin could mean millions of dollars generated or saved. This difference in talent will thus be reflected in different salaries, since high productivity workers have a higher demand for their labor.

Difference in Non-Pecuniary Benefits

Seldom is a job defined exclusively by the income earned. For most jobs, there are differences in the work environment. Is the job inside or outside? Does it involve chemicals that could be harmful, dangerous machinery, or obnoxious people? Do the windows in the office open up? Some jobs include benefits like dental and extended health coverage. Other jobs require lots of travel or commitments to overtime workloads. Issues like location of work, chance of relocation, and the size of office often matter a lot to people. In order for there to be an equilibrium in the labor market, incomes adust to these differences in non-pecuniary benefits and costs. As with risk, differences in non-pecuniary benefits work through the labor supply function. If a job has a host of negative attributes, then the wages will be relatively higher. If a job comes with many amenities, then the wages will be relatively lower.

Differences in wages across the Sexes

In the 21st century, the wage rates of women are still lower on average than those of men occupying the same job. That is, if you take cross sections of female employees in almost any occupation, from secretaries and clerks to sales workers and painters, you will find that they earn less (as much as 40% less) than the men in those jobs. This is not a recent phenomenon, and has been observed throughout the ages. In fact, it is often called the Levitical curse, based on the following Biblical passage: "When a man shall clearly utter a vow of persons unto the Lord, according to thy valuation, then thy valuation shall be for the male from 20 years old even to sixty years old, even thy valuation shall be fifty shekels of silver ... And if it be a female, then thy valuation shall be thirty shekels." (Lev. 27:1-4). Why would this difference in wages be so pervasive?

There is an on-going debate in economics over what explains this difference in the pattern of wages. This debate is not settled yet, and we do not resolve it here. However, we will articulate the debate in terms of the competitive supply and demand model for inputs. In this way, we can see how our model helps to articulate and better understand the issues of the debate. In the competitive labor model, wages are determined by the intersection of the demand and supply for labor, where the demand curve reflects the value of the marginal product of labor, and the supply curve is determined by the trade-off between work and leisure. Given that the interaction of supply and demand determine wages, there are only two potential general explanations for the wage differences. First, the supply of female labor could be larger for women, and men and women compete in separate labor markets. Second, the demand for female labor is lower in labor markets where men and women compete together. The first explanation simply does not fit the facts. Universally men participate in the work force at a much higher rate than women, so the first explanation should be rejected. Hence, the only general explanation left is that the demand for female labor must be lower. But why would the demand for female labor be lower than for men? Here again, there are a number of explanations. First, there may be wide spread discrimination on the part of firm owners (both male and female) to offer lower wages to female workers. Second, consumers may be willing to pay more for products made by men than by women. Finally, women may have lower marginal products than men.

The second explanation would appear to be rejected immediately. Consumers generally have no idea whether men or women were used as inputs in the production of a good, nor is it obvious why they should care. Hence it is unlikely that the lower wages for women are the result of a lower price of their output. A more plausible explanation of the wage difference is that there is widespread discrimination against female workers. However, there are a number of problems with this explanation when applied to women. First, suppose that this were true, and that the degree of discrimination varied among firms. If there were small amounts of women in the labor market, women would work for the firms that discriminated least among them, and female wages would be close to those of men. As the number of women in the market increased, though, more women would be forced to work for firms that discriminated more at the margin, and the wage rate would tend to fall. This grinds against the experience of the last forty years, which has seen the large increases in female labor force participation and the move of female wages a little closer to male wages.

Many economists find a simple discrimination model like this implausible because a firm that indulges in a taste for workers that is not reflected in productivity, pays more for labor than a firm that takes advantage of the lower wage rate for women. If women were equally productive on average as men, an owner of a firm would be forgoing huge profits by not hiring them at lower wage rates. Recall the movie *Schindler's List*, where the main character, Oskar Schindler, hires Jewish prisoners not because he likes them, but because he can get an unlimited supply at virtually a zero wage rate.

Employers tend to keep a close eye on the bottom line, because the discipline of a competitive market stands ready to punish firms with higher costs. Competition among firms forces the wage rate of women up when they are equally productive because employers are more concerned with the tastes of their customers than with their own preferences for workers. Hence, in a competitive model, simple discrimination seems unlikely. It should be mentioned that in models of incomplete information, or in markets where there is a monopsony employer, discrimination of workers can make more sense.

The final explanation for a lower demand for female labor is that women on average, have lower marginal products than men. On the surface this seems as silly as some of the other explanations, unless one is talking about purely physical occupations. However, this argument usually revolves around the fact that women often take time out of the work force to bear and raise children. This directly handicaps them against men since continuity in the job is a valuable attribute of an employee. In anticipation of being absent from the work force, women may invest less in their own human capital, which further lowers their productivity. Finally, as an empirical matter, mothers are more likely to stay at home when children are sick, less likely to work late and travel away from home, and are more likely to work part time. All of these factors lower the marginal productivity of women on average, and therefore, lower the wages of all women — even though any given woman may not behave this way.

To sum up, lower wages for woman can best be explained by a lower demand for their labor. This results from either widespread discrimination or widespread lower productivity. Of the two explanations, the later seems more likely. In occupations where the effects of having children on a woman's human capital are less severe, the wages of men and women should be closer together.

12.5 Prostitution[1]

In the summer of 2007 an SFU criminology graduate student created a stir on campus when she defended her thesis. Contrary to what many people believe about prostitution, violence, and low income, Tamara ODoherty found that 80-90% of Vancouver prostitutes do not work on the street. Of these off-street sex workers, 63% stated they experienced no violence while the majority of violence the others experienced dealt with arguments over payments and condom use. The off-street workers earned on average $60,000 per year, which is equal to the average earnings of all teachers in British Columbia.

Prostitution is a difficult market to study because its illegal status in most countries forces it underground. As a result, for most individuals their only experience with the worlds oldest profession is through contact with street walkers, who are often drug addicted and generally low income earners. This has created a biased impression of the true distribution of income across the profession.

It turns out that ODohertys findings are consistent with the smattering of other empirical studies done on prostitution. In a recent study, Edlund and Korn (2007) found several interesting facts about prostitution. First, it is relatively common, with as many as 2% of American women having sold sex at one point in their lives. Second, it is lucrative on average. In some countries prostitution can count for as much as 14% of GNP, and average earnings worldwide can be multiples of what women could earn in their next best profession. Edlund reports on some studies that claim high end prostitutes can make as much as $2000 per day and earn over 20 times the average wage in their country. Third, prostitution is not a particularly dangerous profession. Many other professions have accident and death rates that are much higher than prostitution.

If these facts are true, then prostitution poses an interesting puzzle. Why does an occupation that is low-skill, labor intensive, and female dominated generate such high income? Other occupations that are characterized by these features (such as being a waitress, hairdresser, or secretary) generally have low incomes.

The resolution of the puzzle proposed by Edlund and Korn is based on stylized facts of the marriage market. Their story goes as follows. Because women are fertile for much shorter periods of their life than men, fecund women are scarce. This sexual bias means that men are generally the buyers of sex, while women are the sellers. Given that women sell sex, and given that women have better information on the paternity of their children, women have historically had custodial rights to children. Men would like to have children, then, but must transfer wealth to women in order to have them. Edlund and Korn argue that marriage has been the traditional way in which women have given rights to fathers over children in exchange for financial security. Hence wives provide sex and to their husbands, and the husbands pay a premium for this because they get legally legitimate children. On the other hand, the prostitute market cannot provide children to men of known paternity, and as a result a prostitute does poorer in the marriage market and sacrifices the high flow of consumption that a wife would receive in marriage. In order to compensate for this, the equilibrium in the prostitute market provides a premium. This premium is analogous to premiums that are paid to other workers for dangerous work or other work related hardships. Essentially it amounts to a shift left of the supply curve for female prostitution labour. Interestingly enough, with

[1] This application is mostly taken from Edlund, *Journal of Political Economy*(2007).

male (homosexual) prostitutes where the production of children is impossible there is no observed prostitution premium.

12.6 Unions and Minimum Wages

Unions are legalized labor cartels, whose purpose is to advance the economic interests of its members. Although unions attempt to do this in a number of fashions, here we will look at two general methods. First is the restriction on entry into the labor market. Figure 12-5 shows what happens to wages and the gains from trade when workers are restricted from entering an industry.

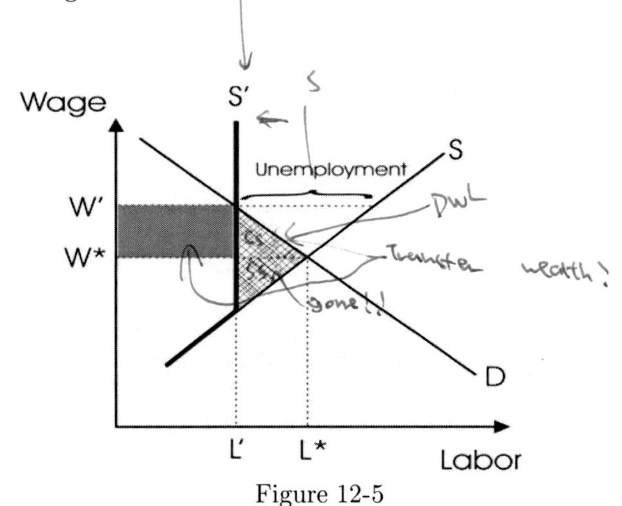

Figure 12-5
Restrictions on Entry Into the Labor Market

Restrictions on entry essentially create a new supply curve — at least a new supply curve as far as the firm is concerned. With the new supply curve S', increases in wages are not met with increases in labor supply. As a result, the restriction on entry raises the wage rate of workers in the industry to W', and creates a transfer of wealth from firms to workers of an amount equal to the grey shaded area. The grey shaded area was surplus to the firm before the restriction was put on. After the restriction, this surplus is captured by the workers in terms of higher wages. The crosshatched area is the deadweight loss caused by the restriction placed on labor supply. This happens because the total amount of labor employed falls from L^* to L'. Thus, firms that used to earn surplus on these workers no longer do, and some workers who earned a supplier's surplus from working are now out of work. Finally, notice that at this higher wage rate, more workers are attracted to the industry, but fewer are able to get work. Hence the restriction on entry creates unemployment.

A second method unions use to benefit their members is to raise the price of substitutes. When the price of non-union labor increases, this increases the demand for union labor. Higher demands mean higher wages for the members. Two of the ways unions accomplish this is to support restrictions on the age of employment and minimum wage laws. Unions have always been huge supporters of minimum ages of employment. In the province of British Columbia children under the age of 15 are essentially prohibited from working ... not even a paper route is allowed. Unions have also supported minimum wage laws, even though those laws are essentially irrelevant for most of their workers. However, both of these policies discourage firms from finding uses for low wage

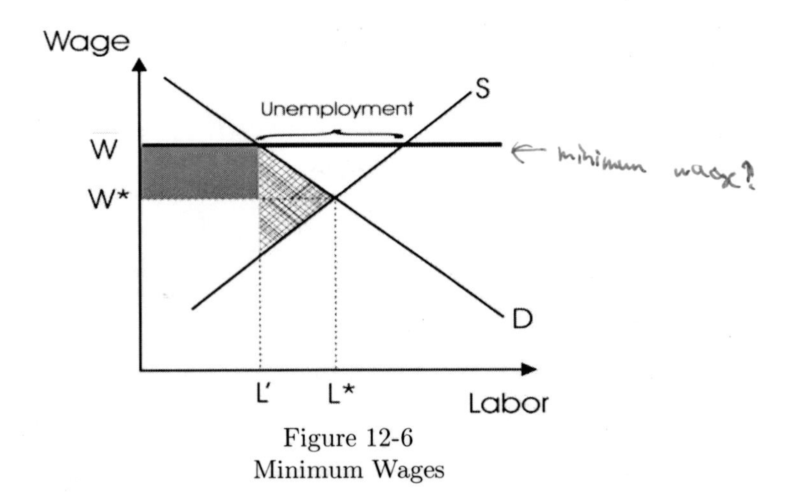

Figure 12-6
Minimum Wages

employees that might substitute for the more expensive wage labor. Figure 12-6 shows the effect of a minimum wage.

The graph is very similar to the one on restrictions on entry. Rather than working on the supply of labor, though, a minimum wage has a direct impact on the wage rate by creating a wage floor. Minimum wage laws create a transfer of wealth to those workers who manage to keep their jobs, but create a deadweight loss from reduced employment. Because the minimum wage increases the wage rate, it also induces more unemployment. There has been a considerable amount of debate over the past few years over the actual size of these changes. Some economists have argued that they are not very big, others suggest they are. What is not in dispute is that employment is lowered when minimum wages are introduced.

12.7 Summary

As humans, we naturally find labor markets more interesting than markets for most other goods. Unless your income depends on coffee beans, its hard to get excited about the bean market. But labor is important for other reasons. Eighty per cent of national income is generated in labor markets, and this sheer size makes it one of the most critical markets. Furthermore, many government policies influence labor markets, and therefore the incomes of many people.

Despite this inherent appeal, it is important to realize that labor markets are fundamentally ruled by economic principles, the way other markets are. Many object to treating labor as a commodity, but by using demand and supply analysis to understand how incomes are determined and change, we are not dehumanizing people. A supply and demand model is meant to understand the price of things and how much gets traded. It is a fact of life that labor is used to produce goods. By analyzing the demand and supply of labor we come to understand the level of employment and the level of wages — nothing pejorative is implied.

REVIEW QUESTIONS

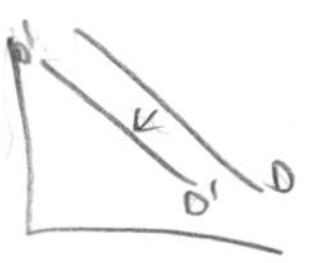

1. What happens to the demand for labor if workers become less productive?

2. Why is it meaningless to talk about unemployment independent of a wage rate?

3. If we observe two people with different incomes, does that mean their skill sets are different?

4. Why might unions support minimum wage laws?

5. When machines are used instead of labor for the production of some good, we often hear the phrase "capital replaced labor." Why is this phrase misleading?

6. Would unions that are successful in raising their wages above the competitive level be more or less likely to racially discriminate in their hiring than the owner of a competitive firm?

7. If the minimum wage is set below the market equilibrium wage in a particular labor market, will the minimum wage will be ineffective?

8. In *1 2 3 4 (Sumpin' New)* by Coolio he states:
   1 2 3, it's like A B C
   if hip hop didn't pay, I'd rap for free
   slide, slide, but that's that past
   *I got sumpin' brand new for that a***

   What would Coolio's supply curve for rap look like?

PROBLEMS

1. Some industries are dominated by women because women are more productive than men in those industries. For example, mushroom pickers tend to be women because their smaller hands don't bruise the mushrooms. Often men are able to compete with women in this market by working for lower wages. What would happen if mushroom workers formed a union and required all workers to be paid the same wage rate?

2. The following question is about minimum wages. Treating labor as a commodity traded in the economy at some price (wage), determined by the supply and demand for various types of labor,

    a. What types of workers are likely to be most affected by min. wages? Eg. teenagers, skilled craftspersons, handicapped workers, etc.

    b. Explain the effect on wages, levels of employment, and possible unemployment in the market most directly affected by this law. Also, what forms of competition among workers might be more prevalent with the higher minimum wage?

    c. Consider that unionized workers generally earn much more than the minimum wage. Unions, however, have always strongly advocated increases in the minimum wage. Are the unionists just interested in the welfare of their poor cousins?

3. A proposition known as "comparable worth" states that people engaged in similar work should receive similar pay. Consider that salaries for professors in different fields at SFU and elsewhere vary considerably, even though faculty in these various disciplines on average work equally hard and are held to the same standards. What accounts for these pay differences, and can one conclude from these data that we value the study of economics more than say, literature? What famous paradox is relevant here?

4. "There are too many jobs." Comment.

5. The following question is dedicated to Don James, former coach of the Washington Huskies. Do the relative salaries of humanities professors and football coaches at major state universities reflect the relative value of football and humanities? Do they reflect the number of years that professors and coaches must spend acquiring an education? The number of hours they work? The difficulty or unpleasantness of their work? Why do the football coaches usually receive salaries that are so much higher?

6. Until the program was abolished in 1987, the government of Holland paid a stipend to artists, based on such factors as marital status and number of children, and took in return a selection of the artists' work deemed equivalent in value. Most of the work so purchased disappeared into warehouses.

    a. Do you think a program like this raises the average income of artists?

    b. How might it actually lower the average income of artists?

7. Should college students be required to pay the full cost of their own education?

a. Who benefits from a person's obtaining a college education?

b. If only low-income students are to receive educational subsidies, where would you place the ceiling on low incomes?

c. If education is an investment designed to secure a higher future income, why don't people who want to acquire years of expensive education simply borrow the money — the way business firms borrow to finance investment?

8. Consider the lyrics from *Some Days You Gotta Dance* by the Dixie Chicks. In the song the singer says it is quitting time on a Friday night, everyone is ready to go, the boss is screaming at the singer saying she has to stay. She can't take it, she's got to get away:
Some days you gotta dance
Live it up when you get the chance
'Cause when the world doesn't make no sense
[...]
Gotta loosen up those chains and dance

   In our popular culture we think of "jobs" as goods. For example, a government always proudly annouces that "we've created more jobs" than the previous administration. As a new economist, is it better to think of jobs as goods or bads? How does the song reflect in your answer?

9. Samuel works for a farm that produces table grapes. The women on the farm are paid more than Samuel because they don't damage the fruit as often (finer fingers, no grape fights, ... whatever). Suddenly the workers become members of a union which insists male workers receive the same wage as female workers. Will this be a good thing for Samuel?

10. You're 20 years old, and you're trying to decide which career path to take based on the future expected streams of income. Occupation A has you earning $15,000 for 5 years, then $25,000 for then next 30 years. Occupation B has you earning only $1000 for 4 years, then $10,000 for 6 years, and finally $50,000 for the next 25 years. You plan to retire when you are 55.

    a. Write out a formula to calculate the present value of each of these income streams, assuming the interest rate is r. [Hint: you don't have to write out all 35 terms, you can use "..." when it is obvious what the next term is in a sequence.]

    b. What occupation would be better if the interest rate was zero? If it was extremely high?

11. According to Henry David Thoreau, in his book Walden, "...it is not necessary that a man should earn his living by the sweat of his brow, unless he sweats easier than I do." How would you interpret this quote with our economic principles? Or does it just make no sense?

12. Why do so many sport leagues, like the NBA, NFL, MLB, and the NHL have "all-star" games? Why would an all star game never result from ordinary allocation of players across teams?

13. Generally speaking, if you were told there was an occupation that was i) low skilled, ii) labor intensive, and iii) dominated by women, what would you predict the wage rate to be? These three features are characteristics of prostitution markets. However, on average wages for pros-

titution are very high. Edlund and Korn (JPE 2002) note that prostitutes can earn as much as 30 times the earnings of women in other professions with comparable skill requirements. How could we explain this with our equilibrium wage model?

14. A mother has been killed in a car accident, and her family is suing the other driver for damages. The defense has put together a report that says "the implicit wage of mothering is $25 per hour. Mothering takes 9 hours per day, and so the value of a mother is $225 per day." Suppose the court has accepted the hourly wage and hours of work. They've also accepted that this sufficiently covers the good "mothering." The mother's family feels there is still something missing and that their mother was worth more than the sum calculated. What is missing? Why is $225 an underestimate.

15. On March 21, 1963 the boxer Davey Moore died from injuries he sustained in the ring with Sugar Ramos. Bob Dylan wrote a classic song called *Who Killed Davey Moore?* in which he goes through a long list of all the people involved. The referee says "not I", even though he could have stopped the fight, but the crowd would have booed him. The crowd says "not us", they just wanted to see a fight and not have him meet his death. "Not me" says the manager, who says it was hard to tell if he was sick or not. "Not me" says the gambler, boxing writer, and everyone else. In fact:
Who killed Davey Moore,
Why an' what's the reason for?
"Not me," says the man whose fists
Laid him low in a cloud of mist,

    From a legal point of view, of course, none of these people killed Davey Moore. However, how is Dylan's point related to the fact that the demand for labor is "derived" from the demand for the output being produced?

16. Government announcements constantly make the claim that "this year we have created [so many] jobs." Why does this statement make no sense if we live in a world of scarcity?

17 Over the past decade the number of men working in the BC labor market increased by 6.2%, while the average real wage increased by 20%. Could this be consistent with our demand and supply model?

18. Airlines in the United States were regulated in the 1970s. The regulations mostly restricted the ability of airlines to compete on specific routes.

    a. What would this regulation have done to the elasticity of demand for a given airline on a specific route. What would this have done to the price consumers paid?

    b. What would this regulation have done to pilot salaries? Explain briefly.

Review Question Answers

1. *When workers become less productive their marginal product falls, and the demand for their services also falls.*

2. *Unemployment is the difference between the quantity supplied and demanded of labor. These quantities depend on the wage rate. Thus, there may be large amounts of unemployment at a wage of $200 per hour, but very little at a wage of $1.*

3. *No. Wages vary for many reasons, some of which are mentioned in the text. Individuals choose occupations based on many different factors, not just the incomes. Thus, two identical people in terms of skill levels could choose different career paths and thus different income streams.*

4. *They don't like low wage competition.*

5. *It took labor to make the machines. When refrigerators replaced the iceman, it took workers to make refrigerators. Thus capital replacing labor is really "labor replacing labor."*

6. *They are more likely to racially discriminate. Since the wage is above the competitive level, there will be an excess demand to join the union, allowing the union members to exercise their preferences in hiring. A competitive market forces the employer to hire the most efficient worker, independent of racial characteristics.*

7. *Yes. If the minimum wage is $6.50, but all workers are earning $10 per hour, then the minimum wage is not binding.*

8. *It would be flat along the horizontal axis (until he some type of time constraint).*

Odd Numbered Problem Answers

1. *At the same wage rate women are more attractive to the employer. Hence only women will be hired.*

3. *The pay differences reflect the value of different human capital in the market place. Universities must pay accounting, computer, engineering, and finance professors much more than the average salary because these fields have market firms bidding for their services. Since the demand for history professors is low, they are willing to work at the university for low salaries.*

5. *Football coaches, like Don James in the 80s and 90s, earn large sums of money because they generate large sums for the university. Universities are willing to pay large salaries because the marginal products of these people is so high. Don James brought the University of Washington tens of millions of dollars by producing a series of winning football teams. Your average professor brings less than this.*

7.

    a. *Most of the benefit goes to the student. Some argue there is an positive externality to society. However, universities add very little to citizen characteristics.*

    b. *I don't know.*

    c. *The problem is one of collateral. Who would lend money to someone who is unlikely to pay it back given slavery is illegal.*

9. *Probably not. At the same wage rate Samuel is a poor substitute for the female workers. He might just find himself out of work.*

11. *Thoreau got it right. Most of us don't make a living with our backs. We earn income (usually much more income) from developing our human capital.*

13. *Generally speaking, women have the option of becoming a prostitute or entering some other profession. Becoming a prostitute, however, almost always means forgoing marriage and the resulting family. This is not the case with other occupations. Thus, prostitution must pay much higher wages to compensate for this negative feature of the job.*

15. *Davey Moore wouldn't have been fighting in the boxing ring had there not been prize money. There wouldn't be any prize money if people weren't entertained by boxing. The demand for boxers is dervied in part from the demand for boxing entertainment. In this sense, Dylan is claiming, all connected with the sport are guilty. What do you think?*

17. *Yes this is easily explained by an increase in the demand for labor. If the supply was relatively inelastic the percentage change in wage would exceed the percentage change in quantity supplied.*

CHAPTER 13

PRICE SEARCHING

13.1 Facing a Downward Sloping Demand Curve

For many problems of human behavior, the assumption of competitive markets and price taking is a decent approximation. Most workers in the job market face competition from other workers who offer services identical to their own. Most firms compete with other firms, both existing and potential, which provide goods essentially equivalent to theirs. Men and women compete for spouses in competitive marriage markets, churches compete for attendance in competitive religious markets, and on and on it goes.

And yet, as good as the price taking model is for analyzing some problems, it is inadequate for others. There are markets where firms supply products for which there are not immediate substitutes. There are markets where consumers are not well aware of prices. And there are markets for which firms have various advantages over other firms. In such markets, when a firm raises the price of its product, not every customer abandons the firms and buys elsewhere. Some customers remain behind and purchase at the higher price. In these markets, the firms are no longer price takers, since the amount of output they produce determines the price they can charge. These types of firms are called *price searchers.*

> *A price searching firm faces a downward sloping demand curve.*
> ↳ price they charge depend on amount of output produce

You've probably noticed that the price of milk is not the same at your neighborhood corner store and your closest Safeway. No doubt Safeway is cheaper. Though your corner store no doubt sells less milk at the higher price, they do manage to sell enough milk to stay in business. Your corner store is a price searcher ... it faces a downward sloping demand curve for its products. You've also no doubt noticed that Microsoft products also sell for different prices at different locations, and that Microsoft has engaged in all types of complicated pricing practices, some of which have cost them a great deal of money in anti-trust lawsuits. Microsoft is also a price searcher and also faces a downward sloping demand curve for its products. Although the two firms are price searchers, they obviously behave differently. This is because the reasons for why they are price searchers are so different. Why would a firm face a downward sloping demand curve.

Costly Product Information

We have been quite silent about assumptions of information in our model. In the competitive model it is assumed that consumers know the products they are buying, they know the price at all stores, and they know firms are unable to cheat in product quality. Of course, no one knows all there is to know about anything, let alone goods purchased. Consider all the things you do in just a simple grocery store that reflect your poor information on product quality. You inspect the apples you buy because you don't want any with bruises or worms. If you knew everything about the apples you wouldn't have to inspect them. You sort through the oranges and mangos for the same reason. If the product is new you might buy a smaller quantity than normal just to "try it out" or the store might have tables set up with samples for you to try. If you knew everything, you would know what the taste and texture was like; you wouldn't need a sample. When you buy a car you take it for a test drive, get it inspected, and make sure a knowledgeable friend is with you. You phone around for the best price, don't trust fly-by-night salesmen, and ask for warranties. All because you need to aquire information to make decisions.

When information is costly, consumers don't switch brands or stores completely due to a price changes. When different firms offer different prices, consumers often suspect that the difference actually reflects something they simply don't know about. Perhaps the service is lacking; perhaps the good is of lower quality; perhaps it really is a good deal. Some consumers switch, but not everyone. Hence, a firm might raise its price, and not all of the customers leave. As information improves, firms find the elasticity of demand for their products increases. And with perfect information they become price takers.

Locational Advantage

Recall the old real estate adage "what are the three most important things in buying a house: location, location, location. In the competitive model, little attention was paid to the fact that we live in a three dimensional world where everything is located in a specific space. When location becomes important, then firms will face downward sloping demand curves because travel across space is not free. When a store is located close to my home, I spend less time traveling to that store compared to a store farther away. If the stores have equal nominal prices, the store farther away has a higher total cost once the travel time is included, and as a result, I will shop at the closer store. This means, however, that the closer store can raise the price of its goods, and I'll still shop there. Some marginal customers may go elsewhere, but the closer customers remain. As a result the firm keeps some of the customers with an increase in price and thus faces a downward sloping demand.

Slightly Different Products

One day I took my wife shopping for a jointer. A jointer is a specialized woodworking tool used for getting a straight edge and a flat surface. A wonderful tool. When we got to the "House of Tools" there were three jointers available. All were the same size, but not all were the same price. I bought the more expensive one, much to my wife's chagrin. When I pointed out the differences (the six inch longer bed, the better fence adjustment, and the fancy chrome knobs) she was not impressed. If she had to choose one of the three jointers, she would have gone with the cheapest version.

In our competitive model, we assumed that the products of all firms were homogeneous; that is, they were all the same. However, if you pick any product, whether blue jeans, frozen juice, or jointers, there is always a slight difference. As similar as they are, Pepsi and Coke don't taste exactly the same *and* not everyone ranks the difference the same. Some people like just like Pepsi, as hard as that is for a Coke drinker to understand, and vice versa.

When products are viewed as different by consumers, then again, the firm will not face a perfectly elastic demand curve, but will face one that is downward sloping. When Pepsi raises the price of its cola, the marginal consumers who think Pepsi and Coke are close substitutes switch and consume Coke, but the die-hard Pepsi drinkers stick with the product.

Monopoly

The extreme case of a price searcher is a monopolist. A monopoly firm is literally the only firm in the market, and a firm that faces the entire market demand of the product. A monopoly doesn't exist just because the market is too small to support more than one firm, a monopoly could exist for a number of reasons. First, a monopoly might exist because the government has granted the firm a special license. This might take the form of a special charter, like in the case of the original Hudson's Bay Company or Wheat Board in Canada, or the East India Company. Similarly, the government might provide a firm with a patent, which is an exclusive license to sell a product innovated by the firm. Or the firm might be in an industry where there are such huge fixed costs, average total costs are always falling. In such an industry, larger firms are always able to charge lower prices than smaller firms, and as a result only one firm ends up surviving in the market. This is called a "natural monopoly." Still a firm might end up a monopoly due to some unique superior input that other firms have no access to. When a firm is a monopoly, they obviously face a downward sloping demand curve, because the market demand curve is downward sloping.

13.2 Marginal Revenue Curve

Figure 13-1 shows a very simple downward sloping demand curve that a firm could face.

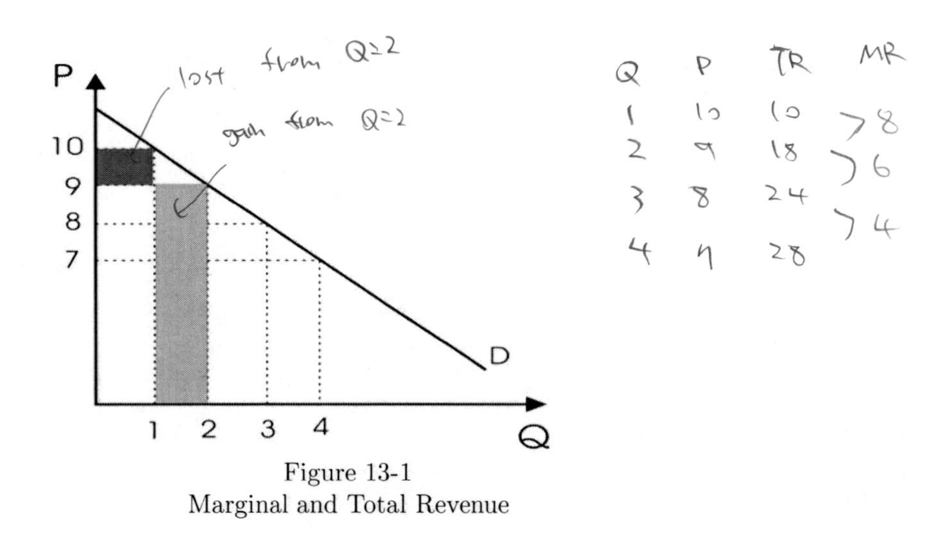

Figure 13-1
Marginal and Total Revenue

When the price of the good is \$10, the firm sells 1 unit, and has a total revenue of \$10. When the firm lowers the price to \$9 the firm sells 2 units, and total revenue becomes \$18. For the third unit sold, the price falls to \$8, and total revenue is \$24. Notice what is happening. In the price taking case the marginal revenue was always equal to the price, but here the marginal revenue is lower than the price. When the firm sells the second unit, the marginal revenue is \$8 (18-10), which is less than the \$9 price. When the firm sells the third unit, the marginal revenue is \$6 (24-18), which is again less than the price of \$8.

This happens because the firm faces a downward sloping, rather than a flat demand curve. Every time the firm lowers its price, it must lower the price for all of the goods it is selling. In Figure 13-1, consider the shaded areas. When the firm goes from selling 1 to 2 units, the firm earns \$9 on the sale of the second unit. However, it must lower the price of the first unit from \$10 to \$9. Hence the firm gains the light shaded region (\$9), but loses the dark shaded region (\$1), which nets out to \$8.

Notice also that as the price falls by \$1 for each extra unit sold, the marginal revenue is falling by \$2. In other words, the marginal revenue is falling twice as rapidly as the price. This is a general result. The marginal revenue curve will always lie below the demand curve and it will always have a slope twice that of the demand curve. Figure 13-2, shows the marginal revenue curve and the demand curve together.

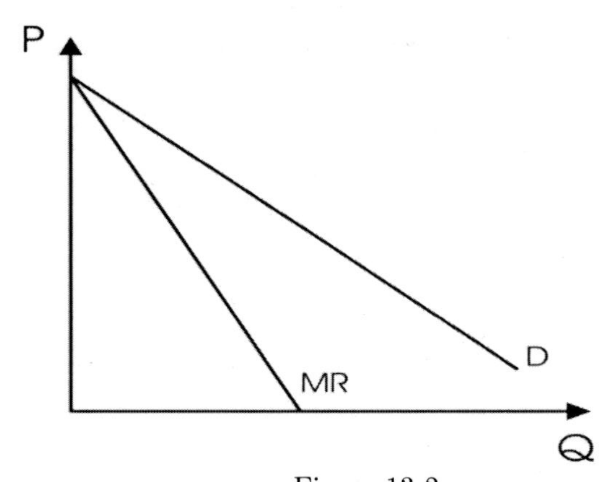

Figure 13-2
Marginal Revenue and The Demand Curve

13.3 The Price Searching Equilibrium

If the price searching firm had no costs of production, what would be the profit maximizing price to charge and output to produce? Think about this for a moment. If you recall from the discussion of elasticity, when we move down a demand curve, the total revenue is not constant. As the price falls, total revenue increases, is maximized, and then begins to fall. If a firm had no costs of production, then that firm would want to maximize revenues, because this would also maximize profits. This would be at a quantity of Q_R in figure 13-3. As always, profit maximization implies that marginal revenues should equal marginal costs. Since marginal costs are zero for a firm with no costs, such a firm would maximize revenues, and this occurs when marginal revenue equals zero.

Total revenue is maximized when marginal revenue equals zero: $MR = 0$.

Fortunately, when a firm has production costs, the price searching solution is very similar to the price taking one. In particular, it is still true that a profit maximizing firm sets marginal revenue equal to marginal cost. Just because a firm is a price searcher, doesn't mean they are any more or less interested in making money. Hence the profit maximizing rule remains. Figure 13-3 shows the equilibrium for a firm with costs.

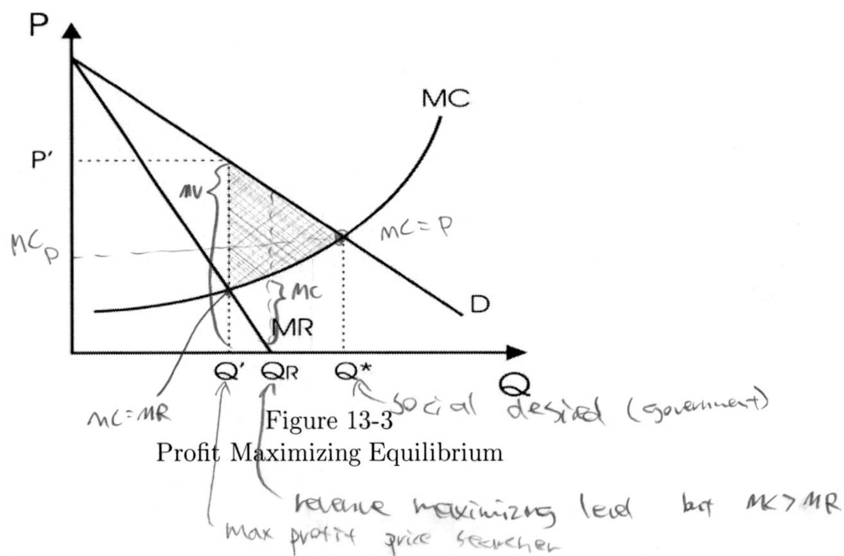

Figure 13-3
Profit Maximizing Equilibrium

The firm produces Q' output, and sells at price P'. This is the highest price the firm can charge for that level of output. Notice that this level of output is less than both the revenue maximizing level of output Q_R and the socially desired level of output Q^*. This latter level of output deserves some elaboration. From a social point of view, output should be produced as long as the marginal value (height of the demand curve) is greater than the marginal cost (height of the marginal cost curve). This condition is true until Q^*. The firm does not produce to this level because to produce that much means that marginal revenue is below marginal costs. The firm wants to maximize profits, not the gains from trade. Hence, because the marginal revenue is less than the price, a price searcher creates a deadweight loss equal to the crosshatched area. The deadweight loss results because the value of this lost production was greater than its costs.

A profit maximizing price searcher chooses a quantity which equates the MC and MR. As long as MC is positive, this quantity is not the quantity that maximizes total revenue, which is maximized when MR is zero, which is at a lower price and higher quantity than the price searching. This fact explains the behavior of many artists with respect to the price of their products. A few years ago Bono, the lead singer of the rock group U2, complained in an interview that his record company charged a price for CD's that he thought was too high. He was not alone. Musicians, authors, and actors often complain that the price of their music, books, and plays are set too high. Indeed, the author of this book complains that the price of his conventionally published book is too high! The question is, are these people (me included) altruists or are they actually acting in their own self interest?

The key to resolving this puzzle is that performers and authors are usually paid a royalty based on the revenue generated from gross sales. Artists are not paid based on profits. When someone is paid a fraction of the revenues, then their income is maximized when revenues are maximized, not when profits are maximized. As a result, their interests are at odds with the firm selling the product. In particular, an artist, or author, or singer, will want a lower price in order to sell a larger volume. In this way, they personally would make more money. Since artists do not bear the costs of production, they do not care that profits are not maximized when revenues are. Bono, and company, are not altruists — after all he didn't make the case that records should be given away!

If you understood the equilibrium with price takers, this one is not much different. You may be wondering where the firm's profits are? As with the price taking firm, the definition of profits remains the same: TR-TC. In order to tell how large profits are, we need to know what the average costs of the firm are. Figure 13-4 shows two situations.

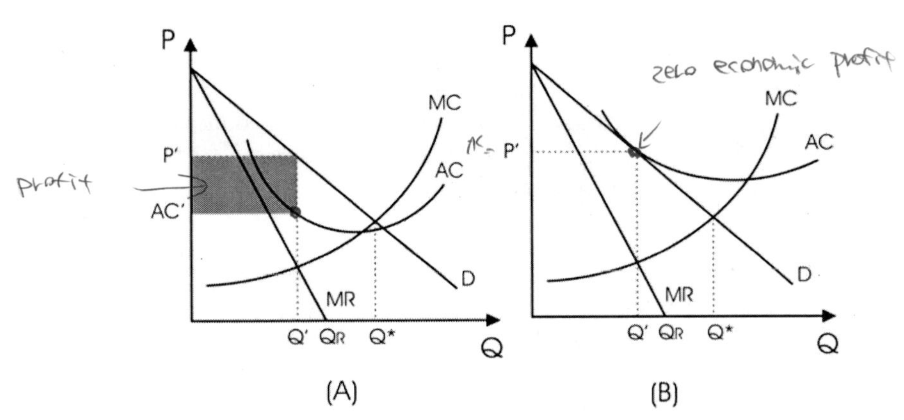

Figure 13-4
Profits For A Price Searching Firm

In panel (A) on the left, the firm has an AC curve that lies below the price when the firm produces Q' output. At this level of output, the firm's average costs are AC'. The difference between $P' - AC'$ is the profit the firm makes per unit of output. If we multiply this by the amount of output the firm produces, Q', we get the total amount of profit, equal to the shaded area. Just because a firm is a price searcher, however, doesn't mean the firm earns a profit. In panel (B) on the right, we see a firm with average costs that just equal price at the profit maximizing level of output. This firm would be making zero economic profit.

Like the case of price taking, the long run equilibrium for a price searcher must also have profits equal to zero. The firm is a price searcher for a special reason. Perhaps the firm has a great location, a trade secret, a franchise monopoly, or a special input. Whatever the reason, if the firm is earning a profit as in panel (A) of Figure 13-4, then the value of this special input must increase. As the value of this input increases, the average costs of the firm increase until the profits are zero. If the firm had been earning a loss, then the value of the asset allowing the price searching would have to fall. Hence, panel (B) represents the ultimate equilibrium for a price searcher.

13.4 Price Discrimination and Other Pricing Practices

The key interesting result of the price searcher model is the deadweight loss that results when a firm prices in such a way as in Figure 13-3. Normally a deadweight loss is produced when the government puts on a tax, subsidy, or some other type of market interference. Yet here we have a profit maximizing firm, trading with utility maximizing consumers, but still not maximizing profits! Something is wrong here. The crosshatched area in Figure 13-3 represents money on the table that is not realized. What is going on?

What has happened is an assumption has been sneaked into the model. The simple price searching model we've been learning about assumes that the firm can only charge one price. Presumably there is a cost to charging more than one price, and so the firm *cannot* capture the deadweight loss. If the firm cannot capture it, it seems silly to call it a loss, but that's the history of the model.

If we relax this assumption, we see that a price searching firm has a tremendous incentive *not* to charge a simple single price to everyone. When simple pricing is done, the gains from trade are not exhausted. By using more complex pricing schemes, the firm can capture more of the gains from trade and make more money. We now turn to this incentive.

Price Discrimination

Economists usually view cases of price discrimination as falling into three broad theoretical categories. The first category is perfect price discrimination: an "ideal," but usually unrealizable case. Here the firm successfully extracts the maximum possible profit from each customer and therefore captures the entire gains from trade. The second category is ordinary price discrimination. This is the familiar case in which the firm identifies potential customers by groups and charges each group a separate price. For example, the pervasive phenomenon of charging different admission prices for groups called "seniors," "adults," "students," and "children" is one instance of ordinary price discrimination. The third category, block or multipart pricing, is the case in which the monopolist charges different rates for different amounts, or "blocks," of a good or service. For instance, it is common practice to charge one rate for the first block of so many kilowatt-hours of electricity in a period and lower rates for subsequent blocks.

Perfect price discrimination results when every consumer pays their total value for the good. Consider the market demand curve in Table 13-1 (note that the numbers under MR lie in between the quantities sold because marginal revenue is the change in revenue for a change in quantity). For simplicity it is assumed that each individual only demands one good; that is, we'll consider the case of unit demand curves discussed in Chapter 6. Hence when the price is $14, one unit is sold, and when the price falls to $13, two units are sold to two individuals. The market demand curve falls with increased quantity because lower prices induce more people to enter the market.

Elasticity and Total Revenue

Quantity	Price	Total Revenue	MR	AR
0	15	0		
			14	
1	14	14		14
			13	
2	13	27		13.5
			12	
3	12	39		13

etc.

Assume for the moment that the monopolist firm facing this demand curve knows each individual's reservation price and can prevent the resale of the product through perfect market segmentation. Furthermore, assume that the firm exploits this knowledge by perfectly price discriminating. What becomes of the marginal revenue curve? From Table 13-1 it is clear that the marginal revenue equals the demand curve, which also equals the price. This is shown in Figure 13-5.

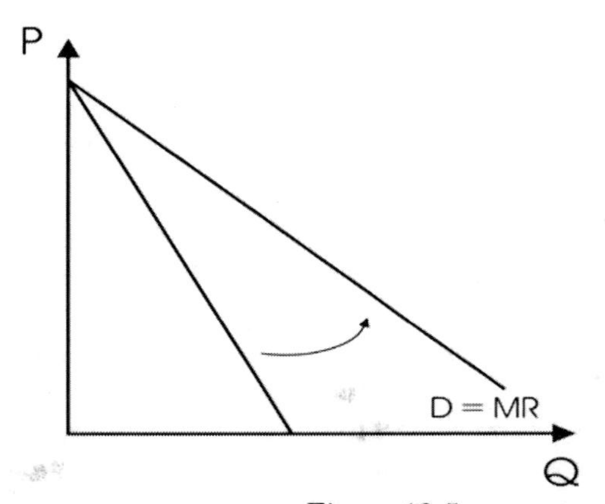

Figure 13-5
Marginal Revenue for Perfect Price Discrimination

In the simple monopoly case, MR fell faster than the price because a reduction in price at the margin meant that all the intramarginal units were reduced in price as well. This is no longer the case. With perfect price discrimination the firm can lower the price to the marginal customer, but those already purchasing continue to pay their reservation prices. Figure 13-6 shows the new equilibrium. As long as $MR > MC$ the firm continues to produce. When MR=MC, as always, the firm reaches the profit maximizing level of output. Since MR now equals the price, at output Q^* $MR = MC =$ price. In other words, the perfectly price discriminating firm produces the efficient level of output. At this level of output, however, the consumer's surplus is zero since each consumer pays their total value. The shaded area of Figure 13-6 is the rent to the firm. Notice as well, that in a market like this there is no single price; every consumer pays a different amount.

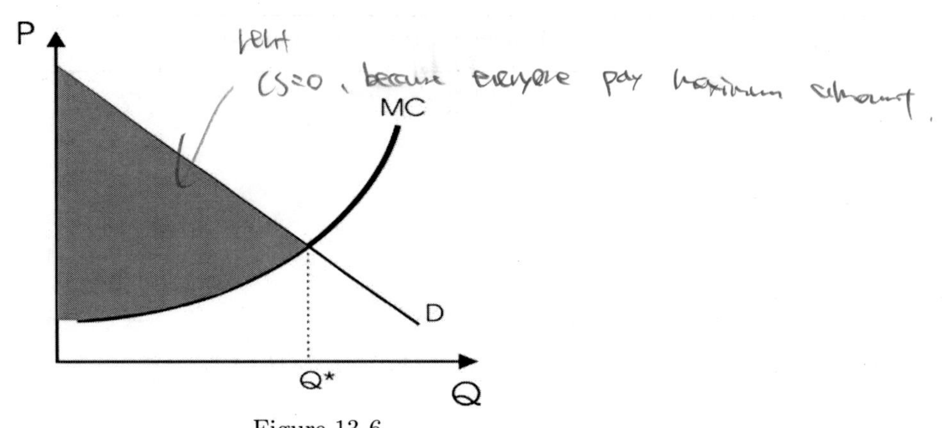

Figure 13-6
Perfect Price Discrimination Gains From Trade

The ability to extract the maximum amount of surplus through perfect price discrimination probably has no precise real world counter part because the conditions necessary for it are too extreme. Seldom do firms have perfect knowledge of their customers individual demands, and seldom can they perfectly segment the market to prevent resale. However, there may be examples that come close. For example, some people have interpreted Dutch auctions as a method of perfect price discrimination. Unlike an English (or ordinary) auction where the price starts out low and is bid higher, in a Dutch auction the price starts out high and then falls. The first person to bid takes the lot for sale at that price. Because there is only one bid, there is an incentive to bid close to the reservation price, and because the high marginal value users bid first, there is a built-in mechanism to prevent resale.

Another example of perfect price discrimination might occur in the provision of accounting services by small firms. Accountants routinely charge their clients different prices for the same service. Given their unique knowledge of their clients books, the professional restrictions on advertising prices, and the inability of a client to resell the accounting service, this type of industry appears to meet the requirements for perfect price discrimination. Accounting firms are not monopolists, but restrictions on advertising and the nature of the business gives each firm some market power.

Ordinary Price Discrimination

Now let us look at ordinary price discrimination by considering first the theory and then the circumstances in which this strategy is feasible. To keep matters simple, we will ask how a firm sets price in a market divided into just two segments. Suppose one segment of the market is characterized by low elasticity of demand, while the other segment has a high elasticity of demand. When a firm decides which market to sell in, it must ask: in which market will there be a larger contribution to profits? The answer to this question is: the market with the higher marginal revenue. So, a profit maximizing firm will sell products in the market with the higher marginal revenue. But when a firm sells in that market the marginal revenue falls, and so it will keep selling until the marginal revenue in each market is the same. Furthermore, the firm will make goods until the total marginal revenue is just equal to their marginal costs, since this is the condition for overall profit maximization.

> *Ordinary Price Discrimination involves: equalizing the marginal revenues across markets, and setting the total marginal revenue equal to the marginal costs.*

This is shown in Figure 13-7. The graph in panel (c) on the far right side shows the joint market situation, where the firm's total demand curve is not shown. What is shown is the sum of the marginal revenues in each of the separate markets. Thus the heavy line marked MR is the horizontal summation of MR_1 and MR_2. The firm equates this marginal revenue with the total marginal costs and ends up producing a total output of $Q_1 + Q_2$. This output is divided between the two segmented markets. To determine what price is charged, a straight line is drawn across to panels (A) and (B). Where this line intersects the individual marginal revenue curves determines the quantities sold in that market. The price in each market is determined by the demand in those separate markets.

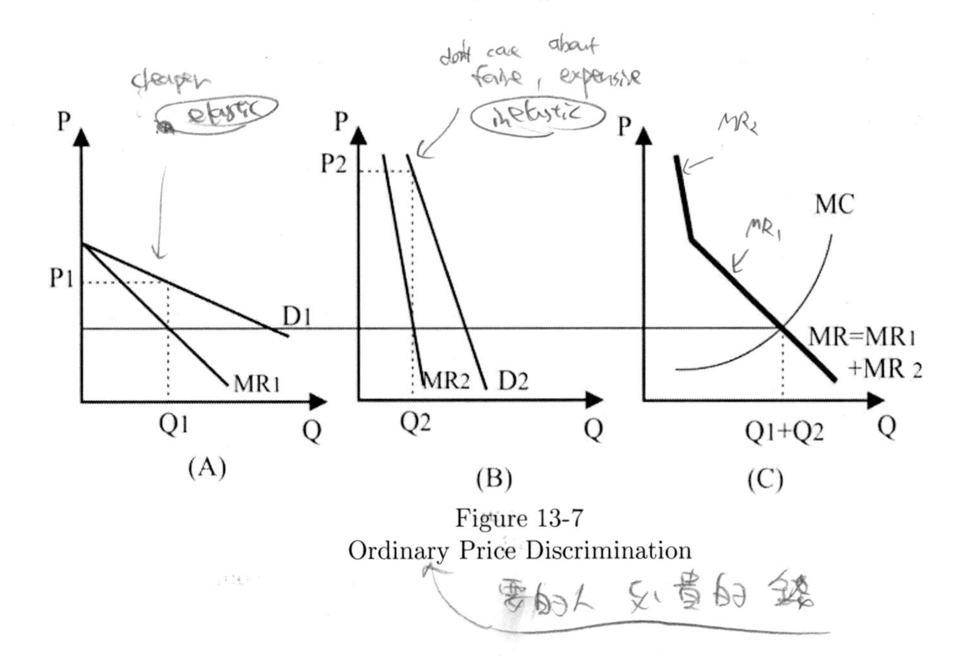

Figure 13-7
Ordinary Price Discrimination

The key result in this simple two sector model is that the price is higher in the market segment with the lower price elasticity of demand. This result makes good sense of ordinary observations. If one of your parents falls desperately ill in Paris, or if your branch plant in London is threatening to close, you will catch the next flight out, of say Canada, almost regardless of the fare. Your demand for airline travel is relatively price inelastic. By contrast, if you have decided to treat yourself to a holiday next spring, but do not care whether you go to Aruba or Mazatlan or Saskatoon, you can pick and choose your flights and airfares. Accordingly, your demand on any of these routes is relatively price elastic. Airline companies respond to these differing elasticities by discriminating — by charging the traveler who wants to depart tomorrow one price and the traveler who wants to depart sometime in the next month or two another, much lower price. The next time you're on a plane, ask the person beside you what price they paid and when they booked their flight ... one of you will feel better.

> *With ordinary price discrimination, the market with the lower elasticity of demand has the higher price.*

To be successful at ordinary price discrimination, the price searching firm must be able to identify different price elasticities of demand and to segment its market accordingly by isolating one portion of the market from the other in order to prevent resale. If the firm cannot separate the markets this way then someone will arbitrage over the price difference: which means buying in the cheap market and selling in the expensive one until the price difference disappears. Where arbitrage can occur, market segmentation cannot be achieved effectively.

In some markets arbitrage is virtually impossible. For example, in a wide range of cases characterized by what we might call personal services, arbitrage is impossible. Although "seniors" get a discount on movie admission prices, for example, they cannot arbitrage in this market because they cannot transfer the good — a movie they have seen — to someone else. Similarly, children cannot arbitrage in the market for haircuts — even though they can buy them more cheaply than adults — because haircuts are not transferable. All sorts of personal services from massage therapy and fitness classes to dental and medical services are markets in which arbitrage between customers cannot occur.

In other cases, arbitrage is possible but unprofitable. For example, the retail price of a new car in Oshawa, Ontario, is sometimes lower than the price of the identical model in Regina, Saskatchewan. But, relative to the price differential, the cost of transporting a car from Oshawa to Regina is high enough to discourage significant arbitrage. If a price differential is large enough, however, arbitrage will occur. Thus, the possibility of arbitrage limits the degree to which prices can diverge in the two markets. In general, where arbitrage costs — the costs of buying, selling, and transporting — are significant, arbitrage will be unprofitable.

In still other cases, arbitrage may be both possible and potentially profitable, but the price discriminator may be able to subvert it effectively. A classic example is the case in which the duopolists Du Pont and Rohm and Haas sold the plastic molding powder methyl methacrylate to general industrial users for $0.85 per pound and to dental manufacturers for $22 per pound. When arbitragers began buying methyl methacrylate at the industrial price and reselling it to denture manufacturers at a price below $22 per pound, Rohm and Haas considered cutting the ground out from under the arbitragers by mixing arsenic with the plastic powder sold for industrial use so that it could not be used for denture work. Although the firm ultimately rejected the idea, it did circulate rumors suggesting that the industrial methyl methacrylate had been adulterated.

The contamination of products is not that uncommon actually. For example, grain intended for seed use only is often poisoned to prevent its use in consumption. An unusual example involved Alcoa, the monopolist aluminum company of America. Alcoa was selling aluminum to aircraft manufacturers at a very high price. Simultaneously, they were selling aluminum to electrical cable companies, and household appliance companies at a significantly lower price. Alcoa quickly found out that the latter group were reselling their inventories of raw aluminum. To counteract this, Alcoa began its own production of cable and pots and pans. Alcoa even had to go to the extreme lengths of adding plastic handles, steel rivets, and copper bottoms to its pots in an effort to stop firms from melting them down in an effort to resell the aluminum.

Damaging goods to prevent resale is quite common in the high-tech software industry. Some financial service firms offer software that provides either real time or delayed stock prices. The delayed price service actually costs more to provide than the real time service because of the added storage capacity required. However, firms incur this higher cost in order to price discriminate between users. Another interesting example is Intel's creation of the 486SX computer chip, which was the regular 486DX chip with its math coprocessor disabled. These software developers are reducing the gross value of some of their products in order to prevent customers from capturing the rents in the high end market.

A final example of product tampering to prevent resale is "purple gas". Most Canadians are unaware that farmers are able to purchase gasoline for their farm vehicles (including their trucks) at a price well below the market level. Farmers could not only exploit this by using this gas in the family car, but could clearly set up a "Farmer Doug's resale gas station" behind the barn to sell gas to their urban cousins. One method used to police this is to dye the gas purple. Police occasionally set up road blocks in rural areas and test the gas in the tank. Those found driving a non-farm vehicle with purple gas face a fine. The threat of the fine then segments the market and reduces the amount of resale.

In cases where arbitrage is either impossible or not profitable, how can the monopolist achieve market segmentation? One method is to sort the individuals in different segments of the market by requiring them to identify themselves. For example, for "seniors" to receive lower prices on prescription drugs or movie tickets, they must somehow certify their age. When the accountant does a clients books, the client obviously must hand the books over to the accountant and reveal his financial status. Requiring direct identification is the most obvious way to isolate market segments from one another. Another method is to rely on self-selection; that is, to induce individuals to sort themselves into the appropriate market niche voluntarily. In the Dutch auction case above, the high demanders sort themselves by bidding first. A more conspicuous example is the two-segment market for airline travel. In the business travel segment of the market, demand is likely to arise on relatively short notice and to be relatively price inelastic. In the holiday travel segment, demand is usually anticipated well in advance and is likely to be relatively price elastic. A standard discriminatory mechanism is the "advanced booking discount," often hedged by such other restrictions as requiring the traveler to stay at least a week or to stay over at least one Saturday night. Because only holiday travelers are able to plan well ahead and stay for at least a week — and are therefore able to take advantage of the discount, the airline's customers reveal their identity as business people or vacationers simply by their response to its price structure.

Another form of market segmentation is intertemporal. Many individuals love the "newest" and "latest" models of everything from cars and stereos, to books and movies. Firms that have some market power over their commodities can price discriminate over time by charging a high price at the product's launch and then lower the price over time. Books are first printed in hard copy versions, and then later sold as paperbacks. Movies are first sold through theaters, and then later through videos. New products in general, whether they are calculators, computers, or water beds, often have prices that fall through time. As with the case of sales, the market is segmented through time, with those willing to pay the highest prices purchasing first.

Mickey Mouse Pricing

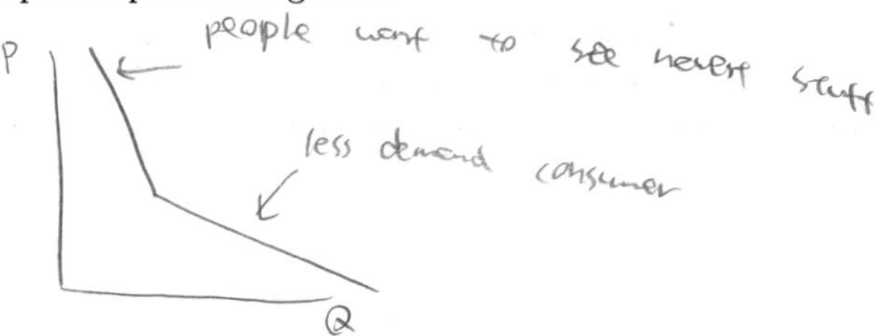

When you go to Disneyland you pay an entrance fee to get in, but once in you get to ride everything for free. When you go to your favorite nightclub, you might pay a cover charge at the door, and then pay for your drinks inside. If you want to shop at Costco, you pay a yearly fee and then purchase the goods inside for a certain price. All of these examples are of what is often called a *two part price* or a *compound price*. Essentially the price has two components: a "fee" for the privilege of consuming the good, and a price per unit.

The question is, if a price searching firm is going to use this type of pricing, what should the fee and per unit price be to maximize profits? To keep things very simple, suppose the firm faced customers that all had demand curves like the one in figure 13-8. As shown in figure 13-8, the firm also has flat marginal costs.

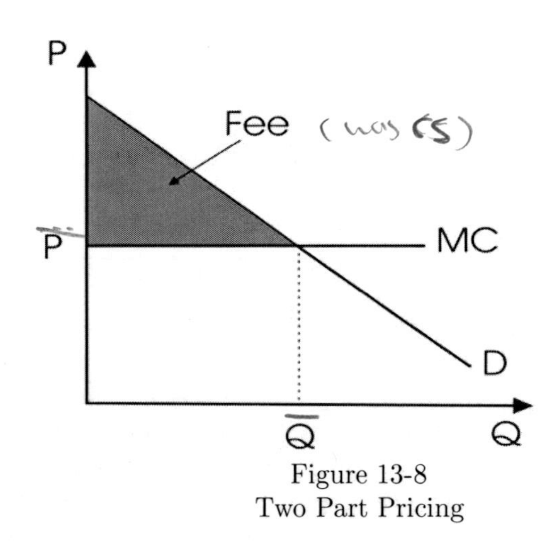

Figure 13-8
Two Part Pricing

Let's start with the profit maximizing combination, shown in figure 13-8. The fee is essentially a transfer of consumer's surplus to the firm, so what the firm wants to do is create as much consumer's surplus as is profitable, and then "tax" it away with the fee. The best way to maximize consumer's surplus, as we've seen from our discussion of competitive markets, is to charge a price equal to marginal costs. In figure 13-8 the firm charges a price equal to $\bar{P}$ and sells $\bar{Q}$. The fee would then be the shaded area. Notice that the firm would completely capture all of the surplus with this pricing scheme, and would produce the optimal amount of output. In this regard, two part pricing is like perfect price discrimination.

Figure 13-9 shows what would happen if the firm charged a per unit price higher than marginal costs. If the price is P', then only Q' is demanded. At this lower quantity, the consumer's surplus is lower, and hence the fee is also lower. This is shown by the smaller light shaded region. Since the firm is charging a higher price, the dark shaded region is rent to the firm. However, the firms overall profits are lower by the crosshatched area. Hence the best thing for the firm to do is set the per unit price equal to the marginal costs.

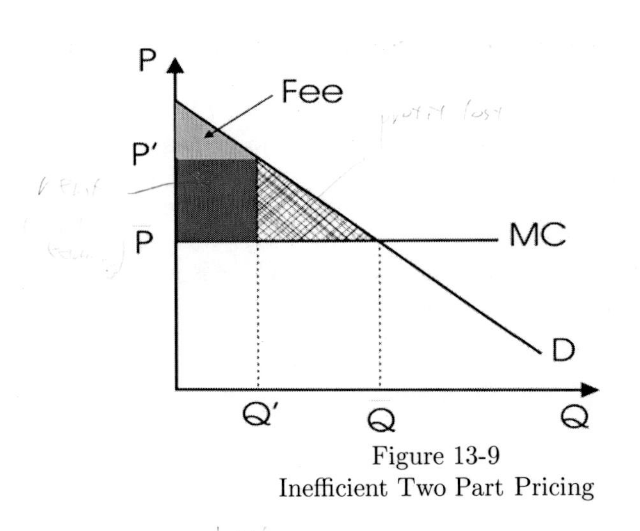

Figure 13-9
Inefficient Two Part Pricing

> *The optimal two-part pricing strategy is to set P=MC, and charge an entry fee equal to the consumer's surplus.*

The major advantage of this type of pricing is that, unlike the situation with price discrimination, the firm does not have to worry about market segmentation and the problem of resale. Here everyone pays the same price. This type of pricing strategy explains the pricing at such firms as Disneyland and Polaroid. Other examples include golf courses that charge a membership fee and green fees, car rental firms that charge a daily fee and a charge per mile, night clubs that charge a cover charge and prices for food and drinks inside, and telephone and cable TV companies that charge a hookup fee and a monthly rental fee.

Two-part pricing is more profitable than ordinary price discrimination because all of the consumer's surplus is transferred to the firm. If two-part pricing brings in more revenue and avoids the problem of having to police resale, why would firms ever bother with price discrimination? Why wouldn't two-part pricing be even more popular? As with all complex pricing practices, two-part prices have their costs. The problem is one entry price is charged to everyone, and not everyone is necessarily willing to pay that price. Suppose there are two types of customers: high demand types and low demand types. If the firm charges the same per unit price to both types of customers, then the high demand types generate a higher consumer's surplus. If the firm decides to extract this surplus through the use of an entry charge, then the low demanders drop out of the market. If there are enough low demand types in the market, the firm may find it more profitable to price discriminate between the two types.

Two-part prices work best when the consumers are homogeneous, or tend to be similar in the demand for the product. As the consumers become more heterogeneous, it will become more profitable to price discriminate. Hence we observe the wholesale distributor Costco charging and entry fee, while ordinary grocery stores do not. Costco caters to large families and small businesses, and has a more homogeneous set of customers than does a store like Safeway. Night clubs charge entry fees because individual clubs create atmospheres that cater to similar types of people. Neighborhood pubs on the other hand do not charge fees because their clientele are quite varied.

In economic circles, the most famous example of two-part pricing is popcorn at the movies. The example is famous because the price of popcorn is apparently too high. Before you read this book, you might have explained this high price as follows. "Once you enter the theater, the theater owner is a monopolist popcorn seller, so he sets a high price." But you know now that this does not make any sense. Setting a high popcorn price lowers the price one is willing to pay at the door. If the movie house is engaged in simple two-part pricing in an effort to extract more surplus from movie goers, surely they could do better by lowering the price of the popcorn and charging a higher price for the movie. One explanation is that perhaps the marginal cost of the popcorn is $4 for a small bag. ... Not. A better explanation might be that popcorn is used as a tie-in sale.

Tie-In Sales

Tie-in sales are another possible way for a price searching firm to extract surplus from its customers. A tie-in sale is where a firm has a monopoly over good 1, but refuses to sell it to you unless you also buy good 2 from them, even though it is available in a competitive market. Tie-in sales have a special history in the folklore of anti-trust cases because of the infamous IBM case. IBM was founded in 1911, and changed its name to IBM in 1924 — long before the invention of computers! IBM made a great deal of money on tabulating machines, and in order to purchase a machine IBM required its customers to purchase "punch cards" through IBM. These cards could also be purchased through the market at prices substantially below what IBM was charging. A law suit was brought against IBM, charging that a tie-in sale was "extending the monopoly power" of IBM into a market that was competitive.

The IBM case launched an entire industry as economists and lawyers developed defenses against the charge. Here we will not consider other explanations for tie-in sales, but simply consider how it could be a method of extracting surplus. Suppose we have a firm that has a monopoly on an adding machine, and that the demand for this machine is given in Figure 13-10, panel (a). For simplicity we can assume that the marginal cost and average cost of producing these machines is zero, and that it is not profitable to price discriminate or use a two-part tariff. If the firm acted as a simple monopoly it would maximize total revenue and charge a price P' and sells Q', generating consumer's surplus equal to the shaded region.

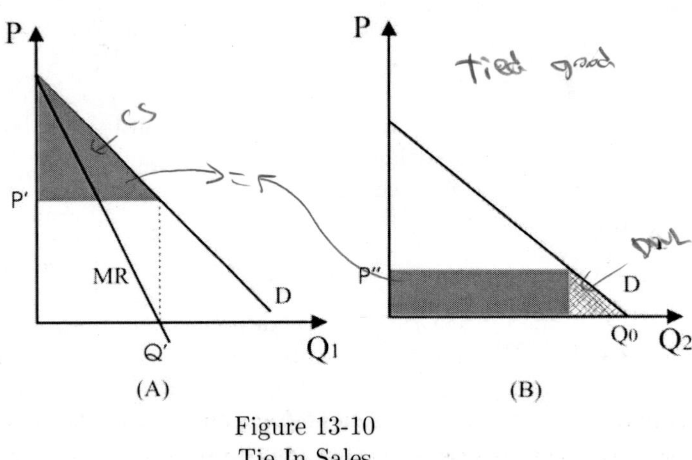

Figure 13-10
Tie In Sales

Now suppose there is another good called "paper" that sells in the competitive market. For simplicity, assume the marginal costs of paper are also zero, and therefore, that its price in the market is also zero. The demand for paper is given in Figure 13-10, panel (b), and at the market price of 0, Q_0 is the amount consumed. One strategy for the monopolist firm is to tie the sale of paper to its adding machines and charge a price of paper above marginal costs. If the firm sets its price for adding machines equal to P', then it can charge a price of paper equal to $P'' > 0$. The total shaded area in panel (b) must equal the shaded area in panel (a). That is, the loss of consumer's surplus from paying more for the paper will just equal the gain in consumer's surplus from consuming the adding machines.

By tying in the paper, the firm is able to extract the consumer's surplus; however, it is unable to extract all of it. The revenue from paper is equal to the entire shaded area of panel (b), but the firm only gets the dark shaded area. That is, the tie-in sale creates a deadweight loss by charging above marginal cost for the tied good. It turns out that the situation in panels (a) and (b) do not represent the equilibrium prices, because the firm can still do better. Do you see how? If the firm lowers the price of the adding machines it increases the consumer's surplus. This means that there is more surplus to extract, and as a result the firm can charge more for the paper. As the price of the paper increases though, the deadweight loss increases. Hence it will never pay for the firm to give its own good away and try to extract all of the surplus away through a tied in good. For us, however, the point is simply that a firm can do better using a tie-in than it can using simple pricing.

> *With a tie-in sale the firm lowers the price of the monopoly good and raises the price of the tied-good.*

So why is popcorn so expensive at the movies? One explanation is that popcorn is used as a tie-in sale in order to extract the surplus from people who really like movies. In order for this argument to work, there must be different tastes for movies and popcorn among the population. Suppose there are two types: movie lovers and marginal movie goers, equally distributed in the population. Further, let's suppose that the movie lovers also love popcorn, but the movie goers just watch the movie. Perhaps the movie lovers are willing to pay \$12 to see a movie, while the movie goers are only willing to pay \$7. What are some pricing strategies that the theater can charge? Once again, we see that a two-part price probably won't work because there is too much heterogeneity in the population. Setting a large entrance fee at \$12 will lose half of the customers. Straight price discrimination is unlikely because the movie lovers and goers may not be part of an identifiable group, and so market segmentation is too costly. A tie-in sale might work, however. By setting a low price of admission, the theater extracts the maximum willingness to pay from the marginal movie goers, but leaves a \$5 surplus to the movie lovers. Once inside, however, the movie theater charges an above marginal cost price for its popcorn in an effort to extract the \$5 from the movie lovers. Notice that in this context, a tie-in sale is a subtle form of price discrimination.

All-or-Nothing Demands and the Exploitation of Affection

An all-or-nothing demand curve is different from an ordinary demand curve. An ordinary demand curve tells us the marginal value of a given quantity, while an all-or-nothing demand curve tells us the average value of a given quantity. Another way of putting this is that an all-or-nothing demand curve tells us the maximum amount per unit a customer would be willing to pay for a given amount of some good, rather than have nothing at all. When a consumer pays the average value for a good, rather than the marginal value, then the consumer's surplus is zero. If a monopolist can charge an all-or-nothing price, then, it is able to extract the entire consumer's surplus.

In Figure 13-11 we have drawn an ordinary demand curve (the marginal value line, MV), and an all-or-nothing demand curve (the average value line AV). Under normal circumstances, at a price P_2, the consumer would set price equal to marginal value in order to maximize utility and would consume Q_1 units. At this level of consumption the consumer would earn a consumer's surplus equal to the light shaded triangle above the price P_1 plus the white area below P_1 and above P_2. However, a price searching firm could offer the following deal to the consumer: pay price P_1 for the quantity Q_1, or receive nothing at all. Even at the price P_1, the consumer receives the light shaded surplus for the first units consumed; however, for the last units consumed the level of surplus is the dark shaded negative area. The light shaded triangle above P_1 is the positive consumer's surplus, while the dark shaded triangle below P_1 is the negative surplus. When these two triangles are equal the firm has found the maximum *average* price the consumer is willing to pay for Q_1, and this price exhausts the surplus. If we calculate this price for every potential level of output, then we get the average value curve AV, which is the all-or-nothing demand curve.

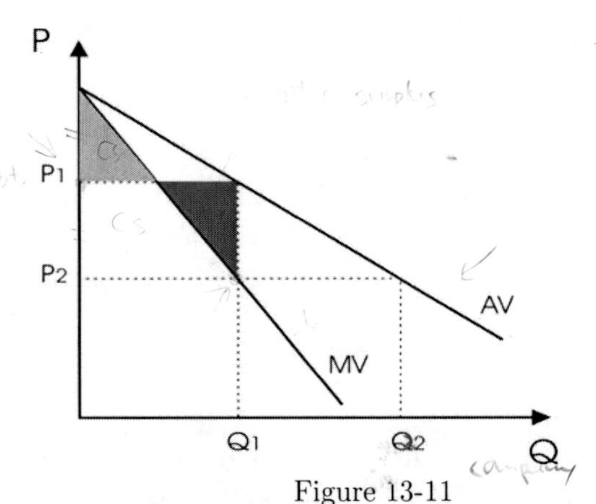

Figure 13-11
The All-Or-Nothing Demand Curve

Another way of interpreting the all-or-nothing demand curve is that it tells us the maximum amount a consumer will purchase at a given price rather than have nothing at all. For example, at price P_1, the consumer, if left on his own, would maximize utility at quantity Q_1. However, the firm could force the consumer to purchase Q_2 units rather than have nothing at all. Again, at this higher quantity, the consumer's surplus is completely transferred to the firm. All-or-nothing pricing, then, is yet another form of perfect price discrimination, and as such can only exist when there is knowledge of the demand curve, and perfect market segmentation.

All-or-nothing pricing may not seem very common, but it occurs all of the time in personal relationships where people generate affection towards one another. Suppose we use a fictitious couple, call them Pat and Heidi. Suppose Heidi loves Pat, and loves doing little favors for him.

She buys him clothes, cooks his favorite meals, and even scratches his balding head every now and then. She does these things because they generate utility for her, but her marginal value for head scratches, like all marginal values, diminishes the more she does it. To keep matters simple, call all of these acts of kindness "gifts". The marginal value of gifts to Pat by Heidi is given in Figure 13-12, along with the marginal costs.

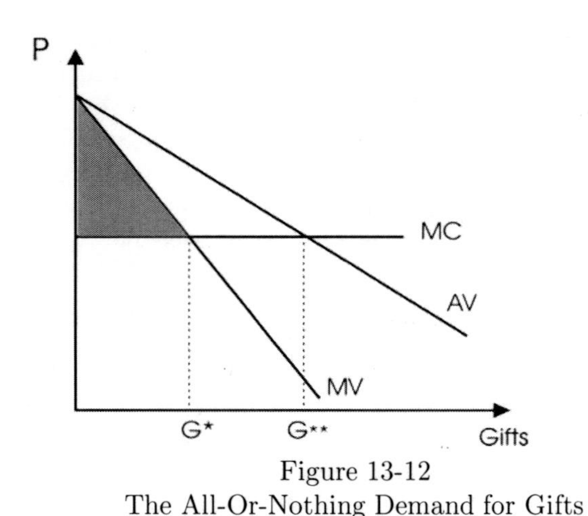

Figure 13-12
The All-Or-Nothing Demand for Gifts

As a maximizing gift giver, Heidi would like to supply Pat with G^* gifts. In doing so she would generate a consumer's surplus equal to the shaded area. However, now let's bring Patrick into the picture. Pat is, in fact, a monopolist with respect to Heidi — it is only his head she likes to scratch. What can Pat do? He can exploit Heidi's affection by demanding G^{**} gifts or threaten to accept none at all. Heidi may only want to scratch Pat's head 3 nights a week, but Pat may be able to extract 6, by threats of not participating at all.

Several things are apparent from this example. The more inelastic is the marginal value of gift giving, the more affection can be exploited. In any interpersonal relationship it is never a good idea to be too dependent on any one person. If you only have one friend in the whole world, that friend will be able to exploit great rents from you. In a marriage relationship, if the wife is homebound, without a car, and has few contacts with the outside world, while the husband is out working and playing golf with his buddies on the weekend, then the wife will be the one with the exploited affection.

Since asymmetries in a relationship lead to one party being exploited to the advantage of the other, we might expect that people enter into relationships with others that are similar in terms of their outside relationship opportunities. This certainly seems to hold for marriage. In a marriage it is uncommon for one partner to continue to have friends of the opposite sex. In fact, the marriage vows often state that each partner promises to "forsake all others." Having friends of the opposite sex, puts one at an advantage in bargaining for gifts, and so will be discouraged. Casual observation also suggests that when individuals engage in adultery, they do so with someone who is also married. Having an affair with an unmarried person is just asking to be blackmailed. Recognizing that affection is potentially exploitable explains why couples fight more as their relationship progresses. When a man and woman first meet, their marginal value curves for gift giving to each other is perfectly elastic, because the number of substitutes for each other is huge. As time progresses, though, each person becomes more specific to the other, and love between the couple develops. As affection grows, however, so does the opportunity to exploit it. No one likes to be exploited, though, and as a result fights arise. On the other hand, any attempt to exploit affection on a first date doesn't lead to fighting; it just leads to the other party telling you to take a hike.

The exploitation of affection also explains some aspects of sibling rivalry. Anyone who has ever seen a proud parent of a first born child has met someone who has an extremely inelastic demand for affection towards the child. For a first time parent, there is no substitute for the new child. As a result, the only child is in a unique monopoly position, and can exploit the affection of the parent to no end by making statements like "If I can't have a pony, I won't love you anymore!" The solution to this problem is to introduce competition in the market for affection. By having more children parents create rivalry for their attention, which increases the elasticity of demand. When a child threatens to withhold affection if they don't get a pony, the parent can now reply "fine, I'll go play with your sister." The model presented would predict that only children would tend to be more spoiled than children from large families.

13.5 Summary

This chapter introduced a major change in one of our key assumptions in the neoclassical model. Rather than assuming firms were price takers, we assumed that firm were price setters. This condition meant that firms could raise their prices and not lose all of their customers. There are many reasons for why a firm might be a price setter: locational advantage, differentiated product, and monopoly being just three. This major change in assumption manifested in only one key difference in our model: price no longer equals marginal revenue for the firm. When price is greater than marginal revenue, the profit maximizing firm ends up producing less than was optimal. This provides the firm with a strong incentive to use complex pricing to capture more of the gains from trade and increase the volume of trade. Several of these pricing schemes were looked at, including price discrimination, two part pricing, tie in sales, and all or nothing pricing.

REVIEW QUESTIONS

1. If a firm wants to make as much money as is possible, does this mean it sets a price as high as possible?

2. Why would a price searching firm try to charge different prices to its customers?

3. Does a profit maximizing price also maximize revenue?

4. How would you explain "Ladies Day" at bars, clubs, and on-line dating services, where women usually get in for free, but men still pay admission?

5. What is the problem with using two-part (Mickey Mouse) pricing?

6. What is the consumer's surplus along the all-or-nothing demand curve?

7. If the government forces a monopolist firm to produce the socially efficient level of output, and the monopolist has a constant (flat) marginal cost, then will the firm necessarily make a loss at this level of output.

8. In his novel, "The Godfather," Mario Puzo makes the following observation about the leader of a crime syndicate: "...like many businessmen of genius he learned that free competition was wasteful, monopoly efficient." In what sense is Puzo using the word "efficient?" Contrast this with the economist's use of the term.

PROBLEMS

1. Suppose the demand function is $P = 100 - Q$ and that the cost function is $TC(Q) = 40Q$. On one diagram, carefully construct the average revenue, marginal revenue, average cost, and marginal cost functions. Then show that the optimal quantity Q^* is 30 and the optimal price P^* is \$70. Construct the profit rectangle and show that profit is equal to \$900.

2. Canadian Tire offers a 4% discount for cash payments. Instead of taking 4% off the total bill, however, the firm gives customers the equivalent in Canadian Tire money. This "money" then can be presented in lieu of cash the next time customers make a purchase at a Canadian Tire store. Can you identify the form of price discrimination through self-selection at work here?

3. What would a theater company using popcorn as a tie-in sale do if the movie lovers didn't snack while watching movies, and it was the marginal movie goers that had the high demand for popcorn?

4. Using Figure 13-12, under what circumstances would a divorce occur? How would the feminist movement have effected the exploitation of affection in a marriage? Given this, what effect on the divorce rate would the feminist movement have had?

5) Answer the following questions about price searchers as True or False, with an explanation.

   a. A price searcher may not always earn a profit, but it always earn a rent.

   b. The profit maximizing rule to choose output for a price searcher who can only charge one price is different from the rule used by a price searcher who can charge more than one price.

   c. All natural monopolies are price searchers, but not all price searchers are natural monopolies.

   d. Two part pricing, when all consumers are identical, exhausts consumer's surplus.

   e. Two-for-one pizza is an example of first degree price discrimination.

   f. A price searcher sets price and quantity independently, while a price taker just sets quantity.

   g. Sequential monopolies make more profit than single monopolies because they charge two monopoly prices rather than one.

   h. When Kodak offers film along with developing they are engaging in two part pricing.

   i. Bowlers pay by the frame; that is, the more frames they bowl, the more they pay. This is an example of price discrimination.

6. Suppose a price searching firm can only charge one price to all of its customers. Also it has a flat marginal cost of \$5. If MC increases to \$6, how much will the price increase by? Use a

graph in your answer.

7. "A monopolist always sets price equal to the unitary elastic point on its demand curve." True or false, use a graph in your answer.

8. A restaurant sells the same meal at dinner and lunch, but charges twice as much for the dinner. It has been sued for price discrimination, and has hired you to defend it. You can make one argument before the judge, what is your defense?

9. "Monopolist will not produce durable goods because they decrease the units sold and therefore the revenues of the firm, and they cost more and therefore also reduce profits." T/F/U. Explain.

10. A monopolist faces the following demand curve and cost function:

$$P = 50 - .5Q \qquad TC = 2Q + 1000$$

   a. Find the following equations: Marginal Cost: Marginal Revenue: Aver. Total Cost: Now carefully graph them, along with the demand curve on the same graph.

   b. What is the optimal price and quantity if the firm can only set one price for all units?

   c. Calculate the elasticity of demand at the profit maximizing price.

   d. If the government forced the firm to produced the socially efficient level of output, and set a per unit subsidy in order to compensate for any losses, what would the per unit subsidy be? (Assume the firm can still set only one price per unit).

   e. What would be the total amount of the subsidy assuming nothing else changes?

11. Suppose a market can be separated into two distinct markets, where $P_1 = 42 - 4Q_1$ and $P_2 = 22 - 2Q_2$ are the demands in each market. Total costs are given by $TC = 5 + 10(Q_1 + Q_2)$

   a. Find the profit maximizing level of output and the price per unit in each segment of the market.

   b. Find the elasticity of demand at the profit maximizing price.

12. Suppose there is a monopolist that has constant (flat) MC=1, and he faces two sets of consumers:

   * Set I consists of 100 buyers, each with the demand curve $p = 16 - q$.

   * Set II consists of 50 buyers, each with the demand curve $p = 10 - q/2$.

   a. Determine the profits and price with simple monopoly; that is, where the firm cannot discriminate between the two types. Hint: add up the demands to find the total market demand.

b. Now determine the profits and price when the firm can charge one different price between the two groups.

c. Finally, what are the profits and prices if the firm can charge an entry fee for each market and a price for q at $p = 1$ for both groups. Rank the three pricing schemes in terms of profitability.

13. Why might camera retailers so often sell the cameras themselves at prices very close to their own wholesale cost, while marking up the price of accessories (carrying cases, extra lenses, filters, and so on) by 100 percent or more?

14. Why are there "Ladies nights" at certain bars, and "Ladies days" at many professional sports events where entrance fees for the female patrons are radically reduced? At what type of events might there be "Gentlemen days"?

15. Following are cost and revenue tables for a price searcher.

Q	P	TR	MR	AC	TC	MC
0	10					
1	9			4		
2	8			4		
3	7			4		
4	6			4		
5	5			4		
6	4			4		
7	3			4		
8	2			4		
9	1			4		
10	0			4		

a. Complete the table.

b. Graph the demand curve, the MR, AC, MC curves all on the same graph.

c. What is the monopolist's P and Q?

d. What are its profits?

e. What is the value of consumer's surplus?

f. Suppose the monopolist is forced to determine his price and output by the competitive criterion. What output and price does this imply? In doing this, what assumptions are you making about costs?

g. At this new output level, what is the value of the monopolist's profits?

h. What is the new level of consumer's surplus?

i. What is the 'deadweight loss' due to this monopoly?

j. Suppose (instead of f), the government imposes a profits tax (99%) on the monopolist that extracts most of the profits, and later redistributes the money back to the customers. What is the new output level? What is the actual price paid, and what is the effective price? What is the 'deadweight loss' now? What is the consumer's surplus?

16. Suppose a price searching firm faces a demand curve given by $Q = 30 - .5P$, and has an average cost curve given by $AC = 8$.

a. Find the equations for the marginal revenue curve and the marginal cost curve.

b. Find the profit maximizing level of output and the profit maximizing price. At this combination, what is the level of firm profit? What is the level of deadweight loss?

c. Now suppose the marginal cost curve becomes $MC = Q - 5$. What is the new profit maximizing price and quantity?

d. Using the new marginal cost function in (c), suppose now the government imposes a \$10 per unit subsidy on the firm. What is the elasticity of demand at the new profit maximizing level of output?

e. Still assuming that the true marginal cost is given by $MC = Q - 5$, does the firm produce the socially optimal level of output in part (d)? Explain

17. Suppose a movie theatre is able to act like a simple price searching firm. The demand it faces for movies is given by $p = 41 - 2q$ and its total costs are given by $TC = 20 + q$.

a. Find the firm's marginal revenue and marginal costs.

b. Find the optimal level of output for the theatre and the optimal price.

c. What are the firm's profits at this level of output?

d. If the total costs of the firm actually turned out to be $TC = 190 + q$. Would anything happen to your answer to (b)?

e. Suppose the theatre figured out that its audience could be divided into two groups: adults, with demand equal to: p=37-6q; and children, with demand equal to: p=13-3q. What would the optimal price and quantity be if the total costs were still $TC = 20 + q$?

18. Sam-the-Man is the only shoe seller in his small, homogeneous town. Every consumer in Sam's town has an identical demand for his shoes, equal to $p = 15 - 3q$, where q is the number of units of shoes.

a. Draw a consumer's demand for Sam's shoes, and show what the marginal value would be for three pairs.

b. Sam decides to bundle his shoes in groups of three units, and to use an all-or-nothing pricing strategy. What is the highest price that Sam can charge for this package, if the consumer's only option is nothing? Draw another graph to show your answer.

19. A price searching firm faces the following demand curve and cost function:

$$P = 100 - Q \qquad\qquad TC = 10Q + 10$$

a. What is the optimal price and quantity for this firm?

b. What profit or loss is the firm making?

c. Suppose the firm could set an entry fee as well as charge a price for the good. What would be the optimal fee and price?

d. What are the profits now under scheme (c)?

20. Both price taking firms and price searching firms maximize profits. If this is true, then why does one set price equal to marginal cost, while the other sets a price that is greater than marginal cost?

21. A monopolist faces a demand curve equal to $P = 100 - Q$. The firm has a fixed cost equal to F, and a variable cost equal to $20Q$.

a. If the firm can only charge one price, what is the largest value for F, such that the firm earns a zero profit.

b. If the firm could costlessly perfectly price discriminate, what is the largest value of F, such that the firm earns a zero profit?

22. Injet is the only Canadian producer of a specific part for Feller-Bunchers (a logging machine). The Canadian government has provided such high tariff protection to Injet that they have a monopoly in Canada. However, this part is sold internationally, and Injet is a price taker on the international market. In the figure below "Dd" is the domestic demand for Injet parts, and MR is the corresponding domestic marginal revenue. The horizontal line "Di" is the international demand curve for Injet's part. The "MC" curve is the marginal cost of Injet for producing its part.

On the graph show what the domestic and international prices are. Also, show how many parts Injet sells in Canada and how many (if any) it sells internationally. Briefly explain your answer.

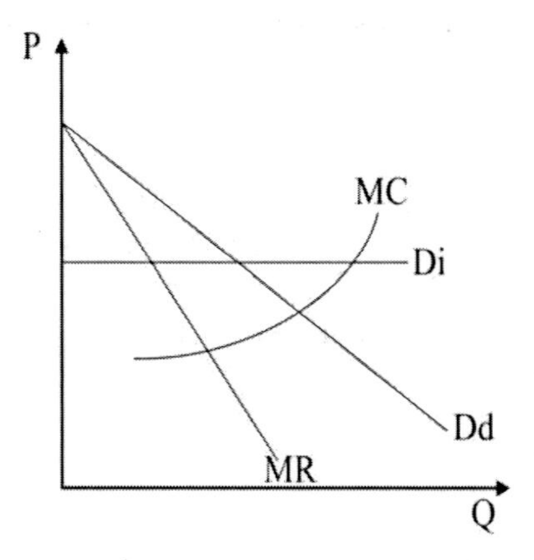

Figure 10–22: Injet's Demands

Review Question Answers

1. *No, if you set the price as high as possible, you'll sell nothing and have no revenue. Maximizing profits is not the same as maximizing price ... or sales.*

2. *Ordinary price searching leads to a deadweight loss. This represents lost profits to the firm. Hence the firm may try some type of compound pricing in order to capture this wealth.*

3. *No, except in the rare case it has no costs.*

4. *This is a form of ordinary price discrimination. There are high demanders (men) and low demanders (women), and the bar has set prices accordingly.*

5. *If different people have vastly different demands, then setting too high of an entry fee will result in a loss of customers. The scheme works best when the customers all have similar demands.*

6. *Zero.*

7. *Not necessarily. It depends on the firm's level of fixed costs. If the fixed costs are positive, then the AC curve will lie above the MC curve and the firm will earn a loss. However, if the firm has zero fixed costs, then the MC=AC curve and the firm would earn zero profits at the socially optimal level of output.*

8. Puzo is meaning that competition hurt the businessman's bottom line. It was "efficient" from the Godfather's point of view to have a monopoly over his crime syndicate. The economist thinks of efficiency from the social point of view. No businessman likes competition. However, for society as a whole it is a good thing.

Odd Numbered Problem Answers

1.

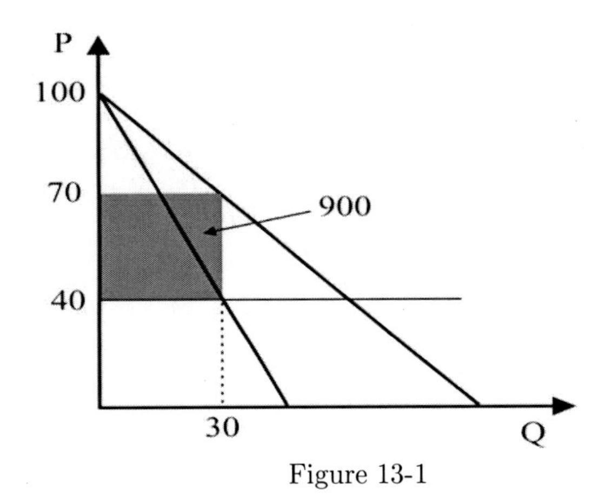

Figure 13-1

3. *It would set a higher price for movies and a lower price for popcorn.*

5)

a. *True. A price searcher doesn't necessarily earn a profit. Though it could earn a zero rent, if the rent is negative it would go out of business.*

b. *True. It will be different. For example, if the firm uses two part pricing it sets P=MC and charges a lump sum equal to the consumer's surplus. This is different from setting MR=MC.*

c. *True.*

d. *True.*

e. *False. First of all, this would not transfer all of the consumer's surplus.*

f. *False. A price searcher sets price and quantity simultaneously.*

g. *False. They make less, since the mark up is magnified and the total gains are lower.*

h. *False. It could be interpreted as a tie in sale.*

i. *True. Better bowlers play faster and therefore pay more per hour.*

7.

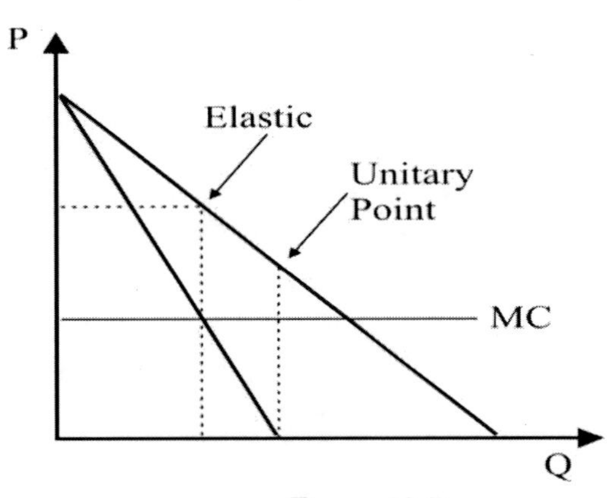

Figure 13-7

False. The price will always be in the elastic portion.

9. *False. Monopolists don't care about the number of units sold. If it is more profitable to sell durable goods, they'll do so.*

11.

a. *In market 1 P=26, Q=4. In market 2 P=16, Q=3.*

b. *In market 1* $E = -1.63$. *In market 2* $E = -2.66$.

13. *They are exploiting the consumer's surplus of the camera through tie in sales.*

15.

Q	P	TR	MR	AC	TC	MC
0	10	0				
1	9	9	9	4	4	4
2	8	16	7	4	8	4
3	7	21	5	4	12	4
4	6	24	3	4	16	4
5	5	25	1	4	20	4
6	4	24	-1	4	24	4
7	3	21	-3	4	28	4
8	2	16	-5	4	32	4
9	1	9	-7	4	36	4
10	0	0	-9	4	40	4

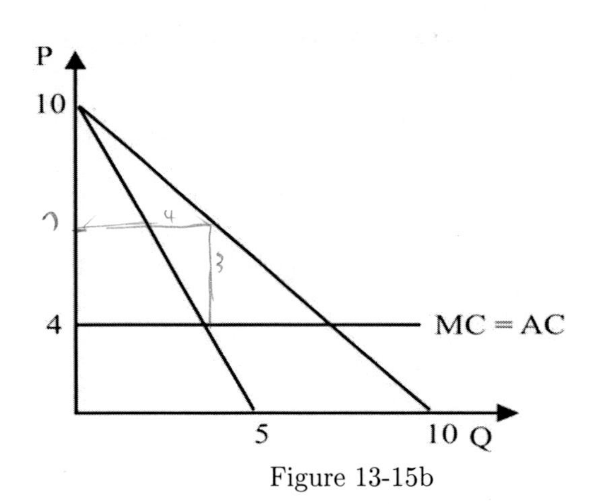

Figure 13-15b

b.

c. *P=7, Q=3.*

d. *Profit is $9.*

e. *Consumer's surplus is $4.5.*

f. *P=4, Q=6. We're assuming nothing happens to the firms cost curves.*

g. *Zero.*

h. *Consumer's surplus is $18.*

i. *$4.5*

j. *The firm still produces 3 units. Consumer's now pay $7, but the effective price is $4.03. The DWL is still $4.5, but the consumer's surplus is now $13.41.*

17.

a. *The marginal revenue curve would be given by* $MR = 41 - 4q$ *and the marginal cost curve would simply be* $MC = 1$.

b. *Set the MR=MC and solve for q=10, then plug this back into the demand curve to find p=21.*

c. *Profit equals total revenue minus total costs, or* $210 - 30 = 180$.

d. *Now the firm's profit would fall to $10, and so nothing would happen to the answer in (b).*

e. *Now the price to adults will be \$19, with 3 sales, and the price to children will be \$7, with two tickets sold.*

19.

a. *The firm sets MR=MC to find Q=45, and P=55.*

b. *The firm makes a profit of \$2015.*

c. *P=\$10, Fee= \$8100*

d. *Profits are now \$8090.*

21.

a. *If the firm can only charge one price then the marginal revenue curve is* $MR = 100 - 2Q$, *and the optimal level of output is 40. At this output the firm charges \$60 per unit, and the rent is \$1600. Hence, F could be as high as \$1600.*

b. *Now the value of F can be as high as the entire consumer's surplus. This is \$3200.*

CHAPTER 14

GAME THEORY, COLLUSION, AND COMPETITION POLICY

A few years ago a group of Fraser Valley raspberry growers were holding a meeting to discuss methods to restrict raspberry production and raise the price. An economist in the audience, who happened to also grow raspberries on the side, stood up and raised the objection that it wouldn't work since the farmers sold some 90% of the crop into the U.S. in direct competition with Washington and Oregon growers. To which an elderly man rose up and said "don't listen to him, we just want to make money!" The old man's sentiments carried the day, but in the end no raspberry cartel was ever forthcoming.

That's a great story for a number of reasons. First, it doesn't take a genius to figure out that an increase in price can be accomplished if the entire industry collectively restricts output. This increase in price, accompanied by a decrease in costs (since output is lower) will mean greater profits for those still producing. Second, as attractive as this is, it seldom comes about because the costs of enforcing the collusive agreement are so high. Like the raspberry farmers, there are failed cartels spread all over the economic landscape. Third, the raspberry cartel failed in part because there were simply too many raspberry producers to bring together. This chapter discusses these issues. However, we first consider a few famous elements of game theory, a branch of mathematics concerned with the interactions of small numbers of people. In this first section we will deal with a game called the prisoner's dilemma, and we will use this result to understand when and why some firms are able to collude together and when they cannot.

14.1 Simple Game Theory: Interactions With Others

Until this point in the book, we've been able to ignore how different individuals interact with one another. In our model of the competitive firm, each firm was so small it had no direct impact on anyone else. Thus this firm ignored other firms, and other firms ignored it. In our model of price searching, the firm faced a downward sloping demand function, and this was independent of the behavior of other firms. Thus this firm could again ignore all others.

But quite often in life interactions between people and firms is very important. Have you ever been watching a baseball game when an announcer starts to say something like this: "Johnny is at the plate, he's got a man on second, the count is three and one you just know he's going to get a slider to the outside." Perhaps that's what the batter is actually thinking. He's saying to himself "when there's a man on second, and the count is three and one, there's only one obvious pitch to do the slider to the outside of the plate!" But perhaps our batter thinks a little harder. If the batter knows a slider to the outside is the best pitch, and the announcer knows a slider to the outside is the best pitch, then it isn't too much of a stretch of the imagination to believe the pitcher also knows a slider to the outside of the plate is the best pitch. If the pitcher knows this, thinks the batter, and if the pitcher knows the batter knows this, then perhaps the pitcher will throw a fastball instead! As you can imagine, this type of thinking could go on forever. At the very least, unlike our announcer, we have to admit the solution over which pitch to throw is not so obvious.

Jim Bouton, a New York Yankee pitcher in the 1960's, was often frustrated by the sort of 20/20 hindsight thinking sports announcers and coaches would often use. In his book *Ball Four* he has the following humorous story:

> These pearls are of a special kind, absolutely valueless at best, annoying enough to upset your concentration at worst. ...Old Chicken Colonel Turner was a master at this. He' sit in the dugout and shout to Stan Bahnsen, "Now, keep the ball down, Bahnsen," and Stan would throw a letter high fastball that would get popped up into the infield and The Colonel would look down the bench and say, "The boy's fastball is moving. The boy's fastball is rising." Two innings later, same situation, the very same pitch, home run into the left-field seats. The Colonel looks up and down the bench and says very wisely, "Got the ball up. You see what happens when you get the ball up?" Then you'd get a weak lefthanded hitter up in Yankee Stadium and somebody would throw him a change-up and he'd hit it for a home run into the short porch and The Colonel would say, "You can't throw a change-up to a lefthanded hitter, boys. Not in this ballpark." A week later a guy would throw the same pitch to the same kind of hitter and the guy would be way out in front and The Colonel would say, "Change-up. One of the best pitches in baseball. You can really fool the hitter with it." Whatever the result, The Colonel always knew the cause.
>
> [pp. 59–61, 1970]

Whenever there are a few players interacting with one another, the behavior of other players cannot be ignored because their actions affect the outcome. Life is often characterized by situations where the interactions cannot be ignored. If you play squash, tennis, or badminton you cannot ignore the strengths of your opponent. Perhaps your forehand is your best shot, but you might never use it because your opponent knows this and keeps the ball away from your forehand. If you are in a sailing race you try to find the best point of sail for the wind conditions, but you must also watch what the boats behind and ahead of you are doing. Quite often boats in the lead of a race simply copy the tactics of the boat behind them, not because the second place boat chooses a better point of sail, but because by copying them there is no way for the second place boat to catch them. And, of course, for many firms changing the price of their product or changing the volume of sales cannot be done without considering how other firms in the industry will respond.

Whether we are talking about the decisions of Ford, Honda, and Toyota, or the decisions of a husband and wife, the interactions of decision makers often can be important. Game theory provides a language for articulating the issues of such cases, and provides a solution concept to resolve them.

14.2 Dominated and Dominant Strategies

We're going to examine one extremely simple game. This game is simple because it contains *dominated strategies.* A strategy is simply something you can do like move your price up or down, or invest or not invest. It could be anything really. A dominated strategy is one which is worse than all other choices you have, *no matter what the other players in the game are doing.*

> *A dominated strategy is worse than all other choices you have, independent of what others do.*

Suppose you're playing baseball and you've made it to first base. There are two outs, and there's a full count on the batter. In this situation everyone knows the runner on first will run, no matter what. If the batter swings and strikes out, running doesn't hurt. If the batter walks, then running doesn't hurt. If the batter hits the ball, then running helps the situation because a jump start might prevent being put out on second. When you're on first base in this situation, running is the dominant strategy, and every other strategy you might have (staying put, waiting to see what the batter does, etc), is dominated by this one. Not only this, it doesn't matter what the actions of the other team are, running is always the dominant strategy.

Examples of Dominant Strategies

In most democracies the right to vote in a free election is one of the most treasured rights held by citizens. Yet in many elections as few as 20-30% of the eligible voters ever bother to show up to cast their ballot. Recently the city of Vancouver held an election on whether or not to support the bid for the 2010 Olympic games. The voter turn out was around 60% of registered voters and this was hailed as a remarkable achievement in civic elections. A 60% turn out is a remarkable achievement? What is going on here? If voting is such a sacred right, why do so few individuals not bother to exercise it?

The answer comes from dominant strategies. Suppose it costs something to vote. You might have to take time off work, you have to travel to the polling station, and you may want to investigate something about the candidates. On the other hand, if you assume large numbers of other people are going to vote, the benefit to voting is close to zero unless you like voting for its own sake. The benefit is close to zero because your single vote is likely to have no impact on who is elected. Thus if you vote you incur costs and have no impact on the election. If you do not vote you save on costs and you still have no impact on the election. Thus it is a dominant strategy to not vote in elections. If everyone thinks this way, then very few people vote, which is what generally happens. Once we understand dominant strategies, perhaps the real question should be "why does anyone actually vote?" The answer must be that for some people there is an intrinsic value to voting. For some it is a patriotic duty, and to not vote causes guilt. Sometimes the margin of victory is almost as important as the victory in an election. When Quebec has a vote on sovereignty, the outcome would mean much more if 60% turn it down rather than just 51% turn it down. In such cases there is a benefit to voting, and if this outweighs the cost one might vote. Finally, some elections are very close, and an individual's vote might be very important.

In 1989 Harrison Ford and Sean Connery teamed up in the movie *Indiana Jones and the Last Crusade.* In the movie Connery plays father to the adventuresome Indiana Jones as they seek out the Holy Grail. In one of the last scenes Connery has been mortally wounded and is about to die. Jones recognizing the situation for what it was, realizes he must get his father to drink from the Holy Grail and be healed. He enters a large room where the Grail is, but is confronted with thousands of cups ... which one is the Holy Grail? This is a mighty problem for Jones because to drink from the wrong cup would mean instant death. Just as he finally selects a cup, Jones has a second thought: "What if I'm wrong?" He quickly fills the cup with water and says "There's only one way to find out" and then proceeds to drink from the cup himself! When nothing happens he realizes he's actually found the Grail. He refills the cup and gives it to his father, his father lives, and they both live happily ever after.

What is wrong with the actions of Indiana Jones? The problem is he's ignored his dominant strategy! The strategies for Jones are to drink of the cup first, or give the cup first to his father. When Jones picks the right cup it doesn't matter what he does ... his father lives either way. But if Jones had picked the wrong cup, it matters a great deal. If he has the wrong cup and Jones drinks first then he dies from the drink and his father dies of his wounds. If he gives the bad drink to his father, then his father dies but he lives. Clearly, the dominant strategy is for Jones to let his father drink first. Failure to follow the dominant strategy ruined the whole movie!

The Prisoner's Dilemma

The most famous game in the world just happens to be a game of dominated strategies. The setting of the prisoner's dilemma is a police station. Two suspects have been arrested on charges of a serious crime, and they've been placed in separate rooms. There isn't enough evidence to convict both of the crime and so the police are trying to get a confession out of them. In order to do this, they've offered each prisoner the following deal. Any prisoner who finks on his partner will be let go if the other suspect won't talk and confess. If a prisoner does not confess, but his partner does, then the book will be thrown at silent prisoner. If they both confess they'll spend a lot of time in jail, and if they both remain silent they'll be convicted of a minor charge.

Suppose our two thieves are Ryan and Petra. Ryan and Petra had the great idea to steal Brian's car one night. In the middle of the theft Brian caught them just as they got the car started and drove down the road. The next day the police caught up with Ryan and Petra with possession of the car. They have enough evidence for the charge of possession of stolen property, but they'd really like to convict them of theft as well. Brian got a look at both of them, but he's only 80% sure he can make a positive identification, not enough to be assured of a conviction. The police have separated the two and made the standard prisoner's dilemma pitch. The payoffs being offered are given in Figure 14-1.

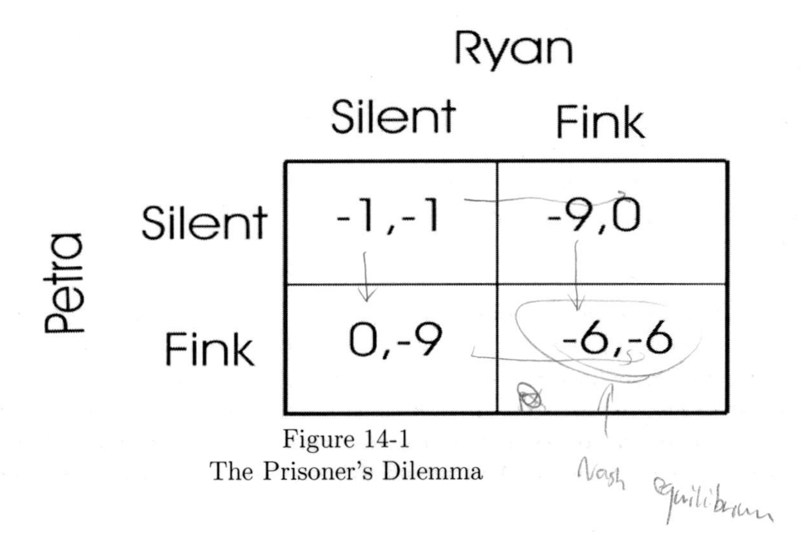

Figure 14-1
The Prisoner's Dilemma

If Petra remains quiet and Ryan finks, then Petra is going to spend 9 months in jail and Ryan is going to walk free. If they both fink, then they will both be convicted of theft and each will spend 6 months in jail. If neither of them fink, then they will only be charged with possession of stolen property and each will spend only one month in prison. What will Ryan and Petra do? In other words, what is the equilibrium outcome of this game?

An easy way to find an equilibrium is to draw arrows showing the direction of preferences over strategies for each player. Horizontal arrows show the preferences of Ryan, while vertical arrows show the preferences of Petra. When two arrow heads meet, then we have what is called a Nash Equilibrium. Figure 14-2 repeats the information of Figure 14-1, except now the arrows are in place.

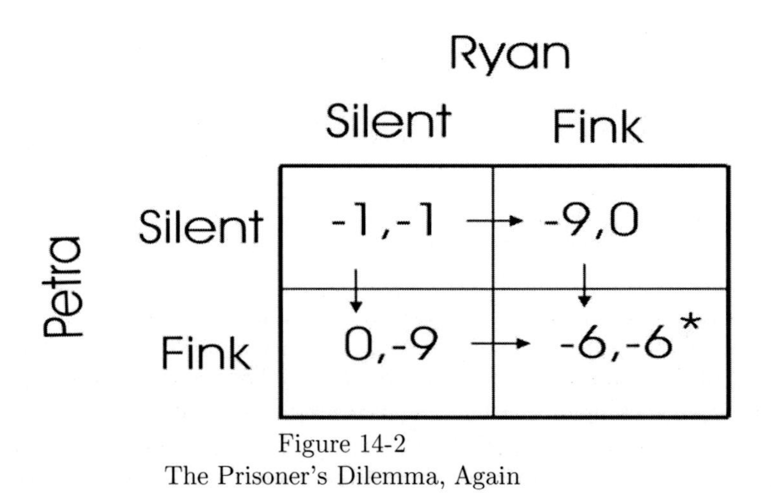

Figure 14-2
The Prisoner's Dilemma, Again

Notice the arrows meet at the cell where both Petra and Ryan fink. (Fink, Fink) then is the equilibrium of the prisoner's dilemma game. There are at least three reasons for why this game is so interesting. First, it has many applications in real life. Below I'll show you how the problem with cartels can be thought of as a prisoner's dilemma game. Second, the equilibrium results from a dominant strategy for both players. As far as Petra is concerned, it doesn't matter what Ryan has in mind, her dominant strategy is to fink. Likewise for Ryan, he's going to fink no matter what Petra does. Finally, the prisoner's dilemma is interesting because the equilibrium outcome is not Pareto optimal. Clearly both Ryan and Petra would be better off if they both remained silent.

14.3 **The Evolution of Cooperation**

Before we move on to examine how the Prisoner's Dilemma game might be applicable to firms, it is worthwhile considering why Ryan and Petra are unable to reach the Pareto optimal result of silence. What would have happened if Ryan and Petra were not in separate rooms? Then, when Ryan was about to fink Petra might give him a look which said "if you fink, my big brother Braun is going to hunt you down and break your legs when you get out." Under such a threat Ryan might think twice about finking. However, if Ryan and Petra are part of a community which often interacts with each other, Ryan might know Braun is going to break his legs for finking, even if Petra isn't there to remind him. Essentially the prisoner's dilemma game assumes the game is a one time thing. That is, there are no consequences to decisions outside the payoffs mentioned in the game. When individuals interact with one another in repeated prisoner dilemma settings, the outcome is usually one of cooperation and Pareto outcomes. However, when there is no ability to punish opposing players for choosing the fink strategy, the outcome is as above.

In the 1979 a political scientist named Robert Axelrod sent a letter to a number of experts in game theory and computers around the world. He told them he was going to hold computer tournament where various programs would play the Prisoner's Dilemma game with each other for 200 rounds. Those receiving the letters were invited to submit their programs. In all, fourteen programs were received, and they varied in complexity and length. The longest program was 77 lines long, the shortest only 4. It turned out that the simplest program won quite easily. What was the strategy for playing the Prisoner's Dilemma over and over again? It was called TIT FOR TAT. TIT FOR TAT simply starts out cooperating (staying silent in our example), and then it does whatever the opposition does in the previous move. Hence, if TIT FOR TAT comes up against a finker, it loses out in the first round, but retaliates in the second.

After Axelrod produced the results of his tournament, he sent them to the fourteen entrants, and invited them to try a second time in another tournament. This time he also opened up the tournament to anyone who wanted to enter, and he advertised it in computer magazines around the country. In the second tournament there were 62 entries, including TIT FOR TAT, sent in by the original author Anatol Rapoport from the University of Toronto. Once again, TIT FOR TAT won. In subsequent tournaments TIT FOR TAT consistently won, and quite often won by a considerable amount.

An interesting feature of TIT FOR TAT is that it is *not* a Nash Equilibrium. If you were playing a TIT FOR TAT strategy, and you run into a non-cooperative player in round one, then you should still cooperate in round 2 if you thought the player would now cooperate. But the TIT FOR TAT strategy says, no, you must retaliate with one defection yourself. The TIT FOR TAT strategy never out performs any other strategy in a single encounter. However, over multiple encounters it starts to rack up points when it meets other cooperative players, and it never gets hurt by players who always defect. Essentially cooperation starts to evolve.

Axelrod came up with four characteristics for strategies that work well over multiple interations. First a strategy should be "nice." This means the first interation should be to cooperate (remain silent in the classic example). Starting off playing nice means that when you run into other nice strategies you get a big payoff. If you keep playing nice with one another, then you do well over time. The second feature of a successful strategy is to be "forgiving." To be forgiving is to not hold a grudge too long. TIT FOR TAT only retaliates once, and then it goes back to being its nice old self. The third characteristic is to be "provocable." That is, one should not get pushed around. When a player uses a non-cooperative strategy (eg. finks) TIT FOR TAT gets mad quickly and doesn't wait around to punish. The final characteristic is to be "clear." TIT FOR TAT is about as simple a strategy you can get, and other players quickly understand it and start cooperating.

> *A successful strategy over a multiple period Prisoner's Dilemma game is characterized by being nice, forgiving, provocable, and clear.*

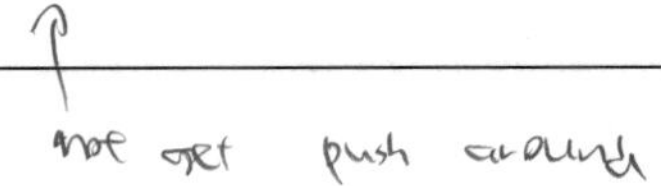

Everyone faces Prisoner's Dilemma like games everyday in life. When you visit a roadside restaurant on vacation, are you ever tempted not to tip the waitress? Why tip, you'll never be back anyway. The dominant strategy is to not tip, but often you tip anyway. Why would you do this? One answer is that we recognize, as a culture, the value of being nice, forgiving, provocable, and clear. If we raise our children to play this way, sure they may tip too much in a roadside restaurant, but they might not get robbed on the roadside when they have a flat tire. Socially, we are all much better off to cooperate with one another, and through multiple interactions this type of behavior can evolve into an equilibrium.

The ancient Hammurabi code, "an eye for an eye, a tooth for a tooth," is essentially a TIT FOR TAT strategy. The Bible certainly teaches us to be nice and forgiving, and some would say even provocable when it comes to the sinful actions of others. Even the concept of a "just war," so much in the news when the U.S. invade Iraq, resembles the characteristics of a socially winning strategy. Wars should be defensive (ie. nice and provocable), they should be proportional (ie. forgiving), and wars should be declared (clear). During the war of 1812, as their ships blocked the American ports for months at a time, the British would have to leave their stations and head to Halifax in Canada or Bermuda for supplies. They did this even though they were often within throwing distance of the American shore, where water, wild and domestic animals were everywhere. They did not take these American provisions because that would violate the "rules of war" at the time. Rules of War? Just another example of how cooperation can evolve, even among countries at war.

14.4 **Theology and Game Theory**

In the next section we'll use some simple game theory to understand the incentives behind colluding firms. In this section we take a brief digression to apply game theory to theology. The purpose is to show you how broad and powerful these tools are, and to have a little fun.

Game I: Free Will versus Predestination

At one time, the study of theology was a major component of a university education. In modern secular times interest in theology, by definition, has waned a little to say the least. Still, it is fun to use our game theory concepts to articulate a few classic theological issues. One of those issues is whether humans have "free will" to choose God or are "predestined" to choose. The debate over free will continues around us all the time. For example, when some one is convicted of a crime, but found "unfit" to stand trial, the court is essentially saying their will was not "free" and therefore responsible for their act. In order to examine this issue with game theory, we need to structure the choices.

Suppose there is a supreme all-knowing God whose primary goal is that he wants a person, Karim, to believe in his existence, and as a secondary goal prefers not to reveal himself. Suppose the primary goal of Karim is to have his belief confirmed by revelation (or his disbelief confirmed by a lack of revelation), and his secondary goal is to prefer to believe in God's existence. Figure 14-3 shows the payoffs of this game, where each outcome is ranked from 1 to 4, with 4 being the best. Under the assumptions we've made, God has a dominant strategy not to reveal himself. Given this, the Nash equilibrium is clearly for Karim not to believe. This set-up would appear to be refuted by the existence of religions all over the world.

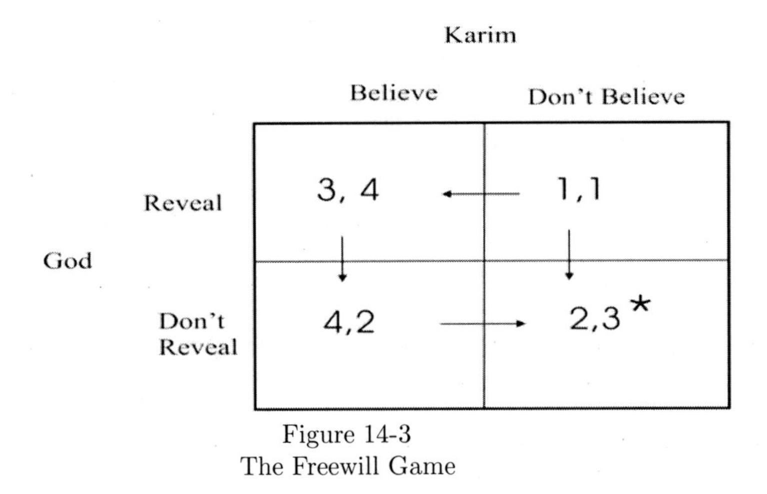

Figure 14-3
The Freewill Game

Now let's consider a change in the goals of the players. Let God's primary goal be the same as above, but now let his secondary goal be to prefer revelation. Second, the primary goal of Karim is to not believe, while Karim's secondary goal is to prefer confirmation. Now the payoffs of the game are given in Figure 14-4, where again the outcomes are ranked from 1 to 4. Now the Nash equilibrium is for God to reveal himself and for Karim to not believe! No one would get to Heaven (assuming you have to believe in order to go) if everyone were like Karim. This situation reminds us of a story about an interaction between God and an atheist. The two meet, and God introduces himself as God. The atheist responds that he doesn't believe in God, and asks for some proof. God immediately turns the bottled water the atheist is holding into a bottle of wine. The atheist then responds, "Hey, what's the trick?"

Finally, let's consider a third game where everything is the same as the second one, but now Karim's primary goal is to prefer to believe. This game's payoffs are shown in Figure 14-5. Clearly in this last game, both players have a dominant strategy, and the outcome is that God reveals himself and Karim believes.

Game theory doesn't provide any of the numbers in these games; they come from particular theologies. According to these games, no one ever goes to Heaven kicking and screaming. One either believes and goes, or does not believe and ... well, goes somewhere else. This is a principle in most

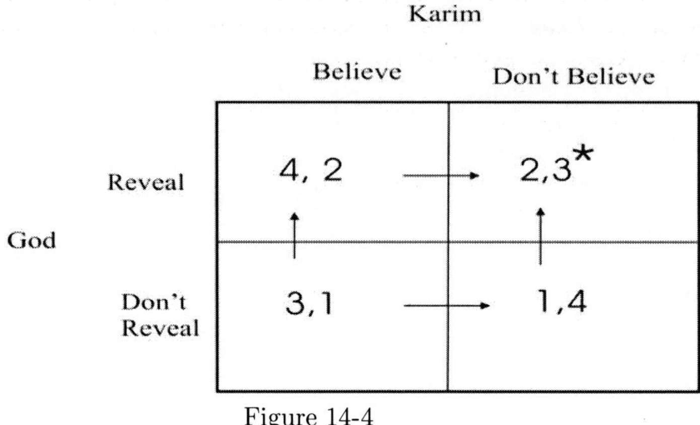

Figure 14-4
The Modified Freewill Game

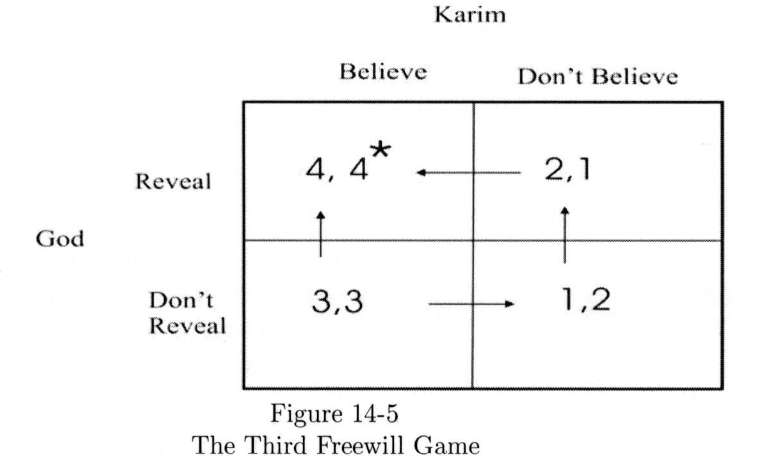

Figure 14-5
The Third Freewill Game

major religions of the world. Also consistent with major religions of the world, no one would have any chance at heaven if God never revealed himself. Finally, although the games do not resolve the issue of free will versus predestination, they do allow for a nice articulation of the debate. Those believers who think some people are predestined to go to Heaven would say everyone is born with a nature described in game 14-4, and God works in some lives to change them into natures described by game 14-5. On the other hand, those believers who think there is free will would suggest we get to choose between the games in Figures 14-4 and 14-5.

Game II: If Omniscient, then God Must Be Holy

Most of the religions of the world have a number of characteristics which are similar. For example, their god is omniscient (all-knowing), requires a standard of behaviour or code of conduct, and is capable of exercising mercy at will. So, in the Christian faith, God gave Moses the Ten Commandments, and yet forgave his people over and over again for their transgressions. On the other hand, in almost all religions individuals can either behave according to the rules or disregard the rules. For ease, let's call the actions of both parties Compromise, Not Compromise.

If neither player compromises the outcome is bad for both (say 1, 1). If one compromises but the other doesn't, the stubborn one gets 4 and the other gets 2. If both compromise they each get 3. These payoffs are set out in Figure 14-6.

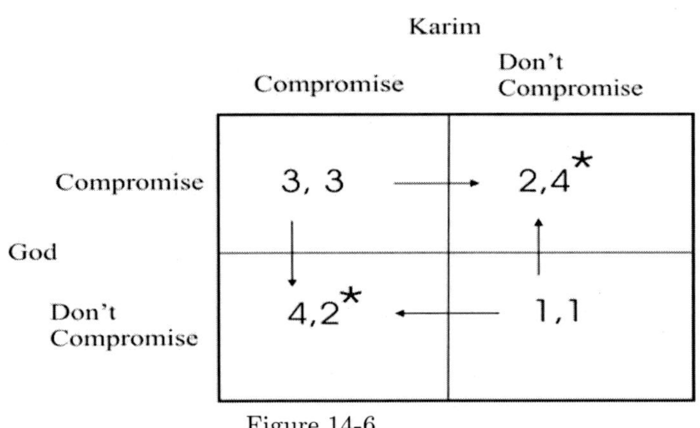

Figure 14-6
Playing Chicken with God

As you can see, Karim is playing a game of chicken with God. In a classic game of chicken two teenage males drive their cars towards each other. The first to swerve (compormise) is the loser. Both swerving is not bad, but neither swerving is a disaster. Of note to us is that in the game of chicken there are two equilibria, not just one. Interestingly, God's omniscience works against him in a situation like this. By being all-knowing, God knows what Karim will do. But Karim knows God is all-knowing, and knows that if he compromises and goes against the rules, God will compromise and exercise his mercy to Karim. Thus, when God is omniscient, the game of chicken has one unique equilibrium, namely (Compromise, Don't Compromise). From God's point of view, this is a bad equilibrium. A solution for God is to announce he is holy and just, and cannot compromise. If Karim believes this, he may want to avoid testing God and follow the rules. This forces a new equilibrium ... which one?

14.5 The Incentive to Collude For Firms

When firms act independently of one another in order to maximize their profits, they do not act in the interests of the group. If the market is generally competitive, we've seen that this leads to the competitive equilibrium, where price is equal to marginal costs and all firms earn zero profits. When there are only a few firms, if they act independently they will still end up producing an amount of output that does not maximize the rents to the individual firms. The incentives to collude then, come from the increased rents that arise from a group of firms acting as a monopolist. As we saw in the last chapter, when a firm is a monopolist, it will set the marginal revenue equal to the marginal costs, and it will maximize the rent to the firm.

Firms want to collude in order to make money.

We can see the incentive to collude in Figure 14-7. The left hand side graph presents the market situation. Suppose this is our raspberry market. The market demand and supply for raspberries produces an equilibrium price and quantity of P^* and Q^*. If all of the raspberry producers were able to get together and somehow restrict raspberry production, they might be able to restrict output to $\bar{Q}$. At this lower level of output, the price rises to $\bar{P}$, and the rents to the industry increase by the dark shaded region. A deadweight loss is also created, although this is not marked on the figure.

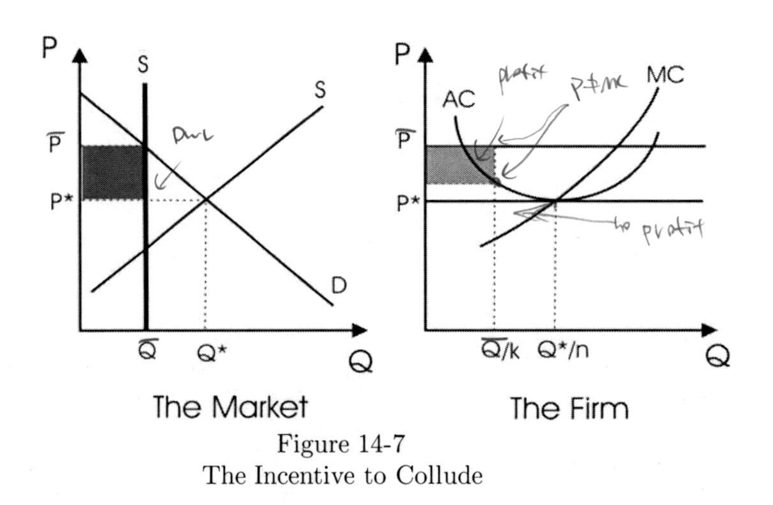

Figure 14-7
The Incentive to Collude

The right hand side graph in figure 14-7 shows the situation for a given raspberry firm. Before the restriction on output the price taking raspberry farmer faced the equilibrium price of P^* and produced until his marginal cost equaled this price. Assuming all raspberry farmers have equal marginal costs, the farmer produces Q^*/n berries, where n is the number of farmers in the market when there is no collusion to restrict output. When the output is restricted, however, this is accomplished in two ways. First, every farmer will have to restrict output. Second, some farmers may be bought out or simply not allowed to farm. In the right hand graph, both have occured. The individual farmer reduces his output, and the number of farms falls from n to k. The farmer earns the light shaded area as an economic profit.

14.6 The Problem of Collusion

Almost as soon as we see the firm graph in figure 14-7, we can tell this outcome cannot be an equilibrium. Just because a group of farmers are able to agree to limit competition among them, does not mean that competition is eliminated. Every farmer is just as much of a maximizer as he always was. The problem with the firm graph in 14-7 is that the firm's marginal costs are below the price, and that means the farmer's private personal incentive is to increase output, hoping that everyone else will stay the course and hold to the agreement. In other words, the dominant strategy for the individual firm is to choose an output where price equals marginal costs. Consider Figure 14-8, which shows the incentive of the individual firm.

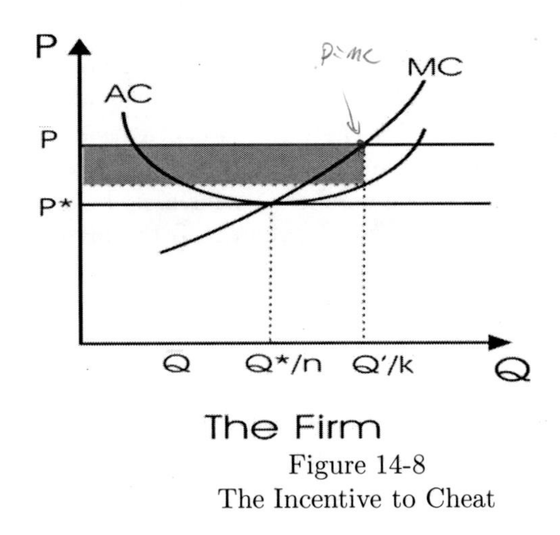

Figure 14-8
The Incentive to Cheat

When the firm produces where marginal costs equal the price $\bar{P}$, the profits to the firm are equal to the light shaded region. These profits are clearly higher than those when the firm cooperates. Hence the major problem with a cartel is that the agreement is not *self enforcing* because the dominant strategy is to cheat. In other words, each firm has an incentive to cheat, and unless something is done about this, each firm *will* cheat. In cheating on the agreement, the price and quantity simply revert back to the original competitive equilibrium. For most industries this cheating problem is so great cartels are simply never formed.

The history of the OPEC cartel illustrates this problem. OPEC is a cartel of oil-exporting countries that operates by assigning export quotas to individual member countries in an attempt to reduce the supply of crude oil to the world market. At various times, particularly during the mid-1970s, the cartel has been successful in restricting supply and thereby raising prices. At other times, however, many OPEC member countries have cheated on their collusive agreement by exporting more than their allotted quotas. For instance, in the late 1980s and early 1990s, newspapers often carried reports about individual OPEC countries that were "keeping their spigots wide open" — that is, exceeding their quotas on the sale of crude oil in the international oil market.

OPEC has not been a successful cartel. Most price shocks to oil have come from Saudi Arabia reducing its supplies while the other smaller countries free ride on this restriction and produce as much as they want. Saudi Arabia is such a large producer that even with this cheating it finds it is in the country's private interests to restrict oil production. Saudi Arabia would like the other producing countries to cut production as well, but has never been able to enforce the agreements.

14.7 Conditions for Collusion

In order for collusion to happen, an enforcement mechanism must be in place to prevent the cheating which ultimately breaks the cartel. Economists have come up with a number of conditions that could foster collusive agreements.

Small Numbers of Firms

When there are vast numbers of suppliers in an industry, collusion is virtually impossible. Imagine all of the corn farmers in the United States, coming together and attempting to reach an agreement on the amount of corn to be grown. There isn't a convention center in the world that could accommodate them. Not only this, how could any of them be policed in terms of the output they produce. In order for collusion to work, the number of firms must be small, and the smaller the better. Evidence seems to suggest that even as few as five firms is too many to effectively enforce a cartel.

No Fringe of Small Firms

Although there may be a small number of firms accounting for perhaps 90% of industry output, in many industries there are often "fringe" firms. These firms may produce goods in the cartel industry as a secondary product, or they may simply be small independent producers. Such firms pose a huge problem for cartels. On the one hand, no cartel wants to include them on the agreement because their individual outputs are so small, any reductions have little impact on price. If they are brought into the agreement, the firms essentially hold the larger firms hostage by demanding larger shares of the rents than there size warrants. The demands for large rents are serious because fringe firms have a credible threat ... they can break the cartel. When a group of large firms restricts output, they raise price. Fringe firms benefit from this by, like our raspberry farmer above, increasing output until their marginal costs equal the new higher price. This increased output, reduces the effectiveness of the cartel.

When US Steel was formed by J.P. Morgan's merger of the twelve largest steel plants in the United States, it became the largest firm in the world, controlling 80% of U.S. steel producing capacity. At that time there was a little known steel firm called Bethlehem Steel. As US Steel restricted output and raised prices, Bethlehem increased output. Since US Steel was not pricing where marginal costs equaled price, but Bethlehem was, the profit margins at Bethlehem Steel were greater. Over a period of twenty years, US Steel lost market share and Bethlehem and other small fringe firms grew. By the 1920s, US Steel no longer had the size to be a dominant firm in the industry.

Costly Entry

Related to the role of fringe firms is the cost of entry. When a group of firms forms a cartel, they not only have to worry about existing small firms, but also potential firms. High returns attract entry, and when entering firms are not part of the cartel agreement, they destroy the cartel. Collusion is often found in industries like oil, or other natural resource commodities, where entry is restricted to those firms with access to the resource.

Standard Products

One method of cheating on a cartel is to slightly alter the good and sell the new quantity. Firms involved in collusive agreements will attempt to monitor the inventories and sales of the group members. When products are complicated and not similar across firms, this monitoring of output becomes more difficult. New products, changes in quality, upgrades, all make the monitoring process difficult. When output is difficult to monitor, the cartel again breaks down. Hence, collusion is much more likely in industries with simple one dimensional products.

Inelastic Demand

When an industry restricts output, it must generate more total revenue at the lower level of output in order for the cartel to work. If less revenue is generated, then there's no point in forming a cartel. This means that there cannot be close substitutes for the product. If raspberry farmers restrict output and consumers simply buy strawberries and blueberries, there will be no increase in revenues. One fundamental problem for collusive agreements is the second law of demand. It states that over time demand curves become more elastic. When a cartel is successful in raising prices, consumers and other individuals seek out substitutes and invent new ones. This raises the elasticity of demand, and eventually terminates the cartel.

There are other conditions that help cartels police their agreements. For example, it helps if all firms are selling at the same level of distribution. But the point is that collusion is difficult to muster. Consider the unsuccessful raspberry farmers once again. They had a lot going against them. First, there's just too many farmers. Not only are there lots of farmers in the Fraser Valley, there are lots of farmers in British Columbia, Washington state, and other parts of the world. There are no major tariffs on raspberries, and so the number of producers is huge. Second, entry is easy and every farmer is a fringe firm. There are no monster raspberry farms, and berries grow on all types of land that at any given time is not in berry production. Increasing the price of raspberries would bring lots of land into raspberry production. Finally, there a many, many great substitutes for raspberries. A cartel is never going to work for raspberries.

Unless, that is, the cartel is formed the way most agricultural cartels are formed: through government protection and quotas. As we'll see below, most often forming a cartel is illegal. The exception is when the government acts as the enforcer of the cartel. As mentioned in chapter 10, a quota is one method of restricting output and raising prices. A quota works for farmers because the government prevents fringe and potential firms from competing, the government policies the output of each farmer, and the government monitors the quality of the goods produced. Now the light grey area in the right hand graph of figure 14-1 is earned by the farmer producing the good.

The Transitional Gains Trap

But does the farmer really earn this grey area? A quota involves a transfer of wealth from consumers to producers equal to the shaded area. This transfer results from the higher price that consumers now face for purchasing the raspberries. Hence consumers are unambiguously hurt by the quota. On the other hand, the farmers benefit from the quota because presumably the transfer from the higher price is greater than the loss from reduced output.

Yet quotas introduce a problem for farmers. Suppose the quota is introduced as a complete surprise to a group of farmers. Overnight they find that if they obey their quota and reduce their production the price will rise and their incomes will increase. To these farmers, the quota is like a gift from Heaven. The quota allows them to earn an economic rent equal to the grey shaded area of figure 14-3, year-in, year-out. If the farmer wished to sell the quota, however, what price would he set for it? Clearly he would charge what it is worth: the *present value* of the stream of rents. But if he charges this amount, this means that the subsequent farmer who purchases this quota is now earning a zero profit return. The quota has simply increased his costs of entering the business, and in fact, the quota is now necessary for him to avoid losses. Hence, when a quota is sold to another farmer, the value of the quota is transferred completely to the original farmer. This problem is called the *transitional gains trap*, and points to how difficult it is to actually improve the incomes of farmers with quotas.

The transitional gains trap is not limited to quotas or farmers. Any time the government generates a transfer of wealth to someone through the creation of a license, permit, or quota, the transfer is capitalized into the value of the paper that gives the right to earn the transfer. Those who purchase these rights only earn a normal rate of return. This explains much of the perpetual plight of the farmer. After decades of government aid, farmers in the US and Canada still claim that they are constantly living on the edge. Droughts, too much rain, and other abnormal weather patterns make national news because of the effect they have on farmers. Surely, with all of the help farmers have received over the years, they can stand some bad weather now and then? The problem is that those farmers helped by the transfers are no longer there. They sell their quota rights to new farmers. These new farmers not only make a normal rate of return, they also have large debts to cover the cost of the price of quota!

14.8 Competition Policy

Both the United States and Canada have laws that presumably are intended to protect consumers against monopoly practices and collusion. In Canada the Combines Investigation Act was enacted in 1889, while in the U.S. the Sherman Antitrust Act was enacted in 1890. In both cases the law was aimed at solving the problem of collusion, but in both cases the wording of the law was less than precise. In Canada the law stated it was a "criminal offense to conspire to unduly lessen competition." By making collusion criminal, a strong burden of proof was required. By using the word "conspire" the prosecution had to show intent, and no one has ever figured out what "unduly" actually means. In the U.S. the law stated that "every contract, combination ... or conspiracy, in restraint of trade ... is illegal." In the U.S. court cases arose immediately and over time the competition laws (called anti-trust laws in the U.S.) were modified by these decisions and other legislation. In Canada, there was relatively little litigation, although the law was modified over time to include a whole host of business practices, including mergers, predatory pricing, price discrimination, resale price maintenance, and the like. In 1986 the law in Canada changed substantially when the cartel clauses were strengthened, circumstantial evidence was allowed, and no intent had to be shown. Furthermore, a civil tribunal was set up to review cases.

In both countries, the law takes a dim view of "collusion." This would make sense from an economic point of view. Collusion is simply an effort to lower output for the sole purpose of transferring wealth to producers. Since collusion creates a deadweight loss, it is socially harmful and should be illegal. Much of the economic reasoning in these cases comes from one of the most famous anti-trust cases: *Addyston Pipe & Steel* (1898). This case involved six firms spread throughout the eastern U.S. who had agreed not to compete with one another in their various home regions. The case is not only famous for the outcome, but also because the judge hearing the case was William Taft the future president, and because the only reason the cartel got caught was because the accountant finked. You need to choose your accountant as carefully as you choose your spouse!

Taft argued that there are two types of "restraints of trade": naked and ancillary restraints. A naked restraint of trade is one that is done for the sole purpose of transferring wealth. These types of collusion, Taft argued, should be *per se* illegal. If caught in such an agreement, the perpetrators are guilty and have no excuse. An ancillary restraint of trade, on the other hand, was merely a by-product of some productive endeavor. These types of restraints are not *per se* illegal, but rather a "rule of reason" is to apply. This means the guilty party is allowed to justify the restraint. If an efficiency reason is found for the practice, the firm is allowed to continue. For example, a firm might be using a tie-in sale form of pricing, and might argue that it does so for quality control purposes. If the court agrees, the firm will be allowed to continue. What Taft realized is that much of economic activity restrains trade, and not all of these restraints are bad. If I provide you with a one year lease to my home, this prevents me from renting it to someone else three months later. This type of restraint on trade is a good thing, however, and should not be illegal.

The notion of a "rule of reason" has carried through much of competition policy, and as a result there are all types of legal collusive behavior. Unions are legal collusive agreements among workers. Medical doctors, teachers, and other professionals cannot practice without the approval of their respective professional associations. These associations are legal entities that restrict the number of practioners in their fields. The NHL, NBA, and NFL are all sports leagues that legally prevent teams from setting up a sports franchise in any city they want. On and on the list goes.

For those industries where collusion is illegal, barring an accountant finking, courts often look at circumstantial evidence for collusion. First courts consider many of the conditions mentioned earlier. If a market is not conducive to collusion, courts will not hear the case. If the industry is conducive to collusion, then the courts often look at other evidence to infer collusion took place. For example, are their trade associations, sealed bids for jobs, stable market shares, formal exchanges of price information between firms, identical or suspicious bidding, excess capacity in the plants, or some other behavior indicating collusion. When a firm is found guilty in Canada the usual penalty is an injunction against the practice and an order to sell off assets to induce competition and eliminate excess capacity. In the U.S., firms are ordered to pay damages, which are then tripled. In the U.S. many of these damage awards are absolutely enormous.

Other Pricing Practices

Competition laws address all types of pricing behavior, most of which we have not discussed at all. In general the rule of reason is applied to these cases. Consider the case of price discrimination. In Canada, price discrimination became an offense under the Act in 1935. It turns out, however, that price discrimination is not as easy to prosecute as it is to observe. The problem is one of taking proper account of costs. If a firm charges two separate prices to different customers, but this difference in price is completely the result of differences in the cost of servicing the customers, then under the law this is not price discrimination. For example, one can purchase a perpetuity that pays an annual income until the time of death. Firms charge women higher prices than men, but this is not price discrimination. The difference in price is a reflection of the longer life expectancy of women over men. Allowing differences in costs to excuse differences in prices is like opening up Pandora's box. In most of the examples of price discrimination it is relatively easy to come up with a cost difference explanation.

Consider the case of airline travel. When airlines offer lower fares to customers who book in advance, they could be passing the savings of advanced planning on to their customers. If airlines could only book customers on the spot, they would be required to hold larger inventories of planes, flights might leave either half full or with passengers left on the ground. In effect, by booking early the passengers are providing the airline information about the demands for different routes and times. This information lowers costs, and hence this is reflected in the price. Is the difference in price worth 1/3 the business fare? It is not obvious, which is what makes price discrimination cases so difficult. Thus when firms are charged with price discrimination, they are allowed to make the case that differences in prices are a reflection of differences in costs. This is an efficiency argument that sometimes works and sometimes doesn't.

The IBM case of tie-in sales was also mentioned in the last chapter. IBM was sued for "extending its monopoly power." This is another violation of the Sherman Act in the U.S. In the case, a rule of reason was applied, and so even though IBM admitted that it did indeed tie the use of its adding machines to the paper cards used, it claimed that this was an efficient practice. IBM claimed that if it allowed its customers to choose their own paper cards they would select the cheapest material they could find. The cheap paper cards would bind in the machine and customers would blame IBM for a bad machine, rather than themselves. IBM lost that argument, but many other firms charged with the same offense have successfully used it since.

14.9 **Summary**

This brief chapter has intended to provide a short introduction to the issue of competition policy. These types of laws came into being at the end of the 19th century over the concern of "restraints of trade." The big concern of the time were trust practices used to form collusive agreements. Early on it was recognized by the courts that some agreements restrain trade in good ways while some practices definitely reduced social welfare. The hard part is to distinguish such practices. As mentioned in the chapter, naked collusive actions are illegal per se, but again the hard part is to actually catch some firm in the act. Courts have adopted a series of methods to deal with this, and some of these were mentioned in the chapter. Competition policy becomes even harder when dealing with forms of compound pricing. Almost any pricing practice has an efficiency rationale, and generally courts have developed a rule of reason to judge whether or not the practices are efficiency enhancing or not. In any event, the entire area is laced with economics, and provides a rich ground of consulting work for economists.

REVIEW QUESTIONS

1. Is walking on the right side of a sidewalk a Nash Equilibrium? Is walking on the left side?

2. Why is it difficult for firms in an industry to collude?

3. Safe driving courses always say "drive defensively." Is this a Nash Equilibrium?

4. "Dumping" is a phrase firms use when foreign firms sell here at prices less than what they charge in their home country. What are these foreign firms doing? Why would local firms be upset by this? Should the domestic government try to stop this?

5. Are dominant strategies Nash Equilibriums?

PROBLEMS

1. Why would a cartel among diet sodas be less likely to work than a cartel among breweries?

2. In the interior of the province of British Columbia there is a toll highway called the Coquihala. Trucks on the Coquihala highway are charged a higher toll to use the road than cars are. Is this price discrimination? Briefly explain.

3. Why are public washrooms so dirty and often disgusting? Are there any dominant strategies in using such facilities?

4. Your brother has taken your Halloween candy and is consuming it in his bedroom. You pound on the door and say you're coming in and you expect the candy to be shared 50–50. Your brother yells back "if you come in this room, I'll punch you in the nose and throw the candy out of the window!" You and your brother are about equal in strength, and you're sure that if a fight breaks out you'll both have sore noses and no candy. You also know that your brother doesn't like a sore nose, and that he understands your relative strengths as well. What to do?

   The payoffs in the game below show the possible outcomes from each of your two strategies. The first number in each cell is your payoff, the second your brother's.

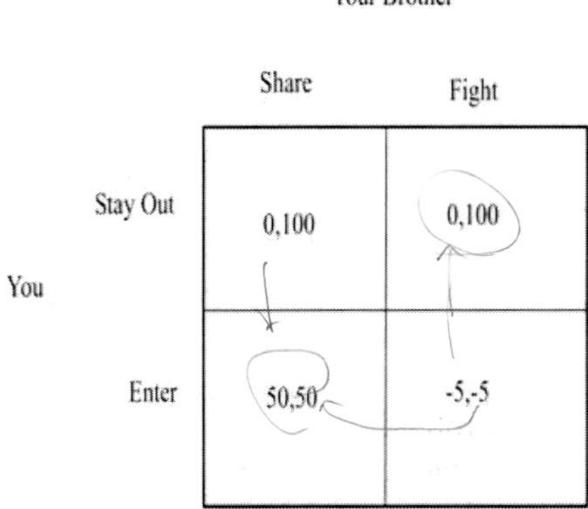

   a. There are two Nash Equilibrium in this game, find them.

   b. From an economic point of view, is there anything odd about one of the equilibriums?

5. The level of noise at a party often gets so loud that you have to shout to make yourself heard. Surely everyone would be better off if everyone kept his voice down. Explain this behavior in terms of dominant strategies.

6. One of the implications of the neoclassical model is that private vice often leads to public virtue. That is, the pursuit of maximization on the part of individuals and firms often leads to socially efficient outcomes. Every Fall, British Columbia starts a new flu season. During this time there are advertisements and public health announcements in all media outlets encouraging

everyone to get a flu vaccination shot. The cost is nominal, and for those most vulnerable, the shot is actually free. However, fewer than 30% of people ever get their shot.

a. What is the economic name given to this type of situation?

b. Explain why, if socially we're all better off to be vaccinated, so many people decide not to?

7. Suppose everyone taking your course had two choices when it came to studying for the final exam. You could study "hard" or take it "easy". If you study hard, and everyone else takes it easy, then you'll get a great grade. Suppose this grade is worth 6 "utils" to you. Because you make everyone look so bad, they get a bad grade worth −4. If you study hard, and everyone else studies hard, you end up with a good grade, and this grade is worth 4 utils to everyone. If no one studies, and everyone takes it easy, then everyone gets an average grade worth 2 units to you. Now the thing is, if you study hard, it will cost you "3" utils.

   a. Write out a two-by-two game, with the relevant strategies and payoffs.

   b. Find the Nash equilibrium of this game.

8. The following game is called the Traveler's Dilemma.

   > "Lucy and Pete, returning from a remote Pacific island, find that the airline has damaged the identical antiques that each had purchased. An airline manager says that he is happy to compensate them but is handicapped by being clueless about the value of these strange objects. Simply asking the travelers for the price is hopeless, he figures, for they will inflate it. Instead he devises a more complicated scheme. He asks each of them to write down the price of the antique as any dollar integer between 2 and 100 without conferring together. If both write the same number, he will take that to be the true price, and he will pay each of them that amount. But if they write different numbers, he will assume that the lower one is the actual price and that the person writing the higher number is cheating. In that case, he will pay both of them the lower number along with a bonus and a penalty — the person who wrote the lower number will get \$2 more as a reward for honesty and the one who wrote the higher number will get \$2 less as a punishment. For instance, if Lucy writes 46 and Pete writes 100, Lucy will get \$48 and Pete will get \$44."

   a. What is the Nash Equilibrim of this game?

   b. What number would you write? Would you play the NE? It turns out that most people don't play the NE, they play a number in the high 90s. Does this suggest there is something wrong with the concept of NE?

9. Mother Mary has decided to play a game with her children Martha and Mark. She gives them each \$9 and an envelope. She puts them in a room and says "You have a choice, you can put the money back in the envelope or keep it. Once you've decided, I'll collect the envelopes and we'll all move to the kitchen. If you put the money back in the envelope I will add \$7 for each person who puts back, and then divide the \$16 between you. So if you both put it back, you'll each end up with \$16. If neither puts it back you'll end up with \$9. etc."

		Mark	
		Put	Share
Martha	Put		
	Share		

a. In the game below, fill in the payoffs.

b. Using arrows and a star, find any Nash Equilibrium. Is this game likely to teach the kids how to share?

10. Ben is the only producer of shirts with a picture of Montana on them. His average and marginal costs of production are $AC = MC = 10$, and the demand for his shirts is given by $Q = 60 - P$.

    a. Calculate the profit-maximizing price and quantity for Ben. What are his profits?

    b. Now Shauna comes along and produces shirts with pictures of Saskatchewan on them. Remarkably, they look the same and consumers view them as perfect substitutes. What will the price be now and how many shirts will be sold in total?

    c. Ben and Shauna get together and decide to collude in the shirt market. What total number of shirts should they produce and at what price? If they split the profits, how much does Ben earn now?

11. Fred and Barb are brother and sister. Their mother uses the rule "one splits, the other chooses" whenever a choice has to be made. For example, if a the last cookie must be split between two the children, then Fred gets to split it, and Barb gets to choose which piece she wants. Let's analyze this cookie splitting method as a game in the following way: Fred can either spilt the cookie evenly (meaning both pieces are the same size) or unevenly (meaning there is a large piece and a small piece.) Fred holds the pieces in his right and left hand so that Barb can see them. If the split is uneven, then Fred puts the larger piece in his right hand. Barb can either choose the cookie in the left or right hand. Assume both children prefer to receive a larger piece of the cookie. Assigning relevant nubers between 1 and 3, draw the game matrix. Place a star next to any Nash Equilibria of the game?

12. There is a new small residential development in South Langley. It is big enough to support one coffee shop. Investing in a coffee shop costs something, and two firms are interested in setting one up. The payoffs are given below:

    a. Find any Nash equilibrium using our arrow technique and show it on the table.

		Esquires	
		Stay Out	Enter
Starbucks	Stay Out	0,0	500,0
	Enter	500,0	-1000,-1000

b. Is this a game of dominant strategies?

13. In the summer of 2008, when gasoline prices were almost \$1.50/liter, there were thoughts of governments cutting their retail taxes by \$.15/liter. One commentator said that this should result in a price of "... about \$1.35/liter, or else the oil companies are conspiring to keep the price high." If the price fell by less than the reduction in taxes, would this mean there was collusion among the oil companies?

14. You're at a pub. You've had a beer and a hamburger for a total of \$15, and you're about to ask for the bill when the pub manager suddenly announces that for tonight only, the bills will be shared by the 100 people in the pub. That is, you only have to pay 15 cents on your bill. The others in the restaurant will each pay 15 cents as well.

    a. What is your dominant strategy now when it comes to ordering more food? Will you stop as you were planning to, or will you do something else?

    b. What will the other patrons do with respect to their ordering choice?

    c. What can we expect to happen to the total amount of revenue the restaurant collects that night?

    d. Is this a prisoner's dilemma type game? __________

Review Question Answers

1. *Yes. Yes. If you think others will walk on the right (left), then you should walk on the right (left). If you walk on the right, then others will walk on the right (left).*

2. *Because collusion is not a Nash Equilibrium. This means, unless the cartel is enforced, individual firms will not follow the instructions to reduce output.*

3. *No it is not. If everyone is going to be defensive, then I will drive aggressively, knowing everyone else will get out of my way. A lot of public "norms" are this way. You may hear an environmental group say "boycott Shell gasoline" or some such thing. But if enough follow this course of action, the price will fall and others then have an incentive to buy.*

4. *They are price discriminating. They don't like low price competition. No. Hurt us more this way!*

5. *Yes.*

Odd Numbered Problem Answers

1. *The demand for diet sodas is likely to be much more elastic. This means reduced output is likely to lead to reduced industry revenue, defeating the purpose of the cartel.*

3. *The dominant strategy in a public washroom is to incur no costs of clean up, and to use the facility in a manner minimizing contact. This often leads to the disgusting level of filth in public washrooms. Washrooms where the clientele are more transient and more often one time users (such as in bus and train depots) are in worse shape than washrooms used by small numbers of people (for example, in an office complex).*

5. *Same answer as in (4). Everyone wants to talk just a little louder than the person beside him. Therefore, everyone ends up yelling.*

7. The Nash Equilibrium is for everyone to study hard, even though everyone would be better off taking it easy.

		Others	
		Study Hard	Take it Easy
You	Study Hard	1, 1	3,-4
	Take it Easy	-4, 3	2, 2

9.

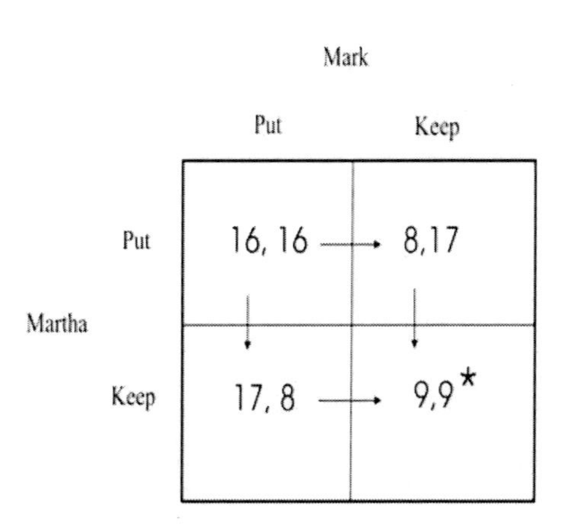

This game will do the opposite and teach Mark and Martha not to share.

11.

		Barb	
		Right	Left
Fred	Even	2,2 *	2,2
	Uneven	1, 3	3,1

13.

A cut in taxes is the same as a subsidy. Generally speaking, a $1 subsidy will lead to a less than a $1 fall in price. Hence the comment is logically wrong.

PART III
THE ORGANIZATION OF MARKETS AND INSTITUTIONS

In his book on Trust, Francis Fukuyama states that:

> Over the past generation, economic thought has been dominated by neoclassical or freemarket economists ... The rise of the neoclassical perspective constitutes a vast improvement from earlier decades in this century, when marxists and Keynesians held sway. We can think of neoclassical economics as being, say, eighty percent correct: it has uncovered important truths about the nature of money and markets because its fundamental model of rational, self-interested human behavior is correct about eighty percent of the time. But there is a missing twenty percent of human behavior about which neoclassical economics can give only a poor account.
>
> [p. 13, 1995]

In Part III of this book we concern ourselves with this extra "twenty" percent. Until now, we have essentially assumed that markets worked for free, and therefore, that prices were always the best way of coordinating production and consumption. Throughout the next part of the book this assumption is relaxed. When markets are costly to use, at times other forms of organization are seen as more effiecient methods of coordination.

CHAPTER 15

ECONOMIC PROPERTY RIGHTS AND TRANSACTION COSTS

Thus far we have examined a very simple but powerful model. One of the assumptions of our economic model has been that markets work for free. In such a world, individuals never leave mutual benefits unclaimed. To do so would be to go against the fundamental principle of maximization. Yet casual observation suggests that many important situations exist where this is not true. For example, when I go to restaurants, movies, and the grocery store, I quite often have to wait in line. You have no doubt experienced this yourself. Why does the price of a dinner not rise to eliminate the queue? Quite often a particular restaurant will habitually have a long line outside, and so we cannot argue that customers showed up unexpectedly. Not only this, but have you noticed that some people are unemployed? Why do wage rates not adjust to eliminate this surplus? And it is worse. As you read this book, at school or at home, look around you and see all of the capital that is unemployed! Chairs sit empty, books collect dust on the shelf, toilets are unused. In fact, during class time most of the toilets on campus are unemployed, but in between classes there is often a shortage! Why are there no markets, as described in earlier chapters, to eliminate these problems?

If you're thinking economically (and by now you should be), you should have no problem thinking up examples that refute our basic model. For example, individuals persistently drive their own cars to work, congesting the streets and highways, even though car pooling or rapid transit would reduce commute times dramatically. Tariffs are levied which raise the prices of domestic goods to an extent that often produces larger loses to consumers than the total gains to the protected industries. Pollution, health care, and the decimation of the Atlantic cod industry are all examples where pure price allocation is not (or was not) used.

It may appear from the examples just stated that "prices couldn't be used in cases like these". But if prices are free to use, why not? If you don't like that answer, consider cases where prices are explicitly and conscientiously not used. As much as you might try, you probably can't buy a grade in your economics class. The penalties are such that trade on this margin is usually eliminated. Not only can you not buy a grade, but you cannot sell your student card to one of your high school buddies. When your future boss tells you to do some task, you are unlikely to respond "what's it worth to you". Your father, if he is like mine, probably didn't bid for your labor services around the house. In firms and families, direction (being told what to do) is used more often than prices to allocate resources.

And so as we come to this last section of the book, we also come to the end of our simple model where information is free, the cost of transacting is zero, and ownership is always perfectly defined. In this chapter we'll begin to explore what happens when these assumptions are relaxed a little. The answer is quite fascinating, but first we must seek to understand the nature of a term called "transaction costs."

15.1 The Coase Theorem

So you think you understand the principles of economics? Let's see. Consider two worlds, both made up of farmers, ranchers, and no fences. Everything in the two worlds is exactly the same —

except one thing. In one world the rancher is liable for the damage his cattle cause as they trespass on the farmer's field. In the other world he is not liable. Both worlds are characterized by zero transaction costs; that is, it costs nothing for the farmer and the rancher to trade with one another. Would the number of cattle be different in either world?

Think about it. Would the production of cattle depend on who had the property right over where cattle should roam? This was the question posed by the Nobel economist Ronald Coase in 1960, and if you answered "No, it would not matter" then you're in very good company.

This is such an outrageous claim, it requires further development. To make the analysis more concrete, consider the data in Table 15-1. Column 1 indicates an amount of cattle produced, and column 2 indicates the marginal cost of producing each additional steer.

Table 15-1
The Coase Cattle Example

(1) Number of Steers	(2) Marginal Private Cost	(3) Marginal Crop Damage	(4) Marginal Social Cost
1	$100	$100	$200
2	150	100	250
3	200	100	300
4	250	100	350
5	300	100	400
6	350	100	450

The figures in column 2 indicate the "private" cost to the rancher of producing steers. These would include, for example, feed, cowboys, etc., meaning all the costs to the rancher of raising cattle to maturity and bringing them to market. According to the table, it costs the rancher $100 to raise one steer, an additional $150 to raise a second, $200 more to raise a third, etc. Not included in these costs, however, are the damages imposed on the neighboring farmer. Each steer tramples $100 worth of crops during its lifetime. These costs, which are "external" to the rancher, are often referred to as "externalities". Thus, the actual cost to society of raising 1 steer is not just the $100 diverted from other uses by the rancher, but also the $100 in crops that never get harvested, yielding a true marginal cost of $250. The complete, actual cost to society of producing a good is generally referred to as its "social cost". Likewise, "marginal social cost" refers to the true, complete cost of producing an additional increment of the good. The "private" cost is really a misspecification of cost; it leaves out part of the true effects of producing this good: in particular, the costs imposed on someone else. We consider private costs because it often seems that producers do not in fact always bear all of the costs of their decisions.

> *The total cost of producing a good, regardless of who bears this cost, is called the "social cost"*

Suppose now the market price of mature steers is $300. How many steers will the rancher produce, and how does the answer depend, if at all, on the rancher's liability for crop damage caused by his steers? Assume first that the rancher is liable for all such crop damage. In this case, the figures in column 4, marginal social cost, are also the rancher's own marginal costs of production. For each steer produced, the rancher must compensate the farmer $100 to cover the cost of the ruined crops. The rancher produces 3 steers under these constraints. Production is carried out until marginal cost rises to the market price. The rancher makes $100 on the fist steer, $50 on the second, and zero on the third, but, as usual, we assume production is carried out to this limit. He receives total rents of $150 on this production.

Suppose now the rancher is not liable for crop damage. In this case, the rancher does not have to compensate the farmer for the $100 of crops each steer destroys. It appears the "private" marginal cost figures in column 2 will determine output. In that case, the rancher would produce 5 steers, where the private marginal cost equals the market price. Coase showed, however, that this conclusion depends on the assumption that the farmer and rancher are unable to negotiate a mutually beneficial contract with each other.

When the rancher produces a fourth steer, his rents are potentially $50: the difference between the market price, $300, and the private marginal cost of that steer, $250. However, this steer produces a greater amount of damages, $100, than the rents received. The farmer would benefit by $100 if the steer were not produced; the rancher gains only $50 from producing it. In this situation, where the loser loses more than the gainer gains, the loser can pay the gainer something greater than the potential gain and less than the potential loss, and the position of both parties will be improved. For example, if the rancher accepts a payment from the farmer of $75 to not produce the fourth steer, then the farmer and the rancher each gain $25. Similarly, since the rancher makes no rents on the sixth steer, any small payment from the farmer will induce him not to produce it, thereby saving the farmer almost $100 in the process. If damages are being produced by someone's actions, those costs must be weighed against the benefits of the actions. If the costs are larger than the benefits, the parties can contract with each other to avoid these losses. Assuming, therefore, that the cost of transactions is sufficiently low that the farmer and the rancher can negotiate, resource allocation is the same, regardless of the assignment of liability. In this example, the rancher produces 3 steers under either assignment of liability. The wealth of the farmer and rancher are of course affected by who has to pay whom. If the rancher is liable for crop damage, he is worse off and the farmer is better off than if the rancher were not liable. The production outcome is the same, however, in either case: 3 steers. This remarkable insight has been dubbed the Coase Theorem. It follows because, in the absence of transactions costs, the gains from trade must be exhausted. Inefficient outcomes violate the axioms of behavior.

> **The Coase Theorem:** *The allocation of resources is independent of the distribution of property rights, when transaction costs are zero.*

Notice, however, that there is nothing the farmer can do to induce the rancher not to produce up to 3 steers. The gains from the rancher, e.g., $200 for the first steer, exceed the crop damage. The farmer could offer the rancher $100 to not produce the fist steer, for example, but the offer will be rejected. More importantly, in terms of producing net benefits for consumers, it is appropriate that the offer be rejected. The market price of $300, after all, measures consumers' marginal value of resources in the form of a steer. If the resource cost of producing that steer is only $200, production of the steer raises the net value of resources by $100 over their next best alternative, even including the crops that are inadvertently trampled. The efficient amount of "externalities" of damage to third parties is not likely to be zero. Sometimes the costs may be less than the benefits generated.

15.2 No-Fault Divorce and the Coase Theorem

If you're like most students, you probably think the Coase Theorem is obvious by now. Let's try another example and see how you fare. In 1969 California was the first state to switch to no-fault divorce. In 1985 South Dakota became the last state to switch to no-fault divorce. In Canada the entire country switched to no-fault divorce in 1968. In fact, most of the western world switched to no-fault divorce in the 1970s.

What is no-fault divorce? Well, prior to these laws, in order for a divorce to take place one party had to commit a "fault". These varied from state to state, but they usually included things like adultery, cruelty, criminal behavior, and other such things. One of the realities of fault divorce was that it was often hard to prove a fault had been committed, especially if the guilty party didn't wish to be caught. What tended to happen was that couples would agree to a fault and then perjure themselves in court. Why would someone agree to a fault? Because they are compensated, of course!

Suppose the husband wanted to leave the marriage. Under the old fault law he would have to "pay" his wife to agree to some fault. This payment often took the form of a certain percentage of the marital assets. For example, the wife might consent to a ground for divorce for full possession of the house, or custody of the children. The point is that the individual *most* wanting the divorce had to pay the individual who *least* wanted to divorce. We could say the "property right" over divorce belonged to the one who least wanted the divorce — in our example the wife.[1]

When the law switches to no-fault divorce, no grounds are required. It is enough that there are "irreconcilable differences", and these differences need only be established by *one* party. In our example, if the husband decides to end the marriage under a no-fault regime, he can just leave. If the wife wants him to stay them she must pay him! Hence the property right to divorce switches from the one who *least* wants a marriage to the one that *most* wants it.

This would appear to provide a nice Coase Theorem experiment. We have two worlds, one where the wife holds the property right, while in the other the husband holds the right. Let's ask

---

[1] Most divorces are filed for by the wife. Who actually causes the divorce is a more difficult question to answer. The best estimates are that men and women seem to instigate divorce at the same rate. Of all divorces, about half appear to be "opportunistic", that is, where one party is trying to gain at the other's expense. Of these types of divorces, husbands tend to go after the financial resources of the marriage, while women tend to go after the children.

the Coase question: will the divorce rate be the same in those states where the law is fault as in those states where the law is no-fault? The answer is, according to the Coase theorem, there should be no difference. But can you see why? Consider Table 15-2.

	Husband	Wife
Married	\$50	\$50
Divorced	\$60	\$30

Table 15-2
Joint Values Married and Divorced

Table 15-2 describes a situation where we have an efficient marriage. That is, the marriage is worth more (\$100) than the joint value of the divorce (\$90). This is a couple who should stay together given our notion that more is better than less. However, it is also a situation where the husband would prefer a divorce to marriage because his wealth is higher when divorced. For the wife, the opposite is true, she prefers being married.

Suppose the state that this couple lives in is a fault state. This means that the husband must pay his wife to agree to a divorce. What is the maximum he is willing to pay (ie. what is his marginal value for the divorce)? Ten dollars? Right. However, the wife will require at least \$20 to agree to a divorce. The husband is unwilling to pay this amount, the wife does not consent, and the efficient result happens — no divorce.

Now suppose this couple had lived in a no-fault state. Now the husband decides to leave and does not require his wife's permission. Will the wife be able to convince her husband to stay? Yes, indeed. She is willing to pay \$20 to have him stay, while he only requires \$10 to be convinced. The efficient result happens again, the husband remains and there is no divorce. To see if you understand this, switch the numbers around so that you have an inefficient marriage; that is, one where the joint value together is lower than the joint value apart. It should be easy for you to show that this couple always divorces, no matter what the law is. So the decision to divorce is independent of the distribution of property rights between the couple. Just like in the cattle example where liability did not matter, here the divorce law didn't matter. The outcome is the same, and it is always efficient. That's the Coase theorem.

The Coase theorem states that the allocation of resources is independent of the distribution of property rights. That means, when transaction costs are zero, it doesn't matter what laws we have, it doesn't matter what types of contracts we make or firms we work in. Every rule is irrelevant. Why? Because individuals respond to costs and benefits, and the rules of the game do not change these fundamental things.

If this is the Coase theorem, you may be thinking like many people think at this stage: "let's take that Nobel prize back!". It doesn't take a genius to realize that rules, laws, contracts, and organizations all matter a great deal. Yet this is the most important feature of the Coase theorem, namely that it is always wrong in practice! For you see, Coase did not stop writing after the cattle/farmer example — he kept on going. The key to the Coase theorem is that it holds for when "transaction costs are zero," which is never true in the world we live in. When they are positive, rules and property rights do matter. Hence, if we are to understand rules, laws, organizations, and all of these sorts of things that cannot be explained by our simple model we must understand transaction costs.

15.3 What are Transaction Costs?

Ironically, before we get started defining transaction costs, we need to define property rights.

Economic Property Rights: *are one's ability to freely exercise a choice.*

The words "Property Rights" get bantered about quite a bit, and different disciplines tend to use the word quite differently. In particular, the legal profession has long used the words to define that body of law which applies to what they call "real property," something like land, a car, or a book. Others talk about "human rights," "natural rights" or even "power," and they often have meanings which overlap with the economists notion of rights. So before we begin discussing property rights, perhaps we should consider the differences in interpretation.

Let's consider the difference between legal property rights, natural rights, and economic property rights. Let's define the former as the right *under the law* to freely exercise a choice.[2] We can define natural rights as the right under Nature or God to freely exercise a choice. These three definitions may have considerable overlap, and it is useful to consider the diagram in Figure 15-1 where each definition is represented by a circle.

Consider section A. Here are a set of choices where one has the economic, legal, and natural right to do something. That is, the person is able, allowed, and morally justified in making such a decision. Many things in life fall into this category. When you go to a store, buy a candy bar and eat it you have all these rights in line. Consider section B, however. Here you have the economic and legal right to do something, but not the natural right. Some might consider abortion to fall into this category. It is legal and available in most North American jurisdictions, but many would consider it a violation of the natural right to life. In section C an individual has the economic and natural rights, but not the legal ones. This might apply to some religious sect which believes in polygamy and is tolerated by the state (there is such a community in Southwestern British Columbia). They are able to have this type of polygamous marriage, they obviously feel it is right, but they do not

---

[2] This definition would not satisfy many legal scholars. Some would add that legal property is a right to real things, belonging to one person against the whole world. For us we will focus on the distinction between *rights under the law* and *rights through possession.* Thus, I may have the legal property right to sell my car, but if it was stolen last night I no longer have any economic property right to the car.

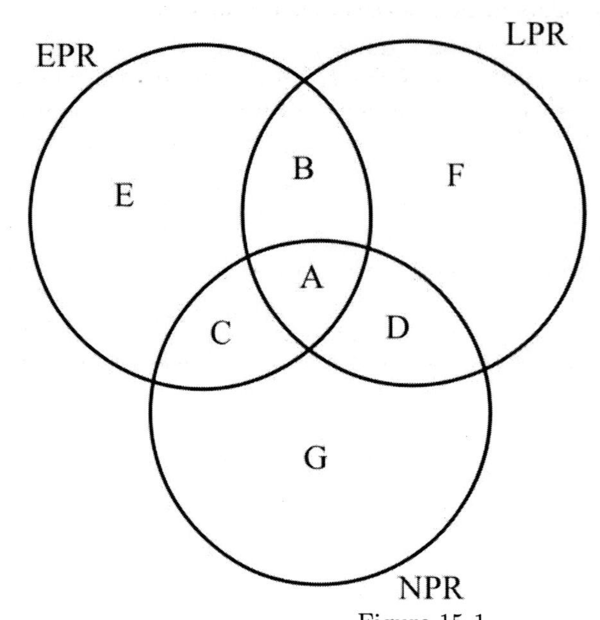

Figure 15-1
Different Definitions of Property Rights

have the legal right to the behavior. How about section D? Can you think of an example of this type where you have the legal and natural right to do something, but not the economic right? You have the legal and natural right to walk through Central Park in New York City at 11:00PM, but if you try to do it you might find yourself robbed and prevented of the pleasure. Section E is quite opposite to this. This is where a thief has possession of some goods and is able to use it, even though it is not his legal or natural property. Section F might apply to abortions in Prince Edward Island. They are legal, but no hospitals perform them. Thus many would consider them a violation of natural law, and the inability to receive one means the economic right is missing. Now that you're getting the hang of it, can you think up some examples that would fit in section G?

Let's return to the discussion of economic property rights (I'm going to start dropping the term "economic"). A property right relates to making choices, and these choices can be over many dimensions. For example, you might decide to possess, use, or improve something, you might exclude others, destroy or sell, you might transform, donate, bequeath, lease, mortgage, consume, or develop, there is a very long list of decisions you could make with respect to something you consider "your property." A property right is *complete* if you are able to make all of the decisions with respect to the good. A property right is *perfect,* if on the demension you are choosing, there is no infringement on the choice you are making. The important thing to realize is that the degree of completeness and perfectness of property rights hinges on the *ability* to make choices. Quite often our ability to make choices is limited, and in these cases we would say our property rights are limited. If our choices are totally limited, then we have no property rights at all. Economic property rights are not an all-or-nothing affair.

It is interesting to think of how limited our property rights really are. We say things like "I own this house". But what happens when you decide to park three cars on blocks in the front yard, or build a ten foot high brick wall around the property, or dig for gold, or start up a soup kitchen? Very quickly you realize that there are many choices with respect to "your" house that you cannot make, and as a result your property rights in that house are not complete.

Quite often property rights are limited by simple facts of nature. If I consumed some wood yesterday by burning it in my fireplace, my choices (hence property rights) over the wood today are severely limited — they are incomplete. More interestingly, my economic property rights are often incomplete because somebody else is the true holder of the rights. You cannot legally sell "your" student card because it legally belongs to the school. All laws and regulations ultimately distribute economic property rights to various individuals, and the simple truth is, none of us end up with all of them. Other times our rights are imperfect because it just doesn't pay to enforce them. Every now and then one reads the bumper sticker "As a matter of fact, I do own the road". Well, as a matter of observation, you don't. Even on private roads, trespass is common, and to the extent you can use logging roads for your weekend pleasure without paying for it, you have the economic property right, not the forest company. When rights are too costly for anyone to own, the asset in question is said to be in the public domain.

The Public Domain is the state where property rights do not exist

There are two important points to be made with respect to property rights. First, when there are no property rights, there is no trade and no wealth. Think about this for a moment. What would a world be like without property rights? That would mean no one could make any decisions. No one would produce anything because as soon as it was made it would be stolen. No one would save for the same reason. It would be literal anarchy. This is one of the reasons why economic rights are so closely linked with legal rights. It is very difficult to trade when one person holds one type of right and someone else holds the other. I have a friend who had his car stolen. This is a situation where my friend has a legal right to the car, but the thief had the economic rights. (When the police found the car it was locked!) Imagine if the thief tried to sell the car back to my friend. The conversation might go something like this "Oh, hello, I'm the fellow who stole your car last night, and I'd like to sell it back for $10,000. Just leave the money in small bills in a paper bag under the third bench at the park." "Oh, well thanks for calling. Unfortunately I have hay fever and the park is really bad for me. Perhaps you could meet me at my house around 10:00 o'clock." This is a transaction that's not going to happen.

The second point regarding property rights is that at the other end of the spectrum, when they are complete and perfectly defined, the gains from trade are maximized. This is the Coase theorem again. And so we see there is a spectrum of rights ranging from zero to perfect completeness, and corresponding to this there are wealth levels that range from zero to some maximum. We live in a world that is at neither extreme. Individuals own property but never completely. This is shown in figure 15-2.

Given that wealth is always higher when property rights are better defined, however, it is always true that individuals prefer better defined rights to poorer ones, other things equal. As a result, individuals will make efforts to establish property rights, and once established, efforts will be made to maintain those rights. This finally leads to a definition of transaction costs.

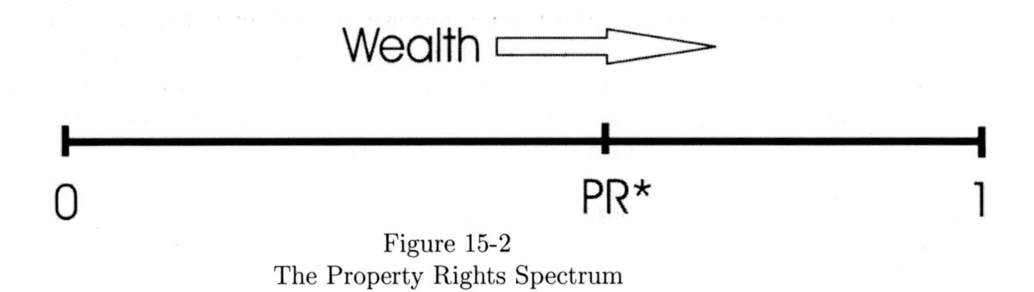

Figure 15-2
The Property Rights Spectrum

Transaction Costs: *The costs of establishing and maintaining property rights.*

These costs include the costs of protection, stealing, and any concomitant losses that result from such efforts. We see immediately that property rights are linked in a fundamental way to transaction costs. When property rights are perfectly defined, no effort is required to establish or protect them, and as a result transaction costs are zero. When transaction costs are prohibitive, no one would engage in them and property rights are zero. Finally, when transaction costs are positive, property rights will be incomplete.

15.4 Back to the Coase Theorem

Now let's return to the no-fault divorce example. It is common knowledge, and it has been shown, that the divorce rate increased with the change in the law. Why might it have increased? What was wrong with the simple numbers in Table 15-2?

In the simple discussion above we assumed that the property rights of the wife and the husband were perfect because transaction costs were zero. Recall, however, that property rights are limited in the world we live in. For example, some states had property laws which stated the owner of a marital asset was the individual whose name was on the title. If a husband divorces after the law has changed, and the home and other major assets are in his name, then the wife may have no wealth to compensate the husband to stay. This would be true despite the wife having made some economic contribution to those assets. The law effectively allows the husband to take the wife's wealth. Positive transaction costs in this situation mean her property rights are incomplete, and this leads to the Coase theorem breaking down. Or as another example, perhaps the wife put her husband through medical school and was expecting a return on this investment. Until recently, courts did not recognize a medical diploma as property, and therefore it could not be divided at divorce. Again, when the law switches to no-fault, the wife might be unable to compensate her husband because her investment is in his head and there is no legal remedy to get it back. As a final example, the wife might have remained in the home and out of the workforce for the entire duration of the marriage, and at the time of divorce may have no liquid assets to compensate her husband. Transaction costs arise in this situation on the part of banks, which will unlikely provide a loan when human capital is the only collateral, since default is likely and slavery is illegal.

Thinking about transaction costs within a marriage reminds one of the story of the married couple who are driving along a highway at a steady forty miles per hour. The wife is behind the wheel when her husband suddenly looks across at her and speaks in a clear voice. "Darling," he says. "I know we've been married for twenty years, but I want a divorce." The wife says nothing, keeps looking at the road ahead, but slowly increases her speed to 45 mph. The husband speaks again. "I don't want you to try and talk me out of it," he says, "because I've been having an affair with your best friend, and she's a far better lover than you are." Again the wife stays quiet, but grips the steering wheel more tightly and slowly increases the speed to 55 mph. He then pushes his luck. "I want the house," he says insistently. The car's now up to 60. "I want the car, too," he continues. 65 mph. "And ," he says, "I'll have the bank accounts, all the credit cards and the boat." The car slowly starts veering towards a massive concrete bridge. This makes him a wee bit nervous, so he asks her "Isn't there anything you want?" The wife at last replies — in a quiet and controlled voice. "No, I've got everything I need." she says. "Oh, really?" he inquires, "what have you got?" Just before they slam into the wall at 75 mph, the wife turns to him, smiles, and says ... "The airbag."

This is what makes transaction costs so special: they are the only costs that break the Coase theorem down. Once they exist, it is no longer true that rules, laws, contracts, etc., no longer matter. They matter indeed. One young lady once wrote Miss Manners and asked her if she should move in with her boyfriend. She wrote "He tells me he loves me, and what's in a piece of paper anyway". Miss Manners wrote back simply "Gentle reader, tell your young friend that Miss Manners has a safety deposit box full of pieces of paper, and they matter a great deal".

Earlier we noted that individuals maximized utility, and that firms maximized profits. None of this changes with the introduction of transaction costs. However, there is a slight modification in that individuals now maximize utility net of transaction costs, and firms maximize profits net of transaction costs. Firms, for example, are not indifferent to the *way* they pay their workers, because different methods of payment lead to different levels of output when it is costly to monitor employees. For example, wage workers take longer to do a given task than a piece rate worker. When firms are not indifferent to organizational forms, then they chose the one that helps to maximize profits. As a result, we have a theory of organizations.

And transaction cost economics is even broader than this. When condominium developers are designing the constitution for the apartments they want to sell, they are not indifferent to the laws they establish. Giving votes based on square footage, results in different behavior of the tenants, that one vote per person, or one vote per apartment. The developers pick those rules that allow them to charge the most for the homes. As a result, we have a theory of rules. And on and on. Transaction cost economics has been used to explain the nature of the common law, regulations, the nature of the firm, and just about every type of rule you can imagine.

This leads us to the last principle of economics:

PRINCIPLE #7

Optimal Organization: *All economic organization is designed to maximize the gains from trade net of transaction costs.*

For our purposes, this will amount to saying that all organizations are organized to minimize the transaction costs involved in the production of their enterprise.

15.5 What Causes Transaction Costs[3]

The underlying theme in understanding transaction costs is the notion of ignorance. Let's face it, if you knew everything, you wouldn't be reading this book ... or attending college. In life, knowledge is scarce and costly to come by. Negotiation, fraud, communication, and contract stipulation all come about because knowledge is incomplete and not common. However, information costs are not the same thing as a transaction cost. An information cost is the cost of obtaining information. For transaction costs to exist, it must be costly to acquire information about anything: goods, people, institutions.

This means information costs are a *necessary* condition for a transaction costs to exist. Information costs, to repeat, are not necessarily transaction costs. You might have no idea if it will rain tomorrow, and this is an information problem. That doesn't mean that you necessarily have a transaction cost problem. The acts of finding a trading partner, determining the correct good for a particular need, or searching for the "best price" are information costs, not transaction costs. All kinds of behavior seems to depend on information costs and not transaction costs. Unemployment, search, and clearance sales are all events that only require costly information.

It is necessary, however, to do more than assume costly information in order to generate transaction costs, because costly information merely makes for risky events. An additional assumption is required that enhances the problem of costly information. Goods are not simple, but are both *variable* and *alterable.*

	Alterable	Non-Alterable
Variable	Everything else	Earthquakes Hurricanes
Non-Variable	a rose	God

Table 15-1
Variable and Alterable Goods

The distinction between variability and alterability can be thought of as those changes brought about by nature and by man. Consider the taxonomy of Table 1. God and the speed of light, for

[3] This section is advanced and can be skipped without paying a price in following chapters.

example, do not vary in nature, nor are they alterable by man. The weather changes constantly, but despite accusations against the Russians and rain dancers, weather storms are probably independent of human manipulation. It is difficult to imagine something that does not vary in nature but that can be altered by man — although Gertrude Stein must have thought a rose fit this category.

The distinction is important. When goods are both variable and alterable (and, of course, information is not free), then cheating becomes possible. Consider the purchase of an apple. Suppose apples never varied in nature, but could be manipulated in some way — for example, hollowing out the apple and filling it with foam. Could a merchant sell a foam-filled apple and not be accused of cheating? No, because any change in the quality of the apple is, by assumption, blamed on the seller. Likewise, if apples came in all different shapes, sizes, and insides, but were impossible to alter, then no suspicion of cheating would exist. All bad apples would be attributed to nature. When both conditions exist, that is, when a bad apple may be produced by the weather or the seller — only then can cheating occur *without* detection. That it is so difficult to think of examples of goods that are non-variable or non-alterable tends to imply that the possibilities of cheating, and therefore transaction costs, are ubiquitous.

When a good contains attributes that are either alterable or variable, but does not contain both, then transaction costs are zero or negligible. Both alterability and variability are needed in order for transaction costs to arise, because these costs stem from the inability to attribute changes in product quality directly to random events or non-random exploitation. When nature and humans play a role in the ultimate quality of a good, then there is confusion on the part of the buyer over who is to blame for the differences in quality. Under these circumstances transaction costs can exist.

15.6 Private Property, Common Property, and Open Access

Let's use the discussion of property rights and transaction costs to examine three types of property found everywhere. Private property is a concept familiar to all of us. The owners of private property decide how an item is to be used, who is to use it, and what happens to the income or utility of the item. As we've mentioned in the discussion of the property rights spectrum, nothing is perfectly private, but there are many things in life we consider our private property. Common property is where access to a good or resource is limited to some group, but within the group no one has the right to exclude others. In an office, the workers may have equal access to the photocopy machine, the washroom, or the secretaries time, but someone off the street doesn't have access to these things. Open access is a situation where no one has the right or ability to exclude anyone. The high seas are an open access resource, as were the bison on the American frontier. Each one of these different property right regimes has different benefits in terms of the wealth they generate. However, each one has different transaction costs associated with them as well. Which one is chosen as the optimal form of ownership depends on which one maximizes the value net of these transaction costs. Let's consider each one in turn.

Private Property

Let's consider a famous example in economics. Suppose there is a lake with fish in it, and there is one boat available for fishing. A community lives on the edge of the lake, and the people make their living off the fish. When someone stands on shore to fish, they catch 4 fish in a day. But if they use the boat to fish, then the number of fish caught per person depends on the number of people in the boat according to our normal production function. Every fisherman in the boat, therefore, contributes to the number of fish caught. The marginal and average product of fish caught is given in Figure 15-3. We've seen marginal products before, but we haven't talked about average products. The average product is just the total amount of fish caught divided by the number of people in the boat. If the people in the boat share the fish caught, then each will get the average product.

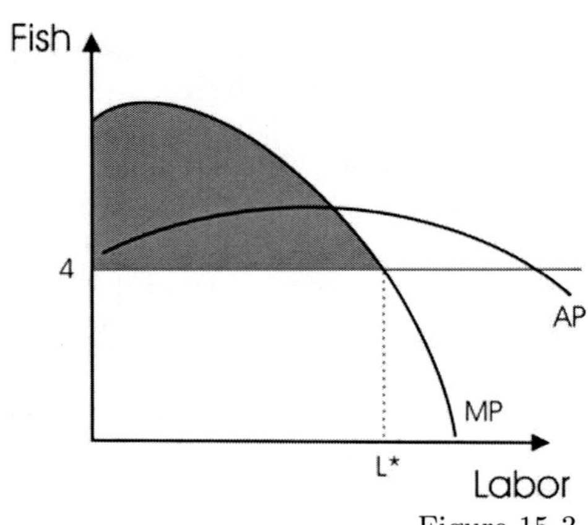

Figure 15-3
Private Property for the Boat

When the boat is privately owned, the owner of the boat decides how many workers will be allowed on. We can think of the boat owner as hiring workers for the boat. Since workers can catch 4 fish on shore, the boat owner must pay each fisherman 4 fish to come fish on the boat. How many fishermen will be hired? We know the answer to this question is determined by where the marginal product just equals the wage. In this case the boat owner hires L^* fishermen. Notice when this is done, the surplus of fish, equal to the light grey shaded area, is maximized. We can think of this area as the value of the boat. If the boat were for sale, the boat owner could receive this area as its price, since that is how many extra fish are capable of being caught with the boat. Hence, ignoring any transaction costs, private property maximizes the wealth of the little village.

> *Private property maximizes the gross value of the resource.*

Common Property

Suppose now that no single person owns the boat, but the boat is owned in common by a small group of fishermen. These fishermen share the catch, and decide how many fishermen should enter the boat. Under these circumstances, the owners of the boat don't want to put men in the boat

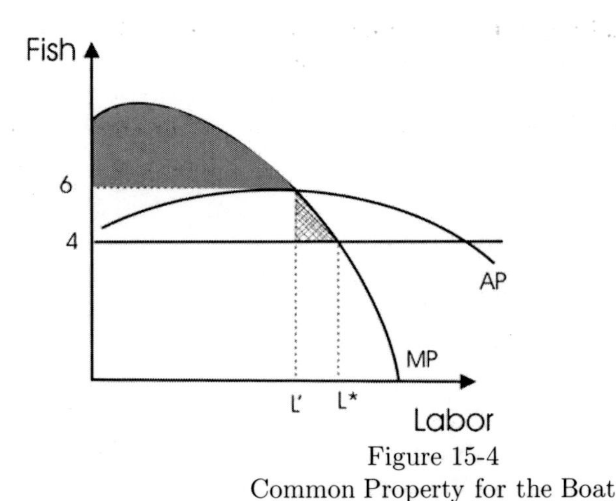

Figure 15-4
Common Property for the Boat

until the wage equals the marginal product. What they want to do is maximize the *average product* because that's what each one of them gets. Figure 15-4 shows this situation.

Now the number of fishermen in the boat equals L', not L^*. This reduction in the number of fishermen comes about because the fishermen want to maximize the average product. At this lower number of men, the average catch is 6 fish, not 4. This extra income for the fishermen comes from the value of the boat, which is now reduced to the light grey shaded area. But there is more than a transfer from capital to labor involved here. Because the number of fishermen has been reduced, along with the total catch, there is a deadweight loss associated with the common property ownership of the boat.

Common property does not maximize the value of the resource

Open Access

With open access, no one owns the boat. Any one who wants to jump in and go fishing can do so. When this property right structure exists, people will enter the boat as long as the average number of fish they catch on the boat is equal to the number they can catch on shore, in this case 4 fish. Figure 15-5 shows this result, which is often called "the tragedy of the commons."

Now too many people hop onto the boat. In fact, L'' fishermen get on, and at this level the deadweight loss, equal to the crosshatched area, is large indeed. In fact, it turns out that the size of the deadweight loss is just equal to the value of the boat under private property. This means the value of the resource is driven to zero! The boat is worthless, which makes sense because incomes with the boat are the same as if there were no boat.

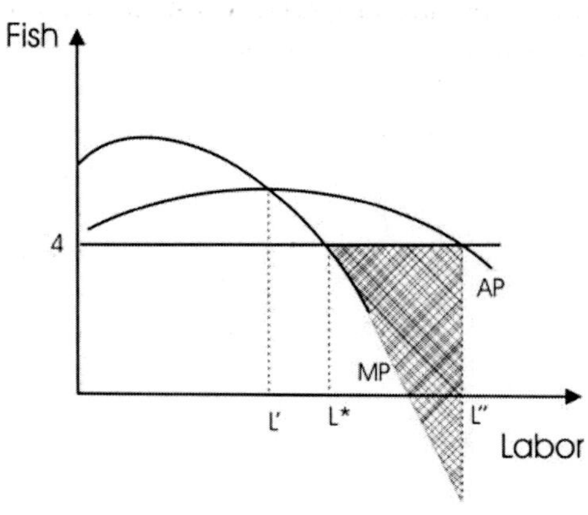

Figure 15-5
Open Access for the Boat

> *Open access drives the value of the resource to zero.*

The Optimal Property Right Rule

If this were all there was to the story, then clearly private property would be the best of all possible worlds. Many believe this to be true. Yet when we look around, we see common property rights all over the place, and even open access property rights, though rarer, can be found. If we believe in maximization, and if we believe that private property is the best system, then how can we explain the choice of common property? People are leaving $500 bills on the sidewalk again.

The reason why we observe all types of property right rules is that the transaction costs of each regime are not the same and they vary depending on the nature of the good. In the real world, owned goods must be protected, and these protection costs are costly. Since private property generates a lot of wealth societies are always trying to find inexpensive ways of enforcing private property. Courts and police are designed to protect private property, for example. For some goods though, the benefits of private ownership are small, and the costs might be enormous. When this is the case, common property often develops. Small groups band together to keep outsiders ... well, out. The groups are often designed to make sure any individual within the group doesn't treat the resource as open access. This usually amounts to making sure the group is homogeneous, or held together by some common bond.

The Swiss Alps are pastures high in the mountains and used for summer cattle grazing. These Alps are owned in common by the local village. Members of the village have access to the Alps and must follow rules for its use, but members of other villages do not have access. The Alps have been managed for centuries this way. Lobsters on the east coast of North America are harvested by groups of fishermen called "lobster gangs" (I'm not making that up!). These gangs police outside fishermen from interloping on their fishing grounds, and they share the catch within their grounds. When gold was discovered in California in 1849, the miners set up common fields in which a group would mine an area and band together to defend the mines. When private or state enforcement comes along, most of these common property regimes disappear. In the case of the California miners, when

U.S. marshals finally moved in the mines became private property. Until then, however, common property is one method of protecting a resources from becoming open access.

Open access occurs when it is simply too costly to keep anyone out of the resource. At one time, virtually the entire ocean was an open access resource. As navies developed, and as cannon fire from shore improved, countries laid claims to the water off their shores. At first countries established sovereignty over two miles; now it is common for countries to claim 200 miles off shore. Still, no country lays claim to the middle of the Pacific. As a result, the resources there are exploited to the limit and the value of fisheries there are close to zero. If the world wasn't the way it is, we could say that open access was inefficient. However, since it costs too much to defend private property at times, on occasion the best we can do is have open access.

Homesteading: The Optimal Property Right Rule?

During the first half of the 19th century a small, debt ridden, loosely held together, sparsely populated new country called the United States had a difficult problem to solve. On paper it claimed ownership to vast tracks of land to the west, yet this land was occupied by native Indians, Mexicans, British trappers, and a host of other minor interests. How were they to actually take possession?

At the very beginning of the 19th century the U.S. government sold public lands in the areas of Ohio, Kentucky and Tennessee, but they quickly switched over to a system of first come, first served called homesteading. A homestead was 160 acres that could be had by the first person to claim it, pay a small registration fee of $10 and improve the land for five years. The advantage homesteading had over land sales was the settler had to occupy the land. Occupation was important because the government did not have the resources to defend the land against others claiming it.

Homesteading allocated the land on a "first come, first served" basis, and this forced individual settlers to show up early and claim the land. Someone purchasing land could buy it, and not show up to farm for many years when it is optimal to show up. A homesteader who waited to show up, would find his plot had long been taken by someone else who got there earlier. The advantage of homesteading was it got people onto the frontier in a hurry, and gave these people an incentive to defend the land against those also claiming possession.

When it came time for Canada to settle its western frontier the new country faced a similar problem, only this time the threat was not Mexicans or Indians, rather it was Americans moving north. Selling the land to private interests would not improve the Canadian claim to sovereignty on the prairies if there were no guns to back it up. Thus the Canadian government adopted the identical homesteading laws the U.S. had used to settle their frontier. By providing an incentive to settlers to "rush" to the prairies and stay to improve the land, the area was populated by Canadians who quite naturally kept the Americans out.

Homesteading was not free. Suppose the optimal time to arrive in say, Lone Spruce, Saskatchewan, in order to start farming was 1920. The problem for a young family living in Ontario in 1900 was that if they waited until 1920, the homestead would be gone, and so the settlers would plan to move out west a year early. Other potential farmers would think the same way and would plan on moving two years early. This process continues until it was just barely worth moving at all. By allocating the frontier this way both governments forced settlers to move too soon and wait for development to catch up. This meant many settlers waited years for railways, schools, and the rest of civilization. As one settler put it "there ain't no such thing as free land." Still, homesteading was the optimal thing to do in light of the threat of enemy invasion.

15.7 The Optimal Value of an Asset

Let's suppose, for sake of argument, that an asset can either be in the public domain, where open access reigns, or it can be held as private property. In other words, let's ignore the option of common property for a moment. We might ask two questions: what happens to the optimal ownership of an asset as the value of an asset increases, and is there an optimal value for an asset to be?

The first question was initially raised by Harold Demsetz who argued that private property rights are established when the benefits of establishment exceed the cost of establishment. Figure 15-6, captures this idea. On the horizontal axis is the zero transaction cost value of an asset, determined by underlying demand and supply conditions. This gross value is independent of transaction costs and is set by a competitive market. On the vertical axis are the dollar benefits and costs of ownership over the asset. Assuming ownership is complete, meaning the owner of the asset receives all of its value, the benefit of property rights is simply the 45^0 line. The total cost function in figure 15-5 gives the cost of establishing and maintaining property rights over the asset. In other words, this is the *transaction cost* function. This function incorporates *all* of the costs of ownership.

The vertical distance between the two lines represents the asset's actual value. That is, this is the amount of money someone would actually pay for the asset. For example, if the zero transaction cost value of an asset was V', then the actual value would be given by distance AB. The critical point made by Demsetz and others was that, assuming these functions had an intersection, a critical zero transaction cost value, V^C, determines whether property rights exist or not. To the left of V^C the asset is in the public domain because the costs borne by those attempting to establish ownership exceed the benefits and wealth maximizers exert no rights to the asset. The asset remains in the public domain and has no value. To the right of V^C private property exists.

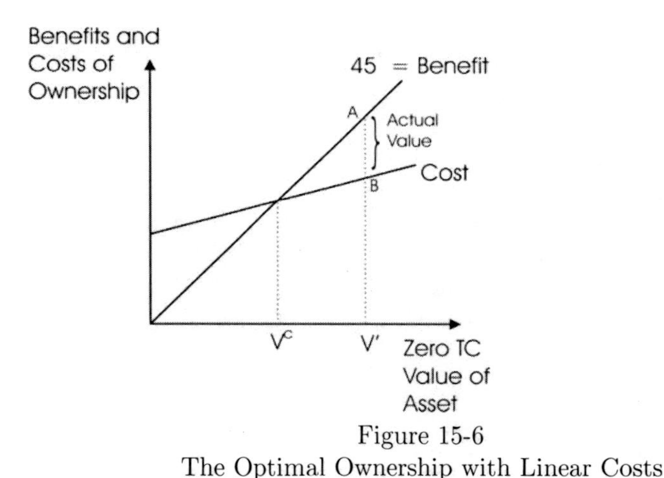

Figure 15-6
The Optimal Ownership with Linear Costs

The key implication from figure 15-6 is that as an asset's value increases from zero — that is, as we move from left to right in the figure — at some point it becomes worthwhile to protect the asset and it moves from open access to private property. History is full of examples of this happening. The western frontier was, for the most part, an open access resource in the first half of the 19th century. Settlers would move out to the frontier and lay claim to the land, but often interlopers would come along and ignore these claims. Sometimes the outcomes were tragic, like the near extinction of the bison. Other times fights broke out, like the disputes between cattle and sheep ranchers. As the value of the frontier increased over the century, protection of private claims increased. Eventually barbed wire was invented, and this allowed a cheap way to fence off claims. Violence on the frontier fell, as did over grazing and other misallocations of resources.

Non-linear Transaction Costs

In figure 15-6 the transaction cost function is linear, but this violates our principle of diminishing marginal products. It would be more realistic to assume marginal costs of protection are increasing. The more valuable an asset is, the more it costs at the margin to protect it. Making this modest change in the model leads to several predictions. First, it is still the case that for low valued assets, as their zero transaction cost value exogenously increases they are likely to move from the public domain to private ownership. In other words, in the neighborhood of V^L in figure 15-7 the original Demsetz prediction still holds. A second observation is just as apparent. It is possible that assets may have zero transaction cost values that are so high the transaction costs of ownership again exceed the benefits and the asset reverts back to the public domain. Hence, paradoxically, in principle the public domain may contain extremely valuable (in a zero transaction cost sense) and extremely low valued assets. Pebbles on the side of the road are low valued and in the public domain. Practical examples of high valued assets in the public domain are rare, but an example of the "urban legend" variety, is of an owner of a convertible who leaves his top down when parking on public streets because he does not want the top damaged by a thief. This would place the valuable interior of his car in the public domain. A third implication from the model is that there exists a finite optimal second-best value of an asset, V^*.

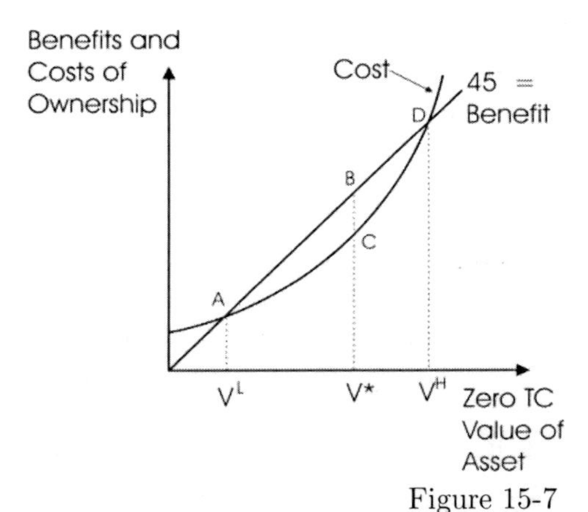

Figure 15-7
The Optimal Ownership with Non-Linear Costs

Wealth maximizers do not like assets in the public domain. When assets are in the public domain because they are too costly to protect given their high zero transaction cost value, there are two general solutions available. The first is to innovate on the transaction cost margin. As shown in Figure 15-8, a fall in transaction costs brought about by an innovation in policing technology allows the high valued asset to be removed from the public domain. This type of innovation is common. For example, the innovation of barbed wire mentioned above brought vast amounts of land in the arid west out of open grazing to enclosed pasture. Another example from the old west comes from innovations in western water law. Historically, ownership of fresh water was limited to use rights in England and the Eastern U.S. These poorly developed rights reflected the low value of water in wet climates. In the arid western states, however, water is an extremely valuable resource. Hence changes in the law developed to create a low transaction cost legal framework for trading water rights. A modern example of protection innovation is the new DVD technology. Although DVD provides a higher quality video and audio output, the driving force behind its development was the ability to prevent pirated copies of the contents through various encryption devices. DVD's are capable of a "Regional Lock" that prevents a DVD from North America being used in any of five other world regions. DVD's carry extra signals, called Macrovision, that prevent the contents being copied to video tape. DVDs also contain a "content scrambling system" that encrypts data and requires a reader decoding key. Ironically, all of these measures were "broken" rather quickly and "patches" can easily be downloaded from the Web to avoid them. History is full of examples of innovations that reduce transaction costs, and therefore, increase net wealth. However, innovation takes time, and its success is always uncertain. In the short run another option may be more profitable.

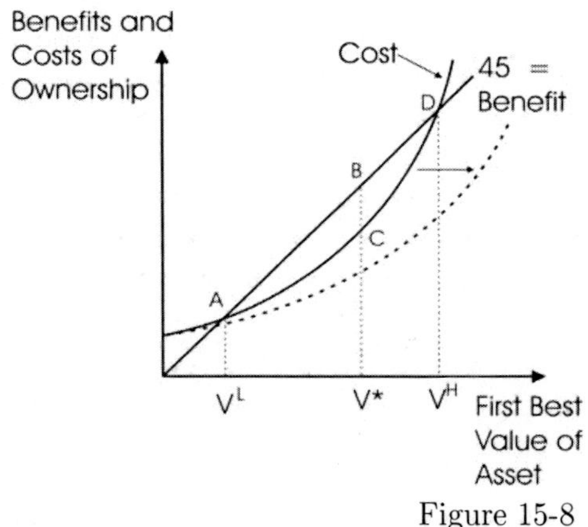

Figure 15-8
Changes in the Transaction Cost Function

A second solution to removing assets from the high zero transaction cost valued end of the public domain is to lower their *gross value.* Lowering the gross value makes the asset less attractive to theft, and given the non-linear transaction costs, the costs of enforcing the property right falls by more than the value of the property right. The net result is private ownership and a positive second-best value. The asset should be reduced in value to the level of V^* in figure 15-7, where the second best value is maximized. Here we can focus on the dramatic case of actual wealth destruction, but a more common practice is simply hiding or disguising wealth. Wealth can be hidden through non-conspicuous consumption, trade-secrets, and off-shore holdings. Apparently it was not uncommon during the Renaissance, when public protection of private wealth was minimal, for elaborate palaces to be constructed behind a ghetto facade. It is critical to note that this type of behavior is different from efforts at protection that raise *both* gross and net values. For example, we are *not* referring to cases such as putting locks on doors, "the club" on car steering wheels, or security strips in currency. We're talking about actually destroying some gross wealth to make the net wealth higher. Let's turn to two examples to show there are many examples in life where the cost of maintaining a property right are higher than a good's value.

The Rhino's Horn.

Let's begin with the example of the rhinoceros because it provides such a stark and simple example of the model. The wild rhinoceros is valued for many attributes, not the least of which is its horn. The horn is essentially made of compressed hair (keratin), and is similar in makeup to a human fingernail. The horn continually grows, and achieves its shape from constant sharpening. Although the horn is used to decorate ceremonial dagger handles in the Middle East, its chief use is in Far East medicine where it is ground into a powder for the relief of fevers.

Generally speaking the governments of Africa manage rhinos as a common property resource in conservation areas and on public lands. In North America, where legal property rights to land are well developed and where state regulation is often enforced, many migratory and wild specie attributes are owned by private landowners, conservation groups, or local, state, and federal governments. In some parts of Africa, most notably South Africa, there are large private reserves for mammals such as rhinos. Over the entire continent, however, rhinos are generally managed as open access.

Since the 1970s there has been an international ban on the trade of rhino horn, making it costly to develop private ranges to farm the animal. In light of the ban a black market trade in horns has developed, which has encouraged poaching. As a consequence rhinoceros populations fell considerably between 1970 to 1990 as poachers killed rhinos for the valuable horn. For example, Black Rhinos numbered between 65,000-100,000 in 1970 and today population estimates are between 3,000-4000. Similar reductions have occured in other rhino species both in Africa and Asia.

To date no one has developed a method or technology to lower the transaction cost function for rhinos. Given the nature of the beast they require vast amounts of territory and are difficult to relocate to safe places. Rhinos require special bacteria to digest food and relocation means that new bacteria must develop when there are small changes in diet. The time lag involved means that rhinos often "starve" to death when moved. However, a solution has been found that appears to be working — dehorning. Dehorning involves the drugging of the rhino and sawing off the horn just above the skin line. The horn eventually grows back and the procedure is repeated every 18–24 months. Dehorning, like having fingernails cut, does not hurt the rhino, nor does it appear to seriously reduce the rhinos ability to forage, defend, or breed. Apparently rhinos often lose their horns in the wild with no major side effects. This is quite different from detusking elephants, whose tusk is essentially a tooth and full of nerves. Although removal of tusks has been done to elephants to reduce poaching, because it destroys other attributes of the animal, it has been less successful.

There is no question that removing a rhino's horn lowers the value of the rhino. However, given that the poacher only values the horn and that the state values the rhino for other attributes (tourism, biodiversity, etc.), removal of the horn lowers the cost of enforcement by much more than the fall in the gross value. The result is an increase in the net value of the rhino. Although it is still early in the program, it appears the policy has reduced poaching. Reports are that dehorning essentially eliminated poaching in northwest Namibia when it was first introduced. Dehorning lowers the gross value of the rhino by systematically eliminating the attribute that the thief values highly.

Built in Obsolescence

On March 3, 1998 the USDA in partnership with Delta and Pine Land, a small Louisiana cotton seed company, announced a new patent for the control of germination in seeds. Monsanto, the largest seller of genetically modified seeds in the world, later purchased Delta and Pine Land and acquired the patent. Called the "terminator gene" the modification essentially makes plants sterile and unable to germinate. Almost immediately there was a massive public campaign against the use of such technology and in 1999 Monsanto announced that it would not commercially use the terminator gene, although it reserved the right to use it in the future.

From a neoclassical perspective the terminator gene presents itself as an economic puzzle: a case of built in obsolescence if ever there was one. The gene itself does not increase output or change the plant in anyway. Its sole purpose is to prevent reproduction and the storage of seed. Forcing farmers to buy seed that lasts only one period over seed that can perpetuate itself only lowers the price of the seed. Since seed is costly to produce, destroying the reproduction capabilities of the plant can only reduce profits — at least in a zero transaction cost world.

The problem for producers of genetically modified seed is that the seeds become stolen and future crops are not captured by the current price. "Seed pirates" are a common problem in third world countries, but the case of a Saskatchewan farmer, though trivial in terms of the revenue to Monsanto, demonstrates the magnitude of the problem. Percy Schmeiser, age 68, lives in Bruno, a small town close to Saskatoon, where he has farmed all of his life. He recently was found guilty by the Federal Court of Canada where he was accused of stealing 320 acres worth of "Round-Up ready canola".[4] Mr. Schmeiser, despite having a field of Monsanto product, never paid Monsanto the $37/ha annual fee for growing it, and claimed the seeds floated onto his property from passing grain trucks. Most remarkable about the case was the extent to which Monsanto had gone to protect its property. Monsanto employees entered the farm without permission to take crop samples for genetic testing; they obtained permission from local flour mills to test Schmeiser's seeds that had been left at the mill for cleaning; and they tried to hire the flour mill owner to report on other local farmers that might be cheating. All of this for a farmer growing a 1/2 section of canola. Clearly, the problem with genetic crops is that they are "too valuable" and encourage theft.

Contracts with farmers to forgo storage and private sales, along with inspection of crops, and tours of flour mills are expensive. The lowering of the first best value of the seed by introducing sterility is not a corporate trick to exploit farmers, but a method to increase the second-best value of the crop by reducing the transaction costs of protection. Interestingly enough, outcries in the press against the use of the terminator gene have not come from farmers using Monsanto seeds, but from farmers who do not use it (many in the third world). One wonders at how many of these farmers, like Mr. Schmeiser, actually are using stolen seed? Although it is yet to be seen if the strategy is feasible, by having a seed that cannot reproduce, problems of theft over future crops are eliminated.

The terminator gene provides an excellent example of attributes that are valuable to seed pirates, but not the legitimate farmers who purchase the seed. Assuming there are some economies of scale in growing and storing seeds, an "honest" farmer who pays for his Monsanto seed would prefer to buy one time seeds each year from Monsanto, rather than produce and store seeds himself. On the other hand, seed pirates highly value a seed's germination qualities. Without the ability to replicate, stolen seeds are only worth the bread they can make. Monsanto did not willy-nilly lower the value of its seed. Rather it lowered the value by eliminating the attribute that was valued more by the thief than by the farmer.

The general issue with the terminator gene is one of built-in obsolescence. Built-in obsolescence may not be as rare as neoclassical textbooks claim it is. By lowering the value of a product the

---

[4] Round-Up is a Monsanto product that farmers use to kill weeds. The Court ruled on March 27, 2001.

benefits of theft are also reduced. Lowering the value in a way that targets the thief increases net value. Consider the case of computer software. A frequent complaint about such software is that there is "excessive upgrading"; that is, producers of software are inefficiently inventing upgrades that consumers would prefer not be invented given the cost.

But there may be another reason. Software for computers is extremely easy to steal and the better the product the more likely the chance that it will be pirated. One strategy to protect the investment of the firm is to continually issue upgrades, or to postpone improvements, *even if the improvements are currently known!* Learning how to use a new upgrade or being incompatible with other users are costs of not upgrading. By offering legal owners of the software easy and cheap upgrades the software company lowers the value of theft of the early versions.

An interesting example comes from one of the most popular typesetting packages for scientific writing. TEX, was released by Donald Knuth into the public domain virtually complete in the 1970s. At the time TEX was capable of producing mathematical expressions, tables, and publisher quality typesetting that privately owned word processor packages only developed in the 1990s. Word processing packages that came later, and that have been notorious for failures and constant upgrades cannot be explained by a lack of knowledge over how to program mathematical expressions, tables, or other features that were in the public domain. Rather, the inferior products and constant upgrades reduced the amount of stolen software revenue and increased profits. Software companies lowered the cost of upgrades to legitimate users by offering lower prices for registered users, with manuals, and phone support.

15.8 **Summary**

This chapter has introduced you to a much more complicated model than the neoclassical model of the first 14 chapters. A standard assumption about the neoclassical model is that markets work for free. This assumption is adequate for most applications, especially in the analysis of price movements and changes in the volume of trade. However, since prices allocate goods freely, there is no room for other types of mechanisms to organize exchange and production. Yet even a casual look around not only suggests markets do not work for free, but other institutions are used to allocate resources as well. The start to understanding organizations is to understand the concept of transaction costs. Transaction costs are a special type of cost: they are the cost of establishing and maintaining ownership over an asset, a stream of income, or anything else you might value.

When transaction costs are zero, any distribution of property rights lead to the same efficient outcome. This is the Coase Theorem. When transaction costs are not zero, then every distribution of property rights lead to a different outcome and the one that provides the most wealth is the optimal organization. This model was applied to different types of ownership. Private property is valuable because it provides the right incentives to use resources, but also requires private protection. Common property and open access are alternative methods of ownership that provide worse incentives, but mitigate protection costs. We also saw that as an asset increases in value it is more likely to be owned. However, given that extremely valuable assets might to too costly to protect, there is an optimal value of assets. In the next chapter we take this transaction cost notion of optimal ownership and apply it to firms.

REVIEW QUESTIONS

1. Is a fence a transaction cost?

2. What is the point of the Coase Theorem?

3. Are property rights human rights? Are human rights property rights?

4. In feminist theories there is the concept of "power." How might this fit into the discussion of property rights offered here?

5. If mother nature didn't exist, would there be transaction costs?

6. A squash partner always leaves his dirty old boots outside the court when he plays. Every time he comes out and says "Look, my boots are still here, that shows you once again how honest people are. I just don't see how you can believe people are always greedy." What is an alternative explanation for the lack of theft?

7. Barbed wire was invented by Joseph F. Glidden in 1874, and it was an immediate commercial success because it allowed cattle ranchers to cheaply fence vast areas of land. Can you think of some ways barb wire changed ordinary production costs and how it changed transaction costs?

PROBLEMS

1. When something is stolen ransom seems like the obvious thing for the thief to always do. The original owner must be the high marginal valued user of the good, so why not sell it back? Can you think of why children tend to be ransomed rather than automobiles?

2. A common explanation for the breakdown of the Coase theorem in family negotiations is that the husband may simply beat his wife to accepting the poorer circumstance. How is this also a problem of transaction costs and incomplete property rights?

3. The golden rule states that "we should do unto others, as we would like others do unto us". Is this a low or a high transaction cost rule for social interactions? Briefly explain.

4. In a world of zero transaction costs, what will the effect of changing liability for accidents be due to the amount of safety equipment in a coal mine? That is, suppose initially workers are responsible for accidents, but courts later switch this to employers being responsible. Explain your answer briefly.

5. Why might a gallery owner who sells a painting create more economic surplus than the artist who painted it? (Provide a supply and demand graph in your answer).

6. Would there not be any violence in a world of zero transaction costs?

7. Why did the bison die out, but cattle didn't?

8. Why do shopping centers often provide free parking — even to people who don't shop in the stores?

9. Using the ideas we learned in the "neoclassical model" what would be the best thing to send to an area that has been devastated by a flood or other similar tragedy? Why? Using the ideas from this chapter; that is, considering that the world is always characterized by positive transaction costs, why do we seldom send the good you just mentioned to victims of natural disasters? What do we tend to send instead and why?

10. In Europe, if you go to a public washroom, most of the time you have to pay for the toilet paper or pay some form of user fee. This never happens in North America. Why?

11. Everyone in my house loves pumpkin pie, and there is often an argument at the dinner table over who got the biggest piece. The solution was to use the simple rule that one child gets to cut the pieces of pie, while the other children get to decide which piece they want. What economic principle is being exploited here? Can you think of a problem that results from this allocation rule?

12. If it was illegal for anyone to own pigs, what would happen to the price of pork?

13. What would be an example of a transaction cost in using money? Do your examples explain why gold was so commonly used as money? (Hint: Think about why diamonds were seldom used as money.)

14. Why did domestic turkey's survive, but wild turkey's became practically extinct, given that the latter is much smarter than the former?

15. Seattle is made up of many small communities. One of these communities, Innes Arden, was on a hill overlooking the Puget Sound, and was developed in the 1950s by the Boeing company for its executives. At one point there were over 30 court cases pending — all of them over the height of trees. Supposedly trees planted 50 years ago were now blocking views. Why was the Coase theorem not working here? That is, (and you should be able to answer this in one sentence) why were the neighbors not bargaining over the trees? If the views were worth more than the trees, then the trees should come down. If they were not, then the trees should stand. Eventually one of the cases was settled in court. What do you suppose happened to the remaining 29 cases when the first case was decided?

16. Consider the following four cases:

    a. A man speeds and wipes out a fence of yours worth \$100. The man gets fined.

    b. A man steals \$100 from your house, is caught, and thrown in jail.

    c. A man plants a tree on his property that blocks your view and reduces the value of your property by \$100. The police just tell you to take him to court.

    d. A man opens a business just like yours and draws \$100 worth of customers away. The man gets a pat on the back.

In each case you lose \$100, yet the social rules used to respond to each loss is different. Questions:

   i) Why is there no penalty in (d)?

   ii) In (a) and (b) laws were broken. Why might some crimes have fines and others internment? (Don't say that everyone speeds).

   iii) Why does the Coase theorem not apply in (c)?

17. Many economists have argued that there is a property right problem with the fisheries. Since no one owns the fish, more than an optimal level of effort is applied to the fishery, and the rents from fishing are driven to zero. Now, consider retailing. A retailer is just like a fisherman, he fishes for customers. Since entry into retailing is open to anyone, there is too much retailing — just as there is too much fishing. Do you agree? Why or why not?

18. Why would a local residential community often have flower beds or other physical interruptions in street intersections that slow down traffic?

19. When you look around most of the furniture on a university campus, especially the furniture in the public spaces, it isn't very comfortable, and it certainly isn't very pretty. This is a common aspect of most public furniture. Why would this be?

20. What is the relationship between transaction costs, sunk costs, and opportunity costs?

21. During the Klondike gold rush of 1898, thousands of people flooded the small tent city of Dawson, Yukon in an attempt to find gold. Since there was no civilization on the spot only 2 years earlier, the town lacked any currency. Goods were traded for gold. Consider the following quote on the problems of using gold as a medium of exchange, taken from Pierre Berton's book *Klondike.*

> ... the great medium of exchange continued to be gold dust, and because of its uncertain quality a continual tug-of-war was maintained between merchant and customer. Most men used the so-called "commercial dust," heavily laced with black sand, to pay their bills. As the bank valued this commercial dust at only eleven dollars an ounce, a customer using it to buy groceries or whiskey could reckon that he was saving five dollars an ounce, since the normal price of clean Klondike gold ran around sixteen dollars — and the tradesmen tacitly accepted all dust at this price. This profit was increased by some who judiciously salted their pokes with fine brass filings. On the other hand, the bartenders and commercial businessmen weighed the dust carelessly, so that a poke worth one hundred dollars was usually empty after seventy dollars' worth of purchases were made. Thus, as was often the case in the Klondike, the gain was largely ephemeral.

  a. From this quote, what are some examples of transaction cost behavior?

  b. Throughout history, gold has been used as a medium of exchange. Why do you think other commodities were not used as a medium of exchange? Why do you think paper fiat currency replaced gold? Is there a transaction cost problem with paper money?

  c. If the miners were cheating the sellers by using padded gold dust, and the sellers were cheating the miners with loose measurements, does that mean in the end we obtain an outcome equivalent to one where there was no cheating going on?

22. Tort law is a body of law that deals with "harms." If you buy a bottle of coke, and it explodes, you sue Coke under tort law. If your neighbor cuts a tree down and it lands on your house, you would sue under tort law. In order to sue under tort an actual harm must take place. Interestingly, harms caused by competition are not considered a "harm" under torts. That is, if I own a shoe store, and another shoe store opens up and takes all of my business, the loss I suffer is not a tort. Does this aspect of tort law make sense from an economic point of view?

23. The countries that border the North Sea have established legal property rights over the rights to oil under the sea. However, they have not done this for other resources in the sea. Why not?

24. Fact #1: Husbands have to worry about the paternity of their wife's children because they only want to raise their own. Given the nature of pregnancy we always know who the mother is, but the father ... could be the milkman. Fact #2: The gene for blue eyes is recessive. This means that two blue eyed parents will have blue eyed children. If the parents have brown eyes,

they may or may not have blue eyed children. Question: If you were a blue eyed male, why might you prefer blue eyed women, all else equal?

25. A new branch of the Royal Bank opened up in Langley in the past year. As a special promotion patrons in the first 3 hours of operation were able to purchase a $100 bill for only $50. Before the branch opened its doors, a line up had formed. Suppose, for the sake of argument, everyone in the line has a time cost equal to $10 per hour. Suppose also that each customer can only purchase one bill, and that the bank has a limit of 200 bills to sell. Finally, suppose the bank can sell the bills instantly once the doors open.

    a. What will the line look like? That is, when do people form the line and how many people are standing there?

    b. Suppose there was no limit to how many bills a customer could purchase. That is, one person could buy all 200 bills that are for sale. How many people would be in the line and how long would the line be in terms of time.

    c. Is waiting in line a transaction cost?

26. *The Guess Who* were one of Canada's greatest bands. In *Share The Land* they claim that people should shake hands and share the land. If they do this people will help one another, there will be no more sadness, sorrow, or bad times. Everybody will be:
    walking together by the river, walking together and
    laughing, everybody singing together, everybody singing and
    laughing, good times good times, everybody walking by the
    river now, walking singing talking smiling laughing loving each other.

    Do you think if we all just "shared the land" that we'd end up laughing and singing together?

27. In the province of BC, when you purchase a land property you register your ownership with the government land titles office. In other jurisdictions across Canada and the US, other types of systems of keeping track of ownership are used. Having said this, generally speaking, when you cross a provincial or state border you don't notice any change in the way land is being used, transfered, or enjoyed. Why might the different legal systems of land ownership have no effect on how land is used?

28. Krista was out shopping one day for a new Star Wars collectible doll with her chubby boyfriend Tom. They had been dating for a year, and when they first met Tom was in great shape. Krista encouraged his eating to the point where he put on a few extra pounds. She eventually drew a line in the pudding and said he had to level out after awhile. The scenario is a common one, men tend to put on weight in relationships, especially after they are married. After a divorce, men tend to lose weight. Assuming that the female in the relationship prefers her man to have a trim body to a heavier one, why might allowing her man to "let himself go" be a solution to a transaction cost problem? [Hint: let's make the assumption that men are less monogamous than women are].

29. Krista has a brand new white Honda Civic she's named the Millennium Falcon. She loves the car and looks after it very well. The surprising thing is that she lets her boyfriend Tom drive it when they are together. What makes this odd is that Tom doesn't really like to drive, and

when she drives with her brothers, father, and other males, she always drives. Assume that Tom and Krista are equally good at driving. How might Krista be trying to get around a transaction cost problem serious dating couples face?

Review Question Answers

1. *Yes. In our world, where property rights are not perfect, a fence is certainly a transaction cost. We put them up to protect what we own.*

2. *Coase was trying to argue that the neoclassical model leads to what we call the "Coase Theorem." He did not suggest that this is how the world is. Rather, he was arguing that since property rights do matter, we must look towards transaction costs to explain why they matter.*

3. *I believe property rights include human rights. Historically human rights were synonymous with natural rights: the right to life, free speech, liberty. More recently they have included such things as rights to education and minimal standards of living. To the extent one is able to obtain these things, they are economic property rights. To the extent they are defined under law they are legal rights.*

4. *"Power" and "economic property rights" would appear to be the same thing.*

5. *No, at least nothing of significance. If there were no nature, then there really can be no confusion over outcomes and actions. We would always be able to trace back why we were cheated, and as a result, there would be no cheating.*

6. *Who wants a pair of used ugly boots.*

7. *First, barbed wire lowered labor costs since fewer people were required to supervise the daily activity of cattle. Second it lowered the cost of keeping weight on cattle because the cattle roamed less. Wandering cattle use up calories. Third it lowered the cost of protecting cattle from cattle thieves. However, the major savings came from reduced fighting between ranchers over open grazing fields and water sources. On the open range rangers would have to be present to keep other herds away from grazing and water resources. The reduced time spent protecting cattle was devoted towards husbandry. Thus most development of cattle breeds takes place with fenced in cattle, not cattle on the open range.*

Odd Numbered Problem Answers

1. *The problem with selling it back is the original owner knows the good is stolen. When the economic property rights are separated from the legal rights, trade is very difficult. In the case of children, the next best offer will be extremely low, probably zero. So there is an incentive to sell them back to the original parents.*

3. *If everyone were to obey it, it would lower transaction costs. The problem is one wolf in the fold can destroy a lot of sheep. So unless we can identify and trust people to follow this strategy, it is a high cost rule.*

5. *Bringing buyers and sellers together is valuable. This value could be greater than the good being traded. In Figure 15-5, the artist on his own has a cost of* $p_2 - p_1$ *per unit to bring customers together. At this high cost, only* q' *units of art are sold. The dealer's costs might be* $p_4 - p_3$*, at which trade increases to* q''*.*

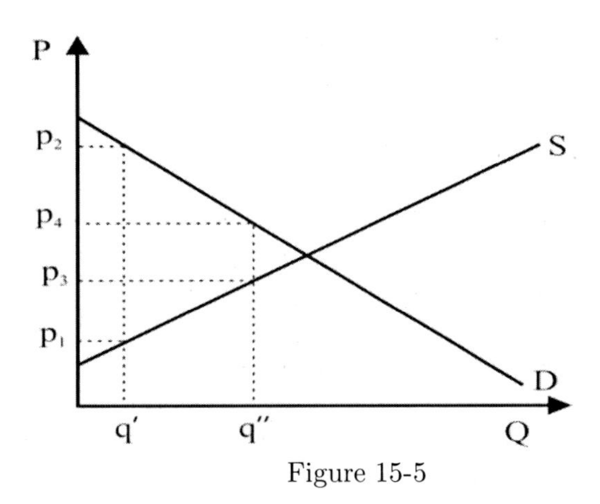

Figure 15-5

7. *The bison were controlled as common property by the Indians for their valuable robes. This meant killing them in the fall. The early hunters also exploited them for their robes. Later, the bison became valued for their leather hides and were killed in the summer while they were in large herds. Because cattle also provided leather, there was no price change as the bison were falling in number, and no great incentive to privatize them. The bison hunt soon became open access. Bison were also hindered by the fact no one in the 19th century really knew how to raise bison in captivity, and attempts to raise them as cattle were huge failures. Thus the lack of knowledge and incentive lead to no ownership over bison and over exploitation. With cattle the opposite was true. They were domesticated, valuable, and privately owned. As a result they were not exploited the extinction.*

9. *The standard economic response would be to send money. The people in trouble know better what they need than we do, so we should provide cash. We don't send cash, however, because it is too easy to steal, and often doesn't get to the people who need it. Therefore, aid is almost always in the form of goods.*

11. *It exploits maximization. The problem is too much time is spent in measurement. This isn't such a big deal with dessert, but it becomes a big problem with other valuable goods. As a result, this method is not used for expensive goods.*

13. *The big cost is in verifying the quality, that is, in measuring the money. Diamonds are very hard to measure, and therefore have always made a poor currency. Gold is relatively easy to measure and difficult to fake.*

15. *The Coase theorem couldn't work because it was not clear who had the property right to the view. Once the first case was settled, the other cases negotiated.*

17. *The problem with the analogy is that customers are not fish. They only buy when it makes them better off. Too much retailing would be punished by consumers and so it doesn't happen.*

19. *This is the same answer as in number 18. They lower the value of the furniture to prevent theft.*

21.

    a. *Using sand and brass to increase the volume of material in liu of gold is a form of cheating on the part of miners. No doubt they would claim less sand was in the mixture than was actually there. The brass would never be claimed, and it was used to hide in the gold. This problem is cheaply eliminated by the use of proper assay equipment, but in the early days of the Klondike rush, it was not available. The slippery methods of measurement on the part of the merchants is another transaction cost problem.*

    b. *A medium of exchange must be easy to measure, because the commodity must be measured for each exchange. Basically gold was used as a medium of exchange because it was the lowest cost commodity to measure. Still, it was not perfect, and fiat money replaced it. The problem with fiat money is counterfeiting ... another transaction cost problem.*

    c. *Both sides know the other side is going to try to cheat. Both sides take efforts to police this behavior. This raises the cost of the exchange and lowers the amounts traded. Hence, both sides would be better off if there was no transaction cost problem.*

23. *The more valuable an asset, the more likely efforts will be made to establish ownership over the asset. Oil is more valuable than the fish.*

25.

    a. *The offer is worth £50, which means everyone is willing to wait 5 hours. Therefore, 200 people line up 5 hours before the bank opens.*

    b. *Now being the first person in line is worth £10,000. Therefore one person will wait in line 1000 hours before the bank opens.*

    c. *Absolutely.*

27. *Even though there are different forms of keeping track of land ownership, they all work relatively the same in terms of costs. The costs of registering land is a transaction cost. If the different methods have similar and low transaction costs then the Coase Theorem states that the general land usage should be the same. If land is best used as a gravel pit, then this will be the use regardless of the method used to register title.*

29. *Krista, like all women, has to solve a hidden information problem: what type of person is Tom? Women make large investments in long term relationships because they have to bear the major costs of children. They want to know that the husband is a "good guy" and will be honest with them. Of course, men know this is what women are looking for, and so while dating they pretend to be better than they actually are. By placing Tom behind the wheel of her car Krista can watch how he treats it, especially when something unexpected happens like there is ice on the road or another driver cuts him off. She doesn't let other males drive because she is not planning on making a specific investment in them.*

CHAPTER 16

THE ECONOMICS OF ORGANIZATION: FIRMS

16.1 The False Dichotomy of Firms and Markets

In 1937 Ronald Coase published a paper that was, in today's language, his undergraduate senior's thesis. In that paper he made the following observation: if prices work for free, why do we see so much allocation in life not using prices? In particular he focused in on firms. Within a firm prices are not always used. Many times allocation is by direction; that is, the boss tells the workers what to do, and his boss tells him what to do, and the stockholders tell that boss what to do. Coase's answer to the question was that the assumption of free prices was wrong; markets don't work for free — they have transaction costs. He also noted that firms don't work for free either; there are transaction costs within firms. This was a brilliant insight.

Unfortunately the notion that allocation is either done through firms or markets is really a false dichotomy. Most of us think we know a firm when we see one; likewise for markets. But even when looking closely it is often hard to tell where the firm begins and the market ends. Take, for example, your local horse racetrack. The track is a firm. There are owners of the track and they hire people to sell tickets, meals, and clean the barns. Horse owners use the track and they rent barns and pay for feed often supplied by the track or sub-contractors who bring the feed in. The track hires some people to inspect the horses and make sure the correct horses are running, and aren't drugged or injured. The track also uses a system of claiming races whereby any member of the racing community can buy any horse running in a race for a prespecified price. The track runs claiming races in order to monitor honesty in horses. Horses sell all the time at the races, and when a certain number of sales are expected in a race, and none are sold, the track becomes suspicious that something dishonest has happened and they investigate. The potential buyers of horses who snoop around the barns inspecting horses end up providing a great service to the track in helping it police honesty and therefore promote betting.

Of all these people, which ones are part of the firm and which ones are part of the market? Some seem pretty obvious. The owners of the track, the wage workers like the ticket seller and the janitor, they are all part of the firm. The person delivering feed, who is paid by the load, probably isn't part of the firm. But what about the people who snoop around the horse barns? The track can manipulate their behavior by changing the purses and claiming prices. They provide a service to the firm like the workers in the kitchen, and they are residual claimants just like the owners of the track. Are these people part of the firm or part of the market? It really is impossible to say.

It is better, again, to think of organization along a spectrum, as shown in figure 16-1. At the right end of the spectrum prices work almost freely and the transaction costs are minimal. Perhaps this is because the nature of the good simply allows for trivial monitoring. Many of these types of exchanges are simple on the spot transactions. We conduct these types of exchanges everyday, hardly giving them a second thought. For example, buying a chocolate bar, renting a video, and taking the bus are simple pure exchanges. At the other end of the spectrum we have pure direction. Here we would observe situations that everyone would agree are production within firms. When Starbucks hires a person to make coffee, the owner of the outlet tells the person when to show up for work, how much whipped cream to put on the moccas, and all the other little tasks involved.

In between these two extremes there are a host of examples that are sort of firms, sort of market transactions. For example, a short term contract between me and Safeway when I rent one of their rug cleaners, is pretty close to a pure exchange. Yet, the contract we sign prohibits me from using the machine in various ways, and protects my rugs to some extent if any damage is done. There is a certain amount of non-price allocation of the surplus in this exchange through the conditions and warranty of the contract. A long term contract between a coal mine and a steel mill, will have many more restrictions. A franchise contract even more. At some point we recognize a "firm" happens, but we also need to acknowledge that a simple choice between firms and markets doesn't exist.

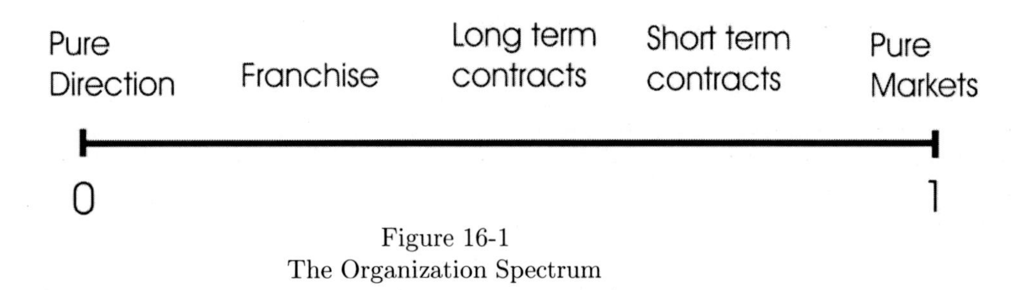

Figure 16-1
The Organization Spectrum

In this chapter we're going to start with the left hand side of the spectrum. We'll talk about the advantages of a firm, and its costs. Then we'll slowly start moving across the spectrum, each time in the context of a specific example. In the next chapter we'll take up exchanges that are more closely related to market exchanges.

> *There is a spectrum of control in all exchanges, ranging from pure direction to pure market exchanges.*

16.2 The Nature of the Firm

In the earlier chapters on production, we assumed production takes place within firms. At the time, nothing much was said about the character or nature of the firm because we were only concerned with the volume of output produced. But as we consider more realistically the act of production, we realize that production takes place in buildings and factories, that these physical places have managers and different types of workers, and that people within these places of employment are paid in many different ways.

In principle, production could be organized anywhere along the spectrum in figure 16-1. Consider what production would be like if organized through markets; one owner of a resource meets with the owner of some other resource, the resources would be exchanged at a certain price, and some output is produced. For example, a landowner might contract with a laborer to rent his land and grow some crops. When production is organized through a firm, one owner of a resource combines other resources through direction, not prices, and produces some output. For example, a wheat farmer might buy his own land, apply his own labor in combination with some hired labor, purchased seeds, and the like, and produce a crop. As another example, if someone wanted to use the market to produce cars they could contract independently for labor, rent equipment, hire consultants to instruct individuals as to how to run the machines and coordinate activities, and the like. This doesn't usually happen. Instead, workers, managers, and capitalists come together in some sort of institutional structure with rights and duties either specifically assigned or informally agreed to. Within a firm, there is a great deal of direction, and people are told what to do, when to arrive and leave work, and their actions are monitored.

How do people decide whether to produce things using a market, a firm, or some type of hybrid? The answer comes from the last chapter. The distribution of property rights leading to the maximum gains from trade, net of transaction costs, will be chosen. A firm is nothing more than a distribution of property rights. Within a firm certain people have rights to control the way the firms assets are used, everyone has rights to certain parts of the revenues of the firm, and the ownership of the assets are defined in a specific way. What makes firms different is the different ways these rights exist. When using a market to produce goods there are certain benefits and certain costs. When using firms to produce goods there are different benefits and costs. The one system that provides the largest net difference is the one that is chosen.

Firms exist for one general reason: they avoid transaction costs that might arise in terms of market production. As we saw in the chapters on production, output is increased when resources are brought together. When large numbers of workers are brought together, they are able to specialize in certain ways that allows output to expand tremendously. However, when large numbers of people come together, they might not work very hard. They might steal other inputs, sleep on the job, or run away with the output. A firm is designed to minimize these transaction costs. When it succeeds production takes place in a firm, when it fails production takes place in a market. Many times organization within the firm involves "bosses" and "direction." Workers put up with this because in solving the transaction cost problem, the net gains from trade are higher and therefore the wages of the workers are higher as well. Shirking, and other forms of individual maximizing behavior not in the interests of the firm, lowers the wages to all workers. A firm is a team, and like a sports team, when someone is not pulling their weight, the whole team suffers. Although every worker might engage in some type of shirking, that worker would wish no one else was engaged in that type of behavior. A firm that fails to get its workers to act in the interests of the owners, is a firm that will ultimately fail. Those firms successful in finding solutions to the cheating problems among workers, are the firms that will survive.

Firms are designed to make the incentives of the workers compatible with those of the owners.

16.3 The Nature of the Farm

Farms are nice firms to study in order to get a handle on incentives and transaction costs. Because they are small firms, the incentives are fairly easy to understand. Also, most of us have some type of connection with a farm somewhere, and well ... wheat is just so darn interesting. Let's consider the history of wheat farming in North America.

Have you ever noticed that farms are organized around the family. Two hundred years ago, if you looked around at the firms in any town, they would have been organized around families as well. That is, the bakery, blacksmith shop, general store, etc. were small firms owned by a husband, and run with the assistance of the wife and children. Now, about the only industry where family production really amounts to anything is in farming. All other industries have long switched over to corporate forms of organization. Why would this be?

Part of the answer is in the gains from specialization. As technology has changed, workers in virtually all industries have been able to specialize more and more into well defined tasks. These specialized tasks not only allow for great leaps in levels of output, but they often are easily monitored. Hence, large firms can hire masses of workers, and pay them simple wages knowing they cannot cheat the firm easily. When it is easy to monitor workers, cheating is hard and seldom takes place. Consider an assembly line for automotive workers. Assembly lines are extremely specialized. Every one has a specific job to do, and everyone knows whose job it is to do what. If one person decides to take it easy and not keep up with the line, or does a job poorly due to lack of attention, this causes problems on the line that are easily attributed to the poor worker. On most assembly lines, when a worker performs a duty improperly, such that the line must be shut down, that worker is sent home without pay. If it happens a second time, then the worker is usually fired. In terms of the definition of transaction costs, on an assembly line Nature plays a very minor role, and as a result, the transaction costs of a firm are small.

Consider now a farm. On a farm the role of Nature is huge. The actions of any one farmer influence output, but the weather plays a large role as well. Better soil, better timing of rains and sun, and a lack of storms during harvest, mean a much higher crop. When Nature plays such a large role, it is almost impossible to hire a "farmer." I'm not talking about hiring a worker to clean a barn, I'm talking about hiring a worker to plant, cultivate, and harvest the crop. Such a worker could shirk until the cows came home and he'd be unlikely to get caught ... he'd just blame the weather for the bad outcome.

The history of farming and the rise and fall of family farms can be explained by this role of nature and the effect it has on transaction costs in conjuction with the role of specialization. When the gains from specializing increase, family production is less likely. When the role of nature increased, family production was more likely. Let's look at three cases of this evolution: the shrinking of tasks done by the family farm; the rise and fall of the great Bonanza farms; and the industrialization of livestock farming.

The Shrinking Family Farm

Until the middle of the nineteenth century, the family farm did virtually everything. They made the farm by clearing land and raising buildings, they processed cheese and milk and made sausage, and they did just about everything in between. The one thing the family never did was grind the grain. This was done at a local gristmill. Gristmills were the first of many firms that specialized in what would otherwise be a single stage of the farm production process, and ultimately evolved into large firms that developed factory production techniques. Because grains are easily stored and a mill can be operated continuously, milling grain for flour is almost completely removed from seasonal forces of nature, and the gains from specialization are high. These factors reduce the value of family production and favor large-scale, factory production. Thus the gristmill was the first stage of production in farming that was not done by the family.

But it was not the last. After the early 1800s dramatic changes in technology led to the rise of separate firms that specialized in single stages of production and operating all year round. New technologies such as refrigeration and railroads limited Nature and allowed seasonal tasks to be performed throughout the year. Overwhelmingly, the new firms engaged in production at either the beginning (equipment, fertilizer, and seed) or the end (marketing, processing, transportation, and storage) of the agricultural production sequence. In the late nineteenth century these firms included flour mills, cheese factories, creameries, early equipment manufacturers (plows, reapers), grain brokers, meat packers, slaughterhouses, livestock breeders, canneries, and other food processors. This process has continued throughout the twentieth century as advances in biological and chemical technology and new product developments in artificial insemination, feeds, fertilizers, pesticides, and seeds that result in gains from specialization and reduced seasonality for certain stages of production. Accordingly, the family farm has abandoned these stages and now controls only the purely biological growth stages of farm production. The biological stage of production is the one where nature still plays a large role. In this stage monitoring is costly, and thus the family is the efficient form of firm.

The Great Bonanza Experiment

In the last quarter of the 19th century, an experiment in farm organization took place on the virgin prairie of the Red River Valley dividing Minnesota and North Dakota. Between 1870 and 1890 a number of extremely large wheat farms were established, some exceeding 50,000 acres (roughly 78 square miles). Even by modern standards these farms were enormous, but their main distinguishing feature was not their size, but rather their factory-corporate organization. The owners were typically businessmen with little or no farm experience. These owners raised capital in eastern markets and organized these farms along the lines of contemporary manufacturing firms typically as corporations with professional managers and a specialized wage labor force. The"bonanza farms,"as they came to be known, were hailed as the future of agriculture. Yet after only one generation, nearly all the bonanza farms were gone, systematically replaced by family farmers.

Most bonanza farms focused exclusively on wheat production and kept virtually the entire production sequence within the firm: from sod-busting, seed development, machine repair, and hardware supply to blacksmithing, seed cleaning, grain storage, and flour milling. The farms were also highly mechanized and used the latest large-scale equipment. Labor was organized in a complex hierarchical system common to industrial manufacturing. Managers were paid a combination of a salary and a commission that depended on farm profits. The farms were broken into 5,000-acre divisions headed by superintendents and 1,200-acre stations headed by foremen. Most of the manual labor force worked out of the stations and were hired in monthly increments and paid a daily wage. Accountants, blacksmiths, mechanics, and hands involved in grain cleaning and storage worked at the farms headquarters. The labor force varied greatly in size over the seasons, with harvest crews typically twice the size of seeding crews.

The bonanzas combination of modern technology, specialized labor, and professional management practices seemed unstoppable. Yet Bonanzas began to disappear as early as 1890, and by 1910 they were virtually extinct. Why? Because the costs of monitoring such large labor forces in an industry where Nature played a large role was simply too costly. These large firms had managers, superintendents, and foremen to monitor workers. All of these men were paid, and these salaries raised costs. Grain from every field was weighed and recorded so that responsibility could be assigned to foremen and superintendents. Labor was performed in crews one task at a time (such as plowing or seeding) to make supervision easier for the foremen; and rigid rules governed the daily routines of the field hands at work and in the bunkhouse. All of this raised costs, ... but more importantly there were no large gains in output. Thus 10 small family farmers could jointly produce as much as a Bonanza farm 10 times as big, but they could do it at much lower costs. Hence, the large farms were broken up and replaced by hundreds of small family farmers.

The Industrial Chicken

Nowhere in farming have firms moved more from family firms to factory-farms than in livestock. This has been especially true for chickens, feedlot cattle, and hogs. The general trend has been to remove stock from an open environment and rear them in climate-controlled barns. This has happened because once animals are moved indoors, the role of Nature is reduced, and monitoring wage employees becomes feasible as firms take advantage of specialization gains.

The chicken industry has its roots in small farms. In fact, the industrialization of chicken production preceded that in cattle feedlots. Prior to the 1930s, most chickens were raised in relatively small flocks on family farms. During this period eggs, not meat, were the primary products and most chickens were slaughtered in the spring. The reorganization of the poultry industry began in the 1930s, and today virtually all broilers (2 to 3 pound chickens) are produced by large, factory-corporate firms. The introduction of antibiotics and other drugs have allowed poultry to be bred, hatched, and grown in highly controlled indoor environments in which disease, climate, food, water, vitamins and other inputs are regulated to the point where poultry barns are virtual assembly lines. At the various stages of production, broiler companies employ wage laborers who undertake specialized but routine tasks such as cleaning, feeding, and immunizing.

A striking example of factory-corporate livestock production is in feedlot cattle. In the first half of this century "farmer-feeders," located primarily in the Corn Belt in the US, supplied the overwhelming majority of finished cattle to slaughterhouses. These farmers typically had less than 1,000 head of cattle that were purchased in late summer or fall and fattened during the late fall and winter (an off season for grain farming). During the last 40 years, the fed cattle industry has been almost completely transformed into one dominated by large corporate firms that employ highly specialized wage labor. In the last two decades, the hog industry has followed the path of the broiler industry. Hog production is increasingly dominated by large, factory-corporate firms that breed and farrow (birthing) pigs in confinement in huge indoor facilities.

The contrast between industrial livestock and grain farming could hardly be more dramatic. This difference results from the elimination of Nature and the reduction of random forces in the production of animals. The driving force in modern livestock production is to reduce the role of nature by bringing production indoors to control climate and disease. As result the livestock industry is perhaps the most specialized of any farm commodity, and the most dominated by companies organized in the corporate-factory form.

16.4 The Success of the British Navy

What could be more different from the family farm in Nebraska or Saskatchewan than the British Navy during the age of fighting sail? The British Navy was the largest firm in England in the 18th century, and also the most successful navy. The King of England, however, had the same basic problem that the owner of any firm has: how to get the most out of his workers? The navy is an interesting example because the transaction cost problem in monitoring a captain or admiral was so severe. The British were successful because they were able to keep the incentives of the officers in line with the incentives of the King.

All navies during the age of fighting sail (approximately 1580 – 1827) faced a serious transaction cost problem. Ships of war were expensive, powerful, and critical for the protection of overseas trade. Yet they were put in the hands of a captain who was sent out with the most general orders: to blockade a port, patrol for pirates and privateers, escort merchant vessels, and in times of war, engage the enemy. The captain had a large informational advantage over the Admiralty in terms of local conditions; in fact, it is hard to imagine a more severe case of asymmetric information. During the age of sail, communication was intermittent, slow, and limited; the world was still generally unexplored, with shoals, waterways, and trade winds not mapped; and even methods for finding positions of longitude were only developed towards the end of the Eighteenth century. Worse, given that ships were propelled by wind, disasters, losses in battle, and other failures of duty could be blamed on the ill fortunes of nature. Added to the severe information asymmetry was the temptation of a captain or admiral to seek out private wealth and safety rather than engage in more dangerous and less profitable assignments. For example, a captain always had the incentive to seek weak, but wealthy, merchant prizes rather than enemy frigates. They also preferred avoiding monotonous and dangerous blockades for profitable raids on shore. Hence, as in the case of farming, we have a situation where Nature played a huge role, and the incentives of the workers were not in line with the owners of the firm. Unlike farming, though, a family cannot run a battleship, and so a family firm was not the solution.

Although the British Navy dominated the open seas for most of the age of fighting sail, the obvious explanations are refuted: their ships were not better; their tactics were 'flawed' according to the experts of the time; and the raw material of their sailors and officers had no distinct advantage over the navies of Spain, France, or Holland. It turns out the British Navy was an effective fighting force because of the set of rules under which the British fought. The British Admiralty created a set of clever monitoring devices that were only slowly copied by their opponents, and which worked even for single ships thousands of miles from home.

Before looking at a couple of these devices, one must understand that the central compensation scheme in the British Navy was a wage system which revolved around the taking of prizes or spoils of war. Unlike on land, where prizes are located in specific places, enemy prize vessels float about. Thus the use of prizes in the navy was a two-edged sword — it motivated captains to be active at sea, but encouraged them, at the margin, to hunt for lucrative prizes instead of pursuing more strategic objectives.

In order for this system to work, some form of monitoring was necessary. Thus, in conjuction with the system of prizes the British Navy used several clever rules to monitor their captains, and which encouraged British captains to fight rather than run. The creation of an incentive to fight led to an incentive to train seamen in the skills of battle. Hence, when a captain or admiral is commanding a ship that is likely to engage in fighting, then that commander has an incentive to drill his crew and devote his mental energies to winning.

So what were these rules? There were lots, so let's just consider a couple. First there was the Weather Gage, which meant to fight windward of the enemy ship — a tactic that was considered inferior by the military intelligentsia of the time. Through out the 18th century French strategists discussed the general benefits of fighting *leeward* of the wind (without the weather gage). When fighting leeward the ship is tilted by the wind away from the enemy and all of the ships gun ports are above the water line. In heavy seas a ship with the windward position might not be able to open its lower gun decks and as a result its fire power was drastically reduced. This is shown in the sad drawing of figure 16-2.

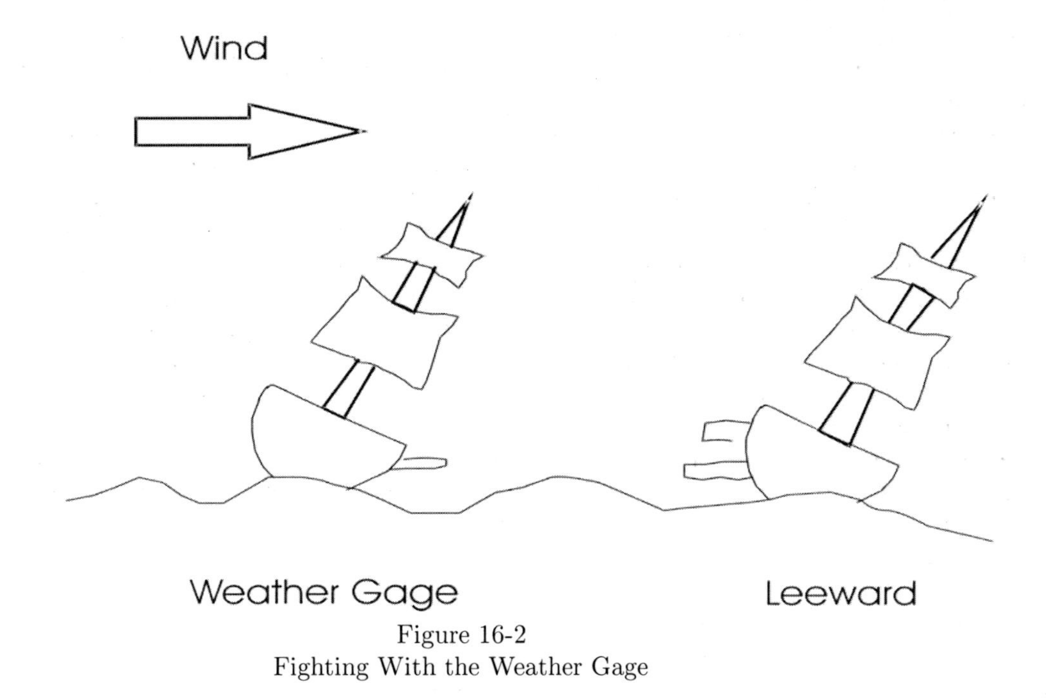

Figure 16-2
Fighting With the Weather Gage

A more important advantage of the leeward position was that if the battle was going poorly, the fleet had the opportunity of simply sailing downwind to escape. Likewise, if an individual vessel became severely damaged it stood a chance of escaping behind its own line. The French proclivity for shooting the masts and rigging of the enemy ships, as opposed to the hull, increased the opportunity of escape and increased their preference for the leeward position. Given the advantages of not having the weather gage, why were the British so insistent upon having it? The answer lies in that it both increased the incentive to fight, and prevented captains from drifting away from battle.

A square rigged ship from the age of fighting sail, was difficult to maneuver, and could could not sail well into the wind at all. Not only could it not sail into the wind at any great angle, but the ship would often drift backwards as well, often making no progress at all. Hence, when attacking from the weather gage a square rigged ship had little choice but to drift upon the enemy. It would have been very difficult for a captain of a British ship in the fleet to casually or inadvertently not engage the enemy once the fleet had formed a line with the weather gage. Whereas this was not generally true with the leeward position. The incentive mechanism of the weather gage is that once engagement is certain, it was in the interests of the British ship to fight most effectively. Just as the weather gage ensured engagement, failure to fight well meant that the ship would eventually drift into the enemy fleet where it would certainly be captured. Thus the weather gage was an easily monitored action that encouraged engagement and effective fighting.

A second rule the British fought under was that an English ship *must* attack an enemy ship of the same class. If the captain failed to do so, the punishment was death! This led to some interesting situations. For example, there was the fateful meeting between the British *Guerriére* and the USS *Constitution* on August 19th 1812. The *Guerriére* was small frigate, totally outclassed by the larger American frigate. The *Guerriére* had only 38 18-pound guns to the *Constitution's* 44 24-pounders, and only 244 men to the *Constitution's* 460. Furthermore, the *Guerriére* was in desperate need of refitting. It was leaking and had recently been hit by lightning. The *Constitution* on the other hand, was recently out of home port. If ever there was an unfair fight, this was it. Still Captain Dacres of the *Guerriére* engaged rather than flee, with the inevitable result of defeat. Dacres managed to live, and though he was no hero for surviving, he was given another ship to command. Just to see how different this rule was, consider the French rule for engagement. For the French, if an enemy ship was spotted, and the captain didn't have overwhelming superiority of force, he was to flee upon the penalty of death.

So the British had a number of rules that essentially forced their captains to fight. But how did the British navy know what the captain was up to? After all the captain was just floating around in the big ocean somewhere. Here's where the British crown was even more clever ... they had spies, and the spies were the lieutenant and the master. The actual system was quite complicated, but essentially the job of the lieutenant was to watch the captain and report on his every move. The job of the master was to watch both of the others, and report on their actions. The lieutenant had an incentive to catch the captain in an error because promotion to captain depended, in part, on a vacancy in the captain's list. The master was essentially an independent observer who could not be removed by the captain, and was there to keep the system honest.

Once again we see that a firm is designed to make the incentives of the worker compatible with those of the owner of the firm. With the navy, the use of the prize system to pay captains created an incompatible incentive. Thus the navy was structured in such a way as to restrict the captain from going after the wrong prizes. The system worked. In the next section, we'll look at the British Army and see how a few differences in logistics made a big difference in the way the Army was organized versus the Navy.

16.5 The Purchase System in the British Army

As mentioned way back in the opening chapter of this book, 1st Duke of Wellington, Arthur Wellesley, purchased his first commission as ensign in 1787, and by 1794, after purchasing seven further commissions and having seen no military action nor having received any military training, had reached the rank of colonel and was in charge of his own regiment. Were it not for his subsequent victories, such a process of purchase over merit and formal training might seem folly both on the part of Wellington and the British Army. Yet Wellington was hardly alone since the purchase system, crudely founded in Medieval times and continued until 1871 in Britain, was the central means by which the European armies staffed their officer corps.

Most historians appear to have a dim view of the purchase system, and it is common in the historical record to find the purchase system blamed for the excesses, foibles and disasters of military history, and seldom given any credit for victories. Yet this conclusion must be premature and result from a myopic view of the role purchase played, given that it was an integral part of successful armies for great lengths of time.

On the surface, the thought that anyone would *pay* to be a soldier seems illogical. After all, it seems illogical for someone with no formal training in war, to actually pay to lead a company. Furthermore, added to the illogic of the general scheme were the large sums paid for an army commission when by all accounts the official wages were so low. For example, in 1832, Lord Brudenell bought a Lieutenant Colonelcy for between £35,000 and £40,000. Higher ranked officers also incurred other expenses in addition to the purchase of their commissions. Although the Crown subsidized them, Colonels were required to pay for all regiment expenses. These included the costs of recruitment, uniforms, wages, equipment, and any welfare paid to the wounded or widows. Yet, among the commissioned soldiers there was no serious and persistent grumbling or revolts about the low pay, nor was there any increase in pay over the last 200 years of the system. All of which points to the fact that there is more to the system of purchase than the simple selling of offices. If the purchase of commissions was part of some *rational* scheme designed to best staff the army, then there was clearly more to the method of compensation than straight wages.

A Little Background

The practice of purchasing a position in an army dates back to the 13th century, peaks in the 17th and 18th centuries, and dies out in the 19th century. Throughout this time the purchase system evolved, and thus the purchase of command in 1200 was considerably different from purchase in 1870. Although the purchase system was used by all European powers, the focus here is on the British Army.

The purchase system has its beginnings when Henry II (1133–1189) relieved the landed class of a medieval tradition introduced by William the Conqueror which required landowners to supply the King with knights for 40 days of the year. Instead, Henry II began a form of taxation with which he hired mercenary companies. The modern commercial connotation of the word "company", in part, reflects the commercial nature of these armies. In addition to pay, the companies received a fraction of the plunder of war, including any ransom from captured prisoners and contributions for protected property. Shares in these companies were determined by the capital investment of its members and were tradable. The purchase of shares by active soldiers was the institutional forerunner of the formal purchase of commissions, which fully developed in the 17th century.

Initially these corporations were composed mostly of foreigners. Eventually, they became dominated by nationals, and by the time of the Tudors the Crown was granting commissions only to landed subjects who then raised a company in service to only the British King. Until the late 1600s, the British never had a standing army. In time of war the King would raise an army in the fashion just mentioned, and it would be disbanded in peacetime. After the Restoration in 1680 and the Glorious Revolution in 1687, there was great debate over the necessity of a standing army. However, perpetual problems with France and colonial struggles resulted in a de facto standing army. The practice of purchasing commissions, begun by Henry II, carried through to the standing army.

The institution of purchased commissions meant that the Crown and Parliament did not have total control over the staffing decisions of the army because each commission was owned in large part by the buyer who had the right to resell it. This led to several conflicts, and attempts by the government to regulate resale. For example, the government established various prices for the different ranks. In practice a black market arose and the traded prices varied considerably, often being much higher (and lower) than the stipulated prices. This was despite the fact that selling above the regulated price (cashiering) was against the law. Furthermore, over time rules were imposed on minimum ages, minimum times between ranks, and conditions for transfer.

Why Were Commissions Purchased?

We can think of the Army as a firm, but not a firm at the far right of the spectrum in figure 16-1. Rather it was a firm somewhere in the middle. Kings at the time could not monitor their soldiers very well, and so the prize system they developed created an incentive for soldiers to fight without being monitored. Thus the military constraints faced in Europe from 1400 to 1800 were best matched with the set of incentives created by the purchase system, in order to minimize the cost of raising an army. In general two major incentive problems existed: how to recruit high quality officers; and how to provide incentives to actually fight in battle in a way that increased the net gain from war.

The first problem in raising an army is to find highly qualified soldiers and officers. An army that experiences no disincentives among its soldiers, but whose soldiers are totally inept at fighting is a losing army just the same. Prior to the 19th century, it was generally thought that a great soldier was born, not made. This implicitly reflected the fact that the inputs for a good soldier were unobservable. What makes a great military leader? One who can motivate troops, ensure they are fed, take some risks but not others, make the right decision in the heat of battle. The question is fundamentally unanswerable, and is similar to "what makes a great entrepreneur?". Furthermore, direct supervision of inputs in battle was also difficult because officers essentially made their decisions in isolated situations where communication was difficult. Furthermore, nature played an extremely large role and soldier efforts were mostly matched against opponents in hand-to-hand combat. In addition, easily observable signals that may have been correlated with ability did not exist. There were no military schools, nor were there obvious skills that could be measured.

Under these conditions military officers can best be paid in terms of output as residual claimants. In this way the purchase of commissions acts in the same manner as the purchase of any business, with soldier entrepreneurs self-selecting what type of fighting they were best suited for. Those who were correct in their personal assessments were rewarded by large residuals and continued to purchase higher positions which in turn led to larger shares of prizes. Those who were incorrect were likely to exit the industry ... permanently and horizontally. The key to the success of such a market structure to the officer corps would be the process of self-selection. Only those who truly thought they could command successfully would advance in ranks.

Throughout the time of purchased commissions, successful regiments were paid in part through the spoils of war. This in effect made the soldiers residual claimants. A key feature of the purchase system is the actual payment for the commission, because it established a property right over the expected residuals from battle. Were the spoils in the public domain, too many individuals would enter the army and the average quality of soldier would have fallen. By introducing a pricing mechanism, only those officers that anticipated a future stream of earnings higher than the marginal soldier entered service.

Having high quality soldiers, however, is only half the battle. Soldiers require the proper incentives to perform. These include not only the incentives to fight, but also to fight in the interests of the entire army. Due to the extreme situations and opportunities for being killed, incentive problems abound in armies at war. The private desire to preserve one's life, regardless of the effect this might have on the overall mission, is a problem of first order that armies must overcome. Transaction cost problems are no doubt extremely high in army regiments where one's life is on the line.

The key aspect of the purchase system — namely that officers were ultimately rewarded through residual claims — is also an important mechanism for establishing incentives to fight. Soldiers received minimal levels of pay for supplies, but their incomes could only grow through actual battle. Residuals mostly arose from the spoils of battle, and rewards from the crown for victory. In paying officers this way, the Crown encourages soldiers to engage the enemy. The common theme in the historical record is that the hope of treasure was a major motivator of the officer corps.

The purchase system was not perfect. The payment to soldiers with prize money was useful in attracting quality soldiers, but could still have hindered the army if the private incentives it provided jeopardized the object of the mission. Premature or excessive looting that prevented the army from victory, should be discouraged. If looting or extortion in themselves begin to affect the overall agenda of the army, then the purchase system should not survive. "Too much" fighting as well may hinder success if regiments have strategic value in containing or defending an enemy rather than attacking.

The purchase system was obviously part of the incentive structure of the individual soldier. Its Achilles heel was that under some circumstances, the incentives of the individual soldiers did not match those of the army. When the incentives reasonably matched those of the Crown, all was well, but when they did not, the system failed.

To reiterate then, the system of purchasing a military commission was used to self-select officers into the military given the general difficulty in observing military talent and the lack of alternative screens or signals of quality. Secondly, the purchase system, by paying with prize money, provided an incentive to engage the enemy in battle. With this form of payment there is a tendency for "too much fighting". This acted as a cost of the system, and in order for it to function properly, the incentives to fight of the individual soldier and commander must match those of the Crown.

Why were commissions sold in the Army but not in the Navy? In the Army the purchase of commissions generally created a compatible incentive with the King, and so the King did not have to have the complicated rules for fighting and promotion that were found in the Navy. In the Navy, the prize system created the incentive for captains to seek after the wrong prizes, and this led to rules over promotion that helped to police this. Thus, commissions in the Navy could not be purchased. The British Army and Navy provide a nice example of movements along the figure 16-1 spectrum. The Navy was more of a "firm" than the Army because it involved more direction, and less use of the price mechanism. The Army more closely resembled a market transaction because the transaction costs involved in the prize system were less severe. They were less severe because prizes on land do not float about like prizes on water!

16.6 Franchising and the Big Mac

Perhaps you don't know much about farming, the British Navy in the 18th century, or the military purchase system, but one firm you're bound to be familiar with is McDonalds. It all started with a man named Ray Kroc who was a peddler of milkshake machines in the early 1950s. He met up with brothers Mac and Dick McDonald who had opened the "Speedee Shakes and Burgers" drive-in in 1953 in St Bernadino, California. They were persuaded to sell the name to "McDonalds" to the milkshake salesman, Kroc, who opened the first store of the McDonald's Corporation in 1955 in Des Plaines, Illinois. The rest is history. McDonald's now has over 20,000 stores in 90 countries, serves 29 million people a day, and opens a new store opens every seven hours. The real genius of Ray Kroc was to figure out how get an employee to sell a decent 5¢ hamburger, and he did this with the use of a franchise contract.

What would be the transaction cost problem of selling an idea? Suppose I come to you and say "Hey, if you give me $30,000 I'll tell you the secret to making a great 5¢ hamburger ... you'll be rich!" Maybe you're dumb enough to give me the money. If you do, you can bet I'll tell you something, but it sure won't be how to make a great 5¢ burger. Maybe you're smart enough to say "Well, you tell me, and if I think its a good idea I'll pay you the money." If I'm dumb enough to tell you the truth, you sure won't tell me its a great idea. You'll just go off and make your fortune on cheap burgers. Information is a strange good to sell. How can I let you look at my "information product" without letting you have it? Also, just because you have the information, doesn't mean that I still don't have it. How can you trust that I'll sell you the right information? After all, you don't know what I'm selling. This is the problem that Ray Kroc faced. He didn't want to flip burgers himself, he wanted to tell others how to do it, and he wanted to be paid for the knowledge.

The franchise was the key. A franchise essentially makes the local manager of the McDonalds restaurant a part owner. When Ray Kroc sells the idea to a franchisee, the latter can trust Kroc because if the wrong information is given the restaurant won't succeed and Kroc won't make any serious money. Also, since Kroc makes money when the local outlet makes money, he won't sell the idea to someone who will open up right next door. Since the local franchisee has a financial interest in his local outlet, he has an incentive to make sure it is run the way it is supposed to.

The problem with the franchise contract is that the local owner of McDonalds can still try to steal the idea and open up his own restaurant that looks the same but just happens to be called "Dougs" or "Burger King." The solution is for a series of restrictions placed on the contract. The parent company, McDonalds corporation, supplies all of its outlets with the food, napkins, manuals, ... everything. The local owner usually has little more than a list of phone numbers for supplies. By keeping the local owner a little in the dark, the corporation prevents him from stealing the idea.

Another way the local owner could cheat the corporation is to tell them he made no money, and therefore their share is zero. The McDonalds corporation gets around this problem by sharing revenues with the local outlet, not profits. It is easy for the corporation to know how many burgers and fries are being sold. Since they set the prices, they know the revenues. Costs on the other hand, are more difficult to keep track of. Since they are harder to keep track of, the local owner could exaggerate them, and cheat the parent company. By using just revenues, this is prevented.

One last way a local McDonalds owner could cheat the parent company is to free ride on the brand name. In most cases your local McDonalds restaurant is just that: local. If they provide bad food or service you just stop going there. But what about a McDonalds on the interstate or trans-Canada highway. For these locations most of the customers are just passing through. They stop because their kids saw the golden arches three miles away and wanted to eat. The customers go to this new McDonalds because they've experienced other local McDonalds restaurants ... not this one. The McDonalds on the interstate could cut costs and free ride on this reputation. The customers won't go back to McDonalds given the poor food and service, but they weren't coming back to this restaurant anyway ... they're from out of town. How does McDonalds solve this problem? For those restaurants that are located in places where there are few repeat customers, the corporation runs the restaurant directly. They hire a manager who gets paid a wage, and they monitor his performance.

16.7 Summary

This chapter has analyzed, mostly through examples, the organization of firms and quasi firms. Some production takes place within very centralized organizational structures, and these institutions we call firms. Firms can increase output using direction of resources without prices because they allow gains from specialization without incurring the transaction costs that arise using prices in a market. In the chapter we saw how various aspects of farming have moved from within the control of the family to the market, and back again depending on the transaction costs involved. The modern movement to industrial farming is the result of changes in transaction costs allowing large firms to out produce small family farmers. We also contrasted the historic organization of the British army and navy, and showed that the army was less of a firm than the navy was because the prize (price) system provides the proper incentives in the army, but not in the navy. We also argued that the navy had superior incentives than the other navies at the time, and this lead to their huge successes over a long period of time. Finally, we considered the incentive structure of a franchise firm. A franchise is a contract that lies in between a market and a firm.

REVIEW QUESTIONS

1. If there were no transaction costs, would there be firms?
2. If there were no transaction costs, what types of markets would there be?
3. Are family farms disappearing, or are there just fewer farms?
4. Why was their purchase in the army, but not in the navy?
5. Is a farmer a capitalist or a laborer?

PROBLEMS

1. "At Segal Furniture we offer you the lowest prices because we sell direct from the factory and bypass the middleman." Under the assumptions of the neoclassical model with zero transaction costs, what is wrong with the logic of this statement? If there are positive transaction costs, can this statement make sense?

2. Suppose a new device is developed which allows your employer to determine at zero cost who is using the photocopying machine for non-business copying. Would that make the typical employee better or worse off?

3. The use of mercenaries paralleled the use of the purchase system in European armies. That is, when armies were staffed with officers who purchased their commissions, these officers were very likely foreigners. With the introduction of professional soldiers paid on a wage basis came the introduction of armies staffed only with nationals. Why would this be?

4. Emily likes to buy her produce at a local store called "Ralph's Market". The store has a common practice of offering its produce for a lower price if it is pre-bagged by the store. For example, apples might cost 89¢ per pound unbagged, but only 79¢ per pound if bagged. Given that the store must pay someone to bag the apples (ie. the cost is higher) why would the price be lower if bagged?

5. The showers in the men's change rooms at most university gyms have only a single faucet for each shower head. That is, it basically turns on or off, and the showeree can't adjust the pressure or temperature. I've noticed that this is very common in public male showers (I'm assuming ... really ... that it is also true of public female showers), but almost never happens in private homes. Why would this be?

6. As economists we naturally think the best way to induce people to supply goods and services is to offer a sufficient price for them. However, sometimes, like in the provision of blood, the good is asked in the form of a donation.

   a. Why would volunteer blood donation be able to out compete for profit blood clinics?

   b. What are some economic problems that arise with volunteer blood giving?

   c. How are these handled?

   d. Every time you give blood, no matter where, they give you a sweet drink and some cookies afterwards. Never a stick of celery or some food with low sugar levels. Can you guess how this might be related to part (b)?

7. "When one company has made specific investments in the manufacture of another company, then a merger is likely." Under what circumstances will this be true, and when will it be not true? Provide an example of each case?

8. Once upon a time a poor graduate student and his wife had a baby. Of course, this was the most beautiful child ever born, and so of course, the wife says, "we must get a professional picture of her." So the couple and child went to Sears. When they returned to look at the

pictures there were a number of options. For $9.95 they could have a package that consisted of the ugliest poses ever seen. The child's parents can't believe their child could look so bad. "But wait!" says the clerk, who pulls out the largest, and most lovely picture of a baby ever taken in the history of the world, "take a look at this!" "Great, we'll take these", say the proud parents. "Fine" says the clerk, "that'll be $179.95". (Parents fall down). Now Sears has a problem here. Sure the couple are willing to pay $180, but no one else in the whole world is willing to pay $2 for this picture. Sears know that, the couple knows that. Question: what is the problem for Sears, and how do they solve it by having the couple deal with a clerk making $6.50 per hour, and who could care less if the couple buy the picture or not?

Review Question Answers

1. *No.*

2. *There would only be simple "spot" trades. We certainly wouldn't see organized markets, or markets with security or other complexities.*

3. *There are fewer farms as the optimal size increases. Most farms, however, are still organized as family firms.*

4. *The navy had the problem that they never knew the conditions of the wind or the exact location of their ships. Thus, if they sold their commissions, they would only attract captains who planned to go after the enemy merchant vessels. In other words, the incentives of the captain would have been incompatible with the king.*

5. *He's both, which points to the natural ambiguity of using such terms.*

Odd Numbered Problem Answers

1. *With zero transaction costs, this makes no sense. The middleman is providing a service, and presumably he has a comparative advantage in doing it. The Segal company must now be doing it, and they must be doing it at a higher cost. With positive transaction costs this could make sense. For some reason, using a middle man could increase the transaction costs considerably.*

3. *Mercenaries fight because there are big pay outs to winning. When the soldiers are paid by a wage, this incentive is mostly gone. Therefore it needs to be replaced. The solution was to use motives of national pride.*

5. *In a public shower where you are not paying for the water or the heat you use too much. In a private home you don't behave this way. So the option is removed.*

7. *The merger is more likely if it solves a transaction cost problem between the two firms without increasing costs of production.*

CHAPTER 17

THE ECONOMICS OF ORGANIZATION: CONTRACTS AND MARKETS

In the last chapter we analyzed exchanges that took place within the context of what we would generally consider firms. At least they were organizations with considerable hierarchy. In this chapter we start off by looking at situations where agents contract with one another over a specific asset. In such cases individuals are linked together, but not as formally as within firms. The focus will be on the contract for land in farming, but after going over this case in considerable detail, examples in other areas of life will also be dealt with. After this, we will move onto the organization of market transactions. Most market exchanges are not simple on the spot trades, and we want to look at how some more complicated trades are organized.

17.1 Contract Choice in Farm Land Leases

Farming, as mentioned before, is a simple type of production relatively familiar to most of us. Farming a crop like wheat or oats requires human capital embodied in the farmer. A farmer needs to know when and how to plant, cultivate, and harvest. The farmer usually needs to know a number of other skills in order to maintain his equipment, keep accounts, and the like. Farming requires equipment. Sometimes this equipment is general, like a tractor, and can be used for all types of farming. Other times the equipment is very specific, like a cherry picker, and can only be used for one type of farming. Farmers tend to always own their equipment. They do this because of the large role the weather plays on production. Perhaps you've heard the phrase "make hay when the sun shines." For a farmer, when the weather provides a window for a task, he needs to perform it right away. A delayed harvest, for example, can mean the crop might get hailed on, blown over by storms or snow, and generally might lower the total yield. Thus farmers own their own equipment so they can work the fields on their own schedule. The last major input in all farming is land. For some types of farming, like grain, land is a huge input. For other types of farming, like chickens, it plays less of a role in total costs.

Interestingly, across Canada and the United States, about 50% of the land farmed is actually owned by the farmer; the rest is rented. When the land is rented, it is rented in one of two ways: cash rent or cropshare. A cash rent contract is where the farmer pays the landowner some fixed amount of rent in dollars. For example, the farmer might pay $150 per acre for the year to use the land. When a farmer rents the land on a cash rent basis, he keeps all of the crop for himself and sells it on the market. A cropshare contract on the other hand, is where the farmer uses the landowners land, harvests the crop, and then pays the landowner with a share of the output. Normally these shares take on a few values. Shares of 1/2, 1/3, and 2/5 to the landowner are the most common. Thus, a wheat farmer might give the landowner 40% of the crop at the end of the season. The puzzle we want to solve is "what explains the use of the different contracts?"

As we will see, the answer will again come down to the transaction costs of each contract under different circumstances. Sometimes the cash rent contract provides the best incentives, and other times the cropshare contract provides the best incentives. Let's start by noting the level of output from a farm depends on a few things. It certainly depends on the level of effort of the farmer — no effort, no crop. But the quality of soil, the weather, pests, and other random features all play a role in the level of crop. Furthermore, output depends on how well the farmer looks after his soil. When a farmer owns his own land he manages his soil, even when it means a lower crop in the current year. Soil is a resource that contains nutrients like nitrogen, moisture, and the like. When a farmer uses too many of these things, he reduces the ability of the soil to produce crops in the future. A farmer who owns his own land will use the nutrients efficiently and will use them until the cost is equal to the value of the marginal product of the nutrient. Furthermore, a farmer who owns his own land will provide the optimal amount of labor on his farm as well. That is, he will supply labor until the value of his marginal product is equal to the wage he could earn off the farm. A farmer does not maximize the size of the current crop, he maximizes the value of his farm. This is shown in figure 17-1, where the farmer chooses the level effort and soil nutrients optimally. The wage w^* is determined in a labor market off of the farm, while the cost of using nutrients n^* can be thought of as the opportunity cost in terms of lost future crops of using nutrients today.

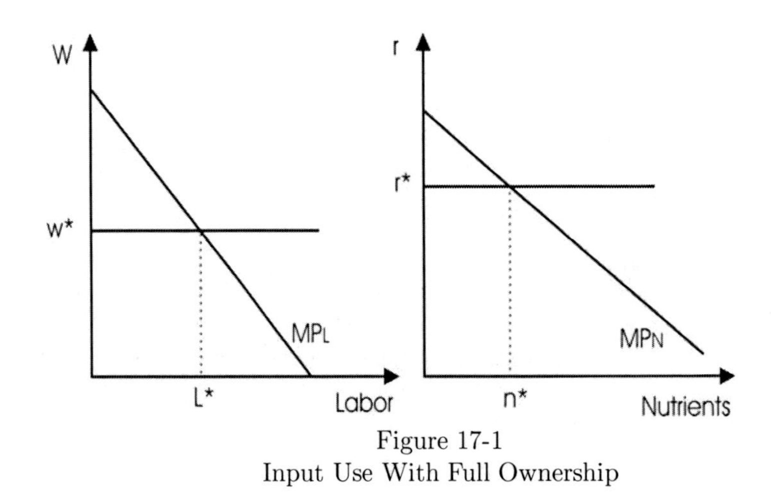

Figure 17-1
Input Use With Full Ownership

Suppose now that instead of owning his land, the farmer rents the land from a landowner. A renter on the other hand, cares less about the soil than the farmer does. This is a common problem with renters. When you rent an apartment from a landlord you treat the place differently than if it was your own. If you spill coffee on the rug, you might mop it up, but you're unlikely to clean the rug. In fact, you probably just move the couch over the stain. You slam doors, overload the dishwasher with unrinsed dishes, leave the water on when you leave for the weekend, and tell your guests to leave their shoes on. When you rent a car, you drive differently than when you own a car. It's what renters do. Economists have a name for this type of behavior, it is called *moral hazard.* Whenever someone doesn't bear the full costs of their decisions, they tend to overuse and abuse the goods they don't fully own.

For the farmer who rents the land by cash, any crop that comes off the land is income to him, and soil be damned. A cash renter has an incentive to mine the soil, and although the landowner may try to directly police this, many soil exploitation techniques are very hard to detect. When the farmer does this he increases the crop he receives this year, but future crops are hurt because the value of the soil is reduced. This type of behavior is shown in figure 17-2, where the cost to the farmer of using soil attributes is r', which is lower than the true cost the landowner bears. When faced with this lower cost, the farmer uses too much of the soil nutrients, and now uses n'. Since the value of the marginal product of these extra nutrients is lower than their true cost, a deadweight loss is created, and is equal to the crosshatched area. We can think of this as being the cost of a cash rent contract.

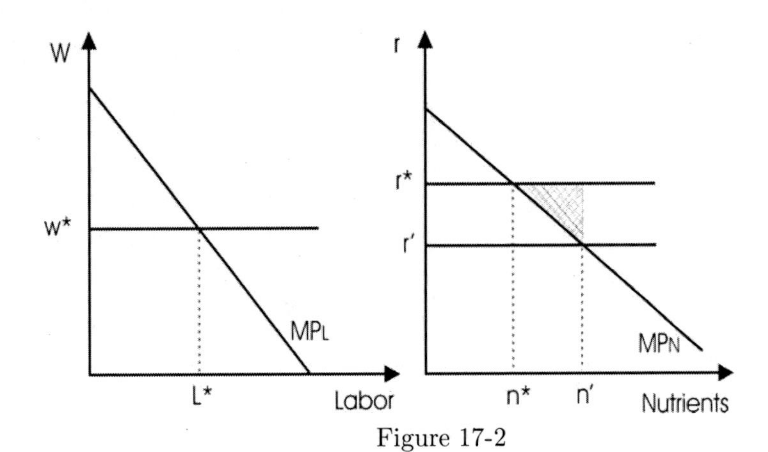

Figure 17-2
Input Use With Cash Rent Contracts

One way to mitigate this moral hazard problem is to slow the farmer down in his desire to use the land by using a share contract rather than a cash rent contract. In many ways a share acts like a tax on behavior. Every time the farmer puts effort into farming, or uses soil nutrients, the landowner takes a cut. This reduces the incentive of the farmer to put effort into the farm and use the soil. Technically what the share does is lower the marginal product of the input to the farmer. This is shown in figure 17-3.

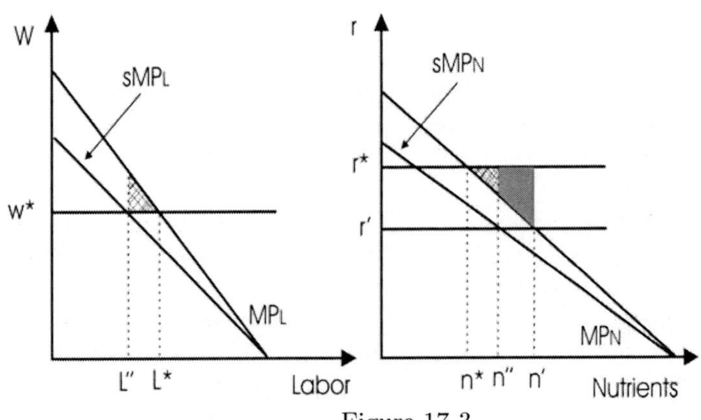

Figure 17-3
Input Use With Cropshare Contracts

The share to the farmer is s, and so as far as the farmer is concerned the value of the marginal product of each input is sMP under the cropshare contract. When the farmer equates his new marginal product curve with his costs we see that he provides less effort (e'') and uses fewer soil nutrients (n'') than he would have under the cash rent contract. The farmer still uses more nutrients that a pure owner would, but he uses less than under the cash rent. Hence the cost of the cropshare contract includes the two crosshatched triangles, but the contract saves the dark shaded region.

You may be wondering, "if the share benefits the landowner (and ultimately the tenant) by getting him to back off on his land abuse, why would a landowner ever use a cash rent contract?" Can you think of a transaction cost problem that arises with a share contract that doesn't arise with a cash rent contract? The problem is that a share contract creates an incentive for the farmer to lie about the amount of crop harvested. Every part of a shared crop that is under reported counts as income to the farmer. For example, suppose the crop is bales of hay, and suppose a field produces a 1000 bales and the share to the landowner is 50%. If the farmer is honest, his income will be 500 bales. But if he reports that only 800 bales came off the field he pays the landowner 400 bales and keeps 600. In other words, his income is higher by 100 bales. Notice that this incentive to under report is missing from the cash rent contract, because there the farmer keeps everything. Just as with the case of soil exploitation, the landowner anticipates this problem and will make some effort to avoid under reporting. However, if the problem of under reporting is serious enough, a cash rent contract solves the problem.

Hence when crop theft is important it is expected that a cash rent contract will be chosen; when soil exploitation is a problem share contracts should be used. This holds for many crops, but consider grass crops versus row crops. Hay, alfalfa, and other grass crops are planted and then harvested several times a year. These crops require little soil manipulation and the output can be sold many ways as well as being used on the local farm for feed. Row crops, like corn, require extensive soil manipulation, and are generally sold through a local elevator. Which do you think is grown with cash rent contracts and which with cropshare? If you said grass and row, respectively, then good for you, you're starting to think like an economist.

Almost all grass crops grown under a land lease are contracted with a cash rent contract. Grass crops are easy to steal and the soil is hard to exploit. Hence they are perfect for a cash rent contract. The costs of these contracts are minimal. Almost all row crops on leased land are grown under cropshare contracts. Row crops are hard to steal, and yet the soil is easily manipulated and exploited. If you grew row crops with cash rent contracts, there simply would be no soil left after a couple of years. Hence we see that contracts are designed to maximize the value of the exchange, taking into account the transaction costs involved. Once you understand what the cheating problems are, the contract solutions seem rather obvious.

Contract choice issues are quite common. Anytime individuals enter into a contract there usually are a number of types of contracts available. For example, when an owner of a stand of trees sells his trees to a logging company he either sells them on a lump sum basis or by the amount of timber that comes out of the forest. That is, the landowner might say "I'll charge you $100,000 and you can go in and cut whatever you want." Or the landowner might say "If you cut down a Douglas Fir tree, you'll pay me $30 for every cubic foot that comes out of the forest." Each contract will have its own specific transaction cost problems. With a lump sum payment the logging company is going to spend a lot of time measuring what quality and volume of trees exist in the forest, and this type of measurement is costly. With a per unit fee for trees the company doesn't have to measure before they commit to logging, but the problem is the company won't want to take all of the trees out. The per unit fee again acts as a tax because it lowers the net price the firm gets per tree. Thus the landowner will have to monitor the logger to induce the optimal level of logging. Hence in stands of forests where all the trees are the same and measurement is easy, lump sum fees are used.

In second growth, heterogeneous stands of trees, the per unit contracts are used.

Movie contracts are another area where we see contract choice. When an actor works on a movie they are either paid a fixed sum or they are paid a share of the film revenues. Payment by a fixed sum is simple, but it requires monitoring. The actor cares less about his performance because his income doesn't depend on how well the film does. When the actor is paid by a share of the revenues, he cares more and puts more effort in. Thus, when the actor's input is more important, he is more likely to be paid by a share than a fixed sum. Actors in sequels, actors who've won an Oscar, and actors whose films have done well in the past, all tend to be paid a share of revenues rather than a fixed sum.

17.2 **Market Enforced Quality Control**

When you walk up to a vending machine, drop some change into the slot, and then punch the button for an *Oh Henry* candy bar, what guarantee do you have that it will be fresh and tasty? If the candy bar is old, lacking peanuts, or for some other reason is generally unsatisfactory, what is a consumer to do? You could write to the Hershey company and demand your money back, but this hardly seems worthwhile. How is a guarantee, guaranteed?

Here is a more general problem. If my car is defective, it is valuable enough that I will pursue the manufacturer until it is fixed. Because I behave this way I am even willing to purchase a guarantee from the automotive company, but when it comes to small time purchases like a chocolate bar or a T-shirt, why would I believe a seller's guarantee of quality when I know it will never pay me to act on it? Furthermore, if firms know that there is little or nothing I will do in response to being cheated, and if cheating is more profitable than being honest, then they will always cheat by promising high quality goods but not delivering them. If consumers anticipated this behavior then they would never be willing to pay more than a low quality price for goods and that is all that would get produced. When quality cannot be guaranteed, it would appear that many markets would simply fall apart! The general market solution to this problem is for the firm to establish a reputation for selling high quality goods. Reputations, therefore, are a market response to a transaction cost problem between buyers and sellers.

Suppose we have the following situation. A number of price-taking firms are selling refrigerators, with every firm deciding whether to sell high quality units that will last for 10 years or sell low quality units that will only last for 1 year. The problem for the consumer is that he cannot tell them apart, and will not know until one year after the purchase which type he has. The problem for the firms is that a high quality refrigerator sells for more than a low quality one, but also costs more to produce. Figure 17-4 shows the three options available for a given firm. Point A represents the case for a firm that decides to produce the low quality refrigerator and announce this truthfully. The firm receives the low quality price P_L, and earns zero profit. Point B is the outcome for a firm that decides to sell a high quality refrigerator, announces its intentions truthfully, and is believed by its customers. In this case, the firm produces along the higher cost functions and again earns zero profit. Point C represents the case of a firm that produces low quality, lies and announces that it has produced high quality, and is believed by its customers. In this case the firm receives the high quality price P_H, but faces the low quality costs, and so earns a profit equal to the shaded area.

Of these three cases, only one is an equilibrium, can you tell which one? If you picked point A, you are right. Clearly the most profitable thing for any firm to do is to lie and announce it

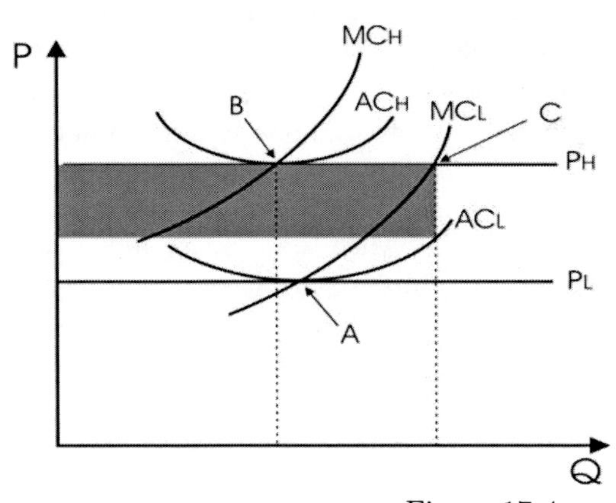

Figure 17-4
The Cheating Equilibrium

is producing a high quality product when in fact, it is producing low quality. However, every customer knows that this is the dominant strategy of the firm and therefore never offers to pay a price higher than P_L. If a firm is honest and produces a high quality refrigerator, no one believes the announcement and the firm loses money because it still receives the low quality price. Hence the only equilibrium is at point A.

Notice punishing a cheating firm by never shopping there again has no impact on their behavior because the firm is better off cheating than being honest. True, the firm will go out of business if it is discovered to be dishonest, but in the meantime it earned a rate of return greater than the return to being honest. Since we do observe firms producing high quality goods, what is the solution? The answer is for the honest firm to be paid a premium for producing high quality. Once this is done, then consumers can punish cheating firms by never buying from them again and this punishment has some bite.

Suppose customers could pay a higher price for the high quality good, such that the honest quality producer could now earn a profit. Figure 17-5 shows if the price of high quality products is raised to P'_H then the honest firm will earn a profit equal to the shaded region. At this higher price there is an even larger gain to cheating, but when a firm cheats it only gets the gain one time and then is "fired" by the consumers. An honest firm gets the shaded region year in year out. As long as the present value of the shaded region from being honest is greater than the one time gain from cheating, firms will be honest, and high quality goods can exist in equilibrium.

The one last thing needing to be resolved is that at point E the high quality firm is earning profit, and in equilibrium we know that profits must be driven to zero. Unfortunately, if prices fall, the firms begin to cheat again. The solution is for the firms to invest in sunk capital until profits are zero. Because the capital is sunk, the shaded region is a rent. Profits are zero, but if the firm cheats it loses its sunk investment. In effect, the sunk investment acts as a bond or a guarantee of quality.

Now we can see the role of a reputation. Reputations are not cheap, and they are always in some form of sunk investment. When a firm advertises, spends money in the community, or takes a costly action that informs customers about itself, it incurs sunk costs. If the firm cheats customers, then it loses these investments, and as a result the existence of a reputation enforces a firm's claims

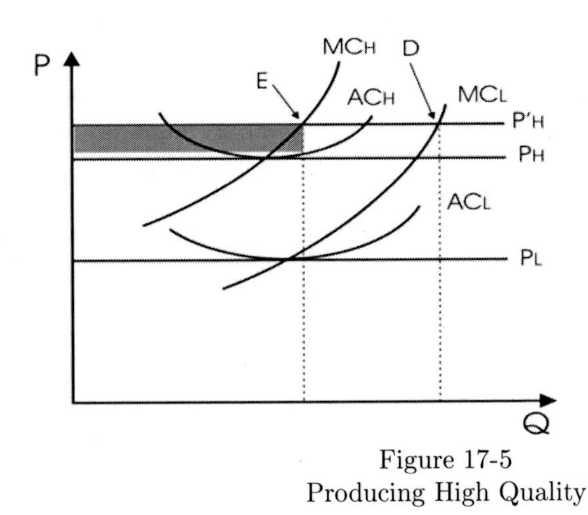

Figure 17-5
Producing High Quality

of high quality.

This provides an interesting explanation for several puzzling observations. How many times have you watched an advertisement on TV for General Motors or Nike running shoes, where there was almost no informational content to the ad? Perhaps the ad showed a beautiful lady on a sailboat in tropical waters, with the camera circling the boat, coming closer and closer. As the picture focuses in on the face of the woman, she turns and says "GM". What information could this possibly convey? The standard reply is that General Motors is playing with our sub-conscious. If we buy a GM car, the story goes, then we will also have a great boat in sunny waters. The answer provided by this model suggests a totally different solution. What the consumer really needs to know is whether they can trust GM or not. If GM is willing to "throw" money away on useless advertisements, then they must be earning a rent. If they are earning a rent then they must be planning on staying in business for a while, and that means they must be planning on producing high quality. Hence General Motors is indirectly advertising that they are honest. Banks are often chastised for having elaborate buildings and expensive interiors. If you travel from city to city you will find the major local bank often owns the nicest place in town. Why would this be? Suppose that a new bank was set up just outside your university. We could call this bank "The Allen Bank". The main feature of this bank would be that it operates out of a motor home (with the motor running). Are you going to put your money in a bank like that? Of course not. Banks, historically, have been required to invest in sunk physical assets in order to guarantee their customers that they will not abscond with their money. Once again, the sunk investment backs up the reputation of the firm and tells customers that they are dealing with an honest firm. On one occasion I was walking down Chicago's "miracle mile", a street with extremely expensive stores. I came upon a Rolex store that was unlike any other. The walls were marble, the door handles were gold, the carpet six inches deep (well, not quite, but it was thick!), and inside were watches that cost up to $25,000. Ironically, around the corner was a gentleman in a long overcoat who was selling Rolex watches for $25! To my eye the watches looked the same. Clearly Rolex had to make extreme investments to guarantee that the watches they were selling were not fakes.

17.3 Signals of Quality Type

Have you ever worn a nice suit to an interview? If you have, you are signaling. It's not clear what you are signaling, but it must be important since everyone who goes to an interview always wears a new suit. Every year around Christmas time economists have their annual meeting, and at this meeting first interviews are done with all of the new Ph.D.'s. Now picture your average Ph.D. student. Perhaps you have one for a teaching assistant. The last thing you would ever picture that person in is a suit right? But at the annual meetings he or she will have one on. In fact, you can always tell the interviewees, and not just be the sweat on their palms ... they're the only ones with new suits!

Signals provide information. In a world where information is costly, and where people take advantage of other's lack of knowledge, signals can be very useful. In order for something to be a good signal it must be difficult to imitate *and* it must be more costly to acquire for the low quality commodity. Hence, dressing in a suit is a lousy signal. Any one can dress in a suit, and good job candidates have no advantage over the bad ones.

An interesting example of signaling was provided by the Air Traffic Controllers (ATC) during the 1970's. In 1972 Congress passed a disability act that allowed "stress" and "burn out" to count as a disability. This act also increased the disability pay so that for some government employees the tax free disability was higher than their after tax wage. In 1974 Congress modified the rules to allow a worker to chose their own physician. Claims made by ATC jumped by 150%. Now this could have been due to the fact that they really were under stress, and the new laws simply lowered the cost of making a claim, but there appears to be more to it. In order to increase the probability of a successful claim ATC's could signal that they were under stress. Planes suddenly started to come closer together. There are several degrees of closeness, and all of them qualify as evidence of stress. Interestingly, planes were brought closer together, but not to the point where there was a near mid air collision! Most of these errors occurred in the daytime, when the weather was nice, with passenger jets, and at non-peak times. This increased the probability that some one else (like a passenger or pilot) would report the error and that the ATC could devote all of his energy to sending the signal. Relax though, Congress changed the rules again in 1978, so the skies are friendly once again.

That was an example of a signal that dissipated wealth. Signals are not always like that. The veal market provides an example of a simple signal that saves resources. Veal is produced from a milk and grain fed steer of 6-12 months old. By feeding the calf heavy doses of milk and grain, and no hay, the farmer produces meat that is pale, soft and valuable. Beef that is fed hay, is red and tougher. Unfortunately it is expensive to feed only milk and grain. Furthermore, veal is almost exclusively sold through auctions where the seller is unknown to the buyer. Can you see a potential transaction cost problem here? A less than honest farmer could feed his calf cheap hay, and try to pawn it off as veal. No one could catch him because the auction doesn't reveal the seller. But, of course, buyers would anticipate this and so they would only offer the red meat price. But we do see veal being sold through the auction. The reason is that there is one breed of cattle that provides a signal for what it has been fed.

The Holstein breed is bred to produce milk not meat. It is a tall skinny animal compared to its beef cousins. The Holstein is the black and white cow most people think of when they think of a cow. However, when this animal is fed hay, it develops a "pot-belly" that any farmer can recognize from one end of the barn to the other. Other breeds do not develop this unique signal. The result is that if you go to a cattle auction, and you hear the auctioneer announce that the veal calves on coming, the only breed you'll see are the Holsteins. Well, you may see some others, but you watch what happens their price!

If you're following this argument, you probably recognize that the reputation argument discussed above is an example of "brand name" signal. When a firm invests in a reputation and announces it as such, this investment acts as a bond for good performance. The consumer sees the brand name signal and recognizes the firm will be worse off if it cheats the consumer. Speaking of posting bonds. Your mother and grandmother probably have very nice diamond engagement rings, but your great-grandmother, and certainly your great-great-grandmother probably didn't. Not only this, your grandmother's ring is probably bigger than you mother's ring, and in terms of the fraction of marital wealth, both will be bigger than your's or your wife's. About 50 years ago it became popular to make substantial investments in diamond engagement rings. Since then it is still customary to buy such rings, but now it is possible to simply purchase 5 point diamonds or high quality Cubic Zirconiums at very modest prices. Why did this happen?

Before you read this book you might have said "It happened because tastes changed; DeBeers came along and told everybody that diamonds are forever, and they just believed them." If you still think this way then you should consider a career in dentistry or accounting. If you're becoming an economist, you should be unsatisfied with theories that cannot be refuted, and you should be trying to think up an explanation based on changing constraints. At one time a broken engagement meant more than embarrassment. Quite often couples would lose their virginity during the engagement, and a broken engagement meant a serious loss of human capital for the woman since this was a serious offense for women 50-100 years ago. A broken engagement meant fewer and poorer options in the marriage market.

Prior to the 1930's women had legal redress through the courts and could sue for breach of promise to marry. Most of these suits were settled out of court, and mostly with the result being a marriage. After 1930, however, different states started to strike these laws from the record. In order to prevent "sleeping and running," diamond rings were used as a promise to fulfill the contract. The more serious the loss of virginity, the more serious the diamond!

17.4 Screening and the Duel of Honor

When a person does something like "dress for success" or tatoo their body, they are trying to signal what type of person they are. Sometimes, however, firms take an action to "screen" or "filter" some types of people from others. When you apply for a job it is often limited to individuals who have completed certain levels of education, or who pass some type of exam. A fascinating screen was used by the aristocracy of Europe during the premodern era to filter out trustworthy people for civil service. This screen was the "duel of honor" seen so often in hollywood movies.

From 1500 to 1900 AD thousands of aristocrats lost their lives in duels of honor. Dueling had a long history before this time, but earlier duels were nothing like the duel of honor. In medieval times justice was often metered out in a judicial duel. These duels took the place of court actions, and the winner was considered chosen by God to be innocent of whatever crime was committed. In addition to these duels, there were the chivalrous duals between knights. These contests were public events used to raise the profile of brave fighters.

Unlike the judicial and chivalrous duels, duels of honor were held in secret and were illegal. Duels of honor were not fought over serious crimes, but of issues of honor (a bad look, a slap to the face, or an accusation of lying). More interestingly, they were conducted with a limited set of lethal weapons (rapiers, sabers, and later pistols), and along a specific set of rules. When an aristocrat was caught dueling no legal action would take place unless the rules were not followed. If someone outside the ruling class was caught dueling they were charged with attempted murder.

There have been many famous duels of honor between many famous people. Abraham Lincoln was in a duel, although a rather humorous one. He had been challenged by a rather small individual, and as the challenged he had the right to choose the weapon. On seeing the stature of his opponent he opted for a set of extremely heavy broad axes (an unconventional weapon). The duel was unable to get off the ground when the opponent was unable to lift the weapon! Another president, Andrew Jackson, was in a duel early in his career. His duel is most remembered for his use of a large overcoat. Normally duelers would strip to the waist in a duel to avoid infection caused by dirty cloth. Jackson kept his large coat on, and when the bullet passed through the coat at a spot where his heart should have been, the witnesses were shocked to see Jackson rise and return a fatal shot to his opponent. The skinny Jackson had apparently shifted his body to one side inside the large coat. Such behavior, if caught was very frowned upon.

The most famous duel of all time was between Alexander Hamilton, one of the founding fathers of the United States, and Colonel Aaron Burr, Vice-President of the United States under Jefferson. Hamilton, a federalist, had lobbied against Burr for the presidency in the election of 1800. When Burr, who did not get along with Jefferson attempted to join the federalist party, Hamilton started a secret campaign to stop him. When Burr discovered some of the things Hamilton had said at a dinner party about him, he challenged Hamilton to a duel. Hamilton did not want to fight the duel, and in a letter to a friend he outlines several reasons why he should not fight: "My religious and moral principles are strongly opposed to the practice of Duelling ...; My wife and children are extremely dear to me ...; I feel a sense of obligation towards my creditiors; I am conscious of no ill-will to Colonel Burr ...; Lastly, I shall hazard much, and can possibly gain nothing by the issue of the interview." Yet he went ahead with the duel, and died from a shot to the abdomen the next day.

So here's the question: why would someone like Alexander Hamilton, or the Duke of Wellington or the Duke of Marlborough (both dueliests), put their valuable lives at stake for such petty issues? The answer is the duel of honor was acting as a screen to enter and stay in the ruling class. Bureaucracies are a modern invention, and in the pre-modern era governments were run by aristocrats with strong reputations for honesty. Reputations were made through sunk investments in the aristocratic society, and the duel was the method by which this reputation was tested. If any aristocrat ever turned down a duel, they became a social outcast, removed from any position of influence. By entering a duel an aristocrat was demonstrating his investment in society and his trustworthiness.

There are many facts about dueling consistent with its role as a screen. First, the outcome of a duel was irrelevant. Win or lose, the participant in a duel was allowed to continue on in the aristocratic world because they demonstrated they had made an investment into society and could be trusted. Only those who turned down the duel and failed the screen were expelled. Ironically, many duelist rekindled friendships after a duel. Aaron Burr was allowed to finish his term as Vice President and had a successful career as a lawyer afterwards. Second, there was a serious attempt to make the outcome of a duel random. As mentioned, duels of honor were fought under specific rules. Many of these rules attempted to make the duel mostly a game of chance. This was necessary, because a duel based on skill could not act as a screen. Someone who was a good duelist could go around challenging people, and pretend they were a trustworthy person. Thus, in pistol duels, for example, the aiming beads were removed, the barrel was shortened, and the barrel was not rifled. All of these efforts made the weapon inaccurate. Furthermore, the participants could not take much time in aiming. These efforts essentially randomized the outcome, and better allowed the duel to act as a screen for reputation. Finally, it didn't matter who made or accepted the challenge. All that mattered in dueling was whether or not one entered or declined.

17.5 Summary

This final chapter has considered the organization of markets. It began with a section on farm land lease contracts. Contracts are not pure market trades, but neither are they firms. A contract, like a franchise firm, lies in between pure firms and markets. We saw that the choice of the type of contract depended on the incentives each one created. Every contract creates different incentives, and lead to different allocations of resources. The contract with the highest value is chosen. Next we looked at how firms make commitments to produce high quality goods. Because firms always have an incentive to cheat customers when customers can't measure the quality of goods, firms invest in specific forms of sunk capital to convince customers of their honesty. We saw that this sunk capital acts as a reputation for the firm. This model explained why so much advertising we observe contains so little informational content. Its sole purpose is to demonstrate the firm's investment in sunk capital. We then looked at how individuals signal quality in veal markets where information is not very good. Finally, we briefly discussed how dueling in the pre-modern era functioned as a screen of trustworthiness in the civil service of the day.

REVIEW QUESTIONS

1. What would happen to the optimal share to a farmer is there was another input besides land attributes and labor (say seed). Suppose this input is supplied by the farmer, not the landowner.

2. Suppose some farmland was to be converted to a shopping center in two years. What type of contract would be used, a share or cash rent?

3. Would the role of reputation would if the firm in figure 17-4 was a price searcher rather than a perfect competitor?

4. Why would ordinary citizens not be allowed to duel?

5. Does the breed of cow matter in private veal sales?

PROBLEMS

1. Mail order firms send out catalogues and then receive orders from their customers. What is a serious transaction cost problem for a mail order firm to overcome? Can you think of methods that might be used to overcome this problem? Can this explain why Sears, when it first started as a mail order business, placed a picture of their new Chicago warehouse on their early catalogs, with each brick stamped with "Sears" on it.

2. Mules are a cross between a horse and a donkey. Mules are very tough and robust. Mules have a tendency to not hurt themselves (they don't overeat or drink, and they simply quit working if worked too hard). On the other hand, mules are less productive than horses on a farm. Mules were heavily used in the American South before tractors, but were never that common in the American North or in Canada where horses were used. In the South most agriculture was done on plantations where many wage workers were employed, while in the north farms were operated by families. Can you use this last fact to explain the use of the mule over horses in the south?

3. In a certain developing country, wheat farms have the following production function, where L=labor input and TP=total product. Labor can earn $4 per day in the nonagricultural sector of the economy.

L	TP
1	10
2	18
3	25
4	31
5	35
6	38
7	40
8+	40

   a. Suppose the farms are owned by landlords who hire workers to farm the land. How many people will work on each farm? Explain.

   b. Suppose the land is "common property": the land is farmed by communes, where the commune is a closed group that decides it own size and then shares equally among its own members. How many people will work on each farm? Explain.

   c. Suppose that the land is still common property, but also the commune cannot prevent anyone from joining and sharing the benefits. How many people will work on each farm? Explain.

   d. If the demand for wheat increased substantially in the economy, so that many additional farms entered into wheat production, what would happen to the rents received by the owner of this land?

As mentioned in this chapter, share tenancy is a common form of rental agreement in agriculture. In this contract, the farmer agrees to pay some fraction of his or her output to the landlord as payment for rent. The system has been likened by some to a tax on labor.

e. Using the numbers derived above, explain why a tax on labor would lead to "too little" labor being used on the land, and why the rent on the land would decrease.

f. A share contract, however, is not a tax. It is a voluntary contract between the landlord and the tenant. The landlord keeps this "tax". Would landlords enter into a contract which gave them less rent than a fixed wage contract as in part a. above?

4. Cars come in every color, independent of brand make. Likewise, street motorcycles also come in any color independent of who made them. But tractors do not. Ford's are blue, John Deere's are green and yellow, International Harvester are red and gold, Case are yellow, etc. Furthermore, off road motorcycles tend to have colors that depend on brand: Honda's are red, Kawasaki's are green, Yamaha's are yellow (I think). Why would this be?

5. Far fewer babies are currently offered for adoption in the United States than couples want to adopt. Would you call this a shortage? Why doesn't the price of an adopted baby rise? By what criteria are the scarce babies rationed to prospective adopters? Why do you think we aren't allowed to sell babies?

6. When I shop at Safeway, there are a number of tellers, each with their own queue. When I shop at the Royal Bank, there is one queue and you go to the first teller available. Why?

7. Here are some lyrics from Fleetwood Mac's *Hold Me*, off their 1982 Mirage Album.
   I don't want no damage
   But how'm I gonna manage with you
   You hold the percentage
   But I'm the fool payin' the dues

   The song is in the context of a personal relationship, but from the lyrics we can see the cause of the problem is a general transaction cost one. What is the general problem that is being referred to? Can you provide your own example of this type of problem?

8. Another song, this time from Donna Summer and *She Works Hard for the Money*
   Its a sacrifice working day to day
   For little money just tips for pay
   But its worth it all
   Just to hear them say that they care

   Clearly in the song the waitress is working hard. What role do you think the "tip" plays in making a waitress work hard?

Review Question Answers

1. *The share will increase to the farmer. You can see this if you draw a figure like that in 17-3, but with three inputs.*

2. *It would be a cash rent contract because you wouldn't care about the lost nutrients, and you'd avoid monitoring the under reporting problem.*

3. *With price searching it plays an even more effective role, since the falling demand curve makes it harder to sell a lot of the low quality product as good quality.*

4. *Dueling was a way for the aristocrats to screen for social capital. Commoners were not allowed into their social circle, so there was no purpose in them dueling. By allowing them to duel it would have simply added noise to the screen.*

5. *No. All breeds are used in private, non-auction veal sales.*

Odd Numbered Problem Answers

1. *The problem is people send in their money, and nothing comes back. Mail order firms have to make some type of reputation investment to convince people they won't rip them off. Sears sunk a lot of money into a building it would never recover if it went out of business.*

3.

    a. *Workers will be hired until their marginal product equals their marginal cost. In this case 5 workers will be hired on each farm.*

    b. *The commune wants to maximize the average product. In this case each farm only has one worker. Some commune!*

    c. *Now people will arrive until the average product is equal to the $4 cost. This happens when 10 people are on each farm.*

    d. *It would depend on which regime we're talking about. In case (a), if the price of wheat increased then the rents to the land would increase.*

    e. *The share would lower the marginal product, this would lower the number of workers on the farm and lower the rent earned.*

    f. *No. So it must be the share contract has some type of value. Workers on a farm tend to exploit the soil of the landowner. The share contract slows this down.*

5. *Yes, it is a shortage. There is no explicit price for babies, so it cannot rise. However, there is an implicit price. People now wait, for example, much longer than before to adopt. There are many non-price allocation mechanisms ... race, religion, stability of couple, etc. I think making babies for sale would increase the number of baby thefts. People would then go to great lengths to protect their children.*

7. *The issue is sharing benefits and costs. Clearly from the song one party gets a share of benefits, while the other bears all of the costs. Just as in the example of the author versus the publisher, this will lead to conflicts over all kinds of things.*